Nuclear and Particle Physics

Universities Press

Nuclear and Particle Physics
An Introduction

Satadal Bhattacharyya
Associate Professor
Department of Physics
Scottish Church College, Kolkata

Universities Press

NUCLEAR AND PARTICLE PHYSICS: AN INTRODUCTION

UNIVERSITIES PRESS (INDIA) PRIVATE LIMITED

Registered Office
3-6-747/1/A & 3-6-754/1, Himayatnagar, Hyderabad 500 029, Telangana, India
info@universitiespress.com; www.universitiespress.com

Distributed by
Orient Blackswan Private Limited

Registered Office
3-6-752 Himayatnagar, Hyderabad 500 029 Telangana, India

Other Offices
Bengaluru / Chennai / Guwahati / Hyderabad
Kolkata / Mumbai / New Delhi / Noida / Patna

First published 2020
Reprinted 2024

ISBN 978-93-89211-15-3

502072

Typeset in Times New Roman 10 points *by*
Textsoft, Hyderabad 500 033

Printed in India by
B.B. Press, Tronica City Ghaziabad (UP) 201102

Published by
Universities Press (India) Private Limited
3-6-747/1/A & 3-6-754/1, Himayatnagar, Hyderabad 500 029, Telangana, India

Preface

This book is an introduction to Nuclear and Particle Physics, intended primarily for BSc Honours and General students pursuing Physics in various Indian universities. In this book, an attempt has been made to meet the basic requirements of undergraduate students so that they can obtain a clear understanding of the subject and also prepare for different examinations. It covers the entire course of Nuclear and Particle Physics of the newly introduced **CBCS syllabus** in the undergraduate curriculum and thus serves the purpose of a syllabus-oriented textbook – this may be taken as the main objective of writing this book.

The book is divided into eight chapters. Each chapter begins with an overview and ends with a brief summary, followed by a number of problems and questions of undergraduate standard. **Chapter 1** describes the basic characteristics of the nucleus. It includes a discussion on the determination of the size and mass of the nucleus, binding energy and its importance, nuclear spin and parity, and the electric and magnetic moments of the nucleus. The basic properties of nuclear force have also been discussed in this chapter. **Chapter 2** illustrates a few simple theoretical nuclear models such as liquid-drop model, shell model and Fermi model, along with their applications. **Chapter 3** provides a detailed discussion on radioactivity. In this chapter, different aspects of alpha, beta and gamma decay are explained in detail. **Chapter 4** is concerned with nuclear reactions, fission and fusion. **Chapter 5** covers the interaction of charged particles with matter, which includes a discussion on energy transfer in collision, ionisation, range and stopping power. Interactions of radiation with matter including photoelectric effect, Compton effect and pair production are also explained in detail. Various types of detectors such as ionisation chambers, and proportional and GM counters have also been discussed. Accelerators including linear accelerator, cyclotron, betatron and synchrocyclotron are covered in **Chapter 6**. An elementary introduction to Particle Physics has been presented in **Chapter 7**. Finally, a brief discussion on Astrophysics has been incorporated in the last chapter, **Chapter 8**.

Throughout the book, emphasis has been given to a proper understanding of the subject, and the different topics are presented in a very lucid and student-friendly manner. The approach followed in the book resembles that of classroom teaching. Illustrative examples with almost step-by-step solutions are provided at the end of each topic. To involve a student in the process of active learning, some assignment problems, termed **Check Progress**, have been provided along with the illustrative examples. Exact experimental data with complete references have been used in many cases to make students aware of the development of the subject.

An attempt has also been made to include different types of problems that may help the reader to develop an insight into the subject as well as to prepare for the university examinations. Finally, a good number of MCQs have been included to make the book equally useful for different competitive examinations such as NET, GATE, etc.

Despite my best efforts, there may be some errors and mistakes in the book and I am fully responsible for all of them. Readers are kindly requested to bring all such errors and mistakes to my attention (email: sbphys@scottishchurch.ac.in).

I consulted a number of acclaimed textbooks on Nuclear Physics while preparing the manuscript. In fact, the present book contains the essence of many excellent texts on this subject, the complete list of which is provided at the end of the book.

I have benefitted greatly from the students of my college, where I have had the opportunity of taking this course for the last 24 years. I have learnt a lot from my students through their discussions and questions. I owe special thanks to my students of different ages who inspired me to write the book. I thank my colleagues in the department for providing support in different forms while preparing the manuscript. I would like to extend my special gratitude towards Dr. Joydip Mitra, one of the youngest and brightest Professors of our department, who has read several topics and given me many enlightening suggestions for improving the book.

I am also thankful to the staff of Universities Press, especially Thomas Mathew Rajesh (Senior Vice-President), Madhavi Sethupathi (Senior Editor) and Kallol Das (Acquisitions Editor), for their cooperation.

Without the constant affection and support of my mother, it would not have been possible for me to execute this endeavour. A very special thanks to my wife for her encouragement in preparing the book. Finally, I would like to convey my heartiest affection to my two daughters, Aparajita and Dipanwita, who are my real inspiration in every aspect of my life.

Satadal Bhattacharyya
Kolkata

Contents

Preface v

1. PROPERTIES OF NUCLEI **1**

1.1 Constituents of the Nucleus 1

1.1.1 Electron–Proton Model of the Nucleus 2

1.1.2 Inconsistency with Uncertainty Principle 2

1.1.3 Inconsistency with Nuclear Spin 3

1.1.4 Inconsistency with Magnetic Moment 3

1.1.5 Neutron–Proton Model 4

1.2 Nuclear Size 4

1.2.1 Estimation from Alpha-Ray Scattering Experiment 4

1.2.2 Observation from Other Scattering Experiments 6

1.3 Atomic Mass 8

1.3.1 Mass Spectrometry 9

1.4 Density of the Nucleus 14

1.5 Binding Energy 15

1.5.1 Binding Energy (BE) Curve and Its Importance 18

1.5.2 Release of Energy in Fission and Fusion 20

1.5.3 Fall of BE Curve at Small and Large Values of A 20

1.5.4 Mass Defect and Packing Fraction 21

1.5.5 Nucleon Separation Energy 23

1.5.6 Abundance of Stable Nuclei 25

1.5.7 Coulomb Energy of the Nucleus 27

1.5.8 Coulomb Energy Difference of Mirror Nuclei and Charge Symmetry of Nuclear Force 28

1.6 Spin and Parity 30

1.7 Electric and Magnetic Moments 31

1.8 Properties of Nuclear Force 33

Summary 38

Review Questions and Problems 39

Hints/Answers to Selected Problems 43

2. NUCLEAR MODEL **45**

2.1 Liquid-Drop Model of the Nucleus 45

2.1.1 Applicability of Liquid-Drop Model 48

2.2 Nuclear Shell Model 55

2.2.1 Shell Model in Atomic Case 56

2.2.2 Evidence for Nuclear Shell Model 56

2.2.3 Introduction to the Nuclear Shell Model 58

2.2.4 Predictions of the Shell Model 60

2.2.5 Drawbacks of the Shell Model 63

2.3 Nuclear Fermi Gas Model 64

Summary 68

Review Questions and Problems 69

Hints/Answers to Selected Problems 72

3. RADIOACTIVITY **73**

3.1 Radioactive Decay Equation 73

3.1.1 Half-Life and Mean Life 76

3.1.2 Radioactive Series 77

3.1.3 Branching 79

3.1.4 Production of Radioactive Element by Nuclear Bombardment 80

3.1.5 Successive Disintegration and Radioactive Equilibrium 80

3.1.6 Radioactive Dating 90

3.2 Alpha Decay 92

3.2.1 Energetics of Alpha Decay 93

3.2.2 Energy Released in Terms of BE 94

3.2.3 Range of Alpha Particles 95

3.2.4 Basic Experimental Results 96

3.2.5 Theory of Alpha Decay 97

3.2.6 Alpha-Ray Spectrum 102

3.3 Beta Decay 104

3.3.1 Beta Spectrum and the Neutrino Hypothesis 105

3.3.2 Difference between Neutrino and Antineutrino 107

3.3.3 Violation of Parity in Beta Decay 108

3.3.4 Energetics of Beta Decay 110

3.3.5 Selection Rules 113

3.4 Gamma Decay 114

3.4.1 Energetics of Gamma Decay 114

3.4.2 Selection Rule 116

3.4.3 Internal Conversion 117

Summary 118

Review Questions and Problems 120

Hints/Answers to Selected Problems 125

4. NUCLEAR REACTIONS **129**

4.1 Nuclear Reactions and Conservation Laws 129

4.1.1 Representation 129

4.1.2 Types of Nuclear Reactions 129

4.1.3 Conserved Quantities 130

4.2 Energetics of Nuclear Reactions 131

4.2.1 Energetics in the Laboratory Frame 131

4.2.2 Energetics in the Centre-of-Mass Frame 137

4.2.3 Cross-section 140

4.2.4 Compound Nucleus 142

4.2.5 Discovery of Neutron 146

4.3 Fission 151

4.3.1 Mass Distribution of Fission Fragments 151

4.3.2 Energy Released in Fission 153

4.3.3 Spontaneous Fission 154

4.3.4 Bohr–Wheeler Theory of Nuclear Fission 156

4.3.5 Emission of Neutrons in Fission 161

4.3.6 Reaction at High Energy 163

4.3.7 Utilisation of Fission Energy 163

4.4 Fusion 170

4.4.1 Solar Fusion 172

Summary 173

Review Questions and Problems 175

Hints/Answers to Selected Problems 179

5. INTERACTION OF NUCLEAR RADIATION WITH MATTER **180**

5.1 Energy Transfer in Elastic Collision 180

5.2 Interaction of Heavy Charged Particles with Matter 181

5.2.1 Bethe Formula for Stopping Power 186

5.3 Interaction of Electrons with Matter 189

5.4 Range of Charged Particles 190

5.4.1 Range of Alpha Particles: Bragg's Experiment 191

5.5 Interaction of Photons with Matter 193

5.5.1 Photoelectric Effect 193

5.5.2 Compton Effect 195

5.5.3 Pair Production 196

5.5.4 Attenuation of Gamma Rays in Matter 198

5.6 Detection of Nuclear Radiation 200

5.6.1 Gas-filled Detector 201

5.6.2 Ionisation Chamber 203

5.6.3 Proportional Counter 204

5.6.4 Geiger–Müller (GM) Counter 206
5.7 Scintillation Detector 212
Summary 215
Review Questions and Problems 216
Hints/Answers to Selected Problems 219

6. PARTICLE ACCELERATORS **220**

6.1 Need for Higher Energy 220
6.2 Linear Accelerator (LINAC) 221
6.3 Cyclotron 224
6.3.1 Limitations of the Cyclotron 225
6.3.2 Magnetic Focussing 230
6.4 Phase Stability and the Principle of Synchrocyclotron 231
6.5 Betatron: Principle of Operation 233
Summary 237
Review Questions and Problems 238
Hints/Answers to Selected Problems 241

7. PARTICLE PHYSICS **242**

7.1 Fundamental Interactions 242
7.2 Elementary Particles 244
7.2.1 Leptons 244
7.2.2 Hadrons 245
7.3 Conservation Laws 246
7.3.1 Basic Conservation Laws 247
7.3.2 Conservation of Lepton Number 252
7.3.3 Conservation of Baryon Number 254
7.3.4 Strangeness 255
7.3.5 Isospin 257
7.3.6 Violation of Conservation Laws 259
7.3.7 Charge Conjugation 266
7.4 The Eightfold Way and the Quark Model 267
7.4.1 The Eightfold Way 267
7.4.2 The Quark Model 271
Summary 276
Review Questions and Problems 277
Hints/Answers to Selected Problems 281

8. NUCLEAR ASTROPHYSICS **283**

8.1 Expanding Universe 283
8.1.1 A Rough Estimation of the Age of the Universe 285
8.1.2 Application of Newtonian Mechanics 286

8.1.3 The Hot Big Bang 288
8.2 Cosmic Microwave Background Radiation 289
8.2.1 Radiation and Expansion 292
8.3 First Few Seconds after the Big Bang 293
8.3.1 Primordial Nucleosynthesis 297
8.4 Stellar Nucleosynthesis 299
8.4.1 Fusion in Stars 299
8.4.2 Hydrogen Burning 302
8.4.3 Nucleosynthesis for $A < 60$ 304
8.4.4 Nucleosynthesis for $A > 60$ 305
Summary 306
Review Questions and Problems 307
Hints/Answers to Selected Problems 308

Appendix A: Penetration of Rectangular Barrier 311
Appendix B: Parity 314
Appendix C: List of Physical Constants 320
Bibliography 321
Index 323

To the memory of my father,
Dayananda Bhattacharyya

Pitṛbhyaḥ svadhā

CHAPTER 1

Properties of Nuclei

According to Rutherford, at the centre of an atom is a **nucleus**. **Protons** and **neutrons**, collectively known as **nucleons**, are the main constituents of the nucleus. The positively charged protons are confined to a very small region, and thus, the repulsive force acting among them is extremely strong. The existence of a bound nucleus implies that in spite of the strong repulsion among the protons, a strong attractive force must be present among the nucleons to bind them in the nucleus. Understanding the nuclear force acting among the nucleons is a challenging problem. The main objective of studying nuclear physics is to discover the nature of nuclear force, and scientists all over the world have been trying to uncover its mysteries since the birth of this subject.

In this chapter, we first discuss some basic characteristics such as the dimensions, mass and density of the nucleus. Then we try to investigate the basic nature of nuclear force through the study of nuclear binding energy. We also briefly explain electric and magnetic moments, and spin and parity of the nucleus. These discussions are very important as they will help us to build a framework for future understanding.

1.1 CONSTITUENTS OF THE NUCLEUS

We first discuss two experimental facts of great significance:

(a) The early chemical methods of measurement of atomic mass. These measurements suggested that the mass of any atom (M) is

$$M \sim \text{integer} \times M_H,$$

where M_H is the mass of the hydrogen atom. The integer is called the **mass number** and is usually denoted by the symbol A.

(b) The concept of atomic number Z. Following the study of the spectral analysis of X-rays, it was recognised that Z is equal to the number of electrons in the atom, and thus, is equal to the number of positive nuclear charges.

Hydrogen is the most simple atom, for which $Z = 1$. Thus, the number of positive nuclear charges, called protons, is 1 for hydrogen. With the identification of A and Z, the **electron–proton model**, the first primitive model of the nucleus, was developed.

1.1.1 Electron–Proton Model of the Nucleus

Until about 1930, protons and electrons were considered as the fundamental constituents of the nucleus. According to the electron–proton model, a nucleus with mass number A and atomic number Z would consist of A number of protons and $(A-Z)$ number of electrons. It yields the observed mass of the atom ($\approx A \times M_H, M_H$ being very close to the mass of the proton) and $(A-Z)$ electrons in the nucleus, which makes the atom electrically neutral. It was generally believed that electrons existed inside the nucleus, and this belief was strengthened by observations of the electrons emitted during β decay.

Despite the success of the electron–proton model in explaining the mass and charge of the nucleus, there were strong arguments that electrons could not exist inside the nucleus.

Illustrative Example 1.1: Hydrogen: $A = 1, Z = 1$

As $Z = 1$, the number of electrons in the atom is 1 and, to preserve electrical neutrality, the number of protons in the nucleus must also be 1. As the electron is much lighter than the atom, it is expected that the mass of the hydrogen atom will be almost equal to that of the proton.

The number of protons in the nucleus = 1
The number of electrons in the nucleus = 0
The number of atomic electrons in the outer orbit = 1
Total charge $= +e - e = 0$; Total mass of the atom $\approx$ Mass of the proton.

Illustrative Example 1.2: Nitrogen: $A = 14,\ Z = 7$

The mass of a nitrogen atom is approximately 14 times greater than that of a hydrogen atom; thus, $A = 14$. Since the mass of a hydrogen atom is almost equal to that of a proton, it was thought that the nucleus of a nitrogen atom would contain 14 protons. As $Z = 7$, the number of electrons in the atom (outside the nucleus) would be 7. Therefore, the nucleus must contain 7 extra electrons so that the atom as a whole becomes electrically neutral.

1.1.2 Inconsistency with Uncertainty Principle

From Rutherford's scattering experiment with α-rays, it was first observed that most of the space in the atom is empty, and the massive part of the atom is concentrated in a very small region, called the nucleus. The size of the nucleus is $\approx 10^{-14}$ m. Thus, the uncertainty in the position of the electron in the nucleus is $\triangle x \approx 10^{-14}$ m. From the uncertainty principle, the uncertainty in the momentum of an electron can be calculated as

$$\triangle p \approx \frac{\hbar}{\triangle x} \approx 10^{-20} \frac{\text{kg.m}}{\text{s}}$$

Therefore, the momentum p itself must be comparable to this magnitude. Now

$$pc \approx 10^{-20} \times 3 \times 10^{8} \approx 3 \times 10^{-12}\ \text{J} \approx 20\ \text{MeV}$$

Since $pc \ggg m_0c^2$, the electron energy[1] is $\approx pc \approx 20$ MeV.

If the electron existed inside the nucleus, then the kinetic energy of the electron would be of the order of at least 20 MeV. However, experiments have shown that the energy of the electrons emitted during β decay (which is only ≈ 1 MeV) is much smaller than this energy. Therefore, the nucleus cannot contain the electrons.

Check Progress 1.1: From the uncertainty principle, we see that electrons cannot be a constituent of the nucleus. Is this argument applicable to protons as well? (Hint: The energy of the protons inside the nucleus ≈ 1000 MeV).

1.1.3 Inconsistency with Nuclear Spin

Protons and electrons are fermions and have a spin of $\frac{1}{2}$. Nuclei with an even number of nucleons should have 0 or **integral** spin. On the other hand, nuclei with odd nucleons have **half-integral** spin. This prediction is, however, not obeyed if the electron–proton model is assumed to be correct. Let us explain this with the following example.

For a deuteron nucleus, $A = 2$ and $Z = 1$.

Configuration according to the electron–proton model:

Number of protons $= 2$

Number of electrons inside the nucleus $= 1$

Number of nucleons $= 2 + 1 = 3$

Expected spin is $\frac{1}{2}\hbar$. However, the experimental value obtained is $\hbar$.

1.1.4 Inconsistency with Magnetic Moment

The magnetic moment of an electron is of the order of Bohr magneton ($\mu_B = \frac{e\hbar}{2m}$, where m is the mass of the electron). Similarly, the magnetic moment of a proton is of the order of nuclear magneton (μ_N), which is equal to $\frac{e\hbar}{2m_p}$, m_p being the mass of the proton. As $m_p \ggg m$, $\mu_N \lll \mu_B$. If the electrons were a part of the nucleus, the nuclear magnetic moment would be of the order of magnitude of that of the electron. However, the observed nuclear moments are comparable to that of the proton, not of the electron. Finally, the hypothesis of nuclear electrons was rejected with the discovery of the neutron by Chadwick in 1932.

[1] $1\ \text{MeV} - 1.6 \times 10^{-13}\ \text{J}$

1.1.5 Neutron–Proton Model

This is the accepted model[2] of the nucleus and it works well. According to this model, the nucleus is a bound system of neutrons and protons, collectively known as nucleons. The neutron is electrically neutral and has nearly the same mass and spin as that of the proton. A nucleus with mass number A and atomic number Z consists of Z protons and $(A-Z)$ number of neutrons. The conventional symbol for the nucleus is ${}^A_Z X$, where X is the chemical symbol of the element; Z is the atomic number of the element = number of protons in the nucleus; and A is the mass number of the element = number of nucleons in the nucleus.

Check Progress 1.2: The ground state spin of ${}^{14}_{7}\mathrm{N}$ is 1. Explain that this value is consistent with the neutron–proton model of the nucleus.

1.2 NUCLEAR SIZE

1.2.1 Estimation from Alpha-Ray Scattering Experiment

Suppose an α particle of charge $+2e$ (actually an α particle is a doubly ionised helium, that is, helium atom $-2e$) is moving towards a target nucleus ${}^A_Z X$, as shown in Fig. 1.1. The force acting between the α particle and the nucleus is repulsive and it is $\propto \frac{1}{r^2}$. The path of the α particle in such a force field is hyperbolic.

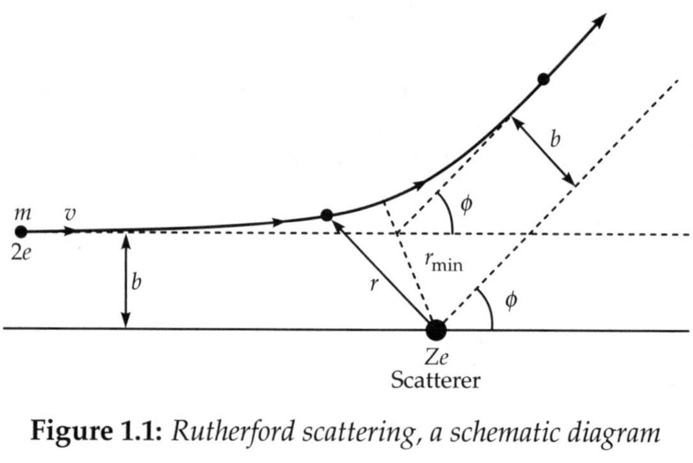

Figure 1.1: *Rutherford scattering, a schematic diagram*

Conservation of energy: Initially, when the α particle is far from the nucleus, the energy is fully kinetic. As the α particle approaches the nucleus, its kinetic energy decreases but its potential energy increases. At the minimum distance of closest approach (r_{min}) to the nucleus, the speed of the α particle becomes minimum (v_{min}) and its potential energy becomes maximum.

[2]For arguments in favour of this model, see Burcham, WE. 1979. *Elements of Nuclear Physics*, Longman Group Ltd., 9:1.

Thus, from the conservation of energy, we get

$$E = \frac{1}{2}mv^2 = \frac{1}{2}mv_{\min}^2 + \frac{1}{4\pi\varepsilon_0}\frac{2Ze^2}{r_{\min}}, \tag{1.1}$$

where m is the mass of the α particle and its initial velocity is v.

Conservation of angular momentum: As the α particle moves in the central force field, the angular momentum (L) about the force centre must be conserved. Far from the nucleus, the angular momentum of the particle about the force centre is mvb, and at $r_{\min}$, the angular momentum is $mv_{\min}r_{\min}$, where b is the impact parameter. Thus

$$L = mvb = mv_{\min}r_{\min} \tag{1.2}$$

Combining Eq. (1.1) and Eq. (1.2), we get

$$E = \frac{Eb^2}{r_{\min}^2} + \frac{1}{4\pi\varepsilon_0}\frac{2Ze^2}{r_{\min}} \tag{1.3}$$

For $b = 0$, the collision is head-on and

$$r_{\min} = D = \frac{1}{4\pi\varepsilon_0}\frac{2Ze^2}{E} \tag{1.4}$$

With an increase in the kinetic energy of the projectile, the distance of closest approach decreases and it may be less than the nuclear radius. In this case, the projectile no longer feels the full nuclear charge; also, the nuclear force, which is much stronger than the Coulomb force, comes into play. In this situation, the Rutherford scattering formula no longer holds. The critical energy at which the scattering law breaks down enables a rough estimate of the nuclear radius of the scatterer.

Illustrative Example 1.3: Estimation of nuclear radius

The Rutherford scattering formula (with the $^{208}_{82}$Pb target) fails at an angle of scattering $\phi = 60^\circ$ when the kinetic energy of the α particle is about 28 MeV (Fig. 1.2).

(a) Find D, the closest distance between the α particle and the nucleus for a head-on collision.

(b) Calculate b, the impact parameter[3] by using the relation $b = \frac{D}{2}\cot\frac{\phi}{2}$.

(c) Calculate $r_{\min}$ for the present case.

Solution (a) $D = \frac{1}{4\pi\varepsilon_0}\frac{2Ze^2}{E}$, $\frac{e^2}{4\pi\varepsilon_0} = 1.44$ MeV.fm, $Z = 82$, and thus, $D \approx 8.4$ fm.

[3] The standard relation between the impact parameter and scattering angle can be found in any textbook of classical mechanics.

(b) $b = \frac{8.4}{2} \cot \frac{60^\circ}{2} \approx 7.3$ fm

(c) $E = 28 = \frac{53.3 \times 28}{r_{\text{min}}^2} + \frac{2 \times 82 \times 1.44}{r_{\text{min}}} = \frac{1492.4}{r_{\text{min}}^2} + \frac{236.16}{r_{\text{min}}}$

Solving this quadratic equation for $\frac{1}{r_{\text{min}}}$, we get $r_{\text{min}} \approx 12.65$ fm.

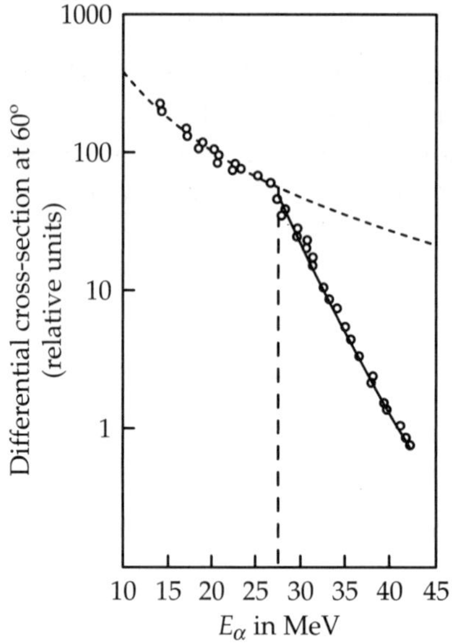

Figure 1.2: *Violation of the Rutherford scattering formula at an angle of scattering* $\phi = 60^\circ$

1.2.2 Observation from Other Scattering Experiments

More sophisticated scattering experiments, using other nuclear particles and electrons, were used to determine the size of the nucleus. The energy of the projectile (either electron or neutron) must be very large so that the de Broglie wavelength of the particle is comparable to the radius of the nucleus under study. An electron interacts with the nucleus through Coulomb force only, while nuclear particles interact mainly through nuclear force. Thus, the electron scattering experiment provides information about the charge distribution (or the electromagnetic properties) of the nucleus. On the other hand, scattering with neutrons provides information about the distribution of nuclear matter and the mass radius of the nucleus. For our present study, we ignore the distinction between the charge radius and mass radius. The data obtained from these experiments suggests that the nucleus is roughly spherical and that the radius of a nucleus of mass number A may be expressed approximately as

$$R = R_0 A^{\frac{1}{3}}, \tag{1.5}$$

where R_0 is a constant determined from the experiment and has a typical value of ≈ 1.2 fm (usually R_0 ranges from 1.2 fm to 1.5 fm).

This, the simplest form of Eq. (1.5), would be obtained if we assume the nucleus to be an assembly of A number of hard spheres. In that case, the volume of the nucleus would be $\frac{4}{3}\pi R^3 = A \times V_0$, where V_0 is the average volume of each sphere. This relation implies that $R = R_0 A^{\frac{1}{3}}$.

Despite the appeal of its simplicity, this model is, in fact, oversimplified. The nucleus is not a hard sphere. Electron scattering experiments show that the nuclear charge density (ρ) does not have a sharp cut-off at the radius R. ρ remains constant over a certain region and then falls gradually to zero. Although nuclei do not have any sharp boundary, the concept of nuclear radius is often useful.

Illustrative Example 1.4: A realistic nuclear charge distribution

A realistic nuclear charge distribution is the Fermi distribution, given by

$$\rho(r) = \frac{\rho_0}{1 + e^{\frac{r-R}{a}}}, \tag{1.6}$$

where ρ_0 is the density at the centre. The parameters R and a are adjusted with the experimental results. R is the distance from the centre to the point where $\rho = \frac{1}{2}\rho_0$ and a is a measure of the skin thickness (t), which is defined as the distance over which ρ drops from 90% of its central value to 10%.

(a) The experimental value of skin thickness is $t \approx 2.3$ fm and it is found to be approximately constant for all nuclei. Assuming $t \approx 2.3$ fm, determine a.

(b) Considering the experimental value of R as $\approx 1.1A^{1/3}$, plot $\frac{\rho}{\rho_0}$ as a function of r for $A = 16$ and $A = 201$.

Solution (a) At $r = r_1$, $\frac{\rho}{\rho_0} = 0.9$. From Eq. (1.6), we get

$$\frac{r_1 - R}{a} = \ln\frac{1}{9}$$

At $r = r_2$, $\frac{\rho}{\rho_0} = 0.1$. From Eq. (1.6), we get

$$\frac{r_2 - R}{a} = \ln 9$$

Thus, $t = r_2 - r_1 = a \times 2\ln 9 \approx 4.4a$ and $a = \frac{2.3}{4.4} \approx 0.5$ fm.

(b) Figure 1.3 shows the required plot.

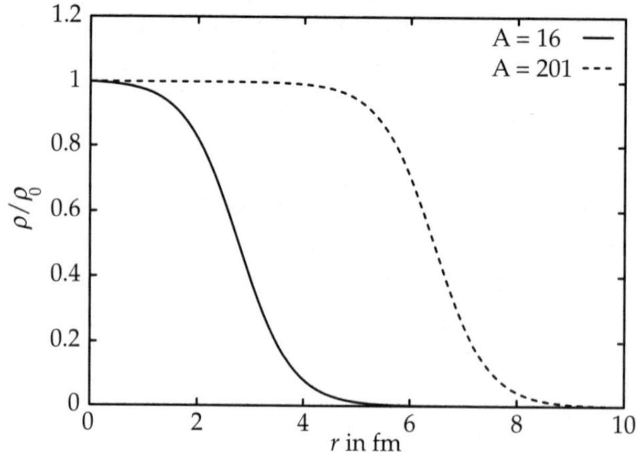

Figure 1.3: *Variation of nuclear charge density with distance for A = 16 and A = 201. It shows that the nucleus has no sharp boundary, where the density drops sharply to zero. Charge density is constant inside the nucleus and decreases smoothly to zero at the boundary.*

Illustrative Example 1.5: Estimate the radius of $^{24}_{12}Mg$.

Solution $R = R_0 A^{\frac{1}{3}} = 1.2 \times 24^{\frac{1}{3}} = 3.46$ fm.

Check Progress 1.3: Calculate the de Broglie wavelength of a proton of 150 MeV.

Check Progress 1.4: Determine the radius of ^{208}Pb and compare[4] it with the result obtained from Illustrative Example 1.3.

Check Progress 1.5: A nucleus with $A = 237$ splits into two new nuclei whose mass numbers are in the ratio 2 : 1. Find their radii.

Check Progress 1.6: The radius of the Ge nucleus is measured to be twice the radius of ^{9}Be. How many nucleons are present in Ge?

The nuclear radius can also be determined by estimating the Coulomb energy difference of mirror nuclei. We will discuss this later in connection with β decay.

1.3 ATOMIC MASS

We cannot measure the mass of a nucleus exclusively, that is, excluding the mass of the electrons. What we can measure is the atomic mass. This always includes the mass of the outer electrons. Atomic mass is expressed in mass units (u). In this unit, the mass of a ^{12}C atom, the most abundant isotope of carbon, is assumed to be exactly 12 u.

[4]The results are different; however, the importance of Rutherford's experiment is that it provides the earliest information about the size of the nucleus.

The weight of 1 atom of ^{12}C $= \dfrac{12}{6.023 \times 10^{23}} = 1.992646 \times 10^{-23}$ g. Thus

$$1\ \text{u} = \frac{1.992646 \times 10^{-23}}{12} = 1.66054 \times 10^{-27}\text{kg} = 931.49\ \text{MeV}/\text{c}^2$$

Mass of electron $= 9.1095 \times 10^{-31}$ kg $= 0.511$ MeV/c^2

Mass of proton $= 1.007276$ u $= 938.28$ MeV/c^2

Mass of neutron $= 1.008665$ u $= 939.57$ MeV/c^2

Mass of hydrogen atom $= 1.007825$ u $= 938.79$ MeV/c^2

1.3.1 Mass Spectrometry

Mass spectrometers are used to measure the mass of an atom. The principle of operation of a mass spectrometer, which was first proposed by JJ Thomson in 1907, is based on the focussing action of electric and magnetic fields with respect to the moving charged particles. All the mass spectrometers developed after 1907 are more or less improved versions of Thomson's method. The atoms under study are first ionised and their motion is controlled by a suitably applied electric or magnetic field. In modern mass spectroscopy, the ions are detected either photographically or electrically. In the first case, the device is known as a mass spectrograph, while in the second, it is called a mass spectrometer.

The first mass spectrograph with a sufficiently high resolution was constructed by Aston in the Cavendish Laboratory in Cambridge in 1919. In Aston's mass spectrograph[5], ions from an ion source were emitted in a given direction but with different velocities. In this spectrograph, the principle of velocity focussing was used to focus ions of the same $\frac{q}{m}$ but with a small velocity spread at a particular point on the photographic plate.

With the help of his instrument, Aston proved the existence of two isotopes of neon, ^{20}Ne and ^{22}Ne. He also proved conclusively that the mass of an atom in atomic mass units is close to an integer. This is the famous **whole number rule**.

The basic principle of operation of another high-resolution mass spectrograph, known as the Bainbridge mass spectrograph, is discussed briefly in the next subsection.

Illustrative Example 1.6: Basic spectroscopy

A beam of singly ionised atomic oxygen ions is passed through a potential difference of 20 kV. It then enters into a region of transverse magnetic field. Find the magnetic field required to bend the ions in an arc of 25-cm radius.

Solution Energy of the ion of charge q and mass m is

$$qV = \frac{1}{2}mv^2 \Rightarrow v = \sqrt{\frac{2qV}{m}}$$

[5]Ghoshal, SN. 1994. *Atomic and Nuclear Physics, Volume II*, S Chand & Company Ltd.

In a magnetic field, the path is circular

$$qvB = \frac{mv^2}{R} \Rightarrow B = \frac{1}{R}\sqrt{\frac{2Vm}{q}}$$

$$B = \frac{1}{0.25}\sqrt{\frac{2 \times 20 \times 10^3 \times 16 \times 1.66 \times 10^{-27}}{1.6 \times 10^{-19}}} \approx 0.3259 \text{ tesla}$$

Illustrative Example 1.7: $R \propto \sqrt{m}$ and $R \propto m$

(a) Two particles, x and y, having equal charge, after being *accelerated through the same potential difference (V)*, enter a region of uniform magnetic field and describe circular paths of radii R_1 and R_2, respectively. Calculate the ratio of their masses $\frac{m_x}{m_y}$. Also find their separation S_1S_2 in the photographic plate, as shown in Fig. 1.4.

(b) Now construct a situation where we have a beam of *ions of the same velocity*. Calculate the ratio $\frac{m_x}{m_y}$.

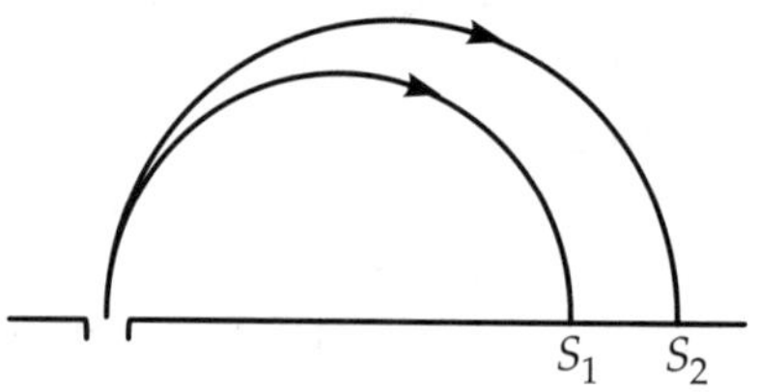

Figure 1.4: *Ions entering into the uniform magnetic field*

Solution (a) In this case, *mono-energetic ions* are produced as the ions have the same charge and the potential difference is fixed:

$$qV = \frac{1}{2}mv^2$$

In the magnetic field, $\frac{mv^2}{R} = qBv \Rightarrow R = \frac{1}{B}\sqrt{\frac{2Vm}{q}} \Rightarrow R \propto \sqrt{m}$.

Thus, $\frac{R_x}{R_y} = \sqrt{\frac{m_x}{m_y}}$ and the separation between the beams is $S_1S_2 = \frac{2}{B}\sqrt{\frac{2V}{q}}(\sqrt{m_x} - \sqrt{m_y})$.

(b) In this case, the ions have *the same velocity*.

$$\frac{mv^2}{R} = qBv \Rightarrow R = \frac{mv}{qB} \Rightarrow R \propto m$$

Thus $\frac{R_x}{R_y} = \frac{m_x}{m_y}$

Bainbridge mass spectrograph: In 1933, Bainbridge devised an improved version of the mass spectrograph, incorporating his new idea of a *velocity filter*, and was able to achieve high precision as well as a convenient linear mass scale to determine the mass of atoms. He carried out a series of precise investigations on the accurate determination of atomic masses.

The velocity filter uses a mixture of electric and magnetic fields to ensure a single velocity stream of ions entering a uniform magnetic field. In a uniform magnetic field, different ions follow circular paths of different radii according to their masses, and thus, a mass spectrum is formed.

Working principle: A schematic diagram of the apparatus is shown in Fig. 1.5. Vacuum is maintained inside the apparatus. The sample is first ionised and then injected into the velocity filter. The velocity filter consists of a crossed electric and magnetic field.

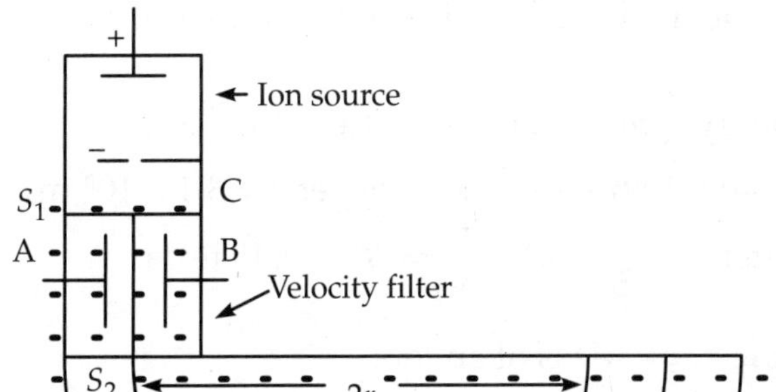

Figure 1.5: *Schematic diagram of Bainbridge mass spectrograph*

Suppose a particle of charge q having arbitrary velocity $v\hat{i}$ enters into the velocity filter, where $\vec{E} = E_0\hat{j}$ and $\vec{B} = B_0\hat{k}$.

The electric force acting on the charge is $qE_0\hat{j}$ and the magnetic force acting on the charge is $qv\hat{i} \times B_0\hat{k} = -qvB_0\hat{j}$. Thus, electric and magnetic forces act on the particle in opposite directions. The two forces will be cancelled if $v = \dfrac{E_0}{B_0}$.

Thus, particles with velocity equal to $v = \dfrac{E_0}{B_0}$ will not be deflected by the fields and pass along the straight line. Particles with velocities other than this specified velocity will be deflected in either direction due to the unbalanced effect of the two opposite forces.

A particle with a charge q and velocity $v = \dfrac{E_0}{B_0}$ will pass through the next slit in a straight line. Thus, all the particles, irrespective of their masses, leaving the filter must have the same velocity. These ions now enter the chamber where a uniform magnetic field B_0 is maintained perpendicular to the trajectories of the ions. Under the influence of this magnetic field, they travel along circular paths of radius R, where

$$m\frac{v^2}{R} = qvB_0, \tag{1.7}$$

m being the mass of the ion and q its charge.

Since v is constant irrespective of the mass of the ion and B_0 is also a constant, $m \propto R$. If these ions are recorded on a photographic plate, then different traces of ions, depending on their masses, will be recorded. *The mass scale is linear, as $m \propto R$.*

Illustrative Example 1.8: Velocity filter

Find the magnetic field required in a velocity filter to filter a 20-keV, singly charged argon ion, if the electric field is $2\frac{\text{kV}}{\text{cm}}$. The mass number of argon is 40.

Solution Kinetic energy $\frac{1}{2}mv^2 = 20 \times 10^3 \times 1.6 \times 10^{-19}$.

Substituting $m = 40 \times 1.66 \times 10^{-27}$ kg, we get $v = 3.1 \times 10^5$ m/s.

In the velocity filter, $v = \frac{E}{B} \Rightarrow B = \frac{E}{v} \Rightarrow B = 0.645$ tesla.

Illustrative Example 1.9: Mass of an ion

In a mass spectrograph, a positive ion is accelerated in a potential 1000 V and it is then passed through a uniform magnetic field of $B = 0.15$ tesla. The trajectory of the ion in a magnetic field is a circle of radius 0.122 m. Find the (i) speed, (ii) mass and (iii) mass number of the ion.

Solution (i) The kinetic energy of the ion in potential V is

$$\frac{1}{2}mv^2 = qV \Rightarrow mv^2 = 2qV$$

Again, in a uniform magnetic field, the path is circular, so that

$$\frac{mv^2}{R} = qvB \Rightarrow mv^2 = qvRB$$

From these relations, we get

$$vRB = 2V \Rightarrow v = \frac{2V}{RB} \Rightarrow v = \frac{2 \times 1000}{0.122 \times 0.15} \approx 1.1 \times 10^5 \text{ m/s}$$

(ii) $mv^2 = qvRB$. Thus

$$m = \frac{qBR}{v} = \frac{1.6 \times 10^{-19} \times 0.15 \times 0.122}{1.1 \times 10^5} = 2.679 \times 10^{-26} \text{ kg}$$

(iii) Mass in atomic mass unit $= \frac{2.679 \times 10^{-26}}{1.66 \times 10^{-27}} \approx 16.13$

The nearest integer to 16.13 is 16, and thus, the mass number is 16.

Illustrative Example 1.10: Separation of isotopes moving with the same velocity

In a Bainbridge mass spectrograph, singly charged ions enter a velocity filter where $E = 5 \times 10^4$ V/m and $B = 0.4$ tesla.

(i) Find the velocity of the ions leaving the filter.

(ii) If the ions enter the magnetic field of 0.8 T, what will be the distance between the ions focussed on the photographic plate for the three isotopes ^{36}Ar, ^{38}Ar and ^{40}Ar?

Solution (i) Velocity $v = \dfrac{E}{B} = \dfrac{5 \times 10^4}{0.4} = 1.25 \times 10^5$ m/s

(ii) For ^{36}Ar, $R_1 = \dfrac{mv}{qB} = \dfrac{36 \times 1.67 \times 10^{-27} \times 1.25 \times 10^5}{1.6 \times 10^{-19} \times 0.8} = 58.74$ mm.

Similarly, for ^{38}Ar, $R_2 = 62.00$ mm, and for ^{40}Ar, $R_3 = 65.27$ mm.
Thus, the required difference is $2(R_2 - R_1) = 6.52$ mm and $2(R_3 - R_2) = 6.54$ mm.

Illustrative Example 1.11: Separation of isotopes moving with the same energy

In a mass spectrograph, singly ionised lithium ions are accelerated by a potential difference of 400 V and then passed through a uniform magnetic field of 0.08 T perpendicular to their direction of motion. The radii of the paths of the ions are 8.83 cm and 9.54 cm, respectively. Calculate the mass number of lithium.

Solution From the relations $\frac{1}{2}mv^2 = qV$ and $\dfrac{mv^2}{R} = qvB$, we get

$$R = \sqrt{\frac{2mV}{q}}\frac{1}{B} \Rightarrow m = \frac{qR^2B^2}{2V}$$

$$\text{Therefore } m_1 = \frac{1.6 \times 10^{-19} \times 8.83^2 \times 10^{-4} \times 0.08 \times 0.08}{2 \times 400} = 998.002 \times 10^{-29}\ \text{kg} \approx 6.012\ \text{amu}$$

$$\text{Similarly } m_2 = \frac{1.6 \times 10^{-19} \times 9.54^2 \times 10^{-4} \times 0.08 \times 0.08}{2 \times 400} = 1164.948 \times 10^{-29}\ \text{kg} \approx 7.018\ \text{amu}$$

Thus, the mass numbers of the isotope are 6 and 7.

Illustrative Example 1.12: Mass resolution

A narrow beam of singly charged ^{10}B and ^{11}B ions of energy 5 keV pass through a slit of width 1 mm into a uniform magnetic field of 0.15 T. After a deviation of 180°, the ions are recorded on a photographic plate. Calculate the spatial separation of the images. Also calculate the mass resolution of the system.

Solution For a beam of mono-energetic ions, the radius of the circular path in the magnetic field is $R = \dfrac{1}{B}\sqrt{\dfrac{2mV}{q}}$ and the separation is

$$2(R_2 - R_1) = \frac{2}{B}\sqrt{\frac{2V}{q}}(\sqrt{m_2} - \sqrt{m_1})$$

$$= \frac{2}{0.15}\sqrt{\frac{2 \times 5 \times 10^3 \times 1.66 \times 10^{-27}}{1.6 \times 10^{-19}}}(\sqrt{11} - \sqrt{10}) = 2.0962 \text{ cm}$$

Since $R = c\sqrt{m} \Rightarrow \frac{dm}{m} = 2\frac{dR}{R} = \frac{2.0962}{R}$, where $R = \frac{R_1 + R_2}{2}$

$$R_1 = \frac{1}{0.15}\sqrt{\frac{2 \times 10.0 \times 1.66 \times 10^{-27} \times 5 \times 10^3}{1.6 \times 10^{-19}}} = 21.47 \text{cm}$$

Similarly $R_2 = 22.52$ cm and the mass resolution is $\frac{m}{dm} \approx \frac{22.0}{2.0962} \approx 10.49$

1.4 DENSITY OF THE NUCLEUS

The density of nucleus ${}^A_ZX$ is

$$\rho = \frac{M}{V},$$

where M is the mass of the nucleus and V is its volume. The mass of the nucleus $M \approx A \times M_p$, where M_p is the mass of proton. Thus

$$\rho = \frac{A \times M_p}{\frac{4}{3}\pi R_0^3 A},$$

and *the density of the nucleus is independent of A and is the same for all nuclei.* Assuming $R_0 = 1.2$ fm and $M_p = 1.67 \times 10^{-27}$ kg, we get [6] $\rho = 2.3 \times 10^{17} \frac{\text{kg}}{\text{m}^3}$.

The fact that nuclear density seems to be independent of the number of neutrons or protons implies that the force between the particles is essentially the same, whether they are protons or neutrons.

Check Progress 1.7: If it were possible to fill up a football of radius 10 cm with nuclear matter, what would be its mass?

Nucleons are contained in a very small dimension ($\sim 10^{-14}$). Coulomb repulsion between the protons is extremely large. However, a stable nucleus exists. How is this possible?

Despite the repulsive Coulomb force, another force must be acting on the nucleons. This force must be attractive and extremely strong compared to the electrostatic repulsion acting among the protons. The aim of studying nuclear physics is to study the properties of this nuclear force that holds the nucleons together.

Illustrative Example 1.13: Neutron density

Estimate the neutron density of a nucleus ${}^A_ZX$.

[6] Compare the result with the density of water ($1000 \frac{\text{kg}}{\text{m}^3}$).

Solution Neutron density $= \dfrac{\text{No. of neutrons}}{\text{Volume of nucleus}} = \dfrac{N}{\frac{4}{3}\pi R_0^3 A}$

Since $N \approx \frac{A}{2}$, neutron density $= \dfrac{3}{8 \times \pi \times R_0^3} = 0.069 \dfrac{\text{neutrons}}{\text{fm}^3}$

Illustrative Example 1.14: Fraction of the nucleons lying on the surface

Suppose the density (ρ) of nucleons in a nucleus varies with radial distance r, as shown in Fig. 1.6. Calculate the fraction of the nucleons lying on the surface of the nuclei for ^{27}Al and ^{216}Pb, if $\rho_0 = 0.17\ \text{fm}^{-3}, c = 1.1A^{1/3}$ and $a = 3.0$ fm.

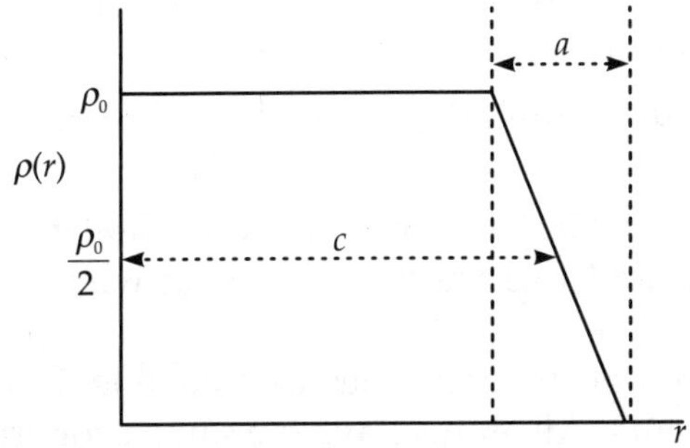

Figure 1.6: *Approximate charge distribution*

Solution Near the surface, the nucleon density drops from ρ_0 to 0 over the radial distance a. Thus, the number of nucleons within the spherical thickness a is

$A_s = 4\pi \int_0^a \rho(r) r^2 dr$, where $\rho(r) = \rho_0 \left(1 - \frac{r}{a}\right)$. Thus

$$A_s = 4\pi\rho_0 \left[\int_0^a r^2 dr - \frac{1}{a}\int_0^a r^3 dr\right] = 4\pi\rho_0 \frac{a^3}{12}$$

Figure 1.6 shows that the density is constant up to $r = c - \dfrac{a}{2}$. Therefore, the total number of nucleons is

$$A = \frac{4}{3}\pi\rho_0 \left(c - \frac{a}{2}\right)^3 + 4\pi\rho_0 \frac{a^3}{12}$$

The fraction of the nucleons lying on the surface of the nuclei is

$$f = \frac{A_s}{A} = \frac{a^3}{a^3 + 4(c - a/2)^3}$$

For ^{27}Al, $c = 1.1 \times 3 = 3.3$ fm and $f = 0.536$.

For ^{216}Pb, $c = 1.1 \times 6 = 6.6$ fm and $f = 0.048$.

Thus, in heavy nuclei, a smaller fraction of the nucleons resides on the surface.

1.5 BINDING ENERGY

We can learn a lot about nuclear force by considering a nucleus in its ground state. One of the most important properties of a nucleus in the ground state is its binding energy.

Hydrogen is the simplest atom. It consists of a single proton in its nucleus and it has no neutron. Its mass is 1.0078 u. Therefore, the mass of the proton is almost equal to the mass of the hydrogen atom, the mass of the electron being negligible. In terms of the level of complexity, the next atom is deuterium. It has a neutron as well as a proton in its nucleus ($^2_1$H). Thus, we expect that the mass of $^2_1$H to be equal to the mass of an ordinary hydrogen atom plus the mass of a neutron.

Mass of $^1_1$H atom $= 1.0078$ u

Mass of neutron $= 1.0087$ u

Thus, the expected mass of $^2_1$H is $1.0078 + 1.0087 = 2.0165$ u. However, the measured value of $^2_1$H is 2.0141 u, which is 0.0024 u less than the combined masses of a hydrogen atom and a neutron. Thus

Mass of neutron and proton in free state > Mass of neutron and proton in bound state

The deficit in mass is 0.0024 u, which is equivalent to the energy of 0.0024×931.49 MeV $= 2.2$ MeV, and this energy is missing when a neutron and a proton form a bound nucleus.

Deuterium atoms are not the only ones that have less mass than the combined masses of their constituents. All atoms have the same property.

In the ^A_ZX nucleus, $ZM_p + (A - Z) \times M_n > M(^A_ZX)$, where $M(^A_ZX)$ is the mass of the ^A_ZX nucleus.

Where does this missing energy go? How do we interpret this?

Interpretation of missing energy: It is reasonable to suppose that the missing energy corresponds to the energy given off when neutrons and protons in the free state combine to form a bound state system. This is explained schematically in Fig. 1.7.

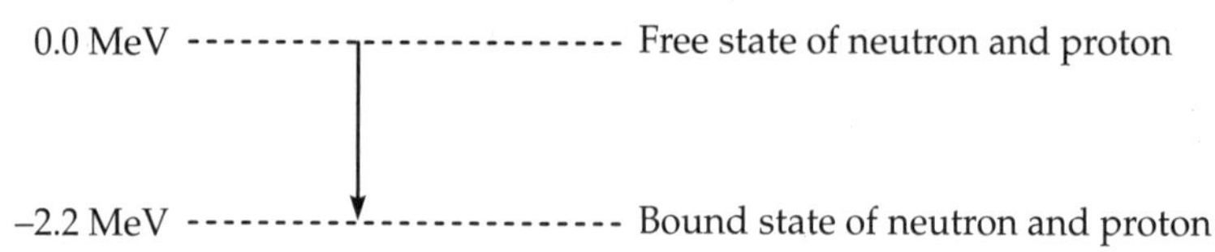

Figure 1.7: *Energy is released when the free nucleons form a bound nucleus*

In another words, if an amount of energy equal to the missing energy is supplied to a nucleus, it will be separated into its constituents. Thus, the binding energy of a nucleus is the energy that holds the nucleons together in the nucleus. This is shown schematically in Fig. 1.8.

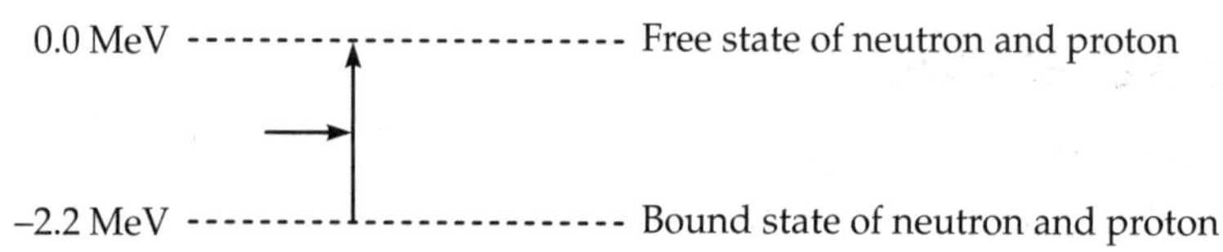

Figure 1.8: *Energy is required to split a nucleus*

To test this interpretation of missing energy, the following reaction may be observed. This reaction is known as the **photo disintegration of deuteron**, where a deuterium nucleus is separated into protons and neutrons by supplying energy in the form of γ rays.

$$\gamma + {}^2_1\mathrm{H} \longrightarrow p + n$$

It is observed that when the energy of the incident γ ray, $E_\gamma < 2.2$ MeV, the deuteron nucleus stays together. However, if $E_\gamma > 2.2$ MeV, the deuteron nucleus splits into protons and neutrons. Thus, the **binding energy of the nucleus** can be defined as the energy required to split the nucleus into its constituent particles. The greater the binding energy of a nucleus, the larger the energy that must be supplied to break it up and the greater its stability. Equivalently, the binding energy of a nucleus is the energy given off when free nucleons combine to form a bound state nucleus. For the bound state system, the binding energy is assumed to be negative because this amount of energy is required to take the system into the free state, which is assumed to be the reference level – the level with zero energy.

Binding energy of ${}^A_ZX$: The binding energy of ${}^A_ZX$ can be written as

$$\begin{aligned} BE(A,Z) &= [ZM_p + (A-Z)M_n - M({}^A_ZX)]c^2 \\ &\approx [ZM({}^1_1\mathrm{H}) + (A-Z)M_n - M(A,Z)_{\mathrm{atom}}]c^2, \end{aligned} \tag{1.8}$$

where the mass of the electrons is neglected.

Illustrative Example 1.15: Error estimation in binding energy

Estimate the error introduced in the approximate relation, Eq. (1.8).

Solution To estimate the error, let us first explain the binding energy of an atom. Binding energy of $(A,Z)_{\mathrm{atom}}$ is

$$BE(A,Z)_{\mathrm{atom}} = [M(A,Z)_{\mathrm{nucleus}} + ZM_e - M(A,Z)_{\mathrm{atom}}]c^2$$

Thus $M(A,Z)_{\mathrm{nucleus}} = M(A,Z)_{\mathrm{atom}} - ZM_e + BE(A,Z)_{\mathrm{atom}}/c^2$

From Eq. (1.8), we get

$$\begin{aligned} BE(A,Z)_{\mathrm{nucleus}} &= [ZM_p + (A-Z)M_n - M({}^A_ZX)]c^2 \\ &= [Z(M({}^1_1\mathrm{H}) - M_e + BE({}^1_1\mathrm{H})_{\mathrm{atom}}/c^2) + (A-Z)M_n \\ &\quad - (M(A,Z)_{\mathrm{atom}} - ZM_e + BE(A,Z)_{\mathrm{atom}}/c^2)]c^2 \\ &= [ZM({}^1_1\mathrm{H}) + (A-Z)M_n - M(A,Z)_{\mathrm{atom}}]c^2 + Z \\ &\quad \times BE({}^1_1\mathrm{H})_{\mathrm{atom}} - BE(A,Z)_{\mathrm{atom}} \end{aligned}$$

The nuclear binding energy $\backsim$ MeV, while the correction term is $\triangle_{BE} = Z \times BE({}^1_1\mathrm{H})_{\mathrm{atom}} - BE(A,Z)_{\mathrm{atom}}$, which is $\backsim$ a few eV only.

Illustrative Example 1.16: Calculation of binding energy

Calculate the binding energy of the ${}^4_2$He nucleus.
Given: $M({}^1_1\mathrm{H}) = 1.0078$ u, $M_n = 1.0087$ u and $M({}^4_2\mathrm{Hc}) = 4.0020$ u

Solution From Eq. (1.8), $BE(^4_2\text{He}) = [2 \times M(^1_1\text{H}) + 2 \times M_n - M(^4_2\text{He})]c^2 = 28.8$ MeV.

Nuclear binding energy is strikingly high. For stable nuclei, it varies from 2 MeV to 1700 MeV. To appreciate this, we may compare it with other energy in a familiar form.

Illustrative Example 1.17: How large is the binding energy!

Calculate the vapourisation energy of 1 kg of water and compare it with the binding energy of 1 kg of $^4_2$He.

Solution Vapourisation energy of 1 kg of water = 540×1000 cal $= 2.26 \times 10^6$ J
BE of 1 kg of $^4_2\text{He} = (6.022 \times 10^{23} \times 10^3)/4 \times 28.8 \text{ MeV} = 6.94 \times 10^{14}$ J

1.5.1 Binding Energy (BE) Curve and Its Importance

In the binding energy curve, the average binding energy per nucleon $\frac{BE}{A}$ is plotted against the number of nucleons A. The curve is shown in Fig. 1.9.

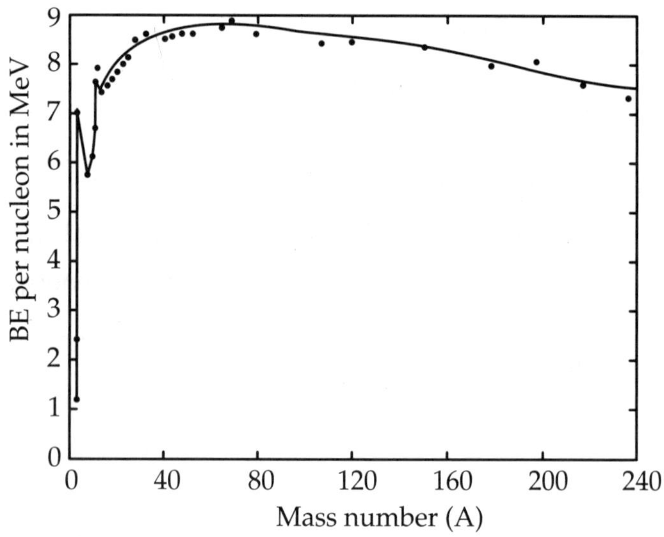

Figure 1.9: *Binding energy per nucleon as a function of mass number A. It is one of the most important curves in nuclear physics.*

A critical observation of this curve shows the following:

(a) $\frac{BE}{A}$ is small for light nuclei. It increases rapidly with increasing A. At $A \approx 30$, it attains a value $\backsim$ 8 MeV. For $20 < A < 200$, the variation in $\frac{BE}{A}$ is quite small; it remains almost constant at $\backsim$ 8 MeV.

(b) The binding energy curve fluctuates for light nuclei, with peaks at $A = 4, 8, 12$ and 16. Peaks are also observed at Z or N equal to $20, 28, 50, 82$ and 126. These are called **magic numbers** and the corresponding nuclei are called **magic nuclei**. The magic nuclei are more stable relative to their neighbours.

(c) The curve reaches its maximum at $A \backsim 56$ (for Fe-group elements). This is the most stable nucleus, as maximum energy is required to pull a nucleon away from it.

(d) For heavy nuclei with $A > 200$, $\frac{BE}{A}$ again decreases below its average value.

Constancy of BE curve and saturation of nuclear force: A striking feature of the curve is the constancy of average binding energy (BE_{av}) for medium-sized nuclei ($20 < A < 200$). This reveals an important property of nuclear force. Suppose the binding energy (just like bonding energy in chemical terms) of each nucleon to every other nucleon in the nucleus is roughly constant ($= C$). Then, the total binding energy of a nucleus containing A nucleons would be

$$BE_{\text{total}} \approx C \times A \times \frac{(A-1)}{2}$$

Thus, BE_{av} would be $\approx C.\frac{(A-1)}{2}$, which is a function of A, contradicting the experimental fact. Thus, the approximate constancy of BE_{av} indicates that each nucleon cannot be bounded equally to other nucleons in the same way.

The constancy of the average binding energy can be explained if we assume that a particular nucleon interacts only with its nearest neighbours, not with all the nucleons present in the nucleus. This is possible only if the range of nuclear force does not extend to more than a few nucleons, that is, *the range of nuclear force is very short*. Since the density of the nucleus is constant, the number of the nearest neighbours surrounding a particular nucleon is always constant, and thus, BE_{av} is also constant.

The constancy of BE_{av} sometimes refers to the *saturation of nuclear force*. **Saturation** means that the binding energy between one nucleon and the rest of the nucleons attains a limit once a certain number of nucleons are assembled.

In this context, we may mention another physical system, namely, a drop of liquid, where the binding energy per particle is constant. Like the binding energy of the nucleus, the vapourisation energy (Q) of liquid can be defined as the energy required to dissociate m g of a substance into its constituent n molecules at a constant temperature.

For water at 100°C, $Q/m = 540$ cal/g = constant. The number of molecules present in 1 g of water is $\frac{6.023 \times 10^{23}}{18}$.

Therefore, the dissociation energy per molecule is $Q/n = \frac{(540 \times 18)}{(6.023 \times 10^{23})}$ cal. ≈ 0.42 eV.

Thus, the average vapourisation energy of water is constant and is of the order of eV.

1.5.2 Release of Energy in Fission and Fusion

The *BE* curve shows that BE_{av} is low for light nuclei as well as for heavy nuclei, and it attains its maximum near $A \backsim 56$. This suggests that we can gain energy in two ways:

(a) By assembling lighter nuclei into a heavy nucleus

(b) By breaking a heavy nucleus into two lighter nuclei

The first method is known as **nuclear fusion** and the second method is called **nuclear fission**.

In the fusion process, two light nuclei combine to form a medium-sized nucleus. The BE curve shows that BE_{av} for the final nucleus is greater than that of the initial nuclei. As a result, a large amount of energy will be released in this combining process. We may illustrate this point with the help of the following example.

Let us consider a fusion reaction

$${}_{1}^{2}\text{H} + {}_{1}^{2}\text{H} \longrightarrow {}_{2}^{4}\text{He}$$

The binding energies of two deuterium nuclei $= 2 \times 2.2 = 4.4$ MeV and the binding energy of ${}_{2}^{4}$He $= 28$ MeV. The binding energies involved in this process are shown schematically in Fig. 1.10. Thus, from energy conservation, we can see that about 23.6 MeV of energy will be released in this process.

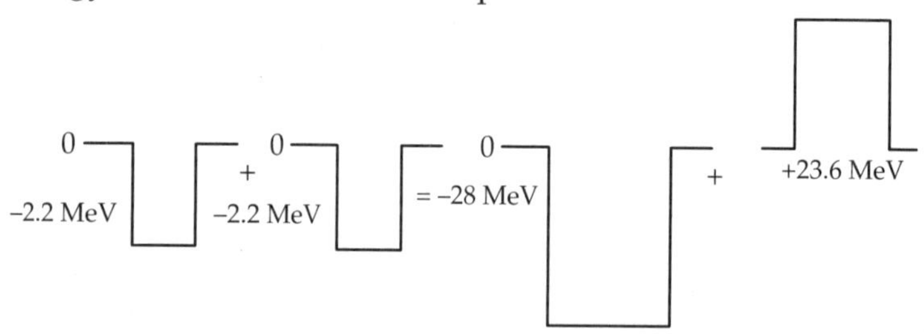

Figure 1.10: *Energy released in fusion, a schematic representation*

In the fission process, a heavy nucleus splits into nuclei of medium size. In this case also, the total binding energy of the product nuclei formed is greater than that of the original nucleus. Therefore, the excess energy is released. For example, consider the following fission process

$${}_{92}^{235}\text{U} \longrightarrow {}_{56}^{144}\text{Ba} + {}_{36}^{89}\text{Kr} + 2n$$

The binding energy of U $\approx 235 \times 7$ MeV and the total binding energy of the product nuclei $\approx 235 \times 8$ MeV. Thus, the gain in energy is $\backsim 200$ MeV.

From the above discussion, we note that *whenever the binding energy in the final state is larger than that of the initial state, energy will be released.*

1.5.3 Fall of BE Curve at Small and Large Values of A

Another feature of the binding energy curve is that it falls at small and high values of *A*. The fall of *BE* at higher *A* can be explained as a Coulomb effect. The

Coulomb repulsion acting between each pair of protons tries to keep them apart. On the other hand, the nuclear force is attractive and also very strong. The strong and attractive nuclear force tries to assemble the nucleons in a small region, while the Coulomb force tries to disrupt the nucleus. Thus, the stability of the nucleus results from the balance between the repulsive force between the protons and the attractive force among the nucleons. The Coulomb energy acting among the protons increases as Z^2, and for larger A, its contribution becomes larger, resulting in a decrease in the binding energy of the nucleus. For a heavy nucleus, the repulsion is too large to disrupt the stability of the nucleus, and as a result, it disintegrates spontaneously.

The fall of BE at small A is due to the fact that full binding is achieved only when each nucleon is completely surrounded by other nucleons. Light nuclei have a greater fraction of their nucleons on the surface. The nucleons lying on the surface are not well surrounded by other nucleons, and thus, full binding is not achieved. As a result, the binding energy is reduced.

1.5.4 Mass Defect and Packing Fraction

The mass of an atom can be measured very accurately. It has been observed that the atomic mass is very close to whole numbers (known as the mass number). For light nuclei with $A < 20$ and for heavy nuclei with $A > 180$, the atomic masses are slightly greater than the corresponding whole numbers, while for $20 < A < 180$, the atomic masses are slightly less than the corresponding mass number. The difference between the measured atomic mass $M(A,Z)$ and the mass number A is known as **mass defect** $\triangle M$ (not mass excess).

$$\triangle M = M(A,Z) - A$$

Packing fraction (f) is the mass defect per nucleon, that is

$$f = \frac{\triangle M}{A} = \frac{M(A,Z)}{A} - 1 \tag{1.9}$$

Thus, f is positive for very light nuclei and decreases rapidly with increasing A. It becomes negative for $A > 20$, with a minimum value at $A \sim 56$. Then it rises slowly with A and again becomes positive for $A > 180$.

Illustrative Example 1.18: Calculation of packing fraction

Calculate the packing fraction of ${}^{4}_{2}He$, ${}^{12}_{6}C$ and ${}^{85}_{37}Rb$.

Solution Mass of ${}^{4}_{2}He$ is 4.002603. Mass defect $= 4.002603 - 4 = 0.002603$ and the packing fraction is $\frac{0.002603}{4} = 0.00065075$.

Mass of ${}^{12}_{6}C$ is 12.000000. Thus, the mass defect is $12.000000 - 12 = 0.000000$ and the packing fraction is 0.00.

Mass of $^{85}_{37}$Rb is 84.911799. Thus, the mass defect is 84.911799 − 85 = −0.088201 and the packing fraction = −0.001037659.

The mass of $^{A}_{Z}X$ can be expressed as $M(A,Z) = (1+f)A$ (1.10)

The relation between the binding energy and packing fraction can be established from Eq. (1.8).

$$\begin{aligned} BE(A,Z) &= [ZM(^1_1\text{H}) + (A-Z)M_n - M(A,Z)]c^2 \\ BE(A,Z)/c^2 &= Z(1+f_H)\times 1 + (A-Z)(1+f_n)\times 1 - (1+f)\times A \\ &= Z\times f_H + (A-Z)\times f_n - f\times A \end{aligned} \tag{1.11}$$

Expressing mass in energy units, we can write

$$\frac{BE(A,Z)}{A} = \frac{Z\times f_H + (A-Z)\times f_n}{A} - f, \tag{1.12}$$

where $f_H = 0.00782$ u and $f_n = 0.008665$ u. The first term on the RHS is nearly constant, and thus, the BE curve and the packing fraction curve, shown in Fig. 1.11, are complementary in appearance.

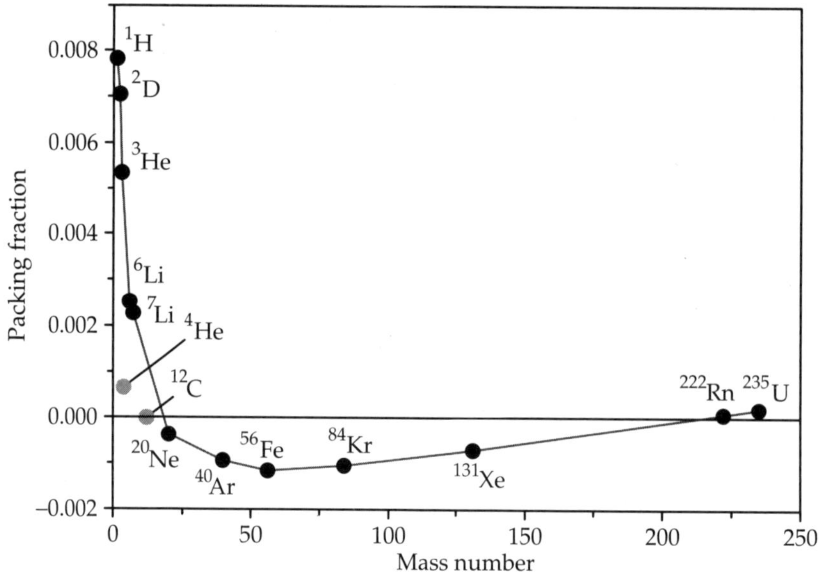

Figure 1.11: *Packing fraction vs mass number: It is negative for* $20 < A < 180$

Illustrative Example 1.19: ^{16}O mass scale

On a physical scale, the masses of the hydrogen atom and neutrons are 1.008142 and 1.008982 amu, respectively. Calculate the packing fraction and the binding energy per nucleon of the ^{16}O nucleus.

Solution In the given scale, the mass of the ^{16}O nucleus is 16. Thus, the packing fraction is zero.

The binding energy per nucleon can be calculated from Eq. (1.12):

$$\frac{BE(A,Z)}{A} = \frac{Z \times f_H + (A-Z) \times f_n}{A} - f$$

$$= \frac{8 \times 0.008142 + 8 \times 0.008982}{16} = 0.008562 \approx 7.97 \text{ MeV}$$

1.5.5 Nucleon Separation Energy

The energy required to separate a single neutron from the nucleus is known as **neutron separation energy** (S_n). Thus

$$S_n = [M(^{A-1}_{Z}X) + M_n - M(^{A}_{Z}X)] \times c^2$$

Using Eq. (1.8), we get

$$M(^{A}_{Z}X) = ZM_p + (A-Z)M_n - BE(^{A}_{Z}X)/c^2$$

And $M(^{A-1}_{Z}X) = ZM_p + (A-1-Z)M_n - BE(^{A-1}_{Z}X)/c^2$

We get $S_n = BE(^{A}_{Z}X) - BE(^{A-1}_{Z}X)$ (1.13)

If $S_n > 0$, the nucleus is stable against neutron decay, and if it is < 0, the nucleus is unstable so that neutron emission is energetically possible.

Similarly, the proton separation energy is given by

$$S_p = BE(^{A}_{Z}X) - BE(^{A-1}_{Z-1}Y) \tag{1.14}$$

And the α separation energy is given by

$$\begin{aligned} S_\alpha &= [M(^{A-4}_{Z-2}Y) + M(^{4}_{2}\text{He}) - M(^{A}_{Z}X)] \times c^2 \\ &= BE(^{A}_{Z}X) - BE(^{A-4}_{Z-2}Y) - BE(^{4}_{2}\text{He}) \end{aligned} \tag{1.15}$$

Illustrative Example 1.20: Comparison of S_n and S_p

(a) Find the energy required to remove a single neutron from the nucleus of $^{42}_{20}$Ca.

(b) Find the energy required to remove a proton from the same nucleus of $^{42}_{20}$Ca.

Given: $m_p = 1.0078$ u, $m_n = 1.0087$ u, $M(^{42}_{20}\text{Ca}) = 41.958622$ u, $M(^{41}_{20}\text{Ca}) = 40.962278$ u, $M(^{41}_{19}\text{K}) = 40.961825$ u

Solution (a) $S_n = M(^{41}_{20}\text{Ca}) + m_n - M(^{42}_{20}\text{Ca}) = 11.51$ MeV
(b) $S_p = M(^{41}_{19}\text{K}) + m_p - M(^{42}_{20}\text{Ca}) = 10.67$ MeV
Note that $S_n > S_p$.

Illustrative Example 1.21: Deuteron separation energy

Find the energy required to remove a deuteron $^{2}_{1}$H from the nucleus.

Solution $S_d = [M(^{A-2}_{Z-1}Y) + M(^{2}_{1}\text{H}) - M(^{A}_{Z}X)] \times c^2 = BE(^{A}_{Z}X) - BE(^{A-2}_{Z-1}Y) - BE(^{2}_{1}\text{H})$, where Eq. (1.8) has been used.

Illustrative Example 1.22: α separation energy for large A

(a) Find the binding energy of ${}^{210}_{84}$Po and ${}^{206}_{82}$Pb.

(b) Calculate the α separation energy of ${}^{210}_{84}$Po.

Given: $m_p = 1.007825$ u, $m_n = 1.008665$ u, $M({}^{210}_{84}\text{Po}) = 209.982876$ u, $M({}^{206}_{82}\text{Po}) = 205.974455$ u, $BE({}^{4}_{2}\text{He}) = 28.80$ MeV

Solution (a) The binding energy of ${}^{210}_{84}$Po is $= [84 \times m_p + 126 \times m_n - M({}^{210}_{84}\text{Po})] \times c^2 =$ 1645.2107 MeV.

Binding energy per nucleon is 7.8343 MeV
Binding energy of ${}^{206}_{82}$Pb is = 1622.3342 MeV
Binding energy per nucleon is 7.8754 MeV.

(b) α separation energy is

$S_\alpha = BE({}^{210}_{84}\text{Po}) - BE({}^{206}_{82}\text{Po}) - BE({}^{4}_{2}\text{He}) = 1645.2107 - 1622.3342 - 28.8 = -5.9235$ MeV

The negative sign implies that ${}^{210}_{84}$Po will emit α particles spontaneously. Note that the *very high binding energy of* ${}^{4}_{2}$He *plays a crucial role in* ${}^{4}_{2}$He *decay*. In fact, α emission is energetically possible in a heavy nucleus[7] when the mass of the parent nucleus is greater than the total mass of the disintegrating particles.

Check Progress 1.8: Why is an α particle, rather than a neutron or proton or deuteron, emitted from an unstable nucleus?

Before closing the discussion on separation energy, we need to mention a typical regularity in observed[8] S_n.

For a given Z, S_n is larger for nuclei with even N than with odd N. Similarly, for a given N, S_p is larger for even Z than odd Z. *This shows another property of nuclear force which produces extra binding between pairs of identical nucleons in the same state.* This effect is called the **pairing effect** and we will discuss it later. Pairing causes even–even nuclei (Z even and N even) to be more stable than even–odd or odd–odd nuclei.

Check Progress 1.9: Find the energies required to remove:

(a) A neutron from ${}^{4}_{2}$He

(b) Then a proton, and finally

(c) To separate the remaining neutron and proton.

Compare the total energy with the binding energy of ${}^{4}_{2}$He.

[7] ${}^{9}_{4}$Be is unstable against α decay (Cohen, BL. 2001. *Concepts of Nuclear Physics*, McGraw-Hill Education).

[8] See figure on neutron separation energy of lead isotopes: (Meyerhof, WE. 1967. *Elements of Nuclear Physics*, McGraw-Hill).

1.5.6 Abundance of Stable Nuclei

In the nucleus, positively charged protons are confined to a small region, so the repulsive force acting among them is extremely large. On the other hand, neutrons interact with other nucleons only through strong attractive nuclear force. Thus, to overcome the repulsion among the protons and to form a stable nucleus, excess of neutrons over protons is necessary. However, all combinations of neutrons and protons do not result in a stable nucleus. Figure 1.12 shows the Segre chart,[9] which presents the stable isotopes in the $Z-N$ plane.

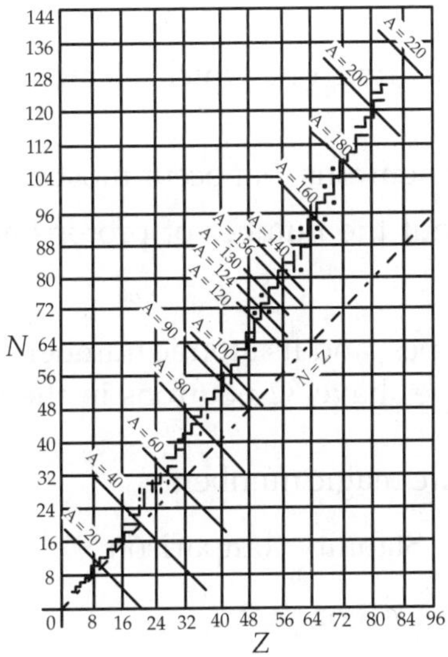

Figure 1.12: *Beta stable nuclei in the $Z-N$ plane*

Significant points

- For light nuclei, the average line of stability clusters around $N = Z$. Thus, they have approximately equal numbers of neutrons and protons. For higher Z, it departs more and more from the $N = Z$ line, showing the greater importance of the Coulomb force.

Table 1.1: *Frequency of occurrence of stable nuclei*

Proton no.	Neutron no.	No. of stable nuclei
Even	Even	160
Even	Odd	53
Odd	Even	49
Odd	Odd	4

- For more than half of the stable nuclides, both Z and N are even numbers. The frequency of occurrence of stable nuclides is shown in Table 1.1.

[9]Evans, RD. 2003. *The Atomic Nucleus*, Krieger Publishing Company.

In nature, even–even nuclei have been found to be the most stable, and hence, more abundant than nuclei with odd A.

- Points to the right of the stability region represent unstable nuclei having excess of protons or a deficiency of neutrons. Their most probable decay is of the β^+ or electron capture type. Points to the left of the stability region represent unstable nuclei having excess of neutrons or a deficiency of protons. Their most probable decay is of the β^- type.

Illustrative Example 1.23: The stability curve

(a) From the stability curve, find out which element has the largest number of isotopes.

(b) Also find the number of neutrons that occur most frequently.

(c) What do you notice about the number of protons and neutrons in each of the above cases?

Solution (a) Tin has 10 isotopes, and its atomic number 50 is a magic number.
(b) A total of 7 stable isotopes have 82 neutrons in the nucleus, more than for any other number of neutrons.
(c) The numbers 50 and 82 are magic numbers.

Illustrative Example 1.24: Stability comparison

Which nucleus is more stable, ${}^{11}_{5}\text{B}$ or ${}^{11}_{6}\text{C}$?

Solution ${}^{11}_{5}\text{B}$ is stable, with $Z = 5$ and $N = 6$. ${}^{11}_{6}\text{C}$ with $Z = 6$ and $N = 5$ is unstable because it has a larger number of protons than neutrons. *In all stable nuclei, $N \geq Z$, except in ${}^{3}_{2}He$.*

Illustrative Example 1.25: Stability comparison

Which nucleus is more stable, ${}^{12}_{5}\text{B}$ or ${}^{12}_{6}\text{C}$?

Solution For ${}^{12}_{5}\text{B}$, $Z = 5$ and $N = 7$. For ${}^{12}_{6}\text{C}$, $Z = 6$ and $N = 6$.

For both of these nuclei, $N \geq Z$. Nucleons, being fermions, obey the Pauli Exclusion Principle. As a result, each nuclear energy level can contain two nucleons of the same type having opposite spins. The energy levels are filled in sequence, just as with the atomic case, to achieve minimum energy configuration.

The boron isotope ${}^{12}_{5}\text{B}$ has more energy than the carbon isotope ${}^{12}_{6}\text{C}$, because one of the neutrons in ${}^{12}_{5}\text{B}$ is in the higher energy level. Thus, ${}^{12}_{6}\text{C}$ is more stable than ${}^{12}_{5}\text{B}$.

Check Progress 1.10: Which nucleus would you expect to be more stable, ${}^{7}_{3}\text{Li}$ or ${}^{8}_{3}\text{Li}$; ${}^{13}_{6}\text{C}$ or ${}^{15}_{6}\text{C}$?

Illustrative Example 1.26: Excess of proton or neutron?

Both ${}^{14}_{8}O$ and ${}^{19}_{8}O$ undergo beta decay. Which would you expect to emit a positron and which an electron? Why?

Solution For ${}^{14}_{8}O$, $Z = 8$ and $N = 6$. So, it has a deficiency of neutrons (or an excess of protons). Thus, it will emit positrons so that the proton number decreases and the neutron number increases. On the other hand, in the ${}^{19}_{8}O$ nucleus, there is an excess of neutrons. So it will emit electrons.

1.5.7 Coulomb Energy of the Nucleus

We may assume that the nucleus ${}^{A}_{Z}X$ is a uniformly charged sphere of radius R with total charge $+Ze$. Therefore, the density ρ of the nucleus is

$$\rho = \frac{Ze}{4/3\pi R^3} = \text{constant}$$

Suppose the sphere is composed of a large number of thin spherical layers. Consider one such layer of radius r. The amount of charge required to form a layer of thickness dr is given by

$$dq = \rho \times 4\pi r^2 dr$$

Now, the work done in forming this layer is

$$dW = \frac{1}{4\pi\varepsilon_0}\frac{qdq}{r} = \frac{1}{4\pi\varepsilon_0} \times \frac{4}{3}\pi \times \rho^2 \times 4\pi r^4 dr$$

Therefore, the total work done in forming a thickness of radius R is

$$W = \frac{1}{4\pi\varepsilon_0}\frac{4}{3}\pi \times \rho^2 \times 4\pi \int_0^R r^4 dr$$

Integrating and substituting the value of ρ, we get $W = \frac{3}{5}\frac{1}{4\pi\varepsilon_0}\frac{Z^2e^2}{R}$.

If $Z = 1$, $W = \frac{3}{5}\frac{1}{4\pi\varepsilon_0}\frac{e^2}{R}$, but there is no field to work against. So this part must be subtracted. Therefore, the energy of the ${}^{A}_{Z}X$ nucleus is

$$\frac{3}{5}\frac{1}{4\pi\varepsilon_0}\frac{(Z^2-1)e^2}{R}$$

For a large Z, it is $\approx \frac{3}{5}\frac{1}{4\pi\varepsilon_0}\frac{Z(Z-1)e^2}{R}$.

Check Progress 1.11: Calculate the Coulomb energy of ${}^{73}_{32}Ge$.

Illustrative Example 1.27: Binding energy without Coulomb energy

(a) Calculate the binding energies of ${}^{3}_{1}H$ and ${}^{3}_{2}He$. Given $m_p = 1.007825$ u, $m_n = 1.008665$ u, $M({}^{3}_{1}H) = 3.016050$ u, $M({}^{3}_{2}He) = 3.016029$ u

(b) Also calculate the Coulomb energy of two protons in the ${}_2^3$He nucleus and show that the difference in the binding energies is of the order of the Coulomb energy of two protons. Hence comment on the dependence of nuclear force on electric charge.

Solution (a) $BE({}_1^3\text{H}) = 1 \times 1.007825 + 2 \times 1.008665 - 3.016050\ \text{u} \approx 8.48\ \text{MeV}$

$BE({}_2^3\text{He}) = 2 \times 1.007825 + 1 \times 1.008665 - 3.016029\ \text{u} \approx 7.72\ \text{MeV}$

Thus, $BE({}_1^3\text{H}) - BE({}_2^3\text{He}) = 0.76$ MeV.

(b) In ${}_1^3$H, Coulomb energy is zero, and in ${}_2^3$He, Coulomb energy is $\frac{1}{4\pi\varepsilon_0}\frac{e^2}{R}$, where $R = 1.2 \times 3^{1/3} = 1.73$ fm. Thus, Coulomb energy is $1.44/1.73 = 0.83$ MeV.

The results show that the difference in the binding energies is of the order of the difference of Coulomb energies, and the Coulomb energy is responsible for the lowering of binding energy in ${}_2^3$He.

Illustrative Example 1.28: Coulomb energy difference of nuclei with the same A

(a) Calculate the binding energies of ${}_8^{15}$O and ${}_7^{15}$N. Given $m_p = 1.007825$ u, $m_n = 1.008665$ u, $M({}_8^{15}\text{O}) = 15.003065$ u, $M({}_7^{15}\text{N}) = 15.000109$ u

(b) Also calculate the Coulomb energy difference between these two nuclei.

Solution (a) $BE({}_8^{15}\text{O}) = 8 \times 1.007825 + 7 \times 1.008665 - 15.003065\ \text{u} \approx 111.96\ \text{MeV}$

$BE({}_7^{15}\text{N}) = 7 \times 1.007825 + 8 \times 1.008665 - 15.000109\ \text{u} \approx 115.49\ \text{MeV}$

Thus, $BE({}_7^{15}\text{N}) - BE({}_8^{15}\text{O}) = 3.53$ MeV.

(b) Coulomb energy of ${}_8^{15}$O is $\frac{3}{5}\frac{1}{4\pi\varepsilon_0}\frac{8^2 \times e^2}{R} = 16.17$ MeV, where $R \approx 3.42$ fm

Coulomb energy of ${}_7^{15}$N is $\frac{3}{5}\frac{1}{4\pi\varepsilon_0}\frac{7^2 \times e^2}{R} = 12.38$ MeV, where $R \approx 3.42$ fm

Thus, the Coulomb energy difference is ≈ 3.79 MeV, which is close to the difference in their binding energies.

1.5.8 Coulomb Energy Difference of Mirror Nuclei and Charge Symmetry of Nuclear Force

Pairs of nuclei for which $Z_1 = n_1, N_1 = n_2$ and $Z_2 = n_2, N_2 = n_1$, where n_1 and n_2 are integers with $n_2 - n_1 = 1$ are called mirror nuclei. Examples include ${}_3^7$Li and ${}_4^7$Be, ${}_7^{15}$N and ${}_8^{15}$O, ${}_6^{13}$C and ${}_7^{13}$N, ${}_{19}^{39}$K and ${}_{20}^{39}$Ca, etc.

The Coulomb energy of the ${}_Z^AX$ nucleus is $\frac{3}{5}\frac{1}{4\pi\varepsilon_0}\frac{(Z^2-1) \times e^2}{R}$ and the Coulomb energy of the ${}_{Z+1}^{A}Y$ nucleus is $\frac{3}{5}\frac{1}{4\pi\varepsilon_0}\frac{((Z+1)^2-1) \times e^2}{R}$.

Therefore, $\triangle E_c = \frac{3}{5}\frac{1}{4\pi\varepsilon_0}\frac{(2Z+1)\times e^2}{R}$. Since Z represents the lower atomic number, the N of that nucleus must be $Z+1$ and the mass number $A = 2Z+1$.
With $R = R_0 A^{1/3}$, we get

$$\triangle E_c = \frac{3}{5}\frac{1}{4\pi\varepsilon_0}\frac{A^{2/3}\times e^2}{R_0} \tag{1.16}$$

The Coulomb energy of mirror nuclei can be measured and be used to determine the nuclear radius[10].

From the study of the Coulomb energy difference of mirror nuclei, we observe that after correcting the Coulomb energy, the binding energies of the mirror nuclei are almost the same. From this observation, we obtain an important insight into nuclear force. Let us explain it with an example.

Charge symmetry and charge independence of nuclear force: Let us consider the schematic presentation of a pair of mirror nuclei, $^7_3$Li and $^7_4$Be, as shown in Table 1.2. For $^7_3$Li, $Z = 3$ and $N = 4$, and for $^7_4$Be, $Z = 4$ and $N = 3$.

Table 1.2: *Arrangement of neutrons and protons in* $^7_3$Li *and* $^7_4$Be

	⊗	○	
○	⊗	○	⊗
○	⊗	○	⊗
○	⊗	○	⊗
$^7_3$Li		$^7_4$Be	

(○ represents protons and ⊗ represents neutrons)

The nuclear bonds in these nuclei are identical, except for those of the last odd nucleon. For $^7_3$Li, the last odd nucleon is a neutron and the interactions with the last nucleon are $3(n-n)$ and $3(n-p)$. For $^7_4$Be, the last odd nucleon is a proton and the interactions with the last nucleon are $3(p-p)$ and $3(p-n)$. Equality of the binding energies (excluding the Coulomb energy) of the two nuclei implies

$$F(p-p) = F(n-n)$$

The **charge symmetry** of nuclear force means that the proton–proton interaction is identical to the neutron–neutron interaction (after correcting for the Coulomb force). Another piece of evidence in favour of this assertion comes from the equality of *pp* and *nn* scattering lengths and ranges.

The notion of **charge independence** is more general. Here, nuclear force must depend on A only and not on N or Z. In other words, after correcting for the Coulomb force between $p-p$, we get

$$F(p-p) = F(n-n) = F(n-p)$$

The experimental evidence for this follows from low-energy two-nucleon scattering.

[10]Please see Chapter 2.

1.6 SPIN AND PARITY

Like electrons, neutrons and protons are also fermions and have an intrinsic angular momentum of $\frac{\hbar}{2}$. The total angular momentum of a nucleus is the vector sum of the angular momenta (orbital plus spin) of its constituent nucleons and is usually called **nuclear spin** (even though it has orbital as well as spin contributions). Nuclear spin is expressed as I (in units of $\hbar$).

For even-A nuclei: I is an integer (including zero)

For odd-A nuclei: I is a half-integer

For example, the spin of ${}^2_1\text{H}$ is $I = 1$ and the spin of ${}^7_3\text{Li}$ is $I = \frac{3}{2}$.

Parity[11]**:** Parity transformation is an inversion of coordinates. Under parity transformation, the point (x,y,z) will be transformed into $(-x,-y,-z)$, that is, a right-handed coordinate system will be changed to a left-handed coordinate system.

The Hamiltonian operator for a nuclear system has the general form

$$H = -\sum_i \frac{\hbar^2}{2m_i}\left(\frac{\partial^2}{\partial x_i^2} + \frac{\partial^2}{\partial y_i^2} + \frac{\partial^2}{\partial z_i^2}\right) + V(x_i, y_i, z_i), \tag{1.17}$$

where the first term represents the kinetic energy operator while the second term describes the potential energy operator of the system. The first term involves the square of ∂x_i, ∂y_i and ∂z_i and the potential energy term depends only on the mutual arrangement of the particles, which will not be changed under the inversion of the coordinates. Thus, the Hamiltonian remains unchanged under the operation

$$(x_i, y_i, z_i) \rightarrow (-x_i, -y_i, -z_i)$$

As the Schrödinger equation is symmetric under the parity operation, we expect the physical properties of the system to be unaffected by such transformation. One such physical result is probability density $|\psi|^2$. The probability of finding a particle in unit volume at any instant must not depend on whether the measurement is carried out using a right-handed or a left-handed coordinate system. Thus, we expect

$$|\psi(x,y,z)|^2 = |\psi(-x,-y,-z)|^2$$

This requirement is satisfied, if

$$\psi(x,y,z) = +\psi(-x,-y,-z) \quad (\text{even parity}) \quad \text{or}$$

$$\psi(x,y,z) = -\psi(-x,-y,-z) \quad (\text{odd parity})$$

Thus, the eigenfunction of the Schrödinger equation must have a definite parity (either even or odd).

In spherical polar coordinates, the parity operation changes the wave function as

$$\psi(r,\theta,\phi) \longrightarrow \psi(r,\pi-\theta,\pi+\phi) \text{ and } |\psi(r,\theta,\phi)|^2 = |\psi(r,\pi-\theta,\pi+\phi)|^2$$

It is equivalent to reflection on the x–y plane followed by rotation about the z axis by an angle of π. Parity transforms a wave function, which is an eigenfunction of the angular momentum operator (L^2), as

[11] Also see Appendix B for a detailed discussion.

$\psi(r,\theta,\phi) \longrightarrow (-1)^l \psi(r,\theta,\phi)$, where l is the orbital angular momentum.
We cannot assign the parity of each nucleon. Like spin (I), we regard parity (π) as an overall parity of the whole nucleus. The parity π is represented as I^π, superscript of the spin I.

Illustrative Example 1.29: Function having a definite parity

Let us consider a function: $f(\theta) = a + b\cos\theta + c\cos^2\theta$. Explain that the function $f(\theta)$ will have a definite parity if $b = 0$.

Solution To have definite parity, $|f(\theta)|^2 = |f(r, \pi-\theta, \pi+\phi)|^2$
Therefore $|a + b\cos\theta + c\cos^2\theta|^2 = |a + b\cos(\pi-\theta) + c\cos^2(\pi-\theta)|^2 = |a - b\cos\theta + c\cos^2\theta|^2$, which holds only when $b = 0$.

1.7 ELECTRIC AND MAGNETIC MOMENTS

Potential, at any distant point due to some arbitrary charge distribution, can be expanded as

$$V = V_{\text{monopole}} + V_{\text{dipole}} + V_{\text{quadrupole}} + \dots,$$

where V_{monopole} represents the potential due to the monopole moment, V_{dipole} represents the potential due to the dipole moment, and so on. The different terms in the expansion thus correspond to the potentials due to monopole, dipole, quadrupole, etc. located at the origin.

The **monopole moment** is a scalar and is given by

$$q = \text{net charge} = Ze,$$

where Z is the atomic number of the nucleus. The potential due to the monopole V_{monopole} drops as $\frac{1}{r}$.

The **dipole moment** is a vector, and for continuous volume charge distribution, the dipole moment is defined by

$$\vec{p} = \int\int\int \rho(\vec{r})\vec{r}\,d\tau \tag{1.18}$$

The potential due to the dipole V_{dipole} drops as $\frac{1}{r^2}$.

The nuclear charge density is

$$\rho(\vec{r}) \propto |\psi|^2,$$

where $|\psi|^2$ refers to the probability density of protons. Since nuclear states have definite parity, $|\psi|^2$ is always even, and thus, the integrand $\rho(\vec{r})\vec{r}$ in Eq. (1.18) is an odd function and the integral vanishes. Therefore, the dipole moment of the nucleus in the ground state must be zero.

Another electrical property of the nucleus is the **electric quadrupole moment**, which gives a measure of the deviation of charge distribution from spherical symmetry. The **quadrupole moment** is a tensor of rank 2 and is defined by

$$Q_{ij} = \int \rho(\vec{r})(3x_i x_j - r^2 \delta_{ij}) d\tau$$

For spherically symmetric charge distribution, the quadrupole moment $Q_{11} = Q_{22} = Q_{33} = 0$. If the charge distribution is extended along the z direction (*prolate shape*), then the quadrupole moment $Q_{33} > 0$, and for *oblate shape* (height < radius) the quadrupole moment $Q_{33} < 0$.

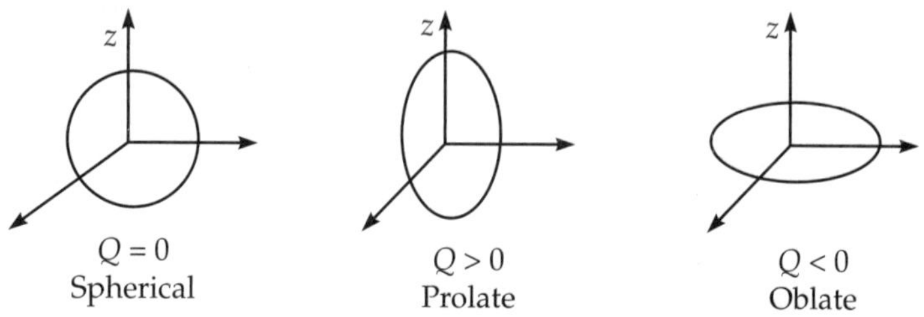

Figure 1.13: *Spherical, prolate- and oblate-shaped charge distributions with respect to the z axis*

To calculate the average value of any electric or magnetic moment, we need to evaluate an integral of the form $\int \psi^* \hat{O} \psi$, where $\hat{O}$ is the appropriate electromagnetic operator. $\psi^* \psi$ is always an even function and does not change under parity operation. However, if $\hat{O}$ has odd parity, then the integrand will be an odd function, and the integral must vanish identically. Therefore *all odd parity multipole moments must vanish.*

The parity of electric moments is $(-1)^L$ and for magnetic moments, it is $(-1)^{L+1}$, where L is the order of the moment. $L = 0$ for monopole; $L = 1$ for dipole; $L = 2$ for quadrupole, etc. All electric moments of odd order ($L = 1, 3,$ etc.) and magnetic moments of even order ($L = 0, 2,$ etc.) must vanish. Thus, the electric dipole moment, magnetic quadrupole moment, and so on, will vanish.

Magnetic moments: Like electrons, protons and neutrons also have intrinsic angular momentum (spin) and corresponding magnetic moments. For an electron, it is given by

$$\mu = g_s s \mu_B, \tag{1.19}$$

where $s = \dfrac{1}{2}$ and $\mu_B = \dfrac{e\hbar}{2m}$ is the Bohr magneton, m being the mass of the electron. The quantity g_s is the spin g-factor and can be determined from relativistic quantum mechanics. For a *spin-$\frac{1}{2}$ particle*, the Dirac equation gives $g_s = 2$. For electrons, the experimental value is very close to the theoretical value.

A relation similar to Eq. (1.19) can be used to define the nuclear magnetic moment as

$$\mu = g_s s \mu_N, \tag{1.20}$$

where $\mu_N = \dfrac{e\hbar}{2m_p}$ is the nuclear magneton, m_p being the mass of the proton. In this case also, the expected value of g_s is 2. However, the experimental values of magnetic moments for free nucleons are far from the expected values:

Proton: $g_s = 5.5856912 \pm 0.0000022$

Neutron: $g_s = -3.8260837 \pm 0.0000018$

Not only is the g_s for protons far from the expected value of 2 for a point particle, the uncharged neutron also has a non-zero magnetic moment! This is perhaps the first evidence that the nucleons are not point particles like electrons; they must have some internal structure. It is interesting to note that the measured value of g_s for protons is greater than its expected value by 3.6, while the measured value of g_s for neutrons is less by almost the same amount from its expected value (0). According to current theories, nucleons are considered to be composed of three quarks, and the magnetic moments of the constituent quarks combine to give the measured value of the magnetic moment for the nucleons.

1.8 PROPERTIES OF NUCLEAR FORCE

We may summarise the different aspects of nuclear force that we have discussed thus far.

(a) **Strong and attractive:** Nuclear force must be very strong and attractive so that it can overcome the large Coulomb repulsion of protons in the nucleus. It is completely different from the electromagnetic or gravitational forces. The larger value of the nuclear binding energy ($\backsim$ MeV) compared to the atomic binding energy ($\backsim$ eV) implies that the nuclear force holding the nucleons together in a small region is much stronger than the electromagnetic force holding the electrons in the atom.

(b) **Saturation of nuclear force:** The most striking feature of the BE curve is that for a medium-sized nucleus, the binding energy per nucleon (BE/A) has an almost constant value irrespective of the number of nucleons in the nuclei. The constancy of average binding energy refers to the saturation of nuclear force. A particular nucleon interacts only with a few nucleons surrounding it, and not with all the other nucleons present in the nucleus. Once a nucleon is surrounded by other nucleons, its energy becomes approximately fixed; it remains almost unaffected by the presence of an additional number of nucleons. In other words, nuclear force, like chemical bonds, saturates. Saturation means that the average binding energy attains a limit once a certain number of nucleons is assembled.

(c) **Extremely short range:** Nuclear force is extremely strong and attractive. Despite the strong attraction among nucleons, the nuclei do not seem to grow to be arbitrarily large. (Compare this with gravitational force, which holds together objects of astronomical size). This implies that nuclear force must have a very short range, that is, the region in which the force acts is limited to nuclear dimensions. Beyond this short range, the force falls off very rapidly.

The range of nuclear force can be inferred by studying the binding energy of deuteron and two-nucleon (n–p or p–p) scattering. It has been found that the range of nuclear force is of the order of 2 fm.

Saturation of nuclear force is closely related to the short-range nature of nuclear interactions. The constancy of BE/A for a medium-sized nucleus suggests that nuclear force cannot have a long range. If the nuclear interaction were long-ranged, then the average binding energy (BE/A) would be a function of A.

Another consequence of the short-range nature of the nuclear force is the constant nuclear density. The density of nucleons (A/V) is approximately constant, irrespective of the number of nucleons present in the nucleus. This means that the number of nucleons surrounding a given nucleon is also constant. This suggests that the average binding energy of a nucleon must be constant, because the nuclear force is of short range and does not act beyond the neighbouring nucleons.

(d) **Repulsive core:** Nuclear force has a repulsive core, when the separation between the nucleons is too short (≈ 0.5 fm). Otherwise, the nucleus would not exist, it would simply collapse. The repulsive term in the nuclear force keeps the nucleons at a certain average separation.

(e) **Charge independent:** The nuclear force between any two nucleons does not depend on whether the nucleons are protons or neutrons.

$$F(p-p) = F(n-n) = F(p-n)$$

In another words, the nuclear force is charge independent.

We now mention some other important properties.

(f) **Spin dependent:** Nuclear force depends on whether the spins of the nucleons are parallel or antiparallel. For example, consider the deuteron nucleus $^2_1$H consisting of a proton and a neutron. The spins of the neutron and proton in this nucleus are always parallel so that total spin is 1. Spin 0 deuteron does not exist. Thus, a neutron and a proton with parallel spins form a bound nucleus, deuteron. However, the same proton and neutron with antiparallel spins do not have a bound state. This implies that nuclear force depends strongly on the spins of the interacting nucleons.

(g) **Non-central part:** The nucleon–nucleon forces have a non-central (called *tensor*) component. This part of the force does not conserve orbital angular momentum, which is a constant of motion under central forces.

The evidence for this non-central nature of nuclear force comes primarily from the study of the deuteron problem. The deuteron nucleus ($^2_1$H) is the simplest nucleus after hydrogen. It is a loosely bound system of a neutron and a proton with a binding energy of 2.22 MeV. It has been observed that the spin (I) and parity (π) of deuteron is $I^\pi = 1^+$ and its magnetic moment is $\mu = 0.8574376\,\mu_N$. It also has a very small positive quadrupole moment: $Q = 0.00288\,b$.

The existence of deuteron in the triplet state (with $S = 1$, that is, a neutron and a proton with parallel spins) and the absence of an analogous nucleus in the singlet state (with $S = 0$, that is, a neutron and a proton with antiparallel spins) leads to an important conclusion about the spin dependence of nuclear force. It reveals that, while describing a nuclear interaction, we will not confine ourselves to a simple central potential $V_0(r)$, but we must introduce a function depending on the spins of the interacting nucleons as well. From the spins $\vec{s}_1$ and $\vec{s}_2$ of interacting nucleons, we can form a scalar $\vec{s}_1 \cdot \vec{s}_2$, which may be used to characterise the interaction between a proton and a neutron (the potential must be a scalar as it is an energy). Thus, taking spin dependence into account, the form of the nuclear potential can be written as

$$V = V_0(r) + V_\sigma(r)(\vec{\sigma}_1 \cdot \vec{\sigma}_2), \tag{1.21}$$

where $\vec{s}_1 = \dfrac{1}{2}\hbar\vec{\sigma}_1$ and $\vec{s}_2 = \dfrac{1}{2}\hbar\vec{\sigma}_2$, $\vec{\sigma}_1$ and $\vec{\sigma}_2$ being the Pauli spin matrices.

The quadrupole moment of deuteron also gives very important information about the nature of nuclear force. The positive quadrupole moment of a deuteron indicates that the distribution of charge is not spherically symmetric. It assumes a prolate shape, where the charge distribution is stretched along the direction of its spin. In other words, a neutron and a proton form a bound state only when the spins of both the nucleons are directed along its axis. Thus, the force between two nucleons depends not only on their separation, but also on the relative orientation of spins with respect to the line joining them. This is explained in Fig. 1.14. This type of interaction is said to be a **tensor interaction**.

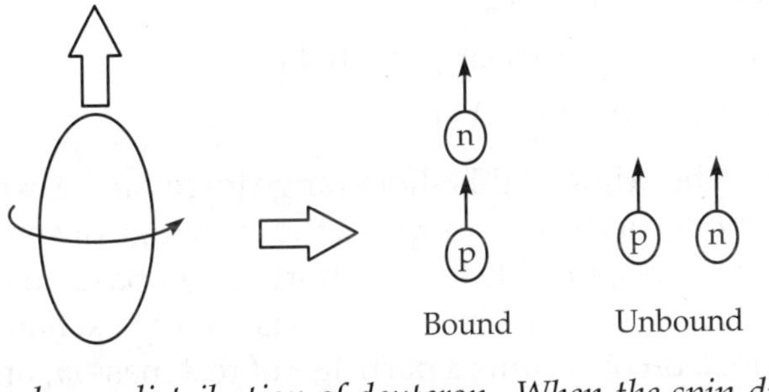

Figure 1.14: *Prolate charge distribution of deuteron. When the spin direction is along the line joining the nucleons, the force is attractive, but when they are perpendicular, the force is repulsive.*

Additional support for the tensor force comes from consideration of the magnetic moment of deuteron. In the ground state of deuteron, $l = 0$, total spin $S = 1$, $I = l + S = 1$ and parity is $(-1)^l = (-1)^0 = +1$. We thus expect that the total magnetic moment of deuteron in the ground state must be the sum of the magnetic moments of proton and neutron. However, it has been observed that

$$\mu_p + \mu_n - \mu_d = -0.0223\mu_N$$

This difference is small but very significant. It implies that the assumption that deuteron is in the $l = 0$ state is not completely correct; there must be some other orbital momentum in deuteron.

In general, the total angular momentum (I) is

$$\vec{I} = \vec{l} + \vec{S}$$

Since for deuteron, $S = 1$ and $I = 1$, l can only be 0, 1 and 2. However, the conservation of parity demands that even and odd values of l cannot both be present in the same wave function. Thus, only $l = 2$ can be present with $l = 0$. The wave function can then be written as

$$\psi = a_0\psi_{1s} + a_2\psi_{1d}, \tag{1.22}$$

where ψ_{1s} and ψ_{1d} correspond to the wave functions in the $l = 0$ and $l = 2$ states, respectively. It turns out that the experimental results of quadrupole moment and magnetic moment can be explained with

$$|a_0|^2 = 0.96 \text{ and } |a_2|^2 = 0.04$$

This implies that the deuteron is in the $l = 0$ state about 96% of the time, while it spends only 4% of its time in the $l = 2$ state.

Wave functions with mixed l result from the non-central potentials. The potential is thus not merely a function of r alone (where l is conserved), it must also be a function of θ. The force corresponding to this potential is called the **tensor force**.

The tensor force of nuclear interaction can be described by a potential

$$V = V_T(r)S_{12}$$

where $S_{12} = 3(\vec{\sigma}_1 \cdot \hat{r})(\vec{\sigma}_2 \cdot \hat{r}) - (\vec{\sigma}_1 \cdot \vec{\sigma}_2)$.

Thus, the general form of nuclear potential is

$$V = V_0(r) + V_\sigma(r)(\vec{\sigma}_1 \cdot \vec{\sigma}_2) + V_T(r)S_{12} \tag{1.23}$$

(h) **Exchange force:** The origin of this short-range force can be explained successfully in terms of the model according to which the exchange of something taking place between nucleons is responsible for the short range. Based on the observed range of the nuclear force, we can estimate the mass of the exchanged particle. Let us assume that a nucleon (N_1) emits a particle x of rest mass m_x and a second nucleon (N_2) absorbs it.

$$N_1 \longrightarrow N_1 + x$$

$$x + N_2 \longrightarrow N_2$$

These relations appear to violate the conservation of energy. However, the uncertainty principle comes to the rescue. We cannot be sure of energy conservation unless we measure it, and we cannot measure it more accurately than $\triangle E$ in time $\triangle t$, where $\triangle E \times \triangle E \approx \hbar$. We can therefore 'violate' the energy by an amount $\triangle E$ for a time interval $\triangle t$, where $\triangle t \approx \frac{\hbar}{\triangle E}$. The amount of energy that can be violated in the process stated above is $\triangle E = m_x c^2$. The longest distance travelled by this particle x is

$$\Delta s = c \times \Delta t = \frac{\hbar c}{m_x c^2} \quad \text{or } m_x c^2 \approx \frac{\hbar c}{\Delta s}$$

Assuming $\Delta s \approx 1.5$ fm, and inserting the value of $\hbar c$, we get $m_x c^2 \approx 130$ MeV. Thus, the expected mass of the exchanged particle is ~ 130 MeV.

The exchanged particles that mediate the nuclear force are called **mesons**. The lightest of the mesons, known as **pion**, is responsible for the long range (1.0 to 1.5 fm) part of the nuclear force. There are three types of pions: π^-, π^0 and π^+. They have zero spin and rest masses of ~ 135 MeV for π^0 and 139.6 MeV for π^- and π^+.

Four types of exchange forces have thus far been proposed to describe the interaction between the nucleons:

(i) **Ordinary or Wigner force:** This simply depends on the separation between two particles. In this case, $V = V(r)w$, where $w = 1$ for all states.

(ii) **Space exchange or Majorana force:** In this case, $V = V(r)M$, where the operator M has the effect of exchanging the space coordinates of two particles and is defined as

$$\begin{aligned} M\psi_{12} = \psi_{21} &= \psi_{12} \text{ for symmetric wave function} \\ &\quad \text{with respect to the exchange of positions of two particles} \\ &= -\psi_{12} \text{ for antisymmetric wave function} \\ &\quad \text{with respect to the exchange of positions of two particles} \end{aligned}$$

(iii) **Spin exchange or Bartlett force:** In this case, $V = V(r)B$, where the operator B interchanges the spins of two particles and is defined as

$$\begin{aligned} B\chi_{12} = B\chi(\sigma_1, \sigma_2) = \chi(\sigma_2, \sigma_1) &= \chi_{12} \text{ in triplet state (S = 1)} \\ &= -\chi_{12} \text{ in singlet state (S = 0)} \end{aligned}$$

(iv) **Space and spin exchange or Heisenberg force:** In this case, $V = V(r)H$, where the operator H interchanges both the spins and the space coordinates of two particles and is defined as

$$H\psi_{12}\chi_{12} = \psi_{21}\chi_{21} = (-1)^{l+S+1}\psi_{12}\chi_{12}$$

Check Progress 1.12:	What limits the size of a stable nucleus?

(Hint: Nuclear force, being short-ranged, falls off rapidly beyond a few nucleons. However, the Coulomb force between protons falls comparatively slowly, and hence, dominates the nuclear force beyond this range. This prevents nuclei from growing larger in size. Nuclear force is not only attractive, but is also repulsive for very small inter-nucleon separation. The existence of the repulsive part is essential to prevent the collapse of the nucleus).

SUMMARY

- **Constituents of the Nucleus**
  - (a) **Electron–Proton Model:** According to this model, a nucleus with mass number A and atomic number Z consists of A number of protons and $(A-Z)$ number of electrons. This model explains the observed mass and charge of the nucleus, but there are very strong arguments that electrons cannot exist inside the nucleus.
  - (b) **Inconsistency with Uncertainty Principle:** Since $\triangle x \approx 10^{-14}$ m, the kinetic energy of electrons would be $\geq$ 20 MeV, which has never been observed.
  - (c) **Inconsistency with Nuclear Spin:** The electron–proton model violates the prediction that nuclei with even A must have 0 or *integral* spin and those with odd A must have *half-integral* spin.
  - (d) **Inconsistency with Nuclear Magnetic Moment:** The electron–proton model predicts the nuclear moment $\backsim \mu_B = \dfrac{e\hbar}{2m}$, where m is the mass of the electron. However, the observed magnetic moment is $\backsim \mu_N = \dfrac{e\hbar}{2m_p}$, m_p being the mass of the proton.
  - (e) **Neutron–Proton Model:** A nucleus ${}^A_ZX$ contains Z number of protons and $A-Z$ neutrons.
- **Nuclear Size:** The radius of the ${}^A_ZX$ nucleus is $R = R_0A^{\frac{1}{3}}$, where $R_0 \approx 1.2$ fm.
- **Mass of Nucleus:** Atomic mass unit: $1\text{ u} = \dfrac{1}{12}M({}^{12}\text{C}) = 931.49\text{ MeV/c}^2$. Atomic mass is measured by the mass spectrograph. Ions of different mass follow circular paths of different radii in a magnetic field. In the Bainbridge mass spectrograph, the ions enter into the magnetic field with the same velocity and the mass scale is linear, as $m \propto R$. The density of the nucleus is very large $\left(\approx \times 10^{17}\dfrac{\text{kg}}{\text{m}^3}\right)$ and is the same for all nuclei.
- **Binding Energy:** It is the energy required to split the nucleus into its constituent particles or the energy released when free nucleons combine to form a bound state nucleus.

  $$BE({}^A_ZX) = [ZM_p + (A-Z)M_n - M({}^A_ZX)]c^2$$

  Essential features of the binding energy curve (BE/A vs A):
  - (a) $\dfrac{BE}{A}$ increases rapidly with increasing A. For a medium-sized nucleus, $20 < A < 200$, $\dfrac{BE}{A}$ remains almost constant at $\backsim$ 8 MeV.
  - (b) The curve has peaks at Z or N equal to $2, 8, 20, 28, 50, 82$ and 126. These are called magic numbers.
  - (c) The curve reaches its maximum at $A \backsim 56$ (for Fe-group elements).
  - (d) Energy will be released in any reaction if the binding energy in the final state is larger than that of the initial state. From this consideration, the energy released in fission or fusion can be explained.
- **Mass Defect and Packing Fraction:** Mass defect (not mass excess) $\triangle M$ = Difference between the measured atomic mass $M(A,Z)$ and the mass number A. Packing fraction (f) is the mass defect per nucleon.
- **Neutron Separation Energy** is $(S_n) = BE({}^A_ZX) - BE({}^{A-1}_{Z}X)$.
- **Proton Separation Energy** is $(S_p) = BE({}^A_ZX) - BE({}^{A-1}_{Z-1}Y)$.
- **Coulomb Energy of the Nucleus** for large Z, $\approx \dfrac{3}{5}\dfrac{1}{4\pi\varepsilon_0}\dfrac{Z(Z-1)e^2}{R}$.

- **Coulomb Energy Difference of Mirror Nuclei** is $\triangle E_c \approx \frac{3}{5}\frac{1}{4\pi\varepsilon_0}\frac{A^{2/3}e^2}{R_0}$.
- **Nuclear Force**
  - (a) Strong and attractive
  - (b) Saturates
  - (c) Short ranged
  - (d) Charge symmetric, $F(p-p) = F(n-n)$
  - (e) Charge independent, $F(p-p) = F(n-n) = F(p-n)$
  - (f) Must have a repulsive core
  - (g) Spin dependent
  - (h) Contains a non-central part
- **Spin and Parity:** Even-A nuclei: integral spin (including zero); Odd-A nuclei: half integral spin. Parity of nuclear state is $(-1)^l$, l being the orbital angular momentum.
- **Electric and Magnetic Moments**
  - (a) Electric dipole moment of the nucleus is zero.
  - (b) Quadrupole moment is zero for spherically symmetric charge distribution, positive for prolate-shaped and negative for oblate-shaped nucleus.

    Nuclear magnetic moment $\mu = g_s s \mu_N$, where $s = \frac{1}{2}$ and $\mu_N = \frac{e\hbar}{2m_p}$ is the nuclear magneton, m_p being the mass of the proton.

    Proton: $g_s = 5.5856912 \pm 0.0000022$

    Neutron: $g_s = -3.8260837 \pm 0.0000018$

REVIEW QUESTIONS AND PROBLEMS

Multiple Choice Questions

1. The intrinsic electric dipole moment of a nucleus ${}_Z^AX$
   (a) Increases with Z, but is independent of A
   (b) Decreases with Z, but is independent of A
   (c) Is always zero
   (d) Increases with Z and A [NET 2013]
2. Which one of the following is a fermion?
   (a) α particle (b) ${}_4^7$Be nucleus
   (c) Hydrogen atom (d) Deuteron [GATE 2014]
3. The radius of the ${}_{29}^{64}$Cu nucleus is measured as 4.8×10^{-13} cm. The radius of the ${}_{12}^{27}$Mg nucleus can be estimated to be
   (a) 2.8×10^{-13} cm (b) 5.2×10^{-13} cm
   (c) 3.6×10^{-13} cm (d) 8.6×10^{-13} cm [NET 2011]
4. The difference in the Coulomb energy between the mirror nuclei ${}_{24}^{49}$Cr and ${}_{25}^{49}$Mn is 6.0 MeV. Assuming that the nuclei have a spherically symmetric charge distribution, the radius of the ${}_{25}^{49}$Mn nucleus is
   (a) 4.9×10^{-15} m (b) 6.9×10^{-15} m
   (c) 5.1×10^{-13} m (d) $11.5 \times 10\ ^{15}$ m [NET 2011]

5. The mass difference of two nuclei ${}^{27}_{14}\text{Si}$ and ${}^{27}_{13}\text{Al}$ is 6.0 MeV. The radius of the ${}^{27}_{14}\text{Si}$ nucleus is approximately
   (a) 0.388 fm (b) 6.47 fm (c) 13.45 fm (d) 4.95 fm
6. Density of nuclear matter is
   (a) $\backsim 10^{17}$ kg/m^3 (b) $\backsim 10^{27}$ kg/m^3 (c) $\backsim 10^{-7}$ kg/m^3 (d) $\backsim 10^{7}$ kg/m^3
7. Density of the nucleus is
   (a) $\backsim 0.14$ nucleons/fm^3 (b) $\backsim 1.74$ nucleons/fm^3
   (c) $\backsim 0.54$ nucleons/fm^3 (d) $\backsim 1.43$ nucleons/fm^3
8. The most stable isotope in nature is close to
   (a) ${}^{4}_{2}\text{He}$ (b) ${}^{56}_{26}\text{Fe}$ (c) ${}^{235}_{92}\text{U}$ (d) ${}^{238}_{92}\text{U}$
9. The charge symmetry of nuclear force means
   (a) $F(n-n) = F(p-p)$ (b) $F(n-n) = F(p-p) = F(n-p)$
   (c) $F(n-p) = F(p-p)$ (d) $F(p-n) = F(n-n)$
10. The energy required to remove a proton or a neutron from a medium-sized nucleus is (mass of proton or neutron is ≈ 1000 MeV)
    (a) ≈ 1 MeV (b) ≈ 100 MeV (c) ≈ 1000 MeV (d) ≈ 10 MeV
11. Choose the **INCORRECT** option. Nuclear force
    (a) Has short range
    (b) Is attractive but becomes repulsive when the distance between any two nucleons approaches zero
    (c) Is central in nature (d) Depends on the spin of the nucleons
12. Suppose two nuclei of A are combined to make a single nucleus of B. Then
    (a) Volume of $B = 2\times$ Volume of A (b) Surface area of $B = 2\times$ Surface area of A
    (c) Radius of $B = 2\times$ Radius of A (d) Density of $B = 2\times$ Density of A
13. Suppose two nuclei of ${}^{12}_{6}\text{C}$ are fused to a single nucleus of ${}^{24}_{12}\text{Mg}$. The total binding energy of ${}^{12}_{6}\text{C}$ is ϕ. What would be the best estimate for the total binding energy of ${}^{24}_{12}\text{Mg}$?
    (a) ϕ (b) $2\times\phi$ (c) $4\times\phi$ (d) $\frac{\phi}{2}$
14. Consider two wave functions: (1) $\phi_1(x) = A_1\sin(3x) + A_2\cos(3x)$; (2) $\phi_2(x) = A_1\sin(3x) + A_2\sin(5x)$. Which of the these functions would be an acceptable wave function for a nucleus in the ground state?
    (a) Only (1) (b) Only (2) (c) Both (1) and (2) (d) Neither (1) nor (2)
15. Packing fraction is $-ve$ for nuclei with approximately
    (a) $12 < A < 180$ (b) $16 < A < 180$ (c) $16 < A < 240$ (d) $20 < A < 180$

16. Two singly charged ions of different masses (m_1 and m_2) but having the same energy enter into a region of transverse magnetic field. The radii of the paths will be related as

(a) $\frac{R_1}{R_2} = \frac{m_1}{m_2}$ (b) $\frac{R_1}{R_2} = \frac{m_2}{m_1}$ (c) $\frac{R_1}{R_2} = \sqrt{\frac{m_1}{m_2}}$ (d) $\frac{R_1}{R_2} = \sqrt{\frac{m_2}{m_1}}$

17. Two singly charged ions of different masses (m_1 and m_2) but having the same velocity enter into a region of transverse magnetic field. The radii of the paths will be related as

(a) $\frac{R_1}{R_2} = \frac{m_1}{m_2}$ (b) $\frac{R_1}{R_2} = \frac{m_2}{m_1}$ (c) $\frac{R_1}{R_2} = \sqrt{\frac{m_1}{m_2}}$ (d) $\frac{R_1}{R_2} = \sqrt{\frac{m_2}{m_1}}$

Short Questions and Problems

Mass of the nucleus

1. Verify that the rest mass energy of an electron is ≈ 0.51 MeV.
2. Verify that 1 u = 931.49 MeV.
3. Use the uncertainty relation to estimate the kinetic energy of a proton in the nucleus. Assume that the nucleus radius is about 5 fm. ($\hbar = 1.054589 \times 10^{-34}$ J.s)
4. Singly ionised ^{20}Ne and ^{22}Ne enter a Bainbridge mass spectrograph with a velocity of 10^5 m/s. If they are deflected by a magnetic field of 0.08 T, determine the separation between the traces produced by them.
5. In a mass spectrograph, singly ionised ^{7}Li ions are accelerated by a potential difference of 400 V and then passed through a uniform magnetic field of 0.08 T perpendicular to their direction of motion. Find the radius of the path of the ions.

   If the slit through which the ions enter into the magnetic field is 1-mm wide, then what is the broadening of the image due to diffraction.

   Calculate the mass resolution $\frac{m}{dm}$ of the system.
6. In the velocity filter of a Bainbridge mass spectrograph, the electric field is 10^4 V/m and the magnetic field is 0.2 T. After crossing the filter, the ions pass through a magnetic field of 0.2 T, perpendicular to the direction of motion.

   (a) Determine the speed of the undeviated ions from the filter.

   (b) If singly ionised ^{12}C and ^{13}C are used, determine the separation between the images formed by them on the photographic plate.

Radius of the nucleus

7. The energy of an α particle emitted from $^{231}_{95}$Am is 5.48 MeV. Find the closest distance it can approach a $^{197}_{79}$Au nucleus.
8. Find the distance of closest approach when a 5-MeV proton is projected on a $^{27}_{13}$Al target.

9. Show that $\dfrac{e^2}{4\pi\varepsilon_0} \approx 1.44$ MeV-fm.

10. Determine the radius of the $^{208}_{82}$Pb nucleus. Assume $R_0 = 1.4$ fm.

11. A stable nucleus has a radius one-third that of ^{189}Os. Identify the nucleus.

12. Estimate the density of nuclear matter in terms of (a) kg/m^3 and (b) nucleons/fm^3.

13. Calculate the density of $^{235}_{92}$U in kg/m^3.

14. Show that the mean square charge radius $< r^2 >$ of a uniformly charged sphere is $\frac{3}{5}R^2$.

Binding energy, packing fraction and nuclear separation energy

15. Calculate the Coulomb energy of the $^{73}_{32}$Ge nucleus.

16. Calculate the binding energy of the $^{39}_{19}$K nucleus.

17. What are mirror nuclei? Calculate the difference in Coulomb energies of two mirror nuclei.

18. (a) Calculate the difference in binding energies of $^{15}_{8}$O and $^{15}_{7}$N.
    Given: $M(^{15}_{8}\text{O}) = 15.003065$ u, $M(^{15}_{7}\text{N}) = 15.000109$ u, $M(^{1}_{1}\text{H}) = 1.007825$ u, $M_n = 1.008665$ u

    (b) Assuming the difference in binding energy is equal to the difference in Coulomb energy, calculate the nuclear radius of $^{15}_{8}$O and $^{15}_{7}$N.

19. (a) Calculate the difference in binding energies of $^{25}_{12}$Mg and $^{25}_{13}$Al.
    Given: $M(^{25}_{12}\text{Mg}) = 24.985837$ u, $M(^{25}_{13}\text{Al}) = 24.990429$ u, $M(^{1}_{1}\text{H}) = 1.007825$ u, $M_n = 1.008665$ u

    (b) Assuming the difference in binding energy is equal to the difference in Coulomb energy, calculate the nuclear radius of $^{25}_{12}$Mg.

20. Estimate the amount of energy required to dissociate completely 1 g of $^{40}_{20}$Ca to its constituent particles. Given: $M(^{40}_{20}\text{Ca}) = 39.962591$ u, $M(^{1}\text{H}) = 1.007825$ u and $M_n = 1.008665$ u

21. $^{236}_{92}$U splits spontaneously into two equal fragments, each of whose $A = 118$. Estimate the decrease in Coulomb energy in the process.

22. Calculate the binding energy per nucleon for $^{7}_{3}$Li, $^{20}_{10}$Ne, $^{56}_{26}$Fe and $^{235}_{92}$U.

23. The mass of $^{2}_{1}$H is 2.014103 u. Calculate its mass defect and packing fraction.

24. (a) Calculate the neutron separation energies for $^{7}_{3}$Li and $^{236}_{92}$U.

    (b) Calculate the proton separation energies for $^{20}_{10}$Ne and $^{197}_{79}$Au.

25. Why does the binding energy per nucleon for medium-sized nuclei remain relatively constant? How do you explain the fall of the binding energy curve for lighter as well as heavier nuclei? Explain from the binding energy curve why energy is released in fission and fusion.

26. Draw the curve representing the variation in binding energy per nucleon as a function of A. Locate the position of the maximum of the curve.

    Consider the symmetric fission of nucleus ^{A}X into two identical nuclei. From the binding energy curve, estimate the energy released. (Assume $A \approx 236$).
27. What is mass defect? What is packing fraction? How is it related to the binding energy of a nucleus? How does the packing fraction vary with the mass number of the nucleus?
28. Is the nuclear binding energy nearly proportional to A or A^2? How can this dependence be explained? (This implies an important property of nuclear force. What is it?)
29. Heavy nuclei emit α particles spontaneously. However, they are stable against the decay of a single proton or neutron or deuteron. Why is α emission favoured over these decays?

General problems

30. A proton is present in the d state ($l = 2$). Calculate its total angular momentum.
31. Lighter nuclei generally have $N \approx Z$, but for massive stable nuclei, N is always greater than Z. Explain why.
32. The magnetic dipole moment of a $^{2}_{1}$H nucleus is $\approx 5 \times 10^{-4}$ μ_B (μ_B is the Bohr magneton). What does it imply about the presence of electrons inside the nucleus?

HINTS/ANSWERS TO SELECTED PROBLEMS

Multiple Choice Questions

1. (c) 2. (b) 3. (c) 4. $\Delta E \approx \frac{3}{5}\frac{e^2}{4\pi\varepsilon_0}\frac{2Z}{R} \Rightarrow 6.9$ fm (b)

5. $M(^{27}_{14}\text{Si}) = 14m_p + 13m_n - BE(^{27}_{14}\text{Si})$

   $M(^{27}_{13}\text{Al}) = 13m_p + 14m_n - BE(^{27}_{13}\text{Al})$; and thus

$$\Delta M = m_n - m_p + BE(^{27}_{14}\text{Si}) - BE(^{27}_{13}\text{Al}) = m_n - m_p + \Delta E_{\text{Coulomb}}$$

$$\frac{3}{5}\frac{e^2}{4\pi\varepsilon_0}\frac{27}{R} = \Delta M - m_n + m_p \approx 6.0 - 1.29 = 4.71\,\text{MeV} \Rightarrow R = 4.95\,\text{fm (d)}$$

6. (a) 7. (a) 8. (b) 9. (a) 10. (d) 11. (c) 12. (a) 13. (b)

14. Nuclear states must have a definite parity (b) 15. (d) 16. (c) 17. (a)

Short Questions and Problems

3. $\Delta p \approx \frac{\hbar}{\Delta x}$ and $\Delta pc \approx 39.547$ MeV. As $\Delta pc << M_0c^2$, which is ~ 1000 MeV, we may use the non-relativistic equation to calculate the kinetic energy of the proton.

   Therefore, KE $= \frac{p^2c^2}{2M_0c^2} = \frac{39.547^2}{2 \times 938.79} \approx 0.83$ MeV.

4. Separation $= 2\times\Delta R = 2\frac{v}{qB}(m_2-m_1) = \frac{2\times10^5\times2\times1.66\times10^{-27}}{1.6\times10^{-19}\times0.08} \approx 0.052$ m.

5. From the relations $\frac{1}{2}mv^2 = qV$ and $\frac{mv^2}{R} = qvB$, $R = \sqrt{\frac{2mV}{q}}\frac{1}{B} \approx 9.52\times10^{-2}$ m. For ^{7}Li ions, $v = \sqrt{\frac{2qV}{m}} \approx 10^5$ m/s and the de Broglie wavelength $\lambda = \frac{h}{p} \approx 10^{-13}$ m. The angular deviation of the beam is $\theta \approx \frac{\lambda}{b} \approx 10^{-10}$, as $b = 1$ mm. Therefore, the broadening of the image due to diffraction is negligible.

$$R = \sqrt{\frac{2mV}{q}}\frac{1}{B} \Rightarrow \ln R = \frac{1}{2}\ln m + c$$

$$\frac{dR}{R} = \frac{1}{2}\frac{dm}{m} \Rightarrow \frac{m}{dm} = \frac{R}{2dR} = \frac{9.52\times10^{-2}}{1\times10^{-3}} = 95.2.$$

6. (a) $v = \frac{E}{B} = 5\times10^4$ m/s, the same for all ions irrespective of their masses.

(b) Separation $= 2\times\Delta R = 2\frac{v}{qB}(m_2-m_1) = \frac{2\times5\times10^4\times1\times1.66\times10^{-27}}{1.6\times10^{-19}\times0.2} \approx 5.19$ mm.

7. $\approx 4\times10^{-14}$ m 8. 3.7×10^{-15} m 10. 8.29 fm 11. $A = 7$, Li 13. $\backsim 10^{17}$kg/m^3

14. $<r^2> = \frac{\int_0^R r^2 4\pi r^2 \rho dr}{\int_0^R 4\pi r^2 \rho dr}$ with constant ρ 15. 146 MeV 16. 333.7 MeV

18. (a) 3.54 MeV (b) 3.66 fm 19. (a) 5.05 MeV (b) $R \approx 4.28$ fm

20. 8.24×10^{11} J 23. $f = 0.00705$ 30. $\frac{3}{2}$ and $\frac{5}{2}$

CHAPTER 2

Nuclear Model

In solving a nuclear system, we face several fundamental difficulties. The main difficulty arises from the mathematics of solving many-body problems. The two-nucleon system (namely, deuteron) is the simplest nuclear system for which the Schrödinger equation is simple and can be solved analytically in an exact way. The three-nucleon system comes next in complexity. However, such a system, even with a simplified form of potential, cannot be solved in an exact way. An exact solution of a many-body system with a realistic nuclear potential is impossible.

The second difficulty, which is actually more serious, is due to nuclear force itself. Nucleon–nucleon interactions are neither very simple, nor are they known precisely. Nucleons interact not only through mutual two-body forces, but through three-body forces as well. Such forces have no classical analogue. As there is no complete theory of the nucleus that explains its different properties, we adopt the following approach for nuclei.

We choose a model that is mathematically solvable and, at the same time, rich in physical insight. If the model works, that is, if it explains at least a few nuclear properties, we can improve it by incorporating additional terms. Through successive steps, we can construct a useful model of the nucleus containing the essential features of nuclear force so that the different properties of the nucleus can be accounted for.

A very simple but useful model is the **liquid-drop model**. Here, we ignore the finer details of nuclear force, and instead focus more on the strong, short-range, inter-nucleon attraction. Another useful model is the **shell model**, which correctly explains some important properties of the nucleus.

2.1 LIQUID-DROP MODEL OF THE NUCLEUS

There are some similarities between a drop of liquid and a nucleus:

(a) From the charge independence of nuclear force, it follows that nucleons have no special identity; they interact among themselves in the same way. Similarly, in a drop of liquid, all the molecules are alike. Thus, the nucleons in a nucleus can safely be treated like molecules in a drop of liquid.

(b) Nuclear density is constant, independent of the size of the nucleus. The density of liquid is also constant.

(c) If we supply energy to a nucleus, it will split into its constituent parts. Similarly, with a supply of energy, the molecules in a liquid are separated; that is, the drop evaporates. The vapourisation energy of liquid is thus similar in nature to the binding energy of a nucleus, and it is proportional to the number of molecules in the drop. Similarly, the binding energy of the nucleus is also proportional to the number of nucleons present in the nucleus.

Essential assumptions

(a) The nucleus consists of incompressible matter, so $R \propto A^{1/3}$.

(b) Nuclear force is charge independent.

(c) Nuclear force saturates.

(d) Nuclear force is strong and short-ranged.

The observed binding energy per nucleon with mass number can be accounted for by considering the different terms of the nucleus when it is treated like a drop of liquid.

Volume term: In this model, the main contribution to binding energy comes from the volume term. From the assumptions listed above, we can write the binding energy of a nucleus containing A nucleons to be proportional to A. This linear dependence of the binding energy (BE) on the mass number (A) is a consequence of the short-range nature of nuclear force (along with its saturation property). If the nuclear force had a long range, the total number of interacting pairs would be $\frac{A(A-1)}{2}$, and thus, BE/A would be a function of A. Thus, it cannot be a long-range force. Since the density of the nucleus is constant, each nucleon has almost the same number of neighbours, and hence, the contribution of BE for each nucleon is roughly constant. Thus, $BE \propto A$, where A is proportional to the volume of the nucleus:

$$BE_v = a_v A, \tag{2.1}$$

where a_v is the proportionality constant.

Surface term: The nucleons lying on the surface of the nucleus are not completely surrounded by other nucelons on all sides. Therefore, full binding is not achieved, and there must be some deficiency in the BE due to these nucleons. This deficit term is usually called the surface term, and it is proportional to the number of nucleons on the surface or simply proportional to the surface of the nucleus. Thus

$$BE_{\text{sur}} = -a_s A^{2/3} \tag{2.2}$$

Coulomb term: Again, BE will be decreased further due to repulsion acting between all pairs of protons. Repulsion acts between all the pairs because the Coulomb force is a long-range force. Considering the nucleus as a uniformly charged sphere,[1] we can write

$$BE_{\text{coul}} = -a_c \frac{Z(Z-1)}{A^{1/3}} \tag{2.3}$$

[1] Please see Section 1.5.7 of Chapter 1

Asymmetry term[2]: This term tends to give the largest BE to nuclei with $N = Z$. We demonstrate this with the help of a simple example.

Let us consider a nucleus with $A = 12$. The neutrons and protons in the nucleus are distributed in different energy levels, assumed to have equidistant spacing ε.

Case 1: $N = Z = 6$. Total energy $= 42\varepsilon$ and the number of excess neutrons is $N - Z = 0$.

Case 2: $N = 7$, $Z = 5$. Total energy $= 43\varepsilon$. The number of excess neutrons is $N - Z = 2$ and the excess energy $\triangle E = E(N > Z) - E(N = Z) = \varepsilon$.

Table 2.1: *Case 1: Arrangement of neutrons and protons for* $N = Z = 6$

○	⊗	6ε
○	⊗	5ε
○	⊗	4ε
○	⊗	3ε
○	⊗	2ε
○	⊗	ε

○ represents protons and ⊗ represents neutrons

Case 3: $N = 8$, $Z = 4$. Total energy $= 46\varepsilon$. The number of excess neutrons is $N - Z = 4$ and the excess energy $\triangle E = E(N > Z) - E(N = Z) = 4\varepsilon$. The transfer of two protons to two neutron states requires an energy of $2 \times 2\varepsilon = 4\varepsilon$.

Table 2.2: *Case 2: Arrangement of neutrons and protons for* $N = 7, Z = 5$

– –	⊗	7ε
– –	⊗	6ε
○	⊗	5ε
○	⊗	4ε
○	⊗	3ε
○	⊗	2ε
○	⊗	ε

○ represents protons and ⊗ represents neutrons

Table 2.3: *Case 3: Arrangement of neutrons and protons for* $N = 8, Z = 4$

– –	⊗	8ε
– –	⊗	7ε
– –	⊗	6ε
– –	⊗	5ε
○	⊗	4ε
○	⊗	3ε
○	⊗	2ε
○	⊗	ε

○ represents protons and ⊗ represents neutrons

Now, suppose $N - Z = 2\nu$. To transfer ν protons to neutron states, the energy required will be

$$\triangle E = \nu \times \nu\varepsilon = \nu^2\varepsilon = \frac{1}{4}(N - Z)^2\varepsilon \tag{2.4}$$

Note that each of the protons will have to be raised in energy by $\nu\varepsilon$. Again, the average spacing of the energy levels can be shown[3] to be $\propto \dfrac{1}{A}$. Thus

$$BE_{\text{asym}} \propto \frac{(N - Z)^2}{A} = -a_{\text{asym}}\frac{(A - 2Z)^2}{A} \tag{2.5}$$

[2]Introduction of this term cannot be explained from the liquid drop model.

[3]Cohen, BL. 1971. *Concept of Nuclear Physics*, Tata McGraw-Hill Education, New York.

Pairing term: It has been mentioned earlier that nuclei with even Z and even N are the most abundant, and thus, the most stable. Thus, nuclear force gives maximum binding for *even–even* nuclei and least binding for *odd–odd* nuclei. This tendency is accounted for by the pairing term δ.

$$\begin{aligned} \delta &= +\Delta \text{ for even–even nuclei} \\ &= 0 \text{ for even–odd nuclei} \\ &= -\Delta \text{ for odd–odd nuclei} \end{aligned}$$

The value of Δ is usually adjusted from experimental data and it is expressed[4] as

$$\Delta = a_p A^{-3/4} \tag{2.6}$$

Combining these five contributions, we get

$$BE(^A_ZX) = a_v A - a_s A^{2/3} - a_c \frac{Z(Z-1)}{A^{1/3}} - a_{\text{asym}} \frac{(A-2Z)^2}{A} + \delta \tag{2.7}$$

Therefore, the mass of ^A_ZX is

$$M(^A_ZX) = Zm_H + (A-Z)m_n - a_v A + a_s A^{2/3} + a_c \frac{Z(Z-1)}{A^{1/3}} + a_{\text{asym}} \frac{(A-2Z)^2}{A} - \delta \tag{2.8}$$

Equation (2.8) is known as the **semi-empirical mass formula**, and it was first proposed by Weizsäcker (1935). It is not an exact theory. It should be regarded as the first attempt to study the binding energy of a nucleus.

The constants must be adjusted to give the best agreement with the experiment data. A specific choice[5] of constants in Eq. (2.8) that gives a result that is closest to the observed behaviour of BE is presented in Table 2.4.

Table 2.4: *Coefficients in semi-empirical mass formula (in MeV)*

a_v	a_s	a_c	a_{asym}	a_p
15.5	16.8	0.72	23.0	34.0

2.1.1 Applicability of Liquid-Drop Model

The semi-empirical mass formula can be used to predict the stability and mass of different nuclei.

Binding energy of nuclei: Equation (2.7), together with the coefficients presented in Table 2.4, can be used to calculate the binding energy of different nuclei. The binding energies of a few nuclei calculated by Eq. (2.7) are presented in Table 2.5. This also shows that the percentage error in calculating the binding energy for medium-sized nuclei is $\lesssim 1\%$.

The relative contributions of different terms in the semi-empirical mass formula to the binding energy are shown in Fig. 2.1. It shows that the binding energy per nucleon can be roughly reproduced by the liquid-drop model.

[4] $\Delta = a_p A^{-1/2}$ is also used.

[5] Krane, KS. 1987. *Introductory Nuclear Physics, Third Edition*, John Wiley & Sons.

Table 2.5: *Contribution of different terms in semi-empirical mass formula (in MeV)*

Contribution of different terms	$^{8}_{4}Be$	$^{40}_{20}Ca$	$^{120}_{50}Sn$	$^{238}_{92}U$
Volume term	124.0	+620.00	+1860.00	+3689.00
Surface term	67.19	−196.44	−408.59	−644.96
Coulomb term	4.32	−80.00	−357.64	−972.70
Asymmetry term	0.0	0.00	−76.67	−281.80
Pairing term	7.15	+2.14	+0.94	+0.56
Total BE	59.64	345.69	1018.04	1790.10
BE/A	7.45	8.64	8.48	7.52
BE from definition	56.50	342.06	1020.55	1801.71
% error	5.56	1.06	0.25	0.64

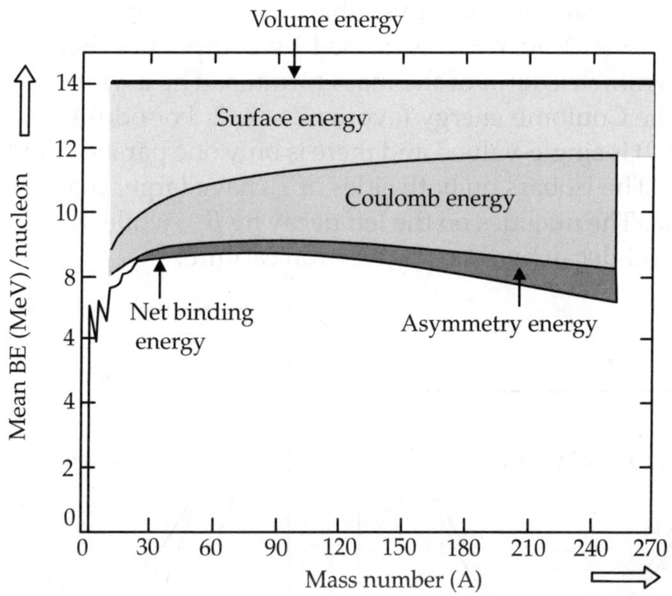

Figure 2.1: *Relative contribution of different terms of semi-empirical mass formula*

Similarly, the relation Eq. (2.8) can be used to calculate the mass of a nucleus $^{A}_{Z}X$, if M_n and M_p are known.

Mass parabola and the most stable isobar: Isobars have the same mass number A. The semi-empirical mass formula can predict the atomic number of the most stable isobar for a given A. From Eq. (2.8), the mass of the $^{A}_{Z}X$ nucleus is calculated as

$$M(^{A}_{Z}X) = A\times\alpha + \beta\times Z + \gamma\times Z^2 - \delta, \tag{2.9}$$

where $\alpha = (m_n - a_v + a_s A^{-1/3} + a_{\text{asym}})$, $\beta = (m_H - m_n - a_c A^{-1/3} - 4a_{\text{asym}})$ and $\gamma = (a_c A^{-1/3} + 4a_{\text{asym}}/A)$ are constants.

For a given A = constant, Eq. (2.9) represents a parabola, known as the **mass parabola**. The minimum of the parabola can be obtained by setting $\frac{\partial M}{\partial Z} = 0$ at $Z = Z_0$. Thus, for the most stable isobar (with lowest mass), $Z_0 = -\frac{\beta}{2\gamma}$.

Using the values of a_c and a_{asym}, we get

$$Z_0 \approx \frac{A}{1.98 + 0.015A^{2/3}} \tag{2.10}$$

And the mass of the stable isobar is

$$M(A, Z_0) = \alpha A - \gamma Z_0^2 - \delta \tag{2.11}$$

Equation (2.10) shows that for a small A, $Z_0 \approx \frac{A}{2}$ as expected, but for a large A, $Z_0 < \frac{A}{2}$. From Eq. (2.10), we can also recognise that the deviation of the stability line (see Fig. 1.14) from $Z = A/2$ or $N = Z$ is caused by competition between the Coulomb term and the asymmetric term of the mass formula. The asymmetry energy favours $Z \approx A/2$, while the Coulomb energy favours $Z < A/2$. For odd-A, $\delta = 0$. The function $M(A, Z)$ in Eq. (2.9) is single-valued and there is only one parabola and only one stable isobar at $Z = Z_0$. The isobars on both sides of Z_0 have larger mass than $M(A, Z_0)$ and are thus unstable. The nuclides on the left decay by β^-, while those on the right have excess protons and decay by β^+ or by electron capture.

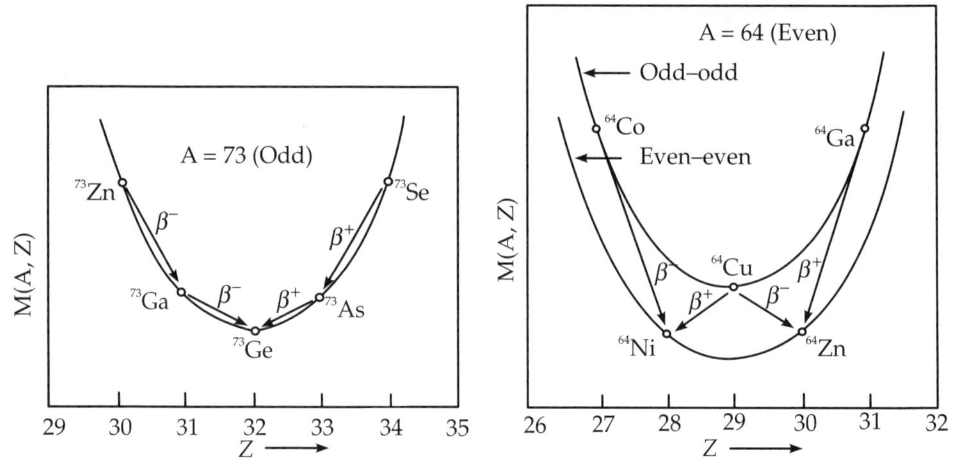

Figure 2.2: *Mass parabola for odd-A and even-A*

For even-A, the function $M(A, Z)$ in Eq. (2.9) is double-valued as δ has different values for even–even and odd–odd nuclei. We thus obtain two parabolas displaced by 2δ: the upper one for odd–odd nuclei corresponds to higher mass and lower stability, while the lower one for even–even nuclei represents higher stability. As a consequence, almost no stable odd–odd nuclei [6] are found in nature.

[6] Exceptions: $^2_1$H, $^6_3$Li, $^{10}_5$B and $^{14}_7$N.

Figure 2.2 for even-A also suggests that for certain odd-A nuclides, both β^- and β^+ are simultaneously possible. For example, this actually occurs for ^{64}Cu. This case also implies that for an *unstable even–even nucleus, double beta decay is allowed*, where Z changes by 2.

Illustrative Example 2.1: Most stable isobar for even-A

Find the most stable isobar for $A = 64$.

Solution From Eq. (2.10), $Z_0 \approx \frac{64}{1.98+0.015\times 64^{2/3}} = 28.8 \approx 29.$
Since the mass parabola for odd–odd nuclei lies higher than that for even–even nuclei, the nucleus with $Z = 29$ is unstable and it can decay either by β^- or β^+ emission.

$$^{64}_{29}\text{Cu} \rightarrow ^{64}_{30}\text{Zn} + e^- + \bar{\nu}_e \quad \text{or} \quad ^{64}_{29}\text{Cu} \rightarrow ^{64}_{28}\text{Ni} + e^+ + \nu_e$$

Therefore, both $Z = 28$ and $Z = 30$ are stable (shown on the right in Fig. 2.2).

Illustrative Example 2.2: Most stable isobar for odd-A

Find the most stable isobar for (a) $A = 109$, (b) $A = 63$ and (c) $A = 73$.

Solution (a) From Eq. (2.10), $Z_0 = \dfrac{109}{1.98 + 0.015 \times 109^{2/3}} = 46.9$. The actual value is 47.
(b) Similarly, for $A = 63$, $Z_0 \approx 28$.
(c) Similarly, for $A = 73$, $Z_0 \approx 32$.

Illustrative Example 2.3: Mass formula for odd-A

Show that for odd-A isobar, $M(Z,A) - M(Z_0,A) = \gamma(Z - Z_0)^2$, where $\gamma = (a_c A^{-1/3} + 4a_{\text{asym}}/A)$ and Z_0 represents the atomic number of the most stable isobar.
Consider the following reactions:

$$^{1}_{1}\text{H} + ^{51}_{23}\text{V} \longrightarrow ^{51}_{24}\text{Cr} + n - 1.53 \text{ MeV} \quad (1)$$

$$^{1}_{1}\text{H} + ^{3}_{1}\text{H} \longrightarrow ^{3}_{2}\text{He} + n - 0.76 \text{ MeV} \quad (2)$$

$$^{51}_{22}\text{Ti} \longrightarrow ^{51}_{23}\text{V} + e^- + 2.44 \text{ MeV} \quad (3)$$

$$^{3}_{1}\text{H} \longrightarrow ^{3}_{2}\text{He} + e^- + 0.02 \text{ MeV} \quad (4)$$

Determine γ and Z_0 for $A = 51$ from the above reactions.

Solution Using Eqs (2.9) and (2.11)
$M(Z,A) = A\alpha + \beta Z + \gamma Z^2 - \delta = A\alpha - 2\gamma Z_0 Z + \gamma Z^2 - \delta$ and $M(A,Z_0) = \alpha A - \gamma Z_0^2 - \delta$

$$\text{Therefore} \quad M(Z,A) - M(Z_0,A) = \gamma(Z - Z_0)^2 \tag{2.12}$$

This relation shows that dependence of the mass of $^{A}_{Z}X$ for fixed A on its atomic number is parabolic, and $M(Z,A)$ becomes minimum at $Z = Z_0$.
The energy conservation in reaction (1) gives

$$M(^{1}_{1}\text{H}) + M(^{51}_{23}\text{V}) - M(^{51}_{24}\text{Cr}) - M_n = -1.53 \text{ MeV}, \tag{2.13}$$

where mass is in energy units. Similarly, from reaction (3)

$$M(^{51}_{22}\text{Ti}) - M(^{51}_{23}\text{V}) - M_e = 2.44 \text{ MeV} \tag{2.14}$$

Equations (2.13) and (2.14) suggest that $M(^{51}_{23}\text{V})$ is smaller than $M(^{51}_{24}\text{Cr})$ and $M(^{51}_{22}\text{Ti})$, and thus, it is a stable isobar ($Z_0 = 23$).

According to Eq. (2.12), $M(^{51}_{24}\text{Cr}) - M(^{51}_{23}\text{V}) = \gamma(24-23)^2$, and thus, Eq. (2.13) can be written as

$$M(^1_1\text{H}) - \gamma - M_n = -1.53 \text{ MeV} \tag{2.15}$$

Similarly, Eq. (2.14) can be rewritten as

$$\gamma - M_e = 2.44 \text{ MeV} \tag{2.16}$$

Subtracting Eq. (2.16) from Eq. (2.15)

$$-2\gamma + M(^1_1\text{H}) - M_n + M_e = -3.97 \tag{2.17}$$

Again, energy conservation in reaction (2) gives

$$M(^1_1\text{H}) + M(^3_1\text{H}) - M(^3_2\text{He}) - M_n = -0.76 \text{ MeV} \tag{2.18}$$

And reaction (4) gives

$$M(^3_1\text{H}) - M(^3_2\text{He}) - M_e = 0.02 \text{ MeV} \tag{2.19}$$

Thus, Eq. (2.18) can be rewritten as

$$M(^1_1\text{H}) + M_e - M_n = -0.78 \text{ MeV} \tag{2.20}$$

Using Equations (2.17) and (2.20), we get $\gamma = 1.595$

Illustrative Example 2.4: Stability against β^- decay

The semi-empirical mass formula is

$$M(A,Z) \approx 924.02937A - 0.7833915Z + 18.33192A^{2/3} + 0.7144605\frac{Z^2}{A^{1/3}} + 92.83329\frac{(Z-A/2)^2}{A} - 34.0A^{-3/4} \text{ (in MeV)}$$

Determine whether $^{27}_{12}\text{Mg}$ is stable against β^- decay or not.

Solution In β^- decay, Z increases by 1. Now, from the given relation

$$M(^{27}_{12}\text{Mg}) - M(^{27}_{13}\text{Al}) = 1.706094 > 0$$

Thus, $^{27}_{12}\text{Mg}$ is unstable against β^- decay.

Mass difference of mirror nuclei: In mirror nuclei, the neutron and proton numbers are interchanged and differ by one. Suppose Z represents the lower atomic number, the neutron number N of that nucleus must be $Z+1$ and the mass number $A = 2Z+1$.

From Eq. (2.7), the binding energy of the ^A_ZX and $^A_{Z+1}Y$ nuclei are

$$BE(^A_ZX) = a_vA - a_sA^{2/3} - a_c\frac{Z(Z-1)}{A^{1/3}} - a_{\text{asym}}\frac{(N-Z)^2}{A} + \delta$$

$$BE(^A_{Z+1}Y) = a_vA - a_sA^{2/3} - a_c\frac{Z(Z+1)}{A^{1/3}} - a_{\text{asym}}\frac{(N-Z)^2}{A} + \delta$$

Therefore, the difference in binding energy is

$$\triangle BE = BE(^A_ZX) - BE(^A_{Z+1}Y) = a_c\frac{2Z}{A^{1/3}} \approx a_cA^{2/3} \tag{2.21}$$

In mirror nuclei, the difference in binding energy is due to their Coulomb energy difference.

In mirror nuclei, $\triangle BE = \triangle E_c$

Here, E_c represents the Coulomb energy.

The semi-empirical mass formula of Eq. (2.8) can thus be used to determine the mass difference of mirror nuclei. The mass of ^A_ZX is

$$M(^A_ZX) = Zm_H + (A-Z)m_n - a_vA + a_sA^{2/3} + a_c\frac{Z(Z-1)}{A^{1/3}} + a_{\text{asym}}\frac{(N-Z)^2}{A} - \delta$$

$$M(^A_{Z+1}Y) = (Z+1)m_H + (A-Z-1)m_n - a_vA + a_sA^{2/3} + a_c\frac{Z(Z+1)}{A^{1/3}} + a_{\text{asym}}\frac{(N-Z)^2}{A} - \delta$$

From these two relations, we get

$$M(^A_{Z+1}Y) - M(^A_ZX) = m_H - m_n + a_c\frac{2Z}{A^{1/3}} \approx a_cA^{2/3} - (m_n - m_H) \tag{2.22}$$

In mirror nuclei, $M(^A_{Z+1}Y) - M(^A_ZX) = \triangle E_c - (m_n - m_H)$

The left-hand side (LHS) of Eq. (2.22) can be measured either directly or from the energy of the β^+ decay of the two isobars. This equation suggests that a plot of the mass difference, considering the correction term of $m_n - m_H = 0.78$ MeV versus $A^{2/3}$, is a straight line passing through the origin.

From the slope of this straight line, a_c and hence the R_0 term in $R = R_0A^{1/3}$ can be determined.

Illustrative Example 2.5: Radius of mirror nuclei from Coulomb energy difference

The binding energies of $^{41}_{21}$Sc and $^{41}_{20}$Ca are 343.143 MeV and 350.420 MeV, respectively. Estimate the nuclear radius.

Solution The Coulomb energy difference between these two nuclei is

$$\triangle E_c = \frac{3}{5}\frac{e^2}{4\pi\varepsilon_0}\frac{1}{R}2Z = \frac{3}{5}\times 1.44\times\frac{2\times 20}{R} = \frac{34.56}{R}\text{ MeV}$$

Thus $\dfrac{34.56}{R} = 350.420 - 343.143 \Rightarrow R \approx 4.75$ fm

Illustrative Example 2.6: Mass difference of mirror nuclei and nuclear radius

Estimate the nuclear radius from the given data: $M(^{15}_{7}\text{N}) = 15.000108$ u and $M(^{15}_{8}\text{O}) = 15.003070$ u, and $m_n - m_H = 0.78$ MeV.

Solution $M(^{15}_{8}\text{O}) - M(^{15}_{7}\text{N}) = 2.7591$ MeV. From Eq. (2.22)

$$2.7591 + 0.78 = a_c \times 15^{2/3}$$

Therefore, $a_c = 0.582$ MeV and $\frac{3}{5}\frac{e^2}{4\pi\varepsilon_0}\frac{1}{R_0} = 0.582$.

Thus, $R_0 = \frac{0.6 \times 1.44}{0.582} = 1.48$ fm and the radius $R = 1.48 \times 15^{1/3} = 3.65$ fm.

Illustrative Example 2.7: Mass difference of mirror nuclei

Estimate the mass difference of ${}^{13}_{6}\text{C}$ and ${}^{13}_{7}\text{N}$.

Solution ${}^{13}_{6}\text{C}$ and ${}^{13}_{7}\text{N}$ are mirror nuclei, and thus

$$M({}^{13}_{7}\text{N}) - M({}^{13}_{6}\text{C}) = \frac{3}{5}\frac{e^2}{4\pi\varepsilon_0}\frac{1}{R_0 A^{1/3}}(7^2 - 6^2) - (m_n - m_H) \approx 3.2\,\text{MeV}, \text{ where } R_0 \simeq 1.2\text{ fm}.$$

β disintegration energy of mirror nuclei: Equation (2.22) can also be used to determine the β disintegration energy of mirror nuclei. For example, consider the following decay

$${}^{A}_{Z+1}X \longrightarrow {}^{A}_{Z}Y + \beta^+$$

The maximum energy released[7] in this decay is $Q_{\beta^+} = M({}^{A}_{Z+1}X) - M({}^{A}_{Z}Y) - m_e$, where M represents the nuclear mass expressed in energy units. Using Eq. (2.22) we get

$$Q_{\beta^+} = a_c A^{2/3} - (m_n - m_p + m_e), \tag{2.23}$$

where m_p is the mass of proton.

Illustrative Example 2.8: β disintegration energy of mirror nuclei

Consider the decay ${}^{15}_{8}\text{O} \longrightarrow {}^{15}_{7}\text{N} + \beta^+$. Estimate the maximum energy released Q_{β^+}. Given $M_n - M_p = 1.29$ MeV.

Solution From Eq. (2.23), $Q_{\beta^+} = a_c \times 15^{2/3} - (1.29 + 0.51)$ MeV.
Assuming $a_c = 0.72$ MeV, we get $Q_{\beta^+} \approx 2.58$ MeV.

Illustrative Example 2.9: β^+ decay of mirror nucleus and nuclear radius

Consider the decay ${}^{27}_{14}\text{Si} \longrightarrow {}^{27}_{13}\text{Al} + \beta^+$. Estimate the radius of ${}^{27}_{14}\text{Si}$, if the maximum energy released is 3.48 MeV. Given $M_n - M_p = 1.29$ MeV.
Solution From Eq. (2.23)

$$Q_{\beta^+} = \frac{3}{5}\frac{e^2}{4\pi\varepsilon_0}\frac{1}{R_0} \times 27^{2/3} - (1.29 + 0.51)\text{ MeV}$$

$$0.6 \times 1.44 \times 9 \times \frac{1}{R_0} = 3.48 + 1.8 = 5.28$$

Therefore, $R_0 \approx 1.47$ fm and $R = 1.47 \times 27^{1/3} = 4.42$ fm.

[7]We will discuss the relation in the context of β decay.

Estimation of energy released in α decay: In α decay, ${}^{A}_{Z}X \longrightarrow {}^{A-4}_{Z-2}Y + {}^{4}_{2}\text{He}$, and the energy released in α decay is

$$Q = BE({}^{A-4}_{Z-2}Y) + BE({}^{4}_{2}\text{He}) - BE({}^{A}_{Z}X)$$

Using Eq. (2.7), we get

$$Q \approx 28.29 - 4a_v + \frac{8}{3}a_s A^{-1/3} + 4a_c Z A^{-1/3}\left(1 - \frac{Z}{3A}\right) - 4a_{\text{asym}}\left(1 - 2\frac{Z}{A}\right)^2 + 3a_p A^{-7/4}, \tag{2.24}$$

where $BE({}^{4}_{2}\text{He}) \approx 28.29$ MeV and we have used the approximation $Z, A \gg 1$.

Illustrative Example 2.10: α decay

Use the semi-empirical mass formula to determine the energy released in α decay:

$${}^{212}_{84}\text{Po} \longrightarrow {}^{208}_{82}\text{Pb} + {}^{4}_{2}\text{He}$$

Solution For ${}^{212}_{84}\text{Po}$, Eq. (2.24) gives 5.07 MeV, which is close to the observed value.

⇒ **Check Progress 2.1:**	Verify Eq. (2.24).

Illustrative Example 2.11: Energy released in α decay

According to the liquid-drop model, the binding energy of ${}^{A}_{Z}X$ is

$$BE({}^{A}_{Z}X) = a_v A - a_s A^{2/3} - a_c \frac{Z(Z-1)}{A^{1/3}} - a_{\text{asym}} \frac{(N-Z)^2}{A} + a_p A^{-3/4},$$

where $a_v = 15.5$ MeV, $a_s = 16.8$ MeV, $a_c = 0.72$ MeV, $a_{\text{asym}} = 23.0$ MeV and $a_p = 34.0$ MeV. Using this relation, estimate the energy released in the decay ${}^{230}_{90}\text{Th} \longrightarrow {}^{226}_{88}\text{Ra} + \alpha$.

Given that the binding energy of α is 28.3 MeV.

Solution Using the given values

$$BE({}^{230}_{90}\text{Th}) \approx 1743.6175 \text{ MeV}, \; BE({}^{226}_{88}\text{Ra}) \approx 1720.857 \text{ MeV}$$

The binding energy of α is 28.3 MeV. Therefore, the total binding energy of the final state is $1720.857 + 28.3 = 1749.157$ MeV.

As the binding energy of the final state is larger than that of the initial state, energy must be released. The energy released is $1749.157 - 1743.6175 = 5.5395$ MeV.

2.2 NUCLEAR SHELL MODEL

We can see that the liquid-drop model of the nucleus explains the binding energy curve to a high degree of correctness. However, it cannot explain many other important properties of the nucleus. For example, it cannot explain

(i) The existence of magic numbers
(ii) Ground state spin and parity
(iii) Magnetic moment and quadrupole moment

We now introduce another model, known as the shell model, which provides an explanation of these properties of the nucleus. Before the introduction of nuclear shell model, a brief discussion of the atomic shell structure may be useful.

2.2.1 Shell Model in Atomic Case

The ionisation energy of an atom is the minimum energy required to remove an electron from the atom. In Fig. 2.3, the ionisation energies of atoms are plotted against their atomic number Z. It can be seen that the curve reaches its peak at $Z = 2, 10, 18, 36, 54, 80$ and 86, corresponding to elements He, Ne, Ar, Kr, Xe, Hg and Rn. Large ionisation implies that these atoms are more stable than their immediate neighbours. Apart from Hg, these are all noble elements and characterised by a closed shell structure. In Hg, there is a closed shell plus two electrons in the s-state. A closed shell configuration is exceptionally stable. It is very easy to remove an excess electron from a filled shell of the atom, and the ionisation energy of such an electron in the unfilled state is very low.

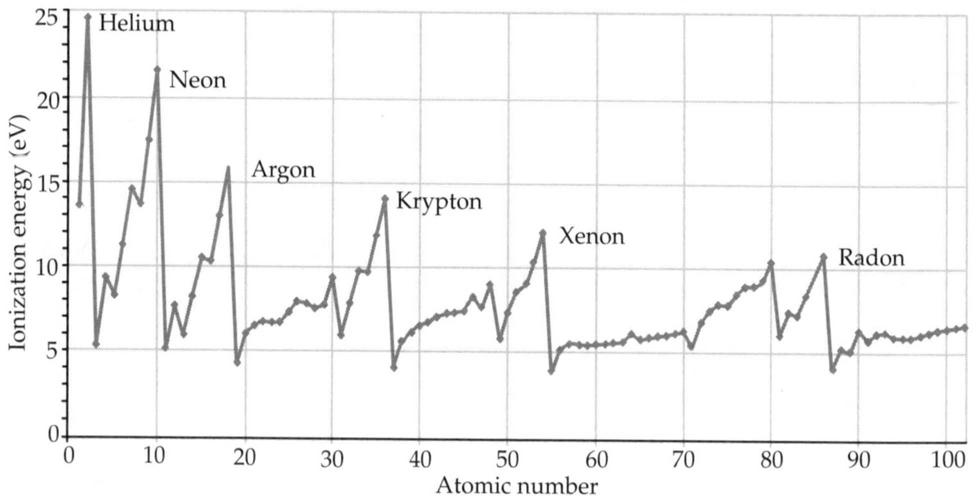

Figure 2.3: *Variation in ionisation energy with atomic number*

In the shell model of an atom, we fill the shells with electrons in the order of increasing energy, so that it is consistent with the Pauli Exclusion Principle, which restricts the number of electrons in each state. This model explains many properties of atoms with remarkable accuracy.

2.2.2 Evidence for Nuclear Shell Model

(a) The most important experimental evidence is the existence of magic numbers. It has been found from the binding energy curve that nuclei whose neutron number or proton number or both are one of the numbers 2, 8, 20, 28, 50, 82 and 126 (known as magic numbers[8]) have large binding energy. They are thus unusually stable compared to their immediate neighbours. Doubly magic nuclei[9] have very large binding energy and are difficult to excite. The exceptional stability of these magic nuclei is evidence of shell closure, as in inert atoms.

(b) Nuclei that have a magic number of protons or neutrons have exceptional stability. The last stable nucleus with $Z = N$ is ${}^{40}_{20}$Ca, which is doubly magic with $Z = N = 20$. The relative stability of different elements is indicated by the number of stable isotopes or isotones. Isotopes having a magic number of protons or neutrons are more abundant. ${}_{50}$Sn with $Z = 50$ has the largest number of isotopes.

On an average, the number of stable isotones for even-N is ~ 3 only. However, this number increases to 5 for $N = 20$, to 6 for $N = 50$ and to 7 for $N = 82$. The largest group of isotones is at $N = 82$. The number of stable isotopes and isotones of some elements with magic numbers are shown in Table 2.6.

Table 2.6: *Number of stable isotopes and isotones*

No. of Z	No. of stable isotopes	No. of N	No. of stable isotones
20	6	20	5
50	10	50	6
82	4	82	7

(c) The stable end products of all four natural radioactive series are the nuclei containing a magic number of protons or neutrons. The lead end products have 82 protons – a magic number – while bismuth has 126 neutrons, also a magic number. ${}^{208}_{82}$Pb is doubly magic, with $Z = 82$ and $N = 126$.

Table 2.7: *End products of natural radioactive series*

Series	First decay	End product
Thorium	${}^{232}\text{Th} \to {}^{228}\text{Ra} + {}^{4}_{2}\text{He}$	${}^{208}_{82}\text{Pb}$
Neptunium	${}^{237}\text{Np} \to {}^{233}\text{Pa} + {}^{4}_{2}\text{He}$	${}^{209}_{83}\text{Bi}$
Uranium	${}^{238}\text{U} \to {}^{234}\text{Th} + {}^{4}_{2}\text{He}$	${}^{206}_{82}\text{Pb}$
Uranium	${}^{235}\text{U} \to {}^{231}\text{Th} + {}^{4}_{2}\text{He}$	${}^{207}_{82}\text{Pb}$

(d) Another piece of evidence comes from the study of absorption cross-sections for neutrons. In a neutron-capture reaction, an atomic nucleus collides with one or more neutrons and they merge to form a heavier nucleus. The neutron-capture cross-sections of the nuclei with a magic number of neutrons are usually low. It appears that the neutron states are filled with these nuclei, so the probability of exciting them with additional neutrons is very low.

(e) Another experimental basis for the nuclear shell model is the study of the neutron separation energy of nuclei (the energy required to remove a neutron from the nucleus). At the magic numbers, the shell is supposed to be "closed", the

[8]The numbers 2, 8, 20, 28, 50, 82 and 126 came to be known as magic numbers because the mystery of their unusual stability could not be resolved for a long time.

[9]For example, ${}^{4}_{2}$He, ${}^{16}_{8}$O, ${}^{40}_{20}$Ca, ${}^{208}_{82}$Pb, etc.

nuclei are more tightly bound, and hence, it is difficult to remove a neutron from the nucleus. If the neutron number $N =$ (magic number) $+ 1$, then the neutron separation energy is particularly low. A similar phenomenon is observed in the ionisation energy of atoms (Fig. 2.3), which is high for inert gases and low for alkali elements. Thus, the high value of neutron separation energy of nuclei with the magic number of neutrons is strong evidence for the shell structure.

(f) The electric quadrupole moment of magic nuclei is practically zero, indicating spherical symmetry.

(g) Consider the following β decay processes:

$${}^{87}_{36}\mathrm{Kr} \longrightarrow {}^{87}_{37}\mathrm{Rb} + \beta^- + Q_1 \text{ and } {}^{87}_{37}\mathrm{Rb} \longrightarrow {}^{87}_{38}\mathrm{Sr} + \beta^- + Q_2$$

In the first case, the decay product is a magic nucleus with $N = 50$ and the energy released $Q_1 \sim 3.6$ MeV. However, in the second case, the energy released is only ~ 0.27 MeV.

The large energy of β decay is observed in transitions to magic nuclei, while the energy of the beta particles emitted by magic nuclei is comparatively much lower.

A similar phenomenon is observed in α decay. For example, the energy released in the α decay of ${}^{212}_{84}\mathrm{Po}$ (which is transformed into a nucleus with $Z = 82$, a magic nuclei) is large (in comparison with that of the neighbouring nuclei).

2.2.3 Introduction to the Nuclear Shell Model

The shell theory is highly successful in atomic physics. Nuclear physicists attempted to introduce a similar theory in nuclear problems, anticipating success, as in atomic physics. Convinced by several experimental results pointing towards the existence of some kind of internal structure in the nucleus, M.G. Mayer in 1948 developed the shell model of the nucleus. However, when we introduce this model in nuclear problems, we encounter some severe objections.

Firstly, in an atom, there is a clear centre of force (the nucleus). So each electron feels a strong attractive force towards the nucleus. The mutual repulsion among the electrons, being weaker, can be considered as a correction term. However, in the nucleus, there is no clear centre of force.

Secondly, nucleons have relatively comparable size to that of the nucleus. Thus, how can we regard the nucleon as moving in a well-defined orbit when a single nucleon may collide many times during an orbit?

Basic assumptions: The basic assumption of the shell model is that each nucleon in the nucleus moves in the mean potential, which is the resultant effect of all the other nucleons on it. Nucleons are considered to move independently of each other in that potential. Assume that each nucleon moves in a random orbit with respect to all other nucleons. If the orbital motions are fast, an individual nucleon will not see the other nucleons but only an average nucleon-cloud produced by the others.

The apparent difficulty in a definite orbit by a single nucleon in an environment crowded with other nucleons is resolved by the Pauli Exclusion Principle. The nucleons moving in an average potential can be in different energy states. In the ground state, all energy levels up to a certain level are filled. In a collision, nucleons transfer energy to one another and, consequently, one of the nucleons will lose a part of its energy and move to a lower level. However, if all the lower energy states are completely occupied, then no additional nucleon can be accommodated, due to the Pauli Exclusion Principle. Therefore, interactions among the nucleons cannot excite a nucleon to a higher level. In another words, nucleons practically do not interact with one another; they move in a common field independently, without any collision.

Choice of potential: In the absence of theoretical guidance, one chooses the simplest form of potential that can be solved analytically. As the nucleus has a spherical shape in the first approximation, we usually assume a spherically symmetric potential[10]. The simplest is an infinite square well of radius R

$$V(r) = 0 \quad r < R$$
$$= \infty \quad r \geq R$$

The solution of the Schrödinger equation for this potential gives a sequence of energy levels (Fig. 2.4). Thus, the magic numbers calculated are $2, 8, 18, 20, 34, 40$, ... etc. Clearly, these are different from the observed magic numbers.

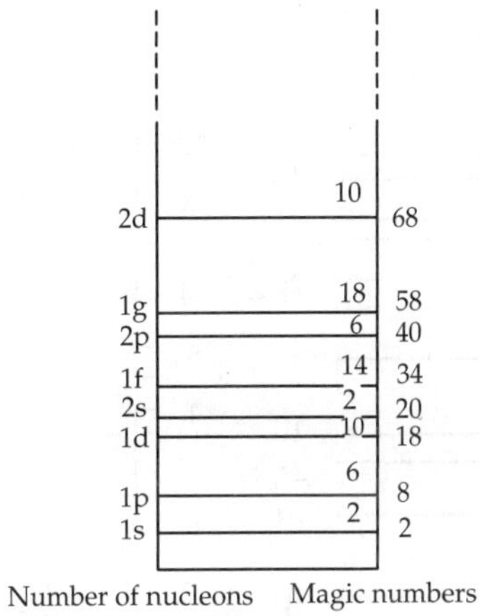

Figure 2.4: *Energy levels in infinite square well potential*

Another important potential is the 3D harmonic oscillator potential $V(r) = \frac{1}{2}kr^2$. The energy can be obtained analytically as $E = \hbar\omega(\Lambda + 3/2)$, where $\Lambda = 2n + l - 2$, with $n = 1, 2, 3, ...$ and $l = 0, 1, 2$. For a given l, there are $(2l + 1)$ different values of m. Each (n, l, m) state can accommodate two nucleons (corresponding to spin up and spin down) of one kind. Thus, the total number of nucleons of one kind (either proton or neutron) that can be accommodated in a particular state is $2\sum(2l + 1)$.

The magic numbers calculated are 2, 8, 20, 40, 70, ... etc. (Table 2.8). Only the first three agree with the observed value.

[10]However, there is good evidence that the potential cannot be completely spherical.

Table 2.8: *Quantum numbers and energy levels of harmonic oscillator potential*

Λ	n	l	State	N_Λ	ΣN_Λ	$\frac{E}{\hbar\omega}$
4	3	0	$3s$	2		
	2	2	$2d$	10		
	1	4	$1g$	18	70	$\frac{11}{2}$
3	2	1	$2p$	6		
	1	3	$1f$	14	40	$\frac{9}{2}$
2	2	0	$2s$	2		
	1	2	$1d$	10	20	$\frac{7}{2}$
1	1	1	$1p$	6	8	$\frac{5}{2}$
0	1	0	$1s$	2	2	$\frac{3}{2}$

Inclusion of spin-orbit coupling: A purely central potential, irrespective of form, cannot produce the observed magic numbers. Once again, we use another idea from atomic physics. In 1949, Mayer and Jensen included a spin-orbit term[11] to the Hamiltonian of the nucleon. The inclusion of this spin-orbit term provides the correct values of the magic numbers (Fig. 2.5). Note that the total energy of a state with given l is lower for the parallel arrangement of orbital angular momentum l and spin s than for an anti-parallel arrangement.

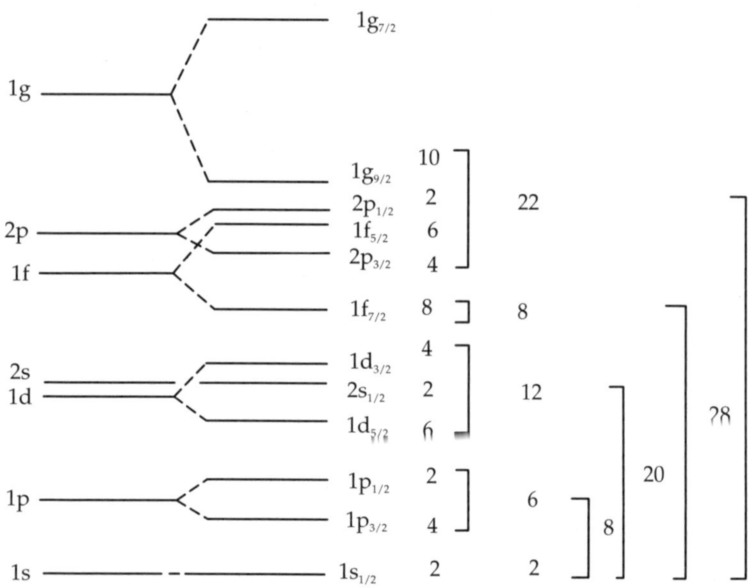

Figure 2.5: *Energy levels in harmonic oscillator potential well with spin-orbit coupling and closed shells with magic numbers of nucleons*

2.2.4 Predictions of the Shell Model

Magic numbers: Shell model energy levels are

$$1s_{1/2}, \overbrace{1p_{3/2}, 1p_{1/2}}, \overbrace{1d_{5/2}, 2s_{1/2}, 1d_{3/2}}, \overbrace{1f_{7/2}}, \overbrace{2p_{3/2}, 1f_{5/2}, 2p_{1/2}, 1g_{9/2}} \cdots$$

[11]Although the spin–orbit interaction in the nucleus seems similar to the atomic case, its origin is not yet clearly understood.

The energy levels are filled by neutrons and protons independently according to the Pauli Exclusion Principle. The desired magic numbers can be reproduced from such an arrangement.

Other than magic numbers, this model can predict many other properties of the nucleus.

Spin: The shell model can predict the spin and parity of a large number of nuclei in their ground state by taking into account the following:

(i) In each completely filled state, the spin and orbital angular momenta of nucleons added together gives resultant zero.

(ii) The resultant angular momentum associated with an even number of neutrons or protons is zero. *In the ground state, the total angular momentum of a nucleus with an even number of protons and an even number of neutrons is zero. There is no known exception to this rule.*

(iii) *The spin of the nucleus is given by its unpaired nucleon.* The particular application of the shell model we have discussed so far is known as **extreme single particle model**. The basic assumption of this is that all nucleons but one are paired and the unpaired nucleon is responsible for different properties of the nucleus. Prediction of nuclear spin from the shell model is in agreement with experimental data, except for heavy nuclei. However, the spin of odd–odd nuclei cannot be predicted from this extreme single particle shell model, as the coupling between the unpaired proton and neutron is not considered.

Unlike in the extreme single particle shell, the coupling of all odd nucleons in the last occupied level is considered in the single particle shell model. The single particle shell model can be used to give information on the spin of odd–odd nuclei.

(iv) To determine the spin of odd–odd nuclei, we need to use the **Nordheim rules**. We define the Nordheim number(N) as

$$N = j_p - l_p + j_n - l_n,$$

where p and n refer to the odd proton and odd neutron, respectively.

If $N = 0$, then $I = \mid j_n - j_p \mid$. If $N = \pm 1$, then $I = \mid j_n - j_p \mid$ or $\mid j_n + j_p \mid$. There are exceptions to these rules, particularly for light nuclei.

Parity: The parity of a nucleus in the ground state is $P = (-1)^l$, where l is the l-value of the last unpaired nucleon. For even–even nuclei, parity is always positive.

Illustrative Example 2.12: The number of nucleons in a particular state

A certain odd parity state can accommodate a maximum of 12 nucleons. Find the j and l of the state.

Solution The state total angular momentum j can accommodate $2j + 1$ nucleons. Thus

$$2j + 1 = 12 \Rightarrow j = \frac{11}{2}$$

Since $j = l + \frac{1}{2}$ or $l - \frac{1}{2}$, the possible values of l are 5 or 6. Again, the parity of the state is $(-1)^l = -1$; thus $l = 5$.

Illustrative Example 2.13: Spin and parity of odd-*A* nucleus

Find the spin and parity of (a) ${}^{13}_{6}C$, (b) ${}^{13}_{7}N$, (c) ${}^{17}_{8}O$ and (d) ${}^{33}_{16}S$.

Solution The spin and parity of these nuclei are presented in Table 2.9.

Table 2.9: *Spin and parity of odd-A nuclei*

Nucleus	Odd nucleon	Arrangement of odd nucleon	Spin and parity	Experiment value
${}^{13}_{6}C$	Neutron	$1s^2_{1/2}1p^4_{3/2}1p^1_{1/2}$	$\frac{1}{2}^-$	$\frac{1}{2}^-$
${}^{13}_{7}N$	Proton	$1s^2_{1/2}1p^4_{3/2}1p^1_{1/2}$	$\frac{1}{2}^-$	$\frac{1}{2}^-$
${}^{17}_{8}O$	Neutron	$1s^2_{1/2}1p^4_{3/2}1p^2_{1/2}1d^1_{5/2}$	$\frac{5}{2}^+$	$\frac{5}{2}^+$
${}^{33}_{16}S$	Neutron	$1s^2_{1/2}1p^4_{3/2}1p^2_{1/2}1d^6_{5/2}2s^2_{1/2}1d^1_{3/2}$	$\frac{3}{2}^+$	$\frac{3}{2}^+$

Illustrative Example 2.14: Spin and parity of even–even nucleus

Find the spin and parity of (a) ${}^{4}_{2}He$, (b) ${}^{16}_{8}O$, (c) ${}^{40}_{20}Ca$ and (d) ${}^{208}_{82}S$.

Solution For all of the above cases, $Z =$ even and $N =$ even; thus spin is 0. Parity for all cases is positive.

⇒ Check Progress 2.2: Predict the ground state spin and parity of (a) ${}^{27}_{13}Al$, (b) ${}^{41}_{18}Ar$ and (c) ${}^{33}_{16}S$.

Illustrative Example 2.15: Spin and parity of odd–odd nucleus

Find the spin and parity of (a) ${}^{30}_{15}P$ and (b)${}^{14}_{7}N$.

Solution (a) In ${}^{30}_{15}P$, $Z = N = 15$ and the arrangement of neutron or proton is

$$1s^2_{1/2}1p^4_{3/2}1p^2_{1/2}1d^6_{5/2}2s^1_{1/2}$$

Thus, $j_p = j_n = \frac{1}{2}$ and $l_p = l_n = 0$. In this case, the Nordheim number (N) is

$N = j_p + j_n - l_p - l_n = +1$ and $I = 0$ or 1; parity is $(-1)^0 \times (-1)^0 =$ positive

(b) In ${}^{14}_{7}N$, $Z = N = 7$ and the arrangement of neutron or proton is

$$1s^2_{1/2}1p^4_{3/2}1p^1_{1/2}$$

Thus, $j_p = j_n = \frac{1}{2}$ and $l_p = l_n = 1$. In this case

$N = j_p + j_n - l_p - l_n = -1$ and $I = 0$ or 1; parity is $(-1)^1 \times (-1)^1 =$ positive

⇒ Check Progress 2.3: Find the spin and parity of (a) ${}^{3}_{1}\mathrm{H}$, (b) ${}^{7}_{3}\mathrm{Li}$, (c) ${}^{25}_{12}\mathrm{Mg}$, (d) ${}^{31}_{15}\mathrm{P}$, (e) ${}^{39}_{19}\mathrm{K}$, (f) ${}^{63}_{29}\mathrm{Cu}$, (g) ${}^{13}_{6}\mathrm{C}$, (h) ${}^{34}_{19}\mathrm{K}$ and (i) ${}^{41}_{20}\mathrm{Ca}$.

Illustrative Example 2.16: Separation between the $1p_{1/2}$ and $1d_{5/2}$ levels

Find the gap between the $1p_{1/2}$ and $1d_{5/2}$ neutron states of ${}^{16}_{8}\mathrm{O}$. Given that the binding energies of ${}^{15}_{8}\mathrm{O}$, ${}^{16}_{8}\mathrm{O}$ and ${}^{17}_{8}\mathrm{O}$ are 111.9556 MeV, 127.6193 MeV and 131.7627 MeV, respectively.

Solution In ${}^{15}_{8}\mathrm{O}$, $Z=8$ and $N=7$. Thus, the neutron arrangement $\Rightarrow 1s^2_{1/2}1p^4_{3/2}1p^1_{1/2}$.
Thus, one neutron is missing in the $1p_{1/2}$ shell.
In ${}^{16}_{8}\mathrm{O}$, $Z=8$ and $N=8$: ⇒ closed shell.
In ${}^{17}_{8}\mathrm{O}$, the neutron arrangement: $\Rightarrow 1s^2_{1/2}1p^4_{3/2}1p^2_{1/2}1d^1_{5/2}$
⇒ one extra neutron in $1d_{5/2}$

The binding energy of the $1p_{1/2}$ neutron in ${}^{16}_{8}\mathrm{O}$ is

$$B_1 = M({}^{15}_{8}\mathrm{O}) + M_n - M({}^{16}_{8}\mathrm{O}) = BE({}^{16}_{8}\mathrm{O}) - BE({}^{15}_{8}\mathrm{O})$$

The binding energy of the $1d_{5/2}$ neutron in ${}^{17}\mathrm{O}_8$ is

$$B_2 = M({}^{16}_{8}\mathrm{O}) + M_n - M({}^{17}_{8}\mathrm{O}) = BE({}^{17}_{8}\mathrm{O}) - BE({}^{16}_{8}\mathrm{O})$$

Therefore, the energy separation of the neutron in the $1p_{1/2}$ and $1d_{5/2}$ shells is

$$\delta = B_1 - B_2 = 2\times BE({}^{16}_{8}\mathrm{O}) - BE({}^{15}_{8}\mathrm{O}) - BE({}^{17}_{8}\mathrm{O})$$

$$= 2\times 127.6193 - 111.9556 - 131.7627 = 11.5203 \text{ MeV}$$

2.2.5 Drawbacks of the Shell Model

The range of applicability of this model is, in fact, very limited. It is mainly used to explain some properties of light nuclei (assumed to be spherical) in the ground state. Even in this narrow range, some discrepancies have been noted between the theoretical and experimentally observed values. Let us mention a few:

(a) There are some discrepancies between the predicted value and the experimental value of nuclear spin. For example, consider the ${}^{6}_{3}\mathrm{Li}$ nucleus. This is an odd–odd nucleus with $Z=N=3$. The arrangement of neutrons or protons is $1s^2_{1/2}1p_{3/2}$.

Thus, $j_p = j_n = \dfrac{3}{2}$ and $l_p = l_n = 1$. In this case, the Nordheim number (N) is

$N = j_p + j_n - l_p - l_n = +1$ and $I = 0$ or 3. However, the experimentally observed value for this is $I = 1$.

(b) Several nuclei with an even number of Z and N have a pronounced structure of rotational levels. This contradicts the assumption[12] that the nucleus is spherical.

[12]Nuclei with closed shells are assumed to be spherical. If a small number of nucleons are added to such nuclei, the shape remains almost spherical. However, for a large number of excess nucleons outside the closed shell, the nucleus becomes non-spherical, which is capable of rotation.

Illustrative Example 2.17: Spin and parity of odd-A nucleus, a few exceptions

Find the spin and parity of (a) ${}^{19}_{9}F$, (b) ${}^{23}_{11}Na$ and (c) ${}^{55}_{25}Mn$.

Solution (a) ${}^{19}_{9}F$: The last odd proton is in $1d_{5/2}$. Expected spin and parity is $\frac{5}{2}^{+}$; however, the experimental result is $\frac{1}{2}^{+}$.

(b) ${}^{23}_{11}Na$: The last odd proton is in $1d_{5/2}$. Expected spin and parity is $\frac{5}{2}^{+}$; however, the experimental result is $\frac{3}{2}^{+}$.

(c) ${}^{55}_{25}Mn$: The last odd proton is in $1f_{7/2}$. Expected spin and parity is $\frac{7}{2}^{-}$; however, the experimental result is $\frac{5}{2}^{-}$.

In this context, we would like to state that the main assumptions of the shell model are as follows: (a) Each nucleon moves in a spherically symmetric potential. (b) Interaction between nucleons is absent, that is, they move independently of each other.

The observed discrepancies between the predicted value and the experimentally observed value indicate the violation of these assumptions. To overcome these drawbacks, we need to introduce non-sphericity associated with the interaction. The model of the nucleus that takes these factors into account is known as the **collective model**.

2.3 NUCLEAR FERMI GAS MODEL

The Fermi gas model is the simplest independent particle model of the nucleus. It pictures the nucleus as a collection of non-interacting nucleons confined to a very small spherical volume V of radius $R = R_0 A^{1/3}$. The neutrons and protons are fermions, and thus, two identical nucleons must be in different states, as required by the Pauli Exclusion Principle. In this model, we also assume that the nucleons of a particular type behave like a fully degenerate gas (all states up to a certain level, known as the Fermi level, are completely occupied). Calculation of Fermi energy is carried out separately for neutrons and protons.

The number of states accessible to the system of volume V with momentum p and $p + dp$ is

$$dn = 2 \times \frac{V}{h^3} \times 4\pi p^2 dp \tag{2.25}$$

This is obtained by dividing the phase space volume by h^3; factor 2 is for spin. Thus, the number of states corresponding to a momentum smaller than the Fermi momentum p_F is

$$n = 2 \times \frac{V}{h^3} \times 4\pi \int_0^{p_F} p^2 dp$$
$$= \frac{8\pi}{3} \frac{V}{h^3} p_F^3 \tag{2.26}$$

Since, at complete degeneracy, the number of states occupied is equal to the number of nucleons in the particular nucleus, the number of neutrons is

$$N = \frac{8\pi}{3} \frac{V}{h^3} p_F^3$$

Therefore $p_F^{\text{neutron}} = (3\pi^2)^{1/3} \hbar \left(\frac{N}{V}\right)^{1/3} = \hbar k_F^{\text{neutron}}$ (2.27)

In crude approximation, $Z = N = \frac{A}{2}$ for light nuclei. Thus, using $V = \frac{4}{3}\pi R_0^3 A$, the Fermi momentum from Eq. (2.27) becomes[13]

$$p_F^{\text{neutron}} \cong \left(\frac{9\pi}{8}\right)^{1/3} \frac{\hbar c}{R_0 c}$$
$$\approx \frac{300}{R_0} \text{ MeV/c} \tag{2.28}$$

This is independent of A (here, R_0 is in fm). The corresponding kinetic energy, known as Fermi energy, is given by

$$E_F^{\text{neutron}} = \frac{p_F^2}{2m}$$

For $R_0 = 1.3$ fm, $E_F^{\text{neutron}} \approx 28$ MeV. This is the maximum kinetic energy of a neutron bound in the nucleus. As the average binding energy of the last neutron is 8 MeV, the depth of the potential well for the neutron is about $V_0^{\text{neutron}} = 28 + 8 = 36$ MeV.

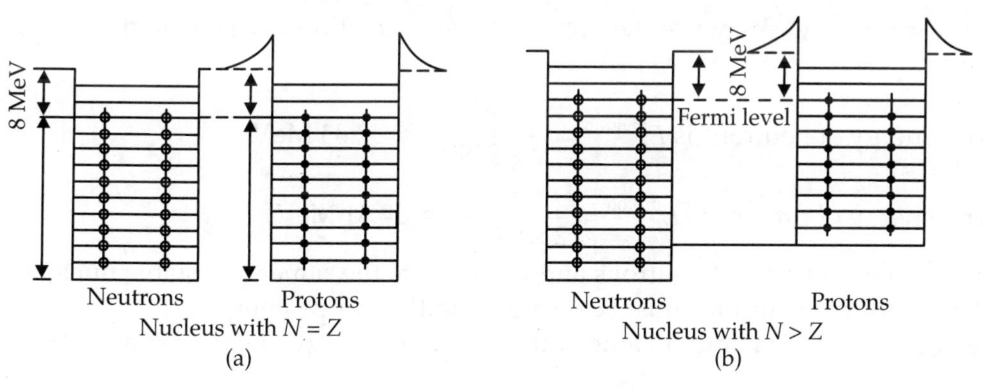

Figure 2.6: *(a) shows the potential well for neutrons and protons separately for a light symmetric nucleus. (b) shows that the depth of the potential well for neutrons is higher than that for protons for a nucleus with $N > Z$.*

[13] $hc = 6.62606957^{-34}$ J.s $\times 3 \times 10^{23}$ fm/s $\Rightarrow \hbar c = 197.326$ MeV-fm.

Similarly, the protons in a light symmetric nucleus[14] have identical parameters, and thus, the depth of the potential well is also about $V_0^{\text{neutron}} = 36$ MeV.

Actually, a nucleus contains fewer protons than neutrons ($N > Z$), and thus, the maximum kinetic energy of the neutrons must be larger than that of the protons. However, the top-most proton level must have the same energy as that of the neutron level, as shown in Fig. 2.6. Otherwise, the higher lying neutrons (protons) could move to the low-lying proton (neutron) states following the transformation $n \to p$ (or $p \to n$), and the nucleus would be β-radioactive. Therefore, the depth of the potential well for neutrons is higher than for protons: $V_0^{\text{neutron}} > V_0^{\text{proton}}$, since an additional repulsive interaction exists between protons.

Illustrative Example 2.18: Calculate the Fermi momentum and energy of neutrons and protons in $^{208}_{82}$Pb. Also estimate the Coulomb energy of a proton lying at the surface of the nucleus and compare the result with the Fermi energy difference between neutrons and protons.

Solution The Fermi momentum, Eq. (2.27), is

$$p_F = (3\pi^2)^{1/3}\hbar\left(\frac{N}{V}\right)^{1/3} = \left(\frac{9\pi}{4}\right)^{1/3}\hbar\left(\frac{N}{A}\right)^{1/3}\frac{1}{R_0},$$

where we have used the relation $V = \frac{4}{3}\pi R_0^3 A$, A being the mass number.

Assuming $R_0 = 1.3$ fm, $p_F \approx 291.31\left(\frac{N}{A}\right)^{1/3}$.

The Fermi momentum of neutrons in $^{208}_{82}$Pb is $291.31\left(\frac{126}{208}\right)^{1/3} \approx 246.48$ MeV/c.

The Fermi momentum of protons in $^{208}_{82}$Pb is $291.31\left(\frac{82}{208}\right)^{1/3} \approx 213.60$ MeV/c.

As $p_F c << mc^2$, we may use the non-relativistic equation to calculate the Fermi energy.

Fermi energy of neutrons is $E_F^{\text{neutron}} = \dfrac{p_F^2}{2 \times 939.57} \approx 32.33$ MeV.

Fermi energy of protons is $E_F^{\text{proton}} = \dfrac{p_F^2}{2 \times 938.28} \approx 24.31$ MeV.

Since the Fermi levels of neutrons and protons are the same for a stable nucleus, the potential for the neutrons must be deeper than that for protons.

The approximate maximum value of the Coulomb energy of a proton at the nuclear surface is $\approx \dfrac{e^2}{4\pi\varepsilon_0}\dfrac{(Z-1)}{R_0 A^{1/3}} = \dfrac{1.44 \times 81}{1.3 \times 208^{1/3}} \approx 15$ MeV.

Difference in Fermi energy is ≈ 10.00 MeV, which is approximately of the same order as of the Coulomb energy of a proton.

[14]The Coulomb repulsion among the protons is assumed to be neglected for a light symmetric nucleus with $N = Z$.

Illustrative Example 2.19: Estimation of asymmetry term in nuclear binding energy

Nucleons are spin-1/2 particles, and thus, obey Fermi–Dirac (FD) statistics. Assume that the nucleus is a degenerated Fermi sphere of radius R and volume V, where the nucleons move independently and freely (molecules of ideal gas without any interaction).

Use the FD distribution to calculate the kinetic energy of the nucleons. Hence estimate asymmetry term in nuclear binding energy. (This is a crude model[15]. As the nucleons are assumed to be non-interacting, the model cannot account for the entire asymmetry term in nuclear binding energy).

The number of states of the proton between momenta p and $p+dp$ is $2\times\frac{4\pi V}{h^3}p^2dp$, where factor 2 is included to consider two spin states of the proton. Since all the states up to the Fermi level are filled, the total number of protons is

$$Z=\frac{8\pi V}{h^3}\int_0^{p_F}p^2dp=\frac{8\pi V}{h^3}\frac{p_F^3}{3} \tag{2.29}$$

Total kinetic energy of protons is

$$\begin{aligned} T_p &= \frac{8\pi V}{h^3}\int_0^{p_F}\frac{p^2}{2m}p^2dp=\frac{8\pi V}{h^3}\times\frac{1}{10m}p_F^5 \\ &= \frac{8\pi V}{h^3}\times\frac{1}{10m}\left(\frac{3h^3}{8\pi V}\right)^{5/3}\times Z^{5/3}=\frac{3h^2}{10m}\left(\frac{3}{8\pi V}\right)^{2/3}Z^{5/3} \end{aligned} \tag{2.30}$$

Similarly, total kinetic energy of neutrons is

$$T_n=\frac{3h^2}{10m}\left(\frac{3}{8\pi V}\right)^{2/3}N^{5/3}, \tag{2.31}$$

where we have assumed the same mass for protons and neutrons. The total kinetic energy is

$$T=T_p+T_n=\frac{3h^2}{10m}\left(\frac{3}{8\pi V}\right)^{2/3}(Z^{5/3}+N^{5/3}) \tag{2.32}$$

Let us now introduce the variables $A=N+Z$ and $\Delta=\frac{N-Z}{2}$. Thus

$$N=\frac{A}{2}+\Delta \text{ and } Z=\frac{A}{2}-\Delta$$

From Eq. (2.32)

$$\begin{aligned} T &= \frac{3h^2}{10m}\left(\frac{3}{8\pi V}\right)^{2/3}\left[\left(\frac{A}{2}-\Delta\right)^{5/3}+\left(\frac{A}{2}+\Delta\right)^{5/3}\right] \\ &= \frac{3h^2}{10m}\left(\frac{3}{8\pi V}\right)^{2/3}\times\left(\frac{A}{2}\right)^{5/3}\left[\left(1-\frac{2\Delta}{A}\right)^{5/3}+\left(1+\frac{2\Delta}{A}\right)^{5/3}\right] \end{aligned}$$

[15] Roy, RR and Nigam, BP. 1996. *Nuclear Physics: Theory and Experiment*. New Age Publications, India.

$$= \frac{3h^2}{10m}\left(\frac{3}{8\pi V}\right)^{2/3} \times 2 \times \left(\frac{A}{2}\right)^{5/3}\left[1+\frac{5}{9}\left(\frac{2\Delta}{A}\right)^2\right]$$

$$T = \frac{3h^2}{10m}\left(\frac{3A}{16\pi V}\right)^{2/3}\left[A+\frac{5}{9}\frac{(N-Z)^2}{A}\right] \tag{2.33}$$

Now, $\frac{A}{V} = \frac{3A}{4\pi R_0^3 A} \approx 0.138\ /\text{fm}^3$, assuming $R_0 = 1.2$ fm and

$$\frac{3h^2}{10m}\left(\frac{3A}{16\pi V}\right)^{2/3} = \frac{3\times 12.4^2\times 10^4}{10\times 938}\left(\frac{3\times 0.138}{16\pi}\right)^{2/3} \approx 20 \text{ MeV}$$

The first term of the RHS of Eq. (2.33) represents the kinetic energy contribution to the volume term in the semi-empirical mass formula. The second term is the symmetry term. Thus

$$T_{\text{asym}} = \frac{3h^2}{10m}\left(\frac{3A}{16\pi V}\right)^{2/3} \times \frac{5}{9}\frac{(N-Z)^2}{A} \approx 11 \times \frac{(N-Z)^2}{A} \text{ MeV} \tag{2.34}$$

Therefore, the asymmetry term varies as $\frac{(N-Z)^2}{A}$. However, it accounts for only about half of the symmetry term. The other half actually comes from the increase in mutual interaction energies when $N \neq Z$.

SUMMARY

- **Liquid-drop Model**
  - (a) Similarity with a drop of liquid
    - Density of nucleus is constant, like in a drop of liquid.
    - Like the molecules in a drop, all nucleons are alike.
  - (b) **Semi-empirical Mass Formula**

    $$M(^A_ZX) = Zm_H + (A-Z)m_n - a_vA + a_sA^{2/3} + a_c\frac{Z(Z-1)}{A^{1/3}} + a_{\text{asym}}\frac{(N-Z)^2}{A} - \delta$$

    Typical values of the constants $a_v = 15.5$ MeV, $a_s = 16.8$ MeV, $a_c = 0.72$ MeV, $a_{\text{asym}} = 23.0$ MeV and $a_p = 34.0$ MeV give the *BE*, which is close to the observed value.
  - (c) **Mass Parabola:** The semi-empirical mass formula represents a parabola for A = constant, known as **mass parabola**. The most stable isobar is $Z_0 \approx \frac{A}{1.98+0.015A^{2/3}}$.
  - (d) β **Disintegration Energy of Mirror Nuclei**: The energy released in β^+ decay is $Q_{\beta^+} = M(^A_{Z+1}X) - M(^A_ZY) - m_e$, where M represents the nuclear mass expressed in energy units. By the mass formula $Q_{\beta^+} = a_cA^{2/3} - (m_n - m_p + m_e)$. This relation may be used to calculate a_c and hence R_0 in the nuclear radius $R = R_0A^{1/3}$.
- **Shell Model**
  - **Assumption**: Each nucleon moves independently in an average potential which is the resultant effect of all the other nucleons present in the nucleus.

- Shell model energy levels (including spin orbit interaction):

$$1s_{1/2},\ \overbrace{1p_{3/2},1p_{1/2}},\ \overbrace{1d_{5/2},2s_{1/2},1d_{3/2}},\ \overbrace{1f_{7/2}},\overbrace{2p_{3/2},1f_{5/2},2p_{1/2},1g_{9/2}}\cdots$$

- **Explanation of Magic Numbers**: Arrangement of nucleons in different energy levels according to Pauli Exclusion Principle leads to shell closure for N or Z equal to $2, 8, 20, 28, 50, 82$ and 126.

- **Predictions of Shell Model**
  - **Ground State Spin (I):** For even–even nuclei $I = 0$. The spin of the nucleus is given by its unpaired nucleons.
  - The parity of the nucleus in the ground state is $P = (-1)^l$, where l is the l-value of the last unpaired nucleon.
  - In odd–odd nuclei

$$\text{If } j_p + j_n - l_p - l_n = 0, \text{ then } I = |j_n - j_p|.$$
$$\text{If } j_p + j_n - l_p - l_n = \pm 1, \text{ then } I = |j_n - j_p| \text{ or } |j_n + j_p|$$

- The Fermi model is the simplest independent nuclear model which considers the non-interacting nucleons confined to a small volume of radius $R = R_0A^{1/3}$. The applicability of this model is not very wide.

Review Questions and Problems

Multiple Choice Questions

1. The binding energy of a light nucleus ${}_Z^AX$ in MeV is given by the approximate formula $B(A,Z) \approx 16A - 20A^{2/3} - 3/4Z^2A^{-1/3} + 30\dfrac{(N-Z)^2}{A}$. The value of Z for the most stable isobar for a given A is

   (a) $\dfrac{A}{2}\left(1-\dfrac{A^{2/3}}{160}\right)^{-1}$ (b) $\dfrac{A}{2}$ (c) $\dfrac{A}{2}\left(1-\dfrac{A^{2/3}}{120}\right)^{-1}$ (d) $\dfrac{A}{2}\left(1+\dfrac{A^{4/3}}{64}\right)^{-1}$

   [NET 2013]

2. The binding energy of a light nucleus ${}_Z^AX$ is given by the approximate formula

$$B(A,Z) \approx a_vA - a_sA^{2/3} - a_cZ^2A^{-1/3} - a_{\text{sym}}\frac{(2Z-A)^2}{A},$$

   where $a_v = 16$ MeV, $a_s = 24$ MeV, $a_{\text{sym}} = 24$ MeV and $a_c = 0.75$ MeV. The value of Z for the most stable isobar with $A = 216$ is

   (a) 68 (b) 72 (c) 84 (d) 92 [NET 2014]

3. Of nuclei with mass number $A = 125$, the binding energy calculated using the liquid-drop model (given that the coefficients for Coulomb and asymmetry energy are $a_c = 0.7$ MeV and $a_{\text{sym}} = 22.5$ MeV, respectively) is maximum for

   (a) ${}^{125}_{54}\text{Xe}$ (b) ${}^{125}_{53}\text{I}$ (c) ${}^{125}_{52}\text{Xe}$ (d) ${}^{125}_{51}\text{Xe}$ [NET 2015]

4. According to the shell model, the spin and parity of the two nuclei ${}^{125}_{51}$Sb and ${}^{89}_{38}$Sr are, respectively

   (a) $\frac{5}{2}^+$ and $\frac{5}{2}^+$ (b) $\frac{5}{2}^+$ and $\frac{7}{2}^+$ (c) $\frac{7}{2}^+$ and $\frac{5}{2}^+$ (d) $\frac{7}{2}^+$ and $\frac{7}{2}^+$

   [NET 2011]

5. A spin-$\frac{1}{2}$ particle A undergoes the decay $A \to B + C + D$, where it is known that B and C are also spin-$\frac{1}{2}$ particles. The complete set of allowed values of the spin of D is

   (a) $\frac{1}{2}, 1, \frac{3}{2}, 2, \frac{5}{2}, 3, \ldots$ (b) 0, 1 (c) $\frac{1}{2}$ only (d) $\frac{1}{2}, \frac{3}{2}, \frac{5}{2}, \ldots$ [NET 2013]

6. According to the shell model, the total angular momentum (in units of $\hbar$) and the parity of the ground state of the ${}^{7}_{3}$Li nucleus is

   (a) $\frac{3}{2}$ with $-$ve parity (b) $\frac{3}{2}$ with $+$ve parity

   (c) $\frac{1}{2}$ with $+$ve parity (d) $\frac{7}{2}$ with $-$ve parity [NET 2013]

7. Let us approximate the nuclear potential in the shell model using a three-dimensional isotropic harmonic oscillator. Since the lowest two energy levels have angular momenta of $l = 0$ and $l = 1$, respectively, which of the following two nuclei have magic numbers of protons and neutrons?

   (a) ${}^{4}_{2}$He and ${}^{16}_{8}$O (b) ${}^{2}_{1}$D and ${}^{8}_{4}$Be (c) ${}^{4}_{2}$He and ${}^{8}_{4}$Be (d) ${}^{4}_{2}$He and ${}^{12}_{6}$C

   [NET 2015]

8. According to the shell model, the spin and parity of ${}^{15}_{7}$N is

   (a) $\frac{1}{2}^-$ (b) $\frac{1}{2}^+$ (c) $\frac{3}{2}^-$ (d) $\frac{3}{2}^+$ [GATE 2010]

9. According to the single particle shell model, the spin and parity of ${}^{17}_{8}$O is

   (a) $\frac{1}{2}^-$ (b) $\frac{3}{2}^-$ (c) $\frac{3}{2}^+$ (d) $\frac{5}{2}^+$ [GATE 2011]

10. Deuteron has only one bound state, with spin parity 1^+, isospin 0 and electric quadrupole moment 0.286 fm^2. This data suggests that the nuclear forces have

    (a) Only spin and isospin dependence

    (b) No spin dependence and no tensor components

    (c) Spin dependence but no tensor components

    (d) Spin dependence along with tensor components [GATE 2012]

11. I^π for the ground state of ${}^{13}_{6}$C is

    (a) 1^+ (b) $\frac{1}{2}^-$ (c) $\frac{3}{2}^+$ (d) $\frac{3}{2}^-$ [NET, GATE 2014]

12. The correct spin-parity and isospin assignments for the ground state of ^{13}C is

(a) $\frac{1}{2}^-, -\frac{1}{2}$ (b) $\frac{1}{2}^+, -\frac{1}{2}$ (c) $\frac{3}{2}^+, \frac{1}{2}$ (d) $\frac{3}{2}^-, -\frac{1}{2}$

13. According to the nuclear shell model, the respective ground state spin-parity values of $^{15}_{8}$O and $^{17}_{8}$O nuclei are

(a) $\frac{1}{2}^+, \frac{1}{2}^-$ (b) $\frac{1}{2}^-, \frac{5}{2}^+$ (c) $\frac{3}{2}^-, \frac{5}{2}^+$ (d) $\frac{3}{2}^-, \frac{1}{2}^-$ [NET, GATE 2016]

Short Questions and Problems

Liquid-drop model

1. What experimental evidence led to the idea of the nuclear shell model?
2. Discuss insertion of the pairing term in the semi-empirical mass formula.
3. Develop the semi-empirical mass formula, discussing the physical basis of each term.
4. (a) Write the Coulomb term in the semi-empirical mass formula. What does it account for?

   (b) What do you mean by mirror nuclei? Give two examples.
5. Write down the semi-empirical nuclear binding energy formula, proposed by Weizsäcker. Obtain the equation of mass parabola from it. Hence explain the stability of nuclei against β decay for the odd-A case.
6. (a) Using the semi-empirical nuclear binding energy formula proposed by Weizsäcker, calculate the atomic number of the most stable nucleus for a given mass number A. (Given: For Coulomb energy term, $a_c = 0.71$ MeV and for asymmetry, $a_s = 22.7$ MeV). Hence show that for light nuclei, $Z \approx \frac{A}{2}$.

   (b) Derive an expression for the Coulomb energy of a spherical nucleus of mass number A and atomic number Z having a uniform charge density. Hence obtain an expression for the Coulomb term occurring in the semi-empirical mass formula.

   (c) Estimate the nuclear radius from the given data $M(^{25}_{12}\text{Mg}) = 24.985837$ u and $M(^{25}_{13}\text{Al}) = 24.990429$ u.

Shell model

7. (a) Write down the nuclear magic numbers. Why are they called so?

   (b) Find the parity for the ground state of the $^{27}_{13}$Al nucleus.
8. Using the extreme single particle shell model, calculate the ground state spin parity of $^{25}_{12}$Mg.
9. In the shell model, the ordering of nuclear energy levels is as follows:

   $1s_{1/2}, 1p_{3/2}, 1p_{1/2}, 1d_{5/2}, 2s_{1/2}, 1d_{3/2}\ldots$

   (a) What is responsible for the splitting of $1p_{3/2}, 1p_{1/2}$?

(b) Predict the ground state spin and parity of $^{7}_{3}$Li, ^{16}O, ^{15}O, ^{17}O, $^{39}_{19}$K and $^{45}_{21}$Sc.

(c) Predict the ground spin and parity of $^{18}_{9}$F.

10. Predict the spin and parity of $^{58}_{27}$Co, $^{59}_{27}$Co and $^{60}_{27}$Co.
11. Obtain the ground state spins and parities of the following nuclei according to the extreme single particle shell model: $^{13}_{6}$C, $^{16}_{8}$O and $^{14}_{7}$N.
12. Explain the basic assumptions of the nuclear shell model.
13. Explain the following statements:

    (a) The motion of an individual nucleon inside the nucleus may be regarded as independent of each other.

    (b) All even–even nuclei have 0^+ spin.

Fermi model

14. Calculate the Fermi momentum and Fermi energy of protons and neutrons in a nucleus with $N = Z$, and hence, estimate the depth of the potential well for neutrons and protons.
15. In a nucleus with $N = Z = A/2$, $p_F \propto \left(\frac{A}{V}\right)^{1/3}$ and thus $E_F = \frac{p_F^2}{2m} \Rightarrow A = kVE_F^{3/2}$.

    Also total energy $U = \frac{3}{5}AE_F = \frac{3}{5}kVE_F^{5/2}$. Show that pressure $p = -\frac{\partial U}{\partial V} = \frac{2}{5}\frac{A}{V}E_F$.

HINTS/ANSWERS TO SELECTED PROBLEMS

Multiple Choice Questions

1. (a) 2. (c) 3. (c)

4. (d) Note that both the nuclei have the same number of odd nucleons, and thus, the same I. Also, the states with higher I will be filled first.

5. (c) 6. (a) 7. (a) 8. (a) 9. (d) 10. (d) 11. (b)

12. $(-1)^{l+s+I_3} = -1$; $l = 1$, $s = \frac{1}{2}$. Thus, $I_3 = \frac{-1}{2}$ (a) 13. (b)

Short Questions and Problems

6. (c) ≈ 4.27 fm 9. (b) $\frac{3}{2}^-, 0^+, \frac{1}{2}^-, \frac{5}{2}^+, \frac{3}{2}^+$ and $\frac{7}{2}^-$ (c) A range of values, in fact 1^+

11. $\frac{1}{2}^-, 0^+$, and 0^+ or 1^+

CHAPTER 3

Radioactivity

Despite the strong force acting among nucleons, the nucleus becomes unstable for certain combinations of neutrons and protons. It has been observed that nuclei that lie away from the stability line $N = Z$ are unstable. By spontaneously emitting particles or radiation or both, an unstable nucleus arrives at its most stable configuration. The spontaneous disintegration of nuclei, leading to a change in their composition and/or energy, from an unstable state is referred to as **radioactivity**. It was discovered accidentally by Henri Becquerel in 1896. He observed an interesting phenomenon while studying the fluorescence and phosphorescence of compounds irradiated with visible light. After illuminating some pieces of uranium salt with visible light, he wrapped them in black paper and kept them in a drawer. He later separated the package from the photographic plates with a piece of silver. It was with great surprise that he noticed the blackening of the photographic plates due to some strong radiation emitted from the uranium salt, without an external source.

Subsequent studies on radioactivity showed that there are three types of radioactive decay: alpha, beta and gamma.

3.1 RADIOACTIVE DECAY EQUATION

All radioactive decay processes are random in nature. It is not possible to predict exactly when an individual unstable nucleus will decay. However, using statistical rules, it is possible to predict the probability of any particular decay.

We now calculate the probability that a given nucleus will survive for a time t or, in other words, the probability of obtaining a nucleus in time t.

Let us divide the entire time interval t in large numbers (n) of small intervals dt, that is, $t = n \times dt$. Radioactivity is a characteristic of the nucleus, and the probability (λ) of decay per unit time of a particular nucleus in a given energy state is constant. Thus, the probability of decay in time dt is λdt.

Therefore, the probability of the nucleus not decaying in time interval dt is $[1 - \lambda dt]$.

The probability that the nucleus will survive for two small time intervals dt and dt is $[1-\lambda dt]^2$. Similarly, the probability of a nucleus surviving a nucleus up to time t is $[1-\lambda dt]^n$.

Therefore, the probability of finding any particular nucleus in time t will be

$$P(t) = \lim_{n\to\infty}[1-\lambda dt]^n = \lim_{n\to\infty}[1-\lambda \frac{t}{n}]^n = e^{-\lambda t} \tag{3.1}$$

Thus, *the probability that a particular nucleus will survive at least up to the time t is* $e^{-\lambda t}$.

If N_0 is the initial number of nuclei and $N(t)$ is the number of surviving nuclei after time t, then

$$N(t) = N_0 e^{-\lambda t} \tag{3.2}$$

This is the **radioactive decay law** and λ is known as the **decay constant**.

Illustrative Example 3.1: Probability of decay between t and $t+dt$

The probability that a particular nucleus will decay between t and ∞ is $e^{-\lambda t}$. Find the probability that a nucleus will decay between the time intervals t and $t+dt$.

Solution Let the probability that a nucleus will decay between the time interval t and $t+dt$ be $f(t)dt$. Thus

$$\int_t^{\infty} f(t)dt = e^{-\lambda t}$$

This gives $f(t) = \lambda e^{-\lambda t}$. Thus, the probability that a nucleus will decay between the time intervals t and $t+dt$ is

$$f(t)dt = \lambda e^{-\lambda t}dt$$

Different approach: Equation (3.2) can also be obtained directly from the definition as follows.

The probability of decay of a single nucleus in time dt is λdt. If $N(t)$ is the number of radioactive nuclei present at time t, then the number of decays is

$$-dN = \lambda N dt \tag{3.3}$$

The negative sign implies that the number of nuclei decreases with time. The rate of decay is

$$\frac{dN}{dt} = -\lambda N \tag{3.4}$$

The equation indicates that the rate at which a particular decay process occurs in a radioactive sample is proportional to the number of radioactive nuclei present at that instant. The proportionality constant, λ, is known as the decay constant. Integrating this equation, we get

$$\int_{N_0}^{N} \frac{dN}{N} = -\lambda \int_0^t dt \quad \text{or} \quad N(t) = N_0 e^{-\lambda t}$$

The **activity or decay rate** is the number of decays per unit time and is given by $A = \lambda N$. Thus

$$A(t) = \lambda N_0 e^{-\lambda t} = A_0 e^{-\lambda t}, \tag{3.5}$$

where A_0 is the decay rate at $t = 0$. The activity[1] of the decaying substance also decays exponentially.

The **unit of activity** that is used frequently is the curie (Ci), where 1 Ci = 3.7×10^{10} decays per second = 3.7×10^{10} becquerel (Bq).

Illustrative Example 3.2: Activity of 1 g of Ra

The half-life of $^{226}_{88}$Ra against α decay is 1622 years. What is the activity of 1 g of $^{226}_{88}$Ra?

Solution Number of atoms in 1 g of $^{226}_{88}$Ra is $\dfrac{6.023 \times 10^{23}}{226} = 2.67 \times 10^{21}$.

$$\lambda = \frac{0.693}{T_{1/2}} = \frac{0.693}{1622 \times 365 \times 24 \times 3600} = 1.355 \times 10^{-11} \text{s}^{-1}$$

Thus, activity is

$$A = \lambda N = 2.67 \times 10^{21} \times 1.355 \times 10^{-11} = 3.61 \times 10^{10} \text{decays per second} \approx 0.97 \text{ Ci}.$$

⇒ Check Progress 3.1: Calculate the activity of 3×10^{-9} kg of gold, $^{200}_{79}$Au, whose half-life is 48 minutes.

Illustrative Example 3.3: Source of strength 5 millicurie

The half-life of $^{210}_{84}$Po against α decay is 138 days. Determine the amount of $^{210}_{84}$Po required to provide a radioactive source of strength 5 millicuries.

Solution The required strength $A = \lambda N = 5 \times 10^{-3} \times 3.7 \times 10^{10}$ decays per second, where $\lambda = \dfrac{0.693}{138 \times 24 \times 3600}$.

Thus, the number of atoms is $N \approx 3.183 \times 10^{15}$

The amount of $^{210}_{84}$Po is $\dfrac{210 \times 3.183 \times 10^{15}}{6.023 \times 10^{23}} \approx 1.11 \times 10^{-6}$g

Illustrative Example 3.4: Unstable parent to stable daughter

Suppose the number of parent nuclei at time $t = 0$ is N_0 and the number of daughter nuclei is 0. The parent nucleus is unstable, but the daughter is stable. Thus, the number of parent nuclei decreases with time, while the number of daughter nuclei increases. What is the number of stable daughter nuclei at any time t?

[1]Note that the activity is defined by $N\lambda$, and not by $-\frac{dN}{dt}$. For a single decay process, both quantities are identical; however, for more complex situations, they may be different.

Solution For the parent nucleus, $\frac{dN_1}{dt} = -\lambda N_1$ (3.6)

Solving the equation with the initial condition, at $t = 0$, $N_1 = N_0$, we get

$$N_1(t) = N_0 e^{-\lambda t} \tag{3.7}$$

Thus, the number of parent nuclei N decreases exponentially with time.

The rate of growth of the daughter nuclei due to disintegration of the parent can be expressed as

$$\frac{dN_2}{dt} = +\lambda N_1 = \lambda N_0 e^{-\lambda t} \quad \text{or, } N_2 = -N_0 e^{-\lambda t} + c$$

At $t = 0$, $N_2 = 0$, and thus, $N_2(t) = N_0 - N_0 e^{-\lambda t}$ (3.8)

Thus, the number of daughter nuclei N_2 increases while N_1 decreases with time. The growth of the daughter and the decay of the parent is shown in Fig. 3.1.

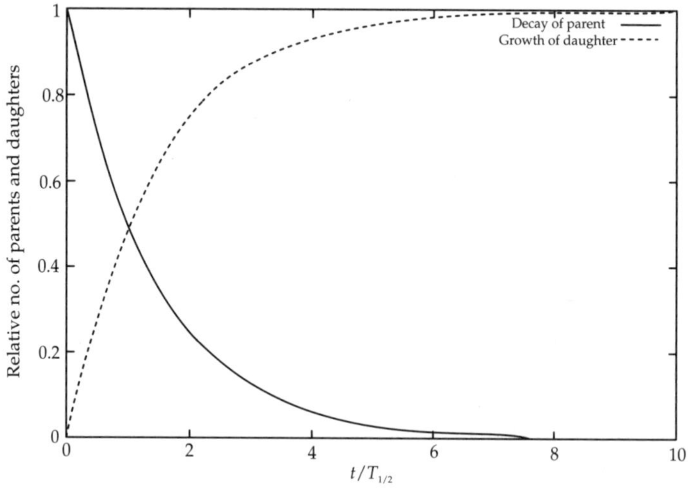

Figure 3.1: *Decay of parent and growth of daughter: Relative number of parent and daughter nuclei as a function of the number of half-lives $t/T_{1/2}$*

3.1.1 Half-Life and Mean Life

Half-life: Another important parameter that characterises the radioactive process is the half-life ($T_{1/2}$). It is the time it takes half of a given number of radioactive nuclei to decay.

Setting $N = \frac{N_0}{2}$ and $t = T_{1/2}$ in Eq. (3.2), we find

$$T_{1/2} = \frac{\ln 2}{\lambda} \approx \frac{0.693}{\lambda} \tag{3.9}$$

Mean life: The distribution function for the exponential decay is

$$f(t) = \lambda e^{-\lambda t}$$

$f(t)dt$ represents the probability of decay of a nucleus between the time intervals t and $t+dt$. In another words, it is the probability that a nucleus will survive up to time t. Thus, the average value of t is

$$<t>= \int_0^{\infty} t\lambda e^{-\lambda t} dt = \frac{1}{\lambda} \tag{3.10}$$

Illustrative Example 3.5: Half-life measurement[2]

The activity of a sample of $^{55}_{24}$Cr at the end of 5-minute intervals is presented in Table 3.1. From this data, find the half-life of $^{55}_{24}$Cr.

Solution The activity follows the exponential law: $A(t) = A_0 e^{-\lambda t}$
Taking log on both sides $\ln A = \ln A_0 - \lambda t$
In Fig. 3.2, $\ln A$ has been plotted for different times. It is a straight line with a slope of 0.198 min^{-1}. Thus, the half-life is $T = \dfrac{0.693}{0.198 \text{ min}^{-1}} = 3.50$ minutes.

Table 3.1: *Activity of* $^{55}_{24}$Cr

Time in m	Activity in mCi
0	19.20
5	7.13
10	2.65
15	0.99
20	0.37

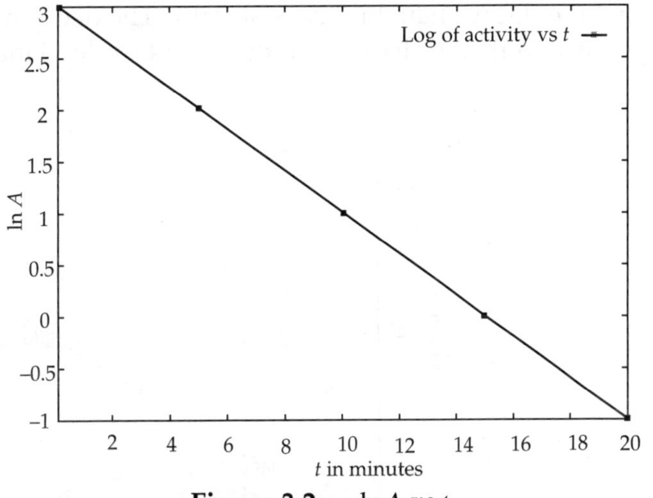

Figure 3.2: $\ln A$ *vs* t

3.1.2 Radioactive Series

Most unstable nuclei do not achieve stability in a single decay. For any decay, the daughter nucleus itself may be unstable and it becomes the parent for a further radioactive decay. After a series of similar steps, a stable nucleus is formed. It has been found after extensive study that most natural radioactive isotopes (with $Z = 81$–92) are members of four radioactive series: thorium, neptunium, uranium and actinium.

[2]For calculation of widely different half-lives of two radioactive nuclei in a sample, see Illustrative Example 3.11.

The reason there are exactly four series follows from the fact that an α decay reduces the mass number (A) by 4, while β decay does not change A at all. Therefore, we have four independent decay series with $A = 4n, 4n+1, 4n+2, 4n+3$.

The four series are listed in Table 3.2. Notice that the half-life of neptunium is quite short compared to the age of the Earth (which is $\sim 10^{10}$ years). As a result, the members of these series are not found on Earth today. They have, however, been produced in the laboratory by neutron bombardment on other heavy nuclei.

Table 3.2: *Radioactive series*

Mass number	Series	Parent nucleus	Half-life of parent (in years)	Final (stable) product
$4n$	Thorium	$^{232}_{90}$Th	1.39×10^{10}	$^{208}_{82}$Pb
$4n+1$	Neptunium	$^{237}_{93}$Np	2.25×10^{6}	$^{209}_{83}$Bi
$4n+2$	Uranium	$^{238}_{92}$U	4.47×10^{9}	$^{206}_{82}$Pb
$4n+3$	Actinium	$^{235}_{92}$U	7.07×10^{8}	$^{207}_{82}$Pb

The decay chain of the ^{232}Th decay series, $A = 4n$, is shown in Fig. 3.3. It shows that the decay chain branches at ^{212}Bi. The decay of ^{212}Bi may proceed either by β^- decay and then α decay or in the reverse order. Finally, both branches lead to ^{208}Pb.

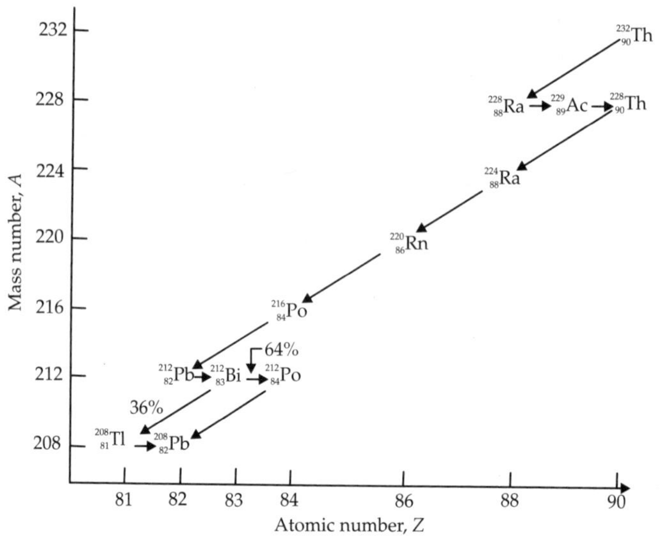

Figure 3.3: *The* ^{232}Th *decay series,* $A = 4n$

There are also other sources of radioactivity of relatively shorter half-life. For example, ^{3}H and ^{14}C, which are formed continuously in the upper atmosphere when cosmic rays strike the atoms of the atmosphere.

3.1.3 Branching

Generally, any radioactive element decays by only one mode. However, there are some radioactive elements for which two modes of decay are possible. For example, ^{212}Bi may decay by emitting α particles or β particles (Fig. 3.3).

The possibility of α decay does not depend on the possibility of β decay. Thus, for a sample of N nuclei, the decrease in N in time dt by both decay modes is

$$-dN = \lambda_\alpha N dt + \lambda_\beta N dt \quad \text{or} \quad -\frac{dN}{N} = (\lambda_\alpha + \lambda_\beta)dt$$

Therefore, the probabilities of the individual decay modes are additive and the probability of the decay is increased. Solving the above equation, we get

$$N = N_0 e^{-(\lambda_\alpha+\lambda_\beta)t} = N_0 e^{-\lambda_{\text{total}} t}, \tag{3.11}$$

where N_0 is the number of parent nuclei at $t = 0$. Equation (3.11) shows that the decay is governed by λ_{total}. This is expected, as the nucleus cannot be prevented from β decay even if α decay is observed. The half-life of the sample is $\frac{\ln 2}{\lambda_{\text{total}}}$. The ratio $\frac{\lambda_\alpha}{\lambda_{\text{total}}}$ is called the **branching ratio for α decay**.

$$\lambda_{\text{total}} = \lambda_\alpha + \lambda_\beta; \quad \frac{\lambda_\alpha}{\lambda_{\text{total}}} + \frac{\lambda_\beta}{\lambda_{\text{total}}} = 1$$

$$\frac{\tau_{\text{total}}}{\tau_\alpha} + \frac{\tau_{\text{total}}}{\tau_\beta} = 1; \quad \frac{1}{\tau_\alpha} + \frac{1}{\tau_\beta} = \frac{1}{\tau_{\text{total}}},$$

where τ_α and τ_α are the partial half-lives.

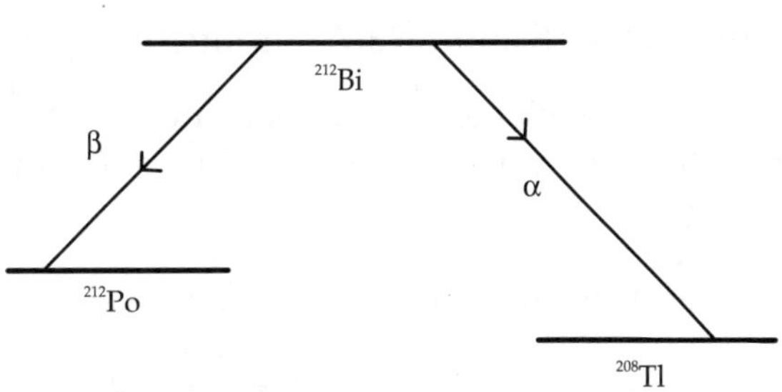

Figure 3.4: *Branching decay*

The α activity is $-\frac{dN_\alpha}{dt} = \lambda_\alpha N = N_0 \lambda_\alpha e^{-\lambda_{\text{total}} t}$. Similarly, the β activity is $N_0 \lambda_\beta e^{-\lambda_{\text{total}} t}$.

Illustrative Example 3.6: Partial decay constants

^{226}Ac can decay by α emission (0.006%), β^- emission (83%) and electron capture (17%). The half-life of ^{226}Ac is 29 hours. Determine the partial decay constants.

Solution The total decay constant of ^{226}Ac is

$$\lambda_{\text{total}} = \frac{\ln 2}{29} h^{-1} \approx 6.6 \times 10^{-6}\ \text{s}^{-1}$$

The partial decay constants are

$$\begin{aligned} \lambda_\alpha &= 6 \times 10^{-5} \lambda_{\text{total}} = 4.0 \times 10^{-10}\ \text{s}^{-1} \\ \lambda_{EC} &= 0.17 \lambda_{\text{total}} = 1.1 \times 10^{-6}\ \text{s}^{-1} \\ \lambda_\beta &= 0.83 \lambda_{\text{total}} = 5.5 \times 10^{-6}\ \text{s}^{-1} \end{aligned}$$

We often specify the branching ratio by partial decay constant or partial half-life.

3.1.4 Production of Radioactive Element by Nuclear Bombardment

Suppose a radioisotope is produced at a steady rate Q by bombarding a sample with neutrons. The radioisotope decays at the rate $-\lambda N$, where N is the number of radioactive nuclei present and λ is its decay constant. The net rate of change[3] of N is

$$\frac{dN}{dt} = Q - \lambda N, \tag{3.12}$$

where Q is constant. Multiplying both sides by the integrating factor $e^{\lambda t}$, we get

$$\frac{d}{dt}(Ne^{\lambda t}) = Qe^{\lambda t}$$

Integrating and considering the initial condition, at $t \to 0,\ N \to 0$, we get

$$N = \frac{Q}{\lambda}(1 - e^{-\lambda t}) \tag{3.13}$$

Equation (3.13) indicates that N grows with time and eventually it becomes constant $(= \frac{Q}{\lambda})$. As soon as the bombardment stops, Q becomes 0 and N decays exponentially according to Eq. (3.12).

Illustrative Example 3.7: Production of radioactive element

An unstable element (with half-life T) is produced in a nuclear reactor at a constant rate Q. How much time, in terms of T, is required to produce half the equilibrium quantity?

Solution From Eq. (3.13) $N = N_{eq}(1 - e^{-\lambda t})$, where the equilibrium value is $N_{eq} = \frac{Q}{\lambda}$.

Therefore $1 - e^{-\lambda t} = \frac{1}{2}$ and $t = \frac{\ln 2}{\lambda} = T$.

Thus, *the result is independent of Q.*

3.1.5 Successive Disintegration and Radioactive Equilibrium

Now, we consider a situation where a parent nuclide decays into a daughter that is also radioactive. Suppose the parent (*Element* 1) decays with decay constant λ_1 and produces a radioactive daughter (*Element* 2), which decays with decay constant λ_2 to *Element* 3. Then, *Element* 3 is assumed to be stable.

Number of daughters (N_2) at a time t: Let N_1 and N_2 be the number of nuclei present in *Element* 1 and *Element* 2, respectively, at any time t. Therefore

$$\frac{dN_1}{dt} = -\lambda_1 N_1 \tag{3.14}$$

The number of *Element* 2 nuclei increases as a result of decays of *Element* 1 and, at the same time, decreases as a result of its own decay. Thus, the net effect is

[3]Note that for this case, $-\frac{dN}{dt} \neq N\lambda$. The activity is defined by $N\lambda$, and not by $-\frac{dN}{dt}$.

$$\frac{dN_2}{dt} = \lambda_1 N_1 - \lambda_2 N_2 \tag{3.15}$$

Initially (at $t = 0$), the number of *Element* 1 nuclei is N_0 and the number of *Element* 2 nuclei is $N_2 = 0$. Integrating Eq. (3.14), we get

$$N_1(t) = N_0 e^{-\lambda_1 t} \tag{3.16}$$

Substituting this value of N_1 in Eq. (3.15), we get

$$\frac{dN_2}{dt} + \lambda_2 N_2 = \lambda_1 N_1 = \lambda_1 N_0 e^{-\lambda_1 t}$$

The integrating factor is $e^{\lambda_2 t}$. Therefore, $\frac{d}{dt}[N_2 e^{\lambda_2 t}] = \lambda_1 N_0 e^{(\lambda_2 - \lambda_1)t}$.

With the initial condition $t = 0$ and $N_2 = 0$, we obtain

$$N_2 = \frac{\lambda_1}{\lambda_2 - \lambda_1} N_0 \left(e^{-\lambda_1 t} - e^{-\lambda_2 t}\right) \tag{3.17}$$

The typical form of the variation of N_1 and N_2 with time is shown in Fig. 3.5. Note that this equation reduces to the case of the previous example of a stable daughter if we insert $\lambda_2 = 0$.

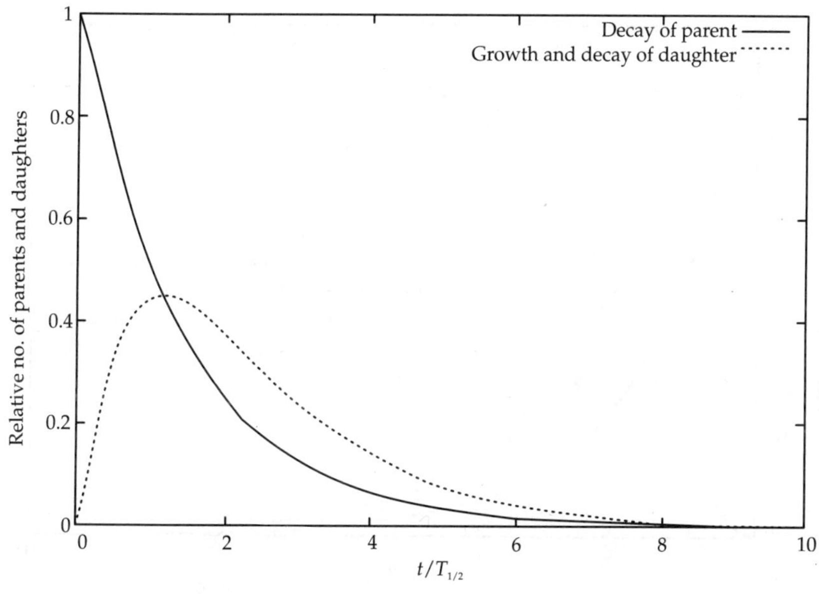

Figure 3.5: *Successive disintegration: Relative number of parents and daughters as a function of the number of half-lives $t/T_{1/2}$ of the daughter*

Time for maximum N_2: N_2 will be maximum at $t = t_m$, when $\frac{dN_2}{dt} = 0$. Using Eq. (3.17), we get

$$t_m = \frac{1}{\lambda_2 - \lambda_1} \ln \frac{\lambda_2}{\lambda_1} \tag{3.18}$$

This relation holds good for both $\lambda_2 > \lambda_1$ and $\lambda_2 < \lambda_1$. Equation (3.15) also suggests that at time $t = t_m$

$$\frac{dN_2}{dt} = 0, \text{ and } \lambda_1 N_1 = \lambda_2 N_2$$

Thus, at this particular time $t = t_m$, the activity of the parent and the activity of the accumulated daughters are equal. *This is perfect equilibrium and is called the ideal equilibrium, but it exists momentarily only at* $t = t_m$.

Number of granddaughters: The daughter (*Element* 3) of *Element* 2 is stable. We want to determine the number of nuclei present in the final product (*Element* 3) at time t. *Element* 3 grows by the decay of *Element* 2.

$$\frac{dN_3}{dt} = \lambda_2 N_2 = \lambda_2 \frac{\lambda_1}{\lambda_2 - \lambda_1} N_0 \left(e^{-\lambda_1 t} - e^{-\lambda_2 t}\right) \tag{3.19}$$

At $t = 0$, $N_3 = 0$, thus $N_3 = \dfrac{\lambda_2 \lambda_1}{\lambda_2 - \lambda_1} N_0 \left(\dfrac{1 - e^{-\lambda_1 t}}{\lambda_1} - \dfrac{1 - e^{-\lambda_2 t}}{\lambda_2}\right)$ (3.20)

Figure 3.6 shows the typical time dependence of N_1, N_2 and N_3.

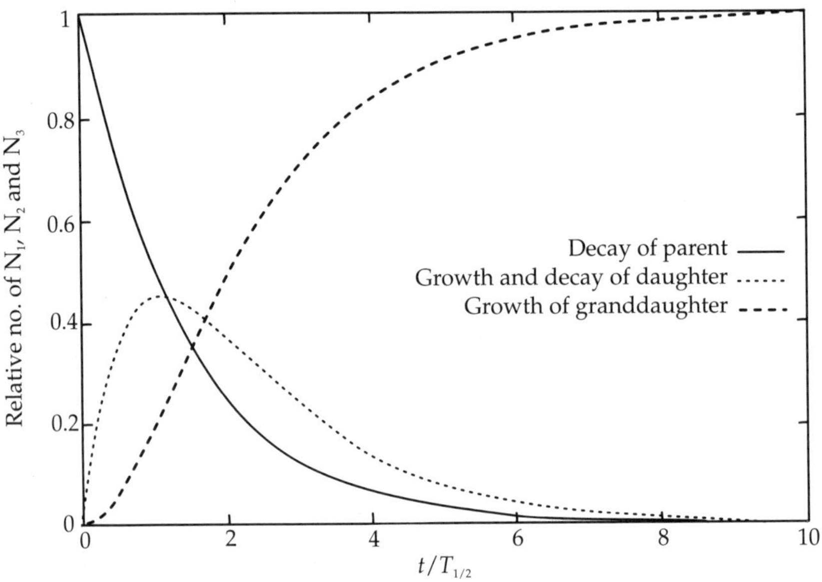

Figure 3.6: *Successive disintegration: Relative number of parents, daughters and granddaughters as a function of the number of half-lives* $t/T_{1/2}$ *of the daughter*

We now introduce the idea of radioactive equilibrium. In radioactive decay, the number of nuclei N present in an element of a radioactive chain always changes with time. However, a state of equilibrium may be attained in many situations.

The number of nuclei in *Element* 2 at any instant is

$$N_2 = \frac{\lambda_1}{\lambda_2 - \lambda_1} N_0 \left(e^{-\lambda_1 t} - e^{-\lambda_2 t}\right)$$

Let T_1 and T_2 be the half-lives of the parent and the daughter, respectively. We will consider the following cases.

Case 1: $T_2 > T_1$ **(No Equilibrium):** First consider the case $\lambda_1 > \lambda_2$, that is, $T_2 > T_1$, where *the parent is short-lived.*

In this case, the $e^{-\lambda_1 t}$ term in Eq. (3.17) decays faster, and thus, after a long time ($t >> T_1$)

$$N_2 \approx \frac{\lambda_1}{\lambda_1 - \lambda_2} N_0 e^{-\lambda_2 t} \tag{3.21}$$

This implies that the daughter decays approximately with its own half-life.
Using Eq. (3.16), the above equation may be rewritten as

$$\frac{N_2\lambda_2}{N_1\lambda_1} = \frac{\lambda_2}{\lambda_1 - \lambda_2}\left(e^{(\lambda_1-\lambda_2)t} - 1\right) \approx \frac{\lambda_2}{\lambda_1 - \lambda_2} e^{(\lambda_1-\lambda_2)t} \tag{3.22}$$

Thus, $\left(\frac{N_2\lambda_2}{N_1\lambda_1}\right)$ increases with time and *there will be no equilibrium.*

Case 2: $T_1 > T_2$ **(Transient Equilibrium):** Now, consider the case $\lambda_2 > \lambda_1$, that is, $T_1 > T_2$, where *the parent is long-lived.*

In this case, the $e^{-\lambda_2 t}$ term in Eq. (3.17) decays faster, and after a long time ($t >> T_2$)

$$N_2 \approx \frac{\lambda_1}{\lambda_2 - \lambda_1} N_0 e^{-\lambda_1 t}$$

This implies that N_2 effectively decays with the decay constant of its parent.
The above relation may also be expressed as

$$\frac{N_2\lambda_2}{N_1\lambda_1} \approx \frac{\lambda_2}{\lambda_2 - \lambda_1} \tag{3.23}$$

Both N_1 and N_2 decrease with time, but the ratio of $\frac{N_2}{N_1}$ eventually becomes constant after a long time, $t >> T_2$. When the ratio of the activities of the daughter to the parent $\left(\frac{N_2\lambda_2}{N_1\lambda_1}\right)$ is constant (> 1), a particular type of equilibrium exists, known as **transient equilibrium**.

Case 3: $T_1 >>> T_2$ **(Secular Equilibrium):** Let us consider the *most important* case when *the parent is very very long-lived*, that is, $\lambda_2 \gg \lambda_1$.

The number of daughter nuclei of *Element* 2 at time t is

$$N_2 = \frac{\lambda_1}{\lambda_2 - \lambda_1} N_0\left(e^{-\lambda_1 t} - e^{-\lambda_2 t}\right) \quad \text{or} \quad N_2 = N_1 \times \frac{\lambda_1}{\lambda_2 - \lambda_1}\left(1 - e^{-(\lambda_2-\lambda_1)t}\right) \tag{3.24}$$

Since $\lambda_2 \gg \lambda_1$, $N_2\lambda_2 \approx N_1\lambda_1\left(1 - e^{-\lambda_2 t}\right)$. Thus, the activity of the daughter increases with time, and finally, it approaches the limiting value of the activity of its parent. At time $t \gg T_2$

$$N_2\lambda_2 = N_1\lambda_1 \tag{3.25}$$

This is called the **secular equilibrium**. Since λN represents the activity or the number of disintegrations per unit time, physically Eq. (3.25) implies the equality of activities

$$A_1 = A_2 \tag{3.26}$$

Thus, if the half-life of the parent is very large compared to that of the daughter, a state of equilibrium is achieved when the rate of disintegration of the daughter is equal to the rate of its formation (that is, the rate of decay of the parent). Equation (3.25) is used to determine the half-lives of the long-lived radioactive elements.

Illustrative Example 3.8: Successive disintegration

Consider the decay: $1 \longrightarrow 2 \longrightarrow 3$, where 3 is a stable element (Fig. 3.7). The number of nuclei of 1, 2 and 3 are given by Eqs (3.16), (3.17) and (3.20), respectively. The activity of 1 is

$$A_1(t) = N_1 \times \lambda_1 = A_0 e^{-\lambda_1 t} \tag{3.27}$$

The activity of 2 is

$$A_2(t) = N_2 \times \lambda_2 = A_1 \frac{\lambda_2}{\lambda_2 - \lambda_1}\left(1 - e^{-(\lambda_2-\lambda_1)t}\right) \tag{3.28}$$

The half-lives of 1 and 2 are, respectively, $T_1 = \dfrac{0.693}{\lambda_1}$ and $T_2 = \dfrac{0.693}{\lambda_2}$.

(a) Assume $\dfrac{T_2}{T_1} = 5$, *the parent is more short-lived than the daughter*. Plot $\dfrac{N_1}{N_0}$ and $\dfrac{N_2}{N_0}$ vs $\dfrac{t}{T_2}$, the number of half-lives of the daughter.

(b) Assume $\dfrac{T_1}{T_2} = 5$, *the parent is more long-lived than the daughter*. Plot $\dfrac{N_1}{N_0}$ and $\dfrac{N_2}{N_0}$ vs $\dfrac{t}{T_1}$, the number of half-lives of the parent.
Also plot $\dfrac{A_1}{A_0}$ and $\dfrac{A_2}{A_0}$ vs $\dfrac{t}{T_1}$.

(c) Repeat (b) for $\dfrac{T_1}{T_2} = 5000$.

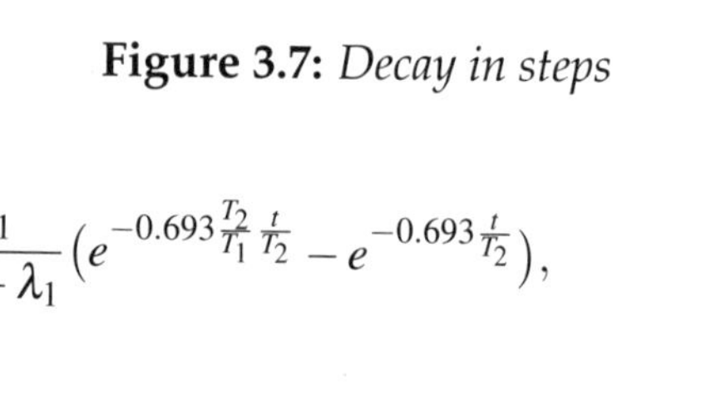

Figure 3.7: *Decay in steps*

Solution (a) *Short-lived parent:*

$$\frac{N_1}{N_0} = e^{-\frac{0.693}{T_1}t} = e^{-0.693\frac{T_2}{T_1}\frac{t}{T_2}} \quad \text{and} \quad \frac{N_2}{N_0} = \frac{\lambda_1}{\lambda_2-\lambda_1}\left(e^{-0.693\frac{T_2}{T_1}\frac{t}{T_2}} - e^{-0.693\frac{t}{T_2}}\right),$$

where $\dfrac{T_2}{T_1} = 5.0$.

In Fig. 3.8, $\dfrac{N_1}{N_0}$ and $\dfrac{N_2}{N_0}$ are plotted as a function of the number of half-lives, t/T_2, of the daughter. This shows that N_2 *increases with time until it attains its maximum value, and then it decays*[4] *exponentially with its own half-life,* T_2.

[4] Suppose $\frac{t}{T_2} = 4$. Thus, $t = 4T_2 = 20T_1$ and the condition $t >> T_1$ is satisfied.

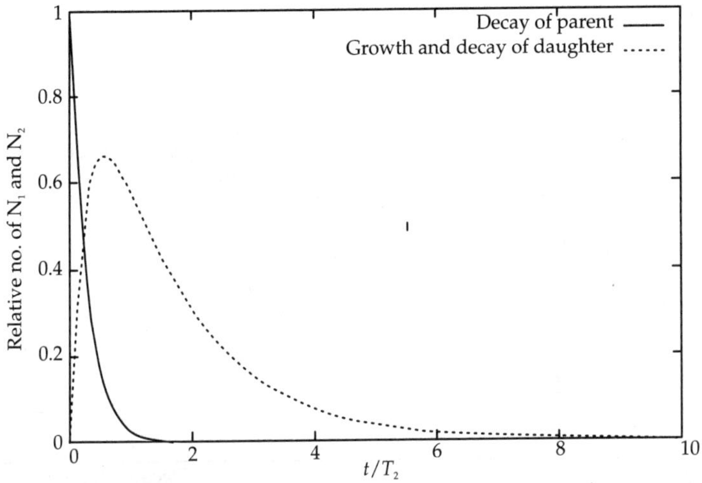

Figure 3.8: $\frac{N_1}{N_0}$ *and* $\frac{N_2}{N_0}$ *as a function of the number of half-lives,* t/T_2*, of the daughter*

In Fig. 3.9, the activities of the parent and daughter have been compared. In this case, the ratio $\frac{A_2}{A_1}$ increases with time, and thus, *equilibrium condition can never be achieved.* However, the figure on the left shows that an ideal equilibrium exists momentarily only at the point of intersection of the two curves.

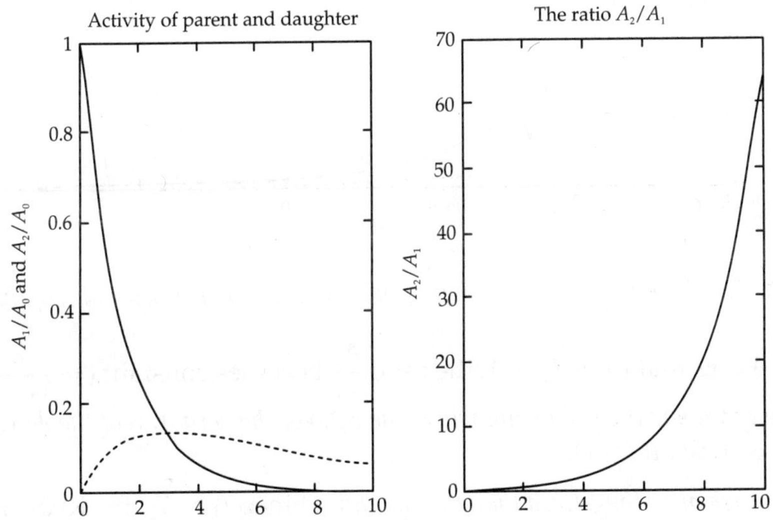

Figure 3.9: *On the left,* $\frac{A_1}{A_0}$ *and* $\frac{A_2}{A_0}$ *are plotted as a function of the number of half-lives,* t/T_1*, of the parent. The figure on the right shows the relative activity* $\frac{A_2}{A_1}$*. For* $t/T_1 \gg 1$*, the ratio* $\frac{A_2}{A_1}$ *increases with time.*

(b) *Parent is more long-lived than the daughter:*

$$\frac{N_1}{N_0} = e^{-0.693\frac{t}{T_1}} \quad \text{and} \quad \frac{N_2}{N_0} = \frac{\lambda_1}{\lambda_2 - \lambda_1}\left(e^{-0.693\frac{t}{T_1}} - e^{-0.693\frac{T_1}{T_2}\frac{t}{T_1}}\right),$$

where $\frac{T_1}{T_2} = 5.0$. The second term of the RHS of $\frac{N_2}{N_0}$ decays faster and, as a result, *decays exponentially with the half-life of its parent* (Fig. 3.10).

The activity of 1 is $A_1(t) = A_0 e^{-0.693\frac{t}{T_1}}$.

The activity of 2 is $A_2(t) = A_0 \frac{\lambda_2}{\lambda_2 - \lambda_1}\left(e^{-0.693\frac{t}{T_1}} - e^{-0.693\frac{T_1}{T_2}\frac{t}{T_1}}\right)$.

Thus, $A_2 = A_1 \frac{\lambda_2}{\lambda_2 - \lambda_1}\left(1 - e^{-0.693\frac{t}{T_1}\left(\frac{T_1}{T_2}-1\right)}\right)$.

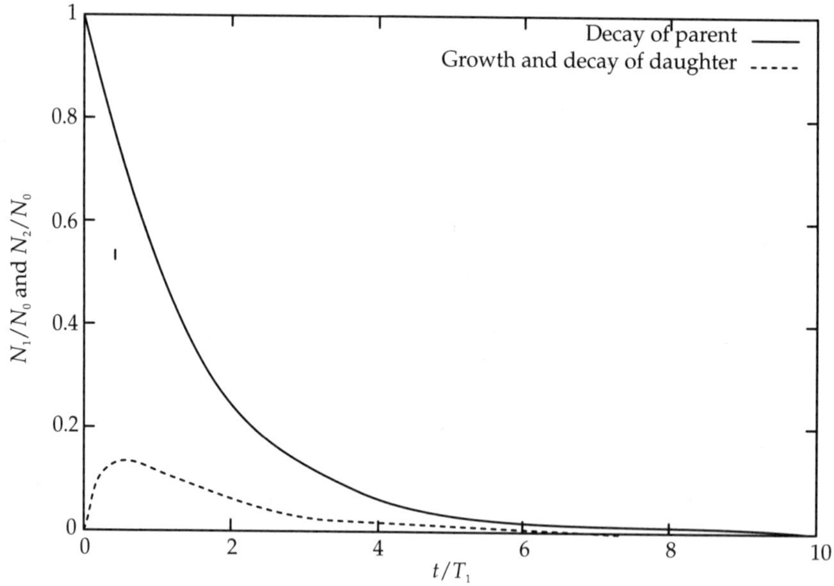

Figure 3.10: $\frac{N_1}{N_0}$ *and* $\frac{N_2}{N_0}$ *as a function of the number of half-lives, t/T_1, of the parent*

Figure 3.11 shows that for $t/T_1 \gg 1$, the ratio $\frac{A_2}{A_1}$ becomes constant $\left(= \frac{\lambda_2}{\lambda_2 - \lambda_1} = 1.25\right)$. *This is a case of transient equilibrium where the ratio of the activities of the daughter to that of the parent is constant (> 1).*

(c) *Parent is much more long-lived than the daughter:* Since $T_1 \gg T_2$, the RHS of $\frac{N_2}{N_0}$ decays very fast. In Fig. 3.12,on the left, the activities $A_1(t)$ and $A_2(t)$ have been plotted as a function of t/T_2 and t/T_1, respectively. The figure on the right shows the variation of $\frac{A_2}{A_1}$. It shows that the ratio is constant ($= 1$). *This is a case of secular equilibrium where both the parent and the daughter decay at the same rate.*

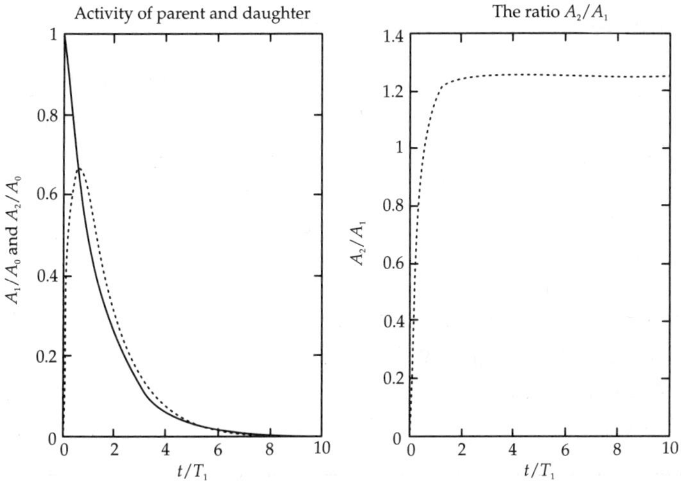

Figure 3.11: *On the left,* $\frac{A_1}{A_0}$ *and* $\frac{A_2}{A_0}$ *are plotted as a function of the number of half-lives,* t/T_1*, of the parent. The figure on the right shows the variation of* $\frac{A_2}{A_1}$*. For* $t/T_1 \gg 1$*, the ratio* $\frac{A_2}{A_1}$ *becomes constant.*

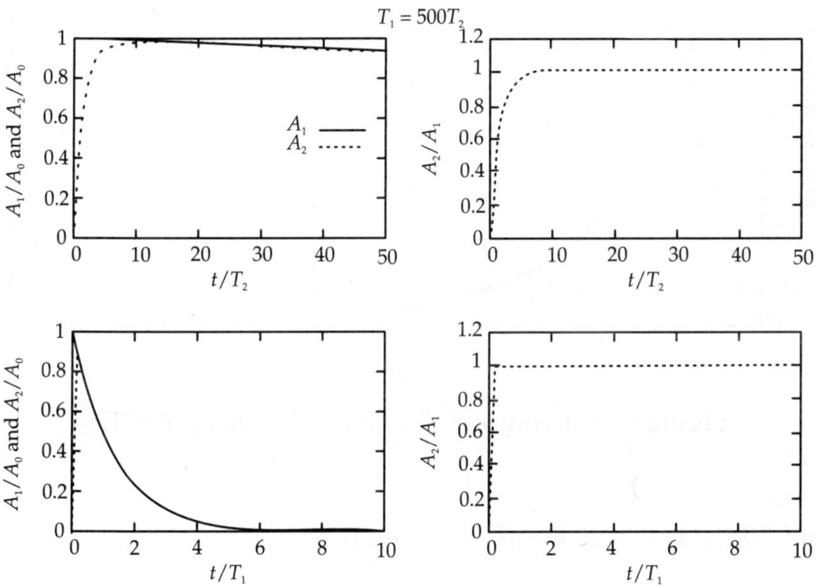

Figure 3.12: *On the left,* $\frac{A_1}{A_0}$ *and* $\frac{A_2}{A_0}$ *are plotted as a function of the number of half-lives,* t/T_2 *of the daughter and* t/T_1 *of the parent. The figure on the right shows the variation of* $\frac{A_2}{A_1}$*. For* $t/T_2 \gg 1$*, the ratio* $\frac{A_2}{A_1}$ *becomes constant* $(= 1)$*.*

Illustrative Example 3.9: Transient equilibrium

Consider an observed decay: $^{139}\text{Cs} \longrightarrow {}^{139}\text{Ba} \longrightarrow {}^{139}\text{La}$. Given: Half-life ($T_1$) of ^{139}Cs is 9.5 minutes, half-life (T_2) of ^{139}Ba is 82.9 minutes and ^{139}La is stable. At $t = 0$, the activity of ^{139}Cs is 1 mCi.
Find the maximum activity of ^{139}Ba. When does it occur?

Solution $N_1(t) = N_0 e^{-\lambda_1 t}$ $N_2 = \dfrac{\lambda_1}{\lambda_2 - \lambda_1} N_0 \left(e^{-\lambda_1 t} - e^{-\lambda_2 t}\right)$

The variation of N_1 and N_2 with time is shown in Fig. 3.13. It shows that ^{139}Cs decays quickly while the daughter grows with time, and after attaining its maximum value, it decays exponentially.

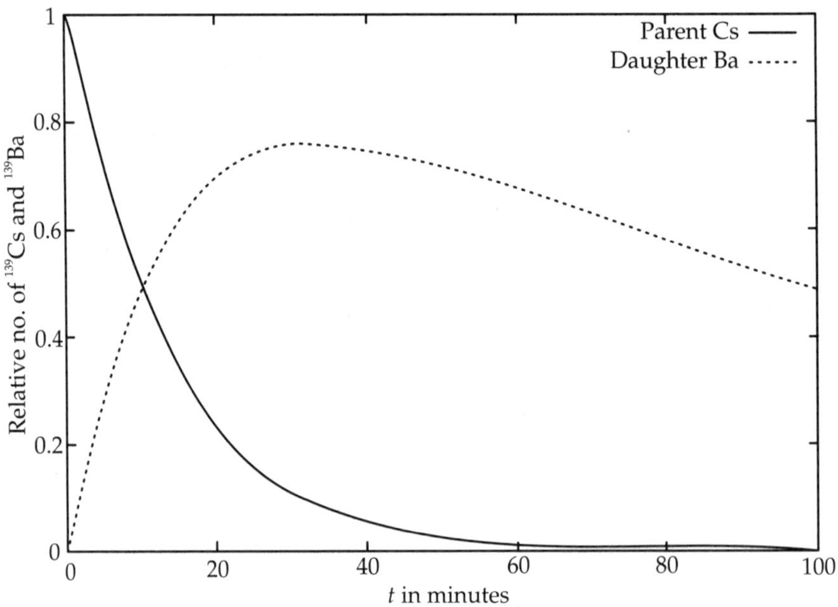

Figure 3.13: *Decay of* ^{139}Cs; *growth and decay of* ^{139}Ba

Activity of ^{139}Ba is $A_2 = N_2 \lambda_2 = N_0 \lambda_1 \times \dfrac{\lambda_2}{\lambda_2 - \lambda_1} \left(e^{-\lambda_1 t} - e^{-\lambda_2 t}\right)$.

The activity A_2 will be maximum at $t = t_m$, when $\dfrac{dA_2}{dt} = 0$. It gives $t_m = \dfrac{1}{\lambda_2 - \lambda_1} \ln \dfrac{\lambda_2}{\lambda_1}$.

Substituting the values of $\lambda_1 \left(= \dfrac{0.693}{9.5}\right)$ and $\lambda_2 \left(= \dfrac{0.693}{82.9}\right)$, we get $t_m = 33.54$ minutes.

Equation (3.15) suggests that at time $t = t_m$, $\dfrac{dN_2}{dt} = 0$, and thus, $\lambda_1 N_1 = \lambda_2 N_2$.
Therefore, the maximum value of the activity will be

$$\lambda_1 N_1 = \lambda_1 N_0 e^{-\lambda_1 t_m} = 1 \times e^{-\frac{0.693}{9.5} \times 33.54} = 0.086 \text{ mCi}$$

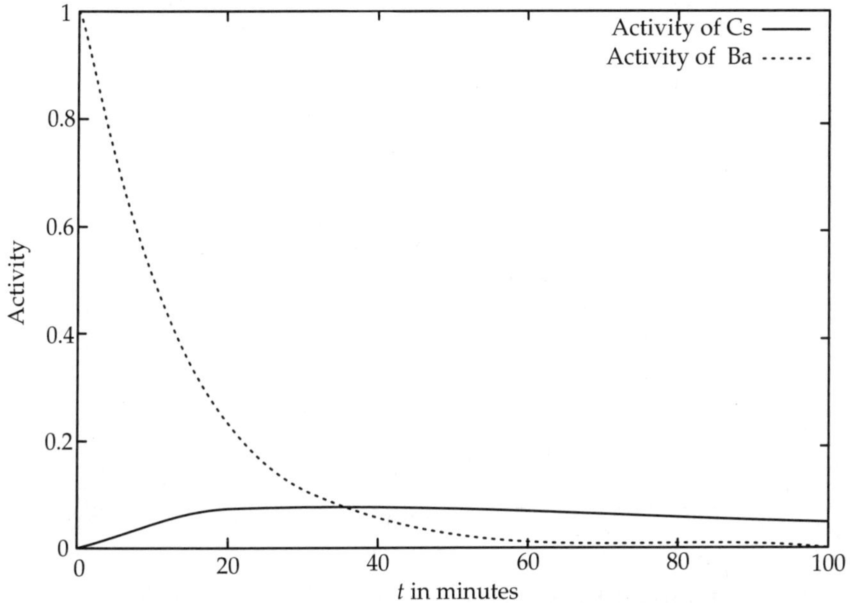

Figure 3.14: *Activity of* ^{139}Cs *and* ^{139}Ba *with time*

Illustrative Example 3.10: Secular equilibrium

Consider an observed decay: $^{235}\text{U} \longrightarrow {}^{231}\text{Th} \longrightarrow {}^{231}\text{Pa}$. Given: Half-life ($T_1$) of ^{235}U is 7.04×10^8 years, half-life (T_2) of ^{231}Th is 25.5 hours and ^{231}Pa is stable. At $t = 0$, the activity of ^{235}U is 1 mCi.

Explain how equilibrium is attained.

Solution Activity of ^{235}U is $A_1 = A_0 e^{-\lambda_1 t}$, where $\lambda_1 = \dfrac{0.693}{7.04 \times 10^8 \times 365 \times 24}$.

Activity of ^{231}Th is $A_2 = A_0 \dfrac{\lambda_2}{\lambda_2 - \lambda_1}(e^{-\lambda_1 t} - e^{-\lambda_2 t})$, where $\lambda_2 = \dfrac{0.693}{25.5}$. Here, we take t in hours.

After large t, the activities of ^{235}U and ^{235}Th are equal ($= 1$), as shown in Fig. 3.15. Thus, the rate of disintegration of ^{231}Th is the same as its rate of creation. *Since the number of* ^{231}Th *nuclei remains constant by regeneration from* ^{235}U*, we essentially have a source of* ^{231}Th *with a half-life of* 7.04×10^8 *years rather than 25.5 hours!*

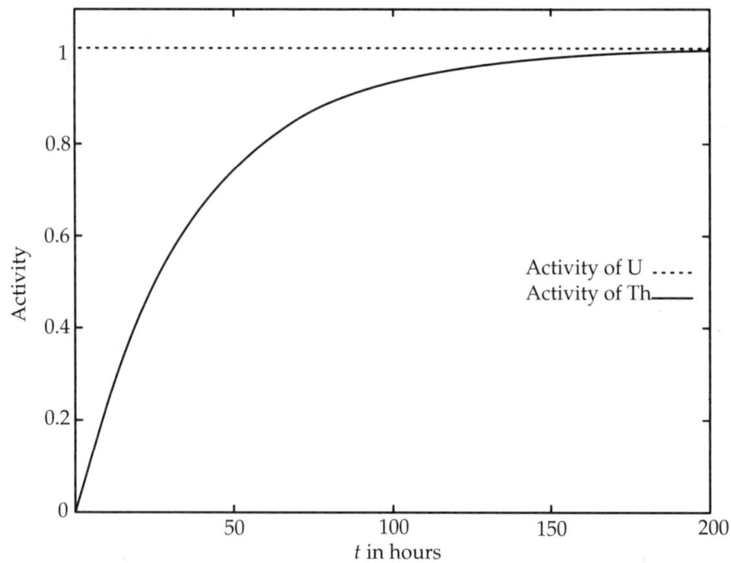

Figure 3.15: *Secular equilibrium of* ^{235}U *and* ^{235}Th

3.1.6 Radioactive Dating

The process of radioactivity is completely random. One cannot predict precisely when an individual nucleus will decay. However, we can predict almost with certainty the time taken by a large number of nuclei to decay to half. Thus, despite the random nature of the radioactive process, radioactive nuclei can be used to measure the passage of time, just like an ordinary clock. The method is often used to determine the age of any biological or geological specimen and is known as **radioactive dating.**

Age of a biological specimen (radiocarbon dating): The **basic principle** of radiocarbon dating is given below.

(a) The carbon isotope $^{14}_{6}$C is radioactive. It is produced at a constant rate in the upper atmosphere by the action of cosmic rays. Cosmic rays hit the earth's atmosphere and produce neutrons. These neutrons collide with atmospheric nitrogen and produce $^{14}_{6}$C as

$$^{1}_{0}n + ^{14}_{7}\mathrm{N} \longrightarrow ^{14}_{6}\mathrm{C} + ^{1}_{1}\mathrm{H}$$

(b) The half-life of $^{14}_{6}$C is about 5730 years. It decays as $^{14}_{6}\mathrm{C} \longrightarrow ^{14}_{7}\mathrm{N} + e^{-} + \bar{\nu}_e$.

(c) Since $^{14}_{6}$C is being continuously produced at a constant rate, the ratio of $^{14}_{6}$C to the stable $^{12}_{6}$C in the atmosphere remains constant.

(d) Plants and animals take up $^{14}_{6}$C along with natural carbon, and thus, maintain a constant proportion of $^{14}_{6}$C to $^{12}_{6}$C when they are alive.

(e) When an organism dies, its intake of carbon stops. Therefore, $^{14}_{6}$C starts to decay from that very moment, but without any replacement (however, the amount of stable isotope ${}^{12}_{6}C$ will remain constant). As a result, its previous content of ${}^{14}_{6}C$ decreases according to radioactive law and its activity at any time will be

$$A(t) = A(t_0)e^{-\lambda(t-t_0)}$$

(f) The age $(t - t_0)$ of the once-living material can thus be determined by measuring the specific activity (activity per gram) of its carbon content.

In this context, it is appropriate to refer to Eq. (3.13), where a radioactive element is continuously produced at a constant rate (Q). After a long time, it becomes constant $\left(=\dfrac{Q}{\lambda}\right)$. As soon as bombardment stops, Q becomes 0 and N decays exponentially. This is the basic principle of radiocarbon dating.

One of the main limiting factors in using this method is our ability to measure the very low activity of the very old specimen under study. After about 10 half-lives have elapsed, the activity will be too weak to measure accurately. This gives an upper time limit, which is $\backsim$ 50,000 years, beyond which it would not be wise to rely on this method.

Illustrative Example 3.11: Age of a biological specimen

A sample of charcoal found in an archaeological expedition shows a ${}^{14}_{6}C$ activity of 11.3 counts per gram per minute. The activity of ${}^{14}_{6}C$ in a living tree is 15.3 counts per gram per minute. Estimate the age of the sample.

Solution Activity decays exponentially as $A(t) = A(0)e^{-\lambda t}$.

Therefore $e^{\lambda t} = \dfrac{15.3}{11.3} = 1.354$, where $\lambda = \dfrac{0.693}{T}$ and $T = 5730$ years. The age of the sample is $t = \dfrac{\ln 1.354}{\lambda} \approx 2505$ years.

Age of a geological specimen: As we have mentioned earlier, there is an upper age limit of about 50,000 years for radiocarbon dating. To a geologist, wishing to date a rock sample, however, this is a very short time period! Fortunately, there are other decays with much longer half-lives that may be used for the dating of such samples. For example

$${}^{87}_{37}Rb \longrightarrow {}^{87}_{38}Sr + e^- + \bar{\nu}_e$$

This has a half-life of 4.8×10^{10} years. The ratio of daughter nuclei to parent nuclei in a sample of rock gives the measure of its age.

Basic principles: Suppose the 'clock' started 'ticking' (usually when the rock condensed) at time t_0, when the number of parent nuclei was $N_p(t_0)$. The parent nuclei will decay and at time t, the total number of parent and daughter (N_d) nuclei will be

$$N_p(t) + N_d(t) = N_p(t_0) \tag{3.29}$$

$$\text{Again} \quad N_p(t) = N_p(t_0)e^{-\lambda(t-t_0)} \Rightarrow (t-t_0) = \frac{1}{\lambda}\ln\frac{N_p(t_0)}{N_p(t)} \tag{3.30}$$

$$\text{Using Eq. (3.29)} \quad (t-t_0) = \Delta t = \frac{1}{\lambda}\ln\frac{N_p(t)+N_d(t)}{N_p(t)} = \frac{1}{\lambda}\ln[1+\frac{N_d(t)}{N_p(t)}] \tag{3.31}$$

Thus, from this knowledge of the ratio of the parent and daughter nuclei in a sample and its decay constant, the age of the sample can be determined.

This method relies on the following assumptions:

(a) Initially, there were no daughter nuclei present, that is, $N_d(t_0) = 0$.

(b) No parent or daughter nuclei have escaped from the sample.

(c) The daughter nuclei have been created within the sample only by one decay process and not as a result of some other radioactive decay.

Illustrative Example 3.12: Age of a rock

In a specimen of rock, the argon/potassium ratio is 2.70. Estimate the age of the rock.
Given: ${}^{40}_{19}\mathrm{K} \longrightarrow {}^{40}_{18}\mathrm{Sr} + e^+ + \nu_e$; half-life of ${}^{40}_{19}\mathrm{K}$ is 1.3×10^9 years.

Solution $\Delta t = \frac{1}{\lambda}\ln[1+\frac{N_d(t)}{N_p(t)}]$, where $\lambda = \frac{0.693}{1.3\times10^9}$ year^{-1} and $\frac{N_d(t)}{N_p(t)} = 2.70$. Therefore,

$$\Delta t = \frac{1.3\times10^9}{0.693}\ln 3.70 = 2.45\times10^9 \text{ years.}$$

3.2 ALPHA DECAY

When a nucleus undergoes α decay, it transforms into a different nucleus. It can be represented by the following process:

$${}^{A}_{Z}X \longrightarrow {}^{A-4}_{Z-2}Y + \alpha$$

Examples of alpha decay:

$${}^{238}_{92}\mathrm{U} \longrightarrow {}^{234}_{90}\mathrm{Th} + {}^{4}_{2}\mathrm{He} + Q \ (4.2 \text{ MeV})$$

$${}^{226}_{88}\mathrm{Ra} \longrightarrow {}^{222}_{86}\mathrm{Rn} + {}^{4}_{2}\mathrm{He} + Q \ (4.9 \text{ MeV})$$

where Q represents the energy released in the decay.

A few properties of α particles:

(a) An α particle is basically a helium nucleus, ${}^{4}_{2}\mathrm{He}$, consisting of two protons and two neutrons (that is, a helium atom that loses both of its orbital electrons).

(b) α radiations are readily absorbed by a thin foil of metal or by passage through a few cm of air at atmospheric pressure. A thin mica sheet or a sheet of ordinary paper will absorb all the α particles from a radioactive material.

(c) Generally, nuclei with $Z > 82$ (heavier than lead) are α-radioactive (a few rare-earth elements are the exceptions).

(d) α particles have very strong ionising power.

3.2.1 Energetics of Alpha Decay

Consider the process ${}^{A}_{Z}X \longrightarrow {}^{A-4}_{Z-2}Y + \alpha$. From energy conservation, we get

$$M({}^{A}_{Z}X)c^2 = M({}^{A-4}_{Z-2}Y)c^2 + T_y + M_{{}^{4}_{2}\mathrm{He}}c^2 + T_\alpha \tag{3.32}$$

From the conservation of momentum, we get

$$0 = \vec{p}_y + \vec{p}_\alpha, \tag{3.33}$$

where T represents the kinetic energy. Usually, atomic mass rather than nuclear mass is measured. It is therefore convenient to express the above relation in terms of the atomic mass. Using the following relation between the atomic mass and the nuclear mass

$$M(A,Z)_{\mathrm{atom}} = M({}^{A}_{Z}X) + ZM_e - BE(A,Z)_{\mathrm{atom}}/c^2$$

From Eq. (3.32), we get

$$M_x c^2 - ZM_e c^2 + BE(A,Z)_{\mathrm{atom}} = M_y c^2 - (Z-2)M_e c^2 + BE(A-4,Z-2)_{\mathrm{atom}}$$
$$+ T_y + M_\alpha c^2 - 2M_e c^2 + BE(4,2)_{\mathrm{atom}} + T_\alpha,$$

where M_x, M_y and M_α represent the atomic masses. The electron masses balance exactly and their binding energies balance within a few eV, so that we can write

$$M_x c^2 = M_y c^2 + T_y + M_\alpha c^2 + T_\alpha \tag{3.34}$$

The energy released in the decay is

$$Q = M_x c^2 - M_y c^2 - M_\alpha c^2 = T_y + T_\alpha \tag{3.35}$$

For spontaneous decay, the energy released (Q) is shared between the daughter nucleus Y and the α particle. The kinetic energies are small compared to the rest masses of the respective nuclei, so non-relativistic expressions may be used to evaluate them. The kinetic energy of the daughter is

$$T_y = \frac{p_y^2}{2M_y} = \frac{p_\alpha^2}{2M_y} = \frac{M_\alpha}{M_y}\frac{p_\alpha^2}{2M_\alpha},$$

where Eq. (3.33) has been used. Therefore, from Eq. (3.35), we get

$$Q = \left(\frac{M_\alpha}{M_y} + 1\right) T_\alpha = \frac{M_y + M_\alpha}{M_y} T_\alpha \approx \frac{A}{A-4} T_\alpha \tag{3.36}$$

Actually, the ratio $\dfrac{M_\alpha}{M_y} \ll 1$ and it is sufficiently accurate to express $\dfrac{M_y + M_\alpha}{M_y}$ simply as $\dfrac{A}{A-4}$ with $A \gg 4$. Therefore, the kinetic energy of the α particle is

$$T_\alpha = \frac{A-4}{A} Q \tag{3.37}$$

Typically, the α particle carries about 98% of the Q value.

Illustrative Example 3.13: Kinetic energy of α particles

Calculate the Q values of the following decays:

(a) ${}^{208}_{84}\text{Po} \longrightarrow {}^{204}Pb + \alpha$ (b) ${}^{230}_{90}\text{Th} \longrightarrow {}^{226}_{88}\text{Ra} + \alpha$

Also calculate the kinetic energy of the emitted α particles and the daughter nuclei in each case.

Given: $M({}^{208}_{84}\text{Po}) = 207.9812$ u, $M({}^{204}_{82}\text{Pb}) = 203.9730$ u, $M({}^{230}_{90}\text{Th}) = 230.0331$ u, $M({}^{226}_{88}\text{Ra}) = 226.0254$ u and $M({}^{4}_{2}\text{He}) = 4.0026$ u.

Solution (a) $Q = (207.9812 - 203.9730 - 4.0026)$ u $= 5.21$ MeV. $T_\alpha \approx \frac{204}{208} \times 5.21 =$ 5.11 MeV and $T_d \approx 0.10$ MeV.

(b) $Q = (230.0331 - 226.0254 - 4.0026)$ u $= 4.75$ MeV. $T_\alpha \approx \frac{226}{230} \times 4.75 = 4.67$ MeV and $T_d = 0.08$ MeV.

3.2.2 Energy Released in Terms of BE

The energy released in the decay is given by Eq. (3.35) as

$$Q = M_x c^2 - M_y c^2 - M_\alpha c^2$$

α decay cannot take place unless Q is positive. The energy released in the decay must come from the net decrease in the mass of the system. Referring to Eq. (1.15) and the definition of α separation energy, we find that

$$Q = -S_\alpha \tag{3.38}$$

Thus, Q can be related to the binding energies of nuclei as

$$Q = BE({}^{A-4}_{Z-2}Y) + BE({}^{4}_{2}\text{He}) - BE({}^{A}_{Z}X) \tag{3.39}$$

To liberate energy, the decay products must be more tightly bound than the parent; that is, the total binding energies of the products must be greater than that of the parent. The exceptionally high value of BE (${}^{4}_{2}$He) plays an important role in making Q positive for nuclei with $A > 150$. For a typical heavy nucleus, $BE/A \backsim 7$ MeV and a large value of BE (${}^{4}_{2}$He) makes Q positive.

Equation (3.39) shows that when the daughter nucleus is magic, that is, it has high binding energy, the energy released, and thus, T_α, is particularly high. Conversely, when the parent nucleus is magic, that is, it has high binding energy, the energy released, and thus, T_α, is particularly low.

Illustrative Example 3.14: Impossibility of decaying a single proton or neutron

Justify that ${}^{238}_{92}$U cannot emit (a) a proton, (b) a neutron, (c) a ${}^{2}_{1}$H, (d) a ${}^{3}_{1}$H or (e) a ${}^{3}_{2}$He but can emit ${}^{4}_{2}$He.

Given: $M({}^{238}_{92}\text{U}) = 238.050785$ u, $M({}^{234}_{90}\text{Th}) = 234.04363$ u, $M({}^{4}_{2}\text{He}) = 4.00260$ u, $M({}^{237}_{91}\text{Pa}) = 237.05121$ u, $M({}^{236}_{91}\text{Pa}) = 237.0$ u, $M({}^{1}_{1}\text{H}) = 1.007825$ u, $M({}^{1}_{0}n) = 1.008665$ u, $M({}^{237}_{92}\text{U}) = 237.048725$ u.

Solution (a) ${}^{238}_{92}\text{U} \longrightarrow {}^{237}_{91}\text{Pa} + {}^{1}_{1}\text{H} + Q$

$$Q = M({}^{238}_{92}\text{U}) - M({}^{236}_{91}\text{Pa}) - M({}^{2}_{1}\text{H}) = 238.050785 - 237.05121 - 1.007825 = -7.68 \text{ MeV}$$

Thus, emission of proton is not allowed.

Similarly, for (b), (c), (d) and (e), Q is negative. However, for (f)

$$^{238}_{92}\text{U} \longrightarrow {}^{234}_{90}\text{Th} + {}^{4}_{2}\text{He} + Q$$

$$Q = M({}^{238}_{92}\text{U}) - M({}^{234}_{90}\text{Th}) - M({}^{4}_{2}\text{He}) = 238.050785 - 234.04363 - 4.002603 \approx +5.40\ \text{MeV}$$

Emission of ${}^{4}_{2}$He is energetically allowed.

Illustrative Example 3.15: Instability against α decay

The binding energies of ${}^{12}_{6}$C, ${}^{8}_{4}$Be and ${}^{4}_{2}$He are 92.16, 56.50 and 28.29 MeV, respectively. Explain why ${}^{12}_{6}$C is stable against the decay of three α particles, but ${}^{8}_{4}$Be is unstable against α decay.

Solution From Eq. (3.39)

$$3 \times BE({}^{4}_{2}\text{He}) - BE({}^{12}_{6}\text{C}) = 3 \times 28.29 - 92.16 = -7.29\ \text{MeV}$$

And decay of ${}^{12}_{6}$C into three α particles is not allowed. However

$$2 \times BE({}^{4}_{2}\text{He}) - BE({}^{8}_{4}\text{Be}) = 2 \times 28.29 - 56.50 = 80.08\ \text{MeV} = 80\ \text{keV}$$

Thus, ${}^{8}_{4}$Be is not stable, as it can decay into two α particles.

3.2.3 Range of Alpha Particles

During their motion in air, the α particles collide with other molecules and are able to ionise them. By such collisions with other particles, they gradually lose their energy[5] and finally, by absorbing other electrons, they become a neutral He atom. *The maximum distance travelled by an α particle before ionisation stops is called its range.* The range of α particles in air at standard atmospheric pressure and temperature is roughly a few cm. However, it depends on the nature of the radioactive elements emitting the particles, and also on the temperature and pressure. With increase in pressure, the range decreases, while it increases with increasing temperature. Typically, the range (R in cm) of an α particle with energy (E in MeV) in air at 15°C and atmospheric pressure is

$$R = 0.318E^{3/2} \tag{3.40}$$

The range of α particles in a gas can be determined by measuring the ionisation produced in the gas at different distances from its source. A typical curve showing the ionisation produced at different distances from the source is shown in Fig. 3.16. It shows that for the greater part of the range, the ionisation current remains constant. The ionisation current then increases and reaches its maximum value just before the end. The peak near the end of the range is due to an increase in the efficiency of ionisation by slow α particles. At the end of its journey, the energy of the α particles becomes low (not too low to ionise the gas) and they remain in close proximity to the molecules in that region for a comparatively longer time. As a result, ionisation increases.

Charged particles lose their energy due to collisions with other particles. Since the process of collision is statistical in nature, the initially mono-energetic particles will exhibit a spread of energy after passage through a certain distance in matter.

[5]Please see Chapter 5.

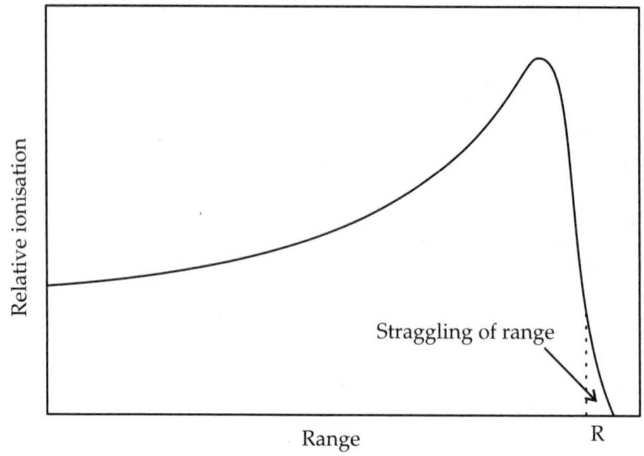

Figure 3.16: *Variation of the relative ionisation produced by α particles with distance from the source. $R \sim a\ few\ cm$ in air.*

The fluctuation in energy transfer leads to variations or spread in range, known as **straggling**.

3.2.4 Basic Experimental Results

From measurement of the energy, range of the α particles, and the half-lives of various α-radioactive nuclides, some regularities in the properties of α decay were discovered.

(a) **Kinetic energy and half-life:** The range of possible values of the kinetic energies (T_α) of α particles is very narrow, while their half-lives ($T_{1/2}$) vary over a wide range.

$$4\text{ MeV} \lesssim T_\alpha \lesssim 9\text{ MeV} \quad \text{but} \quad 10^{-7}\text{s} \lesssim T_{1/2} \lesssim 10^{10}\text{ years}$$

Some α decay energies and their corresponding half-lives are shown in Table 3.3.

Table 3.3: *Energy of some α decays and corresponding half-lives*

Isotope	KE of α particle (in MeV)	Half-life
^{232}Th	4.01	1.4×10^{10} years
^{238}U	4.19	4.5×10^{9} years
^{230}Th	4.69	8.0×10^{4} years
^{241}Am	5.64	433 years
^{230}U	5.89	20.8 days
^{210}Rn	6.16	2.4 hours
^{230}Rn	6.29	56 s
^{222}Ac	7.01	5 s
^{215}Po	7.53	1.8×10^{-3} s
^{218}Th	9.85	1.1×10^{-7} s

Here, α emitters with larger energies have shorter half-lives, and vice-versa.

(b) **Range and half-life:** Short-lived radioactive elements usually emit long-ranged α particles. On the other hand, the long-lived radioactive elements emit short-ranged α particles. For RaC, $T_{1/2} = 1.5 \times 10^{-4}$ s and range $= 6.95$ cm. For U1, $T_{1/2} = 4.5 \times 10^{9}$ years and range $= 2.67$ cm.

(c) **Geiger–Nuttall law:** Geiger and Nuttall in 1911 established a linear relationship between the logarithm of the decay constant and the logarithm of the range of α particles from a naturally radioactive series. It is usually written in the form

$$\log R = A \log \lambda + B, \tag{3.41}$$

where A is a constant with almost the same value for all three radioactive series and B is a constant with a different value for each series.

Since the range and energy are connected (Eq. 3.40), the Geiger–Nuttall law can also be written in a different form as

$$\log \lambda = C \log E + D, \tag{3.42}$$

where E is the energy of the emitted α particle and C and D are two other constants.

The significance of the Geiger–Nuttall law is that it may be used to determine the half-lives of nuclei (for example, nuclei emitting long-range α particles) for which other methods cannot be applied.

3.2.5 Theory of Alpha Decay

Before the discovery of quantum mechanics, scientists trying to account for α emissions faced the following dilemma.

The kinetic energy of an α particle emitted in a typical nuclear decay is $\backsim 5$ MeV. It was found[6] that α particles from a ^{212}Po source having very large kinetic energies of $\backsim 9$ MeV were scattered from a ^{238}U nucleus; they could not penetrate the Coulomb barrier. The maximum height of the Coulomb barrier faced by an α particle while moving towards a heavy nucleus with $A \sim 234$ is about 27 MeV, and it is quite obvious that a 9-MeV α particle cannot overcome this barrier. On the other hand, a low-energy α particle that is bound in a nuclear potential well would encounter the same barrier, but be able to escape. How an α particle could ever escape the nucleus, and cross the potential barrier, was a great puzzle, until it was recognised that the emission of α particles is a quantum-mechanical phenomenon.

The process of α emission was first successfully explained by Gamow, Condon and Gurney (1928) on the basis of quantum mechanics. The simplified theory of α emission may be given as follows.

Assume that an α particle and a daughter exist inside the nucleus prior to its dissociation. The α particle formed inside the nucleus is bound by a strong attractive

[6] In 1927, Rutherford first observed that α particles from a ^{212}Po source with kinetic energies of $\backsim 9$ MeV are scattered by a radioactive nucleus, which emits α particles with a lower energy.

nuclear force of very short range. We may think that the α particle moves inside the nucleus as a free particle with an energy that is much less than the height of the potential barrier, and thus, the Coulomb barrier would prevent it from escaping. Once it comes out of the nucleus, it would feel the Coulomb repulsion of the daughter nucleus, which gives the potential $V(r) \propto \frac{1}{r}$. The force field experienced by the α particle is shown in Fig. 3.17.

The height of the barrier (V_0) is

$$V_0 = \frac{e^2}{4\pi\varepsilon_0}\frac{2(Z-2)}{R}, \tag{3.43}$$

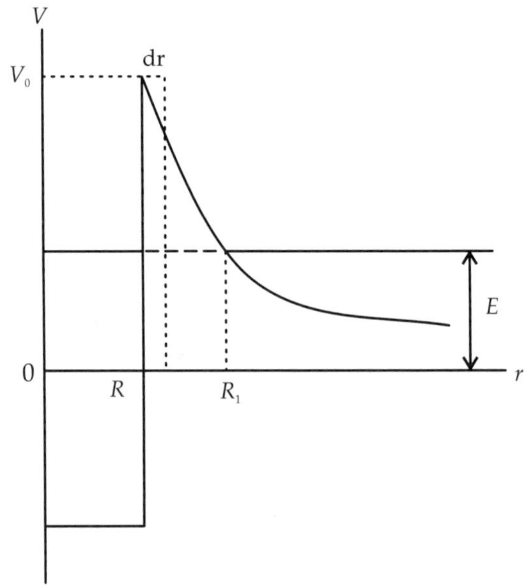

Figure 3.17: *Potential energy of an α particle. Inside the nucleus, the force field is attractive and can be represented by constant negative potential energy, while outside the nucleus, $V(r)$ decreases as $\frac{1}{r}$.*

where Z is the atomic number of the parent nucleus and R is the radius of the daughter nucleus. For a typical heavy nucleus, say $Z = 86$ and $A = 222$

$$V_0 \approx 34 \text{ MeV}$$

Since the kinetic energy of the α particle is much smaller than the height of the potential barrier, it is impossible, classically, for an α particle to surmount the barrier and to escape the nucleus. However, in quantum mechanics, such an α particle could tunnel through the potential barrier and escape from the nucleus with a probability that decreases with the height and thickness of the barrier.

We may summarise the basic notions of the quantum-mechanical theory as follows:

(a) Prior to the decay, an α particle may exist inside the nucleus as a free particle.

(b) It is confined within the nucleus by the potential barrier and strikes the wall of the barrier.

(c) There is a small but finite probability that an α particle may tunnel through the barrier. α decay occurs when it finally tunnels through the barrier after several attempts.

The probability of decay per unit time (which is basically the decay constant, λ) is equal to the number of collisions (ν) per second that the α particles makes with the wall of the barrier multiplied by the probability (P) that the particle will penetrate the barrier.

$$\lambda = \nu \times P$$

If the α particle moves freely with speed v inside a nucleus of radius R, then it will strike the barrier as it bounces back and forth at a time interval of $2\frac{R}{v}$. Therefore

$$\nu \approx \frac{v}{2R}$$

And the decay constant is

$$\lambda \approx \frac{v}{2R}P \tag{3.44}$$

The tunnelling probability through the rectangular barrier[7] is given by

$$P \approx e^{-2\gamma}, \tag{3.45}$$

where $\gamma = \sqrt{\frac{2m}{\hbar^2}(V_0 - E)}\, a$, a and V_0 being the width and height of the barrier, respectively. For the Coulomb barrier

$$\gamma = \sqrt{\frac{2m}{\hbar^2}} \int_R^{R_1} \sqrt{V(r) - E}\, dr, \tag{3.46}$$

where $V(r) = \frac{e^2}{4\pi\varepsilon_0}\frac{2Z}{r}$, Z being the atomic number of the daughter and E the energy of the emitted α particle. In the integral (Eq. (3.46)), R represents the radius of the parent nucleus and R_1 is the classical turning point. Since at the turning point, the total energy is equal to the potential energy, R_1 can be obtained from

$$E = \frac{e^2}{4\pi\varepsilon_0}\frac{2Z}{R_1}$$

$$R_1 = \frac{e^2}{4\pi\varepsilon_0}\frac{2Z}{E} \tag{3.47}$$

[7]Please see Appendix A.

Using this relation, $V(r)=\frac{R_1E}{r}$ and the integral (Eq. (3.46)) can be written as

$$\gamma=\sqrt{\frac{2m}{\hbar^2}}\int_R^{R_1}\sqrt{\frac{R_1E}{r}-E}\,dr=\frac{\sqrt{2mE}}{\hbar}\int_R^{R_1}\sqrt{\frac{R_1}{r}-1}\,dr$$
$$=\frac{\sqrt{2mE}}{\hbar}\left[R_1\cos^{-1}\sqrt{R/R_1}-\sqrt{R(R_1-R)}\right] \tag{3.48}$$

⇒ Check Progress 3.2: Check that $\int_R^{R_1}\sqrt{\frac{R_1}{r}-1}\,dr=R_1\cos^{-1}\sqrt{R/R_1}-\sqrt{R(R_1-R)}$. (Hint: $r=R_1\sin^2 u$).

Typically, $R_1>>R$, and thus, $\cos^{-1}\sqrt{R/R_1}$ is very close $\frac{\pi}{2}$. Let

$$\cos^{-1}\sqrt{R/R_1}=\frac{\pi}{2}-\varepsilon \tag{3.49}$$

$$\text{Therefore}\quad\cos\left(\frac{\pi}{2}-\varepsilon\right)=\sqrt{R/R_1};\quad \sin\varepsilon\approx\varepsilon=\sqrt{R/R_1}$$

Thus $\cos^{-1}\sqrt{R/R_1}=\frac{\pi}{2}-\sqrt{R/R_1}$

$$\text{And}\ \ \gamma=\frac{\sqrt{2mE}}{\hbar}\left[R_1\left(\frac{\pi}{2}-\sqrt{R/R_1}\right)-\sqrt{R(R_1-R)}\right]$$
$$\approx\frac{\sqrt{2mE}}{\hbar}\left[\frac{\pi R_1}{2}-2\sqrt{RR_1}\right]=AZE^{-1/2}-B(ZR)^{1/2}, \tag{3.50}$$

where $A=\frac{e^2}{4\pi\varepsilon_0}\frac{\pi\sqrt{2m}}{\hbar}=1.980\sqrt{\text{MeV}}$ and $B=\left(\frac{e^2}{4\pi\varepsilon_0}\right)^{1/2}\frac{4\sqrt{m}}{\hbar}=1.485\frac{1}{\sqrt{fm}}$.

Using Eq. (3.44), the expression for the decay constant can be written as

$$\ln\lambda=\ln\frac{v}{2R}-2\gamma=\ln\frac{v}{2R}-3.960ZE^{-1/2}+2.970(ZR)^{1/2} \tag{3.51}$$

Since $\ln x=\log x\times\ln 10$

$$\log\lambda=\log\frac{v}{2R}-1.719806148ZE^{-1/2}+1.289854611(ZR)^{1/2} \tag{3.52}$$

This provides a quantitative relationship between the decay constant and the energy, that is, the Geiger–Nuttall law.

The half-life (τ) can be obtained from

$$\log\tau=\log 0.693-\log\frac{v}{2R}+1.719806148ZE^{-1/2}-1.289854611(ZR)^{1/2} \tag{3.53}$$

Figure. 3.18 shows the behaviour of Eq. (3.53) for seven isotopes of $^{238}_{92}$U. It illustrates the huge change in $\log\tau$ (approximately from 15 to -5) when $\frac{1}{\sqrt{E}}$ changes from about 0.50 to 0.36 (that is, E changes from about 4.0 MeV to 7.7 MeV). We will study the variation in the following example.

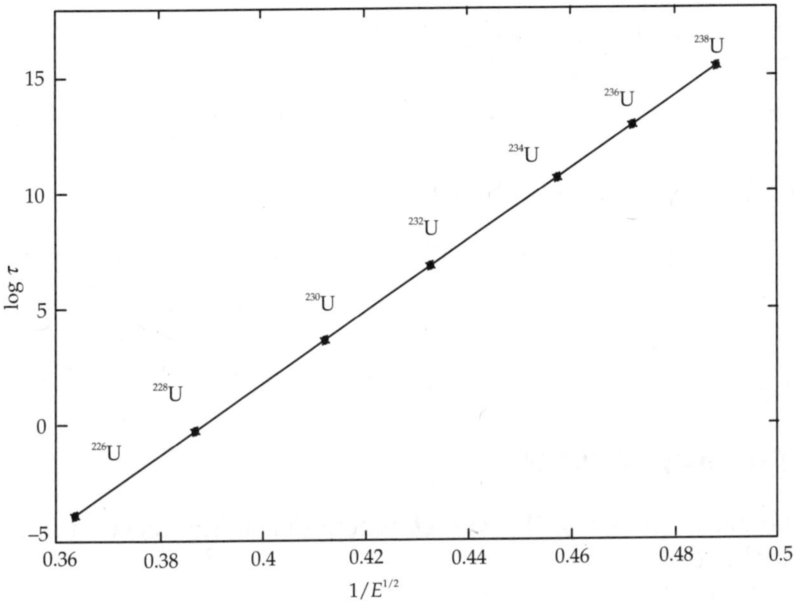

Figure 3.18: *Plot of* $\log\tau$ *vs* $\frac{1}{\sqrt{E}}$ *for seven isotopes of* ${}^{238}_{92}\text{U}$*, where* τ *is the mean life measured in years and E is the kinetic energy of the* α *particle in MeV*

⇒ Check Progress 3.3: Consider ${}^{238}_{92}\text{U} \longrightarrow {}^{234}_{90}\text{Th} + \alpha + Q$.

Given $M({}^{238}_{92}\text{U}) = 238.050784$ u, $M({}^{234}_{90}\text{Th}) = 234.043593$ u and $M({}^{4}_{2}\text{He}) = 4.002603$ u.

(a) Determine the energy(Q) released in the decay.

(b) Show by using Eq. (3.37) that the energy (E) carried by the α particle is ≈ 4.19 MeV.

(c) Estimate the velocity (v) of the α particle from $\frac{1}{2}mv^2 = E$, by ignoring the negative potential inside the nucleus. Justify the use of the non-relativistic equation.

(d) Calculate the radius (R) of ${}^{238}_{92}\text{U}$ (use the relation $R \approx 1.07A^{1/3}$ fm). Show that the frequency (ν) that the α particle makes with the wall of the potential barrier is $\approx 2.14 \times 10^{21}\ \text{s}^{-1}$.

(e) Calculate γ from Eq. (3.50), which is ≈ 50.69, and estimate the tunnelling probability $P \approx e^{-2\gamma}$ (note that Z represents the atomic number of the daughter).

(f) Show that the half-life $T_{1/2} = \ln 2 \times 1.59 \times 10^{15}$ years. The experimental value of $\tau_{1/2}$ is 6×10^9 years, and thus, the above result is only an approximation.

The above problem shows that the α particle has an exceedingly small probability of penetrating the barrier. The α particle knocks at the wall of the nucleus $\sim 10^{21}$ times per second, yet has to wait an average of 10^{15} years to escape!

Figure. 3.18 shows that half-life is extremely sensitive to variations in the energy of the α particle. The next problem illustrates this.

⇒ Check Progress 3.4: Consider ${}^{212}_{84}\mathrm{Po} \longrightarrow {}^{208}_{82}\mathrm{Pb} + \alpha + Q$.

Given $M({}^{212}_{84}\mathrm{Po}) = 211.988842$ u, $M({}^{208}_{82}\mathrm{Pb}) = 207.976627$ u and $M({}^{4}_{2}\mathrm{He}) = 4.002603$ u. Repeat the steps of the previous problem and calculate the average life τ.

Illustrative Example 3.16: Height of the Coulomb barrier

Consider ${}^{238}_{92}\mathrm{U} \longrightarrow {}^{234}_{90}\mathrm{Th} + \alpha + Q$. Calculate the height of the Coulomb barrier.

Solution Height of the barrier

$$V_0 = \frac{e^2}{4\pi\varepsilon_0}\frac{2(Z-2)}{R} = 1.44 \times \frac{2\times 90}{R_0(234^{1/3}+4^{1/3})} = 27.87 \text{ MeV}, \text{ where } R_0 = 1.2 \text{ fm}.$$

3.2.6 Alpha-Ray Spectrum

Consider the decay ${}^{A}_{Z}X \longrightarrow {}^{A-4}_{Z-2}Y + \alpha + Q$, where the energy released in the decay is calculated by Eq. (3.35) as

$$Q = M_x c^2 - M_y c^2 - M_\alpha c^2$$

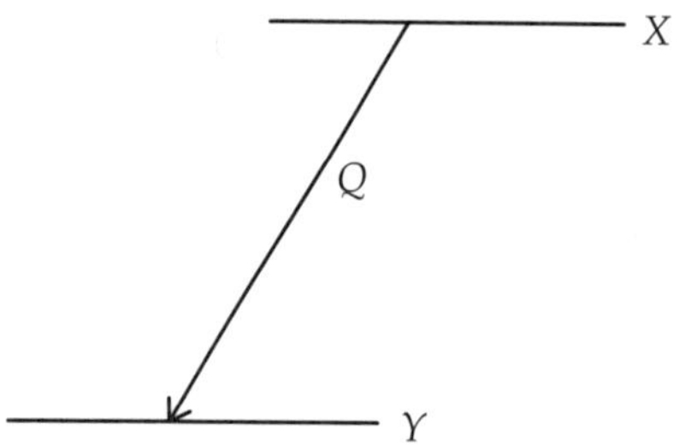

Figure 3.19: *Transition of α particle from parent to daughter*

Since the masses of the parent and daughter are fixed, the Q value must be unique. The α particles emitted from the radioactive elements are thus monoenergetic and the corresponding spectrum is a line spectrum. This is shown schematically in Fig. 3.19. Here, the α particles are emitted during the transition from the definite energy state of the parent nucleus to the definite energy state of the daughter nucleus.

Careful investigations, however, have revealed a fine structure-splitting in the energies of the α particles, that is, closely spaced groups of α particles emitted from any radioactive material. For example, in the decay ${}^{214}_{84}\mathrm{Po} \longrightarrow {}^{210}_{82}\mathrm{Pb} + \alpha$, four groups of α particles with energies of 7.68 MeV, 8.28 MeV, 9.07 MeV and 10.51 MeV are emitted. The most energetic α particles are observed to be produced alone; however, less energetic α decays are always accompanied by the emission of photons. This suggests the presence of discrete energy levels in the daughter nuclei. A parent nucleus can directly transform to the ground state of the daughter nucleus by emitting an α particle with an energy corresponding to the maximum Q value, or it can decay to an excited state of the daughter nucleus, in which case the energy released, Q value, is lower. Finally, as in the case of atomic transitions, the daughter nucleus subsequently comes to its ground state by emitting a photon.

Illustrative Example 3.17: Fine structure of α-ray spectrum

A substance with mass number A undergoes α decay by emitting two groups of α particles with kinetic energies $K_{\alpha 1}$ and $K_{\alpha 2}$. Show that the energy of the accompanying γ ray is $E_\gamma = \frac{A}{A-4}(K_{\alpha 1} \sim K_{\alpha 2})$.

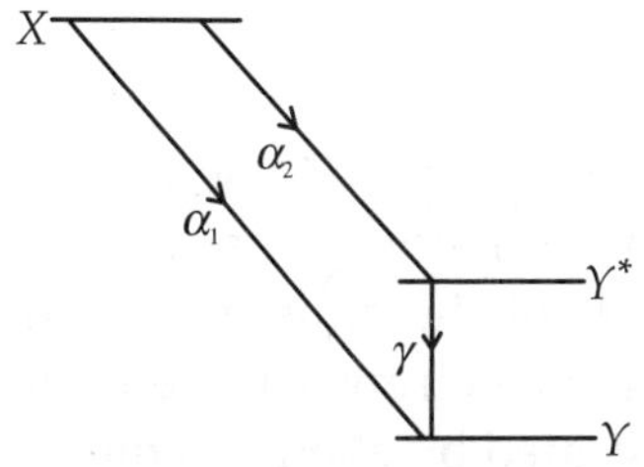

Figure 3.20: *Transition from the parent to different energy levels of the daughter*

Solution In this case, two groups of α particles are emitted. Thus, the transition takes place from the ground state of the parent to two different energy levels of the daughter, as shown in Fig. 3.20. The decay process is given as

$$ {}^{A}_{Z}X \longrightarrow {}^{A-4}_{Z-2}Y^* + \alpha + Q_1 $$

$$ \longrightarrow {}^{A-4}_{Z-2}Y + \alpha + Q_2 $$

And ${}^{A-4}_{Z-2}Y^* \longrightarrow {}^{A-4}_{Z-2}Y + \gamma$, where $Q_2 > Q_1$.

For the transition from the parent to the excited state of the daughter

$$ Q_1 = [M({}^{A}_{Z}X) - M({}^{A-4}_{Z-2}Y^*) - M({}^{4}_{2}\mathrm{He})]c^2 $$

For the transition from the parent to the ground state of the daughter

$$ Q_2 = [M({}^{A}_{Z}X) - M({}^{A-4}_{Z-2}Y) - M({}^{4}_{2}\mathrm{He})]c^2 $$

Since $M({}^{A-4}_{Z-2}Y^*) > M({}^{A-4}_{Z-2}Y)$, $Q_2 > Q_1$. The energy of the emitted γ ray is

$$ E_\gamma = [M({}^{A-4}_{Z-2}Y^*) - M({}^{A-4}_{Z-2}Y)]c^2 = Q_2 - Q_1 \tag{3.54} $$

Using the relations $Q_1 \approx \frac{A}{A-4}K_{\alpha 1}$ and $Q_2 \approx \frac{A}{A-4}K_{\alpha 2}$, Eq. (3.54) can be written as

$$ E_\gamma = \frac{A}{A-4}(K_{\alpha 2} - K_{\alpha 1}) $$

⇒ Check Progress 3.5: Consider

$$ {}^{226}_{88}\mathrm{Ra} \longrightarrow {}^{222}_{86}\mathrm{Rn}^* + \alpha + Q(4.611\ \mathrm{MeV}) $$

$$ \longrightarrow {}^{222}_{86}\mathrm{Rn} + \alpha + Q(4.795\ \mathrm{MeV}) $$

Calculate the energy of the emitted γ ray.

Illustrative Example 3.18: Emission of γ rays from the excited daughter

Consider ${}^{240}_{94}\mathrm{Pu} \longrightarrow {}^{236}_{92}\mathrm{Rn}^* + \alpha$. It is observed that the emitted α particles have energies of 5.17 MeV and 5.12 MeV. Determine the energy of the accompanying γ rays.

Solution Using the relation $Q \approx \frac{A}{A-4}K_\alpha$, we obtain

$$ Q_1 \approx \frac{240}{236} \times 5.17 \approx 5.26\ \mathrm{MeV} \text{ and } Q_2 \approx \frac{240}{236} \times 5.12 \approx 5.21\ \mathrm{MeV} $$

Thus, when $^{240}_{94}$Pu decays with a disintegration energy of 5.21 MeV, the daughter is left in an excited state. Due to the transition to the ground state, a photon of energy $5.26 - 5.21 = 0.05$ MeV is released.

We see from these examples that the spacing between nuclear levels is large (about 100 keV or more), whereas the corresponding spacing in atomic levels is of the order of only 1 eV.

3.3 BETA DECAY

Beta decay is the most common type of radioactive decay because a nucleus with a value of $\frac{N}{Z}$ greater than that for stable nuclei can transform to a more stable nucleus by emitting an electron. The process consists of the emission of an electron directly from a nucleus. Both positive and negative electrons can be emitted from the nucleus. Rutherford and Soddy (1903) demonstrated by chemical means that the atomic number of the nucleus increases by unity during negative beta decay. It was later shown (by Curie and Joliot in 1934) that the atomic number decreases by unity during the decay of positive electrons (called positrons).

In the initial investigation of beta radioactivity, the electrons emitted from the nucleus were confused with the orbital electrons of the atom. However, the electrons emitted during the beta decay cannot be the orbital electrons of the atoms. For atomic electrons, the energy is of the order of a few eV; however, the energy of the electrons emitted during beta decay is very large, of the order of MeV. Unlike atomic electrons, the beta particles have a continuous energy distribution for a given nuclide. Therefore, in beta decay, an electron is emitted directly from the nucleus. It is not that the electron was present previously inside the nucleus[8]. The uncertainty principle forbids electrons of the observed energies to exist inside the nucleus. The electron is produced at the very moment of the decay.

β^- decay: $^{A}_{Z}X \longrightarrow {}^{A}_{Z+1}Y + e^-$. The simplest example of β^- decay is the decay of tritium: $^{3}_{1}\text{H} \longrightarrow {}^{3}_{2}\text{He} + e^-$. From the conservation of charge, it follows that the proton number of the daughter nucleus in β^- decay increases by one unit, while the total nucleon number remains unchanged.

β^+ decay: In this case, a proton-rich nucleus emits a positron [9], thereby reducing the atomic number by one unit. The process can be represented by

$$^{A}_{Z}X \longrightarrow {}^{A}_{Z-1}Y + e^+$$

For example, $^{13}_{7}N \longrightarrow {}^{13}_{6}C + e^+$.

Electron capture (EC): A proton-rich nucleus may also absorb an atomic electron (from the inner K shell of the atom) and reduce its nuclear charge by one unit. This process is referred to as electron capture and may be represented as

$$^{A}_{Z}X + e^- \longrightarrow {}^{A}_{Z-1}Y$$

[8] In contrast is the case of α decay, where the α particle is formed inside the nucleus before decay.

[9] Positrons are antiparticles of electrons that have the same mass as electrons but a positive electric charge.

In this case, the outer electrons of the atom move down to the unfilled K shell and, as a result, X-rays are also emitted. The phenomenon of EC is quite significant for heavy atoms whose K shells are very close to the nucleus.

3.3.1 Beta Spectrum and the Neutrino Hypothesis

Early investigations with beta decay revealed a great puzzle. The conservation principles of energy, linear momentum and angular momentum were all apparently violated in this decay.

Energy conservation: Let us consider the following decay: ${}^{A}_{Z}X \longrightarrow {}^{A}_{Z+1}Y + e^-$.

This is simply a two-body decay. For this decay, where the parent nucleus is at rest, the conservation of energy requires

$$M_x c^2 = M_y c^2 + T_y + M_e c^2 + T_e,$$

where T_y and T_e represent the kinetic energies of the daughter nucleus and the electron, respectively. Therefore, the energy released is

$$Q = (M_x - M_y - M_e)c^2 = T_y + T_e$$

This energy is shared between the daughter nucleus and the ejected beta particle. The maximum energy carried by the electron is

$$(T_e)_{\text{max}} \approx (M_x - M_y - M_e)c^2 \tag{3.55}$$

Therefore, just as in α decay, as $M_e \ll M_y$, most of the energy released is carried away by the lighter emitted particle (the electron) and T_e must have a unique value given by Eq. (3.55).

The energy distribution of electrons emitted by β decay can be investigated with the help of a magnetic beta spectrometer. From the results obtained from such measurements, it has been found that instead of a fixed energy, the electrons emitted during beta decay have a continuous range of energies from 0 to $(T_e)_{\text{max}}$.

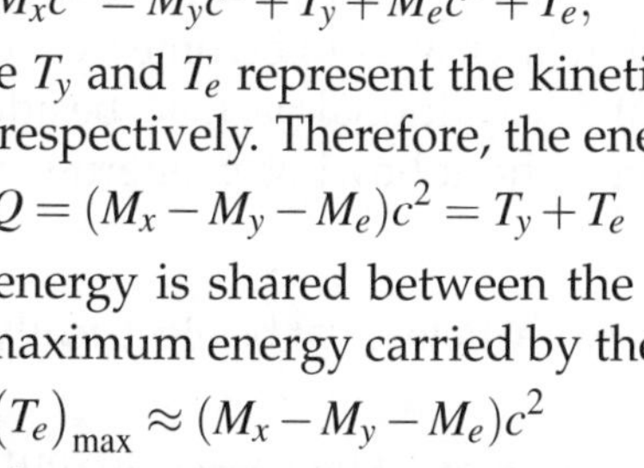

Figure 3.21: *Energy spectrum of electrons in β decay*

The typical shape of a beta decay spectrum is shown in Fig. 3.21. The maximum energy of the emitted electron, known as the **endpoint energy**, is given by Eq. (3.55). We thus conclude that the process of beta decay involves emission of electrons of all energies, ranging from zero to $(T_e)_{\text{max}}$. For most of the electrons, the energies are well below the expected value predicted by energy conservation and, as a result, some energy is *missing* from the spectrum. When this missing energy was first observed, it jeopardised the survival of one of the most cherished conservation laws in physics, namely, the conservation of energy!

Angular momentum conservation: In addition to a possible violation of energy conservation by most of the electrons, the conservation of angular momentum also appeared to be violated. Electrons, as well as each of the nucleons, has a spin angular momentum of $\frac{\hbar}{2}$. Since the parent and daughter have the same number of nucleons, the total angular momenta of the parents and the daughter remain the same. However, the emitted electron has half-spin $\left(\frac{\hbar}{2}\right)$ and it is therefore clear that angular momentum cannot be conserved in this process.

Linear momentum conservation: Beta decay also seemed to violate the law of conservation of linear momentum. When the directions of the emitted electrons and the daughter nuclei were observed in a cloud chamber,[10] they were never seen exactly opposite each other, as required for conservation of linear momentum.

All of the difficulties concerning the conservation laws were overcome by the neutrino hypothesis of Pauli (1933). He proposed that an additional particle, besides the electron, is emitted in beta decay, and he assigned the following properties to the new particle:

(a) The conservation of charge requires that the new particle must be electrically neutral.

(b) To restore the conservation of angular momentum, it must be a fermion with half-spin $\left(\frac{\hbar}{2}\right)$.

(c) This new particle would carry off the missing energy, that is, the difference between the endpoint energy and the actual kinetic energy of the electron.

(d) The observed fact that the energy spectrum extends to a maximum of T_e by Eq. (3.55) suggests that the new particle would be essentially massless.

This new particle is called a **neutrino** (*little neutral one* in Italian). Therefore, the complete decay process is

$$^{A}_{Z}X \longrightarrow {}^{A}_{Z+1}Y + e^{-} + \bar{\nu}$$

$$^{3}_{1}\mathrm{H} \longrightarrow {}^{3}_{2}\mathrm{He} + e^{-} + \bar{\nu},$$

where $\bar{\nu}$ is the antiparticle of ν, called the **antineutrino**. A typical β^+ decay would be

$$^{A}_{Z}X \longrightarrow {}^{A}_{Z-1}Y + e^{+} + \nu$$

$$^{13}_{7}\mathrm{N} \longrightarrow {}^{13}_{6}\mathrm{C} + e^{+} + \nu$$

Applying the neutrino hypothesis, the kinetic energy of the electron in β^- decay would be

$$T_e = (M_x - M_y - M_e)c^2 - E_\nu \tag{3.56}$$

[10]For a cloud chamber photograph of $^{6}_{2}\mathrm{He} \longrightarrow {}^{6}_{3}\mathrm{Li} + e^{-}$, refer to Meyerhof, WE. 1967. *Elements of Nuclear Physics*. McGraw-Hill, USA.

where E_ν is the energy carried off by the neutrino. If $T_e = (M_x - M_y - M_e)c^2 = (T_e)_{\max} =$ *Endpoint energy*, then the energy carried by the neutrino is $E_\nu = 0$. If $T_e = 0$, all this energy is carried off by the neutrino. Therefore, even though the difference in mass between the parent and the daughter is fixed for a given decay, the electrons can have a continuous distribution of energy.

Equation (3.56) can be written as

$$T_e + T_\nu + m_\nu c^2 = (M_x - M_y - M_e)c^2$$

$$\text{or } (T_e)_{\max} + m_\nu c^2 = (M_x - M_y - M_e)c^2 = Q$$

$$\text{Thus } m_\nu c^2 = Q - (T_e)_{\max} \tag{3.57}$$

This relation can be used to estimate the rest mass of neutrinos. Since the experimental value of $Q - (T_e)_{\max}$ with gradual sophistication of measurements is very close to zero, it is assumed that the rest mass of a neutrino is zero.

Illustrative Example 3.19: Most intense point of the β spectrum

The distribution of electrons in the β spectrum may be represented as

$$N(E)dE \propto E^{1/2}(E_{\max} - E)^2 dE$$

Find the energy for which N will be maximum. Also calculate the average energy.

Solution The condition is $\dfrac{dN}{dE} = 0 \Rightarrow E = \dfrac{E_{\max}}{5}$.

$$< E >= \frac{\int_0^\infty E^{3/2}(E_{\max} - E)^2 dE}{\int_0^\infty E^{1/2}(E_{\max} - E)^2 dE} = \frac{E_{\max}}{3}$$

3.3.2 Difference between Neutrino and Antineutrino

Every elementary particle has an antiparticle. The antiparticle of the neutrino is known as the antineutrino ($\bar{\nu}$). The neutrino and the antineutrino are both electrically neutral and massless and, unlike the neutron and antineutron,[11] they have no magnetic dipole moment. Experiments on β decay indicate that *neutrinos are left-handed, whereas antineutrinos are right-handed*. By left-handed, we mean that the spin vector points in the direction opposite the linear momentum (direction of its motion) and right-handed means that its spin points along its direction of motion. The handedness is one of the distinguishing characteristics of neutrinos and antineutrinos, and has far-reaching consequences.

The handedness is represented through a property called **helicity**, which is defined as the projection of spin along its direction of motion

$$h = \frac{\vec{s}.\vec{p}}{|\vec{s}.\vec{p}|} \tag{3.58}$$

[11]The neutron and the antineutron have magnetic dipole moments of opposite sign.

Particles with positive helicity are referred to as *right-handed*, while those with negative helicity are referred to as *left-handed*. For a massless[12] particle, h can only be ± 1. It has been observed that

$$h = -1 \text{ for } \nu \quad \text{and} \quad = +1 \text{ for } \bar{\nu} \tag{3.59}$$

For electrons[13] $h = -\frac{v}{c}$ and for positrons $h = +\frac{v}{c}$.

The neutrino, having no charge and no mass and no magnetic moment, does not produce any ionisation and, therefore, cannot be detected directly. It is a very weakly interacting particle. The neutrino interacts with matter only through inverse beta decay, $p + \bar{\nu} \longrightarrow n + e^+$, where the antineutrinos produced in beta decay interact with a proton to produce a neutron and a positron.

3.3.3 Violation of Parity in Beta Decay

The handedness property of neutrinos described above leads to non-conservation of parity[14] in β decay. The conservation of parity[15] in any process means it does not change under reflection of spatial coordinates; that is, *both the original and the reflected systems must occur in nature. In fact, we could not distinguish the original system from its mirror image in any way.* Let us consider a neutrino travelling to the right, as shown in Fig. 3.22, with its spin pointing to the left. Under mirror reflection, the neutrino would travel to the left and its spin would also point to the left because the angular momentum vector (a pseudo vector) does not change sign under mirror reflection. The situation in the mirror does not occur for a neutrino. Instead, it corresponds to an antineutrino. Therefore, parity conservation is violated in β decay.

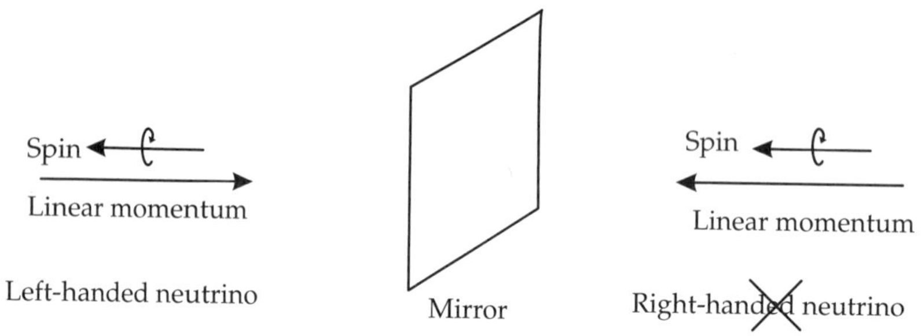

Figure 3.22: *Parity non-conservation of neutrinos*

Until the late 1950*s*, the physical phenomenon was believed to be the same, whether described in a right-handed coordinate system or in a left-handed coordinate system. In another words, it was believed that parity is conserved in all interactions. However, on the basis of certain meson decays, Lee and Young (1956)

[12]Helicity is a well-defined quantity for massless particles for a simple reason: that such a particle must move with the velocity of light. Thus, by making a Lorentz transformation, it is not possible to change the helicity of the particle.

[13]This is not an intrinsic property of all e^- and e^+. Only for e^- and e^+ in beta decay is $h = \pm\frac{v}{c}$.

[14]Feynman, R. et al. 1964. *The Feynman Lectures on Physics*, Addison-Wesley, 1:52.7.

[15]Please see Appendix A.

predicted that parity would not be conserved in β decay. They suggested that it would be possible to observe the parity violation in the beta decay of polarised nuclei. The first such experiment[16] was carried out by Wu et al. which confirmed the parity violation[17] in beta decay.

In the experiment, the nuclear spins of ^{60}Co were polarised by applying a very strong field at an extremely low temperature of about 0.01 K. Such a low temperature is used to minimise the thermal motion leading to depolarisation. The angular distribution of the emitted electrons (θ) relative to the direction of the applied magnetic field was measured. The electrons were found to be emitted preferentially in a direction opposite to that of the applied field, and thus, opposite to the spins of the cobalt nuclei. The preferred emission of electrons with respect to the spin of cobalt is schematically shown in Fig. 3.23. Here, the β decay from ^{60}Co is seen with the spins of the participating particles.

$$^{60}\text{Co}(5^+) \longrightarrow {}^{60}\text{Ni}(4^+) + e^- + \bar{\nu}$$

The numbers within the parenthesis indicate the spins of the nuclei. The conservation of angular momentum requires that the electron and antineutrino must have parallel spin. Since spin and linear momentum are always parallel for antineutrinos, the electron must be emitted in a direction opposite to its spin.

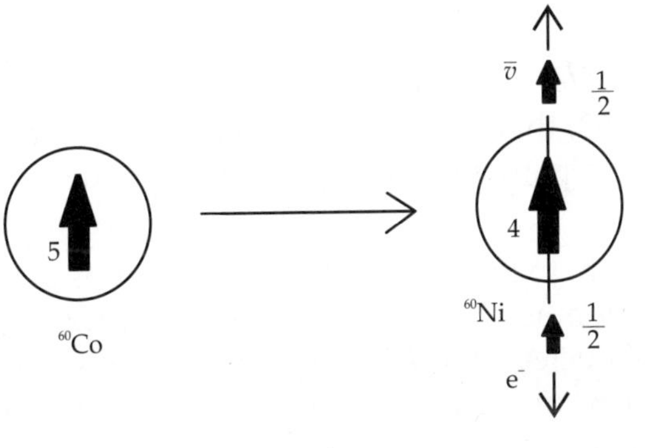

Figure 3.23: *β decay from ^{60}Co. The bold arrows represent the angular momenta while the thin arrows indicate the linear momenta of the participating particles.*

In Wu's experiment, the angular distribution of the emitted electron was measured with respect to the spin of ^{60}Co. The experiment showed that

$$< \cos\,\theta > = < \frac{\vec{s}.\vec{p}}{|\vec{s}.\vec{p}|} > \; < 0, \tag{3.60}$$

where $\vec{s}$ represents the spin of ^{60}Co (or the direction of the applied magnetic field) and $\vec{p}$ represents the linear momentum of the emitted electron.

[16] Wu, CS, et al. 1957. Experimental Test of Parity Conservation in Beta Decay. *Phy. Rec.*, 105:1413.
[17] Burcham, WE. 1973. *Nuclear Physics*. Longman Group.

Since spin $\vec{s}$, being the angular momentum, is an axial vector and $\vec{p}$ is a polar vector, under parity transformation, Eq. (3.60) becomes

$$< \cos\,\theta > = < \frac{\vec{s}.\vec{p}}{|\vec{s}.\vec{p}|} > \longrightarrow - < \frac{\vec{s}.\vec{p}}{|\vec{s}.\vec{p}|} > = - < \cos\,\theta > \tag{3.61}$$

If parity is conserved, the left-hand side and right-hand side of Eq. (3.61) will be identical, and hence, $< \cos\,\theta > = 0$, implying that the angular distribution of the emitted electrons must be isotropic. However, the finite negative value observed for this quantity indicates that the two coordinate systems are not equivalent. Thus, the emission of electrons predominantly against the magnetic field indicates the absence of mirror symmetry and non-conservation of parity.

3.3.4 Energetics of Beta Decay

(a) Let us consider a β^- decay: ${}^A_ZX \longrightarrow {}^{A}_{Z+1}Y + e^- + \bar{\nu}$. This is equivalent to $n \longrightarrow p + e^- + \bar{\nu}$.

From the conservation of energy, we get $M_xc^2 = M_yc^2 + T_y + M_ec^2 + T_e + E$, where M_x, M_y and M_e are, respectively, the masses of the parent nucleus, the daughter nucleus and the electron; and T_y, T_e and $E_{\bar{\nu}}$ represent, respectively, the kinetic energies of the daughter nucleus, the electron and $\bar{\nu}$. Therefore, the energy released is given by

$$Q = (M_x - M_y - M_e)c^2 = T_y + T_e + E_{\bar{\nu}} \tag{3.62}$$

We see from Eq. (3.62) that electron emission can take place only if $Q > 0$, that is, when the mass of the parent nucleus is greater than the sum of the masses of the decay products.

Again, it is convenient to rewrite this equation in terms of the atomic masses. The mass of the (A,Z) atom is $M(A,Z) = M_x + ZM_e - BE(A,Z)/c^2$, where M_x represents the mass of the ${}^A_ZX$ nucleus and $BE(A,Z)$ is the binding energy of the (A,Z) atom. Expressing M_x and M_y in terms of atomic masses in Eq. (3.62), we get

$$\begin{aligned} Q &= [M(A,Z) - M(A,Z+1)]c^2 + BE(A,Z) - BE(A,Z+1) \\ &\approx [M(A,Z) - M(A,Z+1)]c^2 \end{aligned} \tag{3.63}$$

Here, the small difference in atomic binding energies ($\backsim$ eV) has been neglected. Therefore, β^- decay is possible if $M(A,Z) > M(A,Z+1)$.

(b) Let us consider a β^+ decay: ${}^A_ZX \longrightarrow {}^{A}_{Z-1}Y + e^+ + \nu$. This is equivalent to $p \longrightarrow n + e^+ + \nu$.

The energy released is given by $Q = (M_x - M_y - M_e)c^2 = T_y + T_e + E_\nu$, (3.64)

where M represents the nuclear mass. Rewriting this relation in terms of atomic masses, we obtain

$$Q = [M(A,Z) - ZM_e]c^2 + BE(A,Z) - [M(A,Z-1) - (Z-1)M_e]c^2$$
$$- BE(A,Z-1) - M_ec^2$$
$$= [M(A,Z) - M(A,Z-1)]c^2 - 2M_ec^2 + BE(A,Z) - BE(A,Z-1)$$
$$\approx [M(A,Z) - M(A,Z-1) - 2M_e]c^2, \quad (3.65)$$

where, again, the $M(A,Z)$ of Eq. (3.65) refers to atomic masses. Therefore, β^+ decay has a threshold of $2M_ec^2$; in order for the process to occur spontaneously, $[M(A,Z) - M(A,Z-1)] > 2M_e$.

(c) Another process that is similar to positron decay is the electron-capture (EC) process, where the nuclear charge decreases by one unit, $Z \longrightarrow Z-1$. Under certain conditions, a proton in the nucleus captures an atomic electron: $p + e^- \longrightarrow n + \nu$.

The most probable capture is from the K shell because a K electron is closest to the nucleus. The process can be described as

$$^A_ZX + e^- \longrightarrow {}^A_{Z-1}Y + \nu$$

The EC process is shown schematically in Fig. 3.24, where there is a parent atom in the initial state and a daughter atom plus a neutrino in the final state. Since a vacancy is created in the inner shell of the atom, the daughter atom will be in an excited state. The vacancy is quickly filled as electrons from the higher state make a downward transition, resulting in the emission of X-rays.

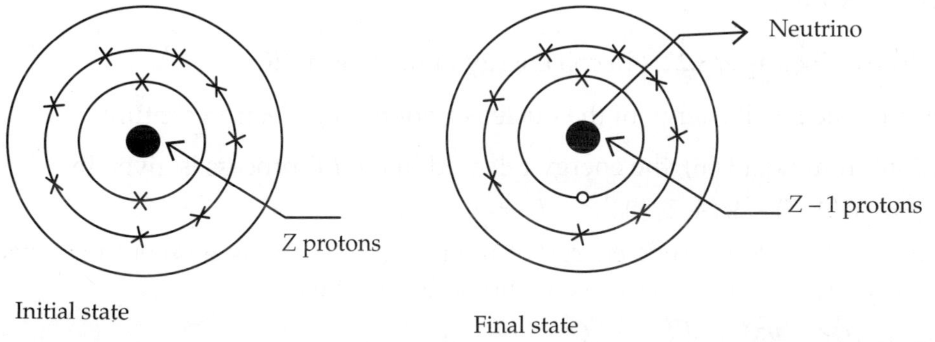

Figure 3.24: *Electron-capture process, where the capture of a K electron is shown*

In the initial state, there is a parent atom of mass $M(A,Z)$. In the final state, there is a daughter atom in an excited state and a neutrino. The conservation of energy requires

$$M(A,Z)c^2 = M^*(A,Z-1)c^2 + E_\nu = M(A,Z-1)c^2 + E_B + E_\nu,$$

where E_B is the excitation energy of the daughter or the binding energy of the K electron (missing). The atomic masses $M(A,Z)$ and $M(A,Z-1)$ refer to the masses in the ground state. The energy released in the EC process is given by

$$Q = [M(A,Z) - M(A,Z-1)]c^2 - E_B \approx [M(A,Z) - M(A,Z-1)]c^2 \quad (3.66)$$

As mentioned earlier, we have neglected a very small binding energy of electrons $\backsim$ eV. Therefore, the EC can take place if $M(A,Z) > M(A,Z-1)$.

Illustrative Example 3.20: β^+ or EC

${}^7_4$Be and ${}^7_3$Li have atomic masses of 7.016929 u and 7.016005 u, respectively. Which of them shows β activity and of what type? Justify your answer.

Solution Since the mass of ${}^7_4$Be is larger, the process is ${}^7_4\text{Be} \longrightarrow {}^7_3\text{Li}$.
The decay mode will be either β^+ or electron capture.

$$M({}^7_4\text{Be}) - M({}^7_3\text{Li}) = 7.016929 - 7.016005 = 0.86 \text{ MeV} < 2M_ec^2$$

Thus, the possible decay mode will be EC.

Illustrative Example 3.21: Energy of ν in EC

Consider an EC process: ${}^{131}_{55}\text{Cs} + e^- \longrightarrow {}^{131}_{54}\text{Xe} + \nu$. Calculate the energy released in the process. Also calculate the energy of the neutrino, if the binding energy of the electron is 35 eV.

Given: $M({}^{131}_{55}\text{Cs}) = 130.905444$ u, $M({}^{131}_{54}\text{Xe}) = 130.905072$ u.

Solution From Eq. (3.66), the energy released in the EC process is $Q = [M(A,Z) - M(A,Z-1)]c^2 - E_B = E_\nu + T_r$, where T_r is the recoil kinetic energy of the nucleus.

$E_\nu + T_r = (130.905444 - 130.905072) * 931.5 - 0.035 \approx 0.312$ MeV. Since the rest mass of the neutrino is zero, almost all the energy is carried by the neutrino. Thus, $E_\nu \approx 0.312$ MeV.

Illustrative Example 3.22: Recoil energy of nucleus in EC

Determine the recoil energy of the nucleus undergoing electron capture.

Solution From Eq. (3.66), the energy released in the *EC* process is given by

$$Q = [M(A,Z) - M(A,Z-1)]c^2 - E_B = E_\nu + T_r,$$

where T_r is the recoil kinetic energy of the nucleus. Also, by momentum conservation, $|p_\nu| = |p_r|$, where p_r is the recoil momentum. Thus

$$T_r = \frac{p_r^2}{2M} = \frac{p_\nu^2}{2M} = \frac{E_\nu^2}{2Mc^2} \approx \frac{Q^2}{2Mc^2}$$

Illustrative Example 3.23: Maximum kinetic energy of β^-

Consider a β^- decay: ${}^A_ZX \longrightarrow {}^A_{Z+1}Y + e^- + \bar{\nu}$. Show that the kinetic energy of the recoil nucleus is $T_y = \dfrac{Q + 2M_ec^2}{2M_yc^2}T_e$, and T_e is the maximum kinetic energy of the emitted electron.

Solution When the kinetic energy of the electron is maximum, the energy carried by the antineutrino is zero. Thus, from Eq. (3.62), the energy released is

$$Q = (M_x - M_y - M_e)c^2 = T_y + T_e,$$

where T_e represents the maximum kinetic energy of the electron and $T_e \gg T_y$ as $M_y \gg M_e$.

From momentum conservation, $|\vec{p}_e| = |\vec{p}_y|$. Since the rest mass of the electron is small (≈ 0.5 MeV), we must use a relativistic result to calculate the kinetic energy of the electron. Therefore

$$p_e^2c^2 = E^2 - M_e^2c^4 = (T_e + M_ec^2)^2 - M_e^2c^4 = T_e^2 + 2M_ec^2T_e$$

Or $\quad p_y^2c^2 = 2M_yT_yc^2 = T_e^2 + 2M_ec^2T_e \qquad (3.67)$

As the rest mass M_y is large, we use the non-relativistic result, $p_y^2 = 2M_yT_y$. Thus

$$T_y = \frac{T_e + 2M_ec^2}{2M_yc^2}T_e \approx \frac{Q + 2M_ec^2}{2M_yc^2}T_e$$

Illustrative Example 3.24: Maximum kinetic energy of β^+

${}^{12}_{7}$N decays to ${}^{12}_{6}$C which comes to the ground state with the emission of 4.43-MeV gamma rays. Find the maximum kinetic energy of the emitted beta particle. Given $M({}^{12}_{7}\text{N}) = 12.018613$.

Solution The decay process: ${}^{12}_{7}\text{N} \longrightarrow {}^{12}_{6}\text{C}^* + \beta^+ + \nu$ and ${}^{12}_{6}\text{C}^* \longrightarrow {}^{12}_{6}\text{C} + \gamma$

Mass of ${}^{12}_{6}$C in the ground state is 12.000000 u; Mass of ${}^{12}_{6}\text{C}^* = 12 + \dfrac{4.43}{931.5} = 12.004756$ u.

Thus, the energy released in the decay is

$$Q = [M({}^{12}_{7}\text{N}) - \text{M}({}^{12}_{6}\text{C}^*) - 2\text{M}_\text{e}]\text{c}^2 \approx 11.89 \text{ MeV}$$

Neglecting the small correction for the recoil kinetic energy of ${}^{12}_{6}\text{C}^*$, the maximum kinetic energy of β^+ will be 11.89 MeV.

⇒ Check Progress 3.6: Consider the decay of a free neutron: $n \longrightarrow p + e^- + \bar{\nu}$. Estimate the recoil energy of the proton when e^- is emitted with maximum kinetic energy.

(Hint: Energy released $Q = (M_n - M_p - M_e)c^2 \approx 0.78$ MeV and the maximum kinetic energy of the electron $T_e = \sqrt{P_e^2C^2 + M_e^2C^4} - M_ec^2 \simeq Q$. Calculating P_eC, apply momentum conservation and finally use $T_p = \dfrac{P_P^2}{2H_p} \simeq 751$ eV).

3.3.5 Selection Rules

The initial and the final states of a nucleus must satisfy certain definite conditions for the allowed β decay. These conditions, known as the *selection rules*, require compliance with the laws of angular momentum conservation and parity. Selection rules are of two types: Fermi (F) and Gamow–Teller (GT).

In β decay, both the electron and the antineutrino are emitted with $l = 0$. However, the electron and the antineutrino each have half-integral spin and the pair may be emitted with parallel or antiparallel spin.

(a) If the electron and antineutrino are emitted with antiparallel spin, then $S = 0$. Therefore, the total angular momentum of the nucleus does not change $(\Delta I = 0)$.

(b) If the electron and antineutrino are emitted with parallel spin, then $S = 1$. Therefore, the total angular momentum of the nucleus can change by $(\Delta I = 0, \pm 1)$ with no $0 \rightarrow 0$ transition.

> **Allowed transitions**
> F selection rule: $(\Delta I = 0)$
> GT selection rule: $(\Delta I = 0, \pm 1)$, but $0 \nrightarrow 0$
> In both cases, the nuclear eigenfunction must not change parity $(\Delta \pi = 0)$.

Illustrative Example 3.25: Fermi or Gamow–Teller

Classify the following transitions:

$${}^{6}_{2}\text{He} \longrightarrow {}^{6}_{3}\text{Li} + e^{-} + \bar{\nu}, (0^{+} \rightarrow 1^{+});\ {}^{14}_{8}\text{O} \longrightarrow {}^{14}_{7}\text{N}^{*} + e^{+} + \nu, (0^{+} \rightarrow 0^{+})$$

Solution The first is a GT transition while the second is an F transition.

3.4 GAMMA DECAY

When a heavy nucleus disintegrates by emitting an α or β particle, the daughter nucleus may be left in an excited state. Like in an atom, the nucleus in the excited state comes to its ground state by emitting high-energy photons or γ rays. Gamma rays typically have energies of ~ 1 MeV, a characteristic of the energy difference between the nuclear states.

The study of the emission and absorption of γ rays forms an essential part of nuclear spectroscopy. The energies of the γ rays can be measured with great precision and they provide a powerful means of studying the energies of the excited states of the nuclei. Also, from the emission of γ rays, the spin and parity of the excited states can be deduced.

3.4.1 Energetics of Gamma Decay

Consider the decay ${}^{A}_{Z}X^{*} \longrightarrow {}^{A}_{Z}X + \gamma$. Energy conservation requires $M_x^* c^2 = M_x c^2 + E_\gamma + T_x$, where M_x^* represents the rest mass of the parent in the excited state, M_x is the rest mass of the daughter in the ground state, E_γ is the energy of the γ ray and T_x is the recoil energy of the daughter.

The energy released is given by $$Q = M_x^* c^2 - M_x c^2 = E_\gamma + T_x \tag{3.68}$$

This is shared by the daughter and the γ ray.

Momentum conservation gives $0 \longrightarrow \vec{p}_x + \vec{p}_\gamma$, where $\vec{p}_x$ and $\vec{p}_\gamma$ represent the momenta of the daughter and the γ ray, respectively. The recoil speed of the daughter is so small that non-relativistic results may be used to calculate T_x. Thus

$$T_x = \frac{p_x^2}{2M_x} = \frac{p_\gamma^2}{2M_x} = \frac{E_\gamma^2}{2M_x c^2} \quad \text{and } Q = M_x^* c^2 - M_x c^2 = E_\gamma + \frac{E_\gamma^2}{2M_x c^2} \tag{3.69}$$

If $E_\gamma = 2$ MeV and $M_x \sim 50$ u, then $T_x = \dfrac{E_\gamma^2}{2M_x c^2} = \dfrac{4}{2 \times 50 \times 931.5} \approx 40$ eV, which is negligible for most practical purposes.

The energy of the emitted γ ray can be obtained from the solution of Eq. (3.69)

$$E_\gamma = M_x c^2 \left[-1 \pm \left(1 + \frac{2Q}{M_x c^2}\right)^{1/2} \right]$$

Since E_γ cannot be negative $\quad E_\gamma = M_x c^2 \left[-1 + \left(1 + \dfrac{2Q}{M_x c^2}\right)^{1/2} \right]$

As $\dfrac{2Q}{M_x c^2} \ll 1, \quad E_\gamma = M_x c^2 \left[-1 + 1 + \dfrac{1}{2}\dfrac{2Q}{M_x c^2} - \dfrac{1}{8}\left(\dfrac{2Q}{M_x c^2}\right)^2 + \ldots \right]$

Thus $\quad E_\gamma = Q - \dfrac{1}{2}\dfrac{Q^2}{M_x c^2}$ $\qquad$ (3.70)

Equation (3.70) can also be obtained directly from Eq. (3.69) by approximation. Since the recoil energy is very small, $E_\gamma \approx Q$.

Thus, the correction term is $\approx \dfrac{Q^2}{2M_x c^2}$. Therefore, from Eq. (3.69), we get

$$E_\gamma = Q - \frac{1}{2}\frac{Q^2}{M_x c^2}$$

Illustrative Example 3.26: Energy of γ rays

The energy of an excited state of ^{14}N (denoted by ^{14}N*) relative to the ground state is 8.62 MeV.

(i) If the excited state is formed by bombarding ^{13}C with protons (p + ^{13}C $\longrightarrow$ ^{14}N*), what must be the kinetic energy of the proton? [Consider the recoil of ^{14}N* in the calculation]. Deduce the formula used.

(ii) If this ^{14}N* at rest decays to the ground state by a single γ-ray photon, what will be the energy of the photon, considering the recoil of ^{14}N? Given: Mass of proton = 938.8 MeV, mass of ^{13}C = 12112.7 MeV and mass of ^{14}N = 13043.9 MeV.

Solution (i) $p + {}^{13}\text{C} \longrightarrow {}^{14}\text{N}^*$

Momentum conservation: $\vec{p}_p = \vec{p}_{N^*}$, ^{13}C is at rest.

Energy conservation: $M_p c^2 + T_p + M_c c^2 = M_{N^*} c^2 + T_{N^*}$, where T represents the kinetic energy. Again

$$T_{N^*} = \frac{p_{N^*}^2}{2M_{N^*}} = \frac{p_p^2}{2M_p}\frac{M_p}{M_{N^*}} = T_p \frac{M_p}{M_{N^*}}$$

Thus $T_p = [M_{N^*} - M_p - M_c]c^2 + T_p \dfrac{M_p}{M_{N^*}} \quad = 1.02 + T_p \times 0.072$

Therefore, $T_p(1 - 0.072) = 1.02 \Longrightarrow T_p = 1.099$ MeV.

(ii) $^{14}N^* \longrightarrow {}^{14}N + \gamma$

From Eq. (3.69), $E_\gamma = 8.62 - \dfrac{1}{2}\dfrac{8.62^2}{13043.9} = 8.6172$ MeV.

3.4.2 Selection Rule

The radiation field produced by the varying charge and current distribution can be analysed like a static field, in terms of its multipole character. From a study of classical electromagnetic radiation, it follows that for each multipole of order L, there are two possible classes of radiation: electric 2^L pole and magnetic 2^L radiation.

For dipole, $L = 1$; $L = 2$ represents a quadrupole, and so on. The parity of the radiation field is

$$\pi = (-1)^{L+1} \text{ for magnetic } 2^L \text{pole radiations}$$

$$\pi = (-1)^{L} \text{ for electric } 2^L \text{pole radiations}$$

The electric and magnetic multipoles of the same order L have opposite parity. For dipole, $L = 1$, and thus, the electric dipole radiation has *odd* parity while the magnetic dipole radiation has *even* parity.

Suppose a transition takes place from initial state i to final state f, $i \longrightarrow f$. The angular momentum of the states are $\vec{I}_i$ and $\vec{I}_f$, respectively. If the parities of the states are π_i and π_f, respectively, then the parity of the radiation field is $\pi = \dfrac{\pi_i}{\pi_f}$.

Conservation of angular momentum requires that the angular momentum ($\vec{L}$) carried away by the photon will be $\vec{L} = \vec{I}_i - \vec{I}_f$.

By the triangular rule, the possible value of $|\vec{L}|$ will be from $|\vec{I}_i - \vec{I}_f|$ to $|\vec{I}_i + \vec{I}_f|$ with $L \neq 0$.

Illustrative Example 3.27: Application of selection rules

Consider the transition from $\dfrac{3}{2}^+ \longrightarrow \dfrac{5}{2}^+$.

Solution The possible value of $|\vec{L}|$ is $\left|\dfrac{3}{2} - \dfrac{5}{2}\right|$ to $\dfrac{3}{2} + \dfrac{5}{2}$, that is, $1, 2, 3$ and 4.

Thus, the radiation field will consist of a mixture of $L = 1$ (dipole), $L = 2$ (quadrupole), $L = 3$ (octupole) and $L = 4$ (hexadecapole) radiation.

Parity of the initial state is $+ve$. Parity of the final state is $+ve$.

Thus, there is no change in parity; $\Delta\pi =$ no change.

Therefore, the radiation field must have even parity.

$L = 1$ Magnetic dipole ($M1$) $L = 2$ Electric quadrupole ($E2$)

$L = 3$ Magnetic octupole ($M3$) $L = 4$ Electric hexasecapole ($E4$)

Illustrative Example 3.28: Electric and magnetic multi-polarities of γ radiation

Determine the type of radiation for the following:

(i) $2^+ \longrightarrow 0^+$ (ii) $1^+ \longrightarrow 0^+$ (iii) $2^+ \longrightarrow 2^+$ (iv) $\frac{1}{2}^- \longrightarrow \frac{1}{2}^+$

Solution (i) Possible value of $L = 2$ and the radiation field must have even parity. Thus, the radiation will be of $E2$.
(ii) Possible value of $L = 1$ and the radiation field must have even parity. Thus, radiation will be of $M1$.
(iii) Possible value of $L = 1,\ 2,\ 3$ and 4 and the radiation field must have even parity. Thus, radiation will be of $M1, E2, M3$ and $E4$.
(iv) Possible value of $L = 1$ and the radiation field must have odd parity. Thus, radiation will be of $E1$.

Illustrative Example 3.29: Nature of radiation field

Find the possible electric and magnetic multi-polarities of the γ rays emitted in the transition between 2.6 MeV (3^-) and 1.2 MeV (1^-).

Solution Possible value of $L = 2, 3, 4$ and as there is no change in parity, the radiation field must have even parity. Thus, the radiation consists of $E2, M3$ and $E4$. The radiation $E2$ is expected to dominate.

3.4.3 Internal Conversion

The emission of internal conversion electron is another mechanism, apart from γ emission, of losing excitation of the nucleus. It is an electromagnetic process where the energy involved in the nuclear transition $\triangle E = E_i - E_f$ is transferred *directly* to an atomic electron and, as a result, the electron is ejected from the atom with a kinetic energy[18] of

$$T_e = \triangle E - E_B, \tag{3.71}$$

where E_B is the binding energy of the electron in the atomic shell from which it is ejected. Unlike β decay, the electron is not created at the time of decay; rather, it is an electron that already exists in the atom. It must be noted very carefully that *internal conversion is not a two-step process*, where the photon is first emitted from the nucleus and then knocks out the atomic electron, like in the photoelectric effect. It is an independent process by which an excited nucleus can release its excitation energy without any γ emission.

[18]The recoil energy of the atom has been neglected.

If an electron from the K shell is ejected, the kinetic energy of the ejected electron will be $T_{e_K} = \triangle E - E_{B_K}$, and that for the L shell electron will be $T_{e_L} = \triangle E - E_{B_L}$, since $E_{B_K} > E_{B_L}$, $T_{e_K} < T_{e_L}$.

If $\triangle E < E_B$, then internal conversion becomes energetically impossible. From the very nature of the process, it follows that internal conversion must always be accompanied by the emission of characteristic X-rays.

Illustrative Example 3.30: Internal conversion

^{203}Hg undergoes β decay to ^{203}Tl, which emits four groups of conversion electrons with kinetic energies of 266.3, 264.2, 263.6 and 193.3 keV. To what shell does each group correspond? The electron binding energies of $K, L1, L2$ and $L3$ are, respectively, 87.7, 15.4, 14.8 and 12.7 keV. Find the γ-ray energy that is concurrent with the decay.

Solution The maximum energy of the ejected electron is 266.3 keV, and for such electrons, the binding energy E_B is the least (Eq. 3.71). Thus

$$\triangle E = (T_e)_{\max} + (E_B)_{\min} = 266.3 + 12.7 = 279.0 \text{ keV}$$

Similarly, for the $L2$ electron, $T_e = \triangle E - E_B = 279.0 - 14.8 = 264.2$ keV, as given.

For the $L1$ electron, $T_e = \triangle E - E_B = 279.0 - 15.4 = 263.6$ keV, as given.

For the K electron, $T_e = \triangle E - E_B = 279.0 - 87.7 = 191.3$ keV, as given.

Since $\triangle E = 279.0$ keV, the energy of the γ ray concurrent with the β decay is 279.0 keV.

SUMMARY

- **Decay Equation:** $N(t) = N(0)e^{-\lambda t}$, where λ is the decay constant or the probability of decaying a nucleus in unit time.
- **Activity**: The *activity or decay rate* is the number of decays per unit time and is given by $A = \lambda N$.

  $$A(t) = A_0 e^{-\lambda t}$$

- **Half-life ($T_{1/2}$), and Mean Life $< t >$**: $T_{1/2} = \frac{0.693}{\lambda}; < t > = \frac{1}{\lambda}$
- **Radioactive Series**: There are four decay series with mass numbers $A = 4n$ (thorium series), $A = 4n+1$ (neptunium series), $A = 4n+2$ (uranium series) and $A = 4n+3$ (actinium series).
- **Branching**: Branching refers competitive decay modes for the same nucleus. In this case, the total probability of decay is $\lambda = \lambda_1 + \lambda_2$ and $\frac{\lambda_1}{\lambda}$ is the branching fraction for the mode 1.
- **Successive Disintegration and Radioactive Equilibrium**: The scheme is $1 \longrightarrow 2 \longrightarrow 3$ Nuclei N_2 produced due to the disintegration of *Element 1* are also radioactive. The basic equations are

  $$\frac{dN_1}{dt} = -\lambda_1 N_1; \quad \frac{dN_2}{dt} = \lambda_1 N_1 - \lambda_2 N_2; \quad \frac{dN_3}{dt} = \lambda_2 N_2$$

Table 3.4: *Radioactive equilibrium*

Type	Condition	Remarks
No equilibrium	$t > T_2 > T_1$	Parent decays quickly and daughter decays with its own half-life
Transient equilibrium	$t > T_1 > T_2$	$\left(\frac{N_2\lambda_2}{N_1\lambda_1}\right)$ is constant (> 1)
Secular equilibrium	$T_1 >> t > T_2$	$\left(\frac{N_2\lambda_2}{N_1\lambda_1}\right)$ is constant ($= 1$)

- **Radiocarbon Dating**: The activity of ^{14}C in a biological specimen attenuates with time after death according to $A(t) = A(0)e^{-\lambda t}$. Thus, the age of the dead sample is $t = \frac{1}{\lambda \ln \frac{A(0)}{A(t)}}$.
- **α Decay**

  (a) $^A_ZX \longrightarrow {}^{A-4}_{Z-2}Y + \alpha + Q$, where $Q \approx 5$ MeV.

  (b) Generally nuclei with $Z > 82$ are α-radioactive.

  (c) The range of possible values of the kinetic energies (T_α) of α particles is very narrow, while their half-lives ($T_{1/2}$) vary over a wide range.

  4 MeV $\leq T_\alpha \leq 9$ MeV and 10^{10} years $\leq T_{1/2} \leq 10^{-7}$ s

  (d) The range (R in cm) of α particles in air and their kinetic energy (T_α) are related by a power law as $R \approx 0.3T_\alpha^{3/2}$.

  (e) Geiger–Nuttall law: $\log R = A \log \lambda + B$ or $\log \lambda = C \log E + D$

  (f) $T_\alpha \approx \dfrac{A-4}{A}Q$. T_α is unique, implying that the process of α decay is a two-body decay.

  (g) Accurate measurement of T_α reveals that T_α is not really unique – it lies in a range. The closely spaced group of α particles (fine structure splitting) suggests the existence of different energy states of the nucleus.

  (h) The features of α decay were established experimentally in the form of the Geiger–Nuttall law and explained theoretically with the help of quantum-mechanical tunnelling through the Coulomb barrier.
- **β Decay**

  (a) The β^- decay process is the spontaneous emission of an electron e^- or a positron e^+ from the nucleus, as well as the capture of an electron from the inner shell of the atom.

  $$^A_ZX \longrightarrow {}^A_{Z+1}Y + e^-; \quad ^A_ZX \longrightarrow {}^A_{Z-1}Y + e^+; \quad ^A_ZX + e^- \longrightarrow {}^A_{Z-1}Y$$

  (b) Unlike discrete α spectra, the β spectra are continuous. The continuous energy spectrum shows that the process of β decay is a three-body problem. An additional particle, called the neutrino ν, is emitted in beta decay along with the electron. The part of the energy released is carried by this neutral particle.

  $$^A_ZX \longrightarrow {}^A_{Z+1}Y + e^- + \bar{\nu}; \quad ^A_ZX \longrightarrow {}^A_{Z-1}Y + e^+ + \nu; \quad ^A_ZX + e^- \longrightarrow {}^A_{Z-1}Y + \nu$$

  Electrons and neutrinos emitted in beta decay do not exist in the nucleus; they appear only at the moment of decay.

  (c) Properties of neutrinos: Mass $= 0$, charge $= 0$, spin $= \dfrac{1}{2}$ and helicity is -1 for ν and $+1$ for $\bar{\nu}$.

(d) Parity is not conserved in β decay. Investigation of β decay in polarised nuclei confirmed parity non-conservation in β decay.

(e) For β^- decay, $Q=[M(A,Z)-M(A,Z+1)]c^2$
For β^+ decay, $Q=[M(A,Z)-M(A,Z-1)-2M_e]c^2$
For the EC process, $Q=[M(A,Z)-M(A,Z-1)]c^2$, where $M(A,Z)$ refers to the mass of the atom (A,Z)

- **γ Decay**

(a) The nucleus in an excited state comes to a less excited state by emitting γ rays.

(b) Energy released $Q=M^*c^2-Mc^2$ and the energy of the γ ray is $E_\gamma \approx Q-\frac{1}{2}\frac{Q^2}{M_xc^2}$.

(c) Selection rule: Consider the transition from initial state i to final state f, $i \longrightarrow f$. The angular momenta and the parities of the states are $\vec{I}_i$, $\vec{I}_f$ and π_i, π_f respectively.
First rule: $|\vec{I}_i-\vec{I}_f| \le \vec{L} \le |\vec{I}_i+\vec{I}_f|$, where $\vec{L}=\vec{I}_i-\vec{I}_f$ is the angular momentum carried away by the photon.
Second rule: The parity of radiation field is $\pi=(-1)^{L+1}$ for magnetic 2^L pole radiation and $\pi=(-1)^L$ for electric 2^L pole radiation, where $\pi=\frac{\pi_i}{\pi_f}$.

(d) Internal conversion: Nuclear excitation is spent on the emission of internal conversion electrons, usually from the K shell. The kinetic energy of the ejected electron is $T_e \approx \triangle E - E_B$, where $\triangle E = E_i - E_f$ and E_B is the binding energy of the electron.

REVIEW QUESTIONS AND PROBLEMS

Multiple Choice Questions

1. ^{24}Na is a β emitter with a half-life of 15 hours. The number of β particles emitted by 1 μg of ^{24}Na in 1 hour is
   (a) 1.13×10^{15} (b) 1.13×10^{18} (c) 1.00×10^{10} (d) 1.13×10^{5}
2. In the β decay of neutron $n \longrightarrow p+e^-+\bar{\nu}_e$, the antineutron $\bar{\nu}_e$ escapes. Its existence is inferred from the measurement of
   (a) Energy distribution of electrons
   (b) Angular distribution of electrons
   (c) Helicity distribution of electrons
   (d) Forward–backward asymmetry of electrons
3. In the β decay process, the transition $2^+ \longrightarrow 3^+$ is
   (a) Allowed both by the Fermi and Gamow–Teller selection rules
   (b) Allowed by the Fermi rule but not by the Gamow–Teller selection rule
   (c) Not allowed by the Fermi rule but allowed by the Gamow–Teller selection rule
   (d) Not allowed by both the Fermi and Gamow-Teller selection rules

4. A nucleus X undergoes a first forbidden β decay to nucleus Y. If the angular momentum (I) and parity (P) are denoted by $I^P = \frac{7}{2}^-$, then which of the following is a possible I^P value for Y?

   (a) $\frac{1}{2}^+$ (b) $\frac{1}{2}^-$ (c) $\frac{3}{2}^+$ (d) $\frac{3}{2}^-$

5. The ground state of the $^{207}_{82}$Pb nucleus has a spin-parity of $J^P = \frac{1}{2}^-$, while the first excited state has a spin-parity $J^P = \frac{5}{2}^-$. The electromagnetic radiations emitted when the nucleus makes a transition from the first excited state to the ground state are

   (a) $E2$ and $E3$ (b) $M2$ or $E3$ (c) $E2$ or $M3$ (d) $M2$ or $M3$

6. The β emitting nuclei lie

   (a) On the line of β stability (b) Below the line of β stability
   (b) Above the line of β stability (d) Below the $N = Z$ line

7. The stable end product of the thorium series is

   (a) $^{208}_{82}$Pb (b) $^{209}_{83}$Bi (c) $^{206}_{82}$Pb (d) $^{207}_{82}$Pb

8. The half-life of an unstable nucleus is τ. What fraction of the original nucleus will be decayed in time 3τ?

   (a) $\frac{1}{8}$ (b) $\frac{3}{8}$ (c) $\frac{7}{8}$ (d) $\frac{3}{4}$

9. The half-lives of elements A and B are τ and 2τ, respectively. Initially, both A and B have the same number of nuclei. After a certain time, 10% of the nuclei of B remain. At the same time, the fraction of nuclei of A that remains will be

   (a) 20% (b) 5% (c) 1% (d) 55%

10. If T_1 and T_2 are the half-lives of the parent nucleus and the daughter nucleus, respectively, then the condition for secular equilibrium is

    (a) $T_2 > t > T_1$ (b) $T_1 >> t > T_2$ (c) $T_2 >> t > T_1$ (d) $T_1 > t > T_2$

11. Which of the following processes is accompanied by mono-energetic X-rays?

    (a) β^- decay (b) β^+ decay (c) α decay (d) Electron capture process

12. The half-life of the ^{198}Au nucleus is 2.70 days. The probability that any ^{198}Au nucleus will decay in one second is approximately

    (a) 2×10^{-6} (b) 1×10^{-6} (c) 3×10^{-6} (d) 3×10^{-4}

13. 5 mg of ^{22}Na ($T_{1/2} = 2.60$ years) will be reduced to 1 mg in approximately

    (a) 6 years (b) 7 years (c) 8 years (d) 9 years

14. The tunnelling probability of an α particle in a decay from ^{238}U is 10^{-38}. The α particle hits the wall of the barrier at about 10^{21} per second. The mean life of ^{238}U is
   (a) 10^{38} s (b) 10^{17} s (c) 10^{-21} s (d) 10^{59} s
15. Radiocarbon dating is done by using the isotope
   (a) $^{12}_{6}$C (b) $^{13}_{6}$C (c) $^{14}_{6}$C (d) $^{14}_{7}$N
16. A nucleus ^{200}Po at rest emits α particles with kinetic energy of 5.77 MeV. The fraction of the total energy released in the process as the recoil energy of the daughter nucleus is
   (a) $\approx 1\%$ (b) $\approx 2\%$ (c) $\approx 5\%$ (d) $\approx 4\%$
17. Consider the reaction $^{11}_{6}\text{C} \longrightarrow {}^{11}_{5}\text{B} + e^+ + \nu_e$. If the maximum kinetic energy of e^+ is 0.98 MeV, the difference in the atomic mass of $^{11}_{6}$C and $^{11}_{5}$B will be
   (a) $\approx 1 \times 10^{-3}$ u (b) $\approx 0.5 \times 10^{-3}$ u (c) $\approx 1.0 \times 10^{-4}$ u (d) $\approx 2 \times 10^{-3}$ u

Short Questions and Problems

Radioactivity decay laws

1. A sealed packet stating that it contains an equal amount of two radioactive elements, *A* and *B*, was found. The half-lives of *A* and *B* are 12 years and 18 years, respectively. When the packet was opened, it was found to contain 0.53 kg of *A* and 2.20 kg of *B*. Determine the time when the packet was sealed.
2. $^{232}_{90}$Th decays to its first daughter $^{228}_{88}$Ra. It is observed that a very thin foil containing 1 g of $^{232}_{90}$Th emits α particles at the rate of 4100/s. Use this data to calculate the half-life of $^{232}_{90}$Th. Also calculate the mean life.
3. A radioactive element with a half-life of 100 days emits β particles with an average energy of 5×10^{-14} joules. It is used to drive a thermoelectric cell, which has an efficiency of only 10%. Determine the amount of the element (in gram molecules) required to generate 5 watts of electricity.
4. A biological specimen (tree) after its death shows $^{14}_{6}$C activity that is one-third of that of a living specimen. Estimate the age of the sample. The half-life of $^{14}_{6}$C is about 5500 years.
5. A sample of charcoal, found in the fire pit of an ancient camp, shows $^{14}_{6}$C activity of 12.9 disintegrations per gram per minute. If the percentage of $^{14}_{6}$C in living trees is $1.35 \times 10^{-10}\%$ of normal carbon and the decay constant is 3.92×10^{-12} s^{-1}, estimate the age of the sample.
6. Consider the decay: $RaE \xrightarrow{\beta} RaF \xrightarrow{\beta} RaG$ (stable). At $t = 0$, the amount of *RaE* is 2.00×10^{-10} g. Calculate the time when the maximum number of *RaF* atoms will be present. Also find this number. Half-lives of *RaE* and *RaF* are 5 days and 138 days, respectively.
7. A radioactive nuclide *A* with decay constant λ_1 decays to another radioactive element *B* with decay constant λ_2. Assume that at $t = 0$, the number of nuclei of *A* is N_0 and the number of nuclei of *B* is 0.

(a) Determine the accumulation of B in time.
(b) Find the time t_m when the the number of B nuclei becomes maximum.
(c) Discuss the special case when $\lambda_1 \approx \lambda_2$.

8. Derive an expression for the growth and decay of a daughter substance from its radioactive parent. Show that radioactive equilibrium is achieved when the daughter's lifetime is much shorter than that of the parent.
How much ^{234}Th would you expect now in a uranium mineral? Given the half-life of ^{238}U $= 42 \times 10^9$ years and ^{234}Th = 24 days.
How does the ratio of daughter to parent vary with time when the lifetimes are nearly equal?
9. It is observed that a solution containing 1 g of ^{226}Ra, which is an α emitter, never accumulates more than 6.4×10^{-6} g of its daughter, which decays with a half-life of 3.825 days. Determine the half-life of ^{226}Ra from this information.
10. Use GNUPLOT or its equivalent to plot all the curves presented in this chapter.
11. The activity of a radioactive sample (containing only one or two types of nuclei) measured at intervals of 4 minutes is presented below.

Table 3.5: *Activity of a radioactive source*

Time (t) in minutes	0	4	8	12	16	20	24	28	32	36	40
Activity(A) in arbitrary units	18.59	13.27	10.68	9.34	8.55	8.03	7.63	7.30	6.99	6.71	6.44

Use GNUPLOT or its equivalent to plot $\ln A$ vs t. Show that the plot is not linear. The source contains two types of radio nuclei of different half-lives. Assuming the half-lives are widely different, estimate the half-lives of the constituent nuclei.

Hint: Figure 3.25 shows the plot. Two straight lines are extrapolated from the two linear parts of the curve. From the slope of the straight lines, λ and the half-lives can be estimated.

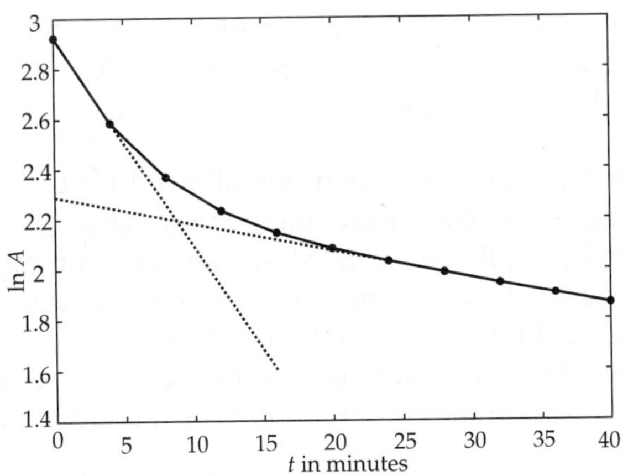

Figure 3.25: $\ln A$ *vs* t

α decay

12. The kinetic energy of the α particles emitted from a ^{210}Po source has been found to be 5.3 MeV. Calculate the α-disintegration energy.
13. The nuclear masses of a parent and its daughter are 226.025 and 222.017 amu, respectively. The mass of the α particle is 4.002 amu. Find out the Q value and the kinetic energy of the α particle emitted in α decay.
14. What is the Geiger–Nuttall law? The range in standard air of α particles from radium (half-life = 1622 years) is 3.36 cm, while the range of α particles from polonium (half-life = 138 days) is 3.85 cm. If radium, polonium and *RaC* are all members of the same radioactive series, calculate the half-life of *RaC* for which the α-particle range is 6.97 cm.
15. The energies of the α particles emitted in the decays of $^{226}_{88}$Ra and $^{226}_{90}$Th are 4.9 MeV and 6.5 MeV, respectively. Find the ratio of their half-lives.
16. Explain the origin of fine structure in the spectrum of α particles emitted by radioactive nuclei.
17. ^{210}Po emits two groups of α particles with kinetic energies of 5.30 and 4.50 MeV, respectively. Calculate the energy of the accompanying γ rays.
18. Calculate the Coulomb barrier (in MeV) when an α particle emitted during the α decay of ^{238}U just touches the ^{234}Th nucleus. Consider the α particle to be a point particle and take $r_0 = 1.2$ fm.
19. Calculate the energy required to force an α particle into the ^{238}U nucleus. (Assume $R_0 = 1.2$ fm).
20. (a) Calculate the height of the Coulomb barrier faced by an α particle while trying to escape from ^{238}U. The highest energy of α particles emitted in the decay of $^{238}_{92}$U to the $^{234}_{90}$Th nucleus is 4196 keV. Is there an apparent anomaly between this and your calculated value? If so, how is this anomaly resolved?

    (b) Assuming a square potential barrier, obtain an expression connecting the decay probability (or the transmission coefficient) and the energy of an α particle.
21. Consider the decay $^{230}_{90}\text{Th} \longrightarrow\, ^{226}_{88}\text{Ra} + \alpha$. Calculate the kinetic energy of the α particle and of the daughter nucleus. ($M(^{230}_{90}\text{Th}) = 230.033128$ u, $M(^{226}_{88}\text{Ra}) = 226.025403$ u, $M_\alpha = 4.002603$ u)

β decay

22. Show that if positron decay is energetically allowed for the nucleus of a neutral atom, electron capture is also allowed, but not vice-versa.
23. Give one example each of β^- decay, β^+ decay and electron capture.
24. Explain why the postulate about the existence of the neutrino was necessary to remove the difficulties in the interpretation of β decay.
25. What is a neutrino? Explain qualitatively how the hypothesis of neutrino solves the apparent breakdown of the conservation principles of momentum and energy in β decay.
26. What do you mean by the endpoint energy of the emitted particles in β decay? Tritium emits negative β particles. Calculate the endpoint energy of the β particles

from the following data. Mass of tritium = 3.01695 amu, mass of ^{3}He = 3.01693 amu.

27. $^{27}_{14}$Si and $^{27}_{13}$Al are mirror nuclei and $^{27}_{14}$Si emits positrons with $E_{\text{max}} = 3.48$ MeV. Assuming the hypothesis of charge symmetry, calculate the radius of $^{27}_{14}$Si.
28. Consider the reaction $^{33}_{17}\text{Cl} \longrightarrow {}^{33}_{16}\text{S} + e^+ + \nu_e$, where the maximum kinetic energy of the positron is $E_{\text{max}} = 4.3$ MeV. Assuming the hypothesis of charge symmetry, calculate the radius of $^{33}_{17}$Cl.
29. $^{64}_{28}$Ni and $^{64}_{29}$Cu have atomic masses of 63.9280 u and 63.9298 u, respectively. Which of them shows β activity and of what type? Justify your answer. Given that $2m_e =$ 0.0011 u.
30. Given the atomic masses of the following:
a) $M(^7_3\text{Li}) = 7.016003$ u and $M(^7_4\text{Be}) = 7.016928$ u
b) $M(^{13}_6\text{C}) = 13.003355$ u and $M(^{13}_7\text{N}) = 13.005739$ u
c) $M(^3_1\text{H}) = 3.016049$ u and $M(^3_2\text{He}) = 3.016029$ u
d) $M(^{34}_{15}\text{P}) = 33.973636$ u and $M(^{34}_{16}\text{S}) = 33.967867$ u.
Which of each pair shows β activity and of what type? Given that $2m_e = 0.0011$ u.

γ decay

31. Show in an energy-level diagram, the following disintegration process:
$$^{27}_{12}\text{Mg} \rightarrow {}^{27}_{13}Al + e^- + \gamma$$
Coincidence experiments reveal that β^- particles with an energy of 1.75 MeV and γ photon with an energy of 0.834 MeV arise from the same transition, whereas γ photons with an energy of 1.015 MeV accompanied the emission of β^- particles, with 1.59 MeV as the maximum energy. Direct transition from the ground state of $^{27}_{12}$Mg to the ground state of $^{27}_{13}$Al is forbidden. Photons with an energy of 0.181 MeV are also realised in this disintegration.
32. Calculate the maximum kinetic energy of the β particles and the frequencies of the emitted γ rays in the decay scheme of Fig. 3.27.
Given $M(^{198}_{79}\text{Au}) = 197.968233$ u and $M(^{198}_{80}\text{Hg}) = 197.966760$ u.
33. $^{226}_{88}$Ra decays to $^{222}_{86}$Rn by emitting three groups of α particles of energies 4.777, 4.503 and 4.342 MeV. Determine the energies of the associated γ rays.

Hints/Answers to Selected Problems

Multiple Choice Questions

1. (a) 2. (a) 3. (c) 4. (c) For the first forbidden β decay $\Delta I = 0, 1, 2$ and parity changes. 5. (c) 6. (b) 7. (a) 8. (c) 9. (a) 10. (b) 11. (d) 12. (c) 13. (a) 14. (b) 15. (c) 16. (b) 17. (d)

Short Questions and Problems

1. $\frac{N_a}{N_b} = e^{(\lambda_b - \lambda_a)t} \Rightarrow t \approx 73.7$ years
2. The activity or decay rate is the number of decays per unit time and is given by $A = \lambda N$, where $N = N_A/232$, N_A is Avogadro's number. $\lambda = 1.579 \times 10^{-18}$. Mean life $= \frac{1}{\lambda}$.

3. Rate of decay: $\frac{dN}{dt} = -\lambda N = -\frac{0.693}{T}N$

The energy released per second $= \frac{0.693}{T}N \times 5 \times 10^{-14}$ joules. The required energy: $0.1 \times \frac{0.693}{T}N \times 5 \times 10^{-14} = 5$

$$N = \frac{100 \times 24 \times 3600 \times 10^{15}}{0.693 \times 6.023 \times 10^{23}} \approx 2.07 \times 10^{-2} \text{ mole}$$

4. ≈ 8719 years.

5. Activity of the old specimen is $A(t) = \frac{12.9}{60}$ per second per gram

Number of ordinary carbon atoms per gram is $\frac{6.023 \times 10^{23}}{12.0}$

Number of ${}^{14}_{6}$C atoms per gram is $\frac{6.023 \times 10^{23}}{12.0} \times 1.35 \times 10^{-12} = 0.6776 \times 10^{11}$

${}^{14}_{6}$C activity in the living sample is $A_0 = 3.92 \times 10^{-12} \times 0.6776 \times 10^{11} \approx 0.265$

$t = \frac{1}{\lambda}\ln\frac{A_0}{A} \Rightarrow \approx 2.032 \times 10^{4}$ years

6. From Eq. (3.18), $t_m = \frac{1}{\lambda_2 - \lambda_1} ln\frac{\lambda_2}{\lambda_1} \Rightarrow t \approx 24.85$ days. $N_2 \approx 5.1 \times 10^{11}$ atoms.

7. $N_2 = \frac{\lambda_1}{\lambda_2 - \lambda_1}N_0(e^{-\lambda_1 t} - e^{-\lambda_2 t})$ and $t_m = \frac{1}{\lambda_2 - \lambda_1}\ln\frac{\lambda_2}{\lambda_1}$

Let $\lambda_2 = \lambda_1(1+\delta)$. Thus $t_m = \frac{1}{\lambda_1\delta}\ln(1+\delta) \approx \frac{\delta - \delta^2/2 + ...}{\lambda_1\delta} \approx \frac{1}{\lambda_1}$ which is equal to the mean life of the parent or daughter.

$N_2 = \frac{N_0}{\delta}e^{-\lambda_1 t}(1 - e^{-\lambda_1\delta t}) \approx N_0(\lambda_1 t)e^{-\lambda_1 t}$; since $\lambda_2 \approx \lambda_1 = \lambda$, $N_2 = N_0(\lambda t)e^{-\lambda t}$

8. $\frac{N_{Th}}{N_U} = \frac{T_{Th}}{T_U} = 1.57 \times 10^{-12}$

9. $N_1\lambda_1 = N_2\lambda_2 \Rightarrow \frac{N_A}{226} \times \frac{0.693}{T_1} = \frac{N_A \times 6.4 \times 10^{-6}}{222} \times \frac{0.693}{3.825} \Rightarrow T_1 \approx 5.92 \times 10^{5}$ days

12. $Q = \frac{A}{A-4}T_\alpha = \frac{210}{206}5.3 \approx 5.40$ MeV 13. $Q = 5.5890$ MeV $T_\alpha = 5.5888$ MeV

14. Geiger–Nuttall law: $\log\lambda = a\log R + b$; $a\log R + \log T = \log 0.693 - b = c$

From the given data, $T \approx 2 \times 10^{-14}$ days

17. ≈ 0.80 MeV 18. The height of the barrier (V_0) is ≈ 35.05 MeV 19. $E \approx 28.4$ MeV

26. ${}^{3}_{1}\text{H} \rightarrow {}^{3}_{2}\text{He} + e^- + \bar{\nu}_e$. The endpoint energy of the β particles corresponds to the energy when the energy carried by the neutrino is zero. Thus, $T_e = (3.01695 - 3.01693) \times 931.5 = 0.01863$ MeV. Note that the masses given are the atomic masses.

27. Please see Illustrative Example 2.7. 29. The decay mode is electron capture.

30. (a) $^7_3$Li is stable. $\triangle M = 0.000925 < 2m_e$. Thus $^7_4$Be is unstable against electron capture. (b) $\triangle M = 0.002384 > 2m_e$. Thus $^{13}_7$N is unstable against β^+ decay and electron capture. (c) $^3_1$H is unstable against β^- decay. (d) $^{34}_{15}P$ is unstable against β^- decay.

31. The decay scheme is represented in Fig. 3.26, where $E_{\beta_1} = 1.750$ MeV, $E_{\gamma_1} = 0.834$ MeV, $E_{\beta_2} = 1.590$ MeV, $E_{\gamma_2} = 1.015$ MeV and $E_{\gamma_3} = 0.181$ MeV

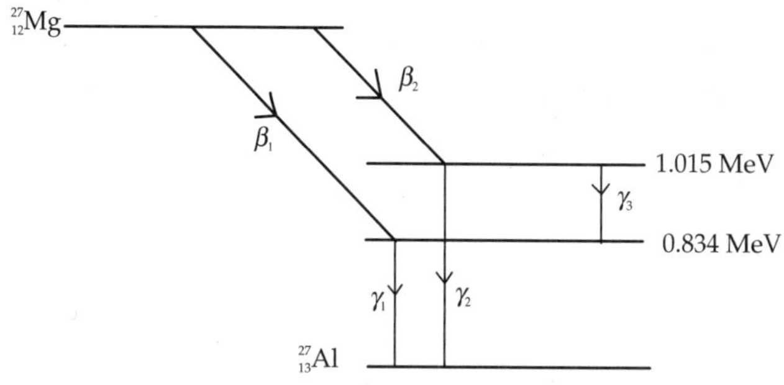

Figure 3.26: *Problem 31: The process* $^{27}_{12}\text{Mg} \rightarrow ^{27}_{13}\text{Al} + e^- + \gamma$

32. $^{198}_{79}\text{Au} \rightarrow ^{198}_{80}\text{Hg} + e^- + \gamma$. $E_{\gamma_1} = h\nu_1 = 0.412$ MeV, $\nu_1 \approx 0.996 \times 10^{20}$

Similarly, $\nu_2 \approx 2.63 \times 10^{20}$ and $\nu_3 \approx 1.63 \times 10^{20}$

Energy released $Q = M(^{198}_{79}\text{Au}) - M(^{198}_{80}\text{Hg}) = (197.968233 - 197.966760) \times 931.5 - 0.412$ $= 0.960$ MeV. Thus, the maximum kinetic energy of β_1 is 0.960 MeV. Similarly the maximum kinetic energy of β_2 is 0.284 MeV.

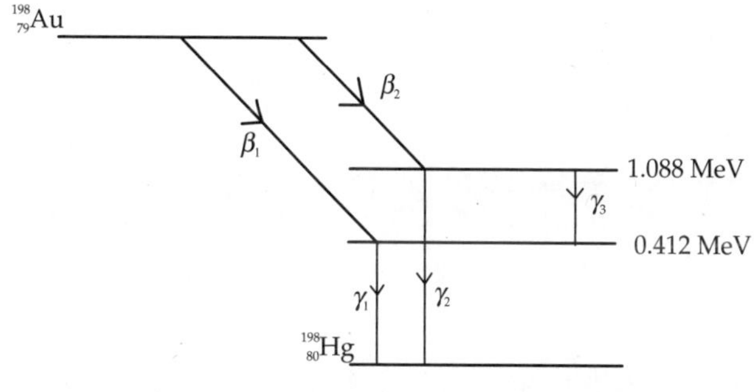

Figure 3.27: *Problem 32: The process* $^{198}_{79}\text{Au} \rightarrow ^{198}_{80}\text{Hg} + e^- + \gamma$

33. $Q_1 = (M_x - M_y - M_\alpha)c^2; \quad Q_2 = (M_x - M_{y^*} - M_\alpha)c^2; \quad Q_3 = (M_x - M_{y^{**}} - M_\alpha)c^2$

$$Q_1 - Q_2 = (M_{y^*} - M_y)c^2 = E_{\gamma_1} \Longrightarrow E_{\gamma_1} = \frac{A}{A-4}(K_{\alpha_1} - K_{\alpha_2})$$

$$Q_1 - Q_3 = (M_{y^{**}} - M_y)c^2 = E_{\gamma_2} \Longrightarrow E_{\gamma_2} = \frac{A}{A-4}(K_{\alpha_1} - K_{\alpha_3})$$

$$Q_2 - Q_3 = (M_{y^{**}} - M_{y^*})c^2 = E_{\gamma_3} \Longrightarrow E_{\gamma_3} = \frac{A}{A-4}(K_{\alpha_2} - K_{\alpha_3})$$

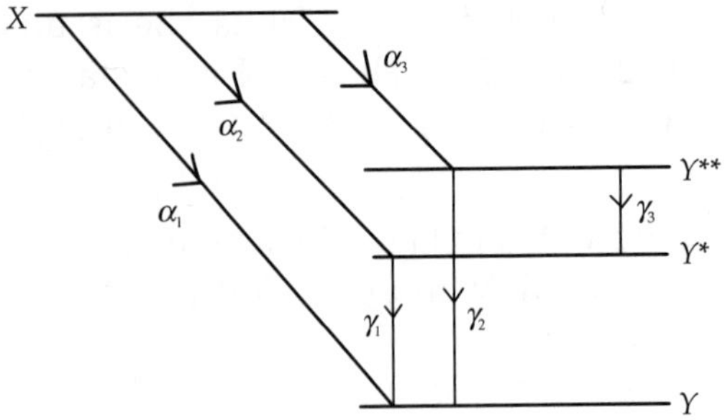

Figure 3.28: *Problem 33: Emission of three groups of α particles*

CHAPTER 4

Nuclear Reactions

Nuclear reaction refers to the process that occurs when a nuclear particle comes in contact with another, during which exchange of energy and momentum takes place. In this process, a change in the composition and/or energy of the target nucleus is brought about through bombardment with different nuclear particles such as neutrons, protons, α particles, and so on. A study of nuclear reactions is important in building up our knowledge of the structure and energy levels of the nucleus and the nuclear force that holds nucleons together.

4.1 NUCLEAR REACTIONS AND CONSERVATION LAWS

4.1.1 Representation

A typical nuclear reaction is represented as

$$a + X \longrightarrow Y + b,$$

where a is the projectile, X is the target nucleus which is usually stationary in the laboratory, Y is the residual nucleus and b is the outgoing particle. Usually, the product Y is heavy and the outgoing particle b, being lighter, is detected.

The above reaction is represented in a compact way as $X(a,b)Y$, which is equivalent to

target (projectile, outgoing particle) residual nucleus

The first nuclear reaction observed by Rutherford in 1919 by using α particles from a radioactive source was

$$\alpha + {}^{14}_{7}\mathrm{N} \longrightarrow {}^{17}_{8}\mathrm{O} + p$$

The reaction can be represented in a compact way as ${}^{14}_{7}\mathrm{N}(\alpha, p){}^{17}_{8}\mathrm{O}$.

4.1.2 Types of Nuclear Reactions

Nuclear reactions may be of different types. If the incident particle a and the outgoing particle b are the same, the process is called **scattering**.

Scattering can be of two types: elastic and inelastic.

(a) *Elastic scattering* $a + X \longrightarrow X + a$: The incident and outgoing particles are the same and the residual nucleus is in the ground state. In this process, the total energy as well as kinetic energy is conserved, and the same particles are scattered in different directions. In the laboratory (lab) frame, elastic scattering results in the redistribution of kinetic energy between the particles; however, in the centre-of-mass (CM) frame, the kinetic energy of each particle is conserved.
(b) *Inelastic scattering* $a + X \longrightarrow X^* + a$: The incident and outgoing particles are the same, but the residual nucleus or the outgoing particle is in the excited state. In this process, the kinetic energy is not conserved.

If nucleons are transferred between the target and the projectile, the reaction is called a **transfer reaction**. This is of two types:

(a) *Pick up*: In this reaction, the projectile picks up nucleons from the target. For example, ${}^{16}_{8}\text{O}\ ({}^{2}_{1}\text{H},\ {}^{3}_{1}\text{H})\ {}^{15}_{8}\text{O}$; ${}^{41}_{20}\text{Ca}\ ({}^{3}_{2}\text{He},\ {}^{4}_{2}\text{He})\ {}^{40}_{20}\text{Ca}$.
(b) *Stripping*: In this case, the bombarding particle loses nucleons to the target. For example, ${}^{23}_{11}\text{Na}\ ({}^{3}_{2}\text{He},\ {}^{2}_{1}\text{H})\ {}^{24}_{12}\text{Mg}$.

There is another type of reaction called **radiative capture,** where b is a γ-ray photon.

Nuclear reactions can also be classified based on the mechanism involved:

(a) *Direct reaction*: In this process, only a few nucleons in the nucleus take part while the rest are passive spectators. The de Broglie wavelength associated with the projectile at high energy is extremely small and is less than the dimension of the whole nucleus. Thus, at high energy, the bombarding particle may interact with a few nucleons of the target without disturbing the others.
(b) *Compound nucleus mechanism*: Here, the target absorbs the incident particle and forms a compound nucleus. All the nucleons of the combined nucleus share the energy of the incident particle, and the compound nucleus is formed usually in an excited state. Finally, the compound nucleus in excited state comes to the ground state by disintegrating particles or γ photons.

4.1.3 Conserved Quantities

The conservation laws impose some restrictions on the occurrence of any reaction, thereby allowing us to determine the reaction correctly. While analysing nuclear reactions, the following conservation laws[1] are generally applied.

(a) **Conservation of energy**: Total energy is always conserved. The sum of the rest mass energy of all the particles taking part in the nuclear reaction and their kinetic energy is always constant.
(b) **Conservation of linear momentum**: Total linear momentum before the collision and after the collision is conserved.

[1]The other conservation laws are discussed in Chapter 8.

(c) **Conservation of angular momentum**: It enables us to relate the spin assignments of the reacting particles and the angular momentum of the outgoing particles.

(d) **Conservation of charge**: Total charge of the projectile and the target is equal to the total charge of the reaction products in all cases. Besides, the total number of nucleons is also conserved.

Check Progress 4.1: Determine the unknown particle in the reactions: (a) ${}^{18}_{8}$O $({}^{2}_{1}\text{H}, p)X$, (b) ${}^{42}_{20}\text{Ca}({}^{6}_{3}\text{Li}, \text{X}){}^{45}_{21}\text{Sc}$.

4.2 ENERGETICS OF NUCLEAR REACTIONS

The conservation of energy and momentum imposes certain restrictions on nuclear reactions. The method of imposing restrictions may be called **kinematics**.

4.2.1 Energetics in the Laboratory Frame

Let us consider a general reaction: $a + X \longrightarrow Y + b$.

Figure 4.1 shows the basic geometry of a nuclear reaction in the laboratory frame. The projectile a hits the target X, which is assumed to be at rest in the laboratory. After the collision, the outgoing particle b is emitted at an angle θ with the original direction of approach and the residual nucleus Y recoils in such a way that energy and momentum are both conserved.

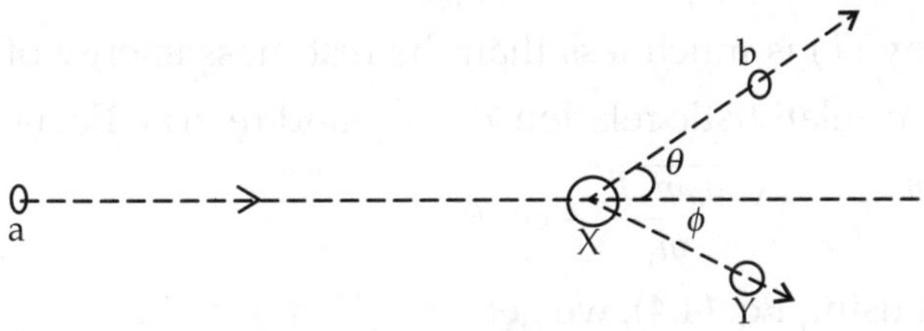

Figure 4.1: *Basic nuclear reaction in the laboratory frame*

The conservation of total relativistic energy gives

$$T_a + m_a c^2 + m_x c^2 = m_y c^2 + T_y + m_b c^2 + T_b, \tag{4.1}$$

where the Ts are the kinetic energies and the ms are the rest masses. Since there is some exchange of kinetic energy and mass energy among the particles, the final kinetic energy may be greater or less than the initial kinetic energy. The excess kinetic energy, which is the difference between the final and initial kinetic energies, is called the Q value of the reaction. Thus

$$Q = T_y + T_b - T_a = [m_a + m_x - m_y - m_b]c^2 \tag{4.2}$$

The Q value is also the difference between the sum of the rest masses of the initial particles and the sum of the rest masses of the final particles. It may be positive, negative or zero.

If $Q > 0$, the reaction is said to be **exoergic**. In this case, $(m_a + m_x) > (m_y + m_b)$ and the excess mass will be converted into energy released.

If $Q < 0$, the reaction is said to be **endoergic**. In this case, $(m_a + m_x) < (m_y + m_b)$, and thus, there is a net deficit of mass. Energy must be supplied from outside to make the reaction possible. The minimum energy required to initiate such a reaction is called the **threshold energy**. This is always slightly greater than Q, as the product particles are always in motion.

If $Q = 0$, then $m_a + m_x = m_y + m_b$ and $T_y + T_b = T_a$. It corresponds to elastic scattering, where the kinetic energy remains unchanged.

The Q value of any nuclear reaction, given by Eq. (4.2) involving the rest masses, is the same in all frames. We now calculate it in the laboratory frame, where the target nucleus is assumed to be fixed. The Q value may be measured experimentally by measuring T_y, T_a and T_b. However, T_y, being much smaller than T_b, is extremely difficult to measure. So, we express T_y in terms of the other quantities involved in Eq. (4.2).

Let us define the reaction plane by the direction of the projectile (a) and the outgoing particle (b). The conservation of linear momentum then requires that the component of the linear momentum of Y perpendicular to the reaction plane must be zero. Therefore, the incident particle, the outgoing particle and the residual nucleus must lie on the same plane, as shown in Fig. 4.1.

The conservation of momentum gives

$$\vec{p}_a = \vec{p}_y + \vec{p}_b \quad \text{or,} \quad p_y^2 = p_a^2 + p_b^2 - 2p_a p_b \cos\theta \tag{4.3}$$

If the kinetic energy (T) is much less than the rest mass energy of the particle, then we may use the non-relativistic relation $T = \frac{p^2}{2m}$, and rewrite Eq. (4.3) as

$$T_y = \frac{m_a}{m_y} T_a + \frac{m_b}{m_y} T_b - 2\frac{\sqrt{m_a m_b T_a T_b}}{m_y} \cos\theta \tag{4.4}$$

From Eq. (4.2) and using Eq. (4.4), we get

$$Q = \frac{m_y + m_b}{m_y} T_b - \frac{m_y - m_a}{m_y} T_a - 2\frac{\sqrt{m_a m_b T_a T_b}}{m_y} \cos\theta \tag{4.5}$$

This is known as the **Q equation**. By measuring T_a, T_b and $\cos\theta$, the Q value can be measured experimentally.

Equation (4.5) can be expressed as

$$T_b - 2\frac{\sqrt{m_a m_b T_a T_b}}{m_y + m_b} \cos\theta - \frac{m_y - m_a}{m_y + m_b} T_a - \frac{m_y}{m_y + m_b} Q = 0 \quad \text{or}$$

$$T_b - 2\alpha\cos\theta\sqrt{T_b} - \beta = 0, \tag{4.6}$$

where $\alpha = \frac{\sqrt{m_a m_b T_a}}{m_y + m_b}$ and $\beta = \frac{m_y - m_a}{m_y + m_b} T_a + \frac{m_y}{m_y + m_b} Q$. By solving Eq. (4.6)

$$\sqrt{T_b} = \alpha\cos\theta \pm \sqrt{\alpha^2\cos^2\theta + \beta} \tag{4.7}$$

$\sqrt{T_b} = \frac{|\vec{p}_y|}{\sqrt{2m_y}}$ is real and positive. Several features of nuclear reactions can be explained from Eq. (4.7).

Case 1: Endoergic reaction: $Q < 0$. In this case, β is not necessarily always positive. If $T_a = 0$, then $\alpha = 0$ and β becomes negative. Thus, $\sqrt{T_b}$ becomes imaginary. Let us now increase T_a, so that $\alpha^2 \cos^2\theta + \beta = 0$. The minimum value of T_a corresponding to $\alpha^2 \cos^2\theta + \beta = 0$ is the threshold energy of the reaction for a particular θ. The minimum of the threshold[2] must occur for $\theta = 0°$, otherwise more energy will be needed to give the momentum of the products transverse to the direction of the incident particles. The minimum energy of the bombarding particle required to initiate the reaction, along $\theta = 0$, is usually known as the **threshold energy**.

The condition $\alpha^2 \cos^2\theta + \beta = 0$ with $\theta = 0°$ gives the threshold energy T_{th} for non-relativistic cases,[3] as

$$T_{\text{th}} = (-Q)\frac{m_b + m_y}{m_y + m_b - m_a} \tag{4.8}$$

Threshold energy supplies the deficit of mass plus the kinetic energy of the outgoing particles. Thus, $T_{\text{th}} > (-Q)$, as given by Eq. (4.8).

If we assume $Q \ll (m_b + m_y)c^2$, which is reasonable for a large m_y, then $m_a + m_x = m_b + m_y + Q/c^2 \approx m_b + m_y$. The threshold energy obtained in Eq. (4.8) then becomes

$$T_{\text{th}} = (-Q)\frac{m_b + m_y}{m_y + m_b - m_a} \approx (-Q)\frac{m_a + m_x}{m_x}$$

For the γ-induced reaction, $T_{\text{th}} = (-Q)$.

Another interesting feature of endoergic reactions is *the double-valued behaviour*[4] *of* T_b for a certain range of T_a. Equation (4.7) shows that for $Q < 0$, the upper limit of β is zero, otherwise $\sqrt{(T_b)}$ would be negative. The energy of the incident particle corresponding to $\beta = 0$ is $T_a = (-Q)\frac{m_y}{m_y - m_a}$.

Therefore, for $T_a = T_{\text{th}}$ to $T_a = (-Q)\frac{m_y}{m_y - m_a}$, both $\alpha\cos\theta + \sqrt{\alpha^2\cos^2\theta + \beta}$ and $\alpha\cos\theta - \sqrt{\alpha^2\cos^2\theta + \beta}$ are allowed for $\sqrt{(T_b)}$, and thus, in this range, T_b is a double-valued function.

In Fig. 4.2, the value of T_b obtained from Eq. (4.7) has been plotted for the endoergic reaction ${}^3_1\text{H}(p,n){}^3_2\text{He}$, for which $Q = -763.75$ keV. For this reaction

$$T_{\text{th}} \approx 1.019 \text{ MeV} \;\text{ and }\; (-Q)\frac{m_y}{m_y - m_a} \approx 1.147 \text{ MeV}$$

The inset in Fig. 4.2 shows that the double-valued situation occurs for $T_a \approx 1.019$ to 1.147 MeV. Except this small range of T_a, T_b depends linearly on T_a for a particular θ. It should also be noted that the range of T_a, corresponding to which the double value of T_b occurs, depends on θ.

[2]Note that threshold energy depends on θ; also see Example 4.6.

[3]The threshold energy for relativistic cases will be discussed in Chapter 7.

[4]Krane, KS. 1987. *Introductory Nuclear Physics, Third Edition*. John Wiley & Sons.

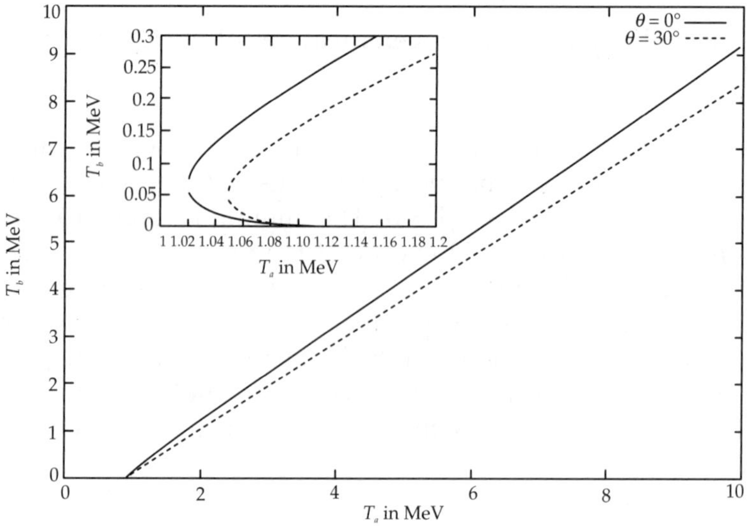

Figure 4.2: *Kinetic energy of the outgoing particle T_b as a function of the incident energy T_a for the reaction ${}^3_1\mathrm{H}(p,n){}^3_2\mathrm{He}$ for which $Q < 0$. The inset shows the double-valued behaviour of T_b near the threshold.*

Case 2: Exoergic reaction: $Q > 0$. Here, β is always positive, and thus, $\alpha^2\cos^2\theta + \beta > \alpha\cos\theta$. Since $\sqrt{(T_b)}$ is positive, we need to consider the positive sign in Eq. (4.7), and $\sqrt{T_b} = \alpha\cos\theta + \sqrt{\alpha^2\cos^2\theta + \beta}$.

This relation holds for any value of T_a, including $T_a = 0$. Reactions with $Q > 0$ have no threshold; also double-valued behaviour does not arise for this case. Figure 4.3 explains the situation for the reaction ${}^3_2\mathrm{He}(n,p){}^3_1\mathrm{H}$ with two values of θ.

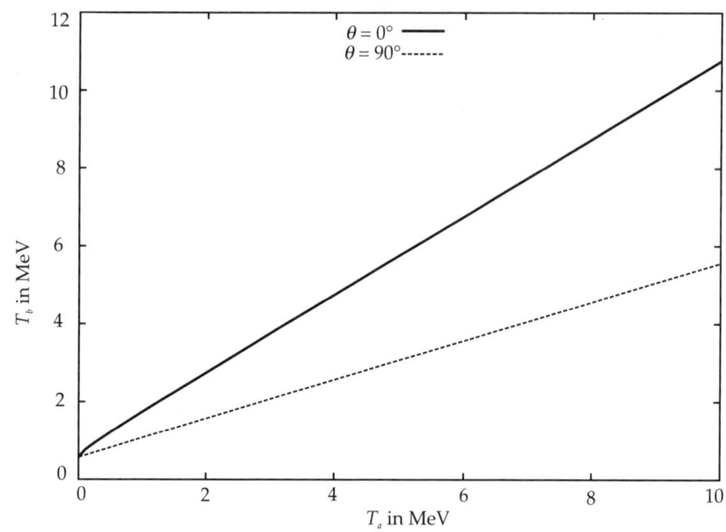

Figure 4.3: *The kinetic energy of the outgoing particle T_b is a function of the incident energy T_a for the reaction ${}^3_2\mathrm{He}(n,p){}^3_1\mathrm{H}$ for which $Q > 0$. No double-valued behaviour of T_b occurs for this case.*

Illustrative Example 4.1: Q value

When ${}^6_3$Li is bombarded with 4-MeV deuterons, two α particles each with energy of 13.2 MeV are observed. Determine the Q value of this reaction.
Given $M({}^2_1\text{H}) = 2.014102$ u, $M({}^4_2\text{He}) = 4.002603$ u and $M({}^6_3\text{Li}) = 6.015121$ u.

Solution ${}^2_1\text{H} + {}^6_3\text{Li} \longrightarrow {}^4_2\text{He} + {}^4_2\text{He}$
The Q value: $Q = M({}^2_1\text{H}) + M({}^6_3\text{Li}) - 2 \times M({}^4_2\text{He}) = 22.37$ MeV
The Q value can also be determined from the difference in kinetic energies as $Q = 2 \times 13.2 - 4 = 22.4$ MeV.

Illustrative Example 4.2: First nuclear reaction by artificially accelerated protons

In 1932, Cockcroft and Walton bombarded lithium with artificially accelerated protons using a linear accelerator. The reaction observed was ${}^7_3\text{Li}(p,\alpha){}^4_2\text{He}$, that is

$$p + {}^7_3\text{Li} \longrightarrow {}^4_2\text{He} + \alpha$$

Calculate the energy released in the reaction. The proton being positively charged will experience Coulomb repulsion while approaching the ${}^7_3$Li nucleus. Calculate the potential barrier faced by the proton when it is very close to the target nucleus. Given $M({}^1_1\text{H}) = 1.007825$ u, $M({}^7_3\text{Li}) = 7.016003$ u and $M({}^4_2\text{He}) = 4.002603$ u.

Solution $Q = 7.016003 + 1.007825 - 2 \times 4.002603\,\text{u} \approx 17.35$ MeV
When the incident proton is very close to the target, the separation is $r \approx 1.2 \times 7^{1/3} \approx 2.30$ fm. Thus, the height of the Coulomb barrier is

$$V_c = \frac{1}{4\pi\varepsilon_0}\frac{3e^2}{r} \approx 1.88\,\text{MeV}$$

Cockcroft and Walton were able to carry out the experiment by artificially accelerating protons to energies of several keV. It was observed that most of the accelerated protons did not split the lithium nucleus. They were simply deflected by the strong Coulomb repulsion (very few of the incident protons tunnelled through the barrier).

Illustrative Example 4.3: Photon-induced reaction

Consider the reaction $\gamma + {}^{16}_8\text{O} \longrightarrow {}^{15}_7\text{N} + {}^1_1\text{H}$.

Calculate the Q value. Given $M({}^1_1\text{H}) = 1.007825$ u, $M({}^{15}_7\text{N}) = 15.000109$ u and $M({}^{16}_8\text{O}) = 15.994915$ u.

Solution $Q = M({}^{16}_8\text{O}) - M({}^{15}_7\text{N}) - M({}^1_1\text{H}) = 12.13$ MeV.

Illustrative Example 4.4: Application of Q equation

Consider the reaction ${}^4_2\text{He} + {}^{14}_7\text{N} \longrightarrow {}^{17}_8\text{O} + {}^1_1\text{H}$.

The α particles have a kinetic energy of 7.70 MeV. The product particles ${}^1_1$H are emitted at 90° to the incident beam and have a kinetic energy of 4.44 MeV. Determine the Q value. Given $M({}^1_1\text{H}) = 1.007825$ u, $M({}^{15}_7\text{N}) = 15.000109$ u and $M({}^{16}_8\text{O}) =$

15.994915 u.

Solution Substituting cos 90° = 0 in Eq. (4.5), we get

$$Q = \frac{M(^{17}_{8}\text{O}) + M(^{1}_{1}\text{H})}{M(^{17}_{8}\text{O})} T_b - \frac{M(^{17}_{8}\text{O}) - M(^{4}_{2}\text{He})}{M(^{17}_{8}\text{O})} T_a \approx -1.19 \text{ MeV}$$

Direct calculation: $Q = M(^{4}_{2}\text{He}) + M(^{14}_{7}\text{N}) - M(^{17}_{8}\text{O}) - M(^{1}_{1}\text{H}) \approx -1.19$ MeV

Illustrative Example 4.5: Neutron production

Find the threshold energy for the reaction $p + ^7\text{Li} \longrightarrow ^7\text{Be} + n$.

Solution The Q value is

$$Q = m_p + m_{\text{Li}} - m_{\text{Be}} - m_n = 1.007825 + 7.016003 - 7.016928 - 1.008665 = -1.64 \text{ MeV}$$

Therefore $T_{\text{th}} = 1.64 \dfrac{7.016928 + 1.008665}{7.016928 + 1.008665 - 1.007825} = 1.87$ MeV

Illustrative Example 4.6: [5] Threshold energy for $\theta = 0$ and $\theta = 90°$

The Q value of the reaction $^3\text{H}(p,n)^3\text{He}$ is -0.764 MeV. Calculate the threshold energy for the appearance of neutrons (a) in the forward direction and (b) in the 90° direction.

Solution Let us consider the reaction $a + X \longrightarrow Y + b$.

(a) *The outgoing particle moves in the forward direction:*

The threshold energy of the incident particle a for the emission of b in the forward direction can be obtained from Eq. (4.8).

$$T_{th} = -Q \frac{m_y + m_b}{m_y + m_b - m_a} \approx 0.764 \times \frac{3+1}{3+1-1} = 1.019 \text{ MeV}$$

(b) *The outgoing particle moves at an angle of 90° to the forward direction:*

Conservation of momentum: $\vec{p}_a = \vec{p}_y + \vec{p}_b$. Thus

$$\vec{p}_y = \vec{p}_a - \vec{p}_b \Rightarrow p_y^2 = p_b^2 + p_a^2$$

Therefore $T_y = \dfrac{p_y^2}{2m_y} = \dfrac{m_a}{m_y} T_a + \dfrac{m_b}{m_y} T_b$ and $Q = T_y + T_b - T_a = \left(\dfrac{m_a}{m_y} - 1\right) T_a + \left(1 + \dfrac{m_b}{m_y}\right) T_b$

$$T_b = \frac{m_y - m_a}{m_y + m_b} T_a + \frac{m_y}{m_y + m_b} Q$$

A plot of T_b vs T_a is a straight line. At the threshold, $T_b = 0$. Thus

$$T_{\text{th}} = -Q \frac{m_y}{m_y - m_a}$$

For the present case, $T_{\text{th}} \approx 1.146$ MeV.

[5]This problem illustrates that the threshold energy for a given nuclear reaction depends on θ. The minimum of the threshold value is obtained for $\theta = 0°$, that is, in the forward direction.

Illustrative Example 4.7: Rough estimation of kinetic energy of the product

In a reaction, $^{235}_{92}$U captures a thermal neutron and releases 175 MeV of energy. The resulting fragments have the mass numbers 138 and 95, respectively. Make a rough estimate of the kinetic energy of the lighter element.

Solution To make a rough estimate, let us consider the reaction as a two-body reaction. For the thermal neutron, $T_a \approx 0$, and thus, $\alpha = 0$, $\beta = \dfrac{m_y}{m_y + m_b} Q$ in Eq. (4.7).

Therefore, from Eq. (4.7,) $T_b \approx \dfrac{m_y}{m_y + m_b} Q \approx \dfrac{138}{138+95} \times 175 \text{ MeV} = 103.65 \text{ MeV}$.

Illustrative Example 4.8: Relativistic collision

A proton of kinetic energy 940 MeV makes an elastic collision with a stationary proton in such a way that after the collision, the protons are travelling at equal angles on either side of the direction of the incident proton. Calculate the angle between the directions of motion of the protons.

Solution The outgoing particles must have the same linear momentum, $|\vec{p}_1|$, otherwise the linear momentum will not be conserved. Thus, the conservation of linear momentum gives

$$p = 2p_1 \cos\theta, \tag{4.9}$$

where $\vec{p}$ is the linear momentum of the incident proton and θ is the angle of scattering of each proton. The kinetic energy of the incident proton is given by

$$\sqrt{p^2c^2 + m_0^2c^4} - m_0c^2 = 940 \text{ MeV} \approx m_0c^2 \text{ or } p^2c^2 = 3m_0^2c^4 \tag{4.10}$$

From the conservation of kinetic energy

$$2\left[\sqrt{p_1^2c^2 + m_0^2c^4} - m_0c^2\right] = 940 \text{ MeV} \approx m_0c^2 \text{ or } 4p_1^2c^2 = 5m_0^2c^4 \tag{4.11}$$

From Eqs (4.9), (4.10) and (4.11), $\dfrac{p}{2p_1} = \cos\theta = \sqrt{\dfrac{3}{5}} = 0.775 \Rightarrow \theta \approx 39.2^\circ$. Therefore, the angle between the scattered protons is 78.4°.

4.2.2 Energetics in the Centre-of-Mass Frame

Experiments are usually carried out in the laboratory frame, where the target is at rest. However, it is convenient for theoretical analysis to use the centre-of-mass (CM) coordinate system.

We define the CM frame as one in which the total linear momentum is zero. Let us now consider the reaction $a + X \longrightarrow Y + b$, where the target X is at rest in the laboratory and the particle a is moving with velocity v_a. Let us assume that the reaction proceeds in two independent steps:

(a) $a + X \longrightarrow C^*$ (formation of the compound nucleus)

(b) $C^* \longrightarrow Y + b$ (decay of the compound nucleus)

For the first step, the conservation of energy in the CM frame gives

$$(m_a + m_x)c^2 + T_{\rm cm}^{\rm in} = m_c^* c^2, \tag{4.12}$$

where $T_{\rm cm}^{\rm in}$ is the kinetic energy of a and X in the CM frame, and is given by

$$T_{\rm cm}^{\rm in} = \frac{1}{2}m_a(v_a - v_{\rm cm})^2 + \frac{1}{2}m_x(0 - v_{\rm cm})^2 = \frac{m_x}{m_a + m_x}T_a, \tag{4.13}$$

where $v_{\rm cm} = \dfrac{m_a v_a}{m_a + m_x}$ and T_a is the kinetic energy of a in the lab frame.

Now, consider the second step. In the CM frame, the compound nucleus is at rest and the particles b and Y move with equal and opposite momentum.

The conservation of energy in the CM frame gives

$$m_c^* c^2 = (m_b + m_y)c^2 + T_{\rm cm}^{\rm out}, \tag{4.14}$$

where $T_{\rm cm}^{\rm out}$ is the energy of the outgoing particles in the CM frame

$$T_{\rm cm}^{\rm out} = \frac{1}{2}m_b v_b^2 + \frac{1}{2}m_y v_y^2 = \frac{m_b + m_y}{m_y}T_b, \tag{4.15}$$

where the condition $m_b v_b = m_y v_y$ has been used.

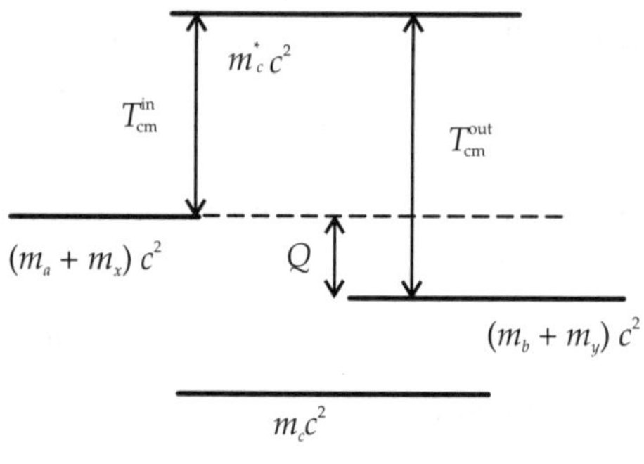

Figure 4.4: *Energy diagram of an exoergic reaction in the CM frame*

The energy diagram for the exoergic reaction is shown in Fig. 4.4. Both the formation of the compound nucleus (Eq. (4.12)), and its decay (Eq. (4.14)) have been presented in Fig. 4.4. Since a and X form a bound compound nucleus, $(m_a + m_x)c^2 > m_c c^2$. For the exoergic reaction, $Q = (m_a + m_x)c^2 - (m_b + m_y)c^2 > 0$, and thus, the level of $(m_a + m_x)c^2$ is higher than $(m_b + m_y)c^2$ by Q. Note that the process is allowed even for $T_{\rm cm}^{\rm in} = 0$; that is, for $T_a = 0$. Figure 4.5 shows a similar energy diagram for the endoergic reaction. It differs from Fig. 4.4 in that $(m_a + m_x)c^2 < (m_b + m_y)c^2$. From the energy diagram

$$T_{\rm cm}^{\rm in} = T_{\rm cm}^{\rm out} + |Q| \tag{4.16}$$

The minimum value of energy for which the reaction is possible is

$$T_{\rm cm}^{th} = |Q| \tag{4.17}$$

Using Eq. (4.13), we obtain the condition for the threshold energy in the laboratory frame

$$\frac{m_x}{m_a + m_x}T_{\rm th} = |Q|;\ T_{\rm th} = |Q|\frac{m_x + m_a}{m_x} \tag{4.18}$$

Note that $T_{\text{th}} > |Q|$: The velocity of the incident particle before collision is v_a and the momentum is $m_a v_a$. After collision, the CM of the combined system of a and X, which can be considered as a compound nucleus, moves with the velocity v_{cm} and the conservation of momentum requires $m_a v_a = (m_a + m_x) v_{\text{cm}}$.

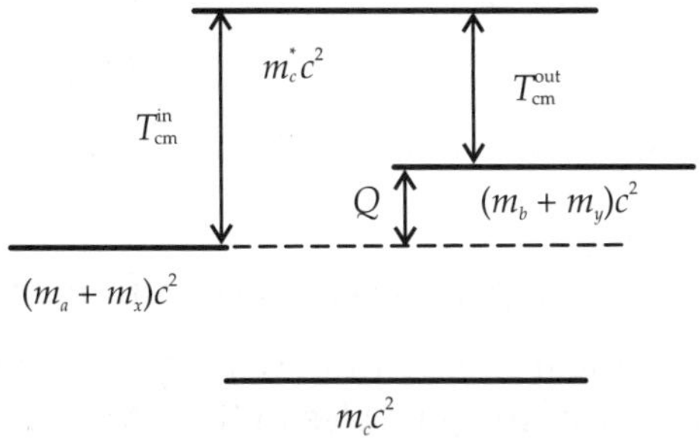

Figure 4.5: *Energy diagram of an endoergic reaction in the CM frame*

For an endoergic reaction, the supplied energy must be used to meet the mass deficit plus the kinetic energy of the combined system. Therefore, from the conservation of energy

$$T_a = -Q + \frac{1}{2}(m_a + m_x)v_{\text{cm}}^2 = -Q + \frac{1}{2}(m_a + m_x)\frac{m_a v_a^2}{(m_a + m_x)^2} m_a = -Q + T_a \frac{m_a}{m_a + m_x} \tag{4.19}$$

At the threshold $T_a = T_{\text{th}}$, Eq. (4.19) gives

$$T_{\text{th}} = -Q \frac{m_a + m_x}{m_x} \tag{4.20}$$

Illustrative Example 4.9: CM frame and lab frame

Let us now consider the reaction $a + X \longrightarrow Y + b$, where the target X is at rest in the laboratory and the particle a is moving with velocity v_a and kinetic energy $T_a = \frac{1}{2} m_a v_a^2$. As the particle a moves towards X, the centre-of-mass also moves in the laboratory frame towards X. We now analyse the reaction in the frame in which the centre-of-mass is at rest. Figure. 4.6 shows the reaction in the lab frame and CM frame.

(a) Show that the total linear momentum in the CM frame is zero.

(b) Derive a relation between the kinetic energy in the lab frame and the CM frame.

(c) Define Q value in terms of the kinetic energy in the CM frame and hence calculate the threshold energy for the endoergic reaction.

Solution (a) The velocity of the CM in the lab frame is $v_{\text{cm}} = \dfrac{m_a v_a}{m_a + m_x}$

The velocity of the particle a in the CM frame is $v_a' = v_a - v_{\text{cm}} = \dfrac{m_x v_a}{m_a + m_x}$

The velocity of the particle X in the CM frame is $v_x' = 0 - v_{\text{cm}} = -\dfrac{m_a v_a}{m_a + m_x}$

In the CM frame, the two particles, therefore, move towards each other.

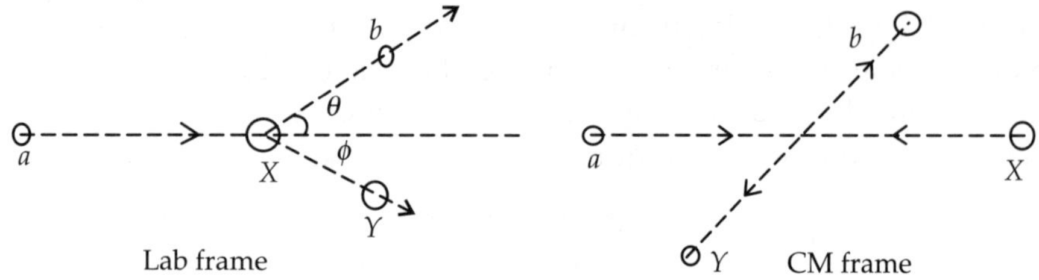

Figure 4.6: *Reaction in the lab frame and CM frame*

Total linear momentum of the particles in the CM frame is $\frac{m_a m_x v_a}{m_a + m_x} - \frac{m_x m_a v_a}{m_a + m_x} = 0$

After collision, the total linear momentum will again be zero, as shown in Fig. 4.6.

(b) Total initial kinetic energy of the particles in the CM frame is

$$KE_i^{\mathrm{cm}} = \frac{1}{2} m_a \frac{m_x^2 v_a^2}{(m_a + m_x)^2} + \frac{1}{2} m_x \frac{m_a^2 v_a^2}{(m_a + m_x)^2} = \frac{1}{2} m_a v_a^2 \frac{m_x}{m_a + m_x} = KE_i^{\mathrm{lab}} \frac{m_x}{m_a + m_x} \tag{4.21}$$

(c) Since the Q value of the reaction depends on the rest masses of the particles concerned, it must be the same in all frames.

$$Q = KE_{\mathrm{final}}^{\mathrm{lab}} - KE_{\mathrm{initial}}^{\mathrm{lab}} = KE_{\mathrm{final}}^{CM} - KE_{\mathrm{initial}}^{CM}$$

The kinetic energy of the reaction products in the CM system is $KE_{\mathrm{final}}^{CM} = KE_{\mathrm{initial}}^{CM} + Q$.

At the threshold, the products are formed with zero mutual velocity in the CM system. Therefore

$$KE_{\mathrm{initial}}^{CM} = -Q; \quad KE_i^{\mathrm{lab}} \frac{m_x}{m_a + m_x} = -Q$$

$$T_{\mathrm{th}} = KE_i^{\mathrm{lab}} = -Q \frac{m_a + m_x}{m_x} \tag{4.22}$$

4.2.3 Cross-section

In any nuclear reaction, we deal with particles of atomic and subatomic dimensions, and thus, it is not possible to follow precisely the track of each projectile or the location of the target nuclei. The situation is very similar to the random firing of a gun on a dark night towards a distant wall on which some tiny targets have been randomly distributed. In practice, it is convenient to study such collisions statistically by analysing a large number of collisions with all the possible values of the impact parameters.

The concept of cross-section is used to express the probability of any particular reaction. *The cross-section of a reaction gives the probability of occurrence of any particular reaction.*

We may associate a fictitious area σ (which need not be related to the actual cross-sectional area of the target nucleus) centred on each target. Any particle entering this area interacts with the target and if a bombarding particle misses this area, there will be no reaction. Hence, the greater the cross-section, the greater the likelihood of an interaction. Thus, the quantity σ, known as the **cross-section**, gives a measure of the reaction probability per target nucleus. The cross-section (σ) varies with the nature of the process involved and with the energy of the incident particles. It may be greater than, less than or equal to the geometrical cross-section of the target.

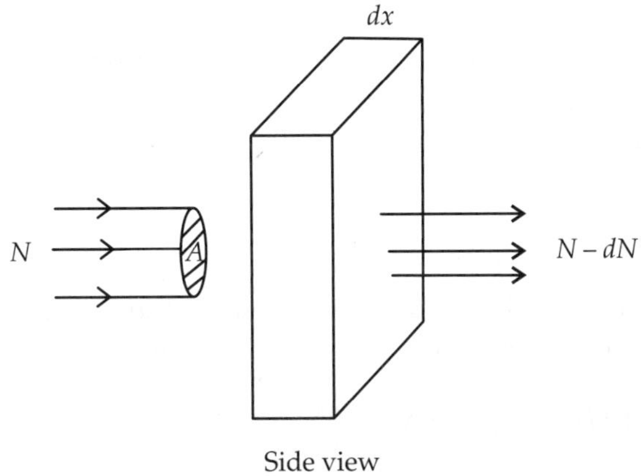

Figure 4.7: *Arrangement to determine the cross-section of a nuclear reaction*

Suppose a homogeneous mono-energetic beam consisting of N particles per unit time distributed uniformly over an area A strikes a thin slab of target material, as shown in Fig. 4.7. The thickness of the slab is dx, and the slab is so thin that a given bombarding particle strikes no more than one target nucleus. Let the number of target nuclei per unit volume of the foil be n. Thus, the total number of available target particles in the foil is $nAdx$. At any time, if an incident particle encounters one of the scattering centres in the foil, the incident particle will be scattered. Suppose the number of particles scattered per second is dN.

Therefore, *the probability that any one bombarding particle has a hit is given by* $\frac{dN}{N}$. The probability can also be expressed in terms of the total projected area of the target nuclei. The probability of any encounter $= \frac{1}{A} \times$ Aggregate cross-section of all target nuclei lying within the area A.

If the effective cross-section of each target exposed to the beam is σ, then

$$\frac{dN}{N} = \frac{nAdx \times \sigma}{A} \tag{4.23}$$

Equation (4.23) can be interpreted in two ways.

First, it can serve as a definition of cross-section, by writing it as

$$\sigma = \frac{dN}{(nAdx) \times \frac{N}{A}} \tag{4.24}$$

This represents the number of scattered particles produced per unit incident flux and per target nucleus. Thus

$$\sigma \equiv \frac{\text{Number of particles scattered per second per target nucleus}}{\text{Number of projectiles incident per second per area}}$$

The unit usually used to measure cross-section in subatomic experiments is the barn, which is defined as 1 barn $= 10^{-24}$ cm^2.

The typical size of a nucleus is about 10^{-12} cm and, therefore, the cross-sectional area for a medium-sized nucleus, assuming it to be a sphere, would be of the order of a barn.

Equation (4.23) can also be used to determine the number of particles scattered from a beam, after it traverses a distance x of the target. As the beam passes a distance dx through the target, dN number of particles are removed from the beam due to scattering. From Eq. (4.23)

$$\frac{dN}{A} = -\sigma n dx \frac{N}{A}, \tag{4.25}$$

where the $-$ve sign is used because an increase in the scattered particle dN corresponds to a decrease of N. Integrating Eq. (4.25), we get

$$\int_{N_0}^{N} \frac{dN}{N} = -\int_0^x \sigma n dx \Rightarrow N(x) = N_0 e^{-n\sigma x}, \tag{4.26}$$

where N_0 is the initial number of particles in the beam. The number of scattered particles is thus given by

$$N_0 - N(x) = N_0(1 - e^{-n\sigma x}) \tag{4.27}$$

Illustrative Example 4.10: Determination of cross-section

For a certain target, 10^{-6}% of an incoming beam is scattered. If the density of the target is 4.1×10^3 kg/m^3, thickness is $= 10^{-8}$ m and the mass number $A = 30$, find the scattering cross-section.

Solution From Eq. (4.27), $\dfrac{N_0 - N(x)}{N_0} = (1 - e^{-n\sigma x})$.

$$10^{-8} = 1 - e^{-n\sigma x}$$

The number of target nuclei per unit volume is

$$n = \frac{6.023 \times 10^{23}}{30} \times 4.1 \times 10^6 = 8.23 \times 10^{28}/\text{m}^3$$

$$e^{-n\sigma x} \approx 1 - n\sigma x = 1 - 8.23 \times 10^{20}\sigma. \text{ Thus}$$

$$10^{-8} = 8.23 \times 10^{20}\sigma \text{ and } \sigma = 0.121 \times 10^{-28} \text{ m}^2 = 0.121 \text{ barn}$$

4.2.4 Compound Nucleus

The compound nucleus theory of nuclear reactions was introduced by Bohr in 1936. According to this theory, many nuclear reactions proceed in two independent steps:

1. Formation of the compound nucleus.
2. Decay of the compound nucleus.

Formation of the compound nucleus: $a + X \longrightarrow C^*$. The target nucleus first captures the incident particle (projectile) and a combined system consisting of the target and the projectile is formed. The projectile entering into the target loses its independent identity and, after several collisions, the incident energy is shared among the nucleons of the combined system. This combined system formed is in the excited state (represented as C^*) and is known as the compound nucleus.

Decay of the compound nucleus: $C^* \longrightarrow Y + b$. The average increase in energy of any single nucleon of the compound nucleus is not enough to free it from the nucleus. However, as random collisions occur among the nucleons, statistically there is a small probability that a single nucleon may have a large enough share of the total energy so that it may escape from the nucleus.

The whole process is represented as: $a + X \longrightarrow C^* \longrightarrow Y + b$, where C^* indicates the compound nucleus.

The average lifetime of the compound nucleus is high ($\sim 10^{-15}$ s), whereas the time taken by an incident particle of moderate energy to traverse the nucleus is very small, $\sim 10^{-22}$ s, and thus, it does not remember how it was formed.

A given compound nucleus may be formed in different ways. Once it is formed, it does not remember how it was formed. The compound nucleus may decay in a number of ways or channels, and the basic assumption of the compound nucleus theory is that the probability for decay into any specific set is independent of the process of formation. The decay process depends only on the excitation energy of the compound nucleus and is governed primarily by statistical rules. In another words, *the formation and the decay of the compound nucleus are independent of each other*. This is known as the **Bohr hypothesis of independence**.

The mean lifetime (τ) of the compound nucleus in any energy level is related to the width of that level through the uncertainty relation as $\tau\Gamma \approx \hbar$.

The probability (w) of decay from any energy level is

$$w = \frac{1}{\tau} = \frac{\Gamma}{\hbar} \tag{4.28}$$

Since a compound nucleus may decay through different ways (that is, in different channels, say, $a, b, \cdots$), the total probability of decay is

$$w = w_a + w_b + \cdots = \frac{1}{\hbar}\sum_i \Gamma_i \tag{4.29}$$

The relative probability of decay in any given channel is

$$\eta_i = \frac{w_i}{w} = \frac{\Gamma_i}{\sum_i \Gamma_i}, \tag{4.30}$$

where Γ_i is the partial width. According to the Bohr hypothesis of independence, the relative disintegration probabilities of a compound nucleus are independent of the manner of its formation.

Compound nucleus energy levels: An analysis of nuclear energy levels shows that for comparatively low excitation energies of a heavy nucleus, its energy levels are spaced rather far apart.

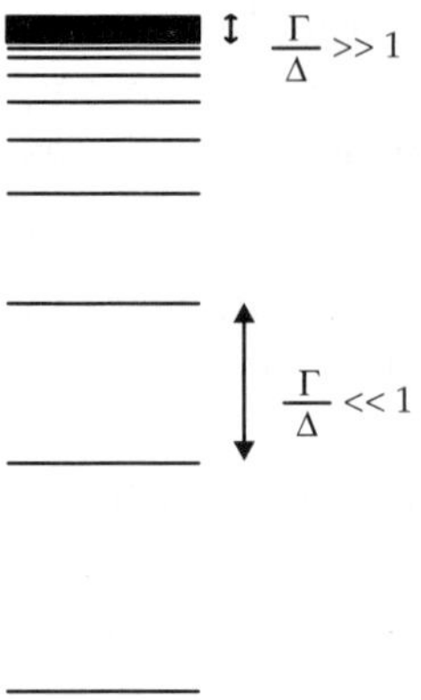

Figure 4.8: *Energy levels of a compound nucleus, a schematic view*

However, for large excitation energies, the levels come closer together and begin to overlap. The energy levels of a compound nucleus have been presented schematically in Fig. 4.8, where Γ is the width of the level and Δ represents the average spacing between the levels. It shows that Δ decreases with increasing energy. In case of high excitation energy of the compound nucleus, $\frac{\Gamma}{\Delta} >> 1$, energy levels are not well-defined and there is complete overlap between them. Under the condition of high excitation, a large number of exit channels are available for the decay of the compound nucleus.

Since the decay of the compound nucleus from a particular level is the property of that level (does not depend on the formation of the level), the independence hypothesis holds for the discrete levels. In this case, the levels are well separated and sharp, so that they do not overlap, that is, the average level spacing is much larger than the width ($\Delta >> \Gamma$).

At low-incident energy, $\Delta >> \Gamma$ and, consequently, decay of the compound nucleus will occur from the well-defined states of the compound nucleus. At high energies, however, the situation changes. The excited states may overlap, and hence, a departure from the independence hypothesis may be expected.

Ghoshal experiment: The Bohr hypothesis of independence was demonstrated by SN Ghoshal[6] in 1950. We now briefly discuss the basic idea underlying the experiment.

Let us first consider the reaction $X(a,b)Y$ through the compound nucleus C

$$a + X \longrightarrow C^* \longrightarrow Y + b$$

The target nucleus X absorbs the projectile a to form the compound nucleus C^* in which all the nucleons share the energy. By the process of chance, sufficient energy may be imparted to the particle b so that it can leave the compound nucleus.

In Ghoshal's experiment, the compound nucleus ${}^{64}_{30}\text{Zn}$ was formed in two different ways:

$$p + {}^{63}_{29}\text{Cu} \longrightarrow {}^{64}_{30}\text{Zn}^* \quad \text{[Channel 1 in Fig. 4.9]}$$

$$\alpha + {}^{60}_{28}\text{Ni} \longrightarrow {}^{64}_{30}\text{Zn}^* \quad \text{[Channel 2 in Fig. 4.9]}$$

It is observed that $[M({}^{1}_{1}\text{H}) + M({}^{63}_{29}\text{Cu})] - [M({}^{4}_{2}\text{He}) + M({}^{60}_{28}\text{Ni})] \approx 7$ MeV.

Thus, to produce the same excitation in ${}^{64}_{30}\text{Zn}^*$, the kinetic energy of α (ε_α) was made larger than that of the proton by 7 MeV.

$$\varepsilon_\alpha - \varepsilon_p \approx 7 \text{ MeV}$$

[6]Ghoshal, SN. 1950. An Experimental Verification of the Theory of Compound Nucleus. *Phys. Rev.*, 80:939.

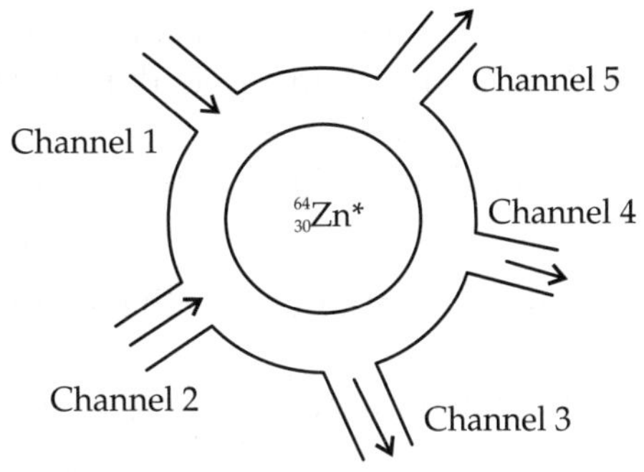

Figure 4.9: *The formation and decay modes of the compound nucleus. The compound nucleus $^{64}_{30}Zn^*$ is formed in two ways, represented as Channel 1 and Channel 2. Channels 4, 5 and 6 represent the decay channels.*

Figure 4.10 illustrates the energy-level diagram of producing the same excitation in $^{64}_{30}Zn^*$.

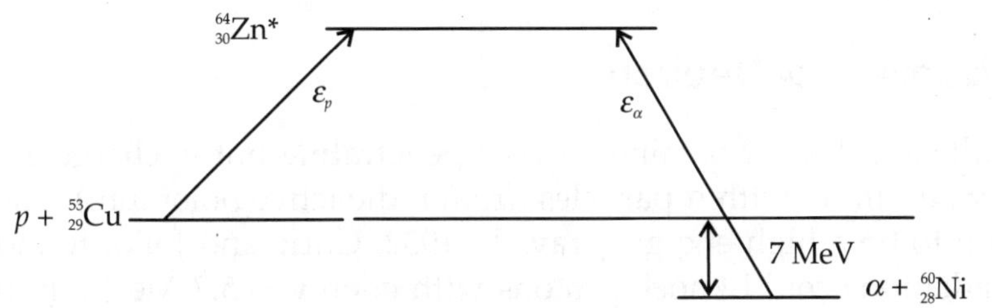

Figure 4.10: *Energy-level diagram showing the same excitation of $^{64}_{30}Zn^*$*

In Ghoshal's experiment, the following decay modes of $^{64}_{30}Zn^*$ were observed:

$^{64}_{30}Zn^* \longrightarrow ^{63}_{30}Zn + ^1_0 n$ [Channel 3 in Fig. 4.9]

$\longrightarrow ^{62}_{30}Zn + ^1_0 n + ^1_0 n$ [Channel 4 in Fig. 4.9]

$\longrightarrow ^{62}_{29}Cu + ^1_0 n + ^1_1 H$ [Channel 5 in Fig. 4.9]

In summary, the three pairs of reactions that occurred through the formation of the same compound nucleus were:

1. $^{60}_{28}Ni(\alpha, n)^{63}_{30}Zn$	4. $^{63}_{29}Cu(p, n)^{63}_{30}Zn$
2. $^{60}_{28}Ni(\alpha, 2n)^{62}_{30}Zn$	5. $^{63}_{29}Cu(p, 2n)^{62}_{30}Zn$
3. $^{60}_{28}Ni(\alpha, pn)^{62}_{29}Cu$	6. $^{63}_{29}Cu(p, pn)^{62}_{29}Cu$

The cross-section of (1), (2) and (3) through the formation of the compound nucleus is

$$\sigma_i = \sigma_1^* \eta_i, \tag{4.31}$$

where σ_1^* is the cross-section of formation of the compound nucleus ${}^{64}_{30}\text{Zn}^*$ through the capture of the α particle (Channel 2) and η_i is the probability of decay through the i-th channel.

Similarly for the reactions $(4),(5)$ and (6), the cross-section is

$$\sigma_i = \sigma_2^* \eta_i, \tag{4.32}$$

where σ_2^* is the cross-section of formation of the compound nucleus through Channel 1.

For identical excitation of the compound nucleus, we expect from Eq. (4.31) and Eq. (4.31)

$$\frac{\sigma[{}^{60}_{28}\text{Ni}(\alpha,n){}^{63}_{30}\text{Zn}]}{\sigma[{}^{63}_{29}\text{Cu}(p,n){}^{63}_{30}\text{Zn}]} = \frac{\sigma[{}^{60}_{28}\text{Ni}(\alpha,2n){}^{62}_{30}\text{Zn}]}{\sigma[{}^{63}_{29}\text{Cu}(p,2n){}^{62}_{30}\text{Zn}]} = \frac{\sigma[{}^{60}_{28}\text{Ni}(\alpha,pn){}^{62}_{29}\text{Zn}]}{\sigma[{}^{63}_{29}\text{Cu}(p,pn){}^{62}_{29}\text{Cu}]} \tag{4.33}$$

The result of Ghoshal's experiment is shown in Fig. 4.11 where two sets of yield curves are superimposed by translating the ε_α scale by 7 MeV with respect to the ε_p scale. Figure 4.11 shows that the experimental results correspond to Eq. (4.33), within the limits of experimental errors, which is thus in agreement with Bohr's hypothesis.

4.2.5 Discovery of Neutron

In 1930, Bothe and Becker obtained a very penetrating but uncharged radiation by bombarding beryllium with α particles (from radioactive polonium). They assumed the radiation to be a high-energy γ ray. In 1932, Curie and Joliot found that these energetic radiations could knock protons with energy ~ 5.7 MeV out of a paraffin slab. If the radiation under study had been a γ ray, the protons could have been knocked out of paraffin by Compton-like collisions. Using the Compton scattering formula, they found that the energy of this γ radiation would be at least 52 MeV. However, the emission of such high-energy γ rays seemed extremely unlikely.

Illustrative Example 4.11: An unknown radiation

Alpha particles of 5 MeV from a polonium source are incident on the ${}^{9}_{4}\text{Be}$ target. It is found that some uncharged but otherwise unknown radiation is produced. Assuming that the unknown radiation is a γ ray, calculate the energy of the γ ray.

Given: $M({}^{4}_{2}\text{He}) = 4.002603$ u, $M({}^{9}_{4}\text{Be}) = 9.012182$ u, $M({}^{13}_{6}\text{C}) = 13.003355$ u.

Solution The assumed reaction is ${}^{4}_{2}\text{He} + {}^{9}_{4}\text{Be} \longrightarrow {}^{13}_{6}\text{C} + \gamma$.
From energy conservation, we get

$$E_c + E_\gamma = E_\alpha + [M({}^{4}_{2}\text{He}) + M({}^{9}_{4}\text{Be}) - M({}^{13}_{6}\text{C})]c^2 = 15.65 \text{ MeV}, \tag{4.34}$$

where the Es represent the kinetic energy.

Momentum conservation gives

$$p_c + p_\gamma = p_\alpha = \sqrt{2M({}^{4}_{2}\text{He})E_\alpha} = 193.09 \text{ MeV/c} \quad \text{or} \quad p_c c + E_\gamma = 193 \text{ MeV} \tag{4.35}$$

We can find an approximate value of E_γ by assuming $E_c \ll E_\gamma$.

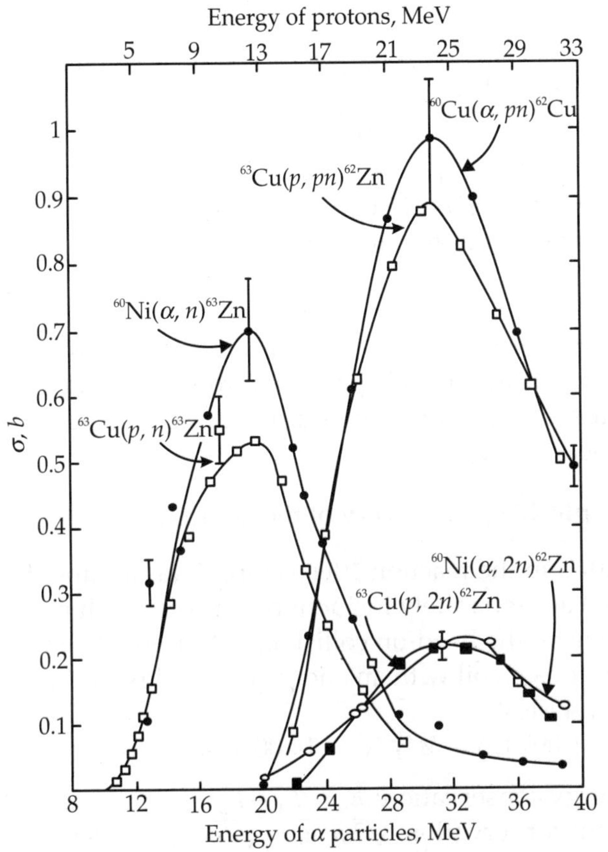

Figure 4.11: *Result of Ghoshal's experiment*

From Eq. (4.34), $E_\gamma \approx 15.65$ MeV. Substituting E_γ in Eq. (4.35), we get $E_c \approx 1.30$ MeV. Again from Eq. (4.34), $E_\gamma \approx 14.35$ MeV.

Illustrative Example 4.12: An inconsistency!

Gamma rays emitted from the reaction ${}^9_4\text{Be}({}^4_2\text{He}, \gamma){}^{13}_6\text{C}$ (assuming the unknown radiation to be a γ ray) are separately incident on a proton-rich paraffin target and on a ${}^{14}_7\text{N}$ target. Determine the minimum energy of the γ ray required to produce the observed 5.7-MeV recoil protons and 1.4-MeV recoil ${}^{14}_7\text{N}$ nuclei.

Given: $M({}^1_1\text{H}) = 1.007825$ u, $M({}^{14}_7\text{N}) = 14.003074$ u.

Solution Energy conservation $h\nu_{\min} = h\nu' + E_x$, where $h\nu'$ is the energy of the scattered photon and E_x is the recoil energy of the target (say X).

Minimum energy corresponds to the head-on collision, and the conservation of momentum gives

$$h\nu_{\min} = -h\nu' + p_x c = -h\nu' + \sqrt{2m_x c^2 E_x}$$

From the above relations, we get $h\nu_{\min} = \frac{\sqrt{E_x}}{2}(\sqrt{E_x} + \sqrt{2m_x c^2}) \approx \frac{\sqrt{E_x}}{2}\sqrt{2m_x c^2}$, assuming $m_x c^2 \gg E_x$.

For the proton target, $h\nu_{\min} = \sqrt{\dfrac{m_x c^2 E_x}{2}} = \sqrt{\dfrac{1.007825 \times 931.5 \times 5.7}{2}} \approx 51.72$ MeV

For the ${}^{14}_{7}$N target, $h\nu_{\min} = \sqrt{\dfrac{m_x c^2 E_x}{2}} = \sqrt{\dfrac{14.003074 \times 931.5 \times 1.4}{2}} \approx 95.55$ MeV.

Both these values are $\gg E_\gamma \approx 15.0$ MeV.

Thus, the assumption that the unknown radiation is a γ ray is inconsistent with the observed value.

Chadwick, in 1932, provided the correct explanation by identifying the unknown radiation as a neutral particle, called the neutron, with a mass nearly equal to that of the proton. Thus, in a head-on collision, a neutron could transfer its energy entirely to the struck proton. By performing additional recoil experiments with neutrons, Chadwick confirmed his hypothesis.

Illustrative Example 4.13: Discovery of the neutron

The neutrons emitted in the reaction ${}^{9}_{4}\mathrm{Be}({}^{4}_{2}\mathrm{He}, n){}^{12}_{6}\mathrm{C}$ (assuming that the unknown radiation is neutrons) are separately incident on a proton-rich paraffin target and on a ${}^{14}_{7}$N target. Considering the head-on collision, determine the mass and energy of the neutron so that protons recoil with an energy of 5.7 MeV and the ${}^{14}_{7}$N nucleus recoils with an energy of 1.4 MeV.

Given: $M({}^{1}_{1}\mathrm{H}) = 1.007825$ u, $M({}^{14}_{7}\mathrm{N}) = 14.003074$ u.

Solution From energy conservation: $E_n = E_x + E_n'$

From momentum conservation: $\sqrt{2m_n E_n} = \sqrt{2m_x E_x} + \sqrt{2m_n E_n'}$ or, $\sqrt{2m_n E_n} - \sqrt{2m_x E_x} = \sqrt{2m_n(E_n - E_x)}$

Simplifying, we get $\sqrt{E_n} = \dfrac{m_n + m_x}{2\sqrt{m_n m_x}} \sqrt{E_x}$.

For the proton target, $\sqrt{E_n} = \dfrac{m_n + m_p}{2\sqrt{m_n m_p}} \sqrt{5.7} = 1.194 \dfrac{m_n + m_p}{\sqrt{m_n m_p}}$.

For the nitrogen target, $\sqrt{E_n} = \dfrac{m_n + m_N}{2\sqrt{m_n m_N}} \sqrt{1.4} = 0.592 \dfrac{m_n + m_N}{\sqrt{m_n m_N}}$.

Equating the two relations, we get $E_n \approx 5.8$ MeV and $m_n \approx 0.98$ u.

Thus, the mass of the neutron is ~ 1 u. The actual mass of the neutron is 1.008665 u.

Illustrative Example 4.14: Mass of the neutron

Consider the interaction of a thermal neutron (with energy 0.0025 eV) with nitrogen:

$${}^{1}_{0}n + {}^{14}_{7}\mathrm{N} \longrightarrow {}^{14}_{6}\mathrm{C} + {}^{1}_{1}\mathrm{H}$$

The kinetic energy of proton is 0.585 MeV. Calculate the mass of neutron.

Given: $M({}^{1}_{1}\mathrm{H}) = 1.007825$ u, $M({}^{14}_{7}\mathrm{N}) = 14.003074$ u, $M({}^{14}_{6}\mathrm{C}) = 14.003242$ u.

Solution The energy released is $Q = T_p + T_c - T_n$. For a thermal neutron, $T_n \approx 0$, and thus, from momentum conservation, $|\vec{p}_c| = |\vec{p}_p|$.

Therefore, $Q = T_p(1+\frac{m_p}{m_c}) \approx 0.627$ MeV. Again, by using the relation $Q = m_n + m_N - m_c - m_p = 0.627$ MeV, we obtain $m_n = 1.00866$ u.

Check Progress 4.2: Calculate the Q value of the reaction ${}^{9}_{4}\text{Be}({}^{4}_{2}\text{He},n){}^{12}_{6}\text{C}$. Also determine the kinetic energy of the emitted neutron. Given: $M({}^{4}_{2}\text{He}) = 4.002603$ u, $M({}^{9}_{4}\text{Be}) = 9.012182$ u, $M({}^{12}_{6}\text{C}) = 12.000000$ u, $M({}^{1}_{0}n) = 1.008665$ u.

Properties and production of neutrons: The neutron is a spin-half neutral particle. It has a negative magnetic moment. The mass of the neutron is 1.008665 u, which is approximately 1.29 MeV larger than the mass of a proton. Consequently, it is β-radioactive and decays with a half-life of 11 minutes according to the scheme

$$n \longrightarrow p + e^- + \bar{\nu} \tag{4.36}$$

Neutrons, together with protons, are the essential constituents of every nucleus. *Unlike protons, the neutrons, being neutral, do not face the Coulomb barrier and can thus interact with the nucleus, even at very low energy.*

Neutrons were first discovered in the reaction involving the interaction of α particles from radium with beryllium:

$${}^{4}_{2}\text{He} + {}^{9}_{4}\text{Be} \longrightarrow {}^{12}_{6}\text{C} + n \quad \text{with Q} \sim 5.5 \ \text{MeV} \tag{4.37}$$

This is also the most common method of obtaining neutrons with a wide energy spectrum. Slow neutrons are usually obtained by surrounding the source with paraffin.

Mono-energetic neutrons can also be obtained by (γ, n) reactions. For example

$$\begin{aligned} \gamma + {}^{2}_{1}\text{H} &\longrightarrow {}^{1}_{1}\text{H} + n \quad \text{with Q} \sim -2.22 \ \text{MeV} \\ \gamma + {}^{9}_{4}\text{Be} &\longrightarrow 2{}^{4}_{2}\text{He} + n \quad \text{with Q} \sim -1.65 \ \text{MeV} \end{aligned} \tag{4.38}$$

Analysis shows that in the first case, a photon with energy $E_\gamma = 2.62$ MeV produces a neutron with kinetic energy $T_n \approx 200$ keV, and in the second case, a photon with energy $E_\gamma = 1.78$ MeV gives a neutron with kinetic energy $T_n \approx 110$ keV.

Neutrons can also be produced by the reaction

$${}^{2}_{1}\text{H} + {}^{2}_{1}\text{H} \longrightarrow {}^{3}_{2}\text{He} + n \quad \text{with Q} \sim 3.2 \ \text{MeV} \tag{4.39}$$

Another method used in the artificial production of neutrons is bombardment of proton beams on a lithium target

$$p + {}^{7}_{3}\text{Li} \longrightarrow {}^{7}_{4}\text{Be} + n \quad \text{with Q} \sim -1.65 \ \text{MeV} \tag{4.40}$$

The threshold energy of a proton is approximately 1.882 MeV and the energy of the neutron produced is approximately 30 keV.

A neutron passing through a material undergoes frequent collisions in which it gives up some energy to the nuclei in its path. Very soon, after several collisions, the neutron attains thermal equilibrium with the atoms of the medium. The elements used for slowing down neutrons are called **moderators**. The neutrons slowed down at room temperature have a Maxwellian distribution of energy, with the most probable energy being $\sim k_BT \approx 0.025$ eV. A neutron with such an energy is called a **thermal neutron**. According to their associated energy, neutrons are classified as:

Thermal	$E \sim 0.025\,\text{eV}$	Slow	$E \sim 1\,\text{keV}$
Epithermal	$E \sim 1\,\text{eV}$	Fast	$E \sim 100\,\text{keV}$ to $10\,\text{MeV}$

Illustrative Example 4.15: Slowing down a neutron

Consider an elastic collision between a neutron of mass m and energy E with a target nucleus of mass M (mass number A). If the energy of the neutron after collision is E', show that $\frac{E'}{E} = \frac{A^2+2A\cos\theta+1}{(A+1)^2}$, where θ is the angle of scattering in the CM frame (but E and E' are in the lab frame).

Solution Figure 4.12 shows the collision in the lab frame and CM frame. Let v_1 be the velocity of the neutron before collision.

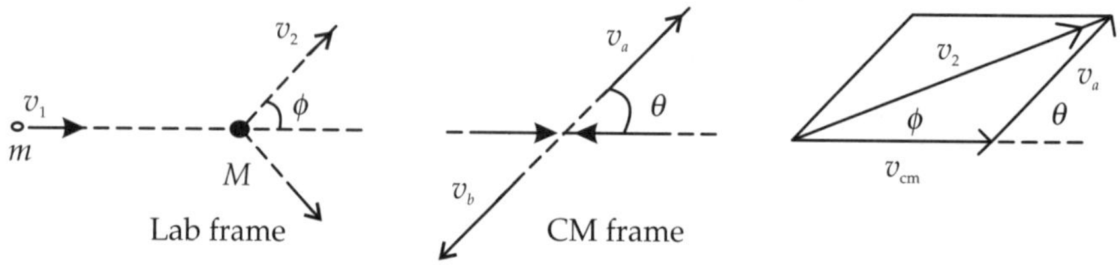

Figure 4.12: *Elastic collision of neutron with stationary target in lab frame and CM frame*

Velocity of the CM is $v_{\text{cm}} = \dfrac{mv_1}{m+M}$. Thus, the velocity of the neutron before collision in the CM frame is $v_1' = v_1 - v_{\text{cm}} = \dfrac{Mv_1}{m+M}$.

Velocity of the target before collision in the CM frame is $v_2' = 0 - v_{\text{cm}} = -\dfrac{mv_1}{m+M}$.

Thus, the total linear momentum before collision in the CM frame is zero. Conservation of momentum after collision in the CM frame requires that

$$mv_a = Mv_b, \tag{4.41}$$

where v_a and v_b are, respectively, the velocity of the neutron and the nucleus after collision in the CM frame. From the conservation of kinetic energy

$$\frac{1}{2}m\left(\frac{Mv_1}{m+M}\right)^2 + \frac{1}{2}M\left(\frac{mv_1}{m+M}\right)^2 = \frac{1}{2}mv_a^2 + \frac{1}{2}Mv_b^2 \tag{4.42}$$

Simplifying these equations, we obtain $v_a = \dfrac{Mv_1}{m+M}$ and $v_b = \dfrac{mv_1}{m+M}$.

Thus, the speed of the particles remains unchanged in the CM frame; however, their directions are changed.

If v_2 and v_a are the velocities of neutron after collision in the lab frame and CM frame, respectively, then

$$\vec{v_a} = \vec{v_2} - \vec{v_{cm}} \text{ or, } v_2^2 = v_a^2 + v_{cm}^2 + 2v_a v_{cm}\cos\theta \text{ or } v_2^2 = v_1^2 \frac{mM}{(m+M)^2}\left[\frac{M}{m} + \frac{m}{M} + 2\cos\theta\right],$$

where θ is the angle of scattering in the CM frame. Substituting $\frac{M}{m} \approx A$, we get

$$\frac{E'}{E} = \frac{A^2 + 2A\cos\theta + 1}{(A+1)^2} \tag{4.43}$$

For no scattering, $\theta = 0$ and $\frac{E'}{E} = 1$ as expected. For head-on collisions, $\theta = \pi$ and $\frac{E'}{E} = \frac{(A-1)^2}{(A+1)^2}$. With $\alpha = \frac{(A-1)^2}{(A+1)^2}$, the maximum energy loss[7] can be expressed as

$$\Delta E = E - E'_{\text{min}} = E(1-\alpha) \tag{4.44}$$

The energy loss of the neutron will be maximum if $\alpha = 0$ or $A = 1$ (hydrogen nucleus). For larger A

$$\alpha = \left(1 - \frac{1}{A}\right)^2 \left(1 + \frac{1}{A}\right)^{-2} \approx 1 - \frac{4}{A} \text{ and thus } \Delta E \approx \frac{4E}{A}$$

This implies that the energy loss is higher for lighter nuclei.

4.3 FISSION

Hahn and Strassmann discovered[8] fission in 1939. By using careful radiochemical techniques, they showed that the bombardment of uranium by low-energy thermal neutrons did not produce a heavier element; instead, the parent nucleus fragmented into two medium-sized daughter nuclei. This process of splitting a heavy nucleus into lighter nuclei is called fission. It may be spontaneous or initiated by the absorption of thermal neutrons. A typical example is given below.

Fission induced by neutrons: $n + {}^{235}_{92}\text{U} \longrightarrow {}^{236}_{92}\text{U}^* \longrightarrow {}^{144}_{56}\text{Ba} + {}^{89}_{36}\text{Kr} + 3n + Q$

Spontaneous fission: ${}^{235}_{92}\text{U} \longrightarrow {}^{144}_{56}\text{Ba} + {}^{89}_{36}\text{Kr} + 2n + Q$

In this process, a relatively large amount of energy is released ($Q \sim$ 200 MeV).

4.3.1 Mass Distribution of Fission Fragments

The two main nuclear products of fission are called the **fission fragments**. One of the most striking features of fission is the distribution of mass among the fission fragments. This depends on the excitation energy at which fission occurs. Figure 4.13 shows the typical mass distribution of the fission products of ${}^{235}_{92}\text{U}$.

---

[7] Compare with Eq. (5.5).

[8] A neutron, being uncharged, will not experience any Coulomb barrier as it approaches a target nucleus. Fermi predicted that the neutron would be a useful projectile, and even a slow neutron would be able to penetrate a massive nucleus.

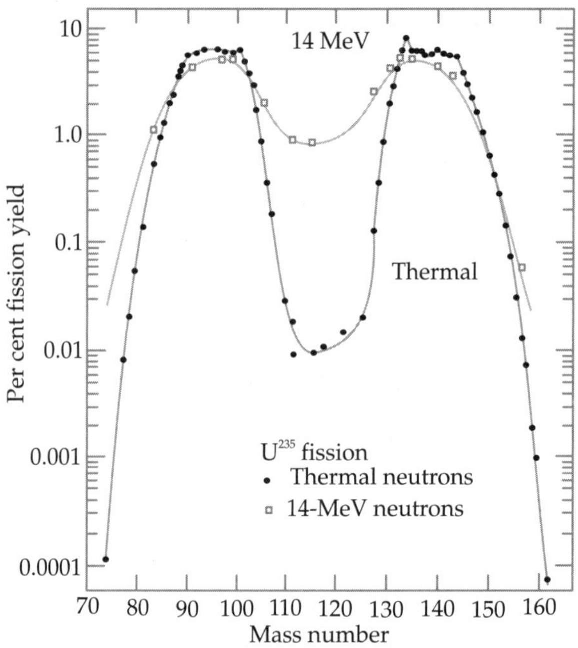

Figure 4.13: *Mass distribution of fission products shows that fission fragments do not have the same mass*

The outstanding feature of this curve is its double peak. The curve shows that the possibility of fission resulting in equal or nearly equal fragments is extremely low. There are two predominant groups of fission fragments (with $A \sim 90$ and $A \sim 140$) for fission with thermal neutrons. The average ratio of the masses of the two fragments is $2:3$. This asymmetry in mass distribution is a unique feature of low-energy fission. However, double peaks gradually disappear with high-energy neutrons, and thus, fission into two fragments of equal mass may be produced with high-energy neutrons.

The mass distribution of fission fragments may be obtained from the distribution of their kinetic energy.

As neutrons carry very little momentum, compared to the fragments, conservation of linear momentum gives $m_1 v_1 = m_2 v_2$, where m_1 and m_2 are the masses of the fission fragments and v_1 and v_2 are their respective velocities. The nucleus undergoing fission is assumed to be at rest. Thus, the ratio of their kinetic energies is

$$\frac{E_2}{E_1} = \frac{m_2 v_2^2}{m_1 v_1^2} = \frac{m_1}{m_2}$$

From the observed energy distribution of fission fragments, it has been found that the average kinetic energy of the lighter nucleus is approximately 98 MeV and that of the heavier nucleus is 66 MeV. Thus

$$\frac{m_1}{m_2} = \frac{66}{98} = 0.67$$

Thus, the ratio of the most probable masses is found to be consistent with the ratio of the kinetic energy of the fragments.

4.3.2 Energy Released in Fission

Like other nuclear disintegration processes, energy is released due to a decrease in mass in the reaction. Consider the reaction

$$n + {}^{235}_{92}\mathrm{U} \longrightarrow {}^{236}_{92}\mathrm{U}^* \longrightarrow {}^{141}_{56}\mathrm{Ba} + {}^{92}_{36}\mathrm{Kr} + 3n + Q$$

Mass of ${}^{235}_{92}\mathrm{U} = 235.04392$ u. Mass of $n = 1.00866$ u. Total mass of ${}^{235}_{92}\mathrm{U}$ and n is 236.05258 u. Total mass of the fission fragments =235.836085 u.

In fission, the difference in mass (≈ 0.216495) is converted to energy (201.66 MeV) and released.

We can also estimate the energy released in fission from the BE curve[9].

For a heavy nucleus with $A \sim 235$, the binding energy per nucleon is ~ 7.6 MeV, which is smaller than that of medium-sized nuclei. If the ${}^{235}_{92}\mathrm{U}$ nucleus splits into two medium-sized nuclei, then total BE increases from 235×7.6 to 235×8.5 MeV. Thus, to conserve energy, $235 \times 0.9 \approx 210$ MeV amount of energy will be released per fission of a single ${}^{235}_{92}\mathrm{U}$ nucleus.

Estimation from semi-empirical mass formula: We can also estimate the energy released in fission using the semi-empirical mass formula. From Eq. (2.8), we get

$$M({}^{A}_{Z}X) = Zm_H + (A-Z)m_n - a_v A + a_s A^{2/3} + a_c \frac{Z^2}{A^{1/3}} + a_{\text{asym}} \frac{(N-Z)^2}{A} - \delta$$

Let us consider a simple case of symmetric fission, where a parent nucleus breaks into two identical nuclei

$$M(A,Z) \longrightarrow M\left(\frac{A}{2},\frac{Z}{2}\right) + M\left(\frac{A}{2},\frac{Z}{2}\right)$$

Neglecting the the quantum-mechanical terms, namely, the asymmetry term and the pairing terms, we can write the semi-empirical mass formula for $M\left(\frac{A}{2},\frac{Z}{2}\right)$ as

$$M\left(\frac{A}{2},\frac{Z}{2}\right) \approx \frac{Z}{2}m_H + \frac{A-Z}{2}m_n - a_v\frac{A}{2} + a_s\left(\frac{A}{2}\right)^{2/3} + a_c\frac{(Z/2)^2}{(A/2)^{1/3}}$$

Thus, the energy released is $\triangle E = \left[M(A,Z) - 2\times M\left(\frac{A}{2},\frac{Z}{2}\right)\right]c^2$

$$\begin{aligned} &= a_s A^{2/3}(1-2^{1/3}) + a_c\frac{Z^2}{A^{1/3}}(1-\frac{1}{2^{2/3}}) = -0.26a_s A^{2/3} + 0.37a_c\frac{Z^2}{A^{1/3}} \\ &\approx -4.37A^{2/3} + 0.27\frac{Z^2}{A^{1/3}}\ \text{MeV} \end{aligned} \tag{4.45}$$

For $A = 236$ and $Z = 92$, Eq. (4.45) gives $\triangle E \approx 200$ MeV.

[9]Please see the discussion on the BE curve in Chapter 1.

Illustrative Example 4.16:

A nuclear reactor using $^{235}_{92}U$ is expected to operate at a power level of 250 MW. If the energy released per fission is $\approx$ 200 MeV, calculate the consumption of uranium per second.

Solution Energy released from the fission of one nucleus ≈ 200 MeV $= 3.2 \times 10^{-11}$ J.

Energy released from the fission[10] of 1 g of $^{235}_{92}U$ is $\dfrac{6.023 \times 10^{23}}{235} \times 3.2 \times 10^{-11}$ J $= 8.2 \times 10^{10}$ J.

To generate 250×10^6 J of energy, the amount of $^{235}_{92}U$ required is $\dfrac{250 \times 10^6}{8.2 \times 10^{10}} = 3.046 \times 10^{-3}$ g. Thus, the consumption of $^{235}_{92}U$ required is 3.046×10^{-3} g/s.

4.3.3 Spontaneous Fission

From Eq. (4.45), the energy released in symmetric fission is

$$\triangle E \approx -4.37A^{2/3} + 0.27\frac{Z^2}{A^{1/3}} \text{ MeV}$$

Thus, the condition for spontaneous fission is $\triangle E > 0$ or $\dfrac{Z^2}{A} > 17$ (4.46)

Nuclei with $Z > 38$ and $A > 85$ satisfy this condition. However, it is quite rare for a nucleus with $Z \sim 38$ and $A \sim 86$ to undergo spontaneous fission. In fact, there are so many nuclei with $Z > 38$ and $A > 85$ that are stable; fission is actually detected for heavy nuclei. So, the condition Eq. (4.46) does not predict the entire picture. The spontaneous fission of such common elements does not take place because they are opposed by the potential barrier, as we will discuss presently.

The process of fission is very similar to α decay, where the α particle encounters a barrier at the time of emission. Immediately after formation, the fission fragments encounter the potential barrier inside the nucleus. It is the potential barrier that prevents the immediate splitting of the parent nucleus. Due to the large size of the fission fragments, the height of the potential barrier encountered by the fragments is very high. When two fragments of equal radius R just touch each other, the Coulomb potential is maximum, and given by

$$V_c = \frac{1}{4\pi\varepsilon_0}\frac{(Z/2)^2e^2}{2R} \tag{4.47}$$

For $A = 238$ and $Z = 92$, $V_c \sim 250$ MeV.

Figure 4.14 shows schematically the potential energy curve of the nuclear fragments. The potential energy of the two fragments is zero at infinity and increases as

[10] Energy released in the chemical process of burning of coal (CO_2) per atom of carbon is about 4 eV. Energy released in the burning of 1 kg of carbon is $\frac{6.023\times10^{23}\times10^3\times4\times1.6\times10^{-19}}{12} \approx 3.2 \times 10^7$ J. Thus, to produce 8.2×10^{10} J of energy, the amount of coal required is $\frac{8.2\times10^{10}}{3.2\times10^7} \approx 2.56 \times 10^3$ kg.

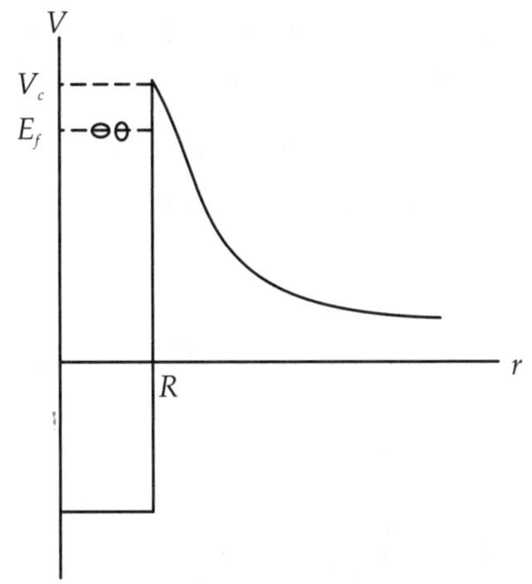

Figure 4.14: *Potential barrier opposing fission. V_c represents the maximum height of the barrier and E_f is the energy released in fission.*

$\frac{1}{r}$ when they are brought closer. It is maximum when the fragments are just touching each other. When the separation is less than their inter-particle distance, the nuclear force becomes dominant. Inside the nucleus, the fragments may be formed instantaneously with the release of energy $E_f = \triangle E$, which is smaller than the height of the Coulomb barrier. As a result, the fragments are prevented from escaping the nucleus.

Let us consider the following situations:

$E_f > V_c$: In this case, the nucleus is clearly unstable.

$E_f < V_c$: In this case, the energy released in fission is not sufficient to overcome the potential barrier. In this situation, tunnelling may occur, but the probability of tunnelling of massive fragments is extremely low. Therefore, *we need to supply ($V_c - E_f$) amount of energy to initiate fission. This minimum energy required to start fission is called the activation energy and its value is typically ~ 6 MeV for nuclei with $A \sim 240$.*

$E_f \ll V_c$: In this case, the probability of spontaneous fission is extremely small and a large amount of energy is required for fission. Such nuclei are relatively stable.

Stability condition: The condition for stability is $V_c - E_f \geq 0$,

where $V_c = \dfrac{1}{4\pi\varepsilon_0}\dfrac{(Z/2)^2e^2}{2R_0(A/2)^{1/3}} \approx 0.189\dfrac{Z^2}{A^{1/3}}$ and $E_F = -4.37A^{2/3} + 0.27\dfrac{Z^2}{A^{1/3}}$.

Thus, $V_c - E_f \geq 0$ gives $\dfrac{Z^2}{A} \leq 54$.

Thus, $\dfrac{Z^2}{A} \approx 54$ is the stability limit against spontaneous symmetric fission.

The values of V_c and E_f used above are not exact. Only approximate values have been considered to illustrate the basic features of the problem. The assumption that a heavy nucleus splits into two equal fragments is also not very realistic. At the distance $r = R$ shown in Fig. 4.14, where two fragments touch each other, the potential deviates from Coulomb's law because of the influence of nuclear forces (actually, at this point, the fragments do not remain strictly spherical). The important point to note here is that this very crude calculation indicates that the parameter $\frac{Z^2}{A}$, which determines stability against spontaneous fission, depends solely on the Coulomb energy and the surface energy.

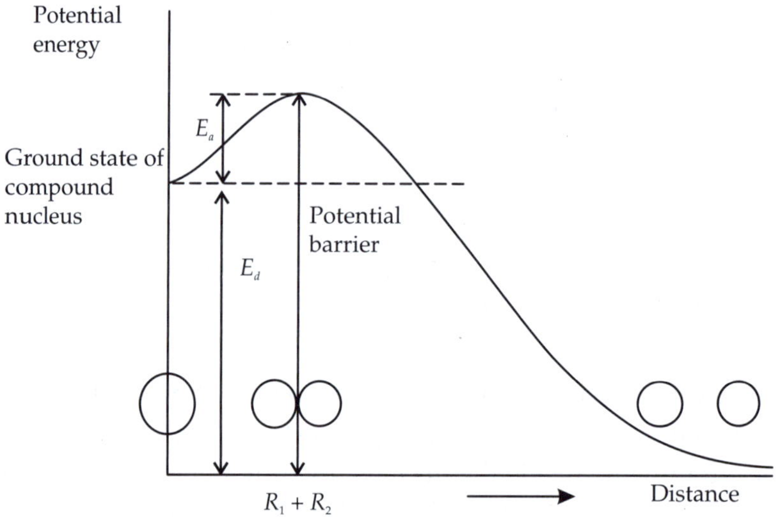

Figure 4.15: *A realistic potential barrier opposing spontaneous fission. The energy difference E_a represents the activation energy.*

A much better estimation of $\frac{Z^2}{A}$ can be obtained, as shown by Bohr and Wheeler, by considering the oscillations of a drop of incompressible fluid under the combined action of the surface and Coulomb forces. The Coulomb barrier for heavy nuclei based on the liquid-drop model is shown schematically in Fig. 4.15. It shows that the potential energy curve passes through its maximum at a certain value of separation (r). In Fig. 4.15, E_d is the ground state of the compound nucleus when the target captures a neutron (that is, the initial energy of the drop excluding the excitation energy due to the captured neutron). The energy required for a nuclear drop to undergo fission, that is, the activation energy (E_a) is $V_c - E_d$.

4.3.4 Bohr–Wheeler Theory of Nuclear Fission

In this theory proposed in 1939, the nucleus is assumed to be a sphere, like a drop of liquid of constant density. The forces in the nucleus are the short-range attractive force among the nucleons and the repulsive Coulomb force among the protons. The attractive nuclear force can be compared to the surface tension force of liquids. The shape of a charged nucleus depends on the balance between the short-range attractive surface tension forces and the repulsive Coulomb forces. If the nucleus is excited by capturing a thermal neutron, the nucleons present within the nucleus are set into oscillations, as a result of which the shape of the nucleus is distorted. Since the surface energy is minimum for a sphere, the surface tension force will tend to restore the original shape of the drop, while the Coulomb force favours deformation. If the deformation is sufficiently large, Coulomb repulsion between the elongated portions of the drop can produce a two-lobe structure that can push the lobes further apart, causing complete splitting of the nucleus. Figure 4.16 illustrates the different stages of deformation leading to two fission fragments.

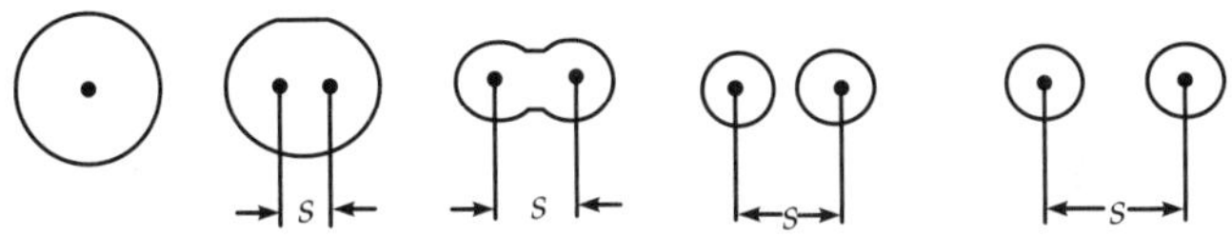

Figure 4.16: *Different stages of deformation leading to fission*

A simple classical calculation may be performed to analyse the stability of a liquid drop under any external perturbation. Let us assume that a spherical liquid drop of radius R deforms very slightly under some external perturbation to an ellipsoid. Since the drop is assumed to be incompressible[11], the volume of the sphere will be equal to that of the ellipsoid. The semi-major axis a and the semi-minor axis b can be written in terms of a small parameter of deformation ε as

$$a = R(1+\varepsilon), \quad b = \frac{R}{(1+\varepsilon)1/2}$$

Such a choice satisfies the incompressibility condition of the nucleus as the volume of the liquid drop remains unchanged

$$V = \frac{4}{3}\pi ab^2 = \frac{4}{3}\pi R^3 \tag{4.48}$$

Since the volume remains unchanged, the volume energy will be the same for both the original and the deformed liquid drops. However, the surface energy and Coulomb energy will be different for the two cases. It can be shown that the surface energy changes from $a_sA^{2/3} \longrightarrow a_sA^{2/3}\left(1+\frac{2}{5}\varepsilon^2\right)$ while the Coulomb energy changes as $a_c\frac{Z^2}{A^{1/3}} \longrightarrow a_c\frac{Z^2}{A^{1/3}}\left(1-\frac{1}{5}\varepsilon^2\right)$.

Thus, the surface energy increases due to deformation, while the Coulomb term decreases with increasing ε. The change in energy due to deformation is therefore

$$\triangle E = \left[a_sA^{2/3}\left(1+\frac{2}{5}\varepsilon^2\right) - a_sA^{2/3}\right] + \left[a_c\frac{Z^2}{A^{1/3}}\left(1-\frac{1}{5}\varepsilon^2\right) - a_c\frac{Z^2}{A^{1/3}}\right]$$

$$\triangle E = \frac{2}{5}a_sA^{2/3}\varepsilon^2 - \frac{1}{5}a_c\frac{Z^2}{A^{1/3}}\varepsilon^2 \tag{4.49}$$

[11]This is justified because the density of the nucleus is constant.

The approximate behaviour of the potential barrier[12] for different values of the parameter $\frac{Z^2}{A}$ have been shown in Fig. 4.17. It shows that the activation energy is less for a nucleus with higher $\frac{Z^2}{A}$. Thus, the nucleus with $\frac{Z^2}{A} = 24$ (with $A = 160, Z = 60$) is more stable than ${}^{235}_{92}$U with $\frac{Z^2}{A} \approx 36$.

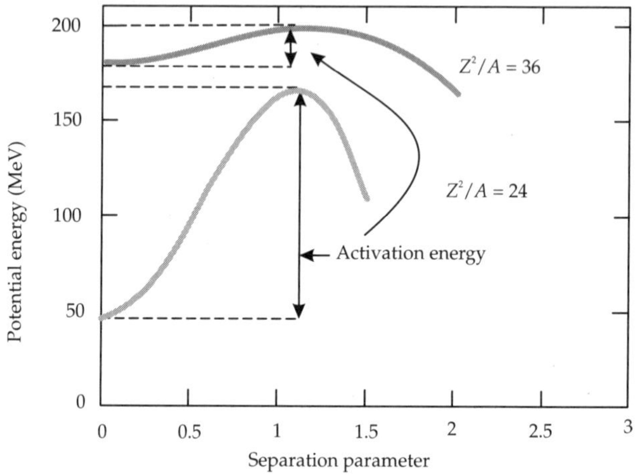

Figure 4.17: *Activation energy for medium and heavy nuclei*

If the second term on the right-hand side of Eq. (4.49) exceeds the first term, then the disruptive effect of repulsive force among the protons will exceed the cohesive effect of attractive surface tension, and the nucleus will then tend to split into fragments. Thus, the *condition that the nucleus will be unstable against fission* is

$$\frac{1}{5}a_c\frac{Z^2}{A^{1/3}} > \frac{2}{5}a_sA^{2/3} \quad \text{or} \quad \frac{Z^2}{A} > \frac{2a_s}{a_c} \approx 47 \tag{4.50}$$

A spherical nucleus will be stable if $\frac{Z^2}{A} < 47$. Figure 4.18 shows the variation of $\frac{Z^2}{A}$ as a function of A. It shows that the elements up to ${}^{235}_{92}$U at least are stable by the criterion given in Eq. (4.50).

Illustrative Example 4.17: If the charge of the proton were doubled!

If the electric charge of the proton were doubled, what would be the heaviest stable nucleus?

Solution For the heaviest stable nucleus, $\frac{Z^2}{A} \approx 47$. If the charge of the proton was doubled, the condition would be $\frac{Z^2}{A} \approx 12$.

[12]To plot the potential energy of the drop, only the first two terms of the expansion are considered. It is not very accurate but has been given only to show the variation of the activation energy with $\frac{Z^2}{A}$.

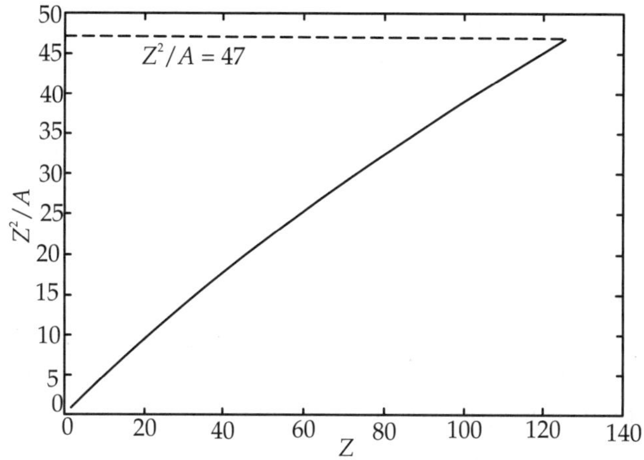

Figure 4.18: *Plot of* $\frac{Z^2}{A}$ *vs A*

As $Z \approx \dfrac{A}{2}$, Z will be ≈ 24; the heaviest stable nucleus would have $Z \approx 24$ and $A \approx 48$.

Illustrative Example 4.18: Fissionability of ^{235}U

Give a simple explanation for why thermal neutrons cause fission in ^{235}U but not in ^{238}U.

Solution The minimum energy required to induce fission is the activation energy, which is supplied to the nucleus in the form of the kinetic energy of the thermal neutron.

Consider the reaction $n + ^{235}\text{U} \longrightarrow ^{236}\text{U}^*$. The excitation energy for the compound nucleus is

$$\begin{aligned}\triangle E &= M(^{236}\text{U}^*) - M(^{236}\text{U}) = M(^{235}\text{U}) + M_n - M(^{236}\text{U}) \\ &= 235.043924 + 1.008665 - 236.045563 = 6.54 \text{ MeV}\end{aligned}$$

The activation energy[13] of $^{235}\text{U} = 6.2$ MeV.

Now, consider the reaction $n + ^{238}\text{U} \longrightarrow ^{239}\text{U}^*$. The excitation energy for the compound nucleus is

$$\triangle E \;=\; M(^{238}\text{U}) + M_n - M(^{239}\text{U}) = 238.050785 + 1.008665 - 239.054290 = 4.81 \text{ MeV}$$

The activation energy of $^{238}\text{U} = 6.6$ MeV. In ^{235}U, the excitation energy is considerably larger than the activation energy, and thus, it is expected to undergo fission with thermal neutrons, which is consistent with its large observed cross-section in the thermal region (Table 4.1). On the other hand, in ^{238}U, the excitation energy is smaller than the activation energy, and the nucleus will not undergo fission with thermal neutrons.

[13]Krane, KS. 1987. *Inroductory Nuclear Physics, Third Edition.* John Wiley & Sons.

Table 4.1: *Fission with thermal neutrons*

Nuclide	Activation energy (in MeV)	Excitation energy (in MeV)	Cross-section (in barn)
$^{235}_{92}U$	6.2	6.5	584 ± 1
$^{238}_{92}U$	6.6	4.8	$(2.7 \pm 0.3) \times 10^{-6}$

Illustrative Example 4.19: Fissionability of ^{235}U and the pairing term

Why does the pairing term make a negative contribution to the energy liberated when a neutron is captured by ^{238}U and a positive contribution in the case of ^{235}U? What are the practical consequences of this situation?

Solution In Illustrative Example 4.18, we saw that the thermal neutrons cause fission in ^{235}U but not in ^{238}U. The difference in fissionability is due to the difference between their excitation energies, which can be explained in terms of the pairing energy of the semi-empirical mass formula.

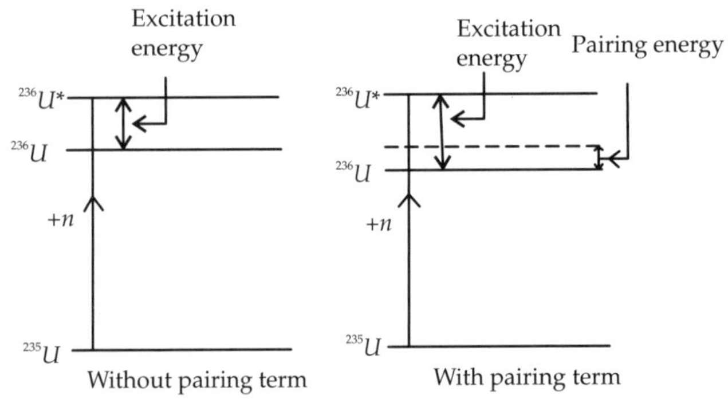

Figure 4.19: *Contribution of pairing energy in* ^{236}U

Figure 4.19 illustrates the role of the pairing term in calculating the excitation energy of ^{236}U. In the ^{235}U nucleus, which contains an odd number of nucleons, the pairing term is zero. On the other hand, ^{236}U is an even nucleus and the pairing term δ is positive, implying that the binding energy of ^{236}U is greater than that of its value without pairing by δ. Thus, the pairing term decreases the ground state energy of ^{236}U by δ and, as a result, the excitation energy is increased by δ over what it would have been without the pairing term.

The importance of pairing term in ^{239}U is explained in Fig. 4.20. In this case, the pairing term does not contribute to the ^{239}U nucleus, which contains an odd number of nucleons. However, the pairing term lowers the ground state of ^{238}U (thereby inreasing the binding energy) by δ. As a result, the energy of the combined state of neutrons and ^{238}U is lowered by δ. The excitation energy is thus reduced by δ relative to its value without pairing.

From this, we can conclude that the excitation energy of ^{236}U increases by δ due to pairing, while the excitation energy of ^{238}U decreases by δ. Thus, the difference in

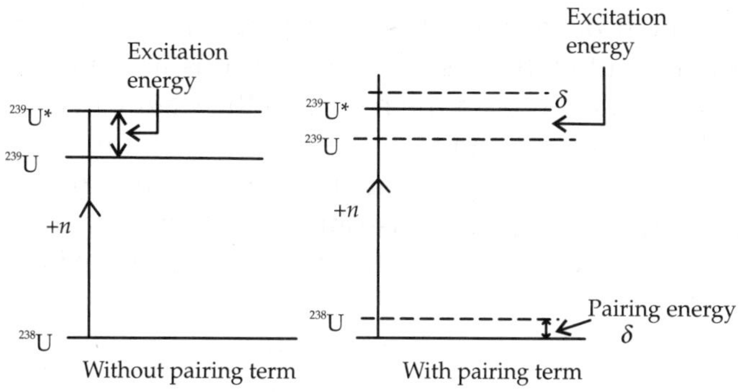

Figure 4.20: *Contribution of pairing energy in* ^{239}U

excitation energy is $\approx 2\delta \approx 2 \times 0.56$ MeV, which accounts properly for the observed result.

4.3.5 Emission of Neutrons in Fission

Fission results in two massive fragments that are extremely rich in neutrons; in fact, they have too many neutrons to be stable. For example, consider a typical neutron-induced fission, where a nucleus of $^{235}_{92}$U splits into two fragments, with $A \sim 95$ and $A \sim 140$.

$$n + ^{235}_{92}\text{U} \longrightarrow ^{236}_{92}\text{U}^* \longrightarrow ^{140}_{55}\text{Cs} + ^{95}_{37}\text{Rb}$$

The fission fragments have $\frac{Z}{A} \sim 0.39$, which is equal to that of the original nucleus, while the most stable nuclei in the range $A \sim 100$–150 have $\frac{Z}{A} \sim 0.41$. Therefore, the fission fragments are neutron-rich and lie above the stability curve, as shown in Fig. 4.21.

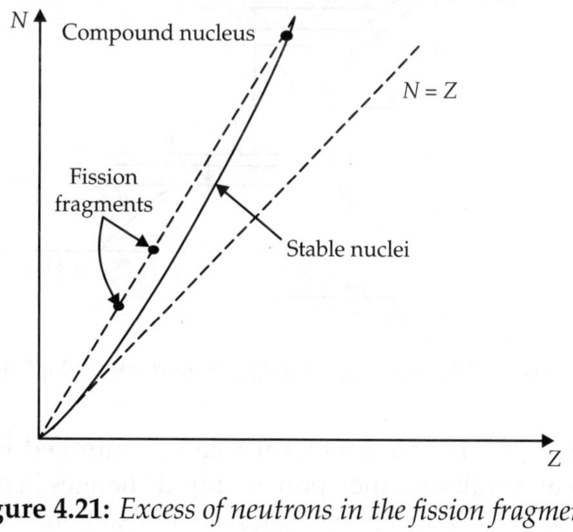

Figure 4.21: *Excess of neutrons in the fission fragments*

Being extremely neutron-rich, the fission fragments emit one or two neutrons at the instant of fission (within 10^{-16} s). These neutrons are known as **prompt neutrons** and their number depends on the nature of the fragments. It has been experimentally observed that, on an average, 2.48 neutrons are emitted per fission of ${}^{235}_{92}$U with thermal neutrons. The energy distribution of these neutrons is approximately Maxwellian. The range of the energy distribution is 0.05 MeV to 17.0 MeV, with an average of about 2 MeV. Thus, in fission, the neutrons are emitted as **fast neutrons**.

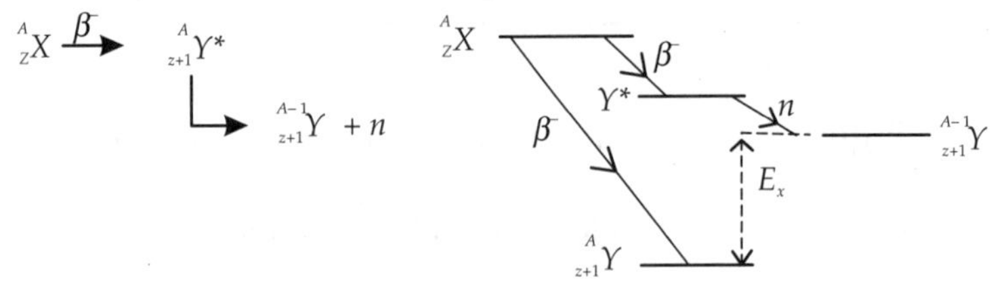

Figure 4.22: *A schematic diagram showing the emission of delayed neutrons*

The neutron-rich fission fragments may reduce their neutron number by β decay. Following β decay, the nucleus may be in the excited state, and if the excitation energy is larger than the neutron separation energy, neutrons will be emitted. The emitted neutrons are then called **delayed neutrons**. The emission of delayed neutrons is explained schematically in Fig. 4.22. Figure. 4.23 shows that the ^{87}Br nucleus decays to ^{87}Kr by emitting β particles. Some of the energy levels of ^{87}Kr are large enough for subsequent neutron decay. The emission of such neutrons is delayed by the half-life of ^{87}Br ($\sim$ 55 s) relative to the emission of the prompt neutrons.

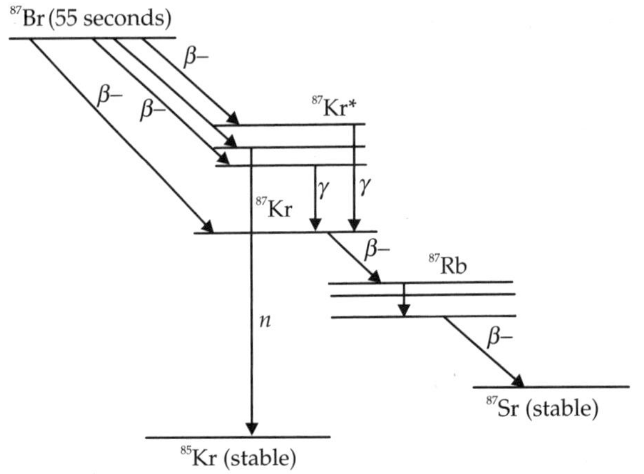

Figure 4.23: *Emission of delayed neutrons from* ^{87}Br

The delayed neutrons play an important role in controlled fission. In a reactor operating near critical conditions, they prevent rapid changes in neutron density and thus help to maintain the self-sustained fission chain reaction.

4.3.6 Reaction at High Energy

Nuclear reactions at energies higher than ~ 50 MeV are quite different in character from those at lower energies. When a particle with such energy strikes a target nucleus, a few nucleons may be knocked out, leaving the daughter in the excited state. The nucleus then splits into different nucleons or into various groups or fragments. This process is referred to as **spallation**.

A typical process of spallation was reported by Batzel and Seaborg[14] in the year 1950. In the course of the detailed investigation of the spallation of copper by the bombardment of protons of energy of 60–70 MeV, they observed a reaction

$$p + {}^{63}_{29}\mathrm{Cu} \longrightarrow {}^{38}_{17}\mathrm{Cl} + {}^{25}_{13}\mathrm{Al} + {}^{1}_{0}n$$

As two fragments larger than ${}^{4}_{2}\mathrm{He}$ are emitted, the reaction may be termed fission. The reaction is endoergic and has a threshold value of about 50 MeV. The cross-section of this reaction is about $10^{-32}\,\mathrm{cm}^2$. The cross-section increases rapidly with increasing energy of the protons.

They also investigated another such process: $p + {}^{63}_{29}\mathrm{Cu} \longrightarrow {}^{24}_{11}\mathrm{Na} + {}^{39}_{19}\mathrm{K} + {}^{1}_{0}n$.

4.3.7 Utilisation of Fission Energy

In fission, emission of neutrons along with a large amount of energy is significant not only from a theoretical point of view, but also from a practical perspective. The neutrons emitted in fission can be slowed down and may be used to further initiate fission in the neighbouring nuclei. In this way, a self-sustaining fission reaction may be developed.

Chain reaction: During the fission of ^{235}U with a thermal neutron, an enormous amount of energy along with a few neutrons is released. Some of these neutrons may now become available to initiate the second generation of fission with the ^{235}U nuclei, accompanied by liberation of more energy and the release of new neutrons. These neutrons will again cause fission of the third generation, and so on. This process is cumulative; thus, under favourable conditions, a self-sustaining fission reaction or *chain reaction* will occur in ^{235}U as soon as any one of the nuclei is disrupted by a thermal neutron.

On an average, it has been found that 2.5 prompt neutrons are produced per fission of ^{235}U by a thermal neutron. These neutrons can ideally initiate fission in 2.5 nuclei, leading to the production of 2.5^2 neutrons, which in turn will again cause fission of the third generation, and so on. After the n-th generation, the number of neutrons produced will be 2.5^n, assuming no neutron loss. The number of uranium atoms in 1 kg of ^{235}U is $\sim \dfrac{6.023\times 10^{23}\times 10^3}{235}$. Setting $2.5^n = \dfrac{6.023\times 10^{23}\times 10^3}{235}$, we obtain $n\log 2.5 = 24.398 \Rightarrow n \approx 60$.

[14]Batzel, RE and Seaborg, GT.1950. *Fission of Medium Weight Elements.* https://escholarship.org/uc/item/2r6137k6

Thus, only 60 fission steps are required to produce enough neutrons to completely disrupt 1 kg of ^{235}U. The velocities of thermal neutrons are such that the time required for the fission of each step is about 10^{-8} s. Therefore, the complete disruption of 1 kg of ^{235}U will take a time of $\sim 60 \times 10^{-8}$ s or ~ 1 μs. Earlier, we had calculated that the complete fission of 1 kg of ^{235}U would yield an energy of about 2.3×10^7 kWh. Dissipation of this enormous energy in a very short time of $\sim 10^{-6}$ s would result in a violent explosion.

The principle of self-sustained fission chain reaction was first realised in practice by the famous physicist, Enrico Fermi. He and his colleagues built the first nuclear reactor in 1942 at the University of Chicago during the Second World War as a prelude to the construction and detonation of the first atom bomb.

For the peaceful use of the enormous energy released in fission, rather than for the manufacture of bombs, it is necessary to control the rate at which the energy is released. The problem of controlling the energy available from fission has been solved in the **nuclear reactor** (also called a **nuclear pile**). The nuclear reactor is basically a device where the fissionable materials, called the **nuclear fuel**, are arranged together with the other materials acting as **moderators** and controlling devices in a structure so that a self-sustained fission chain reaction may be carried out in a controlled way.

In order to determine the feasibility of the fission chain reaction, it is extremely important to know the number of neutrons emitted in a particular fission reaction. For practical purposes, however, this knowledge is not sufficient. A neutron produced in a fission process may undergo various types of interactions with matter. Some of these neutrons may undergo inelastic scattering or radiative capture or may simply leave the reactor. These effects may seriously affect the availibility of neutrons for further fission, and hence, render the chain reaction impossible.

The characteristic parameter that determines the possibility of a self-sustained chain reaction is the **neutron multiplication factor** or **neutron reproduction factor**, usually denoted by the parameter k, which is defined as

$$k = \frac{\text{The number of neutrons causing fission in one generation}}{\text{The number of neutrons in the immediately preceding generation}}$$

Suppose n number of neutrons cause fission in any generation and generate m number of fresh neutrons. If, out of these m neutrons, only N (say) number of neutrons is available for fission in the next generation. Then

$$k = \frac{N}{n} \tag{4.51}$$

If $k = 1$, the pile is said to be *critical* where the self-sustained chain reaction will proceed uninterruptedly at a fixed rate. The reactor will thus generate fixed power.

For $k < 1$, the pile is *subcritical*. In this case, the rate of fission reaction decreases gradually and finally the chain reaction stops after a few generations. Thus, a self-sustaining chain reaction is impossible for this case.

If $k > 1$ even by a very small amount, the pile is *supercritical* and the rate of fission increases from one generation to the next. Since successive generations occur very rapidly, a large number of neutrons along with an enormous amount of energy will be released in a very short period of time. Thus, the system will have explosive tendencies. In the atomic bomb, k is larger than 1 by a considerable amount. However, in a nuclear reactor, k must be controlled to be unity or marginally greater than unity.

Neutron cycle and four-factor formula: It is essential that in a nuclear reactor, the neutron multiplication factor k must be controlled to be unity or slightly larger than unity so that a self-sustained chain reaction takes place at a fixed rate in an uninterrupted way. We now consider different factors on which the multiplication factor k depends.

Suppose the fissile material or the fuel element of a nuclear reactor is natural uranium. It is readily available in considerable quantity and contains both the abundant isotope ^{238}U (99.3%) and the rarer isotope ^{235}U (0.7%). A few spontaneous fission reactions occur in this element with the release of neutrons. The neutrons produced in the process will undergo one of the following processes:

1. Further fission of the uranium nuclei:
   (a) The neutrons (with energy larger than the threshold energy for fission of ^{238}U) may be absorbed by ^{238}U to cause further fission (fast fission).
   (b) The neutrons after being slowed down by the moderator to thermal energy may cause fission in ^{235}U.
2. The neutrons may be captured by uranium without any fission (mainly radiative capture reaction).
3. The neutrons may be absorbed by other materials present in the assembly (for example, moderator, control materials, etc.).
4. The neutrons may escape from the surface (leakage).

The neutrons emitted by fission begin their journey as fast neutrons and, through several processes, get ready for further fission. This is referred to **neutron cycle**. The fate of thermal neutrons from one generation to the next is shown schematically in Fig. 4.24.

To controll k properly, a favourable balance between the process (1) listed above and the others is essential. For an infinte reactor (namely, a reactor of very large size) the leakage of neutrons from the surface is negligible. In this case, the multiplication factor is denoted as k_∞. To arrive at those factors determining the multiplication factor k, a simplified theory was proposed by Fermi[15] (see also Fig. 4.24).

Let us consider the absorption of n thermal neutrons in ^{235}U to produce fission in an infinite reactor using natural uranium as fuel. Let the number of fast neutrons produced per fission be ν. The expected number of fast neutrons emitted as a result of fission with thermal neutrons in n nuclei of ^{235}U is thus $n\nu$. However, the actual number is slightly less. A few thermal neutrons will be captured by both ^{235}U and ^{238}U (or others) without any fission (mostly by radiative capture $[n, \gamma]$ reaction). Let σ_f and σ_a be, respectively, the cross-section for fission with thermal neutrons and the cross-section for other absorptive processes for the thermal neutron. The relative

[15]Fermi, E. 1947. Elementary Theory of the Chain-reacting Pile. *Science*, 105:27.

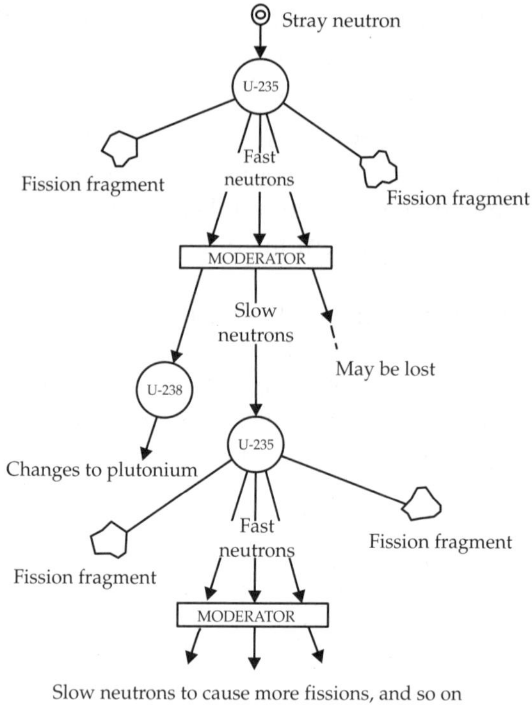

Figure 4.24: *Nuclear chain reaction*

probability for a thermal neutron to cause fission is $\dfrac{\sigma_f}{\sigma_f + \sigma_a}$ and the average number of fast neutrons produced for each fission is $\eta = \nu \dfrac{\sigma_f}{\sigma_f + \sigma_a}$.

Therefore, the average number of fast neutrons emitted as a result of fission with thermal neutrons in n nuclei of ^{235}U is $n\eta$.

Some fast neutrons are also produced due to fast fission of some ^{238}U nuclei (process 1(a)). Thus, the number of fast neutrons produced in one generation is little higher than $n\eta$. Now, we define the **fast fission factor (ε)** as

$$\varepsilon = \frac{\text{Number of fast neutrons produced by all fission reactions}}{\text{Number of fast neutrons generated by thermal fission reactions}}$$

Therefore, the total number of fast neutrons generated is $n\eta\varepsilon$. ε is usually ~ 1.03.

The fast neutrons produced by all fission of reactions are slowed down to thermal energies by a suitable moderator[16](such as graphite). The thermalised neutrons can then initiate fission in ^{235}U. The moderators reduce the kinetic energy of the fast neutrons, but will not absorb them. However, even with the most favourable arrangement of fuel and moderator, some neutrons will be absorbed by ^{238}U (radiation capture). Thus, some of the fast neutrons will simply be lost and the neutrons that

[16]The lightest nucleus to which neutrons transfer the largest possible energy in elastic collision is the best choice for a moderator. Carbon is a reasonable choice as it is solid, inexpensive and easy to handle.

escape radiation capture will finally be slowed down to thermal energies. Now, we define the **resonance escape probability** (**p**) as

$$p = \frac{\text{Number of neutrons that escape resonance capture (thermalised neutrons)}}{\text{Number of fast neutrons that have begun to slow down}}$$

Therefore, the number of thermal neutrons available for the second generation is $n\eta\varepsilon p$. Of these $n\nu\varepsilon p$ thermal neutrons, only a fraction (f) is absorbed by the ^{235}U present. This fraction f, called the **thermal utilisation factor**, is defined as

$$f = \frac{\text{Number of thermal neutrons absorbed in fuel}}{\text{Number of thermal neutrons absorbed in all reactor materials}}$$

Thus, the total number of thermal neutrons absorbed in fuel is $n\eta\varepsilon pf$. The reproduction factor or the multiplication factor for an infinite reactor is

$$k_\infty = \frac{n\eta\varepsilon pf}{n} = \eta\varepsilon pf \tag{4.52}$$

For a natural uranium and graphite pile, the estimated value of k_∞ is about 1.11.

For an actual reactor of finite size, Eq. (4.52) needs to be corrected again by considering the leakage of neutrons from the surface. The leakage both of fast and of thermal neutrons must be considered. If l_f and l_t are the fractions of fast neutrons and thermal neutrons, respectively, that leak out during the process of slowing, then the complete formula for k is

$$k = \eta\varepsilon pf(1-l_t)(1-l_f) \tag{4.53}$$

For an infinite reactor, there is no leakage, and thus, $l_f = 0$ and $l_t = 0$. The schematic diagram showing the different processes[17] by which fission product neutrons produce further fission material is presented in Fig. 4.25.

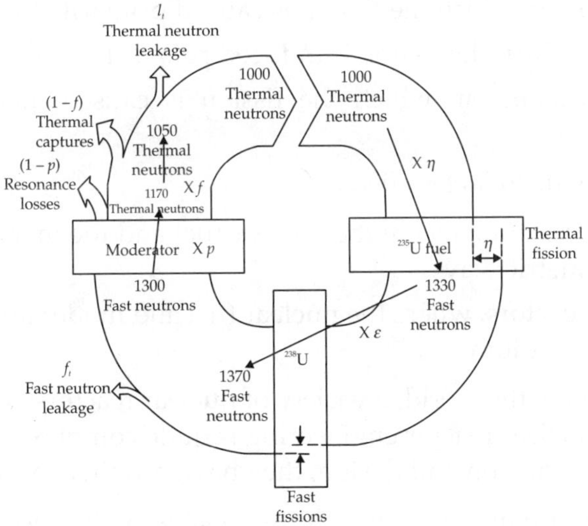

Figure 4.25: *Different processes in a single generation of neutrons. The different parameters used in the reactor cycle are* $\eta = 1.33, \varepsilon = 1.03, p = 0.9$ *and* $f = 0.9$.

[17]Krane, KS. 1987. *Introductory Nuclear Physics, Third Edition.* John Wiley & Sons.

Illustrative Example 4.20:

Given: Fission cross-section for ^{235}U with thermal neutron, $\sigma_f = 584\,b$ and cross-section for other absorptive processes with thermal neutrons, $\sigma_a = 97\,b$.

(a) If the average number of neutrons is $\nu = 2.5$, calculate η, the average number of fission neutrons produced per thermal neutron for ^{235}U.

(b) Also calculate η for natural uranium which contains 99.3% of ^{238}U and 0.7% of ^{235}U. Note that ^{238}U is not fissionable, and thus, $\sigma_f = 0$ but $\sigma_a = 2.75\,b$.

Solution (a) For ^{235}U, $\eta = \nu \dfrac{\sigma_f}{\sigma_f + \sigma_a} = 2.5 \times \dfrac{584}{584+97} = 2.08.$

(b) The effective cross-sections are $\sigma_f = \dfrac{0.7}{100}\sigma_f(^{235}\text{U}) + \dfrac{99.3}{100}\sigma_f(^{238}\text{U}) = 4.09\,b$

$$\sigma_b = \frac{0.7}{100}\sigma_b(^{235}\text{U}) + \frac{99.3}{100}\sigma_b(^{238}\text{U}) = 3.41\,b$$

Thus, $\eta = 2.5 \times \dfrac{4.09}{4.09+3.41} \approx 1.37.$

Check Progress 4.3: An unreflected thermal reactor consists of a lattice of uranium rods surrounded by graphite. The reactor is a cube of a linear dimension of 6.113 m, and the values of the appropriate constants are as follows: $\nu = 2.5$, $\eta = 1.308$, $\varepsilon = 1.0235$, $p = 0.8930$ and $f = 0.8832$. Calculate k.

Nuclear reactors: Reactors are generally used in research in the area of nuclear and solid state physics, and to generate power. The reactors are usually classified as:

(a) **Thermal reactors,** in which the fission is caused primarily by thermal neutrons

(b) **Fast reactors,** in which the fission is induced primarily by fast neutrons

(c) **Intermediate reactors,** in which the fission is caused mainly by epithermal neutrons

Nuclear reactors are further classified as:

(i) **Heterogeneous reactors,** where the nuclear fuel and the moderator are arranged in a regular geometric way

(ii) **Homogeneous reactors,** where the nuclear fuel and moderator are mixed to form a homogeneous medium

In different parts of the the world, a variety of nuclear reactors are currently in operation. The field of nuclear reactor engineering is quite complex. Though the reactors differ widely in construction and design, they have certain common features:

- *Fuel*: Any material that is in principle fissionable with thermal neutrons can be used as reactor fuel. The commonly used fuel element is natural uranium. It is readily available in considerable quantities and contains both the abundant isotope ^{238}U (99.3%) and the rarer isotope ^{235}U (0.7%). ^{239}Pu and ^{233}U are also used as the fuel element.

- *Moderator*: This is an essential component used to thermalise the neutrons (it may not be present in fast reactors). A good moderator must have a very low neutron absorption cross-section and must be capable of slowing down neutrons considerably. The commonly used moderators are water, heavy water, graphite, beryllium and beryllium oxide.
- *Reflector*: A reflector surrounding the core (consisting of fuel and moderators) reflects the neutrons leaking out of the reactor back into the core and thus helps to reduce the critical size of the reactor, with a resultant saving in fuel.
- *Containment vessel*: It is used to prevent the escape of radioactive fission products.
- *Coolant*: The fission chain reaction generates intense heat. Coolants help to remove heat from the core. Some conventional coolants are air, water and heavy water.
- *Shielding*: A reactor must be adequately shielded to prevent harmful radiations. It mainly prevents neutrons and γ rays from causing biological harm.
- *Control system*: Like any other power generating device, a nuclear reactor must have a control unit to control the power level and to ensure steady and smooth operation.
- *Emergency system*: It is designed to prevent accidents or any failure.

Breeder reactor: ^{235}U is the only fissionable species[18] occuring in nature that can be used to cause a self-sustained fission chain reaction in a nuclear reactor. As the process of fission proceeds, the fissile material is consumed and, moreover, neutrons that absorb the fission products are produced. As a result, the neutron reproduction factor (k) tends to decrease from its critial value till finally the reactor ceases to work. In a heterogeneous thermal reactor, it is thus essential that natural uranium (that contains only 0.7% of ^{235}U) be replenished from time to time because the fissile ^{235}U is used up. Thus, to obtain uninterrupted power on a large scale, the problem of availability of nuclear fuel is very serious one. To continue with the nuclear energy programme, to produce electrical power on a large scale, the continual depletion of the world's resources of natural uranium is not desirable. If all the reactors in the world used natural uranium as fuel, then within a few years the entire amount of natural uranium available would be exhausted. Thus, such reactors are not the long-term answer to the power problem. The answer is the *breeder reactor,* which produces not only a large amount of energy, but which will also end up with more fuel than it started with.

Thus, a breeder is a reactor that produces more fuel than it consumes. Materials that can be converted into thermally fissionable materials are said to be **fertile**. Fertile elements are abundant and relatively less expensive. A breeder reactor produces usable fissionable material from comparatively useless fertile material at a greater rate than the fissionable fuel is used up in the fissioning process.

---

[18]Fissionable materials are ^{235}U, ^{233}U, ^{239}Pu and ^{241}Pu (plutonium). Of these, only ^{235}U exists in nature, while the others (present perhaps billions of years ago) have decayed completely. Thus, if we want to use ^{233}U, ^{239}Pu and ^{241}Pu, we would need to produce them artificially.

The main objective of a breeder reactor is thus to convert *fertile material* into *fissile material*. The fertile material is converted into fissionable material when it absorbs a neutron, and thus, the fission process is continued. ^{232}Th, ^{238}U and ^{240}Pu are fertile materials and they can produce fissionable ^{233}U, ^{239}Pu and ^{241}Pu, respectively. Both ^{232}Th and ^{238}U exist in nature, while ^{240}Pu is produced artificially by neutron absorption by ^{239}Pu. For both ^{232}Th and ^{238}U, the process of conversion involves the capture of a neutron followed by two beta decays:

$$^{232}\text{Th} + n \rightarrow {}^{233}\text{Th} \xrightarrow{22 \text{ min}} {}^{233}\text{Pa} + \beta^- + \bar{\nu}$$

$$\hookrightarrow \xrightarrow{27 \text{ days}} {}^{233}\text{U} + \beta^- + \bar{\nu}$$

$$^{238}\text{U} + n \rightarrow {}^{239}\text{U} \xrightarrow{23 \text{ min}} {}^{239}Np + \beta^- + \bar{\nu}$$

$$\hookrightarrow \xrightarrow{2.3 \text{ days}} {}^{239}\text{Pu} + \beta^- + \bar{\nu}$$

Suppose a single neutron striking the nucleus of a fissionable material produces fission fragments along with free neutrons. The number of neutrons released varies, but on an average it is ~ 2.5 to 3.0. Since only one neutron is required to continue the fission chain reaction, the other freed neutrons can be used to produce new fissionable material. These excess neutrons may be absorbed by fertile material to produce new fissionable material, or absorbed non-productively in fission fragments or other materials, or simply escape from the reactor. While developing a breeder, it is therefore necessary to design a reactor in which most of the neutrons are absorbed by the fertile material present. A prerequisite to breeding is that η, the average number of fast neutrons produced for each fission reaction, must be greater than 2.

4.4 FUSION

The BE curve (Fig. 1.9) suggests another method as an alternative to fission, for obtaining energy, where lighter nuclei with less binding energy combine to form a more stable nucleus. The process of joining two lighter nuclei into a heavier nucleus is called fusion. Since the binding energy of the final nucleus formed is larger than the initial binding energies, energy is released. For example, consider a typical fusion process

$${}^1_1\text{H} + {}^1_0 n \longrightarrow {}^2_1\text{H}$$

Energy released is $1.007825 + 1.008665 - 2.014102 = 0.002388$ u $= 2.22$ MeV.

Consider another example where a helium nucleus is formed by the fusion of two deuterium nuclei.

$${}^2_1\text{H} + {}^2_1\text{H} \longrightarrow {}^4_2\text{He}$$

In this case, the energy released is ≈ 24 MeV.

The energy released in fusion is much less than the energy available during fission (~ 200 MeV). However, the fusion process is very important because *the energy released per unit mass is much larger in fusion than that in fission*. As a source of energy, fusion has several advantages over fission. For example, light nuclei are very easy to obtain and the end products of fusion are usually stable. There is, however, a very difficult problem to be solved in fusion. To fuse two nuclei, their mutual Coulomb repulsion must be overcome. Let us estimate the Coulomb barrier in a typical fusion process.

Illustrative Example 4.21: Problem of fusing two deuterium nuclei

Estimate the height of the Coulomb barrier when two deuterium nuclei fuse into helium. Also estimate the temperature required for the fusion.

Solution Both nuclei, being positively charged, repel each other. When two $^2_1$H nuclei touch each other, the Coulomb energy is maximum. Taking the radius of deuterium $R \sim 1$ fm, the maximum Coulomb energy becomes

$$V_c = \frac{1}{4\pi\varepsilon_0}\frac{e^2}{2R} \approx \frac{1.44}{2} \approx 0.72 \text{ MeV}$$

The only practical way to supply such huge energy to the nuclei is by raising their temperature to an excessively high value. The average kinetic energy (E) of a nucleus at temperature T is $\approx k_B T$, where k_B is the Boltzmann constant. Therefore, the required temperature will be

$$T_0 \approx \frac{0.72 \text{ MeV}}{8.617 \times 10^{-11} \text{ MeV/K}} \approx 8.35 \times 10^9 \text{ K}$$

This extremely high temperature is practically unattainable even in the interior of the Sun (which is $\sim 10^7$ K).

There are, however, two factors that make fusion possible at comparatively lower temperatures:

(a) Classically, fusion is possible if the supplied energy (E) is larger than the Coulomb barrier ($E > V_c$) or at temperature $T > T_0$. Quantum-mechanically, however, two nuclei can inter-penetrate even at energy less than V_c or at temperature $T < T_0$.

(b) Since the nuclei have a Maxwellian distribution of energy, a small fraction of the nuclei may have enough energy (much higher than the average energy) required for fusion. These nuclei with a larger amount of energy may fuse together by overcoming the potential barrier.

Another problem associated with the very high temperature ($\sim 10^9$ K) is that matter at such temperature is in a state of ionised plasma[19] (in the form of a mixture of nuclei and electrons). The constituents of plasma have very high kinetic energy and it is extremely difficult to confine them over a sufficiently long period of time.

The problem of confinement is relatively simpler in the *hydrogen bomb*, where enormous energy is liberated within a very short interval of time of $\sim 10^{-6}$ s. A hydrogen bomb is a self-sustained explosion (uncontrolled) reaction (thermonuclear) of transient type.

---

[19]Plasma is a state of matter where a considerable part of the atoms is ionised.

The main reactions that determine rapid liberation of a large amount of energy in a hydrogen bomb are

$$^{2}_{1}\mathrm{H}+^{2}_{1}\mathrm{H} \longrightarrow ^{3}_{1}\mathrm{H}+^{1}_{1}\mathrm{H}+Q(4.04\ \mathrm{MeV})$$

$$^{2}_{1}\mathrm{H}+^{2}_{1}\mathrm{H} \longrightarrow ^{3}_{2}\mathrm{He}+^{1}_{0}n+Q(3.26\ \mathrm{MeV})$$

Another possible process involves cyclic reactions, represented as

$$\begin{aligned} ^{2}_{1}\mathrm{H}+^{3}_{1}\mathrm{H} &\longrightarrow ^{4}_{2}\mathrm{He}+^{1}_{0}n+Q1(17.66\ \mathrm{MeV}) \\ Q2(4.7\ \mathrm{MeV})+^{4}_{2}\mathrm{He}+^{3}_{1}\mathrm{H} &\longleftarrow ^{6}_{3}\mathrm{Li}+^{1}_{0}n \end{aligned}$$

These two reactions keep the number of $^{1}_{0}n$ and $^{3}_{1}\mathrm{H}$ nuclei constant.

Illustrative Example 4.22: Reactions in a thermonuclear reactor

(a) Give three nuclear reactions usually considered for controlled thermonuclear fusion.
(b) Which has the largest cross-section?
(c) How is the resulting neutron used?

Solution (a) Reactions generally considered for thermonuclear fusion are

$$^{2}_{1}\mathrm{H}+^{2}_{1}\mathrm{H}\rightarrow ^{3}_{2}\mathrm{He}+n+3.25\ \mathrm{MeV}$$

$$^{2}_{1}\mathrm{H}+^{2}_{1}\mathrm{H}\rightarrow ^{3}_{1}\mathrm{H}+p+4.0\ \mathrm{MeV}$$

$$^{2}_{1}\mathrm{H}+^{3}_{1}\mathrm{H}\rightarrow ^{4}_{2}\mathrm{He}+n+17.6\ \mathrm{MeV}$$

(b) The cross-section of the last reaction is the largest.
(c) Neutrons resulting from the reactions can be used to instigate fission in a fission–fusion reactor.

4.4.1 Solar Fusion

Fusion requires very high temperatures, like that found at the core of the Sun. Thus, the main source of energy that powers the Sun is fusion. Among the various fusion reactions that may take place inside the Sun (and most of the stars), we will now discuss only two cycles[20].

Proton–proton cycle: The Sun consists primarily of 10^{56} atoms of hydrogen. Consequently, the basic source of energy in the Sun is fusion of hydrogen nuclei. This can take place through the proton–proton cycle, as shown below.

First step: $^{1}_{1}\mathrm{H}+^{1}_{1}\mathrm{H} \longrightarrow ^{2}_{1}\mathrm{H}+e^{+}+\nu_e+Q1$
The energy released is $Q1 = 2\times(1.007825)-(2.014102+2\times 0.00054858)\ \mathrm{u}\approx 0.42\ \mathrm{MeV}$.

Second step: $^{1}_{1}\mathrm{H}+^{2}_{1}\mathrm{H} \longrightarrow ^{3}_{2}\mathrm{He}+\gamma+Q2$

[20]To explain the glow of the Sun, Bethe in 1968 proposed two fusion cycles. These are the proton–proton cycle and the carbon–nitrogen cycle.

The energy released is $Q2 = 1.007825 + 2.014102 - 3.016029$ u ≈ 5.49 MeV.

Third step: ${}^3_2\text{He} + {}^3_2\text{He} \longrightarrow {}^4_2\text{He} + {}^1_1\text{H} + {}^1_1\text{H} + Q3$

The energy released is $Q3 = 2 \times 3.016029 - (4.002603 + 2 \times 1.007825)$ u ≈ 12.86 MeV.

The overall net reaction ($2 \times$ 1st type $+ 2 \times$ 2nd type $+$ 3rd type) is $4{}^1_1\text{H} \longrightarrow {}^4_2\text{He} + 2e^+ + 2\gamma + 2\nu_e + Q$ where $Q = 2Q1 + 2Q2 + Q3 \approx 24.68$ MeV.

For stars heavier than the Sun, another cycle of great importance is the **carbon–nitrogen–oxygen (CNO) cycle** of nuclear fusion. In this process, the carbon nucleus absorbs a proton, leading to

$$
\begin{aligned}
{}^{12}_{6}\text{C} + {}^1_1\text{H} &\longrightarrow {}^{13}_{7}\text{N} + \gamma + 1.95 \text{ MeV} \\
{}^{13}_{7}\text{N} &\longrightarrow {}^{13}_{6}\text{C} + e^+ + \nu_e + 1.20 \text{ MeV} \\
{}^{13}_{6}\text{C} + {}^1_1\text{H} &\longrightarrow {}^{14}_{7}\text{N} + \gamma + 7.55 \text{ MeV} \\
{}^{14}_{7}\text{N} + {}^1_1\text{H} &\longrightarrow {}^{15}_{8}\text{O} + \gamma + 7.34 \text{ MeV} \\
{}^{15}_{8}\text{O} &\longrightarrow {}^{15}_{7}\text{N} + e^+ + \nu_e + 1.68 \text{ MeV} \\
{}^{15}_{7}\text{N} + {}^1_1\text{H} &\longrightarrow {}^{12}_{6}\text{C} + {}^4_2\text{He} + 4.96 \text{ MeV}
\end{aligned}
$$

Therefore, the overall cycle gives $4({}^1_1\text{H}) \longrightarrow {}^4_2\text{He} + 2e^+ + 2\nu_e + 3\gamma + 24.68$ MeV, which is exactly the same as in the proton–proton cycle with the same Q value.

Illustrative Example 4.23: Energy released in the CNO cycle

Determine the energy released for 1 kg of hydrogen that is consumed in the CNO cycle.

Solution The equivalent process of the CNO cycle is

$4({}^1_1\text{H}) \longrightarrow {}^4_2\text{He} + 2e^+ + 2\nu_e + 3\gamma + 24.68$ MeV

The number of hydrogen atoms in 1 kg of hydrogen is $1000 \times 6.023 \times 10^{23}$.

In the fusion of four hydrogen atoms, the energy released is 24.68 MeV. Thus, the fusion of 6.023×10^{26} hydrogen atoms gives energy of $\frac{24.68}{4} \times 6.023 \times 10^{26} \approx 3.72 \times 10^{27}$ MeV.

SUMMARY

- **Characteristics of Nuclear Reactions**

  Types of reactions:

  (a) In *elastic scattering*, total kinetic energy is conserved and both the particles retain the same quantum state. However, in *inelastic scattering*, kinetic energy is not conserved, and one of the nuclei will be in the excited state.

  (b) Depending on the mechanism of interaction, nuclear reactions can be classified as: (i) those proceeding through an intermediate stage of *compound nucleus* and (ii) *direct reactions*.

(c) Reactions involving the transfer of nucleons among the target and the projectile are known as *transfer reactions*. These are of two types: *pick up* and *stripping*.

(d) Nuclear reactions may be induced by charged particles or neutrons or by γ rays.

- **Conserved Quantities**: Besides the conservation of total energy, conservation of angular and linear momenta and the conservation of charge are obeyed in nuclear reactions.
- **Reaction Energy: Q value**
The Q value of the reaction $a+X \longrightarrow Y+b$ is
$Q=(m_a+m_x-m_y-m_b)c^2 == \frac{m_y+m_b}{m_y}T_b - \frac{m_y-m_a}{m_y}T_a - 2\frac{\sqrt{m_a m_b T_a T_b}}{m_y}\cos\theta$
Reactions for which $Q>0$ are exoergic, while those with $Q<0$ are endoergic. $Q=0$ corresponds to elastic scattering. The minimum energy required to initiate an endoergic reaction is called the threshold energy and is given by
$T_{\text{th}} = \frac{m_a+m_x}{m_x}|Q|$
- **Double-valued Nature of T_b:** The kinetic energy (T_b) of the outgoing particle is a double-valued function for $T_a = T_{\text{th}}$ to $T_a = -Q\frac{m_y}{m_y-m_a}$ in case of endoergic reactions. For $Q>0$, T_b depends linearly on T_a.
- **Energetics in the CM Frame:** In the CM frame, $T_{\text{cm}}^{\text{in}} = T_{\text{cm}}^{\text{out}} + |Q|$ and the threshold energy is $T_{\text{cm}}^{th} = |Q|$.
- **Nuclear Cross-section σ**

$$\sigma \equiv \frac{\text{Number of particles scattered per second per target nucleus}}{\text{Number of projectiles incident per second per area}}$$

The unit of cross-section is the barn, which is defined as $1\ \text{barn} = 10^{-24}\ \text{cm}^2$.
The number of particles scattered by being passed through a distance x in matter is $N_0 - N(x) = N_0(1-e^{-n\sigma x})$, where N_0 is the initial number of particles in the beam.
- **Bohr Hypothesis of Independence:** The formation and the decay of a compound nucleus are independent of each other. The most convincing evidence for the correctness of the Bohr hypothesis was obtained in Ghoshal's experiment, where three pairs of reactions through $^{64}_{30}\text{Zn}^*$ were studied.
- **Discovery of Neutrons:** Chadwick in 1932 correctly identified the unknown radiation emitted on the bombardment of beryllium with α particles as a neutral particle, called the neutron. The mass of a neutron is nearly the same as that of the proton.
- **Fission**

(a) Fission is a reaction involving the splitting of a heavy nucleus into two lighter fragments with nearly equal mass. The fission may be spontaneous or initiated by thermal neutrons. The energy released is ~ 200 MeV.

(b) The mass distribution of the fission products is not symmetric. The ratio of the masses of two fragments is roughly $2:3$. With increasing excitation energy, the fission becomes symmetric gradually.

(c) According to the semi-empirical mass formula, fission is favourable if $\frac{Z^2}{A} > 17$.

(d) A much better estimation of $\frac{Z^2}{A}$ can be obtained, as shown by Bohr and Wheeler, by considering the oscillations of a drop of incompressible fluid under the combined action of the surface force and Coulomb force. According to this, the condition of stability of a nucleus is $\frac{Z^2}{A} < 47$.

(e) Thermal neutrons cause fission in ^{235}U, but not in ^{238}U. The pairing term in the semi-empirical mass formula plays a crucial role in this regard.

(f) Fission fragments have a large excess of neutrons and thus emit prompt neutrons at the instant of fission and also delayed neutrons.

- **Fusion**

  (a) The process of formation of a heavier nucleus by joining two light nuclei is called fusion.
  (b) Since the binding energy per nucleon increases with mass number, energy must be released in fusion. The condition of fusion is that the interacting nuclei must have sufficient energy to overcome the Coulomb barrier.
  (c) Thermonuclear reactions take place in the Sun at very high temperature.

REVIEW QUESTIONS AND PROBLEMS

Multiple Choice Questions

1. A spin-1/2 particle A undergoes the decay $A \longrightarrow B+C+D$, where B and C are also spin-1/2 particles. The complete set of allowed values of spin for the particle D is

   (a) $\frac{1}{2}, 1, \frac{3}{2}, 2, \frac{5}{2}, 3, \ldots$ (b) 0, 1 (c) $\frac{1}{2}$ only (d) $\frac{1}{2}, \frac{3}{2}, \frac{5}{2}, \ldots$ [NET 2013]

2. In deep inelastic scattering, electrons are scattered off protons to determine if a proton has any internal structure. The energy of the electron for this must be at least

   (a) 1.25×10^9 eV (b) 1.25×10^{12} eV (c) 1.25×10^6 eV (d) 1.25×10^8 eV

   [NET 2014]

3. Consider the reaction $a + X \longrightarrow Y + b$. If $T_{\text{cm}}^{\text{in}}$ and $T_{\text{cm}}^{\text{out}}$ represent, respectively, the total kinetic energy of the incident and the outgoing particles in the CM frame

   (a) $T_{\text{cm}}^{\text{in}}$ must be greater than $T_{\text{cm}}^{\text{out}}$ for the exoergic reaction
   (b) $T_{\text{cm}}^{\text{in}}$ must be greater than $T_{\text{cm}}^{\text{out}}$ for the endoergic reaction
   (c) $T_{\text{cm}}^{\text{in}}$ is greater than $T_{\text{cm}}^{\text{out}}$ only for elastic scattering
   (d) $T_{\text{cm}}^{\text{in}}$ must be equal to $T_{\text{cm}}^{\text{out}}$ for any type of reaction

4. Consider two reactions: ${}^2\text{H} + {}^4\text{He} \longrightarrow {}^6\text{Li} + Q_1$; ${}^3\text{H} + {}^3\text{He} \longrightarrow {}^6\text{Li} + Q_2$. Choose the correct option (without any calculations).

   (a) $Q_1 > Q_2$ (b) $Q_1 = Q_2$
   (b) $Q_1 < Q_2$ (d) Both are exoergic processes

5. Consider the four reactions:
   ${}^2\text{H} + {}^2\text{H} \longrightarrow {}^4\text{He} + Q_1$ ${}^{40}_{20}\text{Ca} + {}^{40}_{20}\text{Ca} \longrightarrow {}^{80}_{40}\text{Zr} + Q_3$
   ${}^{12}_{6}\text{C} + {}^{12}_{6}\text{C} \longrightarrow {}^{24}_{12}\text{Mg} + Q_2$ ${}^{56}_{26}\text{Ca} + {}^{56}_{26}\text{Ca} \longrightarrow {}^{112}\text{Te} + Q_4$
   What would you expect?

   (a) Q_1 is the maximum (b) Q_3 is the maximum
   (b) Q_2 is the maximum (d) Q_4 is the maximum

6. Energy is released in fission because

(a) Binding energy per nucleon drops from its average value for large A

(b) Binding energy per nucleon is a little bit higher than its average value for large A

(c) Binding energy per nucleon increases with increasing A

(d) Total binding energy of the fission fragments is less than the original nucleus

7. In the reaction $^2\text{H} + ^3\text{H} \longrightarrow ^4\text{He}$

(a) Total binding energy decreases

(b) Total binding energy increases

(c) Total binding energy remains unchanged

(d) Total binding energy may increase or decrease depending on the kinetic energy of the incident ^{2}H

8. Number of fission reactions per second in a 100-MW reactor is

(a) 10^8 (b) 10^{12} (c) 10^{18} (d) 10^{24}

Short Questions and Problems

1. Determine the unknown particle in the reactions (a) $^{27}_{13}\text{Al}(^1_1\text{H}, n)X$ and (b) $^{32}_{16}\text{S}(^4_2\text{He}, \gamma)X$.

2. Complete the following nuclear reactions

$$^6_3\text{Li} + ? \longrightarrow ^7_4\text{Be} + ^1_0 n, \quad ^{35}_{17}\text{Cl} + ? \longrightarrow ^{32}_{16}\text{S} + ^4_2\text{He}, \quad ^9_4\text{Be} + ^4_2\text{He} \longrightarrow ^{12}_6\text{C} +$$

3. Define the Q value of a nuclear reaction. Calculate the Q value of the reaction $^{14}_7\text{N}(\alpha, p)^{17}_8\text{O}$ in MeV. Given $M(^{14}\text{N}) = 14.007518$ u, $M(^4\text{He}) = 4.003873$ u, $M(p) = 1.008144$ u and $M(^{17}\text{O}) = 17.004527$ u.

4. Consider the fusion reaction (D-T fusion) $^3_1\text{H} + ^2_1\text{H} \longrightarrow ^4_2\text{He} + ^1_0 n + Q$.

   (a) Calculate the Q value.

   (b) Also calculate the rate of consumption of deuterium and tritium to produce 1MW of power.

   Given $M(^3_1\text{H}) = 3.016049$ u, $M(^2_1\text{H}) = 2.014102$ u, $M(^4_2\text{He}) = 4.002603$ u, $M(^1_0 n) = 1.008665$ u.

5. The Q value for the reaction $p + ^4_2\text{He} \longrightarrow ^3_2\text{He} + ^2_1\text{H}$ is -18.4 MeV, where α is at rest. Calculate the threshold energy of the reaction.

6. Consider the fusion reaction (D-D fusion) $^2_1\text{H} + ^2_1\text{H} \longrightarrow ^3_2\text{He} + ^1_0 n + Q$. Calculate the Q value.

   Given $M(^2_1\text{H}) = 2.014102$ u, $M(^3_2\text{He}) = 3.016029$ u, $M(^1_0 n) = 1.008665$ u.

7. Consider the fusion reaction $^4_2\text{He} + ^4_2\text{He} + ^4_2\text{He} \longrightarrow ^{12}_6\text{C} + Q$. Calculate the Q value.

   Given $M(^4_2\text{He}) = 4.002603$ u and $M(^{12}_6\text{C}) = 12.000000$ u.

8. Calculate the mass of ${}_{2}^{4}$He from the following data, the Q value of the reaction:

$$^{16}\mathrm{O}(d,\alpha)^{14}\mathrm{N}: Q = 3.112 \text{ MeV} \qquad ^{13}\mathrm{C}(d,\alpha)^{11}\mathrm{B}: Q = 5.160 \text{ MeV}$$
$$^{14}\mathrm{N}(d,p)^{15}\mathrm{N}: Q = 8.615 \text{ MeV} \qquad ^{11}\mathrm{B}(p,\alpha)^{8}\mathrm{Be}: Q = 8.567 \text{ MeV}$$
$$^{15}\mathrm{N}(d,\alpha)^{13}\mathrm{C}: Q = 7.68 \text{ MeV} \qquad ^{8}\mathrm{Be}(\alpha)\alpha: Q = 0.089 \text{ MeV}$$

Mass of ^{2}H nucleus 2.014102 u and mass of ${}_{8}^{16}$O is 15.994915 u.

9. In the following deuterium reactions, the reaction energies are

$$^{14}\mathrm{N}(d,p)^{15}\mathrm{N}: Q = 8.615 \text{ MeV} \qquad ^{13}\mathrm{C}(d,\alpha)^{11}\mathrm{B}: Q = 5.160 \text{ MeV}$$
$$^{15}\mathrm{N}(d,\alpha)^{13}\mathrm{C}: Q = 7.680 \text{ MeV} \qquad ^{11}\mathrm{B}(\alpha,n)^{14}\mathrm{N}: Q = ??$$

Calculate the Q value of the fourth reaction. Given $M({}_{2}^{4}\mathrm{He}) = 4.00387$ u, $M({}_{1}^{2}\mathrm{H}) = 2.014102$ u, $M(p) = 1.008145$ u and $M({}_{0}^{1}n) = 1.00898$ u.

10. The nuclear reaction $p + {}_{29}^{63}\mathrm{Cu} \longrightarrow {}_{30}^{63}\mathrm{Zn} + n$ is followed by the positron decay ${}_{30}^{63}\mathrm{Zn} \longrightarrow {}_{29}^{63}\mathrm{Cu} + e^+ + \bar{\nu}$. If the maximum energy of the positron is 2.36 MeV, find the Q for the original (p,n) reaction. For the reaction $d + {}_{29}^{63}\mathrm{Cu} \longrightarrow {}_{30}^{63}\mathrm{Zn} + 2n$, $Q = -6.38$ MeV. Estimate the binding energy of the deuteron. Given that the mass of an electron is 511 keV, for proton is 938.272 MeV and for neutron is 939.566 MeV.

11. State the basic assumptions of Bohr's theory of compound nuclear reactions. Describe an experiment that justifies these assumptions.

12. In a nuclear reaction, the bombarding particle a is incident on a target nucleus A. After the reaction takes place, the ejected particle b is emitted at an angle θ and the residual nucleus B recoils such that the momentum is conserved. Show that the Q value is given by

$$Q = K_b\left(1 + \frac{m_b}{m_B}\right) - K_a\left(1 - \frac{m_a}{m_B}\right) - \frac{2}{m_B}\sqrt{K_a K_b m_a m_b}\cos\theta,$$

where the Ks are the kinetic energies and the ms are the rest mass.

13. Consider the reaction ${}_{2}^{4}\mathrm{He} + {}_{7}^{14}\mathrm{N} \longrightarrow {}_{8}^{17}\mathrm{O} + {}_{1}^{1}\mathrm{H}$.

The bombarding ${}_{2}^{4}$He particles have kinetic energy $K_\alpha = 7.70$ MeV. Protons are emitted at 90° to the beam of the bombarding particles and have kinetic energy of $K_b = 4.44$ MeV. Determine the Q value of the reaction.

14. Four hydrogen nuclei are fused to form a helium nucleus according to the reaction $4{}_{1}^{1}\mathrm{H} \longrightarrow {}_{2}^{4}\mathrm{He} + 2e^+ + Q$. Calculate the energy released when a 1-g atom of hydrogen is fused to form helium. (Given the mass of hydrogen = 1.007825 u, mass of helium = 4.002603 u and mass of positron = 0.00054858 u).

15. Chadwick and Goldhaber determined the neutron mass from the following reaction: $\gamma + {}_{1}^{2}\mathrm{H} \longrightarrow {}_{1}^{1}\mathrm{H} + {}_{0}^{1}n$.

They used γ rays of energy 2.62 MeV, and the kinetic energy produced in the disintegration was 0.225 MeV. (Given the mass $^2_1$H = 2.014102 u and mass of $^1_1$H = 1.007825 u). Find the mass of the neutron.

16. Explain the concept of 'cross-section' of a nuclear reaction. What are the factors on which σ depends? 'The value of σ of a nuclear reaction is 10^2 barns' – what is the significance of this statement?

17. The density of iron is about 8×10^3 kg/m^3. The neutron capture cross-section of iron is about 2.5 barns. What fraction of an incident beam of neutrons is absorbed by a sheet of iron 1-cm thick?

18. The cross-section of the ^{207}Pb(n, γ) reaction for neutrons is about 1 barn. By how much will the intensity of a beam of neutrons of this energy be reduced on passing through 10 cm of ^{207}Pb (density = 11g/cm^3)?

19. Give a simple explanation of nuclear fission on the basis of the liquid-drop model of the nucleus.

20. When lithium is bombarded by 10-MeV deuterons, neutrons come out at right angles to the direction of the incident beam. Calculate the energy of these neutrons and the angle of recoil of the associated beryllium atom. Mass of $^1_0n = 1.008665$ u, $^2_1$H = 2.014102 u, $^7_3$Li = 7.016003 u and $^8_4$Be = 8.005305 u.

21. Deduce the relation between the Q value of a nuclear reaction and the threshold energy. Hence calculate the threshold energy for the reaction $^{14}N(\alpha, p)^{17}$O. The Q value of the reaction is -1.19 MeV.

22. Calculate the minimum energy required to be given to a neutron in order that the following nuclear reaction may occur: $^1_0n + ^{31}_{15}\text{P} \longrightarrow ^{31}_{14}\text{Si} + ^1_1\text{H}$.

    Mass of $^1_0n = 1.008665$ u, $^{31}_{15}$P = 30.973766 u, $^{31}_{14}$Si = 30.975349 u and $^1_1$H = 1.007825 u.

23. A nuclear reactor using ^{235}U is to operate at a power level of 250 MW. If the energy released per fission reaction of ^{235}U is 200 MeV, calculate the consumption of ^{235}U per second (assume there is no loss).

24. ^{235}U is bombarded by thermal neutrons and fission occurs. The fragmented products are $^{141}_{56}$Ba and $^{92}_{36}$Kr. Three prompt neutrons are released when fission occurs. Write the nuclear reaction involved. Calculate the Q value of the reaction and hence calculate the energy released from the fission of 1 g of ^{235}U.

25. (a) Describe briefly the type of reaction using which a nuclear reactor operates.
    (b) What is the approximate energy released per fission?
    (c) Why is a moderator necessary? Which type of element, light or heavy, is preferred for the moderator?

26. How many neutrons are there in the 100th generation if the fission is started with $N_0 = 1000$ neutrons in a material for which the neutron multiplication number is $k = 1.05$?

27. Find the number of neutrons generated per unit time in a uranium reactor of power 10 MW. Assume that the average number of neutrons released in each fission reaction is 2.5 and the energy released per fission is 200 MeV.

28. Explain briefly the operation of a breeder reactor. What physical constant of fission is a prerequisite for the possibility of breeding? What is the important constraint regarding the choice of materials in the reactor?

HINTS/ANSWERS TO SELECTED PROBLEMS

Multiple Choice Questions

1. (c) 2. $\lambda_e = \dfrac{hc}{p_e c} \sim 1\,\text{fm} \Rightarrow p_e c \approx 1240\ \text{MeV}$(a)

3. (b) 4. (c) BE of ^{4}He is very large 5. (a) 6. (a) 7. (b) 8. (c)

Problems

1. (a) $^{27}_{14}$Si (b) $^{36}_{18}$Ar

4. (a) 17.6 MeV (b) Rate of consumption of deuterium is $\approx 1.18 \times 10^{-6}$ g/s and rate of consumption of tritium is $\approx 1.77 \times 10^{-6}$ g/s.

5. $T_{th} = 23.0$ MeV 10. Q = −4.67 MeV 14. 3.87×10^{23} MeV

18. $\dfrac{I}{I_0} = e^{-0.32}$ 26. $N = 1000 \times 1.05^{99} = 1.25 \times 10^5$ 27. 7.8×10^{17}

CHAPTER 5

Interaction of Nuclear Radiation with Matter

One of the most important problems in experimental nuclear physics is the problem of understanding how particles slow down as they pass through matter. In this chapter, we will discuss the mechanism by which different nuclear charged particles and radiations interact with matter. A charged particle moving through a medium interacts with the electrons of the atoms of the medium and loses its energy. As a result of this interaction with the incident particle, the electrons may be raised to excited states or may be ionised. In either case, the increase in the energy of the electron comes from the kinetic energy of the incident charged particle.

Knowledge of energy transfer of the incident particle is extremely important in designing nuclear detectors. It is also important to study the effect of radiation on living cells.

5.1 ENERGY TRANSFER IN ELASTIC COLLISION

Let us first consider a simple problem of elastic collision of two particles. Figure 5.1 shows a particle of mass M and velocity V approaching another particle of mass m, which is initially at rest. After the collision, the particles of masses M and m move with the velocities V_1 and V_2, respectively, along the same line of travel as the incident particle. We have considered a head-on collision because, compared to oblique collisions, energy transfer is maximum in head-on collisions.

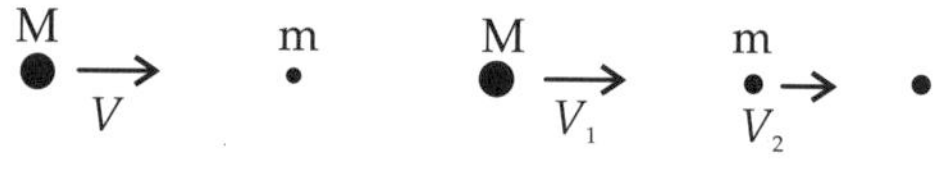

Figure 5.1: *Head-on collision of a particle with a stationary target*

The conservation of linear momentum requires $MV = MV_1 + mV_2$ (5.1)

The conservation of kinetic energy gives $\frac{1}{2}MV^2 = \frac{1}{2}MV_1^2 + \frac{1}{2}mV_2^2$ (5.2)

From Eqs (5.1) and (5.2), we get

$$V_1 = \frac{M-m}{M+m}V \tag{5.3}$$

$$V_2 = \frac{2M}{M+m}V \tag{5.4}$$

The gain in kinetic energy of m, which is equal to the loss of kinetic energy of the incident particle, is

$$\Delta T = \frac{1}{2}mV_2^2 = \frac{4mM}{(m+M)^2}T, \tag{5.5}$$

where $T = \frac{1}{2}MV^2$ is the kinetic energy of the incident particle.

If $M \gg m$, the energy transfer will be small, while for $M \approx m$, the incident particle will transfer its entire energy to the target. Equation (5.5) for maximum energy transfer is kinematic in nature; that is, it follows directly from the conservation of linear momentum and kinetic energy, and thus, does not depend on the nature of the forces interacting between the two particles.

Illustrative Example 5.1:

Calculate the maximum energy that a 10-MeV proton can transfer to an electron.

Solution From Eq. (5.5), the energy loss is

$$\Delta T = \frac{4mM}{(m+M)^2}T = \frac{4\times 0.51\times 938.28}{(0.51+938.28)^2}\times 10 = 0.0217 \text{ MeV}$$

Thus, $\frac{\Delta T}{T} = 0.00217$. Therefore, only about 0.22% of the incident energy is lost.

5.2 INTERACTION OF HEAVY CHARGED PARTICLES WITH MATTER

In 1913, Bohr derived an explicit formula for the energy loss of heavy charged particles in matter. A heavy charged particle moving through a material medium interacts mainly with the electrons of the absorber atoms by Coulomb force. The moving charged particle thus exerts force, and hence, imparts momentum and energy to the electrons passing by. The energy transferred may be sufficient either to raise the electrons to an excited state or to knock the electrons completely out of the atom. In any case, the energy that is transferred to the electron must be obtained from the kinetic energy of the incident particle. As a result, the energy of the incident particle must be decreased.

The loss of kinetic energy (ΔT) of a heavy particle of mass M in a head-on collision with an electron of mass m is $\Delta T \approx \frac{4m}{M}T$.

This is actually a small fraction of the total kinetic energy (T). The incident particle actually loses its energy in many thousands of such interactions with electrons during its passage through the medium. Since the nuclei occupy a very small fraction of the volume of their atoms, the possibility of nuclear encounter is extremely rare. The dominant mechanism of energy transfer of a heavy charged particle is, therefore, through interactions with the electrons of the absorbing material.

Figure 5.2 shows schematically an electron of mass m and charge $-e$, at a distance b, called the impact parameter, from the path of an incident heavy particle of charge ze and velocity v.

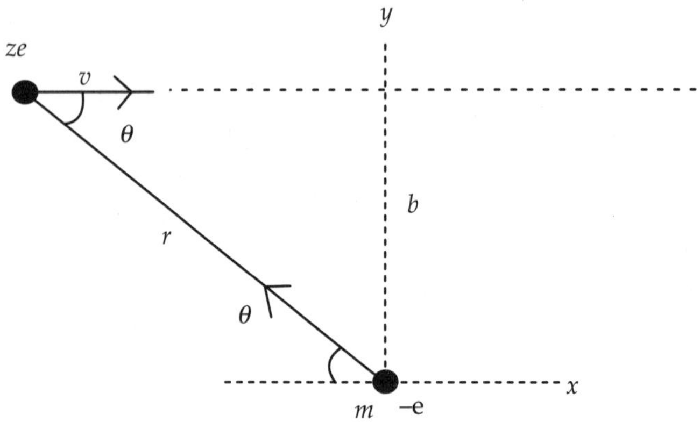

Figure 5.2: *Collision of a heavy charged particle with an electron located at the origin of the xy coordinate system*

The calculation of energy transfer is based on the following assumptions:

- The electron is free and at rest at the origin of the coordinate system, as shown in Fig. 5.2.
- The collision takes place rapidly before any appreciable movement of the electron. Therefore, during the collision, the electric field acting on the electron due to the moving charged particle can be calculated at the initial location of the electron. This assumption is not valid if the velocity of the incident particle is comparable to that acquired by the electron.
- The incident heavy particle is not deflected from its initial straight path.

The components F_x and F_y of the Coulomb force acting on the electron at any instant, as shown in Fig. 5.2, are

$$F_x = \frac{1}{4\pi\varepsilon_0}\frac{ze^2}{r^2}\cos\theta; \quad F_y = \frac{1}{4\pi\varepsilon_0}\frac{ze^2}{r^2}\sin\theta$$

Let us set the time $t = 0$, when the heavy particle crosses the y axis. Considering $r^2 = b^2 + v^2t^2$, we get

$$F_x = \frac{ze^2}{4\pi\varepsilon_0}\frac{vt}{(b^2+v^2t^2)^{3/2}}; \quad F_y = \frac{ze^2}{4\pi\varepsilon_0}\frac{b}{(b^2+v^2t^2)^{3/2}}$$

The component F_x acts symmetrically: on the left of the origin, it acts towards the $-ve$ x axis, while on the right side, it acts towards the $+ve$ x axis. Variation of F_x and F_y with time is shown in Fig. 5.3, where the dimensionless parameters, $F_x \frac{4\pi\varepsilon_0 b^2}{ze^2}$ and $F_y \frac{4\pi\varepsilon_0 b^2}{ze^2}$, have been plotted against a dimensionless parameter, $\frac{vt}{b}$.

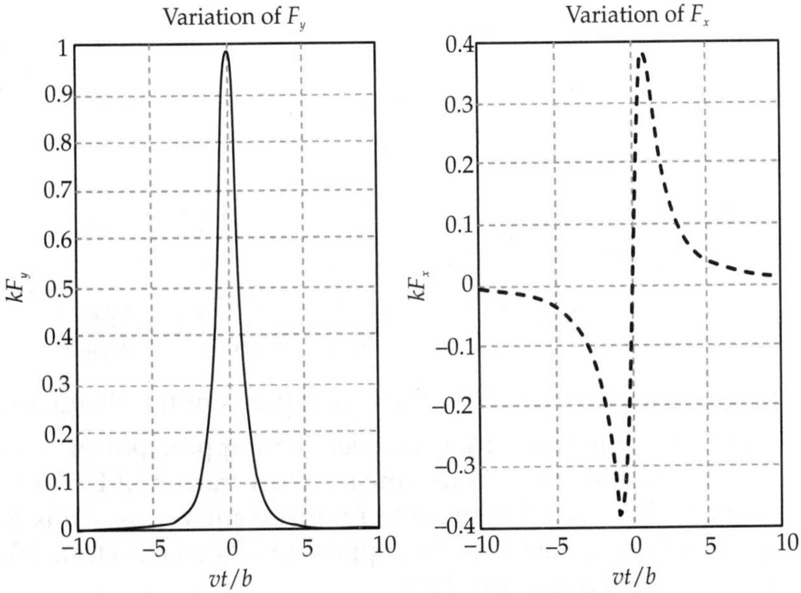

Figure 5.3: *Variation of the dimensionless parameters $F_x k$ and $F_y k$ with time (in terms of the dimensionless parameter $\frac{vt}{b}$). Here, $k = \frac{4\pi\varepsilon_0 b^2}{ze^2}$.*

Figure 5.3 shows that $\int_{-\infty}^{\infty} F_x dt = 0$. The total momentum imparted to the electron is

$$p = \int_{-\infty}^{\infty} F_y dt = \int_{-\infty}^{\infty} \frac{ze^2}{4\pi\varepsilon_0} \frac{b}{(b^2 + v^2t^2)^{3/2}} dt$$

$$= \frac{ze^2}{4\pi\varepsilon_0} \frac{2}{bv} \left[\frac{vt}{\sqrt{(b^2 + v^2t^2)}} \right]_0^{\infty} = \frac{ze^2}{4\pi\varepsilon_0} \frac{2}{vb}$$

The energy transferred to the electron in a single collision is

$$\varepsilon = \frac{p^2}{2m} = \left(\frac{1}{4\pi\varepsilon_0} \right)^2 \frac{2z^2 e^4}{mb^2 v^2} \tag{5.6}$$

It shows that the faster the particle is, the less energy is transferred to the electron (the less time it spends to impart energy to the electron).

Let n be the number of electrons per unit volume of the medium. In traversing a distance dx in the medium, the heavy particle encounters $n\ 2\pi b\ db\ dx$ number of electrons in the range b to $b + db$, as shown in Fig. 5.4.

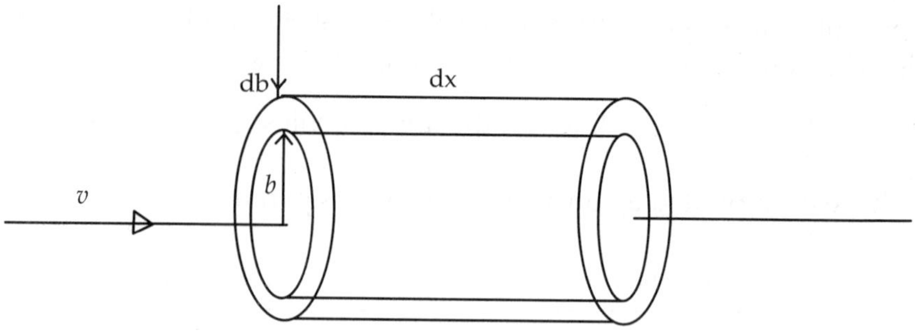

Figure 5.4: *Cylinder of thickness db and length dx centred about the path of the incident particle*

Thus, the energy loss due to these electrons is $dE = \left(\frac{1}{4\pi\varepsilon_0}\right)^2 \frac{2z^2e^4}{mb^2v^2} \times 2\pi n\, b\, db\, dx$

Total rate of energy loss is

$$-\frac{dE}{dx} = \left(\frac{1}{4\pi\varepsilon_0}\right)^2 \frac{2z^2e^4}{mv^2} 2\pi n \int_{b_{min}}^{b_{max}} \frac{db}{b} = \left(\frac{1}{4\pi\varepsilon_0}\right)^2 \frac{2z^2e^4}{mv^2} 2\pi n \ln \frac{b_{max}}{b_{min}} \tag{5.7}$$

The quantity $-\frac{dE}{dx}$, which is the differential energy loss of the charged particle divided by the corresponding path length, is called the **stopping power** of the material for the particle. It is also referred to as the **linear energy transfer (LET)** of the particle. The integral in Eq. (5.7) would diverge both for $b \to 0$ and $b \to \infty$. Thus mathematically, the necessity of using the lower and upper cut-offs on b is clear. We will now try to explain the physical reason for that.

Limit b_{max}: Figure 5.3 shows that the force F_y imparting momentum to the electron is a pulse of time duration $\tau \approx \frac{b}{v}$. Thus, the duration of collision is $\approx \frac{b}{v}$. It can be shown that the electron absorbs practically no energy if the time period of motion of the atomic electron is less than the time of collision. Thus, the condition for absorption of energy is $\frac{b}{v} < \frac{1}{\nu}$, where ν is the frequency of vibration of the electron. Thus, the maximum value of b is

$$b_{max} = \frac{v}{\nu} \tag{5.8}$$

Limit b_{min}: The minimum of the impact parameter b_{min} is restricted by the uncertainty principle. The electron cannot be located at a distance smaller than its de Broglie wavelength with respect to the incident heavy particle. In the rest frame of the incident particle, the electron moves with the velocity v and the de Broglie wavelength of the electron is $\lambda = \frac{h}{mv}$. Therefore

$$b_{min} \approx \frac{h}{mv} \tag{5.9}$$

Using Eqs (5.8) and (5.9) in Eq. (5.7), we get

$$-\frac{dE}{dx} = \left(\frac{1}{4\pi\varepsilon_0}\right)^2 \frac{2z^2e^4}{mv^2} 2\pi n \ln\frac{mv^2}{h\nu} \tag{5.10}$$

Illustrative Example 5.2:

Justify the statement that for $\frac{b}{v} > \frac{1}{\nu}$, transfer of energy[1] to the electron is practically negligible.

Solution Let us consider the motion of the electron along the y axis, that is, along the direction perpendicular to the path of the incident particle. Let the position of the electron at any instant be

$$y = b + a\sin\nu t,$$

where ν is the frequency of the electron and $a \ll b$. The velocity of the electron is

$$\dot{y} = a\nu \cos \nu t$$

The energy received by the electron is

$$\Delta E = \int F_y \times \text{(velocity)}\, dt = \frac{ze^2}{4\pi\varepsilon_0}\int_{-\infty}^{\infty} \frac{b}{(b^2+v^2t^2)^{3/2}} \nu a\cos \nu t dt$$

$$= \frac{ze^2}{4\pi\varepsilon_0} b\ \nu\ a \int_{-\infty}^{\infty} \frac{\cos \nu t}{(b^2+v^2t^2)^{3/2}} dt \tag{5.11}$$

To evaluate the above integral, let us consider the following integral

$$I = \int_{-\infty}^{\infty} \frac{e^{i\nu t}}{(b^2+v^2t^2)^{3/2}} dt \tag{5.12}$$

Substituting $x = \frac{vt}{b}$, the above integral becomes

$$I = \frac{1}{vb^2}\int_{-\infty}^{\infty} \frac{e^{i\xi x}}{(1+x^2)^{3/2}} dx, \tag{5.13}$$

where $\xi = \frac{\nu b}{v}$. The integrand has branch cuts at $x = \pm i$ and it can be shown that

$$I \propto e^{-\xi}$$

Thus, for $\xi = \frac{\nu b}{v} \gg 1$, the integration goes to zero, implying a negligible amount of energy transfer.

Illustrative Example 5.3:

Make an estimate of $b_{\max}$ and $b_{\min}$ for an electronic collision of a 10-MeV proton. Assume that the orbital frequency of the electron in the absorbing material is the same as that of the electron in the ground state of the He^+ ion.

[1]Fermi, E. 1949. *Nuclear Physics: A Course given by Enrico Fermi at the University of Chicago*. University of Chicago Press, USA.

Solution $b_{\max} = \frac{V}{\nu}$, where V is the velocity of the incident proton and ν is the orbital frequency of the electron in the absorbing material.

Estimation of V: Since the kinetic energy (T) of the proton is much less than its rest mass energy, we can use a non-relativistic result

$$\frac{1}{2}mV^2 = T$$

$$V^2 = \frac{2T}{m} = \frac{2\times 10}{938.27}\times 9\times 10^{16} = 19.2\times 10^{14} \quad \text{or} \quad V = 4.38\times 10^7 \text{ m/s}$$

Estimation of ν: From Bohr's postulate, the angular momentum of the electron about the nucleus is

$$mur = n\hbar, \tag{5.14}$$

where m is the mass of the electron. The condition of rotation in a circular orbit is

$$\frac{mu^2}{r} = \frac{e^2}{4\pi\varepsilon_0}\frac{Z}{r^2} \tag{5.15}$$

From these two equations, we get $\frac{1}{r} = \frac{e^2}{4\pi\varepsilon_0}\frac{Zm}{n^2\hbar^2}$ (5.16)

And $u = \frac{e^2}{4\pi\varepsilon_0}\frac{Z}{n\hbar}$ (5.17)

For a He^+ ion in the ground state, $Z = 2$ and $n = 1$.

From Eq. (5.16), $r = 2.65\times 10^{-11}$ m and from Eq. (5.17), $u = 4.37\times 10^6$ m/s.

Therefore $\nu = \frac{u}{2\pi r} = 2.62\times 10^{16}$/s and

$$b_{\max} = \frac{V}{\nu} = 16.7\times 10^{-10} \text{ m}; \; b_{\min} = \frac{h}{mu} = \frac{6.62\times 10^{-34}}{9.1\times 10^{-31}\times 4.38\times 10^7} = 1.67\times 10^{-10} \text{ m}$$

5.2.1 Bethe Formula for Stopping Power

Bethe, using relativistic quantum mechanics, derived a more precise result of the energy loss of the heavy particle in a uniform medium, which is presented below.

$$-\frac{dE}{dx} = \left(\frac{e^2}{4\pi\varepsilon_0}\right)^2 \frac{2z^2}{mc^2\beta^2}2\pi n\left[\ln\frac{2mc^2\beta^2}{I(1-\beta^2)} - \beta^2\right] \tag{5.18}$$

In Eq. (5.18), z = atomic number of the incident heavy particle, m = mass of the electron, n = number of electrons per unit volume of the medium, $\beta = \frac{v}{c}$ and I = average ionisation potential of the electrons. The multiplicative factor in Eq. (5.18) is

$$\left(\frac{e^2}{4\pi\varepsilon_0}\right)^2 \frac{2z^2}{mc^2\beta^2}2\pi n = 5.11\times 10^{-31}\times\frac{nz^2}{\beta^2} \text{ MeV/cm},$$

where the number density of the electron n is expressed in number/m^3. The term in the bracket can be written as

$$\left[\ln\frac{2mc^2\beta^2}{I(1-\beta^2)}-\beta^2\right]=\left[\ln\frac{2mc^2\beta^2}{(1-\beta^2)}-\beta^2-\ln I\right]=F(\beta)-\ln I,$$

where the average ionisation is expressed in eV unit and $F(\beta)=\ln\frac{2mc^2\times\beta^2}{1-\beta^2}-\beta^2$.

Thus

$$-\frac{dE}{dx}=5.11\times10^{-31}\times\frac{nz^2}{\beta^2}\left[F(\beta)-\ln I\right]\ \text{MeV/cm} \tag{5.19}$$

Important features of Eq. (5.18)

(a) Equation (5.18) shows that $-\frac{dE}{dx}$ *is independent of the mass of the incident particle but is* $\propto z^2$. Thus, particles with larger z will have greater energy loss. For example, α particles will lose energy at a rate larger than that of protons of the same energy (Fig. (5.5)). The z^2 dependence also implies that particles with the same energy but opposite charge must have the same stopping power.

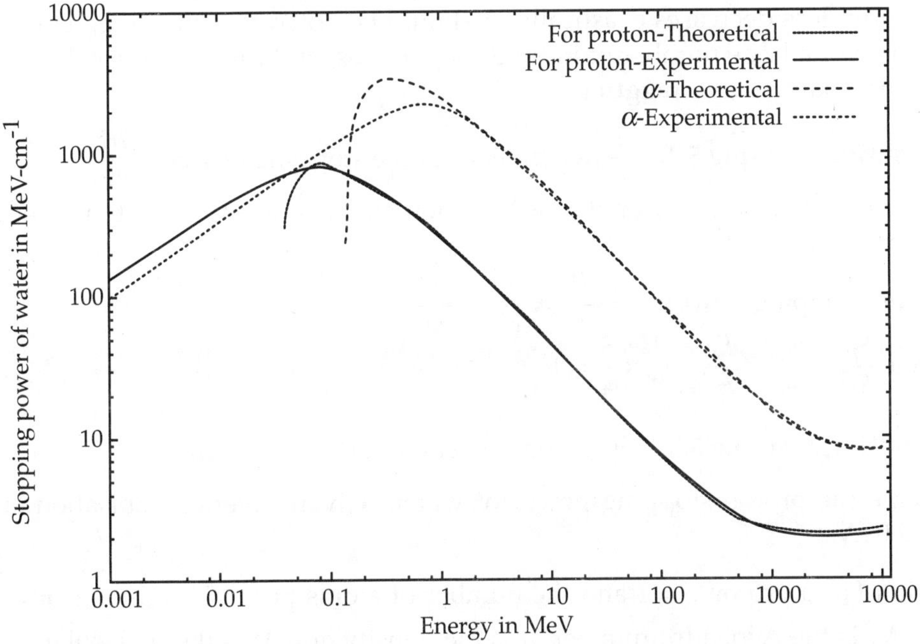

Figure 5.5: *Stopping power of water in MeV.cm^{-1} for protons and α particles*

(b) Since $F(\beta)$ varies slowly with v^2, the general behaviour of $-\frac{dE}{dx}$ can be inferred from the behaviour of its multiplicative factor. *It varies* $\propto \frac{1}{v^2}$ *or varies inversely with the kinetic energy of the particle in the non-relativistic limit. For all particles, the energy loss* $-\frac{dE}{dx}$ *falls as* $\frac{1}{E}$ *and eventually goes through a minimum, and then again increases due to the* $F(\beta)$ *term.*

If each atom of the absorbing medium contains Z electrons, the number of atoms per unit volume is $n = \frac{N_A\rho}{A} \times Z$, where N_A is the Avogadro number, ρ is the density and A is the atomic weight. The energy loss is often represented as $-\frac{dE}{\rho dx}$, which is independent of the physical constitution of the absorbing material.

Experimentally, the energy loss can be determined by the number of ion pairs produced along the path of the moving charged particle. The plot of specific ionisation (the number of ion pairs formed per unit length), which is related to the specific energy loss along the track of a charged particle, is known as the **Bragg curve**. A typical Bragg curve for an α particle of several MeV of initial energy has already been shown in Fig. 3.16 of Chapter 3. It shows that as the α particle moves in the medium, its kinetic energy decreases and specific energy loss increases according to the Bethe formula. At the end of the path, where the energy falls lower than a threshold, the α particle becomes a neutral helium atom by absorbing electrons, and then the specific energy loss decreases drastically. It should be noted that the Bragg curve is an average over a large number of individual particles, and thus, includes the effect of fluctuation, known as **straggling**.

Illustrative Example 5.4: $\frac{1}{E}$ dependence of the stopping power $-\frac{dE}{dx}$

Compare the stopping power of an 8-MeV deuteron and a 4-MeV proton in the same medium.

Solution Stopping power: $S = \frac{dE}{dx} \propto \frac{1}{v^2} \Rightarrow \frac{m}{mv^2}$

Thus $\frac{S_p}{S_d} = \frac{m_p}{m_d} \times \frac{E_d}{E_p} \approx \frac{1}{2} \times \frac{8}{4} = 1$

Illustrative Example 5.5: Stopping power of water for protons

Calculate the proton stopping power of water. Given: average ionisation energy $I = 74.60$ eV.

Solution For a proton $z = 1$ and the number of atoms per unit volume is $n = \frac{N_A\rho}{M}$, where N_A is the Avogadro number, ρ is the density and M is the molecular weight. For water, the number of molecules per unit volume is $= \frac{6.023 \times 10^{23} \times 10^6}{18} = 0.334 \times 10^{29}$ atoms/m^3. The number of electrons in each molecule of water is 10, and thus, the number of electrons per unit volume of water is

$$n = 10 \times 0.334 \times 10^{29} \ /\text{m}^3$$

Therefore $-\frac{dE}{dx} = 5.11 \times 10^{-31} \times 3.34 \times 10^{29} \frac{1}{\beta^2}\left[F(\beta) - \ln I\right]$ MeV/cm

For a proton of kinetic energy T, β can be calculated from the relation

$$T = m_0c^2\left[\frac{1}{\sqrt{1-\beta^2}} - 1\right]$$

For example, $\beta^2 \approx 0.099$, for $T = 50$ MeV and $-\frac{dE}{dx} \approx 12.47$ MeV/cm.

The stopping power of water for a proton and for an α particle has been computed theoretically from Eq. (5.19), and plotted as a function of energy in Fig. 5.5. The theoretical values have also been compared with the experimental values[2]. Figure 5.5 shows the $\frac{1}{v^2}$ dependence of Eq. (5.19), except at very low energy. Agreement between the theoretical and experimental curves is not good at low energy. At very low energy, Eq. (5.19) fails to work because the particle velocity becomes comparable to that of the electrons in the material, and efficiency of energy transfer becomes very poor. At very low energies, the incident charged particle may capture electrons from the absorber, which effectively reduces its charge z and, as a consequence, energy loss is reduced. Finally, the incident charged particle becomes a neutral atom and can lose energy only by collision.

Illustrative Example 5.6: Penetration of muons

The central core of an extensive shower at sea level consists of a narrow vertical beam of muons of energy 60 GeV, which penetrates the interior of the earth. Assuming that the energy loss in rock is constant at 2.0 MeVg^{-1}cm^2 and the density of the rock is 3.0 g/cc, find the depth of the rock through which the muons can penetrate.

Solution Energy loss: $-\frac{dE}{dx} = 2.0\ \text{MeV/g}^{-1}\text{cm}^2 \times 3.0\ \text{g/cm}^3 = 6.0\ \text{MeV/cm}$.

The depth up to which the muon can penetrate is $\frac{60 \times 10^3}{6} = 10^4$ cm.

5.3 INTERACTION OF ELECTRONS WITH MATTER

Like heavy charged particles, fast electrons also interact with atomic electrons through Coulomb force and can excite and ionise the atoms of the absorbing material. A number of important differences, however, should be noted:

- The derivation of Bohr's relation for stopping power, Eq. (5.19), assumes that the deflection of the incident particle is very small – it moves along an almost straight path. However, this is not true for electrons. The incident electron acquires a transverse component of momentum equal to that given to the electron in each collision. Since the mass of the electron is small, the transverse velocity corresponding to this transverse momentum is not negligible for electrons. As a result, the incident electron will be deflected appreciably from its straight path.

[2]Stopping-Power and Range Tables for Electrons, Protons and Helium Ions, NISTIR 4999; https://www.nist.gov

- Because the incident electron and the electron in the stopping material have the same mass, a large fraction of incident energy is transferred in a single collision. In fact, it is difficult to trace which was the incident electron and which was struck.
- The kinetic energy of the electrons emitted in β decay is comparable or larger than its rest mass energy. Thus, the relativistic effect must be taken into account.
- Because the electrons move at high speed and may suffer rapid change in direction, they have large acceleration. Any accelerated charged particle must emit energy, which is known as **bremsstrahlung** (a German word, meaning 'braking radiation'). When a particle of mass m and charge ze moves close to a target nucleus of charge Ze at high speed, it undergoes acceleration that is proportional to $\frac{zZ}{m}$. Thus, radiation loss for electrons is larger than for protons under identical conditions. Therefore, in addition to the collision, electrons also radiate energy by *bremsstrahlung*. This is significant only at high energy.

The interactions of different charged particles in matter (in the range 100 keV to 10 MeV) may be summarised as follows:

- *Electrons:* Electrons lose energy by colliding with the electrons of the absorbing material; that is, by exciting and ionising the atoms along their trajectory. Electrons suffer large deflections in collision and thus follow erratic paths. Energy loss by bremsstrahlung is also important for electrons, particularly at higher energies.
- *α particles:* Since energy loss varies $\propto z^2$, the energy loss of α particles is much larger than that of electrons. As a result, the α particles travel only a few centimetres in air. The path of α particles is almost straight.
- *Protons:* The rate of energy loss for protons is larger than for electrons but lower than that of the α particles. They also follow an almost straight trajectory.

5.4 RANGE OF CHARGED PARTICLES

A charged particle passing through material ionises the atoms along its path and loses its energy. The total distance travelled by a charged particle in a given direction before coming to rest is called its range. It can be calculated by integrating Eq. (5.18) over the energies dE as

$$R = \int_0^R dx = \int_{E_0}^0 \frac{dx}{dE} dE = \int_0^{E_0} (-\frac{dE}{dx})^{-1} dE \tag{5.20}$$

By travelling a distance R, the particle loses its initial kinetic energy E_0 completely. The integration in Eq. (5.20) may be evaluated numerically.

We now make the following observations:

(a) For a rough estimation, we may assume that $-\frac{dE}{dx} \propto \frac{1}{v^2} \propto \frac{1}{E}$. Thus, Eq. (5.20) gives

$$R \propto E^2$$

A more precise consideration gives $R \propto E^{3/2} \propto v^3$.

A rough formula giving the range of the α particle of energy E in air at 15°C and atmospheric pressure is

$$R = 0.318E^{3/2}, \tag{5.21}$$

where R is measured in cm and E is in MeV.

(b) In accordance with Eq. (5.18)

$$-\frac{dE}{dx} = z^2 f(v) \Rightarrow -\frac{d}{dx}\left(\frac{1}{2}mv^2\right) = z^2 f(v)$$

Thus $dx = -\frac{m}{z^2}\frac{vdv}{f(v)}$

Therefore, the range is

$$R = \frac{m}{z^2}\int \phi(v)dv, \tag{5.22}$$

where m is the rest mass of the particle. *It shows that the ratio of the ranges of two charged particles of different mass but with the same initial velocity is*

$$\frac{R_1}{R_2} = \frac{m_1}{m_2}\frac{z_2^2}{z_1^2} \tag{5.23}$$

This relation is helpful for comparing the ranges of different particles (of the same velocity) in the same medium.

(c) To compare the ranges of the same particle in different materials, we may use a rough relation, known as the **Bragg–Kleeman rule**

$$R \propto \frac{\sqrt{A}}{\rho}, \tag{5.24}$$

where A and ρ are, respectively, the mass number and the density of the material.

5.4.1 Range of Alpha Particles: Bragg's Experiment

When a fast moving α particle travels through matter, it loses energy by ionising the atoms of the medium until its energy reduces to a value that is less than the ionisation energy of the atoms concerned. The α particle then becomes a neutral helium atom by capturing two electrons. The length of the path traversed by the α particle before it stops is called its range. This depends on the initial energy of the α particle and on the nature and pressure of the gas through which it moves. Experimentally, the range can be determined by passing a beam of particles at the desired energy through materials of different thickness and measuring the ionisation produced. Bragg and Kleeman[3] in 1904 first performed experiments on the ranges of α particles in gases. A schematic diagram of the apparatus[4] used is shown in Fig. 5.6.

[3]Bragg, WH and Kleeman, RD. 1904. On the Absorption of α Rays and on the Classification of the α Rays from Radiation. *Phil. Mag.*, 8:48.

[4]Yarwood, J. 1958. *Electricity, Magnetism and Atomic Physics, Volume II*. University Tutorial Press, London.

The radioactive source of the α particles is placed on a small platform whose position can be adjusted along the cylindrical tube (T) of length 100 cm. The tube is first evacuated and the gas is then allowed to enter into the tube at various pressures, ranging from a few cm to 76 cm of Hg. The ionisation produced in the gas by the α particles at a distance measured from S can be determined by the ionisation chamber, which consists of the grid A and the plate P. By measuring the ionisation, Bragg obtained a curve, known as the Bragg curve, as shown in Fig. 3.16 of Chapter 3. It has been found experimentally that the range is inversely proportional to the pressure.

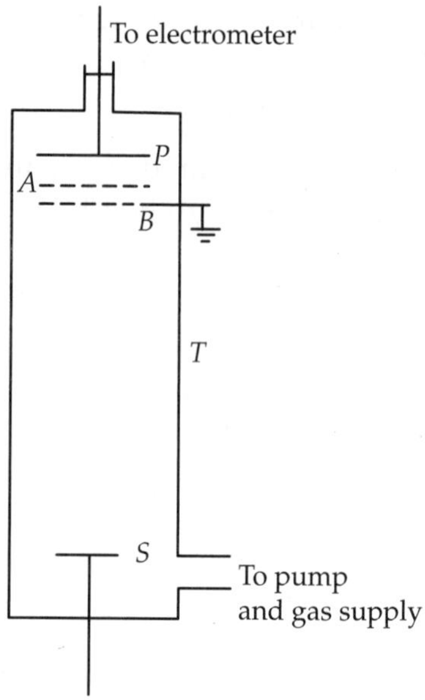

Figure 5.6: *Schematic diagram of the apparatus used to study the range of α particles*

Illustrative Example 5.7: Range of particles with the same velocity

Show that the range of deuteron with energy E is twice that of the proton with energy $E/2$.

Solution For deuteron, $E = \frac{1}{2} m_d v_d^2 \Rightarrow v_d^2 = \frac{2E}{m_d} \approx \frac{E}{m_p}$.

For the proton, $v_p^2 = \frac{2 \times E/2}{m_p} = \frac{E}{m_p}$.

Thus, $\frac{E}{m}$ ratio of the two particles is the same. Since $v_p = v_d$, we may use Eq. (5.23) to get $\frac{R_d}{R_p} = \frac{m_d}{m_p} \frac{z_p^2}{z_d^2} = 2$.

Illustrative Example 5.8: Range of the same particle in different media

Find the ratio of the range of α particles in aluminium and that in air at 15° C and 76 cm of Hg. (Given: $\rho_{\text{air}} = 0.001293$ g/cc and $\rho_{\text{Al}} = 2.7$ g/cc and the mean mass number of air is 14.5 and that of aluminium is 27).

Solution Using the Bragg–Kleeman relation, we get

$$\frac{R_{\text{Al}}}{R_{\text{air}}} = \frac{\rho_{air}}{\rho_{\text{Al}}} \sqrt{\frac{A_{\text{Al}}}{A_{\text{air}}}} \approx 6.534 \times 10^{-4}$$

Illustrative Example 5.9: Range of different particles in the same medium

The range of a 15-MeV proton is 1100 μm in any medium. Another particle having the same initial ionisation as that of the proton has a range of 165 μm. Determine the mass of the particle. (The rate at which a singly ionised particle loses energy E by ionisation along its range is given by $\frac{dE}{dx} = \frac{K}{v^2}$ MeV/μm, where v is the velocity of the particle and K is a constant depending only on emulsion. The mass of the proton is 1837 times the mass of an electron).

Solution $R = \int dx = \frac{1}{K}\int v^2 d\left(\frac{1}{2}mv^2\right)$, since the initial velocities are the same, $\frac{R}{R_p} = \frac{m}{m_p}$. Thus, $m = \frac{165}{1100} \times m_p = 0.15 \times 1837\ \mathrm{m_e} \approx 275.55\ \mathrm{m_e}$.

5.5 INTERACTION OF PHOTONS WITH MATTER

Unlike the charged particles, photons are electrically neutral and do not experience the Coulomb force with the atomic electrons. They interact with matter mainly through three processes, namely:

- Photoelectric effect
- Compton effect
- Pair production

5.5.1 Photoelectric Effect

The photoelectric effect is the process of interaction of γ rays with an electron that is *bound to the atom*. During this interaction, the *entire energy of the photon* is transferred to the electron, as a result of which the electron is ejected from the atom. As energy and momentum cannot be conserved simultaneously, a free electron cannot absorb a photon completely. *Thus, for the photoelectric effect to occur, the electron must be in the bound state.* If the energy required to free a bound electron from the *i*-th state of the atom is I_i (namely, the ionisation energy of the *i*-th state) and the energy of the incident photon is $E_\gamma = h\nu$, the kinetic energy of the emitted electron will be

$$T_e = h\nu - I_i \tag{5.25}$$

We have neglected the recoil kinetic energy (T_a) of the atom. It may be shown that $T_a \sim \frac{m_e}{M} T_e << T_e$, where m_e and M are the rest masses of the electron and the atom, respectively. However, the same conclusion is not true for the momentum of the recoil atom. The atom takes up some of the momentum; this is very significant for the simultaneous conservation of energy and momentum. The photoelectric effect is possible only for electrons bound to the atom. The weaker the binding energy of the electron in comparison with the incident photon energy, the less probable will be the photoelectric effect. From this requirement, we may qualitatively describe different properties of the photoelectric effect.

Important features

(a) *Dependence of the photoelectric cross-section on the atomic number (Z) of the absorbing atom:* Calculating the cross-section for the photoelectric effect is complicated. Roughly, it has been found[5] that

$$\sigma_{\text{photo}} \propto \frac{Z^5}{E_\gamma^{7/2}}, \tag{5.26}$$

where Z is the atomic number of the absorbing atom and E_γ is the energy of the incident photon. The probability of photoelectric effect thus depends very strongly on the charge of the absorbing atom. In light elements (with small Z), the Coulomb force of the nucleus is relatively small and the electrons are bound more weakly than in a heavy nucleus. With increasing Z, the binding between the nucleus and the electron increases, and thus, the probability of photoelectric absorption increases. As the photoelectric effect is dominant for heavy materials with high Z, such materials (for example, lead) are used in γ-ray shielding.

(b) *Dependence of the photoelectric cross-section on E_γ:* The dependence of the photoelectric cross-section[6] on the photon energy E_γ is shown in Fig. 5.7. We can see that *the photoelectric effect is most important for low-energy photons* and not very significant for photon energy ~ 1 MeV. For photons with a large value of E_γ, all electrons appear to be very weakly bound, and therefore, the possibility of photoelectric effect decreases rapidly with increasing photon energy.

(c) Though the probability of photoelectric absorption decreases with increasing photon energy, there are sharp discontinuities, known as *absorption edges*, in the cross-section curve. Figure 5.7 shows that for large values of E_γ (at which electrons can be considered to be weakly bound to the atom), the cross-section is quite small. However, it increases with decreasing E_γ. The cross-section increases rapidly as $E_\gamma \to I_K$, where I_K is the ionisation energy of the K-shell electron (which is ≈ 88 keV for lead). Immediately after this point, $E_\gamma < I_K$, the photoelectric effect is impossible for K-shell electrons. The photoelectric effect may then occur with the electrons in the $L, M, \cdots$ shells. However, the binding of these electrons with the atom is much weaker than for K electrons. Hence, for photons of equal energy, the probability of photoelectric effect for an electron in the L shell is much lower than that for an electron in the K shell. As a result, the cross-section drops sharply at $E_\gamma = I_K$. The discontinuity in the cross-section curve at this point is known as the **K-absorption edge**. Below this energy, the photoelectric cross-section begins to rise once again and then dips as the $L, M, \cdots$ etc. levels are passed. These correspond to the L-absorption edges, M-absorption edges, and so on.

Illustrative Example 5.10: No photoelectric effect with a free electron

Justify that a free electron cannot completely absorb a photon.

[5]Meyerhof, WE. 1967. *Elements of Nuclear Physics*, McGraw-Hill.

[6]Based on Photon Cross Section Database (ver.1.5): http://physics.nist.gov/xcom.

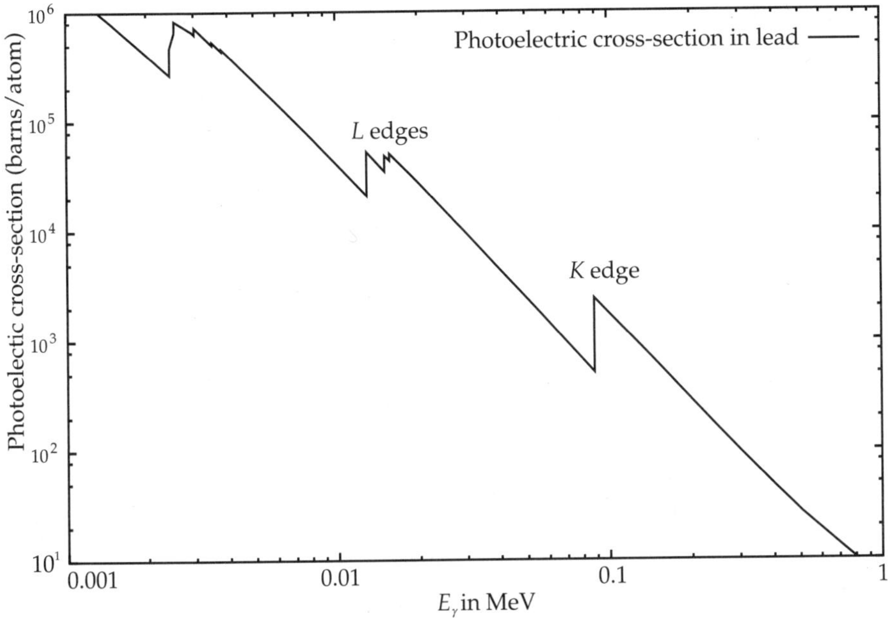

Figure 5.7: *Discrete jumps in the photoelectric cross-section of lead*

Solution Suppose a free electron of rest mass m completely absorbs a photon of energy $h\nu$. Energy conservation gives

$$h\nu + mc^2 = \gamma mc^2 \tag{5.27}$$

And momentum conservation gives

$$\frac{h\nu}{c} + 0 = \gamma mc\beta, \tag{5.28}$$

where $\gamma = \dfrac{1}{\sqrt{1-\beta^2}}$ and $\beta = \dfrac{v}{c}$, v being the velocity of the electron after absorbing the photon. Substituting $h\nu$ from Eq. (5.28) in Eq. (5.27), we get

$$\gamma mc^2\beta + mc^2 = \gamma mc^2$$

$$(1-\beta)\gamma = 1 \tag{5.29}$$

Equation (5.29) has only a trivial solution, $\beta = 0$. Thus, $\gamma = 1$ and Eq. (5.27) leads to the meaningless value of $h\nu = 0$. Thus, we conclude that the photoelectric effect will not occur with a free electron. A free electron will scatter the photon in different directions. We now discuss the scattering of photons by free electrons.

5.5.2 Compton Effect

Photoelectric absorption decreases with increasing energy of the photon. Soon after the K-edge is passed ($E_\gamma > 100$ keV), the dominant process by which the incident photon interacts with the electron is the Compton scattering. In this process, an incident photon with energy $h\nu$ collides with an electron of rest mass m whose binding energy is negligible compared to the energy of the photon. Thus, the electron can be considered as free. For the incident photons of very low energy (below 100 keV), the effects of atomic binding become important, and the electron cannot be assumed to be free. Thus, the Compton effect is not important at low energy. Figure 5.8 shows a schematic view of Compton scattering, where a photon of energy $h\nu$ is incident on a free electron at rest and is scattered at an angle ϕ.

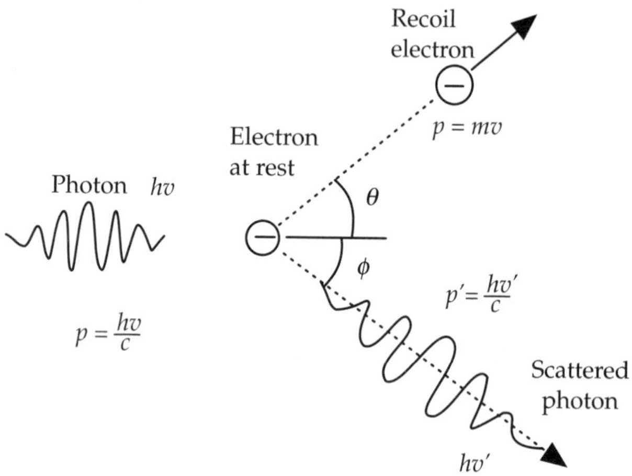

Figure 5.8: *Schematic diagram of Compton effect*

The energy of the scattered photon can be calculated by imposing the conservation of energy and momentum. The energy of the scattered photon is

$$h\nu' = \frac{h\nu}{1 + \frac{h\nu}{mc^2}(1 - \cos\phi)} \tag{5.30}$$

Equation (5.30) shows that the energy of the scattered photon is less than that of the incident one. Thus, the incident photon transfers $h\nu - h\nu'$ amount of energy to the electron. The cross-section for Compton scattering is found to be

$$\propto \frac{Z}{h\nu}, \tag{5.31}$$

where Z is the atomic number of the atoms of the medium. This process is significant in the approximate range of 100 keV to 10 MeV of photon energy.

5.5.3 Pair Production

Another process by which a photon loses its energy is pair production. In this process, a photon creates an electron–positron pair in the field of an atomic nucleus.

$$\gamma \longrightarrow e^- + e^+$$

Since the massive nucleus recoils with negligible energy, the energy balance gives

$$E_\gamma = h\nu = mc^2 + T_- + mc^2 + T_+,$$

where m is the rest mass of the electrons and positrons and T_- and T_+ are their respective kinetic energies. There is a threshold energy of $2mc^2 = 1.022$ MeV for this process. This process is important only for $E_\gamma > 5$ MeV, and its probability increases with atomic number approximately as Z^2.

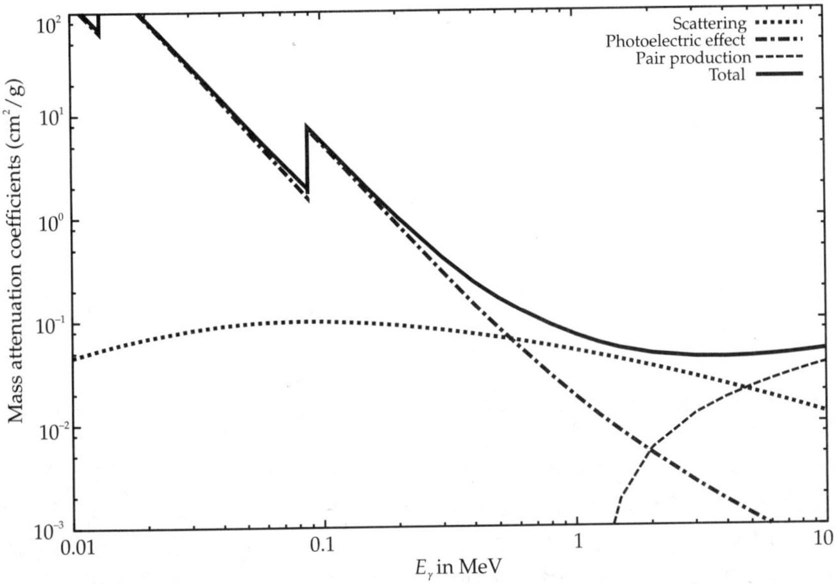

Figure 5.9: *Energy dependence of σ for each of the three mechanisms*

While considering the interaction of γ rays with matter, we must take into account all possible processes, namely, the photoelectric effect, the Compton effect and pair production. The total cross-section for these interactions is

$$\sigma = \sigma_{\text{photo}} + \sigma_{\text{compt}} + \sigma_{\text{pair}}, \tag{5.32}$$

$$\text{where } \sigma_{\text{photo}} \propto \frac{Z^5}{E_\gamma^{7/2}} \tag{5.33}$$

$$\sigma_{\text{compt}} \propto \frac{Z}{E_\gamma} \tag{5.34}$$

$$\text{and } \sigma_{\text{pair}} \propto Z^2 \ln(2E_\gamma) \tag{5.35}$$

Here, Z is the atomic number of the atom of the absorbing material. Figure 5.9 shows the energy dependence of the cross-section for the interaction of γ rays in lead for each of the three possible mechanisms. We can see that the photoelectric effect is the principal mechanism of interaction of γ rays in matter for low energies ($E_\gamma < 100$ keV). The Compton effect is mainly responsible for the intermediate energies (from 100 keV to 5 MeV). Pair production dominates in the high-energy region ($E_\gamma > 5$ MeV).

Figure 5.10 illustrates the relative importance of the three processes described above for different γ ray energies and atomic numbers (Z) of the absorbing material.

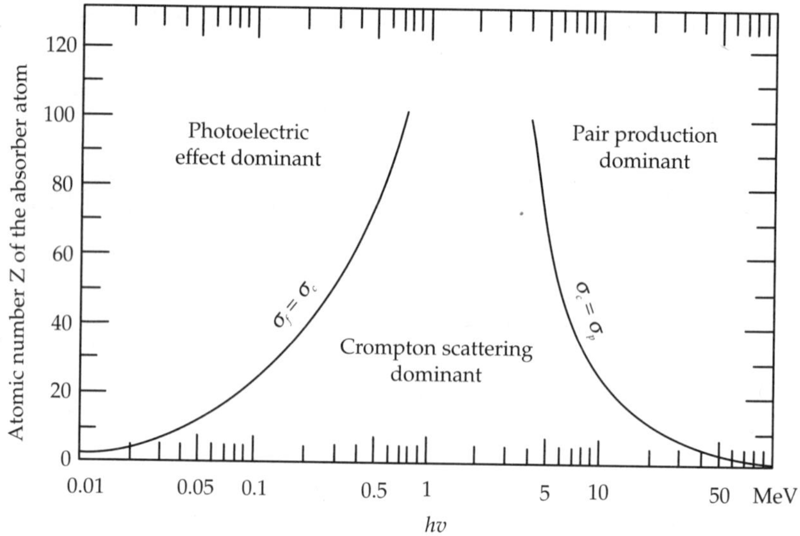

Figure 5.10: *The relative importance of different processes of γ-ray interactions with matter*

For example, consider a γ photon with an energy of 0.1 MeV. If this photon passes through carbon ($Z = 6$), the Compton effect is the predominant mechanism by which this photon interacts. If the same photon travels through lead ($Z = 82$), the photoelectric interaction prevails. For a γ photon with an energy of 2 MeV, the Compton effect predominates for any value of Z. If a photon of 10 MeV travels through carbon, it will interact mainly through Compton scattering. However, the same photon moving through iodine ($Z = 53$) will interact mostly through pair production.

5.5.4 Attenuation of Gamma Rays in Matter

Figure 5.11 shows a collimated beam of γ rays of intensity I_0 incident normally on an absorbing material of thickness t.

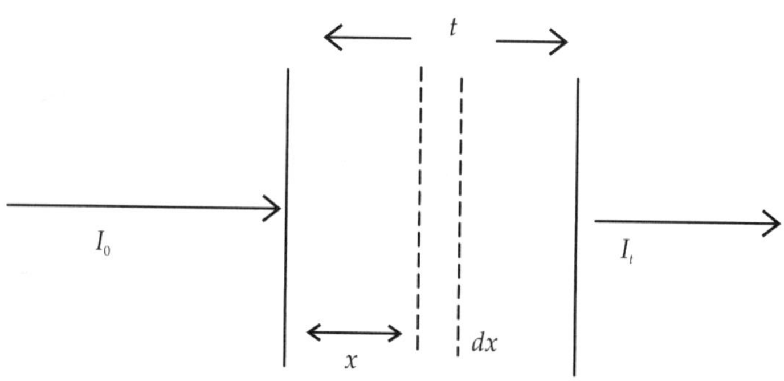

Figure 5.11: *Attenuation of γ rays in matter*

During its passage through the material, the γ rays will undergo photoelectric absorption, pair production or Compton scattering. As a result, some of the photons will deviate from their straight path or be absorbed. Thus, the γ rays will be attenuated gradually in the medium.

Suppose the intensity of the undeviating beam at a penetration depth x is I. The fractional loss in intensity of γ rays $\frac{dI}{I}$ will be proportional to the thickness dx, and thus

$$\frac{dI}{I} = -\mu dx, \tag{5.36}$$

where the proportionality constant μ is called the **linear attenuation coefficient**. Integration of Eq. (5.36) for thickness t gives

$$I_t = I_0 e^{-\mu t} \tag{5.37}$$

The attenuation is caused by three independent processes: Compton effect, photoelectric effect and pair production. Thus, $\mu = \mu_c + \mu_{ph} + \mu_p$, where each partial attenuation coefficient is proportional to the probability of occurrence of the particular process. For a given material, the attenuation coefficient μ depends on the energy of the incident γ ray because different interactions predominate at different energies.

Finally, referring back to our discussion on scattering cross-section in Chapter 4, we can relate the attenuation coefficient to the scattering cross-section. From Eqs (4.26) and (5.37), we find that $\mu = n\sigma$.

Illustrative Example 5.11:

The intensity of an incident γ ray is found to be reduced by a factor of 2 when it penetrates 10 mm of a material. Calculate the absorption coefficient of the material.

Solution: From Eq. (5.37), $\frac{I_t}{I_0} = \frac{1}{2} = e^{-10\mu}$. Solving, $\mu = 0.069$ per mm.

Illustrative Example 5.12:

Calculate the intensity of an incident γ ray absorbed by Compton effect only.

Solution: From Eq. (5.36), the fractional loss in intensity of γ rays due to the Compton effect between x and $x + dx$ is given by

$$\frac{dI_c}{I} = -n\sigma_c dx, \tag{5.38}$$

where σ_c is the scattering cross-section for the Compton effect and $I(x) = I_0 e^{-n\sigma x}$. Therefore

$$dI_c = -n\sigma_c I_0 e^{-n\sigma x} dx \tag{5.39}$$

Solving Eq. (5.39), we get $I_c = I_0 \frac{\sigma_c}{\sigma} e^{-n\sigma x} + c$ (5.40)

At $x = 0$, $I_c = 0$, and thus $I_c = I_0 \frac{\sigma_c}{\sigma}\left(e^{-n\sigma x} - 1\right)$ (5.41)

Similarly, for the photoelectric effect

$$I_{ph} = I_0 \frac{\sigma_{ph}}{\sigma}\left(e^{-n\sigma x} - 1\right) \tag{5.42}$$

Illustrative Example 5.13:

For aluminium and a photon energy of 0.06 MeV, the atomic absorption cross-section due to the Compton effect is 8.1×10^{-24} cm^2, while that due to the photoelectric effect is 4.0×10^{-24} cm^2. How much is the intensity of a given beam reduced by 3.7 g cm^{-2} of aluminium? Also calculate the ratio of the intensities absorbed due to the Compton effect and the photoelectric effect.

Solution: The intensity at thickness t is $I_t = I_0 e^{-n\sigma t}$, where n is the number of atoms per unit volume. Thus, $n \times t$ gives the number of atoms per unit area. 27 g of aluminium contains 6.023×10^{23} atoms. Thus, 3.7 g of aluminium contains $\dfrac{6.023 \times 10^{23} \times 3.7}{27} = 0.825 \times 10^{23}$ atoms. Thus, the number of atoms per unit area $= 0.825 \times 10^{23}$.

$$\frac{I}{I_0} = e^{-0.825 \times 10^{23} \times (8.1+4.0) \times 10^{-24}} = 0.368$$

Therefore, the fraction of the intensity reduced is $1 - 0.368 = 0.632$; or 63.2% of the intensity will be absorbed.

From Eqs (5.41) and (5.42), the ratio of the intensities absorbed by the Compton effect and the photoelectric effect is $\dfrac{\sigma_c}{\sigma_{ph}} = \dfrac{8.1}{4}$.

5.6 DETECTION OF NUCLEAR RADIATION

The operation of the nuclear detector depends on the interaction of nuclear charged particles with matter. Nuclear radiation and charged particles are capable of ionising the material through which they pass. These radiations can be detected by the ionisation they produce in the medium. The various methods of detection are given below:

- Electrical (based on the ionisation produced in the gas by radiation)
- Optical (based on the emission of light, scintillation of a crystal, etc.)
- Photochemical (imprint of a photographic emulsion)

Detectors of the first type involving the ionisation of a gas by nuclear radiation are widely used. They are usually known as gas-filled detectors and can be classified into three main groups:

- Ionisation chamber
- Proportional counter
- Geiger–Müller (GM) counter

Their modes of operation are based on a common principle that we will now discuss.

5.6.1 Gas-filled Detector

The operation of a gas-filled detector is based on the ionisation produced by radiation or the charged particles as they pass through a gas.

Figure 5.12 shows a schematic representation of a typical gas-filled detector. A thin metallic wire is placed along the axis of a gas-filled cylindrical chamber and is made positive with respect to its cylindrical surface. Thus, the central wire acts as the anode and the surface of the cylinder acts as the cathode. When a charged particle enters the detector, it loses energy by repeated collision with the atomic electrons, and the gas inside the chamber becomes ionised. The free electrons will be attracted radially towards the central wire, while the positive ions will move to the cylindrical wall. The flow of charge constitutes a current, and a voltage drop across the resistance (R) is developed. This voltage drop is magnified and the number of pulses is recorded by a suitable counter.

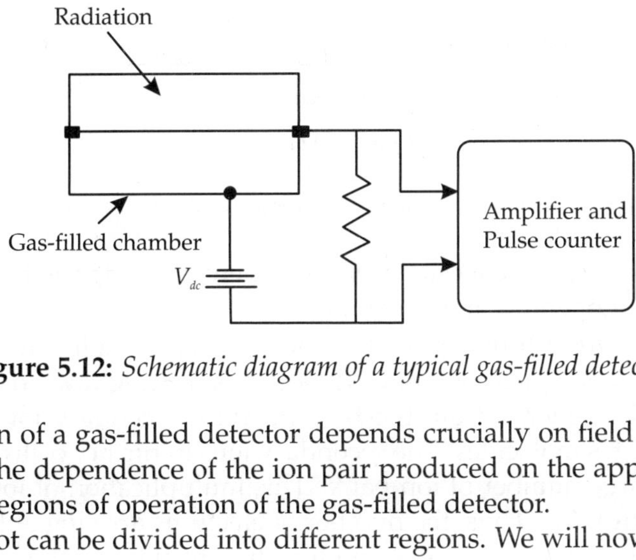

Figure 5.12: *Schematic diagram of a typical gas-filled detector*

The operation of a gas-filled detector depends crucially on field strength. Figure 5.13 illustrates the dependence of the ion pair produced on the applied voltage and shows various regions of operation of the gas-filled detector.

The entire plot can be divided into different regions. We will now discuss each of these.

(a) **Recombination region:** Ion pairs are created by the entry of the radiation into the detector. The number of ion pairs formed inside increases with the energy of radiation. If there is no applied voltage, the ions will again simply recombine soon after they are produced. With application of the applied voltage, recombination of positive ions and electrons will decrease and some of ions will be able to reach the respective electrodes. In this region, the drift velocity of the charges is low and most of them recombine before reaching the electrodes. With an increase in the voltage applied, the number of recombinations reduces, and hence, the number of ions collected increases. No detector operates in this region.

(b) **Ionisation region:** In this region, the electric field is sufficiently large that all of the ion pairs produced are collected by the electrodes. The amplitude of the output pulse is proportional to the energy of thc incident radiation. In this region,

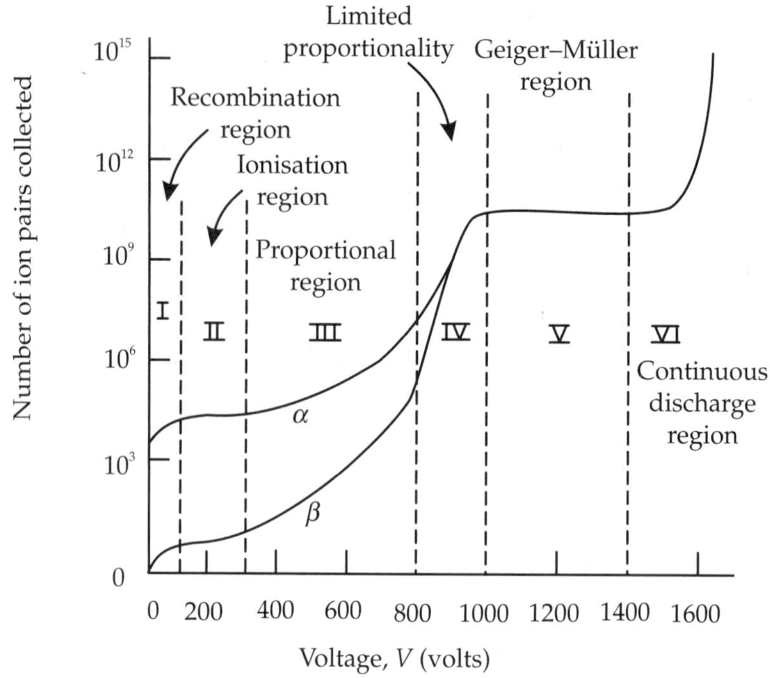

Figure 5.13: *Different operating regions of a gas-filled detector*

the number of ion pairs collected is independent of the applied voltage. The ionisation chamber operates in this region.

(c) **Proportional region:** If the applied voltage is raised to a few hundred volts, the field near the anode increases and the electrons drifting towards the centre wire acquire sufficient energy from the field to cause secondary ionisation by collisions with the gas molecules. The secondary ions in further collisions produce an enormously large number of ion pairs. This multiplication of ion pairs is called **gas amplification** (A). Thus, the number of electrons arriving at the electrode increases exponentially, that is, gas amplification results. Each electron produced earlier, before gas multiplication, acts independently and the amplitude of the output pulse is proportional to the number of ions initially produced by the incident radiation (that is, proportional to the incident energy). This region is known as the proportional region and the proportional counter operates in this region.

(d) **Limited proportionality region:** If the applied voltage is increased further, the number of secondary ions increases, but the proportionality between the ions finally collected and those initially produced disappears gradually. This is the region of limited proportionality. No counter operates here.

(e) **Geiger–Müller region:** If the applied voltage is increased further, then the field becomes so strong that any initial ionisation produced by the incident radiation can trigger a complete gas break-down by producing an avalanche of electrons. Here, all radiations, irrespective of their energies, give the same output. This region is called the Geiger–Müller region, and is used in the Geiger–Müller (GM) counter. As the output pulse is independent of the incident energy, it cannot be used to measure energy.

With a further increase in the applied voltage, the field eventually becomes so strong that it ionises the gas directly, producing continuous discharge.

5.6.2 Ionisation Chamber

An ionisation chamber can be regarded as a parallel plate capacitor, as shown schematically in Fig. 5.14, in which the space between the plates is filled with a gas, often air. Due to the passage of radiation through the chamber, ion pairs are formed. The value of the electric field strength between the plates is such that all the ions formed along the path of the passing particle are collected at the respective plates, but there is no secondary ionisation by collision; that is, gas amplification (A) is unity. The flow of charge constitutes a current that develops a voltage pulse across the resistance R.

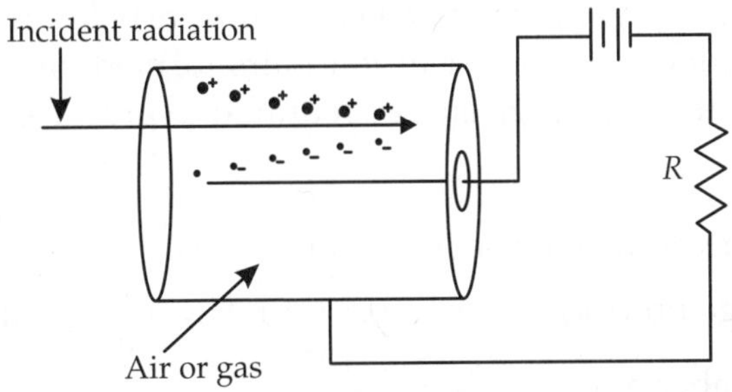

Figure 5.14: *Visualisation of the ion chamber operation*

The output voltage pulse is proportional to the number (n) of ion pairs formed, and hence, proportional to the energy of the incident radiation, but is independent of the applied voltage. The applied voltage determines the speed at which the electrons and ions drift to their respective electrodes. The force on either charge carrier is the same; however, their accelerations are quite different. The collection time with 500 V of applied voltage is $\backsim 1 \mu s$ for electrons and $\backsim$ 1 ms for ions. This duration of collection time is quite long compared to the standard nuclear counting (a weak radioactive source gives on an average 1 decay in 30 μs) and thus, the ionisation chamber is impractical for counting individual pulses.

Any good counter must satisfy the following requirements:

- Every particle entering the detector should produce a pulse at exit.
- The duration of the pulse should be sufficiently short so that particles coming in one after the other in quick succession produce separate pulses.

Illustrative Example 5.14: Estimation of voltage pulse

Assume that the average energy required to produce one ion pair is about $\backsim$ 34 eV. Suppose β particles of energy 1 MeV pass through an ionisation chamber and are absorbed completely. The capacity of the electrodes is 100 pF. Calculate the height of the output pulse.

Solution The energy required to produce one ion pair in the gas is 34 eV. Thus, the number of ion pairs produced by 1 MeV radiation is $n = \dfrac{10^6}{34} \approx 3 \times 10^4$.

The electric charge produced is

$$Q = 3 \times 10^4 \text{ ions } \times 1.6 \times 10^{-19}\text{Coulomb/ion} \approx 5.0 \times 10^{-15}\text{Coulomb}$$

Therefore, the resulting voltage pulse is $V = \dfrac{5.0 \times 10^{-15} C}{100 \times 10^{-12} F} \approx 50\ \mu\text{V}$.

This is quite small and must therefore be amplified considerably using standard electronics.

Illustrative Example 5.15: Estimation of energy

An ionisation chamber is connected to an electrometer of capacitance 0.5 pF and voltage sensitivity of 4 divisions per volt. A beam of α particles produces 0.8 divisions of deflection. Determine the number of ion pairs formed and the energy of the α particles. (Assume that the average energy required to produce one ion pair is about $\backsim$ 34 eV).

Solution The resulting voltage pulse is $\dfrac{0.8}{4} = 0.2$ volt.

Total electric charge produced $= 0.2 \times 0.5 \times 10^{-12} = 10^{-13}$ Coulomb.

Therefore, the number of ion pairs $= \dfrac{10^{-13}}{1.6 \times 10^{-19}} = 6.25 \times 10^5$.

The required energy is $34 \times 6.25 \times 10^5$ eV $= 21.2$ MeV.

5.6.3 Proportional Counter

The geometry of the proportional counter is cylindrical, as shown schematically in Fig. 5.12. This counter differs from the ionisation chamber in having higher electric fields. The electric field in an ionisation chamber with parallel plate capacitor is constant, whereas in the proportional counter, the field at a radius r is

$$E(r) = \frac{V}{r \ln(\frac{b}{a})}, \tag{5.43}$$

where a is the radius of the central anode wire and b is the radius of the cathode cylinder. $E(r)$ becomes large near the anode wire even with moderate applied voltage. In this case, the sequence of events is as follows:

1. An incident radiation forms an electron–ion pair along its path in the volume. In the presence of the electric field, the electrons and ions start to drift towards their respective electrodes. At points far from the anode, the electric field is not large enough; so the electrons can gain, between two collisions, sufficient kinetic energy to ionise other atoms of the gas.

2. As the electrons of the primary ionisation approach the anode, field strength increases and, at a certain distance, the drifting electrons gain enough energy to cause further ionisation, thus liberating more electrons. The secondary ions again produce further ionisation through collisions. The chain of such events leads to an avalanche of electrons (Fig. 5.15) .

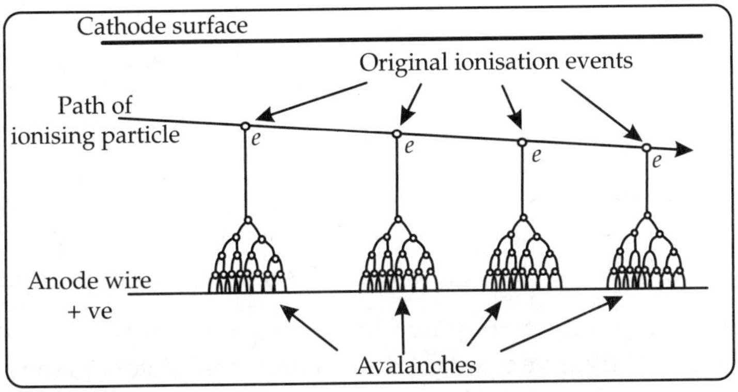

Figure 5.15: *Avalanches in proportional counter*

3. The avalanche occurs in the high-field region near the central anode. Most of the primary ions are formed far from this central region, and the electrons drift slowly until the avalanche begins. Proportional counters operate in the region where each primary electron creates an avalanche separately and the voltage pulse thus generated is proportional to the primary ionisation. In proportional counters, the typical value of gas multiplication (A) is $\backsim 10^3$.

Illustrative Example 5.16: Estimation of electric field

The inner and outer radii of the cylindrical counter are 0.1 mm and 1.0 cm, respectively. Assuming an applied voltage of 1000 V, calculate the field strength at a point very close to the central wire and also at $r = 0.5$ cm.

Solution The field at r is $E(r) = \frac{V}{r\ln(\frac{b}{a})}$.

At a point close to the anode, $r \backsim 0.1$ mm.

$$E(r) = \frac{1000}{0.01 \times \ln\left(\frac{1}{0.01}\right)} \approx 2.2 \times 10^4 \text{ V/cm}$$

At $r = 0.5$ cm

$$E(r) = \frac{1000}{0.5 \times \ln\left(\frac{1}{0.01}\right)} \approx 4.34 \times 10^2 \text{ V/cm}$$

Illustrative Example 5.17: Estimation of gas multiplication (A)

A photon of energy 2 MeV gives up all of its energy to the gas in a proportional counter. Estimate the gas multiplication (A). Assume that the input capacitance of the amplifier in parallel to the proportional counter is 1.5 nF and input sensitivity is 1 mV. Also assume that the average energy required to produce one ion pair is $\backsim$ 34 eV.

Solution The number of primary ion pairs produced is $N = \dfrac{2 \times 10^6}{34} \approx 5.88 \times 10^4$.

If the gas multiplication is A, then $Q = ANe$.

Since $Q = CV$, gas multiplication is $A = \dfrac{CV}{Ne} = \dfrac{1.5 \times 10^{-9} \times 10^{-3}}{5.88 \times 10^4 \times 1.6 \times 10^{-19}} \approx 159$.

Illustrative Example 5.18: Estimation of voltage pulse in proportional counter

Assume that the average energy required to produce one ion pair is $\backsim$ 34 eV. Suppose electrons of energy 14 keV give up all of their energy completely to the gas in the proportional counter. Calculate the height of the output pulse. Given gas multiplication is 500 and the capacitance of the circuit is 1 pF.

Solution The number of primary ion pairs produced is $N = \dfrac{14 \times 10^3}{34} \approx 411$.

Total charge $= 500 \times 411 \times 1.6 \times 10^{-19} = 3.29 \times 10^{-14}$

Therefore, the height of the voltage pulse is $\dfrac{3.29 \times 10^{-14}}{1 \times 10^{-12}} = 3.29 \times 10^{-2}$ V.

5.6.4 Geiger–Müller (GM) Counter

The geometry of the GM counter is cylindrical – the same as in the proportional counter. The only difference is that the applied voltage is very large in this case: $\sim$ 1000 V. Therefore, the electric field near the central wire is very large.

The radiation entering the tube ionises the gas at low pressure. The negative electrons drift towards the central positive wire, while the positive ions move to the negative cylindrical surface. As the electric field near the wire is extremely large, the electrons released in the primary ionisation acquire sufficient energy to release additional electrons from the neutral atoms by collision. These secondary electrons are also accelerated as they move towards the wire and produce further ionisation. This cumulative ionisation is known as the **Townsend avalanche**. The electrons accelerating in the strong electric field may also produce, in addition to the new avalanche of electrons, excitation of the atoms of the gas. These molecules produce photons on de-excitation. These photons, in turn, produce photoelectrons, which participate in further avalanches. Thus, the avalanche that began at a point close to the wire spreads very rapidly to the entire volume of the cylinder. The gas multiplication A becomes extremely large, $A \sim 10^{10}$. The electrons that reach the wire produce a voltage pulse across the resistance R.

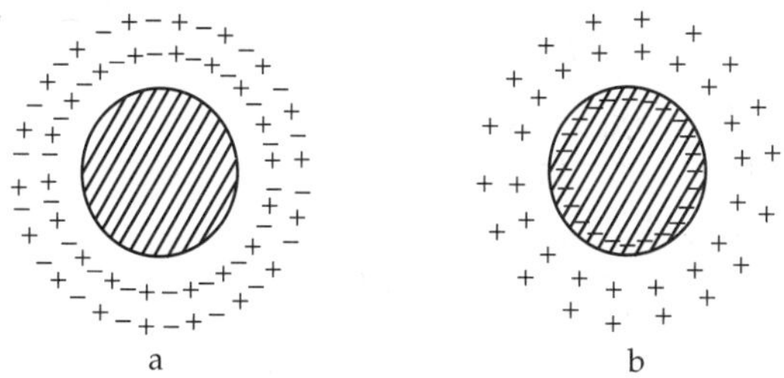

Figure 5.16: *Sheath of positive ions around the anode. (a) represents the situation just immediately after the avalanche and (b) a fraction of a microsecond later.*

Dead time, recovery time and resolving time: The electrons produced during ionisation, being light, reach the central wire very quickly – within a fraction of a microsecond after ionisation occurs. However, the positive ions, being massive, drift relatively slowly when compared to the fast moving electrons. As a result, a sheath of positive charge is developed around the central anode (Fig. 5.16). This layer of positive charge screens the anode electrostatically (many electrons will not be able to reach the anode) and reduces the field to less than the value necessary for Geiger action. A particle entering the counter at this time will thus be unable to produce an avalanche, and no voltage pulse will be formed. The counter becomes insensitive for this period. This insensitivity lasts for a certain period, called the *the dead time of the counter*.

The time interval during which the counter is insensitive for further ionising events, after a pulse occurs, is known as the dead time.

For a fixed voltage applied to the tube, a certain density of positive ions will be needed to reduce the electric field below the minimum value required for further multiplication. Thus, after developing about the same number of total positive charges, each Geiger discharge is terminated regardless of the number of original ion pairs produced by the incident radiation. *All output pulses are therefore about the same size, and their amplitude cannot provide any information about the properties of the incident radiation.*

As the positive sheath of ions moves to the cathode, the field strength near the central wire increases to a critical value sufficient to re-start the Geiger action. If another ionising event triggers the counter at this stage, a pulse smaller than normal is obtained, as the full voltage across the counter is not operative. When the positive ions reach the cylinder, the electric field near the wire recovers to its full value and the full-sized pulse is obtained. These full-sized pulses cannot occur until the positive ions have reached the cylinder.

The time required for the positive ions to reach the counter wall is known as the recovery time.

The minimum time interval within which two pulses must be detected as separate pulses by the counter is called the **resolving time**[7]. Dead time, recovery time and resolving time are illustrated in Fig. 5.17.

[7]Kamal, A. 2014. *Particle Physics*. Springer-Verlag, Berlin.

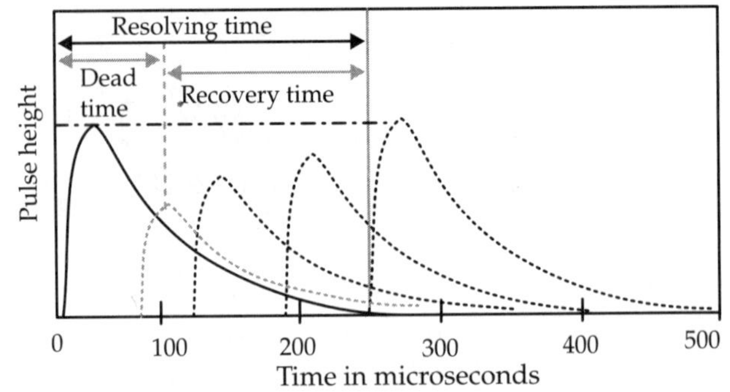

Figure 5.17: *Dead time, resolving time and the time of resolution of the GM counter*

From Fig. 5.17, we note that

Resolving time = Dead time + Recovery time

Let n be the observed counts in unit time when the counter is exposed to N initiating events per unit time. Thus, the true counting rate is N and the observed count rate is n. Let τ be the resolving time, that is, the time interval between two resolvable pulses. In each count, the counter remains practically insensitive for time τ. Thus, the total insensitive time is $n\tau$ per second. The number of counts missed is $N \times n\tau$, which is also equal to $N - n$. Thus

$$N \times n\tau = N - n$$

Or, the actual count rate is $N = \dfrac{n}{1 - n\tau}$ (5.44)

To appreciate the advantages of the GM counter over the ionisation counter, let us consider the following example.

Illustrative Example 5.19: Estimation of voltage pulse in GM counter

Assume that the average energy required to produce one ion pair in a GM tube filled with helium is $\backsim$ 42 eV. Suppose β particles of 0.5-MeV energy pass through the chamber and are absorbed completely. Calculate the height of the output pulse.

If the particle passes through an ionisation chamber with capacitance of 1 nF, calculate the output.

Solution The energy required to produce one ion pair in the gas is 42 eV.

Thus, the number of ion pairs produced by 0.5-MeV radiation is

$$n = \frac{0.5 \times 10^6}{42} \approx 12 \times 10^3$$

The electric charge produced is:

$$Q = 12 \times 10^3 \text{ions} \times 1.6 \times 10^{-19} \text{Coulomb/ion} \approx 19.2 \times 10^{-16} \text{Coulomb}$$

If the detector operates as an ionisation chamber, the resulting voltage pulse will be

$$V = \frac{19.2 \times 10^{-16} C}{10^{-9} F} \approx 2 \times 10^{-6} \text{ V}$$

This is quite small and must thus be amplified considerably using standard electronics.

If the detector operates as a GM counter, the number of ion pairs produced will be $n \approx 12 \times 10^3 \times A$, where the gas multiplication A is very large, ($A \backsim 10^{10}$). Consequently, the voltage pulse developed will also be very large ($\backsim$ a few volts).

Illustrative Example 5.20: Estimation of electric field

An organic quenched GM tube operates at 1000 V and has a wire of diameter 0.2 mm. The radius of the cathode is 2 cm. What is the maximum radial field?

Solution The field at r is $E(r) = \dfrac{V}{r\ln(\frac{b}{a})}$.

At a point close to the anode, $r \backsim 0.1$ mm $= 0.1 \times 10^{-4}$ m. The maximum field is $E_{max} = \frac{V}{r\ln(\frac{b}{a})}$, where $V = 1000$ V, $a = 0.1$ mm and $b = 2$ cm. Thus, $E_{max} \approx 1.89 \times 10^6$ V/m.

Illustrative Example 5.21: Estimation of electric field

A GM counter operates at 1 kV and has a wire of diameter 0.2 mm. The radius of the cathode is 2 cm and the tube has a guaranteed lifetime of 10^9 counts. What is the magnitude of the maximum radial field? If the counter is used on an average for 30 hours a week at 3000 counts per minute, how long will the counter last?

Solution The maximum field is $E_{max} = \dfrac{V}{r\ln(\frac{b}{a})}$, where $V = 1000$ V, $a = 0.1$ mm, $b = 2$ cm and $r \approx 0.1$ mm. Thus, $E_{max} \approx 1.89 \times 10^6$ V/m.

Number of counts per week is $30 \times 60 \times 3000 = 54 \times 10^5$.

Number of counts per year is $52 \times 54 \times 10^5 = 2.808 \times 10^8$.

Therefore, the counter will last for $\dfrac{10^9}{2.808 \times 10^8} \approx 3.56$ years.

Illustrative Example 5.22:

It has been found that in a counter, the average current in the circuit is 1.333×10^{-11} A. Find the counting rate per minute if the counter collects 10^7 electrons per discharge.

Solution Let the number of counts per minute be N.

The number of electrons collected per second is $\dfrac{N \times 10^7}{60}$.

Thus $\dfrac{1.6 \times 10^{-19} \times N \times 10^7}{60} = 1.333 \times 10^{-11}, \quad N \approx 500$

The counting rate is ≈ 500 per minute.

Illustrative Example 5.23: Reduction of field due to space charge[8]

Suppose the positive ion sheath around the anode lies at a distance r_0 from the centre. Find the field strength inside the cylinder.

[8] Kamal, A. 2014. *Particle Physics*. Springer-Verlag, Berlin.

Solution In the absence of space charge, the field inside the tube is

$$E_0 = \frac{V_0}{\ln\frac{b}{a}}\frac{1}{r}, \tag{5.45}$$

where V_0 is the voltage difference between the anode and the cathode.
Now, we want to determine the field in the presence of space charge.
Let λ_- and λ_+ be the charge per unit length on the wire and in the space charge, respectively.

The field inside the ion sheath $(r_0 > r > a)$ is $E_1 = \frac{1}{2\pi\varepsilon_0}\frac{\lambda_-}{r}$.

The field outside the sheath $(r_0 < r < b)$ is $E_2 = \frac{1}{2\pi\varepsilon_0}\frac{\lambda_+ + \lambda_-}{r}$.

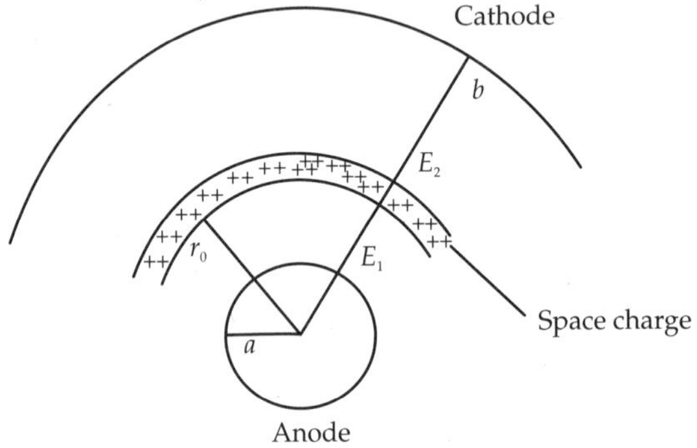

Figure 5.18: *Calculation of field in the presence of ion sheath*

Assuming that the voltage difference remains constant

$$V_0 = \int_a^{r_0} E_1 dr + \int_{r_0}^{b} E_2 dr = \int_a^{r_0} \frac{1}{2\pi\varepsilon_0}\frac{\lambda_-}{r}dr + \int_{r_0}^{b} \frac{1}{2\pi\varepsilon_0}\frac{\lambda_+ + \lambda_-}{r}dr$$

$$= \frac{\lambda_-}{2\pi\varepsilon_0}\ln\frac{b}{a} + \frac{\lambda_+}{2\pi\varepsilon_0}\ln\frac{b}{r_0} \text{ or } \frac{\lambda_-}{2\pi\varepsilon_0} = \frac{V_0}{\ln\frac{b}{a}} - \frac{\lambda_+}{\ln\frac{b}{a}}\ln\frac{b}{r_0}$$

Therefore $E_1 = \frac{V_0}{\ln\frac{b}{a}}\frac{1}{r} - \frac{\lambda_+}{\ln\frac{b}{a}}\ln\frac{b}{r_0}\frac{1}{r}$ or $E_1 = E_0 - \frac{\lambda_+}{\ln\frac{b}{a}}\ln\frac{b}{r_0}\frac{1}{r}$

Thus, the positive space charge around the wire reduces the field. If it is reduced sufficiently, secondary ionisation temporarily becomes impossible and no event can be recorded. This time interval is called the dead time. As the ion sheath moves towards the cylindrical surface, r_0 increases. Thus, the negative term in the above equation decreases, and hence, E_1 again increases and finally the original value is restored.

Illustrative Example 5.24: True count

A GM counter with a resolving time of 2×10^{-4} s registers 10^3 counts per second. Find the actual count rate.

Solution The actual count rate is $N = \dfrac{n}{1 - n\tau} = \dfrac{1000}{1 - 10^3 \times 2 \times 10^{-4}} \approx 1250$

Quenching the discharge: When the positive ions finally strike the cathode eject electrons and since by this time the field has been restored to its original high value, a new avalanche starts and the process just described is repeated. Clearly, there must be some mechanism by which the occurrence of repetitive discharge is permanently stopped or "quenched". This mechanism is referred to as **quenching**[9].

A commonly used method of quenching is to add a small amount of another gas of relatively lower ionisation potential to the inert gas. For example, ethyl alcohol.

When a positive ion of the counter gas collides with a molecule of ethyl alcohol, the latter, because of its lower ionisation potential, can transfer an electron to the counter gas, thereby neutralising it. Positive ions of the quenching gas, on reaching the cathode wall, give up their energy by dissociating themselves into simple molecules rather than producing new electrons. The discharge is thus stopped.

GM characteristics: Figure 5.19 shows the typical behaviour of the count rate with respect to the applied voltage of a GM counter. It shows that unless the applied voltage exceeds a threshold value, no counts will be recorded.

Figure 5.19 has three distinct regions:

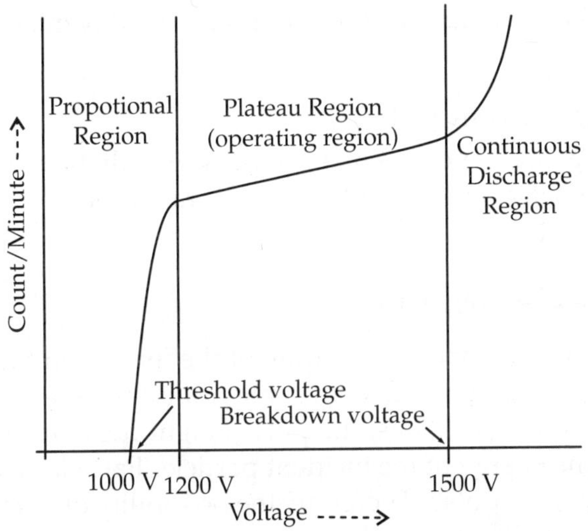

Figure 5.19: *GM plateau*

(a) The proportional region, where gas multiplication takes place. The size of the electrical pulses is proportional to the energy of the incident radiation. This region generally varies from 500 V to 1000 V.

(b) The plateau region, where gas amplification is extremely large. After a sharp rise, the counting rate remains almost constant. This flat region is called the plateau.

[9]Knoll, GF. 2010. *Radiation Detection and Measurement, Fourth Edition,* John Wiely & Sons; Kamal, A. 2014. *Particle Physics.* Springer-Verlag, Berlin.

In this region, the electrical pulses are of the same size, irrespective of the initial energy of the incident radiation and independent of the applied voltage. The length of plateau is generally ~ 300 V.

(c) The continuous discharge region, where the electrical field strength is sufficiently large to produce continuous gas multiplication.

Illustrative Example 5.25: Operating voltage fluctuation

The slope of the plateau of the GM counter working at 1000 V is 2% counting rate per 100 V. Calculate the allowed variation of the operating voltage if the counting rate is to be limited to 0.2%.

Solution Let N_1 and N_2 be the count rate at voltages V_1 and V_2, respectively. The percentage change in counting rate is $\frac{N_2 - N_1}{N_{av}} \times 100$, where $N_{av} = \frac{N_1 + N_2}{2}$.

Given: $\frac{(N_2 - N_1) \times 100}{N_{av}} \times \frac{100}{V_2 - V_1} = 2.$

If $\frac{(N_2 - N_1)}{N_{av}} \times 100 = 0.2,\ V_2 - V_1 = 10.$

Therefore, the working voltage may be varied as 1000 ± 10 V.

Advantages and disadvantages of GM counter: The advantages of a GM counter are as follows:

(a) Technically simple to construct.

(b) Very useful for general measurement of nuclear radiation. It is a very sensitive counter that can detect even very-low-energy radiation.

(c) Low cost

It has two important disadvantages:

(a) There is no information about the nature of the ionisation that caused the pulse. In the GM counter, any particle with some minimum energy can create an electron avalanche in the gas. Thus, the pulse height developed in the output does not depend on the energy of the incident particle. Particles with different energy will produce the same pulse. Therefore, the possibility of determining the energy of the incident particle is lost in this counter.

(b) Because of the large avalanche, the GM counter takes a relatively long time to reset (the recovery time $\backsim$ 1 ms). Thus, it is not sensitive to radiation of high counting rate.

5.7 SCINTILLATION DETECTOR

The scintillation detector is an important particle detection device that is often used in a wide range of high-energy physics experiments today. It was developed from the early scintillation methods as practised by Rutherford and others. This detector makes use of the fact that the excitation of atoms in certain materials, when struck by the incident radiation or particle, results a small flash of light (known as scintillation). These scintillations can be converted to electrical pulses by an amplifying device such as a photomultiplier, which can then be counted electronically to obtain information about the incident particle.

Basic process

1. The incident radiation passing through the scintillator excites its atoms and molecules.
2. The excited atoms come to the ground state by emitting photons (luminescence).
3. The emitted photons strike a photo-sensitive surface, called photocathode, releasing at most one photoelectron per photon.
4. These photoelectrons are then accelerated and multiplied in the photomultiplier tube (PMT) to produced a large pulse.

A schematic sketch of the basic elements of a scintillation detector[10] is shown in Fig. 5.20. It consists of scintillating material which is optically connected to the photomultiplier tube (PMT).

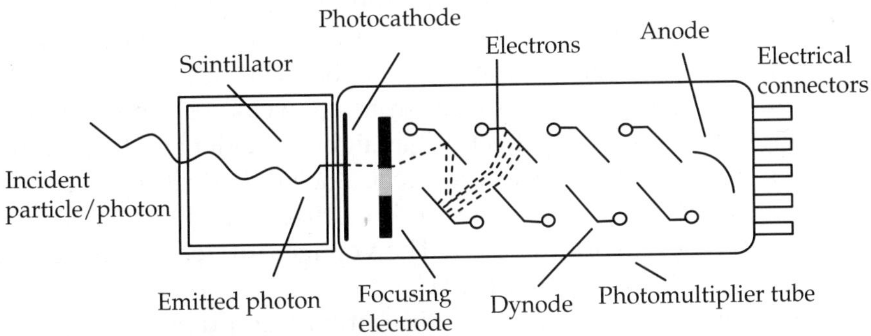

Figure 5.20: *Sketch of a scintillation counter*

Scintillators exhibit *luminescence,* that is, they absorb and re-emit energy in the form of light. The most commonly used scintillators are inorganic single crystal and organic liquids or plastics.

Inorganic crystal scintillators, such as NaI or CsI, are usually doped with activator centres (for example, thallium). Ionising particles traversing the crystal produce free electron-hole pairs, which move around until captured by an activator centre. The activators (dopants) are thus excited and decay with emission of light over a broad spectrum in the visible region. The decay time of de-excitation is of the order of 250 ns.

In **organic scintillators** (for example, anthracene or naphthalene), however, the mechanism of luminescence is completely different. The scintillation mechanism in organic materials is molecular in nature. In this case, the molecules are excited and

[10]Leo, WR. 1994. *Techniques for Nuclear and Particle Physics Experiments*, Springer-Verlag, Berlin.

then decay with the emission of ultraviolet light. Unfortunately, light of such frequency is rapidly attenuated. The conversion from the initially produced ultraviolet ray to the visible ray is achieved through the fluorescent excitation of dye molecules known as the **wavelength shifter**, which is admixed with the primary scintillator. Organic scintillators have a fast decay time of the order of 10 ns.

Good scintillators have the following characteristics:

(a) *High efficiency of converting energy to light*: They must convert the energy of the incident particle or photon efficiently into detectable light. The highest efficiency of about 13% is obtained with sodium iodide.

(b) *Linearity*: They should also have a linear energy response (that is, the light produced and the energy deposited is linear).

(c) *Short decay constant*: The luminescence should be rapid, so that light pulses are generated very quickly.

(c) *Transparency so as to allow transmission of light*: The scintillator must be transparent to the light emitted.

(d) It should have good *optical quality* for coupling to a photomultiplier tube.

Since the intensity of the light emitted by luminescence is low, the photon signal must somehow be amplified in order to be detected. This amplification is achieved by using a photomultiplier tube. It consists of a photocathode made up of Sb coated with alkali metals in which the valence electrons are weakly bound and have a high cross-section for the photoelectric effect. When light is incident on the photocathode, electrons are emitted by the photoelectric effect. The emitted electrons are then multiplied and accelerated by a series of electrodes, called dynodes, which are made of material of relatively low work function. The voltage difference between two adjacent dynodes is typically $V_d \sim 100$ V to 200 V.

Suppose the number of stages of multiplication (the number of dynodes) is n. Let δ be the electron gain (which is the number of secondary electrons generated from each of the primary electrons). The number of electrons obtained from the final electrode is

$$G = \delta^n \tag{5.46}$$

For dynodes with Mg-O, CS_3, $\delta \sim 3$ to 6.

If, for example, there are 10 dynodes with $\delta = 4\,(\text{say})$, then $G = 4^{10} \approx 10^6$.

In a Ga-P dynode, δ is large, ~ 25, thus very high multiplication is achieved by a few dynodes. (Less space is required and it is easy to maintain linearity).

Essential features

(a) *Linearity*: It is a linear device. The output light of the scintillator is directly proportional to the energy of the incident radiation. Since PMT is also a linear device, the final output voltage developed is also proportional to the incident energy. This makes the scintillation detector useful as an energy measuring device.

(b) *Fast time response*: Its recovery time is very low compared to the other detectors. Thus, the time difference between two events may be obtained with greater precision.

(c) *Pulse shape determination*: It is possible to detect different types of particles by analysing the pulses developed at the output.

The two main advantages of the scintillation counter over the GM counter are as follows:

(a) Time of flight of the electrons through the tube is very small and about 10^6 particles per second can be counted. This is about 200 times larger than the possible rate with the GM counter.

(b) The efficiency of γ-ray detection is much higher.

SUMMARY

- **Energy Transfer in Elastic Collision:** Elastic collision is characterised by conservation of total kinetic energy. Loss of kinetic energy of the particle of mass M in a collision with a stationary particle of mass m is shown as $\Delta T = \dfrac{4mM}{(m+M)^2}T$.
  If $M \gg m$, the energy transfer is small, while for $M \approx m$, the incident particle transfers its entire energy to the target.
- **Interaction of Charged Particles with Matter**

  (a) One form of inelastic collision of charged particles with matter is ionisation loss, when the kinetic energy of the incident particle is used either to excite or to ionise atoms of the material through which it passes.
  The stopping power is independent of the mass of the incident particle, but is proportional to the square of its charge and the number density of electrons in the medium.

  $$-\frac{dE}{dx} \propto \frac{nz^2}{v^2}$$

  Here, v is the velocity of the incident particle.

  (b) The range (R) of any charged particle and its energy (E) are related as $R \propto E^{3/2}$.

  (c) The ratio of ranges of two charged particles of different masses with the same initial velocity is $\frac{R_1}{R_2} = \frac{m_1}{m_2}\frac{z_2^2}{z_1^2}$.

  (d) The Bragg–Kleeman rule may be used to compare the ranges of the same particle in different materials

  $$R \propto \frac{\sqrt{A}}{\rho},$$

  where A and ρ are, respectively, the mass number and the density of the material.

  (e) When a charged particle moves close to a nucleus, it accelerates and emits radiation. This inelastic process is known as bremsstrahlung. The energy loss due to bremsstrahlung for particles with the same charge is inversely proportional to the square of the mass. Therefore, the radiation loss is significant for light particles (electrons).

(f) Photons interact with matter through the photoelectric effect, Compton effect and pair production.

In the photoelectric effect, the entire energy of the incident photon is absorbed by one of the electrons that constitute the atom. As a free electron cannot absorb a photon completely, the photoelectric effect cannot occur for free electrons. It is the principal mechanism of absorption of low-energy (long wavelength) γ radiation in matter.

The Compton effect is the process of scattering of γ rays with a free electron, where a part of the energy of the incident photon is transferred to the electron. This process is significant in the intermediate energy range of 100 keV to 10 MeV.

The process of electron–positron pair production (in the field of the nucleus) dominates in the high-energy range. The threshold energy for this process is $E_\gamma = 2m_ec^2$.

The total cross-section for these interactions is $\sigma = \sigma_{\text{photo}} + \sigma_{\text{compt}} + \sigma_{\text{pair}}$, where $\sigma_{\text{photo}} \propto \frac{Z^5}{E_\gamma^{7/2}}$; $\sigma_{\text{compt}} \propto \frac{Z}{E_\gamma}$ and $\sigma_{pair} \propto Z^2 \ln(2E_\gamma)$, Z being the atomic number of the atom of the absorbing material.

The γ ray attenuates in matter as $I_t = I_0 e^{-\mu x}$, where $\mu = \mu_{\text{Compton}} + \mu_{\text{ph}} + \mu_{\text{pair}}$.

- **Gas-filled Detector:** The operation of the gas-filled detector is based on the ionisation produced in the gas by the incident nuclear radiation. Depending on the applied voltage, gas-filled detectors can be classified into three main groups as (i) ionisation chambers, (ii) proportional counters and (iii) Geiger–Müller (GM) counters.

(a) In an ionisation chamber, all ion pairs formed by the passage of radiation are collected at the respective plates and there is no secondary ionisation. Thus, gas multiplication A is 1.

(b) In a proportional counter, the electric field, unlike in the ionisation chamber, at a radius r is $E(r) = \frac{V}{r\ln(\frac{b}{a})}$, where a is the radius of the central anode wire and b is the radius of the cathode cylinder. The counters operate in the region where each primary electron creates n avalanches separately and the voltage pulse thus generated is proportional to the primary ionisation. The typical value of the (A) is 10^3.

(c) In a GM counter, the applied voltage is very large and the gas multiplication (A) is 10^{10}. Here, any particle with some minimum energy can create an electron avalanche, and thus, the counter cannot determine the energy of the incident particle. The time between two recordable pulses is known as resolving time (τ). The true counting rate N and the observed counting rate n are related as $N = \frac{n}{1 - n\tau}$.

REVIEW QUESTIONS AND PROBLEMS

Multiple Choice Questions

1. The energy loss $-\frac{dE}{dx}$ of a heavy particle of mass m in a medium is

(a) $\propto m$ (b) $\propto \frac{1}{m}$ (c) $\propto m^2$ (d) Independent of m

2. The energy loss $-\dfrac{dE}{dx}$ of a heavy particle of mass m and charge ze in a medium is

   (a) $\propto z$ (b) $\propto \dfrac{1}{z}$ (c) $\propto z^2$ (d) Independent of z

3. Let R_p, R_e and R_α be the rate of energy loss of a proton, electron and an α particle, respectively. Then

   (a) R_p is the largest (b) R_α is the largest
   (c) R_e is the largest (d) R_α is the smallest

4. A charged particle moves in air with a velocity v. Its range R will be approximately

   (a) $\propto v^2$ (b) $\propto v$ (c) $\propto v^4$ (d) Independent of v

5. If R_e and R_p represent the radiation loss due to bremsstrahlung for electrons and protons, respectively, under identical conditions, then

   (a) $R_e = R_p$ (b) $R_e >> R_p$ (c) $R_e < R_p$ (d) R_e is slightly larger than R_p

6. Suppose a photon of energy 100 keV is passed through lead. Which one of the following processes is the dominant mechanism of its energy loss?

   (a) Compton effect (b) Bremsstrahlung
   (c) Photoelectric effect (d) Pair production

7. Suppose a photon of energy 100 keV is passed through carbon. Which one of the following processes is the dominant mechanism of its energy loss?

   (a) Compton effect (b) Bremsstrahlung
   (c) Photoelectric effect (d) Pair production

8. The maximum change in the wavelength of Compton scattered radiation is approximately

   (a) 0.486 nm (b) 0.0486 nm (c) 0.00886 nm (d) 0.00486 nm

9. For a Geiger–Müller (GM) counter, which one of the following statements is CORRECT? [GATE 2012]

   (a) Multiplication factor of the detector is of the order of 10^{10}
   (b) Type of the particles detected can be identified
   (c) Energy of the particles detected can be distinguished
   (d) Operating voltage of the detector is a few tens of volts

10. The length (approximate order) of the plateau in a Geiger–Müller counter is

    (a) ≈ 300 V (b) ≈ 30 V (c) ≈ 3 V (d) ≈ 3000 V

11. In the proportional counter

    (a) Avalanche occurs near the central anode
    (b) Avalanche occurs near the central cathode
    (c) Avalanche occurs in the entire region of the tube
    (d) There is no avalanche at all

12. The efficiency of a proportional counter
    (a) Depends on the signal-to-noise ratio
    (b) Does not depend on the primary ionisation
    (c) Depends on total ionisation
    (d) Depends on the primary ionisation
13. A GM counter operates at 2 kV and a wire of diameter 50 μm. The diameter of the tube is 10 mm. The maximum radial field is
    (a) $\approx$ 150 kV/cm (b) $\approx$ 150 kV/m (c) $\approx$ 15 kV/cm (d) $\approx$ 15 kV/m

Short Questions and Problems

1. If the range of 10-MeV protons in lead is 0.316 mm, find the range of 20-MeV deuteron and 40-MeV α particles.
2. Find the ratio of the range of protons in aluminium and protons in air at 15°C and 76 cm of Hg. (Given $\rho_{air} = 0.001293$ g/cc and $\rho_{Al} = 2.7$ g/cc; and mean mass number of air is 14.5 and that of aluminium is 27).
3. Protons and deuterons of the same energy are passed through a medium. Compare their energy loss.
4. The energy loss of protons and deuterons is the same in a medium. Compare their energies.
5. The range of a 5-MeV α particle in air at STP is 3.8 cm. Find the range of a 10-MeV α particle in air at STP.
6. Under identical conditions, α particles and deuterons are accelerated in a cyclotron. The extracted beam of particles is then passed through an absorber. Show that the range of deuteron will be approximately twice that of α particles.
7. What are the different processes by which uncharged particles and gamma rays lose energy when they pass through matter?
8. Compare the energy loss of photons in the following two cases:
    (a) A single Compton scattering through 180°
    (b) Two successive scatterings through 90° each
9. Estimate the thickness of lead ($A = 207$ and density 11.3 g/cc) required to absorb 80% of gamma rays of energy 1 MeV. The absorption cross-section of gamma rays in lead is 20 barns/atom.
10. In a proportional counter, the amplitude of the pulse induced by the entry of a charged particle is proportional to the kinetic energy of the particle, while the pulse is independent of the latter in a GM counter. Explain why.
11. Explain the working principle of a GM counter.
12. Draw the characteristic curve of a GM counter. Define the threshold voltage. Why is it not possible for a GM counter to measure the energy of the incident particle?

13. A GM counter has a dead time of 400 μs. What are the true counting rates when the observed rates are 1000 per minute?
14. Describe the construction of a GM counter. Explain the terms dead time, recovery time and resolving time of a GM counter. A GM counter has a dead time of 60 μs. What is the true counting rate per minute if the observed rate is 1000 per minute?
15. A GM counter operates at 1 kV and a wire of diameter 0.2 mm. The radius of the cathode is 20 mm and the tube has a guaranteed lifetime of 10^9 counts. What is the maximum radial field? If the counter is used on an average for 30 hours per week at 3000 counts per minute, then how long will the counter last?
16. Explain the working principle of a semiconductor detector. What is the main advantage of this detector over others?

HINTS/ANSWERS TO SELECTED PROBLEMS

Multiple Choice Questions

1. (d) 2. (c) 3. (b) 4. (c) 5. (b) 6. (c) 7. (a) 8. (d) 9. (a) 10. (a)
11. (a) 12. (d) 13. (a)

Problems

1. $R_p = R_\alpha = \dfrac{R_d}{2}$ 2. Apply the Bragg–Kleeman relation.

3. Stopping power: $S = \dfrac{dE}{dx} \propto \dfrac{1}{v^2} \Rightarrow \dfrac{m}{mv^2}$. Thus $\dfrac{S_p}{S_d} = \dfrac{m_p}{m_d} \times \dfrac{E_d}{E_p} \approx \dfrac{1}{2}$.

4. $\dfrac{S_p}{S_d} = \dfrac{m_p}{m_d} \times \dfrac{E_d}{E_p} = 1$ 5. 10.75 cm 6. $\dfrac{mv^2}{r} = qvB \Rightarrow v = \dfrac{qB}{m} \Rightarrow v_d = v_\alpha$ and $\dfrac{R_\alpha}{R_d} = \dfrac{1}{2}$.

8. $\Delta E = h\nu \left[\dfrac{2\dfrac{h\nu}{m_0c^2}}{1+2\dfrac{h\nu}{m_0c^2}} \right]$ for both

9. $I(x) = I_0 e^{-n\sigma x}$, $\sigma = 20 \times 10^{-24}$ cm^2/atom and $n = \dfrac{6.023 \times 10^{23} \times 11.3}{207}$ atoms/cc

Thus, $I/I_0 = 0.2 = e^{-0.658x} \Rightarrow x = 2.45$ cm

13. The actual count rate is $N = \dfrac{n}{1 - n\tau} = \dfrac{1000}{1 - 10^3 \times 400 \times 10^{-6}} \approx 1.67 \times 10^3$

CHAPTER 6

Particle Accelerators

Particle accelerators are one of the most important devices in nuclear physics designed to impart high kinetic energies to charged particles such as electrons, protons or heavier ions. The first successful accelerator built by Rolf Wideroe in 1928 was a small, two-stage linear accelerator. It was followed by the invention of the electrostatic accelerator by Van de Graaff in 1931 and the cyclotron by Lawrence in 1932.

Particle accelerators are generally of two types: linear (LINAC) and circular. In the linear accelerator, particles travel a long distance in a straight line and are given a succession of accelerating kicks by proper adjustment of the high-frequency AC voltage. In circular accelerators, particles are propelled repeatedly through a circular or spiral path in the presence of the appropriate field.

Low-energy accelerators operate roughly in the energy range of 10–100 MeV, medium-energy accelerators in the range of 100–1000 MeV and high-energy accelerators produce beams of 1 GeV (= 1000 MeV) and above.

6.1 NEED FOR HIGHER ENERGY

The best way to 'see' the constituents of a body is by hitting it and breaking it into smaller fragments. In order to strike an object, we must use a particle as a projectile whose wavelength is comparable to the size of the object under consideration. The de Broglie relation enable us to find the wavelength of a particle of mass m of a given kinetic energy (T) as

$$\lambda = \frac{h}{p} = \frac{h}{\sqrt{2mT}} \tag{6.1}$$

For a relativistic particle, the relation is

$$\lambda = \frac{hc}{pc} = \frac{hc}{\sqrt{(T+m_0c^2)^2 - m_0^2c^4}} = \frac{hc}{\sqrt{T(T+2m_0c^2)}}, \tag{6.2}$$

where m_0c^2 is the rest mass energy of the particle. The relation Eq. (6.2) shows that the wavelength of a particle decreases with an increase in its energy. The higher the energy of the particle, the shorter will be its de Broglie wavelength and the more closely it can probe into the structure of the matter. Thus, we need particles of very high energy (corresponding to very small wavelength) to probe the tiniest pieces of matter. Therefore, the high-energy particles are used to study the basic structure of matter at the elementary level. *Particle accelerators are used mainly to explore matter on the smallest scale.*

1 keV = 10^3 eV
1 MeV = 10^3 keV
1 GeV = 10^3 MeV
1 TeV = 10^3 GeV

Accelerators also serve another purpose. High-energy particles are also used to produce new particles of larger masses. Energetic particles are made to collide with each other and, in such collisions, some energy is converted to mass, and thus, a new particle is produced.

Illustrative Example 6.1:

The Tevatron at the Fermi National Accelerator Laboratory (also known as Fermilab) in the United States – one of the most powerful synchrotrons in the world – has a circumference of 6 km and accelerates protons and antiprotons to 1000 GeV. Calculate the wavelength of the protons produced by this machine.

Solution Since the energy of the proton is much larger than its rest mass energy ($\backsim$ 1000 MeV), we need to use the relativistic result

$$\lambda = \frac{hc}{\sqrt{T(T+2m_0c^2)}} = \frac{12.4\times10^{-3}\text{ MeV-Å}}{\sqrt{10^6(10^6+2000)}\text{ MeV}} \approx 12.4\times10^{-9}\text{ Å}$$

Illustrative Example 6.2:

Consider the reaction: $p+p \longrightarrow p+\Lambda^0+\Sigma^+$. Estimate the minimum kinetic energy of the proton required to make this reaction possible.

Solution Mass of the proton is ≈ 938.28 MeV, mass of Λ^0 is ≈ 1116 MeV and mass of Σ^+ is ≈ 1189 MeV.

Mass of $p+\Lambda^0+\Sigma^+$ is 3243.28 MeV. Thus, to observe this reaction, the kinetic energy of the proton must be greater than $\approx 3243.28 - 2\times938.28 = 1366.72$ MeV.

6.2 LINEAR ACCELERATOR (LINAC)

In linear accelerators, particles are accelerated to high energies in successive steps. The basic principle of acceleration in a LINAC may be explained with the help of a schematic diagram, as shown in Fig. 6.1. It consists of an evacuated pipe containing a set of coaxial cylindrical metal tubes of increasing length, where alternate tubes are connected to either side of a radio frequency ($f \backsim 10$ MHz) voltage so that alternate cylinders have potentials of the opposite sign. Thus, in one cycle, the first, third, fifth, etc. tubes are $+ve$, while the second, fourth, sixth, etc. are $-ve$. In the next cycle, the polarities of the tubes will be reversed.

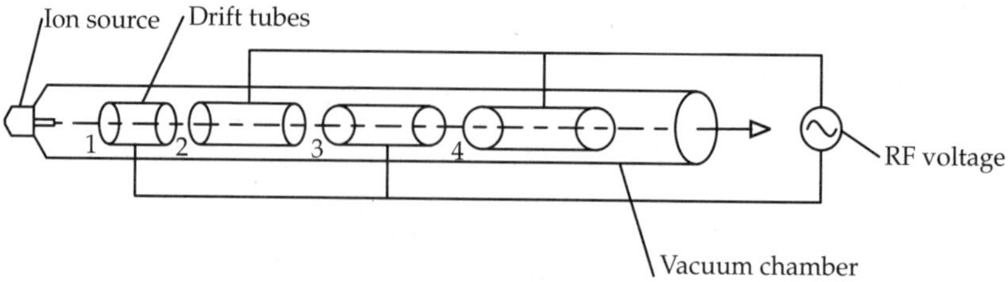

Figure 6.1: *Schematic diagram of a LINAC*

Suppose a positive charge q leaving the source arrives in front of the first tube, when it is at $-ve$ potential (the second tube will then have $+ve$ potential, and so on). The charge will then be accelerated towards the first tube. Since each tube has constant potential, the charged particle will not be accelerated inside the tube. At the moment the charge leaves the first tube, the polarity of the second tube will be reversed; that is, it becomes $-ve$ (the third tube will then be $+ve$, and so on). The positive charge will be accelerated in the gap between first and second tubes. This happens if the time of transit of the charge through the first is exactly equal to the half period of the applied radio frequency voltage. Once again, the electron moves inside the second tube with constant velocity. When the charge exits from the second tube, the polarity of the third tube will be reversed and the charge will again be accelerated in the gap between the third and fourth tubes.

This process will repeat in a regular way, and each time, the charge will receive extra energy. As a result of the energy gain at each step, the ion will move faster in each tube. To make sure that the charge leaves a tube at the right moment, the tubes must be of different lengths and each must be larger than the previous one.

Let m be the mass of a particle with charge q and V be the potential difference between any two neighbouring tubes. The energy acquired by the charge across the first gap is qV. If there are n such gaps, then the energy acquired will be nqV.

Let v_n be the velocity of a particle when it enters the nth tube. Thus

$$\frac{1}{2}mv_n^2 = nqV$$

$$v_n = \sqrt{\frac{2nqV}{m}} \Longrightarrow v_n \propto \sqrt{n} \tag{6.3}$$

The charge will move faster in the second tube than it did in the first, and so on. If L_n is the length of the nth tube, then the time taken by the charge to pass through the nth tube is

$$t_n = \frac{L_n}{v_n}$$

The condition for synchronisation is thus

$$t_n = \frac{L_n}{v_n} \tag{6.4}$$

$$= \frac{T}{2} = \frac{1}{2f}, \tag{6.5}$$

where T and f are, respectively, the time period and the frequency of the RF oscillator. From Eqs (6.3) and (6.5), we can write

$$L_n = v_n \frac{1}{2f} = \frac{1}{2f}\sqrt{\frac{2nqV}{m}} \tag{6.6}$$

Thus $L_n \propto \sqrt{n}$ (6.7)

The final energy acquired by the non-relativistic particle is given by

$$W = nqV = (2fL_n)^2 \frac{m}{2} \tag{6.8}$$

The total length of the accelerator may be calculated from Eq. (6.6). Neglecting the gaps between the tubes, the total length for large n is given as

$$L = \frac{1}{2f}\sqrt{\frac{2qV}{m}}\sum\sqrt{n} \approx \frac{1}{2f}\sqrt{\frac{2qV}{m}}\int_0^n \sqrt{n}dn$$

$$= \frac{1}{3f}\sqrt{\frac{2qV}{m}}n^{3/2} \tag{6.9}$$

The total energy can thus be expressed as

$$W = nqV = (3LfqV)^{2/3}\left(\frac{m}{2}\right)^{1/3} \tag{6.10}$$

Alvarez[1] et al. in 1945 were able to accelerate protons to 32 MeV using LINAC.

Illustrative Example 6.3:

Protons are accelerated in a LINAC to an energy of 100 MeV. If the frequency of the radio frequency voltage is 200 MHz, find the length of the last tube.

Solution From Eq. (6.8), $(2fL_n)^2 \frac{m}{2} = 100$ MeV.

$$\frac{2 \times 200 \times 10^6 \times L_n}{3 \times 10^8} = \sqrt{\frac{200}{938.28}} \Longrightarrow L_n \approx 0.35 \text{ m}$$

Advantages of LINAC

(a) It provides a very well-collimated beam of charged particles.
(b) It is an economical way of obtaining high energy, as no magnet is required.
(c) The radiation loss is low.

Disadvantages of LINAC

(a) It is of an inconveniently large length.
(b) Due to the relativistic variation of mass, it is difficult to accelerate electrons to high energies.

[1]Alvarez, LW. 1946. The Design of a Proton Linear Accelerator. *Phys. Rev.*, 70:799; Alvarez, LW et. al. 1947. *Science*, 106:506.

6.3 CYCLOTRON

The cyclotron was invented by Lawrence[2] in 1929. It consists of two hollow, semi-circular, metallic, D-shaped chambers, commonly known as *dees*, placed between the poles of a powerful electromagnet. There is a narrow gap between the dees, and their edges are parallel to each other (as shown in Fig. (6.2)). The dees are connected to an alternating voltage of frequency $\backsim$ 10 MHz. The applied electric field changes sign appropriately to accelerate the charged particle every time across the gap, and the magnetic field applied in the perpendicular direction propels the particle in a circular path. The radius of the circular path increases gradually with increasing energy so that the path spirals out from the centre.

Consider a particle of mass m and charge $+q$ introduced near the centre of the gap between the dees at point a in Fig. 6.2. If the upper dee D_1 is $-ve$, the particle will be accelerated between the gap $a \to b$. Inside the hollow D_1, there is no electric field, but the particle is subjected to a perpendicular magnetic field, which provides the necessary centripetal force for the particle to move in a circular path with constant speed v.

$$\frac{mv^2}{r} = qvB; \quad r = \frac{mv}{qB} \tag{6.11}$$

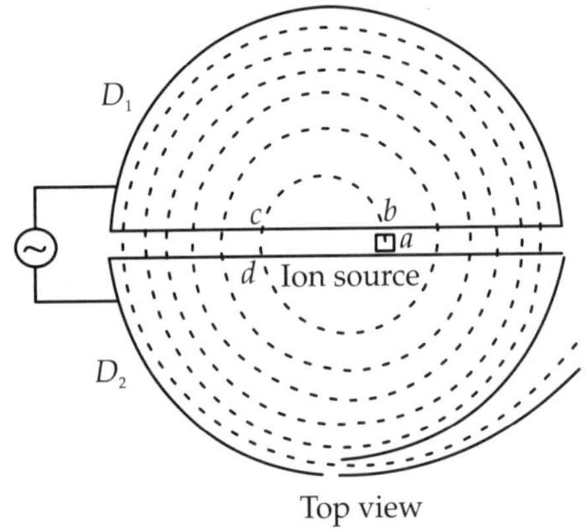

Figure 6.2: *Sketch of a cyclotron. The electric field reverses at the moment when the charge q completes a half-circle. The charge is accelerated across the gap between the two dees.*

Since there is no electric field in the space inside D_1, the particle moves with constant speed along a semicircular path of radius r, given by Eq. (6.11), and will eventually return to the gap between the dees at a time when the polarity of the dees is reversed. Thus, the particle will again be accelerated.

The time required to cover the semicircular path is given by

$$\tau = \frac{\pi r}{v} = \frac{\pi m}{qB} \tag{6.12}$$

The significant point to note in Eq. (6.12) is that the value of τ is constant for the given value of B and $\frac{q}{m}$ and independent of the radius. Thus, the particle reaches the gap after an equal interval of time. The particle will be accelerated between the gap if the time period (T) of the oscillating electric field satisfies the condition

$$T = 2\tau \tag{6.13}$$

[2]Lawrence, EO, and Edlefsen, NE. 1930. On the Production of High Speed Protons, *Science*, 72:376; Lawrence EO, and Livingstone, S. 1931. The Production of High Speed Protons without the Use of High Voltages, *Phys Rev.*, 37:1707.

> **Condition for cyclotron resonance:**
> **Frequency of the RF supply = Frequency of the orbiting particle**

Thus, the frequency of the oscillating field is

$$f = \frac{1}{T} = \frac{qB}{2\pi m} \tag{6.14}$$

This is known as the **cyclotron resonance frequency**.

Energy of the particle: Energy is given by $E = \frac{1}{2}mv^2$.

Substituting v from Eq. (6.11), we get

$$E = \frac{1}{2}m\left(\frac{qBr}{m}\right)^2 = \frac{q^2B^2}{2m}r^2 \tag{6.15}$$

The energy gained by the particle will be maximum when it reaches the periphery of the dees. Thus

$$E_{\max} = \frac{q^2B^2}{2m}r_{\max}^2 \tag{6.16}$$

Equation (6.16) shows that the maximum energy attained depends only on the magnetic field (B) and final radius ($r_{\max}$) but is independent of the amplitude of the AC voltage applied between the dees. It is worth noting that any increase in $r_{\max}$, or in the strength of the magnetic field B, results in a quadratic increase in the final kinetic energy.

The *maximum energy of the proton* is

$$E_{\max} = \frac{q^2B^2}{2m}r_{\max}^2 = \frac{1.6 \times 1.6 \times 10^{-38} \times B^2}{2 \times 1.6721 \times 10^{-27}} \times r_{\max}^2 \approx 47.83B^2r_{\max}^2 \text{ MeV} \tag{6.17}$$

Similarly, the *maximum energy of the deuteron* is

$$E_{\max} \approx 23.92B^2r_{\max}^2 \text{ MeV} \tag{6.18}$$

The *maximum energy of the α particle* is

$$E_{\max} \approx 47.83B^2r_{\max}^2 \text{ MeV} \tag{6.19}$$

Radius at the nth revolution: Let r be the radius of the beam at the nth revolution. If the energy gained in crossing the gap is qV_0, then from Eq. (6.15), we get

$$\frac{q^2B^2}{2m}r^2 = 2nqV_0; \; r = \frac{1}{B}\sqrt{\frac{4mV_0}{q}}\sqrt{n} \tag{6.20}$$

Factor 2 is introduced because the particle crosses the gap twice in one rotation. The radius of the orbiting particle increases as $\sqrt{n}$, and thus, the radial separation (dr) between the adjacent orbits becomes smaller with increasing n, as shown in Fig. 6.2.

In a typical cyclotron: $r_{\max} \sim 50$ cm, $B \lesssim 2\ T, V \sim 200$ kV and $f \sim 10$–20 MHz.

6.3.1 Limitations of the Cyclotron

Relativistic effect: A serious problem arises from the relativistic behaviour of the accelerated particles at large energy. The relativistic variation of mass limits the maximum kinetic energy obtained from the cyclotron. For the relativistic case, the cyclotron condition Eq. (6.14) becomes

$$f = \frac{qB\sqrt{1-\frac{v^2}{c^2}}}{2\pi m_0} \tag{6.21}$$

As the velocity of the particle v increases, the frequency f decreases. Thus, the particle revolves slowly in the semicircular path inside the dee. As a result, the particle will arrive late in the gaps and cannot be accelerated due to time lag. Ultimately, the particle will be out of step with the applied oscillating voltage. To maintain the resonance condition, either the magnetic field B must increase with increasing radius (r) or the alternating radio frequency must be decreased accordingly.

(a) In a *synchrocyclotron*, the magnetic field B is kept constant but the frequency of the external voltage is decreased accordingly so that the frequency f in Eq. (6.21) remains constant.

(b) Accelerators where the magnetic field B is changed, irrespective of whether the frequency of the alternating voltage is changed or not, are called *synchrotrons*. In electron synchrotrons, the magnetic field is changed while keeping the frequency constant, whereas in proton synchrotrons, both the frequency and the magnetic field are varied.

In this context it should be noted that the electron, being the lightest particle, cannot be accelerated by a fixed frequency cyclotron as relativistic variation of its mass is very large even at lower energy. Thus, it goes out of step with the RF voltage very quickly.

Effect of the fringing field near the edge of the cyclotron: The magnetic field near the edge of the cyclotron is not exactly vertical; it becomes curved (it has a vertical and a radial component), as shown in Fig. 6.3. The effect of this fringing field is two-fold: one is beneficial and the other is harmful. The force on the charge due to the radial component of the field is directed towards the median plane, which tends to provide proper focus. At the same time, the vertical component of the field changes at the edge and, as a result, the resonance condition is disturbed.

Decrease in frequency due to relativistic correction: We now calculate the percentage decrease in frequency due to relativistic correction.

With relativistic correction, the frequency becomes

$$f = \frac{qB\sqrt{1-\frac{v^2}{c^2}}}{2\pi m_0} = f_0\sqrt{1-\frac{v^2}{c^2}},$$

where $f_0 = \dfrac{qB}{2\pi m_0}$ is the cyclotron frequency for the non-relativistic particle. Thus

$$\frac{f}{f_0} = \sqrt{1-\frac{v^2}{c^2}} \tag{6.22}$$

$$\text{Again} \quad \frac{m_0c^2}{\sqrt{1-\frac{v^2}{c^2}}} = T + m_0c^2 \tag{6.23}$$

$$\text{From Eqs (6.22) and (6.23), we get} \quad \frac{f_0 - f}{f_0} = \frac{\frac{T}{m_0c^2}}{1+\frac{T}{m_0c^2}} \tag{6.24}$$

Table 6.1: *Relativistic effect on the frequency of circulating protons*

Kinetic energy (T)	% change in frequency ($\frac{f_0-f}{f_0} \times 100$)
10 MeV	$\approx 1\%$
250 MeV	$\approx 21\%$
1000 MeV (1 GeV)	$\approx 52\%$

Since the frequency of the circulating proton is very large ($\backsim$ 10 MHz), a change in frequency of only 1% for a 10-MeV proton is quite sufficient to upset the resonance condition[3]. For electrons of energy $\backsim$ 10 keV, the frequency changes by 1%. Therefore, the resonance condition may be destroyed even for the low-energy electrons. For this reason, the cyclotron is not used to accelerate electrons.

Illustrative Example 6.4: Relativistic correction

Calculate the percentage change in resonance frequency due to relativistic effect for protons with an energy of 20 MeV in a fixed frequency cyclotron. Also determine the percentage increment in the magnetic field required to preserve the resonance condition.

Solution Using Eq. (6.24), $\dfrac{f_0 - f}{f_0} = \dfrac{\frac{T}{m_0c^2}}{1+\frac{T}{m_0c^2}}$.

For protons of energy 20 MeV, the percentage change in frequency $\approx 2\%$.

To make $f_0 = \dfrac{qB_0}{2\pi m_0}$ = constant, B must be increased with m.

$$\frac{qB}{2\pi m} = f_0 \Longrightarrow B = \frac{2\pi m f_0}{q}$$

$$dB = \frac{2\pi f_0}{q} dm = \frac{2\pi f_0}{q} m_0(\gamma - 1) = B_0(\gamma - 1)$$

$$\text{Therefore} \quad \frac{dB}{B_0} = \gamma - 1 \tag{6.25}$$

Again, $m_0c^2(\gamma - 1) = 20$ MeV. Thus, $(\gamma - 1) \approx \dfrac{20}{1000}$ and the percentage increase in B is $\approx 2\%$.

[3]Rotblat, J. 1950. The Cyclotron in *The Acceleration of Particles to High Energies*, HR Lang (Ed.). Institute of Physics, London.

Illustrative Example 6.5: Resonance condition

The diameter of the dee in a cyclotron is 0.5 m and the magnetic field $B = 1.5$ T. Calculate the frequency of the radio frequency voltage required to accelerate protons and the maximum energy gained. What is the frequency required to accelerate a deuteron?

Solution The frequency is given by $f = \dfrac{qB}{2\pi m} = \dfrac{1.6 \times 10^{-19} \times 1.5}{2 \times \pi \times 1.6721 \times 10^{-27}} \approx 23$ MHz.
From Eq. (6.16), the maximum energy of protons is $E_{\text{max}} \approx 47.83 B^2 r_{\text{max}}^2$ MeV $= 47.83 \times 1.5^2 \times 0.25^2 \approx 6.73$ MeV.
The frequency of the supply voltage needed to accelerate a deuteron is 11.5 MHz.

Illustrative Example 6.6: Maximum energy of an α particle

The diameter of the pole pieces of a cyclotron is 0.50 m and the magnetic field $B = 1.5$ T. Calculate the frequency of the radio frequency voltage needed to accelerate protons and α particles. Also determine the maximum energies gained in each case.

Solution For protons, the frequency is ≈ 22.8 MHz.
The maximum energy is given by $E_{\text{max}} \approx 6.74$ MeV.
For an α particle, $f = \dfrac{qB}{2\pi m} \approx 11.5$ MHz.
The maximum energy of an α particle is $E_{\text{max}} \approx 47.83 \times 1.5^2 \times 0.25^2 \approx 6.74$ MeV.

Check Progress 6.1: A cyclotron is designed to accelerate protons to an energy of 10 MeV. Determine the resonance frequency and the maximum radius in terms of the magnetic field B.

Illustrative Example 6.7: Duration of acceleration

The peak voltage of the radio frequency supply of a cyclotron is 50 kV and the frequency is 12 MHz. Determine the magnetic field strength for resonance when deuterons and α particles are accelerated.

If the radius of the orbit at ejection is 30 cm, then how long will the particles be accelerated?

Solution For a deuteron

$$B = \frac{2\pi m f}{q} = \frac{2\pi \times 2 \times 1.67 \times 10^{-27} \times 12 \times 10^6}{1.6 \times 10^{-19}} \approx 1.57 \text{ T}$$

For α particles, m and q are almost doubled. Thus, the resonance frequency remains approximately the same.

Since the particle crosses the gap twice in one rotation, the increase in energy in one rotation is $2qV_0$.

If f is the frequency, then the increase in energy in 1 s $= 2qV_0 \times f$.

The maximum energy is $E = \frac{q^2B^2}{2m}R^2$. Therefore, the time duration for the acceleration is $T_0 = \frac{q^2B^2}{2m}R^2 \times \frac{1}{2qV_0f}$ s $= \frac{\pi B}{2V_0}R^2$.

For both deuterons and α particles, $T_0 = \frac{1.57 \times \pi}{2 \times 50 \times 10^3}0.3^2 \approx 4.43$ μs.

Illustrative Example 6.8: Minimum separation between the neighbouring orbits

The frequency of the radio frequency supply of a cyclotron is 10 MHz. Determine the accelerated voltage applied across the dees if the separation between the neighbouring orbits of protons is not less than 1.0 cm at a trajectory radius of 0.5 m.

Solution Energy after n rotations is $E = \frac{q^2B^2}{2m}R^2 = 2nqV_0$.

Rewriting E in terms of frequency $f = \frac{qB}{2\pi m}$

$$m\pi^2 f^2 R^2 = nqV_0$$

$$2m\pi^2 f^2 R dR = qV_0 dn \tag{6.26}$$

For two neighbouring orbits $dn = 1$, and thus, $V_0 = \frac{2m\pi^2 f^2 R}{q}dR$.

Therefore, minimum of $V_0 = \frac{2 \times 1.67 \times 10^{-27}\pi^2 \times 10^{14} \times 0.5}{1.6 \times 10^{-19}} \times 0.01 \approx 10.30 \times 10^4$V.

Check Progress 6.2: The radius of the dee in a cyclotron is $r_{max} = 0.5$ m and the magnetic field $B = 1.0$ T. Calculate the maximum energy gained by a proton.

Calculate the minimum frequency of the cyclotron oscillator if the maximum energy of the proton is 20 MeV.

Illustrative Example 6.9: Total distance covered by the particle in a cyclotron

The radius of the dee in a cyclotron is $r_{max} = 0.6$ m, the frequency of the RF oscillator is $f = 10$ MHz and the accelerating voltage is 50 kV. If singly charged ions of He^+ are accelerated, calculate: (a) Total time of acceleration (b) Total distance covered by the ion during the acceleration.

Solution (a) Given $f = 10^7$ Hz, $V_0 = 50$ kV and $R = 0.6$ m.

$$E_{max} = \frac{q^2B^2}{2m}r_{max}^2 = 2m\pi^2 f^2 r_{max}^2 \approx 29.67 \text{ MeV}$$

Energy in rotation is $2qV_0 = 2 \times 50 \times 10^3 = 0.1$ MeV
The energy gained in one second is $0.1 \times 10^7 = 10^6$ MeV
Therefore, total time of acceleration is 29.67×10^{-6}

(b) From Eq. (6.20), the radius of the nth orbit is $r_n = \frac{1}{B}\sqrt{\frac{4mV_0}{q}}\sqrt{n}$.

Total distance covered by the ion for large n is

$$L = 2\pi \sum r_n \approx \frac{2\pi}{B}\sqrt{\frac{4mV_0}{q}} \int_0^n \sqrt{n}dn$$

$$L = \frac{2\pi}{B}\sqrt{\frac{4mV_0}{q}} \frac{2}{3}n^{3/2} = \frac{4}{3}\frac{\pi^3 mf^2 r_{\max}^3}{qV_0},$$

where $f = \dfrac{qB}{2\pi m}$ is used. From the given data, $L \approx 0.74$ km.

6.3.2 Magnetic Focussing

In a cyclotron, the charged particles are constrained to move along a spiral path under the influence of a magnetic field perpendicular to the plane of motion. The particles are accelerated in the gap between the dees by a high-frequency electric field. Since both the magnetic field and the electric field act perpendicular to the instantaneous velocity of the particle in the gap between the dees, the path will not be exactly circular – the particle will try to follow a helical path.

The magnetic field in the cyclotron is not exactly uniform near the edge – it deviates from the vertical, as shown in Fig. 6.3.

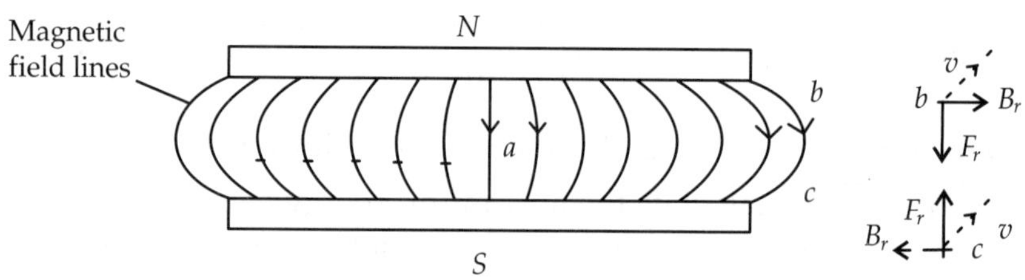

Figure 6.3: *Deviation of the magnetic field lines from the vertical near the edge of the cyclotron*

At the middle point a in Fig. 6.3, the magnetic field is exactly vertical ($B = B_z$ and the radial component $B_r = 0$). The force acting on q due to the vertical component B_z provides the centripetal force for rotation.

At another point b (above the median plane) near the edge, the radial component $B_r \neq 0$. The force on q due to B_r is qvB_r and it is directed in the downward direction, trying to confine the particles in the median plane. At another point c below the median plane, the radial component is directed in the opposite direction, and thus, the force qvB_r is in the upward direction.

Due to the bending magnetic field, a particle deviating from the median plane will experience a restoring force and, therefore, oscillate about the median plane. In the conventional cyclotron, the magnetic field is designed specially to produce the required force towards the median plane.

Assume that the vertical component of the magnetic field (B_z) decreases with r as

$$B_z \propto \frac{1}{r^n},$$

where n is integer. Thus $\dfrac{1}{B_z}\dfrac{dB_z}{dr} = -\dfrac{n}{r}$ (6.27)

In free space $\vec{\nabla} \times \vec{B} = 0 \Rightarrow \dfrac{dB_z}{dr} = \dfrac{dB_r}{dz}$.

From Eq. (6.27), $\dfrac{dB_r}{dz} = -n\dfrac{B_z}{r}$ (6.28)

Solving Eq. (6.28) for small z, $B_r = -\dfrac{nzB_z}{r}$ (6.29)

The vertical restoring force is $qvB_r = -q\omega_0 r\dfrac{nB_z z}{r}$ and the equation of motion for the z direction is

$$m\frac{d^2z}{dt^2} = qvB_r; \quad \frac{d^2z}{dt^2} = -n\frac{qB_z}{m}\omega_0 z$$

$$\frac{d^2z}{dt^2} + n\omega^2 z = 0 \tag{6.30}$$

Thus, the particle will execute simple harmonic motion about the median plane $z = 0$ with frequency $f = f_0\sqrt{n}$.

A similar calculation for radial motion yields $f = f_0\sqrt{1-n}$. Thus, simultaneous stability in both vertical and radial directions exists if $0 < n < 1$.

6.4 PHASE STABILITY AND THE PRINCIPLE OF SYNCHROCYCLOTRON

The relativistic effect cannot be compensated for in fixed frequency and fixed magnetic field cyclotrons. It restricts the upper limit of the energy attained by the particle. To overcome this problem, a variable frequency cyclotron, known as synchrocyclotron, is used. Such an accelerator uses the principle of phase stability[4]. Let us discuss the principle briefly and qualitatively.

Let us consider a particle moving in a circular orbit under the influence of the magnetic field. Figure 6.4 shows a particle arriving at the gap at the instant the accelerating electric field passes through zero (and is about to become a decelerating field), represented by the point *a*. Such a particle will then circulate along the stable orbit of constant radius with constant speed. While moving in this orbit, there will be no loss or gain in the energy of the particle. The particle is called a **synchronous particle** and the orbit is called the **synchronous orbit**. An ideal synchronous particle always arrives at the gap with constant phase.

Phase stability refers to the automatic correction of phase of a particle orbiting slightly out of phase with respect to the synchronous particle.

[4]Yarwood, J. 1965. *Atomic Physics, Volume II*, University Tutorial Press.

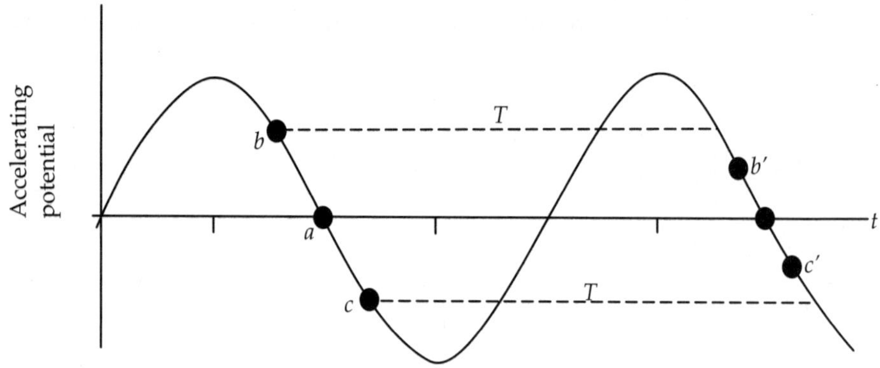

Figure 6.4: *Illustration of phase stability. T represents the time period for one complete rotation of the synchronous particle.*

Now consider another particle arriving at the gap a little earlier (at time smaller than that of the synchronous particle) at point b in Fig. 6.4. This particle will see an accelerating field, and thus, the energy of the particle will be increased while crossing the gap. The radius of orbit of the particle will also be increased. With increasing energy, the mass will increase and the orbital frequency of the particle will be decreased (Eq. (6.21)). Due to decrease in frequency, the particle now moves a bit slowly and will take a longer time to reach the gap the next time (at point b' in Fig. 6.4), which is closer to the synchronous particle.

Similarly, a particle arriving at the gap a little later (at time larger than that of the synchronous particle) at point c in Fig. 6.4 will be decelerated. Thus, the mass will be decreased and the orbital frequency will be increased. The particle now moves faster and arrives at the gap again at a time (at point c' in Fig. 6.4) that is closer to that of the synchronous particle. In this way, the particles tend to oscillate about the point (the point a in Fig. 6.4, that is, with respect to the synchronous orbit) where the condition of phase stability is satisfied.

In a synchrocyclotron, the magnetic field is kept constant but the frequency of the alternating supply voltage is slowly decreased. With increasing energy, the radius of the orbit increases. In this accelerator, the particles moving with different phases ultimately bunch together to a new stable orbit with higher r.

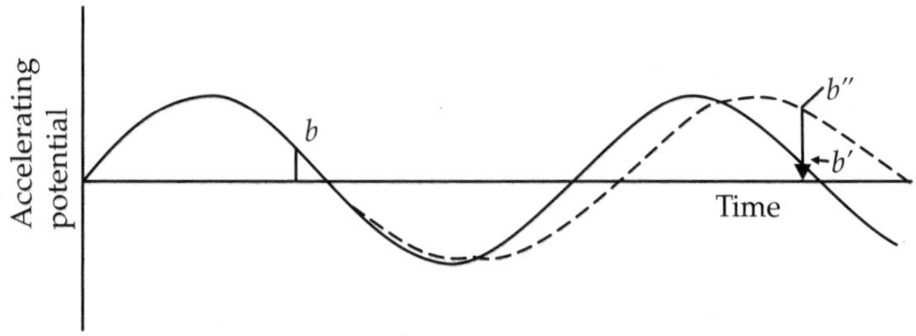

Figure 6.5: *Illustration of phase stability. Effect of decreasing frequency.*

Now consider the effect of decreasing frequency. Suppose the change in frequency takes place after the point b in Fig. 6.5. The particle at b will now reach the gap the next time at b'', when the field is accelerating. It will then gain energy and after a few cycles be settled in a new stable orbit of larger radius corresponding to a larger kinetic energy. In the synchrocyclotron, the frequency is decreased slowly, and thus, at each passage of the gap, the particles appear at an early position with respect to the synchronous orbit. As a result, the particles are accelerated and at the same time bunched by the phase stability effect.

If R is the radius of the circular orbit of the charged particle of mass m moving under the action of a uniform magnetic field, then

$$\frac{mv^2}{R} = qvB \text{ or, momentum (p)} = qBR$$

$$R = \frac{p}{qB} \tag{6.31}$$

The kinetic energy is given by $T = \sqrt{p^2c^2 + m_0^2c^4} - m_0c^2$.

$$T(T + 2m_0c^2) = p^2c^2 \tag{6.32}$$

Thus, from Eq. (6.31), the radius of the circular orbit is

$$R = \frac{\sqrt{T(T + 2m_0c^2)}}{qBc} \tag{6.33}$$

This increases with kinetic energy T.

The frequency of revolution of the particle is

$$f = \frac{1}{2\pi}\frac{qB}{m} = \frac{1}{2\pi}\frac{qBc^2}{T + m_0c^2} \tag{6.34}$$

This decreases with increasing T. To maintain the resonance, the frequency of the applied RF supply must be decreased accordingly.

6.5 BETATRON: PRINCIPLE OF OPERATION

The betatron[5] is used to accelerate electrons to high energy. The electrons in a betatron revolve in a circular orbit of constant radius R under the action of a time-dependent magnetic field $B(t)$. The changing magnetic field induces an electric field and the induced electric field accelerates the electron. Thus, no separate accelerating section is required.

In a cyclotron: $R = R(t)$ and $B =$ constant In a betatron: $R =$ constant and $B = B(t)$

The schematic diagram of a betatron is shown in Fig. 6.6. Electrons are accelerated in the doughnut-shaped (toroidal) tube placed between the pole pieces of an electromagnet.

[5]Kerst, DW. 1941. The Acceleration of the Electrons by Magnetic Induction, *Phys. Rev.*, 60:47.

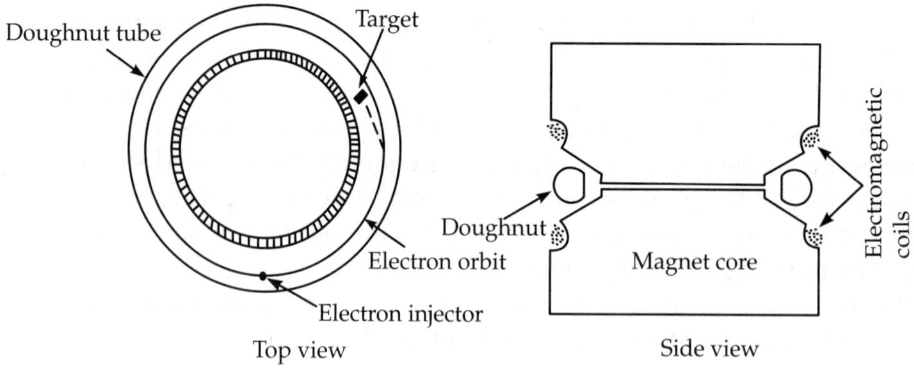

Figure 6.6: *Schematic diagram of a betatron*

Let B_{av} and B_0 be the average magnetic field at the central region and at the location of the orbit, respectively. The perpendicular magnetic field at the orbit provides the necessary centripetal force to the rotating electron. Thus, for circular motion of the electron

$$\frac{m(v)v^2}{R} = evB_0 \tag{6.35}$$

The momentum of the electron is $p = m(v)v = eB_0R$ (6.36)

Due to the changing magnetic field $B_0(t)$, there will be an induced electric field tangential to the orbit of the electron which will accelerate it around the circle.

The induced electric field ($\vec{E}$) is related to the rate of flux change as, by Faraday's law

$$\oint \vec{E}\cdot\vec{dr} = -\frac{d\phi}{dt} \tag{6.37}$$

Since the induced electric field, by symmetry, is directed along the tangent to the circular loop, as shown in Fig. 6.7

$$E \times 2\pi R = -\frac{d\phi}{dt} = -\frac{d}{dt}\int\int \vec{B}\cdot\vec{dS} = -\frac{d}{dt}(\pi R^2 B_{av})$$

$$\text{Therefore } E = -\frac{R}{2}\frac{dB_{av}}{dt}, \tag{6.38}$$

where B_{av} is the average magnetic field in the circular region of radius R. The force on the electron is

$$F = -eE = \frac{eR}{2}\frac{dB_{av}}{dt} \tag{6.39}$$

Using Eqs (6.36) and (6.39)

$$F = \frac{dp}{dt} = \frac{eR}{2}\frac{dB_{av}}{dt} \text{ or } eR\frac{dB_0}{dt} = \frac{eR}{2}\frac{dB_{av}}{dt} \text{ or } B_0 = \frac{B_{av}}{2} \tag{6.40}$$

This is known as the **betatron condition**.

Therefore, to enable the electrons to revolve in an orbit of constant radius R, the average field at the central region of the orbit must be twice the magnetic field at the orbit.

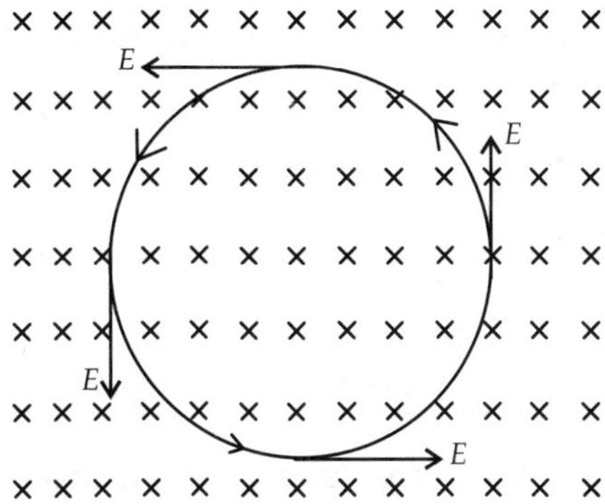

Figure 6.7: *Induced electric field (tangential) due to the magnetic field that increases with time. Induced current is along the anti-clockwise direction.*

Average energy of electrons: From Eq. (6.36), the momentum of the electron at time t is

$$p(t) = eRB_0(t)$$

The maximum possible momentum of the electron is $p_m = eRB_{om}$, (6.41)

where B_{0m} is the maximum value of the alternating magnetic field ($B_0(t) = B_{0m}\cos(2\pi\nu t)$) at the orbit. Therefore, the maximum energy of the electron is

$$W \approx p_m c = ecRB_{om} \tag{6.42}$$

Typically, $B_{0m} \sim 1$ T, $\nu \sim 60$ Hz and $R \sim 1$ m. Thus, $W = pc \sim 300$ MeV, which is much larger than the rest mass energy (0.51 MeV) of the electron.

Average energy gained per cycle: Suppose the flux changes as

$$\phi = \phi_0 \sin\omega t \tag{6.43}$$

The electrons are injected into the obit when the magnetic field is increasing during the first quarter of the alternating cycle of B_0 and are removed at a time corresponding to the peak of B_0. The average energy gained by the electrons per cycle is

$$W_0 = e < \frac{d\phi}{dt} >= e\omega\phi_0 < \cos\omega t >$$

Since the electrons are accelerated only over time $t = 0$ to $t = T/4$

$$W_0 = e\omega\phi_0 \frac{2}{\pi}\int_0^{\pi/2} \cos(\omega t)d(\omega t) \;= e\omega\phi_0 \frac{2}{\pi} = \frac{2}{\pi} \times e\omega \times \pi R^2 \times (B_{av})_{\max}$$

$$= \frac{2}{\pi} \times e\omega \times \pi R^2 \times 2B_{0m} \tag{6.44}$$

The total path described by an electron during acceleration is

$$L = c \times \frac{T}{4} = \frac{c\pi}{2\omega},$$

where the speed[6] of the electron in the orbit is assumed to be $\approx c$. Therefore, the number of turns described is

$$N = \frac{L}{2\pi R} = \frac{c}{4R\omega} \tag{6.45}$$

The energy of the electrons is

$$W = \frac{2}{\pi} \times e\omega \times \pi R^2 \times 2B_{0m} \times \frac{c}{4R\omega} = ecRB_{om} \tag{6.46}$$

The maximum energy of electrons that can be achieved in a betatron is $\backsim$ 300 MeV.

Illustrative Example 6.10: Maximum energy of electrons in a betatron

In a particular betatron, the maximum magnetic field at orbit is 0.4 T, the operating frequency is 60 Hz and a stable orbit diameter is 168 cm. Determine the energy gained by an electron per cycle and the final energy of the electron.

Solution The maximum energy is

$$W = ecRB_{0m} = 3 \times 10^8 \times 0.4 \times 0.84 \text{ eV} = 100.8 \text{ MeV}$$

The number of turns

$$N = \frac{cT/4}{2\pi R} = \frac{1}{4}\frac{c}{2\pi f R} = \frac{3 \times 10^8}{8 \times \pi \times 60 \times 0.84} = \frac{3 \times 10^8}{1266.69}$$

The average energy gained by an electron per cycle

$$W_0 = \frac{100.8 \times 10^6 \times 1266.69}{3 \times 10^8} = 425.61 \text{ eV}$$

Illustrative Example 6.11: Distance covered by electrons in a betatron

In a particular betatron, the diameter of the stable orbit is 25 cm and magnetic flux grows at a constant rate of 5 Wb/s during the accelerating period. If the final energy gained by an electron is 25 MeV, find the number of revolutions of the electron and the total distance covered by the electron during the acceleration.

Solution Energy gained in each rotation $= e\frac{d\phi}{dt} = e \times 5 = 5$ eV.

Number of rotations is $N = \frac{25 \times 10^6}{5} = 5 \times 10^6$ turns.

Total distance covered is $2\pi R \times N \approx 3.93 \times 10^3$ km.

Illustrative Example 6.12: Betatron condition for a specific variation of B

Find the radius of the electron orbit in a betatron if the magnetic field (B) varies with the distance (r) from the axis of the field as $B = B_0 - ar^2$, where B_0 and a are positive constants.

[6]If the kinetic energy of electrons is 1 MeV, then $\frac{m_0c^2}{\sqrt{1-v^2/c^2}} \approx \frac{3}{2}$ MeV and $v = \sqrt{\frac{8}{9}}c$.

Solution The betatron condition, Eq. (6.40), is $B_{\text{orbit}} = \frac{1}{2}B_{av}$, where B_{orbit} represents the magnetic field at the orbit. Now

$$B_{av} = \frac{1}{\pi R^2}\int_0^R (B_0 - ar^2)2\pi r dr = B_0 - \frac{aR^2}{2}$$

Using the betatron condition, we get

$$B_0 - \frac{aR^2}{2} = 2(B_0 - aR^2) \text{ or } B_0 = \frac{3aR^2}{2}$$

Illustrative Example 6.13: *B* growing at a constant rate

The radius of an electron orbit in a betatron is 20 cm. During a time interval of $\Delta t = 1.0 \times 10^{-3}$ s, the magnetic field at the orbit varies at a constant rate from 0 to 0.4 T. Determine the energy gained by the electron in one rotation.

Solution The average value of ΔB is 2×0.4 T. Energy gained by the electron in one rotation is

$$e \times \pi R^2 \times \frac{(\Delta B)_{av}}{\Delta t} = e \times \pi \times 0.2^2 \times \frac{0.8}{10^{-3}} \approx 0.10 \text{ keV}$$

SUMMARY

- **Need for Higher Energy:** The higher the energy of the particle, the shorter its de Broglie wavelength, and thus, we need particles of very high energy to study the basic structure of matter at the elementary level.
- **Basic Designs:** There are two basic designs for particle accelerators: linear (LINAC) and circular. In the first type, the energy gained increases with length while for the second case, high energy is achieved by circulating the particles many times.
- In linear accelerators, the particles are accelerated in steps along the axis of the cylindrical tubes, where the properly synchronised radio frequency voltage provides the accelerating force between the tubes.

  The length of the *n*th drift tube is given by $L_n \propto \sqrt{n}$. And the energy gained is $W = nqV = (2fL_n)^2\frac{m}{2}$.
- **Cyclotron:** It consists of two hollow, D-shaped, metal electrodes connected to radio frequency voltage. Inside the *dees*, there is no electric field and particles are accelerated only when they cross the gap between the *dees*. A constant magnetic field applied perpendicular to the *dees* propels the particle on a circular path.

  Resonance condition: $f = \frac{qB}{2\pi m}$; Maximum energy by the particle $E_{\max} = \frac{q^2B^2}{2m}r_{\max}^2$

  The upper limit of energy is limited by the relativistic variation of mass with velocity, which causes the particle to arrive at the accelerating gap progressively later until finally it will be out of resonance with the applied oscillating voltage.

  The limitation on the energy attainable in a cyclotron due to relativistic effect is overcome by the synchrocyclotron and synchrotron.
- **Synchrocyclotron:** In a synchrocyclotron, the magnetic field is kept constant while the frequency of the external voltage is decreased accordingly so that the resonance condition is maintained.

- **Synchrotron:** Here, the magnetic field is changed, irrespective of whether the frequency of the alternating voltage is changed or not.
- **Focussing:** The magnetic field in a cyclotron is not exactly uniform near the edge. Near the edge, the magnetic field becomes convex and thus has a radial component of the magnetic field B_r, which confines the particles in the median plane.
- **Phase stability:** This refers to the automatic correction of the phase of a particle orbiting slightly out of phase with respect to the synchronous particle.
- **Betatron:** A betatron works on the principle of electromagnetic induction. In this case, the electrons revolve in a circular orbit of constant radius under the action of a time-dependent magnetic field. The changing magnetic field induces an electric field which accelerates the electron.

  Betatron condition: $B_{\text{orbit}} = \frac{1}{2} B_{\text{average}}$, Energy of electrons: $W = eRc(B_{\text{orbit}})_{\max}$

REVIEW QUESTIONS AND PROBLEMS

Multiple Choice Questions

1. The length of the nth drift tube in LINAC is

   (a) $\propto n$ (b) $\propto \sqrt{n}$ (c) $\propto n^2$ (d) $\propto \frac{1}{n}$

2. A LINAC operating at a frequency of 25 MHz accelerates ^{12}C ions to an energy of 80 MeV. The length of the longest drift tube is

   (a) ≈ 0.72 m (b) ≈ 0.92 m (c) ≈ 1.37 m (d) ≈ 0.52 m

3. In a LINAC, the velocity of the particle on entering the nth tube is

   (a) $\propto n$ (b) $\propto \sqrt{n}$ (c) $\propto \frac{1}{\sqrt{n}}$ (d) $\propto \frac{1}{n}$

4. Vertical focussing is achieved by varying the magnetic field as

   (a) $B(r) \propto \frac{B_z}{r}$ (b) $B(r) \propto \frac{B_z}{r^2}$ (c) $B(r) \propto \frac{B_z}{r^3}$ (d) $B(r) \propto \frac{B_z}{r^4}$

5. A 50-kV, 5-MHz radio frequency source is applied to a cyclotron of diameter 1.524 m. The resonance condition for protons will be satisfied if the magnetic field B is

   (a) ≈ 3.3 T (b) ≈ 0.33 T (c) ≈ 33 T (d) ≈ 0.1 T

6. A 50-kV, 5-MHz radio frequency source is applied to a cyclotron of diameter 1.524 m. The resonance condition for deuterons will be satisfied if the magnetic field B is

   (a) ≈ 6.6 T (b) ≈ 0.66 T (c) ≈ 66 T (d) ≈ 0.6 T

7. A 50-kV, 5-MHz radio frequency source is applied to a cyclotron of diameter 1.524 m. The resonance condition for an α particle will be satisfied if the magnetic field B is

   (a) ≈ 6.6 T (b) ≈ 0.66 T (c) ≈ 66 T (d) ≈ 0.6 T

8. In a betatron, electrons rotate in a circular orbit where
   (a) The radius increases as R^3
   (b) The radius increases as R^2
   (c) The radius increases slowly after each rotation
   (d) The radius R is constant
9. The radius of the orbit of electrons in a betatron is 1 m. If the magnetic field changes at the rate of 50 Wb $m^{-2}s^{-1}$, then the energy acquired by the electron in one rotation is
   (a) ≈ 100 eV (b) ≈ 50 eV (c) $\approx 50\pi$ eV (d) $\approx 100\pi$ eV
10. If the changing magnetic field in a betatron suddenly becomes constant, then the electron will
    (a) Keep moving with constant energy
    (b) Stop suddenly
    (c) Keep moving with deceleration
    (d) Keep moving with acceleration
11. The accelerator that works on the principle of electromagnetic induction is
    (a) Betatron (b) Cyclotron (c) Synchocyclotron (d) Synchroton
12. In a synchrocyclotron, the angular velocity of the particle
    (a) Increases with increase in kinetic energy
    (b) Decreases with increase in kinetic energy
    (c) Remains constant
    (d) May increase or decrease depending on the nature of the particle

Short Questions and Problems

1. A cyclotron of diameter 1.524 m is operated by a 50-kV, 5-MHz radio frequency supply. Determine the magnetic field that satisfies the resonance conditions for (a) protons, (b) deuterons and (c) α particles. Also determine the energies attained by these particles.
2. Calculate the radius of the *dees* and the applied magnetic field B of a cyclotron that will accelerate protons to a maximum energy of 5 MeV, if a radio frequency voltage of frequency 8 MHz is available.
3. When a cyclotron shifts from ^{2}H to α particles, it becomes necessary to decrease the magnetic field slightly. If the masses of ^{2}H and α are 2.014102 amu and 4.002603 amu, respectively, calculate the percentage decrease in the required magnetic field.
4. If the frequency of the dee voltage at the beginning of an accelerating sequence is 20 MHz, calculate the final frequency if the protons attain an energy of 469 MeV.

5. Explain the working principle of a fixed frequency cyclotron with a diagram. Show that for a fixed magnetic field, the kinetic energy of a particle in the cyclotron is proportional to the square of the orbit radius.
6. Show that in a synchrocyclotron, the angular velocity of a particle decreases with increase in its kinetic energy.
7. What are the design parameters for a cyclotron that would accelerate α particles to a maximum energy of 20 MeV? The dees have a diameter of 1 m.
8. What are the limitations of a fixed frequency cyclotron?
9. Describe the working principle of a fixed frequency cyclotron and show that the radius of curvature of the path of the particle inside the cyclotron is proportional to $\sqrt{n}$, where n is the number of times the particle has been accelerated across the space between the dees.
10. In a cyclotron, a flux density of 1.4 $\mathrm{Wb/m^2}$ is employed for accelerating the protons. How rapidly should the electric field between the dees be reversed?
11. Give an account of the essential features of a LINAC and explain its action. Explain the principle of phase stability of a LINAC.
12. A cyclotron has an oscillator frequency of 12 MHz and dee radius of 21 inches. Calculate the magnetic induction B needed to accelerate deuterons.
13. Explain the working of a LINAC. Show that the energy of the particles coming out of the LINAC is given by $E = \left(\frac{3LeV_0}{2\lambda}\right)^{2/3} (2mc^2)^{1/3}$, where L is the integrated value for the total length of the accelerator, V_0 and λ are the voltage amplitude and the wavelength of the impressed voltage, respectively, and e and m are the charge and mass, respectively, of the particle accelerated.
14. A fixed frequency cyclotron magnet of radius 1 m produces a maximum magnetic induction of 1.5 T. Calculate the energies of the deuterons and α particles accelerated by it. What are the frequencies of the radio frequency field in both cases? What is the magnetic induction required to accelerate protons by the same cyclotron without changing the frequency?
15. A cyclotron whose magnetic pole faces have a diameter of 1.52 m is operated by a radio frequency field at 10^7 Hz. Show that this machine can accelerate protons to an energy of approximately 10 MeV and α particles to approximately 40 MeV.
16. A cyclotron accelerated deuterons to an energy of 12 MeV. The deuterium is replaced by helium. What will be the energy of the α particles obtained from the same instrument?
17. Assume that the magnetic flux linking the orbit in a betatron varies with time according to the relation $\phi = \phi_0 \sin \omega t$ and the acceleration of the electron occurs during one-fourth of the cycle, that is, during the time interval $\pi/2\omega$. Find the formulae for

(a) The energy per turn available when the flux changes.
(b) The average value of the energy during the accelerating period.
(c) The distance travelled by the electrons under the assumption that the speeds differ by only a negligible amount from that of light.
(d) The number of turns, if the radius of the orbit is R.
(e) The final energy of the electron.

18. Prove the betatron condition that the magnetic field on the orbit is equal to half the average value of that inside the orbit. Also calculate the maximum energy to which an electron can be accelerated by a betatron.

HINTS/ANSWERS TO SELECTED PROBLEMS

Multiple Choice Questions

1. (b) 2. (a) 3. (b) 4. (a) 5. (b) 6. (b) 7. (b) 8. (d) 9. (d) 10. (c) 11. (a) 12. (b)

Problems

1. For protons, $B = 0.328$ T and $E = 3$ MeV. For deuterons, $B = 0.656$ T and $E = 6$ MeV and for α particles, $B = 0.656$ T and $E = 12$ MeV.
2. $f = \dfrac{qB}{2\pi m} \Rightarrow B = 0.52$ T. $E = \dfrac{q^2B^2R^2}{2m} \Rightarrow R = 0.62$ m.
3. $f = \dfrac{eB_d}{2\pi m_d}$ and $f = \dfrac{2eB_\alpha}{2\pi m_\alpha}$. Thus $\dfrac{B_\alpha}{B_d} = \dfrac{m_\alpha}{2m_d}$ and $\dfrac{B_\alpha - B_d}{B_d} = \dfrac{m_\alpha - 2m_d}{2m_d} = -0.006355$. Percentage decrease $= 0.6355\%$
4. $f_0 = \dfrac{eB}{2\pi m_0}$ and $f = \dfrac{eB}{2\pi m}$ where $m = m_0c^2\gamma$. Thus $f = \dfrac{f_0}{\gamma}$ where kinetic energy $T = m_0c^2(\gamma - 1)$. For the given data $\gamma = \frac{3}{2}$ and $f = 13.33$ MHz.
7. $E = \dfrac{q^2B^2R^2}{2m} \Rightarrow B = \sqrt{\dfrac{2mE}{q^2R^2}} \approx 1.29$ T. The resonance frequency is $f \approx 9.88$ MHz.
10. $f = \dfrac{qB}{2\pi m} \Rightarrow T = 1/f \Rightarrow$ time for two switches. Therefore, the time for one switch is $\tau = \dfrac{\pi m}{qB} = 2.3 \times 10^{-8}$ s.
12. $B \approx 1.57$ T
14. For deuterons, $E_{max} \approx 53.89$ MeV and $f = 11.44$ MHz. For α particles, 2×53.89 MeV and $f = 22.88$ MHz.
15. For proton: $E_{max} = 2\pi^2 m f^2 R^2 \approx 11.5$ MeV. For α particles, $E_{max} \approx 46$ MeV.
16. Energy will be doubled.

CHAPTER 7

Particle Physics

During the 1930s, electrons, protons and neutrons were considered as the only elementary particles. By 1960, however, with advances in experiments involving high energy, a large number of new particles that could be regarded as equally fundamental were discovered. It was thought earlier that an elementary or fundamental particle is a point particle without any structure. However, with the development of the high-energy accelerator, it was revealed that the particles that had been considered as elementary are not really so.

Our understanding of elementary particles has changed drastically in last few decades. It is now possible to find a systematic relationship among these particles of apparently diverse character. We now discuss the properties of elementary particles and their interactions from a purely phenomenological point of view.

7.1 FUNDAMENTAL INTERACTIONS

There are only four types of fundamental interactions in nature. All particles interact with one another through these basic forces. The main features of these forces are listed in Table 7.1.

The **gravitational** force is quite familiar to us. It is extremely important in our daily life and also in celestial bodies. However, on the scale of fundamental interactions, it is of the least importance. It is the weakest of all interactions and of long range. All particles, whether massive or massless[1], are subject to the gravitational force.

The **electromagnetic** force acts only on charged particles. It is responsible for the binding of atoms and molecules. The electromagnetic force has infinite range, like the gravitational force. Each of these fundamental forces is mediated by the exchange of a particle. The electromagnetic forces are mediated by massless photons, while the gravitational force is conjectured to be mediated by the graviton, which is also believed to be massless, like the photon.

Strong and **weak** forces were unknown to classical physics. The nucleons in the nucleus interact through the strong force and it is responsible for the binding of

[1]The bending of light in a gravitational field is an established fact.

Table 7.1: *The four basic forces*

Interaction	Property	Range	Mediator	Relative strength	Characteristic time
Strong	Binds the nucleons, in stable form	Short range, ~ 1 fm	Gluon	1	10^{-22} s
Electromagnetic	Binds the atoms and molecules	Long range, $\propto \frac{1}{r^2}$	Photon	10^{-2}	10^{-14} to 10^{-21} s
Weak	Responsible for β decay	Short range, ~ 1 fm	$W^{\pm}$, Z bosons	10^{-7}	10^{-8} to 10^{-13} s
Gravitational	Holds the planets and stars	Long range, $\propto \frac{1}{r^2}$	Graviton	10^{-39}	Years

nucleons inside a nucleus. On the other hand, the weak force is responsible for β decay[2]. Unlike the electromagnetic and gravitational forces, they are exceedingly short-ranged. The strong force is stronger than the electromagnetic force, which in turn, is stronger than the weak force. There are some particles that ignore the strong interaction. For example, protons and electrons never interact through the strong force.

The weak interaction is mediated by the $W^{\pm}$ and Z bosons with masses that are about 100 times the proton mass. These are responsible for the beta decay of neutrons. For example, β^- can be represented as

$$n \longrightarrow p + W^- \text{ followed by } W^- \longrightarrow e^- + \bar{\nu}_e$$

The mediator of strong interactions is the gluon.

A typical relationship between the range of an interaction and the mass of its mediator can be determined from the uncertainty principle. When two particles exchange a mediating particle of rest mass m, the conservation of energy is temporarily violated by an amount, $\Delta E = mc^2$. The mediating particle may exist for the time Δt as long as

$$\Delta E \Delta t \approx \hbar$$

The largest distance the particle can move is then

$$R = c\Delta t \approx \frac{\hbar c}{mc^2} = \frac{\hbar}{mc} \tag{7.1}$$

Thus, the range of the force is inversely proportional to the rest mass of the exchanged particles. For a range of 1 fm, the mass of the exchanged particle is

$$mc^2 = \frac{\hbar c}{R} \approx \frac{197.329 \text{ MeV.fm}}{1 \text{ fm}} \sim 200 \text{ MeV} \tag{7.2}$$

On the other hand, photons have zero rest mass, and thus, have infinite range[3].

[2]It is also responsible for the decay of the pion, the muon and many of the strange particles.

[3]Gluon, the mediator of the strong interaction between quarks, is massless. However, the range of strong interactions is extremely small.

7.2 ELEMENTARY PARTICLES

Depending on the nature of the interactions, all known elementary particles are grouped into four main categories, as presented in Table 7.2.

All the particles in nature can be classified as either bosons or fermions. Bosons have integral spin and they follow the Bose–Einstein statistics. On the other hand, fermions have half-integral spin and they follow the Fermi–Dirac statistics. Leptons and baryons are fermions, and thus, they obey the Pauli Exclusion Principle. Photons have integral spin and mesons have *zero* spin; thus, they are bosons.

Table 7.2: *Elementary particles*

Group	Particle	Classification by statistics
Photons	γ	Bosons
Leptons	$e^-, \mu^-, \tau^-, \nu_e, \nu_\mu, \nu_\tau$	Fermions
Mesons	$\pi^+, \pi^-, \pi^0, K^+, K^-, K^0, \eta^0, \rho^+, \rho^-, \rho^0, \ldots$	Bosons
Baryons	$p, n, \Lambda^0, \Sigma^+, \Sigma^-, \Sigma^0, \Xi^0, \Xi^- \ldots$	Fermions

7.2.1 Leptons

Leptons are fundamental particles with half-integral spin. They have no internal structure and can be considered as points with no finite dimension. Thus, they are elementary particles in the true sense. Leptons participate in the weak interactions and in electromagnetic interactions (only the charged leptons), but they do not sense any strong force. The number of leptons is very limited – there are only six leptons (each having an antiparticle): electron (e^-), muon (μ^-), tau (τ^-), electron-type neutrino (ν_e), muon-type neutrino (ν_μ) and tau-type neutrino (ν_τ).

The implication of the Dirac relativistic quantum theory is that for every particle, there is an antiparticle. The antiparticle has the same mass and spin as that of the particle, but their charge is opposite. The antiparticle of the electron is the positron (e^+), the antiparticle of μ^- is μ^+ and the antiparticle of the neutrino (ν) is $\bar{\nu}$.

As mentioned earlier, ν_e and $\bar{\nu}_e$ are produced during the beta decay of radioactive elements. They are also produced in the solar fusion process. The difference between a neutrino and an antineutrino has already been discussed in the context of β decay. The electron is a stable particle, but μ^- and τ^- decay to other leptons.

It has been observed that the number of fermions in any process is always conserved, whereas the number of bosons (photons and mesons) is not. This suggests that conservation of the number of fermions is a fundamental feature of all interactions.

A quantum number, called the lepton number, is assigned to each lepton. The leptons numbers for different leptons are presented in Table 7.3.

Table 7.3: *Lepton properties*

Particle (Antiparticle)	Mass in MeV	L_e	L_μ	L_{tau}	Stability
Electron (e^-)	0.511	1	0	0	Stable
(Positron (e^+))		(−1)	0	0	
E-neutrino (ν_e)	0	1	0	0	Stable
($\bar{\nu_e}$)		(−1)	0	0	
Muon (μ^-)	105.7	0	1	0	Unstable
(μ^+)		0	−1	0	Unstable
μ-neutrino (ν_μ)	0	0	1	0	Stable
($\bar{\nu_\mu}$)		0	−1	0	Stable
Tau (τ^-)	1784.0	0	0	1	Unstable
(τ^+)		0	0	−1	Unstable
τ-neutrino (ν_τ)	0	0	0	1	Stable
($\bar{\nu_\tau}$)		0	0	−1	Stable

7.2.2 Hadrons

Mesons and baryons are collectively known as hadrons. Hadrons are strongly interacting particles.

In 1935, Yukawa described the short-ranged nature of the nuclear force between protons and neutrons by postulating that the force was due to the exchange of a massive particle. According to Yukawa, the mass of the exchanged particle is

$$m \approx \frac{\hbar}{Rc},$$

where R is the range of the nuclear force. This relation is identical to Eq. (7.1), which is obtained from arguments based on the uncertainty principle.

As the range of the nuclear force $R \sim$ few fm, Yukawa predicted the mass of the exchanged particle as, $mc^2 \approx 100$ MeV. Yukawa called the particle **meson** (meaning middle) as its mass is midway between that of light electrons and heavy nucleons. *Mesons have integral spin and masses intermediate between leptons and baryons.* The pion, observed in 1947, has a mass of ~ 147 MeV and spin 0. A few examples of mesons are listed in Table 7.4.

Mesons are strongly interacting particles. Pions can be produced in reactions with high-energy protons. For example

$$p+n \longrightarrow p+p+\pi^-$$

The decay schemes of mesons are shown in Table 7.4. For example

$$\pi^- \longrightarrow \mu^- + \bar{\nu_\mu} \quad \text{(weak interaction)}$$

$$\pi^0 \longrightarrow \gamma+\gamma \qquad \text{(electromagnetic)}$$

Baryons are strongly interacting particles with non-integral spin of $\frac{1}{2}$ or $\frac{3}{2}$. Proton is the lightest baryon. Like the leptons, they have distinct antiparticles. Proton is the only

Table 7.4: *Meson properties*

Particle	Antiparticle	Mass in MeV	Spin	Decay modes
Pion (π^+)	π^-	140	0	$\pi^+ \longrightarrow \mu^+ + \nu_\mu$
Pion (π^0)	π^0	135	0	$\pi^0 \longrightarrow \gamma + \gamma$
Pion (π^-)	π^+	140	0	$\pi^- \longrightarrow \mu^- + \bar{\nu_\mu}$
Kaon (K^+)	K^-	494	0	$K^+ \longrightarrow \mu^+ + \nu_\mu$ $K^+ \longrightarrow \pi^+ + \pi^0$
Kaon (K^0)	$\bar{K^0}$	498	0	$K^0 \longrightarrow \pi^+ + \pi^-$ $K^0 \longrightarrow \pi^0 + \pi^0$
Eta (η^0)	η^0	549	0	$\eta^0 \longrightarrow \gamma + \gamma$

hadron that is stable in free space. The neutron is stable inside the nucleus, but decays into protons, electrons and antineutrinos in free space.

Table 7.5: *Baryon properties*

Particle	Antiparticle	Mass in MeV	Spin	Decay modes
Proton (p)	$\bar{p}$	938.3	$\frac{1}{2}$	Stable
Neutron (n)	$\bar{n}$	939.6	$\frac{1}{2}$	$n \longrightarrow p + e^- + \bar{\nu}_e$
Lambda (Λ^0)	$\bar{\Lambda^0}$	1115.6	$\frac{1}{2}$	$\Lambda^0 \longrightarrow p + \pi^-$ $\Lambda^0 \longrightarrow n + \pi^0$
Sigma (Σ^+)	Σ^-	1189.4	$\frac{1}{2}$	$\Sigma^+ \longrightarrow p + \pi^0$ $\Sigma^+ \longrightarrow n + \pi^+$
Sigma (Σ^0)	$\bar{\Sigma^0}$	1192.5	$\frac{1}{2}$	$\Sigma^0 \longrightarrow \Lambda^0 + \gamma$
Sigma (Σ^-)	$\overline{\Sigma^+}$	1197.3	$\frac{1}{2}$	$\Sigma^- \longrightarrow n + \pi^-$
xi (Ξ^0)	$\bar{\Xi^0}$	1395.0	$\frac{1}{2}$	$\Xi^0 \longrightarrow \Lambda^0 + \pi^0$
xi (Ξ^-)	Ξ^+	1321.0	$\frac{1}{2}$	$\Xi^- \longrightarrow \Lambda^0 + \pi^-$
Omega (Ω^-)	Ω^+	1672.0	$\frac{3}{2}$	$\Omega^- \longrightarrow \Xi^0 + \pi^-$

Baryons, like the mesons, can be produced from high-energy reactions with nucleons through strong interactions. For example

$$p + p \longrightarrow p + \Lambda^0 + K^-$$

All baryons (except protons) decay in such a way that the end product is always a proton. For example, $\Xi^0 \longrightarrow \Lambda^0 + \pi^0$ and $\Lambda^0 \longrightarrow p + \pi^-$.

7.3 CONSERVATION LAWS

A reaction is allowed energetically if it does not violate any recognised conservation laws. For example, a reaction that violates the conservation of momentum will not take place. In the subatomic domain, we do not have a complete understanding of the forces acting among the particles, and thus, all the relevant conservation laws are not known precisely. We believe that the conservation principles, similar to the classical particles, also hold good for elementary particles. In the case of elementary particles, certain types of reactions are observed while some other processes seem to be forbidden. The conservation laws help us to understand why a particular process is allowed or forbidden.

7.3.1 Basic Conservation Laws

The basic conservation laws universally valid for all interactions are

(a) Conservation of energy

(b) Conservation of linear momentum

(c) Conservation of angular momentum

(d) Conservation of charge

In addition, two other conservation laws are applied in the realm of particle interactions:

(e) Conservation of lepton number

(f) Conservation of baryon number

Illustrative Example 7.1: Decay from rest

A particle a decays from rest as $a \longrightarrow b + c$.
Calculate the energy and momenta of b and c.

Solution From the conservation of energy

$$E_b + E_c = m_a c^2, \tag{7.3}$$

where m_a is the rest mass of a and

$$E_b^2 = p_b^2 c^2 + m_b^2 c^4 \tag{7.4}$$

$$E_c^2 = p_c^2 c^2 + m_c^2 c^4 \tag{7.5}$$

m_b and m_c are the rest masses of b and c, respectively.

The conservation of momentum requires $\vec{p}_b + \vec{p}_c = 0$.
The particles b and c must move in opposite directions. Thus

$$|\vec{p}_b| = |\vec{p}_c| = p \text{ (say)}$$

From Eq. (7.5), $E_b^2 - E_c^2 = (m_b^2 - m_c^2)c^4$.

$$E_b - E_c = \frac{(m_b^2 - m_c^2)c^2}{m_a} \tag{7.6}$$

Using Eqs (7.3) and 7.6)

$$E_b = \frac{(m_a^2 + m_b^2 - m_c^2)c^2}{2m_a} \tag{7.7}$$

$$E_c = \frac{(m_a^2 + m_c^2 - m_b^2)c^2}{2m_a} \tag{7.8}$$

The kinetic energy of b is

$$T_b = \frac{(m_a^2 + m_b^2 - m_c^2)c^2}{2m_a} - m_b c^2 = \frac{(m_a + m_c - m_b)(m_a - m_b - m_c)c^2}{2m_a} \tag{7.9}$$

And the kinetic energy of c is

$$T_c = \frac{(m_a + m_b - m_c)(m_a - m_b - m_c)c^2}{2m_a} \tag{7.10}$$

Eqs (7.9) and (7.10) show that the decay is allowed energetically if $m_a > (m_b + m_c)$. The momentum of b or c can be obtained from Eq. (7.5).

Illustrative Example 7.2: Decay of π^0

A positive pion at rest decays as $\pi^0 \longrightarrow \mu^- + \nu_\mu$.
Determine the kinetic energy of μ^- and the energy of ν_μ.

Solution Momentum conservation gives $\vec{p_\mu} = -\vec{p_\nu}$.

Energy conservation gives $m_\pi c^2 = p_\nu c + \sqrt{p_\mu^2 c^2 + m_\mu^2 c^4}$

$$(m_\pi c^2 - p_\nu c)^2 = p_\mu^2 c^2 + m_\mu^2 c^4$$

Thus, the energy of ν_μ is $p_\nu c = \dfrac{(m_\pi^2 - m_\mu^2)c^2}{2m_\pi}$.

The energy of μ is $E_\mu = \sqrt{p_\mu^2 c^2 + m_\mu^2 c^4} = \dfrac{(m_\pi^2 + m_\mu^2)c^2}{2m_\pi}$.

Kinetic energy μ is $T_\mu = \dfrac{(m_\pi^2 + m_\mu^2)c^2}{2m_\pi} - m_\mu c^2 = \dfrac{(m_\pi - m_\mu)^2 c^2}{2m_\pi}$.

Check Progress 7.1: A pion at rest decays as $\pi^- \longrightarrow \mu^- + \bar{\nu}_\mu$.
If $T_\mu = 4.2$ MeV and $m_\mu = 105.66$ MeV, calculate the mass of π^-.

Illustrative Example 7.3: Decay of Σ^+

Consider the decay $\Sigma^+ \longrightarrow n + \pi^+$.
Determine the kinetic energy of the neutron and pion.

Solution From Eq. (7.10), the kinetic energy of the neutron is

$$T_n = \frac{(m_\Sigma + m_\pi - m_n)(m_\Sigma - m_\pi - m_n)c^2}{2m_\Sigma}$$

$$= \frac{(1189.36 + 139.57 - 939.57)(1189.36 - 939.57 - 139.57)}{2 \times 1189.36} \approx 18.0 \text{ MeV}$$

The kinetic energy of the pion is $T_{\pi^+} = \dfrac{(m_\Sigma + m_n - m_\pi)(m_\Sigma - m_n - m_\pi)c^2}{2m_\Sigma}$

$$= \frac{(1189.36 + 939.57 - 139.57)(1189.36 - 939.57 - 139.57)}{2 \times 1189.36} \approx 92.0 \text{ MeV}$$

Illustrative Example 7.4: Maximum energy of e^+ in μ^+ decay

A muon at rest decays as $\mu^+ \longrightarrow e^+ + \nu_\mu + \nu_e$.
Determine the largest possible kinetic energy of e^+.

Solution Energy conservation requires

$$(m_\mu - m_e)c^2 = T_e + 2E_\nu, \tag{7.11}$$

where m represents the rest masses and T_e is the kinetic energy of the electron.

The kinetic energy of the positron will be maximum when both of the neutrinos move in the same direction, which is opposite to that of e^+, so that

$$\vec{p}_e + 2\vec{p}_\nu = 0$$

Thus, $p_e = 2\dfrac{E_\nu}{c}$. The kinetic energy of the electron is $T_e = \sqrt{p_e^2c^2 + m_e^2c^4} - m_ec^2$

$$(T_e + m_ec^2)^2 = p_e^2c^2 + m_e^2c^4 \Rightarrow p_ec = \sqrt{T_e^2 + 2T_em_ec^2}.$$

And from Eq. (7.11), $(m_\mu - m_e)c^2 = T_e + \sqrt{T_e^2 + 2T_em_ec^2}$.

This gives $T_e = \dfrac{(m_\mu - m_e)^2}{2m_\mu}c^2 \approx 52.5$ MeV.

Illustrative Example 7.5: No pair production in free space

Show that the following process is forbidden in free space: $\gamma \longrightarrow e^- + e^+$.

Solution In the above process, known as pair production, energy and momentum are not conserved simultaneously. It can be easily shown by considering the 4-momenta of photons and electrons separately.

For photons: $p^\mu = \left(\dfrac{h\nu}{c}, \dfrac{h\nu}{c}, 0, 0\right)$

For electrons: $p^\mu = \left(\dfrac{E}{c}, p\cos\theta, p\sin\theta, 0\right)$

For positrons: $p^\mu = \left(\dfrac{E}{c}, p\cos\theta, -p\sin\theta, 0\right)$

$$\text{Therefore } h\nu = 2E = 2\sqrt{p^2c^2 + m_0^2c^4} \tag{7.12}$$

$$\text{And } h\nu = 2pc\cos\theta = 2\sqrt{p^2c^2\cos^2\theta} \tag{7.13}$$

Since $\cos^2\theta \leq 1$, Eqs (7.12) and (7.13) are inconsistent, and thus, the process of pair production in free space is forbidden.

From the invariance principle: For a photon in the lab frame: $p^\mu = \left(\dfrac{h\nu}{c}, \dfrac{h\nu}{c}, 0, 0\right)$.

$$\text{Therefore, the quantity } \frac{E^2}{c^2} - p^2 = \frac{h^2\nu^2}{c^2} - \frac{h^2\nu^2}{c^2} = 0 \tag{7.14}$$

is an invariant, having the same value in all inertial frames.

Let us now calculate the same quantity for the electron–positron pair in the CM frame. Since the total linear momentum is zero in the CM frame, for the pair $p^\mu = \left(\frac{2m_0c^2}{c}, 0, 0, 0\right)$ and $\frac{E^2}{c^2} - p^2 = 4m_0^2c^2$.

From Eq. (7.14), $4m_0^2c^2 = 0$, which is completely wrong.

Illustrative Example 7.6: Pair production in the field of an electron

Determine the threshold energy of a γ photon to produce an electron–positron pair in the field of a stationary electron.

Solution The process is $\gamma + e^- \longrightarrow e^- + e^+ + e^-$.

Total initial energy in the lab frame is $E = h\nu + m_ec^2$ and momentum is $p = \frac{h\nu}{c}$.

Thus, the invariant quantity is $\frac{E^2}{c^2} - p^2 = \frac{(h\nu + m_ec^2)^2}{c^2} - \frac{h^2\nu^2}{c^2}$.

Total momentum of the products in the CM frame $= 0$.

Total energy of the products at threshold in the CM frame $= 3m_ec^2$.

The invariant quantity is $\frac{(3m_ec^2)^2}{c^2}$.

Thus $\frac{(h\nu + m_ec^2)^2}{c^2} - \frac{h^2\nu^2}{c^2} = \frac{(3m_ec^2)^2}{c^2}$ which gives $h\nu = 4m_ec^2$.

Illustrative Example 7.7: Production of a π^+ and π^- pair in the field of a proton

Determine the threshold energy of a γ photon to produce an π^+ and π^- pair in the field of a stationary proton.

Solution The process is $\gamma + p \longrightarrow \pi^+ + \pi^- + p$.

Total initial energy in the lab frame is $E = h\nu + m_pc^2$ and momentum is $p = \frac{h\nu}{c}$.

Thus, the invariant quantity is $\frac{E^2}{c^2} - p^2 = \frac{(h\nu + m_pc^2)^2}{c^2} - \frac{h^2\nu^2}{c^2}$.

Total momentum of the products in the CM frame $= 0$.

Total energy of the products at threshold in the CM frame $= 2m_\pi c^2 + m_pc^2$.

The invariant quantity is $\frac{(2m_\pi c^2 + m_pc^2)^2}{c^2}$.

Thus $\frac{(h\nu + m_pc^2)^2}{c^2} - \frac{h^2\nu^2}{c^2} = \frac{(2m_\pi c^2 + m_pc^2)^2}{c^2}$ which gives $h\nu = 2\frac{m_\pi^2 + m_\pi m_p}{m_p}c^2$.

Illustrative Example 7.8: Threshold energy for relativistic reaction

Consider the reaction $a + X \longrightarrow Y + b$, where the target X is at rest in the lab frame. Determine the threshold energy for this reaction, that is, the minimum energy required for the projectile a to make the reaction possible. (Assume that the total rest mass on the left-hand side is less than that on the right-hand side).

Solution The 4-momenta for the incident particle and the target is

$$P_a^\mu = \left(\frac{E_a}{c}, \vec{P}_a\right); \; P_x^\mu = (m_x c, 0, 0, 0),$$

where m_x is the rest mass of the target X.

Total 4-momenta for the initial pair is $P^\mu = \left(\frac{E_a}{c} + m_x c, \vec{P}_a\right)$.

The quantity $\left(\frac{E_a}{c} + m_x c\right)^2 - P_a^2 = (m_a + m_x)^2 c^2$ is invariant, and thus, will have the same value in all inertial frames. For the RHS, it is easier to work in the CM frame[4].

The 4-momenta for the products is

$$P_y^\mu = \left(\frac{E_y}{c}, \vec{P}_y\right); \; P_b^\mu = \left(\frac{E_b}{c}, \vec{P}_b\right)$$

In the CM frame, the product particles will move with zero velocity

$$P_y^\mu = (m_y c, 0, 0, 0); \; P_b^\mu = (m_b c, 0, 0, 0)$$

Thus, the invariant quantity will be $(m_y + m_b)^2 c^2$.

Therefore $\left(\frac{E_a}{c} + m_x c\right)^2 - P_a^2 = (m_y + m_b)^2 c^2$

$$\left(E_a + m_x c^2\right)^2 - (E_a^2 - m_a^2 c^4) = (m_y + m_b)^2 c^4$$

Simplifying, we get $E_a = \frac{(m_y + m_b)^2 - (m_a^2 + m_x^2)}{2m_x} c^2$.

The kinetic energy of the incident particle is

$$E_{\text{threshold}} = E_a - m_a c^2 = \frac{(m_y + m_b)^2 - (m_a + m_x)^2}{2m_x} c^2$$

$$= \frac{(\sum m_{\text{final}})^2 - (\sum m_{\text{initial}})^2}{2m_x} c^2 = (-Q) \frac{m_a + m_x + m_b + m_y}{2m_x}, \tag{7.15}$$

where $Q = (m_a + m_x - m_b - m_y)c^2$.

Equation (7.15) can be written as

$$E_{\text{threshold}} = -Q\left[\frac{2(m_a + m_x) - Q/c^2}{2m_x}\right] = -Q\left[-\frac{Q}{2m_x c^2} + \frac{m_a + m_x}{m_x}\right]$$

For a non-relativistic case, $Q \ll 2m_x c^2$, and thus $E_{\text{threshold}} \approx (-Q)\left(1 + \frac{m_a}{m_x}\right)$.

[4]"This is perhaps a good place to emphasise the distinction between a conserved quantity and an invariant quantity. Energy is conserved – the same value after the collision as before – but it is not invariant. The clever exploitation of conserved and invariant quantities can save you a lot of messy algebra."- Griffiths, D. 2008. *Introduction to Elementary Particles, Second Edition.* Wiley-VCH, 97.

Illustrative Example 7.9: Production of proton and antiproton pair

Antiprotons are produced by the reaction $p+p \longrightarrow p+p+p+\bar{p}$, where a high-energy proton strikes another proton at rest and a proton–antiproton pair, in addition to the original particles, is produced. Determine the threshold energy for this reaction.

Solution From Eq. (7.15), $E_{th} = \dfrac{(\sum m_{\text{final}})^2 - (\sum m_{\text{initial}})^2}{2m_x}c^2$.

$$E_{th} = \frac{(4m_p)^2 - (2m_p)^2}{2m_p}c^2 = 6m_pc^2 = 5.633 \times 10^3 \text{ MeV} = 5.633 \text{ GeV}$$

Illustrative Example 7.10: Production of π^0

Calculate the threshold energy of γ rays for pion production by $\gamma + p \longrightarrow p + \pi^0$.

Solution From Eq. (7.15), $E_{th} = \dfrac{(m_p+m_\pi)^2 - m_p^2}{2m_p}c^2 = m_\pi\left(1+\dfrac{m_\pi}{2m_p}\right)c^2$.

$$= 135.5\left(1+\frac{135.5}{2 \times 938.5}\right) \approx 144.7 \text{ MeV}$$

Illustrative Example 7.11: Production of π^0

Calculate the threshold energy for the reaction $p+p \longrightarrow p+p+\pi^0$.

Solution From Eq. (7.15)

$$E_{th} = m_\pi\left(\frac{m_\pi + 4m_p}{2m_p}\right)c^2 = 135.5\left(2+\frac{135.5}{2 \times 938.5}\right) \approx 281 \text{ MeV}$$

Illustrative Example 7.12: Pair annihilation

An electron and a positron moving in opposite directions, each with the same kinetic energy of 1 MeV, collide and annihilate: $e^- + e^+ \longrightarrow \gamma + \gamma$.
Calculate the energy of each photon.

Solution The 4-momenta for the electron and positron are

$$P_e^\mu = \left(\frac{E}{c}, +p, 0, 0\right);\ P_{e^-}^\mu = \left(\frac{E}{c}, -p, 0, 0\right)$$

The 4-momenta for the photons is given by $P_\gamma^\mu = \left(\dfrac{2h\nu}{c}, 0, 0, 0\right)$.

To conserve momentum, two photons must fly off in opposite directions. Therefore, the energy of each photon is $h\nu = E = 1 + 0.51 = 1.51$ MeV.

7.3.2 Conservation of Lepton Number

We had mentioned earlier that all leptons have a lepton number, $L = 1$, while the hadrons carry no lepton number.

$L = 1$ for leptons; $L = -1$ for antileptons

There are three types of lepton quantum numbers: electron–lepton number L_e, muon–lepton number L_μ and tauon–lepton number L_τ. The lepton numbers assigned to various leptons are shown in Table 7.3. In any process, L_e, L_μ and L_τ are separately conserved.

Introduction of lepton quantum number is necessary to explain many experimentally observed reactions. For example, consider the reaction: $e^- + e^- \longrightarrow \pi^- + \pi^-$.

In this reaction, the charge and angular momentum (spin) are conserved. The reaction is kinematically allowed at high energy. However, this reaction is never observed. Lepton number conservation prevents this reaction from taking place.

$$e^- + e^- \longrightarrow \pi^- + \pi^-$$

$$L_e : 1 + 1 \longrightarrow 0 + 0$$

Illustrative Example 7.13: Necessity of L_e and L_μ

Explain why the following processes are forbidden:

$$\mu^- \longrightarrow e^- + \gamma;\ \mu^- \longrightarrow e^- + e^+ + e^-$$

Solution $\mu^- \longrightarrow e^- + \gamma$

In this case

Initial lepton number = Final lepton number = 1

However, this decay is never observed. To explain this, different kinds of lepton numbers are assigned for different members of the lepton family.

$$L_e :\ 0 \longrightarrow 1 + 0 \quad \text{Not conserved}$$

$$L_\mu :\ 1 \longrightarrow 0 + 0 \quad \text{Not conserved}$$

For the second case

$$\mu^- \longrightarrow e^- + e^+ + e^-$$

$$L_e :\ 0 \longrightarrow 1 + -1 + 1 \quad \text{Not conserved}$$

$$L_\mu :\ 1 \longrightarrow 0 + 0 \quad \text{Not conserved}$$

In this decay, charge, spin and energy are conserved. However, L_e and L_μ are not separately conserved. Thus, the processes are forbidden. This example shows the importance of introducing two types of lepton numbers. If μ^- and e^- were of the same type of lepton, then we would observe such decay.

Illustrative Example 7.14: Decay of μ^- and π^-

Verify the conservation of lepton numbers in the following decays:

$$\mu^- \longrightarrow e^- + \bar{\nu}_e + \nu_\mu;\ \pi^- \longrightarrow \mu^- + \bar{\nu}_\mu$$

Solution In the first case

$$\mu^- \longrightarrow e^- + \bar{\nu}_e + \nu_\mu$$

$$L_e :\ 0 \longrightarrow 1 - 1 + 0 \quad \text{Conserved}$$

$$L_\mu :\ 1 \longrightarrow 0 + 0 + 1 \quad \text{Conserved}$$

In the second case

$$\pi^- \longrightarrow \mu^- + \bar{\nu}_\mu$$

$$L_e: 0 \longrightarrow 0+0 \quad \text{Conserved}$$

$$L_\mu: 0 \longrightarrow 1-1 \quad \text{Conserved}$$

In both of these processes, charge, spin, energy and lepton numbers are conserved. Thus, both of these decays are allowed. Note that in the second decay, a pion disappears. The validity of the second reaction implies that *there is no conservation rule regarding meson numbers.*

Check Progress 7.2: A μ^- decays at rest and emits an electron. Which other particles will be emitted in the above decay? Use the conservation laws to establish your answer.

Check Progress 7.3: Define lepton number and baryon number. Write down the equation for muon decay. How is a lepton number conserved in this process?

Check Progress 7.4: Check whether the following reaction is allowed or not: $\gamma \longrightarrow e^- + e^+$.
(Hint: In this process, L_e is conserved, but energy and linear momentum are not conserved simultaneously. Thus, the process is forbidden).

7.3.3 Conservation of Baryon Number

Like the lepton number, a baryon number (B) is assigned to each particle. For baryons, $B = +1$; for antibaryons, it is -1 and *zero* for others. In any process, the total baryon number is always constant.

Conservation of baryon number implies that the proton, being the lightest baryon, should not decay.

Illustrative Example 7.15: $p \nrightarrow \pi^0 + e^+$

Consider the decay $p \longrightarrow \pi^0 + e^+$.
Explain why this decay is forbidden.

Solution In this decay, charge is conserved. Since $m_p >> m_e + m_\pi$, the decay is allowed energetically. However, such decay is never observed. This suggests that there is some conservation rule that prevents this decay. The impossibility of the decay can be explained from the conservation of baryon number. For proton, $B = 1$, but on the right-hand side, $B = 0$.

Illustrative Example 7.16: $n \nrightarrow e^- + e^+$

Why does a free neutron not decay into an electron and a positron?

Solution The baryon number will not be conserved, and thus, the decay is forbidden.

Illustrative Example 7.17: $p+p \nrightarrow p+p+\bar{n}$

Verify the conservation of baryon numbers in the following decay: $p+p \longrightarrow p+p+\bar{n}$.

Solution $p+p \longrightarrow p+p+\bar{n}$.

$B: \; 1+1 \longrightarrow 1+1-1$ Not conserved

Charge and spin angular momentum are conserved. But, the baryon number is not conserved. Thus, the process is forbidden, even at high energy.

Check Progress 7.5: Illustrate on the basis of the conservation of baryon numbers whether or not the following reactions can occur: $p+n \longrightarrow p+p+n+\bar{p}$; $p+n \longrightarrow p+p+\bar{p}$.

7.3.4 Strangeness

Let us look carefully at the decay modes of π^0 and η^0 mesons

$$\pi^0 \longrightarrow \gamma+\gamma$$

$$\eta^0 \longrightarrow \gamma+\gamma \tag{7.16}$$

Both π^0 and η^0 decay very rapidly ($\sim 10^{-16}$ s).

On the basis of this systematic behaviour of neutral pions, we expect that another neutral pion (K^0) would decay into two photons in a similar manner. However, its decay mode is completely different: $K^0 \nrightarrow \gamma+\gamma$.

It has been observed from the cloud chamber photograph of cosmic rays that

$$K^0 \longrightarrow \pi^+ + \pi^-$$

$$K^0 \longrightarrow \pi^0 + \pi^0 \tag{7.17}$$

The observed decay mode is also very slow ($\sim 10^{-8}$ s).

Again, consider another example. In the collision of high-energy pions and protons, the following reaction is observed.

$$\pi^- + p \longrightarrow K^0 + \Lambda^0 \tag{7.18}$$

On the other hand, the following reactions with high-energy pions are never observed, although no known conservation laws are violated.

$$\pi^- + p \nrightarrow K^0 + n$$

$$\nrightarrow \pi^0 + \Lambda^0 \tag{7.19}$$

So, there must be some rule of nature that is responsible for the non-occurrence of such reactions.

A group of particles (kaons and hyperons, namely, $K, \Lambda, \Sigma, \cdots$ etc.) were found to exhibit unusual properties:

(a) They were found to produce always in pairs (this is known as the phenomenon of associated production).

(b) They are produced by strong interaction at a high rate (on a time scale of $\sim 10^{-23}$ s). However, they decay very slowly (typically about $\sim 10^{-8}$ s) as the weakly interacting particles.

For example, in the reactions (7.18) and (7.19), K^0 is produced in association with Λ^0, but never with a neutron.

Similarly, for the reaction $\pi^+ + p \nrightarrow \Sigma^+ + \pi^+$

$$\pi^+ + p \longrightarrow K^+ + \Sigma^+$$

$$K^+ \longrightarrow \pi^+ + \pi^0$$

$$\Sigma^+ \longrightarrow n + \pi^+ \tag{7.20}$$

Σ^+ is produced in association with K^+, not with π^+. To explain these unusual properties, Murray Gell-Mann and Abraham Pais proposed a new quantum number, called **strangeness** (S). Leptons, pions and nucleons are non-strange particles, with $S = 0$. Kaons (K^+ and K^0) are assigned $S = +1$.

$$S = +1 \text{ for } K^+ \text{ and } K^0$$

$$S = -1 \text{ for } \Lambda^0, \Sigma^+, \Sigma^0 \text{ and } \Sigma^-$$

Strangeness is conserved in strong and electromagnetic processes. However, it is not conserved in weak interactions.

Illustrative Example 7.18: Strangeness of Ξ^-

The following reaction proceeds through strong interactions (with a large cross-section):

$$K^- + p \longrightarrow \Xi^- + K^+$$

From this reaction, determine the strangeness of Ξ^-.

Solution For K^-, strangeness $S = -1$ and for K^+, strangeness $S = +1$. Thus, strangeness of Ξ^- is $S = -2$.

Illustrative Example 7.19: $K^0 \nrightarrow \gamma + \gamma$

Explain why the following reaction is not observed: $K^0 \nrightarrow \gamma + \gamma$.

Solution $K^0 \nrightarrow \gamma + \gamma$.

Strangeness $\quad 1 \nrightarrow 0 + 0 \quad$ Not conserved

The existence of photons in the products implies that the reaction is electromagnetic in character. Since strangeness is not conserved, the reaction is not allowed.

Illustrative Example 7.20: Decay of K^0

Explain why the following reaction is not observed through the strong interaction:

$$K^0 \rightarrow \pi^+ + \pi^-$$

Solution Here, strangeness is not conserved, so the process cannot be strong. It occurs through weak interaction (the weak interaction does not conserve strangeness).

7.3.5 Isospin

The concept of isospin stems from the charge independence of the strong interactions. In fact, studies of the Coulomb energy difference of mirror nuclei revealed that the force $F(p-p) = F(n-n)$. Furthermore, scattering experiments have demonstrated that if we correct for electromagnetic effects, the scattering cross-section for two protons is the same as that for two neutrons. Thus, $F(p-p) = F(n-n)$. The notion of charge independence implies that the strong nuclear force does not distinguish between protons and neutrons – they are indistinguishable. However, the presence of electromagnetic force removes this degeneracy and allows us to distinguish between a neutron and a proton.

Similarly, as far as strong interaction is concerned, pions behave in the same way. This charge independence of the strong force allows us to assign a quantum number, known as isospin, to all strongly interacting particles or hadrons. If I is the isospin of any hadron, its multiplicity in the charge space is $2I+1$. The z component of I, known as I_3, has values $-I$ to $+I$ in steps of integers (similar to the z component of spin).

The isospin quantum number is found to be conserved in strong interactions. However, this does not hold in electromagnetic and weak interactions. Since the nucleons are found in two charge states, the isospin of nucleons is $I = \frac{1}{2}$. For protons, $I_3 = +\frac{1}{2}$ and for neutrons, $I_3 = -\frac{1}{2}$.

Like nucleons, π^+, π^0 and π^- behave in the same way with respect to strong interactions. Thus, pions have $I = 1$.

Similarly, the (K^+, K^0) doublet can be considered as two manifestations of a single particle K in charge space. In fact, the discussion can be extended to all hadrons participating in strong interactions.

The isospin and strangeness of mesons and baryons are presented in Table 7.6 and Table 7.7, respectively.

Table 7.6: *Isospin and strangeness of mesons*

Particle	Symbol	Isospin (I)	I_3	Strangeness (S)
Pion	π^+	1	+1	0
	π^0	1	0	0
	π^-	1	−1	0
Kaon	K^+	$\frac{1}{2}$	$+\frac{1}{2}$	+1
	K^0	$\frac{1}{2}$	$-\frac{1}{2}$	+1
Eta	η^0	0	0	0

The strangeness quantum number of hadrons is related to its other quantum numbers through the Gell-Mann–Nishijima relation

$$Q = I_3 + \frac{B+S}{2}, \tag{7.21}$$

Table 7.7: *Isospin and strangeness of baryons*

Particle	Symbol	Isospin (I)	I_3	Strangeness (S)
Proton	p	$\frac{1}{2}$	$+\frac{1}{2}$	0
Neutron	n	$\frac{1}{2}$	$-\frac{1}{2}$	0
Lambda	Λ^0	0	0	−1
Sigma	Σ^+	1	+1	−1
	Σ^0	1	0	−1
	Σ^-	1	−1	−1
xi	Ξ^0	$\frac{1}{2}$	$+\frac{1}{2}$	−2
	Ξ^-	$\frac{1}{2}$	$-\frac{1}{2}$	−2
Omega	Ω^-	0	0	−3

where Q is the charge (in units of e), B is the baryon number and I_3 is the z component of isospin. The hypercharge is defined by $Y = B + S$.

The quantum numbers of hadrons are summarised in Table 7.8.

Table 7.8: *Isospin and strangeness of hadrons*

Particle (Antiparticle)	Charge Q	I_3	Baryon number B	Strangeness S	Hypercharge $Y = B + S$
$\pi^+(\pi^-)$	$+1(-1)$	$+1(-1)$	0(0)	0	0
$\pi^0(\pi^0)$	0	0	0	0	0
$\pi^-(\pi^+)$	$-1(+1)$	$-1(+1)$	0	0	0
$K^+(K^-)$	$+1(-1)$	$+\frac{1}{2}(-\frac{1}{2})$	0	$1(-1)$	$1(-1)$
$K^0(\bar{K^0})$	0	$-\frac{1}{2}(\frac{1}{2})$	0	$1(-1)$	$1(-1)$
$\eta^0(\eta^0)$	0	0	0	0	0
$p(\bar{p})$	$+1(-1)$	$+\frac{1}{2}(-\frac{1}{2})$	$1(-1)$	0	$1(-1)$
$n(\bar{n})$	0(0)	$-\frac{1}{2}(+\frac{1}{2})$	$1(-1)$	0	$1(-1)$
$\Sigma^+(\bar{\Sigma}^-)$	$+1(-1)$	$+1(-1)$	$1(-1)$	$-1(+1)$	0
$\Sigma^0(\bar{\Sigma}^0)$	0	0	$1(-1)$	$-1(+1)$	0
$\Sigma^-(\bar{\Sigma}^+)$	$-1(+1)$	$-1(+1)$	$1(-1)$	$-1(+1)$	0
$\Lambda^0(\bar{\Lambda}^0)$	0	0	$1(-1)$	$-1(+1)$	0
$\Xi^0(\bar{\Xi}^0)$	0	$+\frac{1}{2}(-\frac{1}{2})$	$1(-1)$	$-2(+2)$	$-1(+1)$
$\Xi^-(\bar{\Xi}^+)$	$-1(+1)$	$-\frac{1}{2}(+\frac{1}{2})$	$1(-1)$	$-2(+2)$	$-1(+1)$
$\Omega^-(\bar{\Omega}^+)$	$-1(+1)$	0	$1(-1)$	$-3(+3)$	$-2(+2)$

Illustrative Example 7.21:

Find the strangeness of K^+.

Solution $Q = I_3 + \dfrac{B+S}{2}$

Here, $Q = +1, B = 0$ and $I_3 = +\frac{1}{2}$. Thus, $S = +1$.

Check Progress 7.6: Verify the Gell-Mann–Nishijima relation for hadrons.

7.3.6 Violation of Conservation Laws

In the previous section, we mentioned the basic conservation laws that are valid for all interactions. These conservation laws are:

(a) Conservation of energy
(b) Conservation of linear momentum
(c) Conservation of angular momentum
(d) Conservation of charge
(e) Conservation of lepton number
(f) Conservation of baryon number

There are some other conservation laws that are not obeyed by all the interactions. The conserved quantities and different interactions are listed in Table 7.9.

Table 7.9: *Conservation laws*

Conserved quantities	Strong interaction	Electromagnetic interaction	Weak interaction
Energy	√	√	√
Linear momentum	√	√	√
Angular momentum	√	√	√
Charge	√	√	√
Lepton number	√	√	√
Baryon number	√	√	√
Isospin	√	×	×
Strangeness	√	√	×

For example, in high-energy pion–proton collisions, two strange particles might be produced

$$\pi^- + p \longrightarrow K^0 + \Lambda^0;$$
$$\longrightarrow K^0 + \Sigma^0$$

In addition to all of the above conservation rules, the conservation of strangeness number (S) and isospin (I_3) are obeyed in both of these reactions.

$$\begin{aligned} \pi^- + p &\longrightarrow K^0 + \Lambda^0 \\ S:\ 0+0 &\longrightarrow +1-1 \\ I_3:\ -1+\frac{1}{2} &\longrightarrow -\frac{1}{2}+0 \\ \pi^- + p &\longrightarrow K^0 + \Sigma^0 \\ S:\ 0+0 &\longrightarrow +1-1 \\ I_3:\ -1+\frac{1}{2} &\longrightarrow -\frac{1}{2}+0 \end{aligned}$$

However, consider the decay process (*weak* process)

$$\begin{aligned} \Lambda^0 &\to p^+ + \pi^- \\ S: \quad -1 &\longrightarrow 0+0 \Rightarrow \Delta S = 1 \\ I_3: \quad 0 &\longrightarrow \frac{1}{2} - 1 \end{aligned}$$

Such a weak process does not respect the conservation of strangeness and I_3.

Strong interaction: All of the conservation laws including isospin number and strangeness are conserved in strong interactions.

Illustrative Example 7.22: Strong interaction

Verify that the reaction $\pi^- + p \longrightarrow K^0 + \Sigma^0$ is allowed through strong interaction, while the reaction $\pi^- + p \longrightarrow \eta^0 + \Sigma^0$ is not.

Solution $\pi^- + p \longrightarrow K^0 + \Sigma^0$

$$\text{Charge:} \quad -1+1 \longrightarrow 0+0 \quad \text{Conserved}$$

$$\text{Spin:} \quad \vec{0} + \frac{\vec{1}}{2} \longrightarrow \vec{0} + \frac{\vec{1}}{2} \quad \text{Conserved}$$

$$\text{Lepton number:} \quad 0+0 \longrightarrow 0+0 \quad \text{Conserved}$$

$$\text{Baryon number:} \quad 0+1 \longrightarrow 0+1 \quad \text{Conserved}$$

$$S: \quad 0+0 \longrightarrow +1-1 \quad \text{Conserved}$$

$$I_3: \quad -1+\frac{1}{2} \longrightarrow -\frac{1}{2}+0 \quad \text{Conserved}$$

The reaction is allowed through strong reaction.

Now consider the reaction $\pi^- + p \longrightarrow \eta^0 + \Sigma^0$.

$$\text{Charge:} \quad -1+1 \longrightarrow 0+0 \quad \text{Conserved}$$

$$\text{Spin:} \quad \vec{0} + \frac{\vec{1}}{2} \longrightarrow \vec{0} + \frac{\vec{1}}{2} \quad \text{Conserved}$$

$$\text{Lepton number:} \quad 0+0 \longrightarrow 0+0 \quad \text{Conserved}$$

$$\text{Baryon number:} \quad 0+1 \longrightarrow 0+1 \quad \text{Conserved}$$

$$S: \quad 0+0 \nrightarrow 0-1 \quad \text{Conserved}$$

$$I_3: \quad -1+\frac{1}{2} \nrightarrow 0+0 \quad \text{Not Conserved}$$

The reaction is not allowed through strong reaction.

Weak interaction: Both conservation of isospin number and conservation of strangeness number are violated in weak interactions. Weak interaction processes are of three types.

(a) $\Lambda^0 \to p^+ + \pi^-$, where only the hadrons are present in the final state.

(b) $n \longrightarrow p+e^-+\bar{\nu}_e$, where both hadrons and leptons are present in the final state.

(c) $\mu^- \longrightarrow e^-+\bar{\nu}_e+\nu_\mu$, where only leptons are present. Isospin and strangeness are not defined for leptons.

Illustrative Example 7.23: Weak interaction without ν

Verify that isospin and strangeness numbers are not conserved in the following reactions:

(a) $K^0 \longrightarrow \pi^+ + \pi^-$ (b) $\Sigma^+ \longrightarrow p+\pi^0$ (c) $\Xi^- \longrightarrow \Lambda^0+\pi^-$

Solution (a) $K^0 \longrightarrow \pi^+ + \pi^-$

$S:\ 1 \longrightarrow 0+0$ Not Conserved $\Rightarrow |\Delta S| = 1$

$I_3:\ -\frac{1}{2} \longrightarrow +1-1$ Not Conserved

(b) $\Sigma^+ \longrightarrow p+\pi^0$

$S:\ -1 \longrightarrow 0+0$ Not Conserved $\Rightarrow |\Delta S| = 1$

$I_3:\ +1 \longrightarrow +\frac{1}{2}+0$ Not Conserved

(c) $\Xi^- \longrightarrow \Lambda^0+\pi^-$

$S:\ -2 \longrightarrow -1+0$ Not conserved $\Rightarrow |\Delta S| = 1$

$I_3:\ -\frac{1}{2} \longrightarrow 0-1$ Not Conserved

Illustrative Example 7.24: Weak interaction with hadrons and leptons

Show that isospin and strangeness are not conserved in the following reactions:

(a) $K^+ \longrightarrow \pi^0+\mu^++\nu_\mu$ (b) $\Sigma^- \longrightarrow n+e^-+\bar{\nu}_e$ (c) $\Lambda^0 \longrightarrow p+e^-+\bar{\nu}_e$

(d) $\pi^+ \longrightarrow \pi^0+e^++\nu_e$ (e) $n \longrightarrow p+e^-+\bar{\nu}_e$

Solution

(a) $K^+ \longrightarrow \pi^0+\mu^++\nu_\mu$

$S:\ 1 \longrightarrow 0$ Not conserved

$I_3:\ \frac{1}{2} \longrightarrow 0$ Not conserved

(b) $\Sigma^- \longrightarrow n+e^-+\bar{\nu}_e$

$S:\ -1 \longrightarrow 0$ Not conserved

$I_3:\ -1 \longrightarrow -\frac{1}{2}$ Not conserved

(c) $\Lambda^0 \longrightarrow p+e^-+\bar{\nu}_e$

$S:\ -1 \longrightarrow 0$ Not conserved

$I_3:\ 0 \longrightarrow \frac{1}{2}$ Not conserved

(d) $\pi^+ \longrightarrow \pi^0+e^++\nu_e$

$S:\ 0 \longrightarrow 0$ No change

$I_3:\ +1 \longrightarrow 0$ Not conserved

(e) $n \longrightarrow p+e^-+\bar{\nu}_e$

$S:\ 0 \longrightarrow 0$ No change

$I_3:\ -\frac{1}{2} \longrightarrow +\frac{1}{2}$ Not conserved

Electromagnetic interaction: In this case, strangeness is conserved, while isospin is not.

Illustrative Example 7.25:

Verify that strangeness number is conserved, but isospin is not conserved in the following reactions:

(a) $\pi^0 \longrightarrow \gamma+\gamma$ (b) $\eta^0 \longrightarrow \gamma+\gamma$ (c) $\Sigma^0 \longrightarrow \Lambda^0+\gamma$

Solution

(a) $\pi^0 \longrightarrow \gamma+\gamma$

$S:\ 0 \longrightarrow$ Not defined

$I_3:\ 0 \longrightarrow$ Not defined

(b) $\eta^0 \longrightarrow \gamma+\gamma$

$S:\ 0 \longrightarrow$ Not defined

$I_3:\ 0 \longrightarrow$ Not defined

(c) $\Sigma^0 \longrightarrow \Lambda^0+\gamma$

$S:\ -1 \longrightarrow -1$

$I_3:\ 0 \nrightarrow 0$ Not defined

Illustrative Example 7.26:

Identify which of the following weak decay modes is impossible for Ω^-:

(a) $\Omega^- \longrightarrow \Xi^- + \pi^0$ (b) $\Omega^- \longrightarrow \Lambda^0+K^-$ (c) $\Omega^- \longrightarrow \Sigma^- + K^0$

Solution (a) $\Omega^- \longrightarrow \Xi^- + \pi^0$

Charge: $-1 \longrightarrow -1+0$ Conserved

Spin: $\frac{\vec{3}}{2} \nrightarrow \frac{\vec{1}}{2}+0$ Not conserved

Since spin is not conserved, the decay is usually forbidden.

(b) $\Omega^- \longrightarrow \Lambda^0+K^-$

Charge: $-1 \longrightarrow 0-1$ Conserved

Spin: $\frac{\vec{3}}{2} \nrightarrow \frac{\vec{1}}{2}+\vec{0}$ Not conserved

Lepton number: $0 \longrightarrow 0+0$ Conserved

Baryon number: $1 \longrightarrow 1+0$ Conserved

$S:\ -3 \nrightarrow -1-1$ Not conserved

$I_3:\ 0 \nrightarrow 0-\frac{1}{2}$ Not conserved

This decay may not be possible through weak interaction.

(c) $\Omega^- \longrightarrow \Sigma^- + K^0$

Charge: $-1 \longrightarrow -1+0$ Conserved

Spin: $\frac{\vec{3}}{2} \nrightarrow \frac{\vec{1}}{2}+\vec{0}$ Not conserved

Lepton number: $0 \longrightarrow 0+0$ Conserved

Baryon number: $1 \longrightarrow 1+0$ Conserved

$S: \quad -3 \nrightarrow -1+1$ Not Conserved

$I_3: \quad 0 \nrightarrow -1-\frac{1}{2}$ Not Conserved

This decay is not possible through weak interaction.

Illustrative Example 7.27:

Which of the following strong reactions is impossible?

(a) $p+p \longrightarrow p+n+K^+$ (b) $p+p \longrightarrow \Lambda^0+K^0+p+\pi^+$

Solution (a) $p+p \longrightarrow p+n+K^+$

Charge: $1+1 \longrightarrow 1+0+1$ Conserved

Spin: $\frac{\vec{1}}{2}+\frac{\vec{1}}{2} \longrightarrow \frac{\vec{1}}{2}+\frac{\vec{1}}{2}+\vec{1}$ Conserved

Lepton number: $0 \longrightarrow 0+0$ Conserved

Baryon number: $1+1 \longrightarrow 1+1+0$ Conserved

$S: \quad 0+0 \nrightarrow 0+0+1$ Not Conserved

$I_3: \quad +\frac{1}{2}+\frac{1}{2} \nrightarrow \frac{1}{2}-\frac{1}{2}+\frac{1}{2}$ Not Conserved

This reaction is not possible through strong interaction.

(b) $p+p \longrightarrow \Lambda^0+K^0+p+\pi^+$

Charge: $1+1 \longrightarrow 0+0+1+1$ Conserved

Spin: $\frac{\vec{1}}{2}+\frac{\vec{1}}{2} \longrightarrow \frac{\vec{1}}{2}+\vec{1}+\frac{\vec{1}}{2}+0$ Conserved

Lepton number: $0 \longrightarrow 0+0$ Conserved

Baryon number: $1+1 \longrightarrow 1+0+1+0$ Conserved

$S: \quad 0+0 \longrightarrow -1+1+0+0$ Conserved

$I_3: \quad +\frac{1}{2}+\frac{1}{2} \longrightarrow 0-\frac{1}{2}+\frac{1}{2}+1$ Conserved

This reaction is possible through strong interaction.

Illustrative Example 7.28:

Are the following reactions allowed or forbidden?

(a) $\pi^-+p \longrightarrow \pi^0+n$ (b) $\pi^++n \longrightarrow p+\nu_e$

Solution (a) $\pi^-+p \longrightarrow \pi^0+n$

Charge: $-1+1 \longrightarrow 0+0$ Conserved

Spin: $\vec{0}+\frac{\vec{1}}{2} \longrightarrow \vec{0}+\frac{\vec{1}}{2}$ Conserved

Lepton number: $0+0 \longrightarrow 0+0$ Conserved

Baryon number: $0+1 \longrightarrow 0+1$ Conserved

S: $0+0 \longrightarrow 0+0$ Conserved

I_3: $-1+\frac{1}{2} \longrightarrow 0-\frac{1}{2}$ Conserved

This reaction is allowed through strong interaction.

(b) $\pi^+ + n \longrightarrow p + \nu_e$

Lepton number: $0+0 \longrightarrow 0+1$ Not Conserved

This reaction is not allowed.

Illustrative Example 7.29:

Check whether the following processes are allowed or forbidden. If they are forbidden, mention why.

(a) $\pi^- + p \longrightarrow \pi^0 + \Lambda^0$ (b) $K^- + p \longrightarrow K^0 + n$

Solution (a) $\pi^- + p \longrightarrow \pi^0 + \Lambda^0$

Charge: $-1+1 \longrightarrow 0+0$ Conserved

Spin: $\vec{0}+\frac{\vec{1}}{2} \longrightarrow \vec{0}+\frac{\vec{1}}{2}$ Conserved

Lepton number: $0+0 \longrightarrow 0+0$ Conserved

Baryon number: $0+1 \longrightarrow 0+1$ Conserved

Strangeness: $0+0 \longrightarrow 0-1$ Not Conserved

$I_3 : -1+\frac{1}{2} \longrightarrow 0+0$ Not Conserved

This reaction is allowed through weak interaction.

(b) $K^- + p \longrightarrow K^0 + n$

Charge: $-1+1 \longrightarrow 0+0$ Conserved

Spin: $\vec{0}+\frac{\vec{1}}{2} \longrightarrow \vec{0}+\frac{\vec{1}}{2}$ Conserved

Lepton number: $0+0 \longrightarrow 0+0$ Conserved

Baryon number: $0+1 \longrightarrow 0+1$ Conserved

Strangeness: $-1+0 \longrightarrow +1+0$ Not Conserved

$I_3 : -\frac{1}{2}+\frac{1}{2} \longrightarrow -\frac{1}{2}-\frac{1}{2}$ Not Conserved

This reaction is allowed through weak interaction.

Illustrative Example 7.30:

Are the following reactions possible?

(a) $p \longrightarrow n + e^+ + \nu_e$ (b) $p + p \longrightarrow n + p + \pi^0$

Solution (a) $p \longrightarrow n + e^+ + \nu_e$. Since $m_p < m_n$, energy conservation will be violated. So the decay is not allowed.

(b) $p + p \longrightarrow n + p + \pi^+$

Charge: $1 + 1 \longrightarrow 0 + 1 + 1$ Conserved

Spin: $\frac{\vec{1}}{2} + \frac{\vec{1}}{2} \longrightarrow \frac{\vec{1}}{2} + \frac{\vec{1}}{2} + \vec{0}$ Conserved

Lepton number: $0 + 0 \longrightarrow 0 + 0$ Conserved

Baryon number: $1 + 1 \longrightarrow 1 + 1 + 0$ Conserved

Strangeness: $0 + 0 \longrightarrow 0 + 0 + 0$ Conserved

I_3 : $\frac{1}{2} + \frac{1}{2} \longrightarrow -\frac{1}{2} + \frac{1}{2} + 1$ Conserved

This reaction is allowed through strong interaction.

Illustrative Example 7.31:

Explain why a Λ hyperon does not decay into a π^+ and π^- meson.

Solution $\Lambda \longrightarrow \pi^+ + \pi^-$

Baryon number: $1 \longrightarrow 0 + 0$ Not conserved

Thus, the decay is forbidden.

Illustrative Example 7.32:

Identify the unknown particle X.

(a) $\mu^- + p \longrightarrow x + n$ (b) $\pi^- + n \longrightarrow K^0 + x$

Solution (a) Baryon number of the unknown particle is $B = 0$.

Charge of the unknown particle is $C = 0$.

Spin of the unknown particle is $s = \frac{1}{2}$.

L_μ of the unknown particle is $L_\mu = 1$.

Thus, $x = \nu_\mu$.

(b) $x = \Sigma^-$

Illustrative Example 7.33:

Identify the unknown particle X.

(a) $\pi^- + p \longrightarrow K^0 + X$ (b) $K^- + p \longrightarrow K^+ + X$

Assume all reactions are strong.

Solution (a) $\pi^- + p \longrightarrow K^0 + X$

Charge: $-1+1 \longrightarrow 0+q \Rightarrow q=0$

Spin: $0+\frac{\vec{1}}{2} \longrightarrow \vec{1}+\vec{s} \quad \Rightarrow \vec{s}=\frac{\vec{1}}{2}$

Lepton number: $0 \longrightarrow 0+L \quad \Rightarrow L=0$

Baryon number: $0+1 \longrightarrow 0+B \quad \Rightarrow B=1$

Strangeness: $0+0 \longrightarrow 1+S \quad \Rightarrow S=-1$

$I_3: \quad -1+\frac{1}{2} \longrightarrow -\frac{1}{2}+I_3 \quad \Rightarrow I_3=0$

The unknown particle is Λ^0 or Σ^0.

(b) $K^- + p \longrightarrow K^+ + X$

Charge: $-1+1 \longrightarrow 1+q \quad \Rightarrow q=-1$

Spin: $\vec{1}+\frac{\vec{1}}{2} \longrightarrow \vec{1}+\vec{s} \quad \Rightarrow \vec{s}=\frac{\vec{1}}{2}$

Lepton number: $0 \longrightarrow 0+L \quad \Rightarrow L=0$

Baryon number: $0+1 \longrightarrow 0+B \quad \Rightarrow B=1$

Strangeness: $-1+0 \longrightarrow 1+S \quad \Rightarrow S=-2$

$I_3: \quad -\frac{1}{2}+\frac{1}{2} \longrightarrow \frac{1}{2}+I_3 \quad \Rightarrow I_3=-\frac{1}{2}$

The unknown particle is Ξ^-.

Check Progress 7.7: Identify the unknown particle X: $p+p \longrightarrow \Lambda^0 + X + n + \pi^+$.

7.3.7 Charge Conjugation

As the term implies, the operation of charge conjugation (C) reverses the sign of the charge of a particle.

$Q \xrightarrow{C} -Q$; For example, $p \xrightarrow{C} \bar{p}$.

The charge conjugation operator not only applies to the charged particles, but also to neutral particles. It inverts all the internal quantum numbers, such as charge, baryon number, lepton number and strangeness, and thus, converts each particle into its antiparticle. A chargeless particle, for example, a π^0 meson, has an antiparticle that is identical to the particle itself.

$C|\pi^0> = |\pi^0>$

Thus, π^0 has a definite value of $C=+1$.

Under the operation of charge conjugation, strong and electromagnetic interactions are found experimentally to be invariant. For example, consider the reaction

$$p+\bar{p}\longrightarrow\pi^{+}+\pi^{-}+\pi^{0}$$

Under C operation, the left-hand side of the reaction becomes $\bar{p}+p$ and the right-hand side becomes $\pi^{-}+\pi^{+}+\pi^{0}$. Thus, the reaction is invariant under C operation.

Illustrative Example 7.34: C for γ

From the decay $\pi^{0}\longrightarrow\gamma+\gamma$, verify that C for γ is -1.

Also explain why the decay of π^{0} to three γ is forbidden.

Solution C of π^{0} is $+1$, and for $\gamma+\gamma$ it is $(-1)\times(-1)=+1$. Thus, C is conserved in this decay. In the case of $\pi^{0}\longrightarrow\gamma+\gamma+\gamma$, the conservation of C is violated, and thus, the process is forbidden.

Check Progress 7.8: Check that Maxwell's equations are invariant under C operation.
(Hint: Since the charge changes sign under the C operation, the electric and magnetic fields transform as $\vec{E}\overset{C}{\rightarrow}-\vec{E}$; $\vec{B}\overset{C}{\rightarrow}-\vec{B}$).

Illustrative Example 7.35: Charge conjugation and weak interaction

Consider the decay $\pi^{+}\longrightarrow\mu^{+}+\nu_{L}$, where the subscript L means left-handed and, in this case, $\nu=\nu_{\mu}$. Explain how the decay behaves under charge conjugation and parity.

Solution Under parity, $\pi^{+}\longrightarrow\mu^{+}+\nu_{L}\overset{P}{\Rightarrow}\pi^{+}\longrightarrow\mu^{+}+\nu_{R}$.
Under charge conjugation, $\pi^{+}\longrightarrow\mu^{+}+\nu_{L}\overset{C}{\Rightarrow}\pi^{-}\longrightarrow\mu^{-}+\bar{\nu}_{L}$.
However, both $\bar{\nu}_{L}$ (left-handed antineutrino) and ν_{R} (right-handed neutrino) do not exist. The neutrino is always left-handed while the antineutrino is always right-handed.

But, for the reaction

$$\pi^{+}\longrightarrow\mu^{+}+\nu_{L}\overset{C}{\Rightarrow}\pi^{-}\longrightarrow\mu^{-}+\bar{\nu}_{L}\overset{P}{\Rightarrow}\pi^{-}\longrightarrow\mu^{-}+\bar{\nu}_{R}$$

Thus, the above decay, which is a weak interaction, is invariant under CP.

7.4 THE EIGHTFOLD WAY AND THE QUARK MODEL

7.4.1 The Eightfold Way

Gell-Mann in 1961 introduced the Eightfold Way to describe a classification scheme of elementary particles. The term is taken from the Eightfold Path of Buddhism and refers to the eight-member families to which many sets of elementary particles belong.

The classes and properties of the elementary particles appear to be haphazard. However, an underlying order in the hadron family is revealed if we represent various families on a chart showing charge (Q) or isospin component I_3 plotted against strangeness (S). Let us first consider the spin 0^- mesons. The eight members of the spin 0^- mesons, including the antiparticle (excluding $\bar{\eta}^0$), are presented in Table 7.10.

Table 7.10: *Family of spin 0^- mesons*

Mesons	Q	I_3	S	Hypercharge (Y)
π^+	$+1$	$+1$	0	0
π^0	0	0	0	0
π^-	-1	-1	0	0
K^+	$+1$	$+\frac{1}{2}$	$+1$	$+1$
$\bar{K}^+$	-1	$-\frac{1}{2}$	-1	-1
K^0	0	$-\frac{1}{2}$	$+1$	$+1$
$\bar{K}^0$	0	$+\frac{1}{2}$	-1	-1
η^0	0	0	0	0

The charge (Q) vs strangeness (S) of mesons is shown in Fig. 7.1.

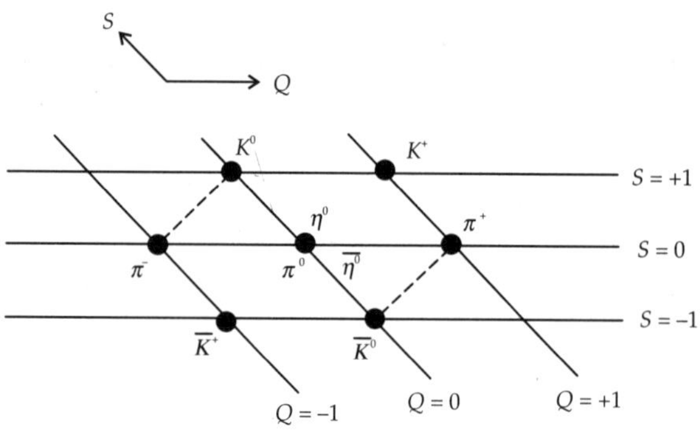

Figure 7.1: *Meson octet: Charge vs strangeness chart for spin 0^- mesons*

A fascinating hexagonal pattern emerges from Fig. 7.1. The diagonal lines determine charge and the horizontals determine the strangeness. The particles and their corresponding antiparticles are at the vertices of the hexagon. The particles having their own antiparticles are at the centre.

A similar pattern is obtained for eight spin $\frac{1}{2}^+$ baryons. The eight members of the spin $\frac{1}{2}^+$ baryons are listed in Table 7.11.

The charge (Q) vs strangeness (S) of spin $\frac{1}{2}$ baryons and spin $\frac{3}{2}$ baryons are shown in Fig. 7.2 and Fig. 7.3, respectively.

Table 7.11: *Members of spin* $\frac{1}{2}^{+}$ *baryons*

Baryons	Q	I_3	S	Hypercharge (Y)
p	+1	$+\frac{1}{2}$	0	1
n	0	$-\frac{1}{2}$	0	1
Λ^0	0	0	−1	0
Σ^+	+1	+1	−1	0
Σ^0	0	0	−1	0
Σ^-	−1	−1	−1	0
Ξ^0	0	$+\frac{1}{2}$	−2	−1
Ξ^-	−1	$-\frac{1}{2}$	−2	1

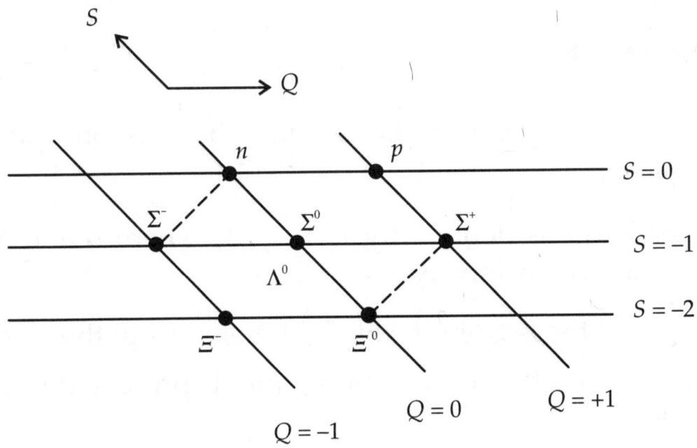

Figure 7.2: *Baryon octet: Charge vs strangeness chart for spin* $\frac{1}{2}^{+}$ *baryons*

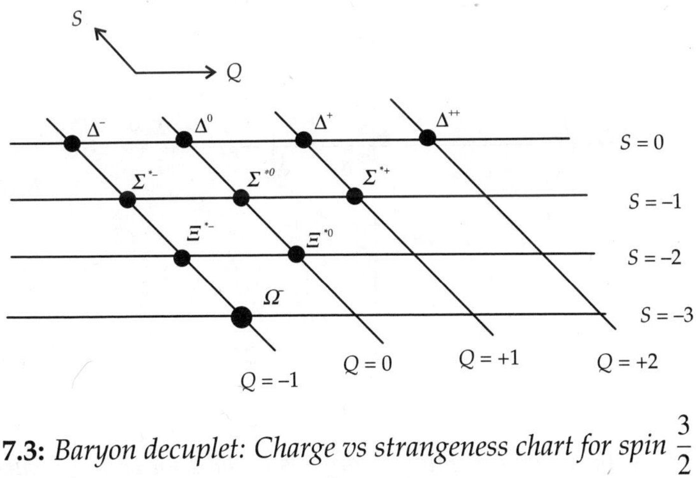

Figure 7.3: *Baryon decuplet: Charge vs strangeness chart for spin* $\frac{3}{2}$ *baryons*

The scheme of representing the hadrons in this systematic way, according to their charge and strangeness, is known as the Eightfold Way. Any vacancy in the arrangement indicates a missing particle in the family. For example, when this scheme was proposed, only nine spin $\frac{3}{2}$ baryons were known. The tenth member of the baryon decuplet (Ω^-) was detected later in accordance with the prediction of the scheme[5].

The leptons are really elementary particles in their true sense. They do not have any internal structure and do not seem to decay into smaller units. They are also very limited in number. Hadrons, on the other hand, are complex particles with definite size and they have been found to decay into other hadrons. They are not limited in number. We also recall that the periodic table in chemistry is a manifestation of the structure of the atom. Similarly, the occurrence of octet and decuplet in hadrons could be a manifestation of some regular pattern underlying the structure of hadrons. Thus, the Eightfold Way also implies that hadrons cannot be truly elementary.

Illustrative Example 7.36:

What is hypercharge? Show the multiplet of spin $\frac{1}{2}$ baryons on a plot of hypercharge versus isospin projection.

Solution The hypercharge is defined by $Y = B + S$, where B and S are the baryon number and strangeness, respectively.

The hypercharge and the isospin (I_3) of eight members of the spin $\frac{1}{2}^+$ baryons are presented in Table 7.11, and the corresponding plot is presented in Fig. 7.4.

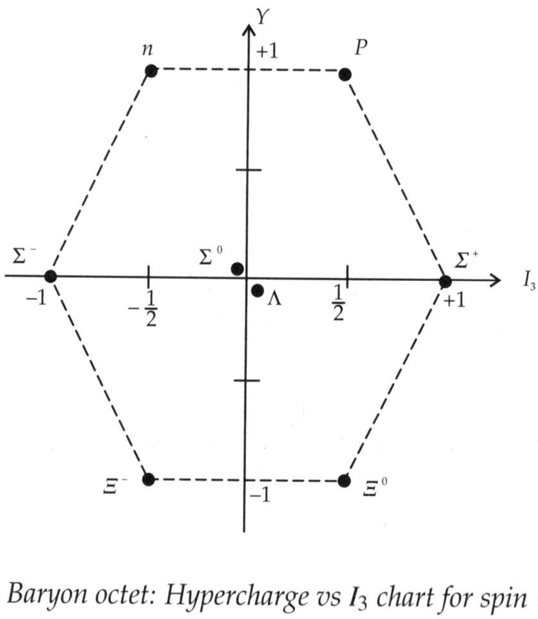

Figure 7.4: *Baryon octet: Hypercharge vs I_3 chart for spin $\frac{1}{2}^+$ baryons*

[5]Griffiths, D. 2008. *Introduction to Elementary Particles, Second Edition*, Wiley-VCH.

Illustrative Example 7.37:

A hadron is symbolised by $\Delta^{++}\left(\frac{3^+}{2}\right)$. Is it a fermion or a boson? What is its spin, parity and isospin?

Solution Since it has half-integral spin, it is a fermion.

Spin is $\frac{3}{2}$, in unit of $\hbar$. Parity is +ve. Its strangeness is $S = 0$.

$$Q = I_3 + \frac{B+S}{2};\; 2 = I_3 + \frac{1}{2} \Rightarrow I_3 = \frac{3}{2}$$

7.4.2 The Quark Model

In 1964, Gell-Mann and Zweig independently proposed that the observed pattern of the hadrons could be reproduced if mesons and baryons were composed of three elementary constituents, which they named **quarks**. The three types of quarks are up (u), down (d) and strange (s). It is customary to refer to u, d and s as the three *flavours* of quarks. The properties of these three quarks are listed in Table 7.12.

The u quark carries a fractional charge of $+\frac{2}{3}e$ and the d and s quarks have a charge of $-\frac{1}{3}e$ each. Strangeness (S) is zero for the u and d quarks, while $S = -1$ for the s quark. Figure 7.5 shows the charge and strangeness of these basic quarks. Antiquarks are those that have all their quantum numbers of the opposite sign to the quarks.

Table 7.12: *Quark properties*

Name	Symbol	Charge (e)	Spin	Baryon number	Strangeness
up	u	$+\frac{2}{3}$	$+\frac{1}{2}$	$+\frac{1}{3}$	0
down	d	$-\frac{1}{3}$	$+\frac{1}{2}$	$+\frac{1}{3}$	0
strange	s	$-\frac{1}{3}$	$+\frac{1}{2}$	$+\frac{1}{3}$	-1

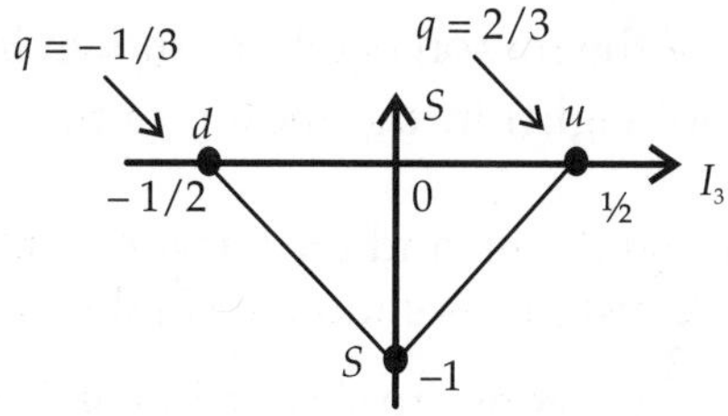

Figure 7.5: *The basic quark triplet*

As mesons have integral (0) spin and baryon number $B = 0$, a combination of quark and antiquark gives a meson. The quark–antiquark combinations representing the mesons are presented in Table 7.13.

Table 7.13: *Possible quark–antiquark combinations of spin 0 mesons*

Combination	Charge	Spin	Baryon number	Strangeness	Meson
$u\bar{u}$	$+\frac{2}{3}-\frac{2}{3}=0$	0	0	0	π^0
$u\bar{d}$	$+\frac{2}{3}+\frac{1}{3}=1$	0	0	0	π^+
$u\bar{s}$	$+\frac{2}{3}+\frac{1}{3}=1$	0	0	+1	K^+
$d\bar{u}$	$-\frac{1}{3}-\frac{2}{3}=-1$	0	0	0	π^-
$d\bar{d}$	$-\frac{1}{3}+\frac{1}{3}=0$	0	0	0	η
$d\bar{s}$	$-\frac{1}{3}+\frac{1}{3}=0$	0	0	+1	K^0
$s\bar{u}$	$-\frac{1}{3}-\frac{2}{3}=-1$	0	0	−1	K^-
$s\bar{d}$	$-\frac{1}{3}+\frac{1}{3}=0$	0	0	−1	$\bar{K}^0$
$s\bar{s}$	$-\frac{1}{3}+\frac{1}{3}=0$	0	0	0	η'

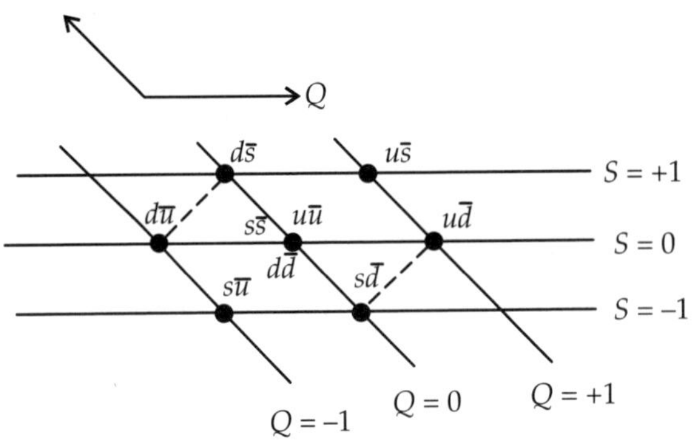

Figure 7.6: *Meson octet: Possible quark–antiquark combinations*

The quark constituents of the meson octet are shown in Figs 7.6 and 7.7. In fact, there are nine members (not eight) in the meson family. The last member η' was discovered later.

As baryons have half-integral spin and the baryon number $B = 1$, a baryon can be represented as a three-quark system, as shown in Table 7.14. The quark combinations of spin $\frac{1}{2}$ baryons and spin $\frac{3}{2}$ baryons are shown in Fig. 7.8 and Fig. 7.9, respectively. The baryon number is −1 for antibaryons, and thus, antibaryons can be represented as a system of three antiquarks.

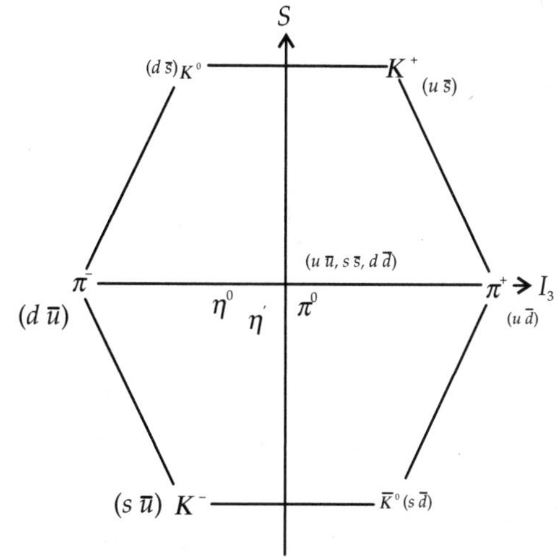

Figure 7.7: *Possible quark–antiquark combinations of mesons in S vs. I_3 diagram*

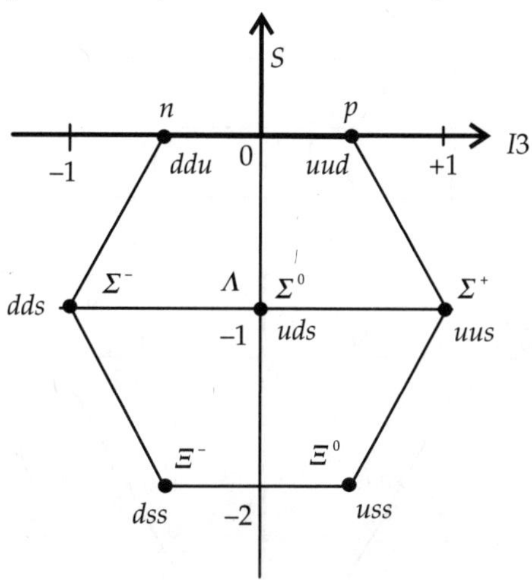

Figure 7.8: *Baryon octet: Possible quark combinations*

All quarks are fermions with half-spin. So they must follow the Pauli Exclusion Principle. However, formation of the Δ^{++} baryon, for example, with three identical quarks (*uuu*), violates this principle. To avoid this difficulty, an additional quantum number is assigned to the quarks. This is known as **colour**. In an analogy to the primary colours, they are labelled red, green and blue. Three *u* quarks in Δ^{++} do not violate the Pauli Exclusion Principle because they have different colours.

$\Delta^{++} \rightarrow u_R u_G u_B$

This occurs in a properly symmetrising fashion. Quarks of different colours combine in such a way as to produce colourless hadrons. The **colour** charge is responsible for the strong interaction between the quarks.

Table 7.14: *Possible quark combinations of spin $\frac{1}{2}$ baryons*

Combination	Charge	Spin	Baryon number	Strangeness	Baryon
uuu	$+\frac{2}{3}+\frac{2}{3}+\frac{2}{3}=+2$	$\frac{3}{2}$	1	0	-
uud	$+\frac{2}{3}+\frac{2}{3}-\frac{1}{3}=+1$	$\frac{1}{2}$	1	0	p
udd	$+\frac{2}{3}-\frac{1}{3}-\frac{1}{3}=0$	$\frac{1}{2}$	1	0	n
uus	$+\frac{2}{3}+\frac{2}{3}-\frac{1}{3}=+1$	$\frac{1}{2}$	1	-1	Σ^+
uss	$+\frac{2}{3}-\frac{1}{3}-\frac{1}{3}=0$	$\frac{1}{2}$	1	-2	Ξ^0
uds	$+\frac{2}{3}-\frac{1}{3}-\frac{1}{3}=0$	$\frac{1}{2}$	1	-1	Σ^0
ddd	$-\frac{1}{3}-\frac{1}{3}-\frac{1}{3}=-1$	$\frac{3}{2}$	1	0	-
dds	$-\frac{1}{3}-\frac{1}{3}-\frac{1}{3}=-1$	$\frac{1}{2}$	1	-1	Σ^-
dss	$-\frac{1}{3}-\frac{1}{3}-\frac{1}{3}=-1$	$\frac{1}{2}$	1	-2	Ξ^-
sss	$-\frac{1}{3}-\frac{1}{3}-\frac{1}{3}=-1$	$\frac{3}{2}$	1	-3	Ω^-

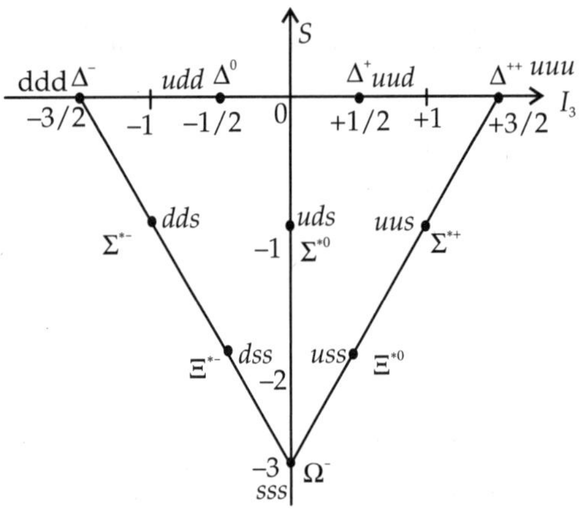

Figure 7.9: *Baryon decuplet: Possible quark combinations*

The current experimental status of particle physics is well established. According to current theory, there are six types (flavours) of quarks: u (up), d (down), s (strange), c (charm), b (bottom) and t (top). The c quark was discovered from observations of massive meson states of the type $\psi = c\bar{c}$ in 1974 and the b quark resulted from observations of the even heavier meson $\Upsilon = b\bar{b}$ in 1977. Finally, the list was completed with observations of the most massive quark, t-quark, in 1995. The properties of these quarks are presented in Table 7.15.

Table 7.15: *Quark properties*

Name	Symbol	Charge (e)	Spin	Baryon number	S	C	T	B
up	u	$+\frac{2}{3}$	$+\frac{1}{2}$	$+\frac{1}{3}$	0	0	0	0
down	d	$-\frac{1}{3}$	$+\frac{1}{2}$	$+\frac{1}{3}$	0	0	0	0
strange	s	$-\frac{1}{3}$	$+\frac{1}{2}$	$+\frac{1}{3}$	−1	0	0	0
charm	c	$+\frac{2}{3}$	$+\frac{1}{2}$	$+\frac{1}{3}$	0	+1	0	0
bottom	b	$-\frac{1}{3}$	$+\frac{1}{2}$	$+\frac{1}{3}$	0	0	0	-1
top	t	$+\frac{2}{3}$	$+\frac{1}{2}$	$+\frac{1}{3}$	0	0	+1	0

Illustrative Example 7.38: Beta decay in the quark model

Interpret beta decay of the neutron in the quark model.

Solution In β decay, $n \longrightarrow p + e^- + \bar{\nu}_e$.
The process of beta decay can be represented as

$$n \longrightarrow p + W^- \Rightarrow W^- \longrightarrow e^- + \bar{\nu}_e$$

Actually, decay of $n \longrightarrow p + W^-$ violates energy as the mass of W^- is large and the existence of W^- is restricted by the uncertainty principle.

In terms of quarks, $udd \longrightarrow uud + e^- + \bar{\nu}_e$.

On each side, one pair of u and d remains unchanged. Thus, removing these spectator quarks (u and d) on both sides, we are left with

$$d \longrightarrow u + e^- + \bar{\nu}_e$$

The complete process may be represented as $d \longrightarrow u + W^- \Rightarrow W^- \longrightarrow e^- + \bar{\nu}_e$.

Illustrative Example 7.39:

The net colour of mesons is white. Explain.

Solution A meson is composed of a quark and an antiquark. The quark of a particular colour combines with its anticoloured antiquark to give a net colour of white.

Check Progress 7.9: The net colour of baryons is white. Explain.

Check Progress 7.10: Find the baryon number, hypercharge and I_3 of the following quark systems: (a) $u\bar{s}$ (b) $u\bar{d}$ (c) $s\bar{s}$ (d) $\bar{u}\bar{u}\bar{d}$

Illustrative Example 7.40:

A hadron has the quark content $u\bar{d}$. Find the baryon number, charge, spin and strangeness of this hadron.

Solution Baryon number: $B = +\frac{1}{3} - \frac{1}{3} = 0$; Charge: $+\frac{2}{3} + \frac{1}{3} = +1$
Spin:$= 0$; Strangeness $= 0$
It is a π^+ meson.

Illustrative Example 7.41:

Explain why you do not find (a) a baryon with strangeness -2 and electric charge $+1$, (b) a meson with strangeness $+1$ and electric charge -1.

Solution (a) As baryons have half-integral spin and the baryon number $B = 1$, a baryon must be formed by three quarks. For a strangeness of -2, two s quarks are required.

Thus, the total charge of the combination is $q - 2 \times \frac{1}{3} = +1$. Therefore, $q = \frac{5}{3}$.
However, a quark with a charge of $\frac{5}{3}$ does not exist.

(b) A quark and an antiquark together make a meson. To achieve a strangeness of $+1$, $\bar{s}$ is required.

Thus, the total charge of the combination is $q + \frac{1}{3} = -1$. Therefore, $q = -\frac{4}{3}$. However, a quark with a charge of $-\frac{4}{3}$ does not exist.

SUMMARY

- **Fundamental Interactions:** The four fundamental interactions are strong, electromagnetic, weak and gravitational. Strong interaction has the greatest strength and takes place in the shortest time ($\sim 10^{-22}$ s).

  Electromagnetic interaction is weaker (10^{-2} times) than the strong interaction and occurs over a time of 10^{-14} to 10^{-21}s.

  The strength of the weak interaction is about 10^{-9} times that of the strong interaction.

  Gravitational interaction is the weakest of all.
- **Elementary Particles:** Elementary particles are categorised as leptons, mesons and baryons.
- **Leptons**: $(e^-, \mu^-, \tau^-, \nu_e, \nu_\mu, \nu_\tau)$ and their antiparticles. Electrons (positrons) and all types of neutrinos are stable, while muons decay according to $\mu^- \longrightarrow e^- + \bar{\nu}_e + \nu_\mu$. All leptons participate in weak interaction. The lepton number (L_e and L_μ) is non-zero only for the leptons corresponding to it, and zero for others. In any process, the total lepton number is always conserved.
- **Mesons**: The lightest mesons are pions. They decay according to $\pi^+ \longrightarrow \mu^+ + \nu_\mu$ and $\pi^- \longrightarrow \mu^- + \bar{\nu}_\mu$ through weak interactions. π^0 decays according to the electromagnetic scheme $\pi^0 \longrightarrow \gamma + \gamma$.
- **Pions** are pseudoscalar, having zero spin and negative parity (0^-). Pions form an isotopic triplet with isospin $\vec{I} = \vec{1}$ and $I_3 = 1(\pi^+), 0(\pi^0)$ and $-1(\pi^-)$.

Kaons, like pions, have zero spin and isospin $\vec{I} = \frac{\vec{1}}{2}$. They form isotopic doublets, $K^+\left(I_3 = +\frac{1}{2}\right)$ and $K^0\left(I_3 = -\frac{1}{2}\right)$.

- **Baryons**: Baryons are strongly interacting particles with half-integral spin. They have +*ve* parity. Proton is the lightest stable baryon. Particles with a mass larger than the mass of nucleons are called hyperons. The hyperons are $\Lambda^0, \Sigma^+, \Sigma^0, \Sigma^-, \Xi^0, \Xi^-, \Omega^-, \ldots$. For baryons, the baryon number $B = +1$ and 0 for others.
- **Strange Behaviour of Kaons and Hyperons**
(a) They always produce in pairs.
(b) They are produced by strong interaction at a high rate; however, they decay very slowly as weakly interacting particles.
These particles are called the strange particles. The kaons (K^+ and K^0) are assigned $S = +1$.
The Gell-Mann–Nishijima relation $Q = I_3 + \frac{B+S}{2}$.
- **Antiparticles:** Every particle has an antiparticle with the same mass but opposite charge, lepton number, baryon number, I_3 and S.
- **Decay from Rest:** $a \longrightarrow b + c$
Kinetic energy of c is $T_c = \frac{(m_a + m_b - m_c)(m_a - m_b - m_c)c^2}{2m_a}$ and kinetic energy of b is $T_c = \frac{(m_a + m_c - m_b)(m_a - m_b - m_c)c^2}{2m_a}$.
- **Threshold Energy:** $a + X \longrightarrow Y + b$
$E_{\text{threshold}} = \frac{(\sum m_{\text{final}})^2 - (\sum m_{\text{initial}})^2}{2m_x} c^2 = (-Q)\frac{m_a + m_x + m_b + m_y}{2m_x}$.
- **Conservation Laws:** The laws of conservation of energy, linear momentum, angular momentum, charge, lepton number and baryon number hold in all processes. Isospin is not obeyed in electromagnetic interactions and strangeness and isospin are both violated in weak interactions while all are conserved in strong interactions.
- **Charge Conjugation:** It is the process of replacing a particle with its antiparticle. The strong and electromagnetic interactions are invariant under C operation.
- **Quarks:** Quarks are structureless spin $\frac{1}{2}$ fermions from which all hadrons are built. They occur with a baryon number, $B = \frac{1}{3}$. The up quark (u) has a charge of $+\frac{2e}{3}$ but the down (d) and strange (s) quarks have a charge of $\frac{-e}{3}$ each. A combination of quark and antiquark gives a meson, and baryons are built with three quarks.

baryon $= qqq$; meson $= q\bar{q}$

Since quarks are confined in hadrons, a free quark cannot be observed.

REVIEW QUESTIONS AND PROBLEMS

Multiple Choice Questions

1. Arrange the four basic interactions in increasing order of strength:
   (a) Strong, weak, electromagnetic, gravitational
   (b) Strong, electromagnetic, gravitational, weak

(c) Strong, electromagnetic, weak, gravitational
(d) Strong, weak, gravitational, electromagnetic

2. Arrange the four basic interactions in increasing order of typical time over which they act:
   (a) Strong, weak, electromagnetic, gravitational
   (b) Strong, electromagnetic, gravitational, weak
   (c) Strong, electromagnetic, weak, gravitational
   (d) Strong, weak, gravitational, electromagnetic
3. The interaction responsible for the decay, $\eta^0 \longrightarrow \gamma + \gamma\,(10^{-8}\,s)$, is
   (a) Strong (b) Electromagnetic (c) Weak (d) Gravitational
4. The basic process underlying the neutron β decay is
   (a) $d \longrightarrow u + e^- + \bar{\nu}_e$ (b) $d \longrightarrow u + e^-$ (c) $u \longrightarrow d + e^- + \bar{\nu}_e$ (d) $s \longrightarrow u + e^- + \bar{\nu}_e$
   [GATE 2010]
5. Match the reactions on the left with the associated interactions on the right:
   A. $\pi^+ \longrightarrow \mu^+ + \nu_\mu$ (*i*) Strong
   B. $\pi^0 \longrightarrow \gamma + \gamma$ (*ii*) Electromagnetic
   C. $\pi^0 + n \longrightarrow \pi^- + p$ (*iii*) Weak
   (a) (A,iii), (B,ii), (C,i) (b) (A,i), (B,ii), (C,iii)
   (c) (A,ii), (B,i), (C,iii) (d) (A,iii), (B,i), (C,ii) [GATE 2010]
6. The isospin and strangeness of the Ω^- baryon is
   (a) $1, -3$ (b) $0, -3$ (c) $1, 3$ (d) $0, 3$ [GATE 2011]
7. The decay process $n \longrightarrow p + e^- + \bar{\nu}_e$ violates
   (a) Baryon number (b) Lepton number (c) Isospin (d) Strangeness
   [GATE 2013]
8. In $\bar{\nu_\mu} + p \longrightarrow n + x$, x is
   (a) e^+ (b) μ^+ (c) π^+ (d) None of the above
9. Consider the decay $K^- \longrightarrow \mu^- + \nu_\mu$. If the rest mass of K^- is 494 MeV and the rest mass of muon is 106 MeV, the energy of ν_μ is
   (a) ≈ 120 MeV (b) ≈ 236 MeV (c) ≈ 300 MeV (d) ≈ 388 MeV
10. The process $\mu^+ \longrightarrow e^+ + \gamma$ is forbidden, because it violates
    (a) Momentum and lepton number conservation
    (b) Baryon and lepton number conservation
    (c) Angular momentum conservation
    (d) Lepton number conservation [GATE 2015]

11. A beam of pions (π^+) is incident on a proton target, giving rise to the process $\pi^+ + p \longrightarrow n + \pi^+ + \pi^+$. Assuming that the decay proceeds through strong interactions, the total isospin I and its third component I_3 for the decay products are

    (a) $I = \frac{3}{2}, I_3 = \frac{3}{2}$ (b) $I = \frac{5}{2}, I_3 = \frac{5}{2}$ (c) $I = \frac{5}{2}, I_3 = \frac{3}{2}$ (d) $I = \frac{1}{2}, I_3 = -\frac{1}{2}$

    [NET 2011]

12. The dominant interactions underlying the following processes are
    A. $K^- + p \longrightarrow \Sigma^- + \pi^+$ B. $\mu^- + \mu^+ \longrightarrow K^- + K^+$ C. $\Sigma^- \longrightarrow p + \pi^0$

    (a) A: strong, B: electromagnetic and C: weak
    (b) A: strong, B: weak and C: electromagnetic
    (c) A: weak, B: electromagnetic and C: strong
    (d) A: weak, B: electromagnetic and C: weak [NET 2012]

13. The recently discovered Higgs boson at the LHC experiment has a decay mode into a photon and a Z boson. If the rest masses of the Higgs and Z bosons are 125 GeV/c^2 and 90 GeV/c^2, respectively, and the decaying Higgs particle is at rest, the energy of the photon will be approximately

    (a) $35\sqrt{3}$ GeV (b) 35 GeV (c) 30 GeV (d) 15 GeV [NET 2014]

14. Consider the four processes
    $i.p \longrightarrow n + e^+ + \nu_e$ $ii.\Lambda^0 \longrightarrow p + e^+ + \nu_e$
    $iii.\pi^+ \longrightarrow e^+ + \nu_e$ $iv.\pi^0 \longrightarrow \gamma + \gamma$
    Which of the above is/are forbidden for free particles?

    (a) Only (ii) (b) (ii) and (iv) (c) (i) and (iv) (d) (i) and (ii) [NET 2014]

Short Questions and Problems

Particle decay and interactions

1. A neutral particle (X) decays from rest as $X \longrightarrow p + \pi^-$.

   If the kinetic energy of the proton is 5.3 MeV, find the mass of X. Identify X. (Given: $M_p = 938.3$ MeV and $M_\pi = 140$ MeV).

2. K^+ at rest decays as $K^+ \longrightarrow e^+ + \pi^0 + \nu_e$.

   Determine the maximum possible kinetic energy of e^+ and of π^0.

3. K^0 at rest decays as $K^0 \longrightarrow \pi^+ + \pi^-$.

   Determine the maximum possible kinetic energy of π^+ and of π^-.

4. Calculate the energy of neutrons produced when a slow negative pion is captured by a proton. Treat the neutron non-relativistically.

5. Determine the threshold energy for the following reactions.

   i. $\pi^- + p \longrightarrow \Lambda^0 + K^0$ ii. $p + p \longrightarrow n + \Sigma^+ + K^0 + \pi^+$

Conservation laws and different interactions

6. Find the missing particle (x) in each of the following decays

   i. $K^0 \longrightarrow \pi^0 + \pi^0 + x$ ii. $K^- \longrightarrow \pi^0 + e^- + x$

7. Find the missing particle (x) in each of the following reactions:

   i. $K^- + n \longrightarrow \Lambda^0 + x$ ii. $\bar{\nu_\mu} + p \longrightarrow n + x$
   iii. $p + \bar{p} \longrightarrow n + x$ iv. $p + p \longrightarrow p + \Lambda^0 + x$

8. Determine whether the following reactions are allowed through strong, electromagnetic or weak processes.

   i. $\pi^- + p \longrightarrow \pi^0 + \Sigma^0$ ii. $\pi^- + p \longrightarrow K^0 + \Sigma^0$ iii. $\pi^- \longrightarrow \mu^- + \bar{\nu_\mu}$
   iv. $p \longrightarrow n + e^+ + \nu_e$ v. $\Xi^- \longrightarrow \Sigma^- + \pi^0$ vi. $\pi^0 \longrightarrow \gamma + \gamma$

9. Verify that the reaction $\pi^- + p \longrightarrow n + \gamma$ is allowed through strong interaction, while the reaction $\pi^- + p \longrightarrow \pi^0 + \Lambda^0$ is not.

10. Which of the following reactions is allowed for strong interaction?

    i. $p + p \longrightarrow K^+ + \Sigma^+$ ii. $p + p \longrightarrow K^+ + p + \Lambda^0$

11. Verify that the reaction $\Sigma^- \longrightarrow \pi^- + n$ is allowed through weak interaction, while the reaction $\Sigma^- \longrightarrow \pi^- + p$ is not.

12. Which of the following reactions is allowed for weak interaction?

    i. $n \longrightarrow p + e^- + \nu_e$ ii. $n \longrightarrow p + e^- + \bar{\nu}_e$

13. Which of the following reactions is allowed for weak interaction?

    i. $\nu_e + p \longrightarrow e^- + \pi^+ + p$ ii. $\nu_\mu + p \longrightarrow \mu^+ + n$
    iii. $K^+ \longrightarrow \pi^0 + \mu^+ + \nu_\mu$ iv. $\Lambda^0 \longrightarrow \pi^+ + e^- + \bar{\nu}_e$

14. A particle X decays weakly at rest as $X \longrightarrow \pi^0 + \mu^+ + \nu_\mu$. Determine the following properties of X:

    i. charge, ii. lepton number, iii. baryon number, iv. spin, v. fermion or boson, vi. isospin, vii. strangeness. Identify X.

15. Determine whether the reaction $K^- + p \longrightarrow \Xi^0 + K^0$ is allowed by the conservation of charge, spin and strangeness.

16. From the reaction $p + \pi^- \longrightarrow K^0 + \Lambda^0$, which occurs through a strong interaction, deduce the strangeness of Λ^0, given $S = 1$ for K^0. Now comment on the fact that the decay $\Lambda^0 \longrightarrow p + \pi^-$ does not occur in nature.

17. Are the following processes possible? Give reasons.

    i. $n \longrightarrow p + e^- + \gamma$ ii. $n + \gamma \longrightarrow p + e^-$

General problems

18. What is resonance?

19. (a) Explain the meaning of isotopic spin and strangeness.

    (b) Explain what is meant by Eightfold Way? What is its importance in the classification of particles?

    (c) What are the hypercharges of the u, d and s quarks?

20. Interpret the reaction $\pi^- + p \longrightarrow \Lambda^0 + K^0$ in terms of quarks.

21. Define hypercharge. Plot the hypercharge against isospin for the quark triplet and the baryon decuplet, with their respective particles and their quark contents properly indicated for the latter.

HINTS/ANSWERS TO SELECTED PROBLEMS

Multiple Choice Questions

1. (c) 2. (c) 3. (b) 4. (a) 5. (a) 6. (b) 7. (c) 8. (b)

9. (b) $T_b = \dfrac{(494+106)(494-106)}{2 \times 494} = 235.6$ MeV

10. (d) 11. (c) 12. (a) 13. (c) $T_b = \dfrac{(125+90)(125-90)}{2 \times 125} = 30$

14. (d) i. energy and ii. charge violation.

Particle decay and interactions

1. $m_X c^2 = m_p c^2 + T_p + \sqrt{m_\pi^2 c^4 + T_p(T_p + 2m_p c^2)} \approx 1115.57$ MeV, and thus, X is Λ^0.

2. For maximum kinetic energies of e^+ and of π^0, energy of the ν_e will be zero, that is, it will be a two-body decay. Thus, $T_e = \dfrac{(m_k - m_e)^2 - m_\pi^2}{2m_k}c^2 = \dfrac{(494-0.5)^2 - 135^2}{2 \times 494}$ ≈ 228 MeV and $T_\pi = \dfrac{(m_k - m_\pi)^2 - m_e^2}{2m_k}c^2 = \dfrac{(494-135)^2 - 0.5^2}{2 \times 494} \approx 130$ MeV.

3. $T_\pi \approx 107$ MeV.

4. $\pi^- + p \longrightarrow n + \pi^0$. Energy conservation: $Q = m_{\pi^-} + m_p - m_n - m_{\pi^0} = T_n + T_{\pi^0}$.

   Momentum conservation: $p_{\pi^0} = p_n$, assuming the proton is at rest and neglecting the momentum of the slow pion.

   Assuming the nonrelativistic collision, $T_{\pi^0} = \dfrac{p_{\pi^0}^2}{2m_{\pi^0}} = T_n \dfrac{m_n}{m_{\pi^0}}$.

   Thus, $T_n + T_n \dfrac{m_n}{m_{\pi^0}} = m_{\pi^-} + m_p - m_n - m_{\pi^0}$. From this equation, T_n can be calculated.

5. i. 3608 MeV ii. 1800 MeV

Conservation laws and different interactions

6. i. π^0 ii. $\bar{\nu}_e$ 7. i. π^- ii. μ^+ iii. $\bar{n}$ iv. K^+

8. i. I_3 and S are not conserved. Only i weak ii. strong iii. weak iv. forbidden as $m_p < m_n$ v. forbidden as energy is not conserved. vi. electromagnetic

10. ii 12. ii

13. i. allowed ii. not allowed iii. allowed iv. not allowed

14. i. $+e$ ii. $L_\mu = 0$ iii. $B = 0$ iv. 0 or 1 v. boson vi. $I_3 = \frac{1}{2}$ as $\Delta I_3 = \pm\frac{1}{2}$ vii. $S = 1$ as $\Delta S = \pm 1$ in weak interaction. K^+.

15. Charge, spin and strangeness are all conserved.

16. $S = -1$ for Λ^0. 17. No, as L_e is not conserved.

General problems

18. The resonance particles, or resonances, are extremely short-lived particles. The lifetime of these particles is $\sim 10^{-23}$ seconds. These particles can only travel about $\sim 10^{-15}$ metres, or about the diameter of a proton, before decaying. Such a small distance cannot be measured by any device.

19. (c) Hypercharge of u, d and s are $\frac{1}{3}, \frac{1}{3}$ and $-\frac{2}{3}$, respectively.

21. Please see Table 7.11 and Figs 7.10, 7.11 and 7.12.

Table 7.16 *Quark properties*

Quark	Charge (e)	I_3	B	S	$Y = B+S$
u	$+\frac{2}{3}$	$+\frac{1}{2}$	$+\frac{1}{3}$	0	$+\frac{1}{3}$
d	$-\frac{1}{3}$	$-\frac{1}{2}$	$+\frac{1}{3}$	0	$+\frac{1}{3}$
s	$-\frac{1}{3}$	0	$+\frac{1}{3}$	-1	$-\frac{2}{3}$

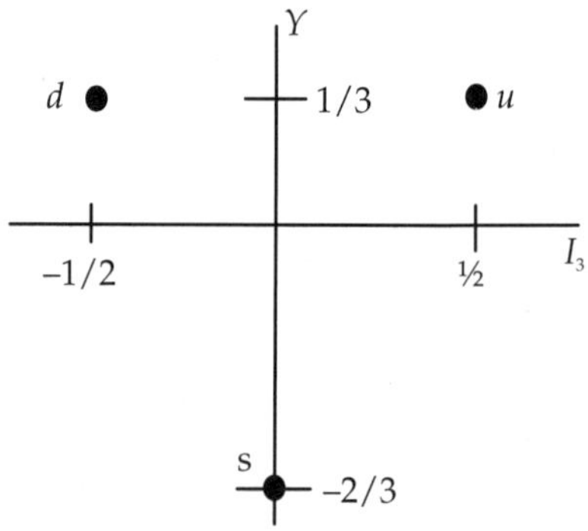

Figure 7.10 *Quark triplet: Hypercharge vs I_3*

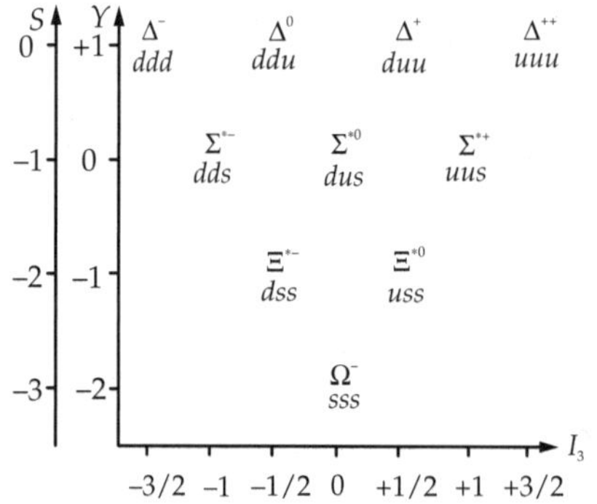

Figure 7.11: *Baryon decuplet: Hypercharge vs I_3*

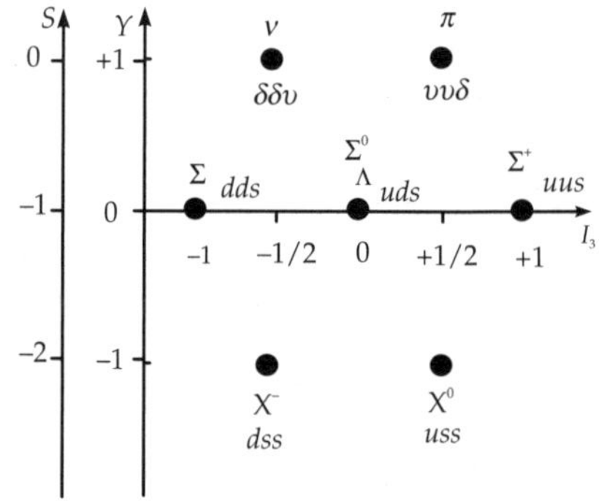

Figure 7.12: *Baryon octet: Hypercharge vs I_3*

CHAPTER 8

Nuclear Astrophysics

By the early 20th century, astronomers had discovered that our Sun is a member of the galaxy known as Milky Way, which contains billions of stars. The universe itself contains an equally vast number of galaxies. Astrophysics is the branch of science that applies the rules of physics to explain the nature of different celestial objects in the universe.

In this closing chapter, we will briefly study the origin and evolution of the universe from our earthly perspective. We will also discuss the basic aspects of stellar nucleosynthesis, explaining the formation of different elements in the stellar interior.

8.1 EXPANDING UNIVERSE

In 1929, Edwin Hubble, an American astronomer, observed that the wavelengths of spectral lines from stars in distant galaxies did not correspond exactly to the wavelengths of the same lines emitted by terrestrial sources. The lines appeared to shift to the long-wavelength (red) end of the visible spectrum. This **red shift** of the spectral lines can be interpreted as the Doppler effect of the electromagnetic waves associated with a moving source. Measuring the red shift, Hubble observed that the more distant galaxies appeared to move faster than the ones nearby, and he concluded that galaxies are receding away from us at a velocity that is proportional to their distance from us. The linear relationship between the velocity of recession and distance can be given as

$$v = Hd \tag{8.1}$$

This is known as **Hubble's law**. The proportionality constant H is called the **Hubble's constant**. Exact determination of H is extremely difficult, as it involves the measurement of very distant galaxies. The best value[1] of H that we have is

$$H = 100\, h_0 \frac{\text{km/s}}{\text{Mpc}}, \tag{8.2}$$

where the value of h_0 is settled at about

$$h_0 = 0.7 \pm 0.1 \tag{8.3}$$

[1]Perkins, DJ. 2000. *Introduction to High Energy Physics, Fourth Edition.* Cambridge University Press, UK.

Here, 1 Mpc = 1 megaparsec = 3.26×10^6 light years (ly) = 3.09×10^{19} km. Note that the uncertainty in H is large.

Figure 8.1 is a modern version[2] of Hubble's plot. It shows that the recession of two objects is proportional to their distance.

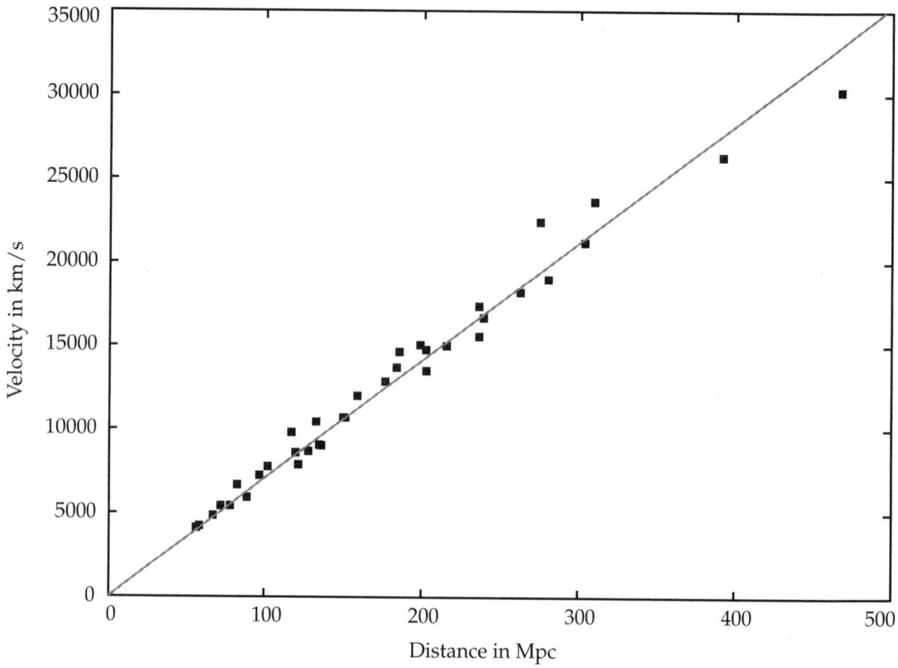

Figure 8.1: *Velocity vs distance for galaxies*

Hubble's discovery of recession of galaxies in all directions marked a turning point in our understanding of the nature of the universe. We interpret the recession of galaxies to mean that the universe is expanding. According to the present model, expansion is the general property of the universe. Observers on other galaxies would find that galaxies were moving away from them according to Hubble's law. As a result of this expansion, any length in the universe, be it wavelength or the separation between galaxies, increases with time.

To explain the time dependence of any typical length, a *scale factor* $R(t)$, is introduced. Any expansion in length can be described by $R(t)$.

Suppose the distance between two points is $l(t_1)$ at time t_1. The distance between them at time t will be

$$\frac{l(t)}{l(t_1)} = \frac{R(t)}{R(t_1)} \quad \text{or} \quad l(t) = \frac{l(t_1)}{R(t_1)} R(t) \tag{8.4}$$

$$\text{Velocity } v = \frac{dl(t)}{dt} = \frac{l(t_1)}{R(t_1)} \times \frac{dR(t)}{dt} = \frac{l(t)}{R(t)} \frac{dR}{dt}$$

[2]Freedman, W, et al. 2001. *The Astrophysical Journal*, 553: 47.

$$\text{Therefore } v = Hl(t) \quad \text{or } H = \frac{1}{R}\frac{dR}{dt} \tag{8.5}$$

In principle, H is a function of time due to the retarding effects of gravity on the expanding objects, but it does not depend on the position. It is an important parameter. It is a measure of the rate at which the universe is expanding. If the universe expands at a constant rate, then H is a constant.

8.1.1 A Rough Estimation of the Age of the Universe

If the galaxies are receding away from each other at the present moment, they were closer together earlier. We may extrapolate the expansion back in time and expect that all the galaxies must have been closer in the past. In the beginning, the density of the universe was extremely large. Extrapolating further at $t \to 0$, we come to a singularity, called the **Big Bang**[3]. Thus, according to the Big Bang Theory, the universe is assumed to have originated as a singularity of infinite energy density at a point in space-time.

Suppose at $t = 0$, the separation between any two galaxies was $d_0 = 0$, and after time t

$$d = vt, \tag{8.6}$$

where we assume that the universe is expanding at a constant rate. Now, by Hubble's law

$$d = Hd \times t \quad \text{or} \quad t = H^{-1} = 15 \text{ Gyr} \tag{8.7}$$

Thus, the present age of the universe (assumed to be expanding at a constant rate) is approximately $t = H^{-1} = 15$ Gyr. By the 'age' of the universe, we mean the time taken by the universe to expand from its initial state at the beginning (at $t = 0$) to the present state.

The universe was created as a Big Bang about 15 billion years ago.

Illustrative Example 8.1: Red shift and Hubble's constant

Calculate the velocity of recession of a galaxy resulting from the expansion of the universe.

Solution Let the wavelength of light at time t_1 be λ_1. The wavelength (λ) at time t will be

$$\frac{\lambda}{\lambda_1} = \frac{R(t)}{R(t_1)} \tag{8.8}$$

Expanding $R(t)$ about t_1, we get

$$\lambda = \frac{\lambda_1}{R(t_1)}\left[R(t_1) + (t - t_1)\frac{dR}{dt}\bigg|_{t_1}\right] = \lambda_1\left[1 + (t - t_1) \times \frac{1}{R(t_1)}\frac{dR}{dt}\bigg|_{t_1}\right] \tag{8.9}$$

[3]Originally proposed by Lemaitre in 1923 and also by Gamow in 1948.

The change in wavelength due to Doppler effect is

$$\lambda = \lambda_1 \sqrt{\frac{1+\beta}{1-\beta}} = \lambda_1(1+\beta), \text{ if } \beta << 1 \tag{8.10}$$

Comparing Eqs (8.9) and (8.10), we get

$$v = c(t - t_1) \times \frac{1}{R(t_1)} \frac{dR}{dt}\bigg|_{t_1} = \frac{l}{R} \frac{dR}{dt} \tag{8.11}$$

⇒ Check Progress 8.1: Table 8.1 shows precise measurements for the distance and velocity of different galaxies.

(a) Plot a graph of velocity vs distance using GNUPLOT. Draw the best fit straight line passing through the origin.

(b) Determine Hubble's constant and estimate the age of the universe.

8.1.2 Application of Newtonian Mechanics

Based on the General Theory of Relativity, Einstein[4] presented a model of the universe in 1917. The time evolution of the universe can be described by the solution of Einstein's field equations of general relativity. For a homogeneous and isotropic distribution of mass, the result of general theory of relativity can be used to connect the rate of expansion of the universe with energy density by the Friedmann equation, as

$$H^2 = \frac{\dot{R}^2}{R^2} = \frac{8\pi G\rho}{3} - \frac{kc^2}{R^2} + \frac{\Lambda}{3}, \tag{8.12}$$

where G is the gravitational constant, ρ is the mass or energy density, and k and Λ are constants. For an expanding universe, $\Lambda = 0$. The constant k is determined by the fundamental geometry of space-time.

It is interesting that the form of Eq. (8.12) can be derived in a straightforward way using Newtonian considerations, without applying the General Theory of Relativity.

Let us consider a spherical region of radius R in the universe. The mass of this cosmic sphere of homogeneous density ρ is

$$M(t) = \frac{4}{3}\pi R^3 \rho(t) \tag{8.13}$$

The force on a galaxy of mass m at a distance R is

$$m\frac{d^2R}{dt^2} = -\frac{GMm}{R^2} \tag{8.14}$$

If no mass is created, M is constant. Thus

$$m\frac{d^2R}{dt^2}\frac{dR}{dt} = -\frac{GMm}{R^2}\frac{dR}{dt} \quad \text{or} \quad \frac{d}{dt}\left(\frac{1}{2}m\dot{R}^2\right) = GMm\frac{d}{dt}\left(\frac{1}{R}\right)$$

Therefore $\frac{1}{2}m\dot{R}^2 = \frac{GMm}{R} + \text{constant}$

[4]Einstein, A. 1917. *Cosmological Considerations in the General Theory of Relativity.* Sitzungsber. Preuss. Akad. Wiss. Berlin (Math. Phys.), 142.

Table 8.1: *Data for Hubble's law*

Distance (d) in Mpc	Velocity in kms^{-1}
134.7	9065
158.9	12012
198.6	15055
238.9	16687
117.1	9801
56.0	4124
183.9	13707
121.5	7880
274.6	22426
102.1	7765
58.0	4227
467.0	30253
262.2	18212
88.6	5935
151.4	10696
202.5	13518
235.9	17371
176.8	12871
77.9	5434
309.5	23646
391.5	26318
280.1	18997
303.4	21190
236.1	15567
215.4	15002
119.7	8604
202.3	14764
71.8	5424
96.7	7241
127.8	8691
66.8	4847
149.9	10715
185.6	14634
82.4	6673
136.0	9024
132.7	10446

This represents energy conservation.

$$\frac{1}{2}m\dot{R}^2 - \frac{GMm}{R} = \text{constant}$$

Therefore, Kinetic + Potential energy $= E =$ constant (8.15)

Since the mass of the galaxy m is arbitrary, we may choose the constant as $E = -\frac{1}{2}mc^2k$. With this choice, the above equation becomes

$$\frac{1}{2}m\dot{R}^2 = \frac{GMm}{R} - \frac{1}{2}mc^2k \quad \text{or } H^2 = \frac{\dot{R}^2}{R^2} = \frac{2GM}{R^3} - \frac{kc^2}{R^2} \tag{8.16}$$

This is the Friedmann equation for $\Lambda = 0$ in the Newtonian limit.

If $k = -1$, total energy E is positive. It represents an open universe with $\dot{R} \to c$ as $R \to \infty$. If $k = +1$, total energy E is negative and the corresponding universe will be closed. In this case, E reaches its maximum and then collapses. Total energy $E = 0$ for the case $k = 0$. It represents a flat universe. In this critical case, Eq. (8.16) becomes

$$\dot{R}^2 = \frac{2GM}{R} \quad \text{using } \dot{R} = HR,\ H^2 = 2G \times \frac{4}{3}\pi\rho_c$$

$$\rho_c = \frac{3}{8\pi G}H^2 \approx 5 \times 10^{-27}\ \frac{kg}{m^3} \tag{8.17}$$

If $\rho > \rho_c$, total energy E will be negative and the universe will be closed. On the other hand, if $\rho < \rho_c$, galaxies will continue to move away from each other.

Illustrative Example 8.2: Age of the universe

For a flat universe dominated by non-relativistic matter of constant mass, estimate the age of the universe.

Solution In this case, from Eq. (8.17), we get $\dot{R} = \sqrt{2GM}R^{-1/2}$.

Integrating $R^{3/2} = \frac{3}{2}\sqrt{2GM} \times t$, (assuming R = 0 at t = 0)

$$= \frac{3}{2}\sqrt{2G\frac{4}{3}\pi R^3\rho_c} \times t = \frac{3}{2}\sqrt{2G\frac{4}{3}\pi R^3\frac{3}{8\pi G}H^2} \times t \text{ or } t = \frac{2}{3}H^{-1} \approx 8 \text{ Gyr}$$

8.1.3 The Hot Big Bang

The matter density of the universe varies as

$$\rho_m \propto \frac{1}{R^3} \tag{8.18}$$

The average energy of each photon in radiation is $h\nu = \frac{hc}{\lambda}$, and it is proportional to $\frac{1}{R}$. Thus, the density of radiation varies as $\rho_r \propto \frac{1}{R} \times \frac{1}{R^3} \propto \frac{1}{R^4}$.

Therefore $\rho_r = \frac{C}{R^4}$, (8.19)

where C is constant. The matter density ρ_m dominates today, but earlier, following the Big Bang with sufficiently small R, ρ_r must have been dominant. Assuming $k = 0$, Eq. (8.16) can be rewritten as

$$\dot{R}^2 = 2\frac{GM}{R} = \frac{8\pi G}{3c^2}\rho_r R^2 = \frac{8\pi G}{3c^2}\frac{C}{R^4}R^2$$

$$R\frac{dR}{dt} = \sqrt{\frac{8\pi GC}{3c^2}} \text{ or } R^2 = 2\sqrt{\frac{8\pi GC}{3c^2}} \times t \tag{8.20}$$

$$\text{Or } t = \sqrt{\frac{3c^2R^4}{32\pi GC}} = \sqrt{\frac{3c^2}{32\pi G\rho_r}} \tag{8.21}$$

The energy density (rather than mass density) is

$$\rho_r = \frac{3c^2}{32\pi G} \times \frac{1}{t^2} \tag{8.22}$$

For a photon gas in thermal equilibrium at temperature T, the energy density is

$$u = \sigma T^4, \tag{8.23}$$

where σ is the Stefan–Boltzmann constant. From Eqs (8.22) and (8.23), we obtain a relation between the temperature of radiation at any time t

$$\frac{3c^2}{32\pi G} \times \frac{1}{t^2} = \sigma T^4 \text{ or } T^4 t^2 = \frac{3c^2}{32\pi G\sigma}$$

$$= \frac{3 \times 9 \times 10^{16}}{32 \times \pi \times 6.67 \times 10^{-11} \times 7.56 \times 10^{-16}} = 5.326 \times 10^{40}$$

$$T \approx \frac{1.52 \times 10^{10}}{t^{1/2}} \text{K} \tag{8.24}$$

Equation (8.20) shows that the radius R of the universe increases with time t as $R \propto t^{1/2}$. However, the temperature drops as $T \propto \frac{1}{t^{1/2}}$. The temperature of the universe was extremely high at the beginning ($t \to 0$), and thus, the universe began as a hot Big Bang.

8.2 COSMIC MICROWAVE BACKGROUND RADIATION

One of the major discoveries of fundamental significance for our understanding of the nature of the universe was the first observation of isotropic cosmic microwave background radiation[5] (CMBR), by Penzias and Wilson in 1964 at the Bell Telephone Laboratory. They were working on a radio receiver, tuned to a wavelength of 7.35 cm, which was built for satellite communication. In this process, they observed a background 'noise' that was found to not vary by day or night or time of year, nor to depend on the direction. Despite their best efforts, they were unable to eliminate the noise from the system. After painstaking measurements, they concluded that the supposed noise was, in fact, a real signal from space.

[5]Padmanabhan, T. 2007. *Resonance, Journal of Science Education*, 12:4.

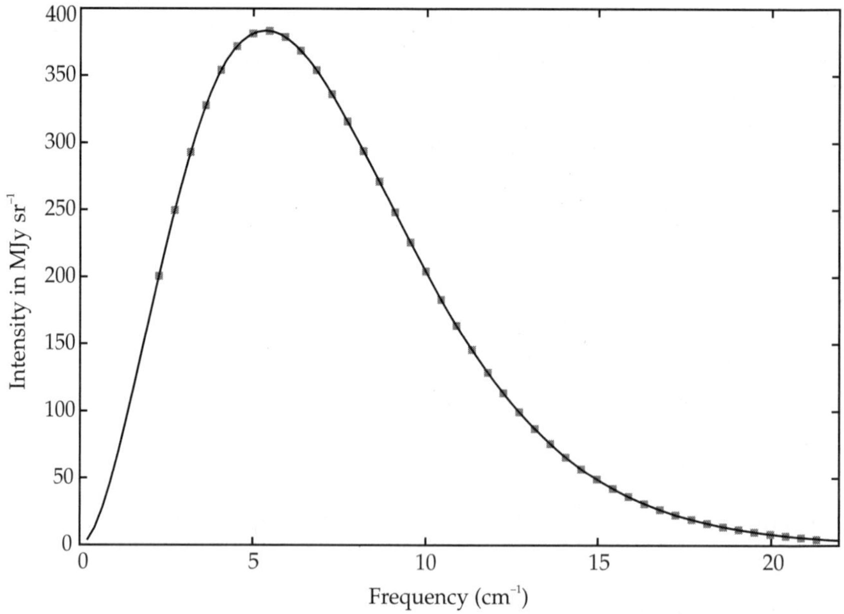

Figure 8.2: *Intensity of cosmic microwave background radiation*

Figure 8.2 shows recent data[6] on the spectral distribution of the radiation measured with the COBE (Cosmic Background Explorer) satellite. The data points fall exactly on the fitted line for Planck's law of black-body radiation. From the best fit, we find that the temperature of radiation is $T = 2.727$ K. By measuring the energy density of the radiation, we can conclude that the whole of space is filled with cosmic microwave radiation at a temperature of about 2.7 K.

At the beginning, just after the Big Bang, the universe was extremely hot and dense. The temperature of the universe began decreasing and the wavelengths of the photons were stretched by the continuing expansion. The microwave radiation can thus be considered a remnant of the Big Bang 'fireball' cooled by expansion to a few kelvins.

⇒ Check Progress 8.2: Table 8.2 shows precise measurements of intensity distribution by the COBE satellite.

(a) Plot a graph of intensity vs frequency using GNUPLOT.

(b) Planck's distribution law can be represented as $u = \dfrac{\bar{\nu}^3}{exp(\frac{hc\bar{\nu}}{k_B T}) - 1}$, where $\bar{\nu} = \dfrac{1}{\lambda}$ and other symbols have their usual meaning. Express $\dfrac{1}{\lambda}$ in cm^{-1} and draw the best fit line passing through the data points.

(c) Verify that $T \approx 2.727$ K.

[6] Fixsen, DJ, et al. 1996. *The Astrophysical Journal*, 476:576; Caruso, F, and Oguri, V. 2009. *The Astrophysical Journal*, 694:151.

Table 8.2: *Data for CMBR*

Intensity (d) in $MJysr^{-1}$	Frequency in cm^{-1}
2.27	458
2.72	605
3.18	770
3.63	956
4.08	1106
4.54	1218
4.99	1346
5.45	1473
5.90	1534
6.35	1588
6.81	1623
7.26	1645
7.71	1619
8.17	1576
8.62	1541
9.08	1490
9.53	1423
9.98	1331
10.44	1234
10.89	1171
11.34	1077
11.80	996
12.25	910
12.71	814
13.16	780
13.61	687
14.07	595
14.52	551
14.97	492
15.43	435
15.88	388
16.34	326
16.79	318
17.24	275
17.70	230

8.2.1 Radiation and Expansion

We will now show that the effect of the expansion of the universe on the radiation is to preserve the form of the black-body spectrum, but to lower the temperature. Suppose the black-body radiation confined in a volume is in thermal equilibrium at temperature T_1 at any given time t_1. Then, the number of photons in volume V in the frequency interval ν_1 and $\nu_1 + d\nu_1$ is

$$N_{\nu_1} d\nu_1 = \frac{8\pi V}{c^3} \frac{\nu_1^2}{e^{\frac{h\nu_1}{k_B T_1}} - 1} d\nu_1 \tag{8.25}$$

With expansion, the frequency will change. At a later time t, the new frequency will, by Eq. (8.8), be

$$\nu = \nu_1 \frac{R(t_1)}{R(t)} \tag{8.26}$$

The distribution of photons at time t will be

$$\begin{aligned} N_\nu d\nu &= \frac{8\pi V'}{c^3} \frac{\nu^2}{e^{\frac{h\nu}{k_B T_2}} - 1} d\nu = \frac{8\pi V}{c^3} \times \frac{R^3(t)}{R^3(t_1)} \times \frac{\nu_1^2}{e^{\frac{h\nu_1}{k_B T_2} \times \frac{R(t_1)}{R(t)}} - 1} \times \frac{R^3(t_1)}{R^3(t)} d\nu_1 \\ &= \frac{8\pi V}{c^3} \times \frac{\nu_1^2}{e^{\frac{h\nu_1}{k_B T_2} \times \frac{R(t_1)}{R(t)}} - 1} d\nu_1 \end{aligned} \tag{8.27}$$

Assuming that we neglect the interaction of radiation and matter, no new photons are created and none are destroyed. Therefore, from Eqs (8.25) and (8.27)

$$T_1 = T_2 \times \frac{R(t)}{R(t_1)} \qquad \text{or} \qquad T_1 R(t_1) = T_2 R(t) \tag{8.28}$$

Thus, expansion maintains the form of the spectrum but lowers the temperature in such a way that

$$RT = \text{constant} \tag{8.29}$$

The number of photons per unit volume at temperature T can be obtained from Eq. (8.25) as

$$n_\gamma = \frac{8\pi}{c^3} \int_0^\infty \frac{\nu^2}{e^{\frac{h\nu}{k_B T}} - 1} d\nu \tag{8.30}$$

Substituting $\frac{h\nu}{k_B T} = x$, we obtain

$$\begin{aligned} n_\gamma &= \frac{8\pi}{c^3} \left(\frac{k_B T}{h}\right)^3 \int_0^\infty \frac{x^2}{e^x - 1} dx = \frac{8\pi}{c^3} \left(\frac{k_B T}{h}\right)^3 \times 2.404 \\ &\approx 2 \times 10^7 T^3 \text{ photons/m}^3 \end{aligned} \tag{8.31}$$

Similarly, the energy density of radiation is

$$\rho_\gamma = \frac{8\pi h}{c^3} \int_0^\infty \frac{\nu^3}{e^{\frac{h\nu}{k_B T}} - 1} d\nu \tag{8.32}$$

Substituting $\frac{h\nu}{k_B T} = x$ again, we obtain

$$\rho_\gamma = \frac{8\pi h}{c^3}\left(\frac{k_B T}{h}\right)^4 \int_0^\infty \frac{x^3}{e^x - 1} dx = \frac{8\pi h}{c^3}\left(\frac{k_B T}{h}\right)^4 \times \frac{\pi^4}{15}$$

$$\approx 4.7 \times 10^3\, T^4 \text{ eV/m}^3 \quad (8.33)$$

At the present temperature of 2.7 K, the energy density of photons is

$$\rho_\gamma = \frac{4.7 \times 10^3 \times 2.7^4}{10^6} \approx 0.25 \text{ eV/cc}$$

The number of photons per unit volume is $n_\gamma = \frac{2 \times 10^7 \times T^3}{10^6} \approx 394$ photons/cc.

Therefore, at present, the mean energy of photons is approximately only 0.0006 eV. This is why we cannot detect them under ordinary conditions.

The present matter density of the universe is difficult to determine. However, the best estimate suggests that the density of the luminous (visible) matter (ρ_{matter}) of the universe is approximately 3×10^{-31} g/cc. To account for the non-luminous matter in the universe, this value may be increased arbitrarily by a factor of 2, as

$$\rho_{\text{matter}} \approx 6 \times 10^{-31} \text{ g/cc} = \frac{6 \times 10^{-34} \times 9 \times 10^{16}}{1.6 \times 10^{-19}} \text{ eV/cc}$$

$$\approx 3.4 \times 10^2 \text{ eV/cc} >> \rho_\gamma \quad (8.34)$$

Therefore, in the present universe, matter density dominates radiation density by a factor of 10^3. However, at the beginning of the universe, the scenario was completely different. We may justify this in the following way.

The radiant energy density is $\rho_\gamma \propto T^4$ (from Eq. (8.33))

$$\propto \frac{1}{R^4} \text{ (from Eq. (8.29))}$$

On the other hand, $\rho_{\text{matter}} \propto \frac{1}{V} \propto \frac{1}{R^3}$.

Therefore, the ratio of these two densities at present time t varies as

$$x(t) = \frac{\rho_\gamma(t)}{\rho_{\text{matter}}(t)} \propto \frac{1}{R(t)}$$

Thus, at an earlier time, t_0 $\frac{x(t_0)}{x(t)} = \frac{R(t)}{R(t_0)} > 1$.

This implies that radiation density dominated matter density in the early universe.

8.3 FIRST FEW SECONDS AFTER THE BIG BANG

Just after the Big Bang, the universe was dominated by radiation – radiation energy density exceeded matter density. In this radiation-dominated universe, the temperature of the universe was related to its age (t in seconds), from Eq. (8.24), as

$$T \approx \frac{1.52 \times 10^{10}}{t^{1/2}} \text{ K}$$

After a few nanoseconds, the temperature became extremely high and matter and radiation were then in equilibrium. The interaction between matter and radiation can be represented as

photons $\rightarrow x+\bar{x}$; $x+\bar{x}\rightarrow$ photons,

where particle(x)–antiparticle($\bar{x}$) pair production occurs as often as annihilation.

Illustrative Example 8.3: Production of nucleon–antinucleon pair

Consider the reactions

$$\gamma+\gamma \leftrightarrows p+\bar{p};\quad \gamma+\gamma \leftrightarrows n+\bar{n}$$

Determine the temperature of the universe at which these reactions occurred. Also estimate the age of the universe when it cooled to that temperature.

Solution Minimum energy required to produce the pair is $E_\gamma \gtrsim 940$ MeV and the corresponding temperature is

$$T=\frac{E_\gamma}{k_B}=\frac{940\times10^6}{8.6\times10^{-5}}\approx 1.1\times10^{13}\,\text{K}$$

The age of the universe at that time would be

$$t^{1/2}=\frac{1.52\times10^{10}}{1.1\times10^{13}}\approx 1.4\times10^{-3}$$

$$t\approx 2\times10^{-6}\,\text{s}$$

Therefore, nucleon production and annihilation were favoured energetically before $t\approx 2\times10^{-6}$ s. After this time, the temperature decreased to the required value so that pair production would stop, but pair annihilation would continue to occur.

Now, we are in a position to describe the main developments in the evolution of the universe. Let us begin from the time when the universe was about 1-μs old.

t $\approx 10^{-6}$ s: At this time, the temperature of the universe was $T\approx 10^{13}$ K and $k_BT\approx$ 1000 MeV.

If t_0 is the age of the present universe, from Eq. (8.29), we get

$$\frac{R(t)}{R(t_0)}=\frac{T(t_0)}{T(t)}=\frac{2.7}{10^{13}} \tag{8.35}$$

Therefore, at time $t\approx 10^{-6}$ s, the scale factor decreased to about 10^{-13} and the radius of the universe was also reduced to a factor of 10^{-13}, implying that the size of universe at this time was almost equal to that of the present solar system. At the age of 1 μs, the universe consisted of neutrons (n), protons (p), electrons (e), neutrinos (ν), muons (μ), pions (π) and their antiparticles, and also photons.

As the average energy of the particles at this temperature was greater than 1000 MeV, neutrons, protons and their antiparticles were continuously created from the photons. However, they were being produced just as quickly as the particles and antiparticles were being annihilated. Therefore, the process of creation and annihilation of nucleons was in equilibrium, and the number of particles was roughly equal to the number of antiparticles for each species. The number of nucleons was high enough at that time and was equal to the number of photons, which in turn, was roughly equal to the number of electrons or positrons. At this time, the neutron-to-proton ratio was almost equal to 1.

As the universe expanded and cooled, the average kinetic energy of the particles dropped below $\sim$ 1000 MeV. As the average energy fell below the minimum energy required to create nucleons and antinucleons, the process of nucleon creation could not continue. However, the process of annihilation of nucleons with antinucleons could continue, until there were almost no nucleons left; but the number of nucleons would not be exactly zero.

t $\approx 10^{-2}$ s: By this time, the temperature of the universe dropped to $T \approx 10^{11}$ K and $k_B T \approx 10$ MeV.

At time $t \approx 10^{-2}$ s, the scale factor increased to about 10^{-11} and the radius of the universe became 100 times larger than its value at $t \approx 10^{-6}$ s.

As the average energy of photons was much less than the rest mass of pions and muons, production of the latter ceased. The average lifetimes of pions and muons is much less than 10^{-2} s, and thus, they all eventually decayed into electrons, positrons and neutrinos. As mentioned earlier, the production of nucleons and antinucleons was not possible at this energy level, but annihilation of nucleons and antinucleons continued. In fact, not all of the nucleons disappeared; a small residue remained. Pair production of electrons and positrons also took place at this energy level. Thus, at this point in time, the universe consisted of neutrons, protons, electrons, positrons, neutrinos and photons.

The relative numbers of neutrons and protons depend on the following factors:

(a) As the expansion proceeded and $K_B T$ fell below $\sim$ 1000 MeV, the nucleons could be considered as non-relativistic. At equilibrium, the ratio of neutrons to protons could be given by

$$\frac{N_n}{N_p} = e^{-(m_n - m_p)c^2/k_B T}, \tag{8.36}$$

where the mass difference between the neutrons and protons is

$$(m_n - m_p)c^2 = 1.293 \text{ MeV} \tag{8.37}$$

At $k_B T \approx 10$ MeV, $\dfrac{N_n}{N_p} \approx 0.88$.

(b) Conversion of neutrons to protons occurs through

$$n + \nu_e \leftrightarrows p + e^-$$

$$p + \bar{\nu}_e \leftrightarrow n + e^+ \tag{8.38}$$

If the numbers of $e^{\pm}$, ν_e and $\bar{\nu}_e$ are sufficient, the n and p will be in equilibrium.

t $\approx$ 1 s: By t $\approx$ 1 s, the temperature dropped to 1.5×10^{10} K and $K_B T \approx 1.3$ MeV. At this time

$$\frac{N_n}{N_p} = e^{-1.293/1.3} \approx 0.37 \text{ or } \frac{N_n}{N_p + N_n} = \frac{0.37}{1.37} = 0.27$$

Therefore, the number of neutrons decreased substantially.

To convert a proton to a neutron, an antineutrino of at least 1.8-MeV energy is required. Thus, at $t \approx 1$ s, neutrinos were no longer important. This was the beginning of the era of 'neutrino decoupling', when the interactions of matter and neutrinos could no longer occur. From this time, the neutrinos continued to expand freely with the universe and remained virtually unaffected by nuclear reactions. These primordial neutrinos today have roughly the same density as the microwave photons. However, it can be shown that the neutrinos have a slightly lower temperature (about 2 K) than that of the photons.

The Boltzmann factor in Eq. (8.36) implies that the ratio $\frac{N_n}{N_p}$ decreased rapidly with decreasing temperature; that is, with the expansion of the universe. However, as the temperature decreased below 10^{10}K, the neutrino reactions were less significant, and neutrons and protons transformed very slowly into one another, through the reactions specified in Eq. (8.38). When the rate of these weak interactions became extremely low, the numbers of neutrons and protons ceased to change. It has been observed that the ratio $\frac{N_n}{N_p}$ is almost frozen at a value of about $\frac{1}{5}$ at temperature $T \approx 9 \times 10^9$ K. This occurred at about $t \approx 3$ s. In fact, this ratio continues to fall slowly because neutrons are unstable. They decay to protons as

$$n \rightarrow p + e^- + \bar{\nu}_e \text{ (half-life of about 10 s)}$$

Illustrative Example 8.4: Formation of deuteron

The first reaction to begin production of heavy nuclei is

$$n + p \rightarrow {}^2_1H + \gamma$$

The binding energy of deuteron is 2.22 MeV. At high temperatures, when $E_\gamma >$ 2.22 MeV, the reverse reaction $\gamma + {}^2_1H \rightarrow n + p$ occurs as quickly as the production of deuteron. Thus, there will be no accumulation of deuteron. The energy of 2.22 MeV corresponds to temperature $T \approx 2.5 \times 10^{10}$ K. We, therefore, expect deuteron accumulation as soon as the temperature drops below 2.5×10^{10} K. However, the emitted photons have a black-body spectrum that extends to large energy. A small fraction of photons in the high-energy tail has energy ≥ 2.22 MeV, and these photons can also produce the photodisintegration reaction of deuteron.

(a) Determine the fraction (f) of photons having energy $E_\gamma > 2.22$ MeV in the high-energy tail of the spectrum at temperature T.

(b) At time $t = 0.01$ s, the ratio of neutrons to photons is about $\frac{1}{6} \times 10^{-9}$. Determine the temperature at which the ratio of the neutron to the photons having energy 2.22 MeV is less than $\frac{1}{6} \times 10^{-9}$. Under this condition, there will be too few photons to inhibit deuteron production.

Solution (a) The distribution of photons with energy E and $E+dE$ with $E >> k_BT$ can be approximated as

$$N(E)dE \approx \frac{8\pi V}{(hc)^3}E^2 e^{-\frac{E}{k_BT}}dE$$

Therefore, the number of photons per unit volume with energy greater than $E_0 = 2.22$ MeV is

$$n_{>E_0} = \frac{8\pi}{(hc)^3}\int_{E_0}^{\infty} E^2 e^{-\frac{E}{k_BT}}dE = \frac{8\pi}{(hc)^3}(k_BT)^3\int_{\frac{E_0}{k_BT}}^{\infty} x^2 e^{-x}dx \quad \text{with } x = \frac{E}{k_BT}$$

$$= \frac{8\pi}{(hc)^3}(k_BT)^3 e^{-\frac{E_0}{k_BT}}\left[\left(\frac{E_0}{k_BT}\right)^2 + 2\frac{E_0}{k_BT} + 2\right]$$

The fraction of photons with energy $E > 2.22$ MeV is

$$f = \frac{n_{>E_0}}{n_{>0}} = \frac{8\pi}{(hc)^3}\frac{(k_BT)^3}{2\times 10^7 T^3}e^{-\frac{E_0}{k_BT}}\left[\left(\frac{E_0}{k_BT}\right)^2 + 2\frac{E_0}{k_BT} + 2\right]$$

$$\approx 0.42e^{-\frac{E_0}{k_BT}}\left[\left(\frac{E_0}{k_BT}\right)^2 + 2\frac{E_0}{k_BT} + 2\right] \tag{8.39}$$

(b) $\frac{1}{6}\times 10^{-9} = 0.42e^{-\frac{E_0}{k_BT}}\left[\left(\frac{E_0}{k_BT}\right)^2 + 2\frac{E_0}{k_BT} + 2\right]$

Numerical solution of this equation gives $\frac{E_0}{k_BT} \approx 28$. With $E_0 = 2.22$ MeV, $T \approx 9\times 10^9$. Thus, at temperature $T > 9\times 10^9$, the formation of deuteron is prevented.

8.3.1 Primordial Nucleosynthesis

Let us summarise the developments in the evolution of the universe in the first few seconds ($t \sim 6$ s) after the Big Bang.

(a) During this time, the temperature of the extremely hot and dense universe, consisting of particles and antiparticles, reduced to $\sim 10^{10}$ K.

(b) At $t \approx 1$ s, the neutrinos decoupled and continued to cool with the expansion of the universe.

(c) Most of the original particles and antiparticles were annihilated by this time, leaving a small number (N) of protons, an equal number (N) of electrons and about $\frac{N}{5}$ number of neutrons.

If nothing else were to happen, the neutrons would die away by $n \rightarrow p + e^- + \bar{\nu}_e$. And the matter of the early universe would consist exclusively of protons and electrons. However, nucleosynthesis begins immediately through the formation of deuteron

$$n + p \rightarrow {}^2_1H + \gamma$$

The emitted photons have a black-body spectrum that extends to large energy. A small fraction of photons in the high-energy tail has energy ≥ 2.22 MeV, and these photons can also produce the photodisintegration reaction

$$\gamma + {}^2_1H \rightarrow n + p$$

Again, the huge preponderance of photons over nucleons implies that the deuterons are not frozen until the temperature drops below $\sim 10^9$ K, corresponding $k_BT \approx 0.08$ MeV. Thus, when T falls below $\sim 10^9$ K (at about $t \approx 250$ s), deuteron nuclei begin to be present in significant numbers. As soon as photodisintegration of deuterium ceases after $t \approx 250$ s, competing reactions leading to helium production take over

$${}^2_1\mathrm{H} + n \rightarrow {}^3_1\mathrm{H} + \gamma;\ {}^3_1\mathrm{H} + p \rightarrow {}^4_2\mathrm{He} + \gamma$$

$${}^2_1\mathrm{H} + p \rightarrow {}^3_2\mathrm{He} + \gamma;\ {}^3_2\mathrm{He} + n \rightarrow {}^4_2\mathrm{He} + \gamma$$

As there is no stable nucleus with $A = 5$, no further reactions of this type are possible. Also, two ${}^4_2$He cannot combine, as ^{8}Be is highly unstable. Reactions of the form

$${}^4_2\mathrm{He} + {}^3_1\mathrm{H} \rightarrow {}^7_3\mathrm{Li} + \gamma;\ {}^4_2\mathrm{He} + {}^3_2\mathrm{He} \rightarrow {}^7_4\mathrm{Be} + \gamma$$

are possible. However, the Coulomb barrier for these reactions is about 1 MeV, which is much larger than $k_BT \approx 0.08$ MeV. Therefore, as ${}^4_2$He is the most stable nucleus, nearly all the neutrons are converted into helium.

Illustrative Example 8.5: Relative abundance of He

Calculate the relative abundance of helium at time $t \approx 400$ s, corresponding to $k_BT \approx 0.05$ MeV.

Solution The exact calculation shows that neutrino decoupling occurs at the critical energy, $k_BT \approx 0.87$ MeV. Thus, initially, at the time of decoupling, the neutron-to-proton ratio from Eq. (8.36) is

$$\frac{N_n(0)}{N_p(0)} = e^{-(m_n - m_p)c^2/k_BT} = e^{-\frac{1.293}{0.87}} \approx 0.23 \tag{8.40}$$

At time t after decoupling, the number of neutrons will be $N_n(t) = N_n(0)e^{-t/\tau}$, where $\tau \approx 896$ s is the mean life of free neutrons. The number of protons will be

$$N_p(t) = N_p(0) + N_n(0)(1 - e^{-t/\tau})$$

Therefore, the ratio of neutrons to protons at $t = 400$ s is

$$r = \frac{N_n(t)}{N_p(t)} = \frac{N_n(0)e^{-t/\tau}}{N_p(0) + N_n(0)(1 - e^{-t/\tau})} = \frac{e^{-400/896}}{4.35 + 0.36} \approx 0.14$$

Once neutrons are bound inside deuterons, they will not decay, and the ratio $r \approx 0.14$ will remain fixed. Suppose N_{He} and N_H number of helium and hydrogen nuclei, respectively, are formed. The *helium mass fraction* (Y) is

$$Y = \frac{N_{\mathrm{He}} \times m_{\mathrm{He}}}{N_{\mathrm{He}} \times m_{\mathrm{He}} + N_H \times M_H} \approx \frac{4N_{\mathrm{He}}}{4N_{\mathrm{He}} + N_H} \quad \text{as } m_{\mathrm{He}} \approx 4m_H$$

Every hydrogen nucleus contains 1 proton, and every helium nucleus contains 2 protons and 2 neutrons. Thus

$$N_p = N_H + 2N_{\text{He}} \text{ and } N_n = 2N_{\text{He}} \tag{8.41}$$

Using these relations in Eq. (8.41), we get

$$Y = \frac{2N_n}{N_n + N_p} = \frac{2r}{1+r} \approx 0.25 \tag{8.42}$$

Therefore, about 25% of the total mass has been converted to helium. The *helium mass fraction (Y)* has been measured at different celestial sites in the solar system. The average value is 0.24 ± 0.01. The close agreement between the calculated value and measured value is indeed a great success for the Big Bang model.

8.4 STELLAR NUCLEOSYNTHESIS

There is general consensus that stars are born when gaseous clouds (mostly composed of hydrogen) contract due to gravity. On contraction, the kinetic energy of the particles constituting the cloud increases and it continues to do so until the temperature of the core rises enough to trigger thermonuclear fusion of hydrogen to form helium (called the 'burning' of hydrogen). Both the gravitational contraction of the gaseous clouds and the thermonuclear fusion reactions play an important role in generating the energy of a star. The tremendous energy released in fusion reactions produces an outward pressure that brings the contraction of the star to a temporary halt. Gravitational contraction resumes when the hydrogen content in the core of the star is exhausted. The internal temperature then rises again until the next available fuel, helium, is ignited and further contraction is arrested. In this way, a star can proceed through a sequence of nuclear burning stages, which prolongs its life, and synthesises heavier atomic nuclei.

8.4.1 Fusion in Stars

The most remarkable fact about fusion in stars is that it happens at relatively low temperatures. When it was first noticed, many scientists expressed their doubt that stars were not hot enough for nuclear fusion to occur. The reason for this can be explained as follows.

Consider two nuclei with charges Z_a and Z_b with masses m_a and m_b, respectively. Classically, fusion of two charged particles is possible only when the nuclei have sufficient kinetic energy to climb over a Coulomb barrier of height

$$V_c = \frac{e^2}{4\pi\varepsilon_0}\frac{Z_a Z_b}{R} \approx \frac{1.44 Z_a Z_b}{R \text{ in fermi}} \text{ MeV}, \tag{8.43}$$

where R is the smallest separation between the centres of the nuclei. Note that V_c is of the order of MeV. On the other hand, the temperature inside a star is $\sim 10^7$ K, and thus, the average thermal energy of the nucleus in a star is

$$k_B T \approx 8.61 \times 10^2 \text{ eV} \sim 1 \text{ keV}, \tag{8.44}$$

which is $<<< V_c$. Also, the fraction of the nuclei having energy $E \sim 1$ MeV is proportional to $e^{-\frac{E}{k_B T}} = e^{-1000}$. Therefore, at first sight, Coulomb repulsion presents an insurmountable barrier to fusion in stars.

Quantum mechanically, however, tunnelling through the barrier may enable fusion to take place. Fusion proceeds at a rate that is proportional to the probability of penetration of the barrier. The probability that nuclei with energy E will penetrate the barrier[7] is given by

$$\text{Probability} \propto e^{-\sqrt{\frac{E_G}{E}}}, \tag{8.45}$$

where E_G is called the **Gamow energy**. It is defined by

$$E_G = (\pi\alpha Z_a Z_b)^2 2m_r c^2, \tag{8.46}$$

where $\alpha = \dfrac{e^2}{4\pi\varepsilon_0\hbar c} = \dfrac{1}{137}$ is the dimensionless fine structure constant and m_r is the reduced mass given by $m_r = \dfrac{m_a m_b}{m_a + m_b}$. For fusion of two protons, $E_G \approx 493$ keV. The probability of penetration at $k_B T \approx 1$ keV is approximately $e^{-\sqrt{493}} \approx e^{-22}$. As it is extremely small, fusion proceeds at a slow pace and, as a result, the nuclear fuel lasts an astronomically long time.

The probability of penetration through the barrier increases with increasing energy (Eq. (8.45)). However, the possibility of having a particle of high energy at a given temperature decreases rapidly with increasing energy. The net result of these two opposing effects is an energy window for the fusion of two charged particles. The rate of fusion of nuclei of types a and b with concentrations n_a and n_b can be calculated as

$$R_{ab} = n_a n_b \left(\frac{8}{\pi m_r}\right)^{1/2} \left(\frac{1}{k_B T}\right)^{3/2} \int_0^\infty S(E) e^{-\frac{E}{k_B T} - \sqrt{\frac{E_G}{E}}} dE, \tag{8.47}$$

where $S(E)$ is determined by the nuclear physics of fusion. To react at energy E, the nuclei need to borrow energy E from the thermal environment, and the probability that a particle has energy E at temperature T is proportional to the Boltzmann factor, $e^{-\frac{E}{k_B T}}$. To fuse, the nuclei must penetrate the Coulomb barrier and the probability of penetration is proportional to $e^{-\sqrt{\frac{E_G}{E}}}$.

The integrand in Eq. (8.47), being the product of an exponential function that vanishes at large E and another exponential function that vanishes at low E, is a sharply peaked function, as shown schematically in Fig. 8.3. The location of the maximum of the product can be determined from the condition

$$\frac{d}{dE}\left[e^{-\frac{E}{k_B T} - \sqrt{\frac{E_G}{E}}}\right]\Bigg|_{E_0} = 0 \quad \text{or} \quad \left[-\frac{1}{k_B T} + \frac{\sqrt{E_G}}{2E_0^{3/2}}\right]\left[e^{-\frac{E_0}{k_B T} - \sqrt{\frac{E_G}{E_0}}}\right] = 0$$

$$E_0 = \left(\frac{E_G (k_B T)^2}{4}\right)^{1/3} \tag{8.48}$$

[7] Phillips, AC. 1999. *The Physics of Stars*. Wiley.

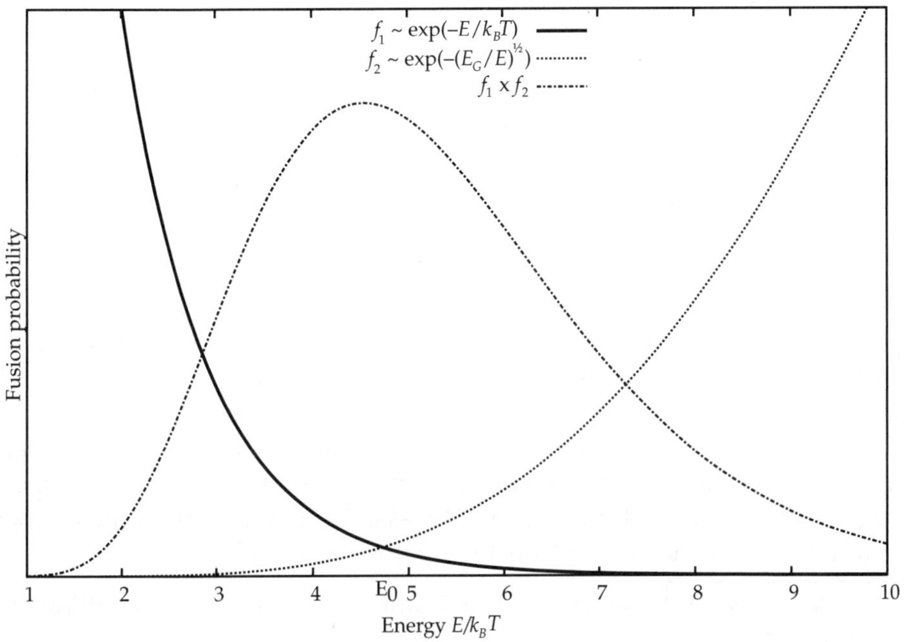

Figure 8.3: *Fusion window with Gamow energy E_G and temperature T*

Particles having energies very close to E_0 are most effective in causing fusion. Figure 8.3 shows that fusion takes place in a narrow energy around E_0. The width of this window can be determined from the Taylor series expansion of the integrand of Eq. (8.47) about E_0

$$e^{-\frac{E}{k_BT}-\sqrt{\frac{E_G}{E}}} \approx e^{-3(E_G/4k_BT)^{1/3}} \times e^{-\left(\frac{E-E_0}{\Delta/2}\right)^2}, \tag{8.49}$$

where Δ, the width of the fusion window, is given by

$$\Delta = \frac{4}{\sqrt{3}\times 2^{1/3}} E_G^{1/6}(k_BT)^{5/6} = \frac{4}{\sqrt{3}}\left(E_0 k_BT\right)^{1/2} \tag{8.50}$$

Equation (8.50) shows that the width of the fusion window is approximately twice the geometric mean of k_BT.

Illustrative Example 8.6: Estimation of Δ

Estimate Δ for the fusion of two protons at temperature 2×10^7 K.

Gamow energy, from Eq. (8.46), is

$$E_G = \left(\pi \times \frac{1}{137} \times 1 \times 1\right)^2 \times 2\frac{m_p}{2}c^2 \approx 493 \text{ keV}$$

At temperature 2×10^7 K, $k_BT \approx 1.7$ keV and from Eq. (8.48), we get

$$E_0 - E\left(\frac{493 \times 1.7^2}{4}\right)^{1/3} \approx 7.1 \text{ keV}$$

Therefore $\Delta = \frac{4}{\sqrt{3}}(7.1 \times 1.7)^{1/2} \approx 8.0$ keV

Usually, the nuclear factor $S(E)$ remains almost constant across the fusion window. Thus, Eq. (8.47) can be simplified to

$$R_{ab} \approx n_a n_b \left(\frac{8}{\pi m_r}\right)^{1/2} \left(\frac{1}{k_B T}\right)^{3/2} S(E_0) \int_0^\infty e^{-\frac{E}{k_B T} - \sqrt{\frac{E_G}{E}}} dE$$

$$\approx 6.48 \times 10^{-24} \frac{n_a n_b}{A_r Z_a Z_b} S(E_0) \left(\frac{E_G}{4k_B T}\right)^{2/3} e^{-3\left(\frac{E_G}{4k_B T}\right)^{1/3}} / \text{sm}^3, \tag{8.51}$$

where the numerical values of the various constants have been inserted. Here, A_r is the relative mass of the nuclei in atomic mass unit and $S(E_0)$ is in keV barns.

Equation (8.51) shows that the reaction rate for fusion depends mainly on three factors: fusion factor $S(E_0)$, Gamow energy E_G and temperature T. $S(E_0)$ depends on the specific reaction taking place. Gamow energy E_G, given in Eq. (8.46), depends on the charge of the nuclei and their reduced mass. E_G, together with the temperature T, determines how the reaction is affected by the Coulomb barrier.

⇒ Check Progress 8.3: Determine the Gamow energies for the following two fusion reactions at temperature $T = 2 \times 10^7$K:

$p + {}^2_1\text{H} \rightarrow {}^3_2\text{He} + \gamma$; $\text{p} + {}^{12}_6\text{C} \rightarrow {}^{13}_7\text{N} + \gamma$

Also show that the reaction rates for these two processes are proportional to e^{-14} and e^{-52}, respectively. Thus, the second reaction becomes much slower for a large Coulomb barrier.

8.4.2 Hydrogen Burning

The main nuclear burning process in a star results in the fusion of four hydrogen nuclei into a helium nucleus. At relatively low temperatures ($T < 2 \times 10^7$ K), hydrogen burns through the **proton–proton chain** (known as p–p chain). Weizsäcker, in 1937, suggested that the only possible reaction for the fusion of two protons is

$${}^1_1\text{H} + {}^1_1\text{H} \longrightarrow {}^2_1\text{H} + e^+ + \nu_e + Q1 \text{ (0.42 MeV)} \tag{8.52}$$

This reaction involving weak β decay is very slow. However, once the deuteron is formed, the way is clear for much faster reactions to synthesise ^{4}He nuclei. The formation of the deuteron, through Eq. (8.52), is followed by fusion of a proton and deuteron, as

$${}^1_1\text{H} + {}^2_1\text{H} \longrightarrow {}^3_2\text{He} + \gamma + Q2 \text{ (5.49 MeV)} \tag{8.53}$$

The reaction is then completed through one of three alternative routes: Branches I, II and III.

Branch I: A ${}^3_2$He nucleus formed by Eq. (8.53) may fuse with another ${}^3_2$He to form ${}^4_2$He.

$${}^3_2\text{He} + {}^3_2\text{He} \longrightarrow {}^4_2\text{He} + {}^1_1\text{H} + {}^1_1\text{H} + Q3 \text{(12.86 MeV)} \tag{8.54}$$

The overall net reaction (2 × First type of reaction, Eq. (8.53) + 2 × Second type of reaction, Eq. (8.53) + Third type of reaction, Eq. (8.54)) thus results in the consumption of four protons to form ^{4}He as

$$4\,{}^1_1\mathrm{H} \longrightarrow {}^4_2\mathrm{He} + 2e^+ + 2\gamma + 2\nu_e + Q,$$

where $Q = 2Q1 + 2Q2 + Q3 = 2 \times 0.42 + 2 \times 5.49 + 12.86 \approx 24.68$ MeV.

Fusion of a ${}^3_2$He nucleus formed by Eq. (8.53) with another pre-existing ${}^4_2$He nucleus leads to the formation of ${}^7_4$Be, which can be processed by Branches II and III.

Branch II: ${}^3_2\mathrm{He} + {}^4_2\mathrm{He} \longrightarrow {}^7_4\mathrm{Be} + \gamma$

$${}^7_4\mathrm{Be} + e^- \longrightarrow {}^7_3\mathrm{Li} + \nu_e$$

$${}^7_3\mathrm{Li} + {}^1_1\mathrm{H} \longrightarrow {}^4_2\mathrm{He} + {}^4_2\mathrm{He}$$

The net energy released in this branch is $Q \approx 25.7$ MeV.

Branch III: ${}^3_2\mathrm{He} + {}^4_2\mathrm{He} \longrightarrow {}^7_4\mathrm{Be} + \gamma$

$${}^7_4\mathrm{Be} + {}^1_1\mathrm{H} \longrightarrow {}^8_5\mathrm{B} + \gamma$$

$${}^8_5\mathrm{B} \longrightarrow {}^8_4\mathrm{Be} + e^+ + \nu_e$$

$${}^8_4\mathrm{Be} \longrightarrow {}^4_2\mathrm{He} + {}^4_2\mathrm{He}$$

For this branch, $Q \approx 19.1$ MeV. Note that a pre-existing ^{4}He acts as a catalyst in Branches II or III, and finally for both branches, two more ^{4}He are produced at the end. Also note that two proton–proton fusions are required to produce a ^{4}He nucleus through Branch I, while only one is required for Branches II and III. According to the Standard Solar Model, the proton–proton chain in the Sun is terminated by Branch I 85% of the time, by Branch II 15% of the time and by Branch III 0.02% of the time. Thus, the average energy released per proton–proton fusion in the Sun is

$$0.85 \times 24.68/2 + 0.15 \times 25.7 + 0.02 \times 19.1 \approx 14.73 \text{ MeV}$$

Carbon–nitrogen (CN) cycle: The proton–proton chain can successfully account for the rate of energy production in Main Sequence stars with masses comparable to that of the Sun, but it fails to explain the enormous increase in luminosity in more massive stars. Bethe, in 1939, established that reactions of protons with carbon and nitrogen nuclei would provide competition to p–p chains and that they acted as the source of energy in massive stars. He showed that in a series of reactions, known as the carbon–nitrogen (CN) cycle, carbon and nitrogen nuclei served only as catalysts for the conversion of hydrogen to helium but were not themselves destroyed. The reactions of the carbon–nitrogen cycle are given below:

$$p + {}^{12}_6\mathrm{C} \longrightarrow {}^{13}_7\mathrm{N} + \gamma$$

$${}^{13}_7\mathrm{N} \longrightarrow {}^{13}_6\mathrm{C} + \mathrm{e}^+ + \nu_\mathrm{e}$$

$$p + {}^{13}_6\mathrm{C} \longrightarrow {}^{14}_7\mathrm{N} + \gamma$$

$$p + {}^{14}_7\mathrm{N} \longrightarrow {}^{15}_8\mathrm{O} + \gamma$$

$${}^{15}_8\mathrm{O} \longrightarrow {}^{15}_7\mathrm{N} + \mathrm{e}^+ + \nu_\mathrm{e}$$

$$p+{}^{15}_{7}\text{N} \longrightarrow {}^{12}_{6}\text{C}+{}^{4}_{2}\text{He} \tag{8.55}$$

The net result of this cycle is

$$4p \longrightarrow {}^{4}_{2}H+2e^{+}+2\nu_e \quad \text{Q} \approx 23.8 \text{ MeV},$$

and ^{12}C is still in circulation as catalyst for hydrogen burning. It has been observed from accurate calculations that about 98.4% of solar energy is due to the proton–proton chain and only 1.6% is due to the carbon–nitrogen cycle. Thus, the CN cycle is not an important source of energy production in the Sun.

8.4.3 Nucleosynthesis for A < 60

Once the hydrogen fuel is exhausted in the stellar core, fusion ceases, and gravitational collapse begins again. The temperature of the star increases further due to contraction, and once the temperature reaches about 10^8 K, the Coulomb barrier for the fusion of two helium nuclei can be overcome. This increase in temperature results in the expansion of the outer surface of the star by a large factor (perhaps by 100 to 1000). The apparent energy density of the surface decreases. This is the **red giant phase**.

The lack of a stable isotope with $A = 8$ hinders the process of helium burning, and thus, blocks the formation of the most abundant nucleus, ^{12}C. In stars, this hurdle is overcome by the **triple-alpha reaction** which occurs in three stages:

The production of very small but unstable ^{8}Be through

$$^{4}\text{He}+{}^{4}\text{He} \longrightarrow {}^{8}\text{Be}^{*} \tag{8.56}$$

The production of ^{12}C in excited state through

$$^{4}\text{He}+{}^{8}\text{Be}^{*} \longrightarrow {}^{12}\text{C}^{*} \tag{8.57}$$

Decay of $^{12}\text{C}^{*}$

$$^{12}\text{C}^{*} \longrightarrow {}^{12}\text{C}+2\gamma \tag{8.58}$$

The net effect of this sequence is

$$^{4}\text{He}+{}^{4}\text{He}+{}^{4}\text{He} \longrightarrow {}^{12}\text{C} \quad (\text{Q} = 7.275 \text{ MeV}) \tag{8.59}$$

The ^{8}Be formed in Eq. (8.56) is very unstable; it decays back to two ^{4}He in 10^{-16} s. The triple-alpha reaction, Eq. (8.59), can occur only if a third ^{4}He is captured by the ^{8}Be nucleus within this short time interval of 10^{-16} s. Hoyle predicted that the reaction in Eq. (8.57) would have negligible probability unless the capture is resonant, where the sum of the energies of $^{8}\text{Be}^{*}$ and ^{4}He is very close to that of an excited state of the resulting ^{12}C nucleus. In the presence of such a resonance, ^{12}C can be formed in an excited state with higher-than-normal probability and then de-excited down to the ground state by emitting photons. The existence of this resonance level of ^{12}C was later confirmed by Fowler and his group.

Once ^{12}C is formed, other fusion reactions involving α particles become possible:

$$^{4}\text{He}+{}^{12}\text{C} \longrightarrow {}^{16}\text{O}+\gamma \quad (\text{Q} = 7.16 \text{ MeV}, V_c = 3.57 \text{ MeV})$$

$$^{4}\text{He}+{}^{16}\text{O} \longrightarrow {}^{20}\text{Ne}+\gamma \quad (\text{Q} = 4.73 \text{ MeV}, V_c = 4.47 \text{ MeV})$$

$$^{4}\text{He} + {}^{20}\text{Ne} \longrightarrow {}^{24}\text{Mg} + \gamma \ \ (Q = 9.31 \text{ MeV}, V_c = 5.36 \text{ MeV}),$$

where V_c represents the Coulomb barrier. As V_c increases with atomic number A of the target, the possibility of fusion reactions decreases for heavier nuclei.

When most of the helium fuel has been used up, helium burning stops and gravitational collapse sets in again. As a result of contraction, the temperature of the star increases further and burning of ^{12}C and ^{16}O begins:

$$^{12}\text{C} + {}^{12}\text{C} \longrightarrow {}^{20}\text{Ne} + {}^{4}\text{He}$$

$$^{16}\text{C} + {}^{16}\text{C} \longrightarrow {}^{28}\text{Si} + {}^{4}\text{He}$$

In addition to these reactions, other α-capture reactions producing the chain

$^{14}\text{N} \rightarrow {}^{18}\text{O} \rightarrow {}^{22}\text{Ne} \rightarrow {}^{26}\text{Mg} \cdots$ can occur.

When the temperature is sufficiently large ($T > 3 \times 10^9$ K), burning of ^{28}Si starts. In this case, however, the Coulomb barrier (V_c) is so high that the direct reaction

$^{28}\text{Si} + {}^{28}\text{Si} \longrightarrow {}^{56}$ Ni is not allowed. The process proceeds as

$$^{28}\text{Si} + \gamma \longrightarrow {}^{24}\text{Mg} + {}^{4}\text{He}$$

$$^{28}\text{Si} + {}^{4}\text{He} \longrightarrow {}^{32}\text{Si} + \gamma \text{ and so on.}$$

The end products of such chains are nuclei with $A = 56$ (^{56}Ni, ^{56}Co, ^{56}Fe).

8.4.4 Nucleosynthesis for A > 60

It has been observed from the binding energy curve that binding energy per nucleon is maximum at $A = 56$. Thus, fusion reactions are not energetically favoured beyond $A > 56$. For these nuclei, neutron capture[8] becomes a dominant process. Neutrons, being uncharged, are not repelled by positively charged target nuclei, and thus, can be captured easily. Nuclei heavier than ^{56}Fe are believed to be formed by the neutron-capture process. Some of the products of neutron-capture reactions are radioactive and other stable nuclei are formed from the successive β disintegration.

Let us consider, for example, ^{56}Fe. In the presence of neutrons, a sequence of neutron-capture process reactions take place:

$$\begin{aligned} &^{56}\text{Fe} + \text{n} \longrightarrow {}^{57}\text{Fe} + \gamma \\ &^{57}\text{Fe} + \text{n} \longrightarrow {}^{58}\text{Fe} + \gamma \\ &^{58}\text{Fe} + \text{n} \longrightarrow {}^{59}\text{Fe} + \gamma \end{aligned} \tag{8.60}$$

^{57}Fe and ^{58}Fe are stable, but ^{59}Fe is β-radioactive, with a half-life of about 45 days.

The neutron-capture process can be carried out in two distinct ways: s-process and r-process. The s- (s for slow) and r- (r for rapid) processes indicate the time-scale of neutron capture and β decay.

[8]In α-particle reactions, if the target is neutron rich – that is, it has relatively weakly bound neutrons – the neutrons are likely to be emitted. For example, $^{13}\text{C}(\alpha,\text{n})^{16}\text{O}, {}^{22}\text{Ne}(\alpha,\text{n})^{25}\text{Mg}$, etc. The emitted neutrons are captured by heavier nuclei.

The process in which neutron capture occurs very slowly compared to the β decay of the product is called the s-process. In the r-process, the capture of neutrons takes place much faster than the β decay of the product.

The speed (s or r) depends on the density of neutrons. If neutron density is low, the probability of capture becomes very low and the daughter undergoes β^- decay before it can capture another neutron. The process shown in Eq. (8.60) will thus continue as an s-process:

$$^{59}_{26}\text{Fe} \xrightarrow{\beta^-} {}^{59}_{27}\text{Co} \text{ (stable)}$$

$$^{59}_{27}\text{Co} + {}^{1}_{0}\text{n} \longrightarrow {}^{60}_{27}\text{Co}$$

The s-process operates at low neutron concentration and at comparatively lower temperature. If the neutron density is very high, the probability of neutron capture is large and the sequence continues as

$$^{59}_{26}\text{Fe} + {}^{1}_{0}\text{n} \longrightarrow {}^{60}_{26}\text{Fe}$$

$$^{60}_{26}\text{Fe} + {}^{1}_{0}\text{n} \longrightarrow {}^{61}_{26}\text{Fe} \quad \text{and so on.}$$

In this case, the nucleus captures several neutrons before a β decay takes place. This process stops when the half-life of the product is shorter than the time required for the next neutron capture.

SUMMARY

- **Hubble's Law:** Galaxies are receding away from us at velocities proportional to their distance from the Earth: $v = Hd$, where H is Hubble's constant.
- Age of the universe is $t = \frac{2}{3}H^{-1} \approx 8$ Gyr.
- In a radiation-dominated universe, the temperature (T) of the universe depends on its age (t) as $T \approx \frac{1.52\times10^{10}}{t^{1/2}}$ K.
- **Cosmic Microwave Background Radiation (CMBR):** The entire universe is filled with CMBR at a temperature of about 2.727 K. The presence of CMBR is another proof of the Big Bang theory, according to which the universe is assumed to have originated as a singularity of infinite energy density.
- Energy density of photons is $U = 4.72 \times 10^3 T^4$ eV/m^3.
- **Primordial Nucleosynthesis:** At $t \approx 10^{-6}$ s, the universe consisted of neutrons, protons, electrons, muons, neutrinos, pions and their antiparticles.

  At $t \sim 1$ s, neutrinos decoupled and continued to cool down with the expansion of the universe. By this time, most of the original particles and antiparticles have been annihilated, leaving a small number (N) of protons, an equal number of electrons and about $N/5$ number of neutrons.
- Nuclear reactions in the early universe led to a universe in which about 25% of the total mass was helium.
- Most of the elements in the solar system are produced from nucleosynthesis during the Big Bang and nucleosynthesis during stellar evolution.
- The p–p chain reactions are the main source of energy for the Sun. Massive stars generate energy by carbon burning.

- In the final stage of stellar evolution, elements heavier than iron are produced by neutron capture.

Review Questions and Problems

Multiple Choice Questions

1. Cosmic microwave background radiation is
   (a) The remnants of the Big Bang
   (b) Created by the collision of galaxies
   (c) Released when atoms were first formed
   (d) Electromagnetic radiation from nearby galaxies
2. The quantity (with symbols having usual meaning) $\sqrt{\frac{hG}{c^5}}$ has the dimension of
   (a) Mass (b) Length (c) Time (d) Dimensionless
3. Red shift measurements of a galaxy yield a recession of 1700 km/s. The distance of the galaxy from us is approximately
   (a) 10×10^6 ly (b) 50×10^6 ly (c) 80×10^6 ly (d) 1×10^6 ly
4. The wavelength of light from a distant galaxy is observed as $\lambda = 1.1\lambda_0$, where λ_0 is the proper wavelength of the emitted light. The approximate distance of the galaxy from us is
   (a) 1.5×10^6 ly (b) 2.0×10^{10} ly (c) 8.0×10^7 ly (d) 1.4×10^9 ly
5. The recessional speed of a distant galaxy is equal to the speed of light. The distance of the galaxy is
   (a) 1.5×10^7 ly (b) 1.4×10^{10} ly (c) 8.0×10^8 ly (d) 1.4×10^9 ly
6. The basic process responsible for the stellar nucleosynthesis of elements with $A > 60$ is
   (a) Thermonuclear fusion (b) Carbon–nitrogen cycle
   (c) Neutron capture (d) Proton–proton cycle

Short Questions and Problems

1. What is Hubble's parameter H? Is it a constant? Explain.
2. Suppose sodium light of wavelength 590 nm is emitted from a distant galaxy. Using Hubble's law, estimate the wavelength of this light as observed from the Earth if the distance of the galaxy from us is (a) 1.0×10^6 light years and (b) 1.0×10^9 light years.
3. The wavelength of a spectral line emitted from a distant galaxy is observed to be red-shifted so that $\frac{\lambda_{\text{observed}}}{\lambda} = 2$. Estimate the distance of the galaxy from us.

4. Calculate the peak photon energy of the microwave background radiation at temperature $T = 2.727$ K.

5. Explain why the age of the universe is approximately $\frac{2}{3}H^{-1}$.

6. Determine the age of the universe when it is cooled below the threshold temperature for (a) nucleon production and (b) pion production.

7. At what temperature was the universe hot enough to produce kaons of mass 500 MeV? Determine the age of the universe at that temperature.

8. Estimate the age of the universe when the neutron-to-proton ratio is $\frac{N_n}{N_p} = \frac{2}{3}$.

9. Estimate the age of the universe when the temperature is 5000 K. Also determine the average photon energy.

10. The Planck time t can be expressed in terms of the fundamental constants h, c and G as $t \propto h^x \times c^y \times G^z$. Find x, y and z.

HINTS/ANSWERS TO SELECTED PROBLEMS

Multiple Choice Questions

1. (a) 2. (c) 3. (c) 4. (d) 5. (b) 6. (b)

Questions and Problems

2. (a) $v = Hd = \frac{70 \text{ km/s}}{3.26 \times 10^6 \text{ light years}} \times 1.6 \times 10^6$ light years. ≈ 34.36 km/s

Therefore, $\beta = \frac{v}{c} = \frac{34.36}{3 \times 10^5} = 11.452 \times 10^{-5}$. The changed wavelength due to Doppler effect is

$$\lambda = \lambda_1 \sqrt{\frac{1+\beta}{1-\beta}} \approx \lambda_1(1+\beta) \ \ (\text{as } \beta << 1) \ = 590 \times 1.00011452 = 590.0676 \text{ nm}$$

(b) = 661.92 nm

3. $2 = \sqrt{\frac{1+\beta}{1-\beta}}$ or $\beta = \frac{3}{5}$

By Hubble's law, $d = \frac{v}{H} = \frac{3 \times 3 \times 10^5 \times 3.26 \times 10^3}{5 \times 70} \approx 8.38 \times 10^6$ light years

4. Microwave radiation follows the distribution law of Planck's black-body radiation law. The energy distribution is maximum at $\frac{h\nu_m}{k_B T} \approx 2.822$.

$$h\nu_m = 2.822 \times 8.62 \times 10^{-5} \times 2.727 \text{ eV} \ \approx 6.63 \times 10^{-4} \text{ eV}$$

6. (a) Minimum energy required to produce a nucleon is $E_\gamma \gtrsim 940$ MeV and the correspond temperature is $T = \dfrac{E_\gamma}{k_B} = \dfrac{940 \times 10^6}{8.6 \times 10^{-5}} \approx 1.1 \times 10^{13}$ K.

The age of the universe at that time is $t^{1/2} = \dfrac{1.52 \times 10^{10}}{1.1 \times 10^{13}} \approx 1.4 \times 10^{-3}$

$t \approx 2 \times 10^{-6}$ s

(b) For pion, $E_\pi \gtrsim 140$ MeV and the correspond temperature is

$$T = \frac{E_\gamma}{k_B} = \frac{140 \times 10^6}{8.6 \times 10^{-5}} \approx 16.3 \times 10^{11} \text{ K}$$

The age of the universe at that time is $t \approx 87 \times 10^{-6}$ s

7. $T = \dfrac{E_k}{k_B} = \dfrac{500 \times 10^6}{8.6 \times 10^{-5}} \approx 58.14 \times 10^{11}$ K

The age of the universe at that time is $t \approx 6.8 \times 10^{-6}$ s

8. $\dfrac{N_n}{N_p} = e^{-(m_n - m_p)c^2/k_BT} = e^{-\frac{1.293}{k_BT}}; \ \dfrac{1.293}{k_BT} = 0.405; \ T \approx 3.70 \times 10^{10}$ K

The age of the universe at that time is $t \approx 0.17$ s

9. The age of the universe at temperature 5000 K is $t \approx 11.56 \times 10^{12}$ s

Energy density of photon at temperature T is $\rho_\gamma = 4.7 \times 10^3 T^4$ eV/m^3

Density of photon is $n_\gamma = 2 \times 10^7 T^3$ photons/m^3

Thus, the average energy of photon is

$$e_\gamma = 2.35 \times 10^{-4} T \text{ eV} = 2.35 \times 5000 \times 10^{-4} = 1.175 \text{ eV}$$

10. $t \propto (ML^2T^{-1})^x (LT^{-1})^y (M^{-1}L^3T^{-2})^z$

$\propto M^{(x-z)} L^{(2x+y+3z)} T^{(-x-y-2z)}$

Thus, $x - z = 0$

$2x + y + 3z = 0$

$x + y + 2z = -1$

Solving, $x = \dfrac{1}{2}, y = -\dfrac{5}{2}$ and $z = \dfrac{1}{2}$. Therefore $t \propto \sqrt{\dfrac{hG}{c^5}}$.

We can not analyse the nature of the universe before the time t, known as the Planck time, where $t \sim 10^{-43}$ s.

APPENDIX A

Penetration of Rectangular Barrier

Let us consider a particle of mass m incident on a rectangular barrier of width a from the left with energy E (Fig. A.1). The barrier potential $V(x)$ is

$$V(x) = \begin{cases} V_0 & 0 < x < a \\ 0 & \text{otherwise} \end{cases}$$

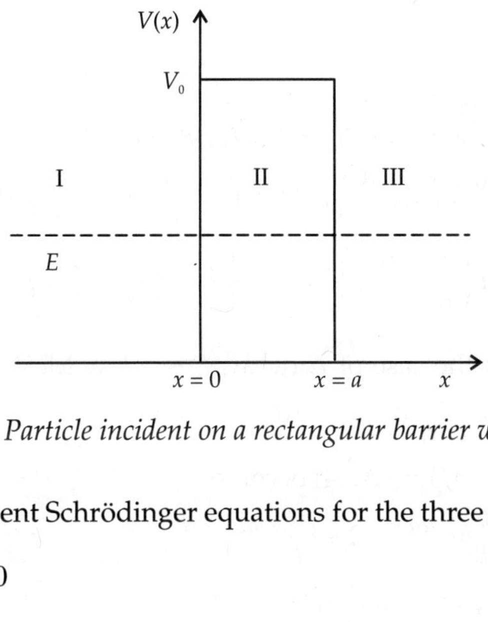

Figure A.1: *Particle incident on a rectangular barrier with energy E*

The time-independent Schrödinger equations for the three regions I, II and III are

$$\frac{d^2u_I}{dx^2} + k^2 u_I = 0 \tag{A.1}$$

$$\frac{d^2u_{II}}{dx^2} - \alpha^2 u_{II} = 0 \tag{A.2}$$

$$\frac{d^2u_{III}}{dx^2} + k^2 u_{III} = 0, \tag{A.3}$$

where $k^2 = \dfrac{2mE}{\hbar^2}$ and $\alpha^2 = \dfrac{2m(V_0 - E)}{\hbar^2}$.

The solutions of these equations are

$$u_I(x) = A_1 e^{ikx} + B_1 e^{-ikx} \tag{A.4}$$

$$u_{II}(x) = A_2 e^{\alpha x} + B_2 e^{-\alpha x} \tag{A.5}$$

$$u_{III}(x) = A_3 e^{ikx}, \tag{A.6}$$

where we have used the fact that there is no reflected wave in region III. The constants $A_1, B_1, ...$ will be determined by making use of the fact that the wave function must be well behaved. Thus, the wave function and its derivative must be continuous across the boundaries $x = 0$ and $x = a$.

$$u_I(0) = u_{II}(0) \Rightarrow A_1 + B_1 = A_2 + B_2 \tag{A.7}$$

$$u_I'(0) = u_{II}'(0) \Rightarrow A_1 - B_1 = \frac{\alpha}{ik}(A_2 - B_2) \tag{A.8}$$

From these two equations, we get

$$A_1 = \left(1 + \frac{\alpha}{ik}\right)\frac{A_2}{2} + \left(1 - \frac{\alpha}{ik}\right)\frac{B_2}{2} \tag{A.9}$$

Again $u_{II}(a) = u_{III}(a) \Rightarrow A_2 e^{\alpha a} + B_2 e^{-\alpha a} = A_3 e^{ika}$ (A.10)

$$u_{II}'(a) = u_{III}'(a) \Rightarrow A_2 e^{\alpha a} - B_2 e^{-\alpha a} = \frac{ik}{\alpha} A_3 e^{ika} \tag{A.11}$$

Therefore $A_2 = \frac{A_3}{2}(1 + \frac{ik}{\alpha})e^{ika}e^{-\alpha a}$ (A.12)

$$B_2 = \frac{A_3}{2}(1 - \frac{ik}{\alpha})e^{ika}e^{\alpha a} \tag{A.13}$$

Substituting the values of A_2 and B_2 in Eq. (A.9), we get

$$\begin{aligned} A_1 &= \frac{A_3}{4}e^{ika}\left[\left(1 + \frac{\alpha}{ik}\right)\left(1 + \frac{ik}{\alpha}\right)e^{-\alpha a} + \left(1 - \frac{\alpha}{ik}\right)\left(1 - \frac{ik}{\alpha}\right)e^{\alpha a}\right] \\ &= \frac{A_3}{4}e^{ika}\left[\left\{2 + i\left(\frac{k}{\alpha} - \frac{\alpha}{k}\right)\right\}e^{-\alpha a} + \left\{2 - i\left(\frac{k}{\alpha} - \frac{\alpha}{k}\right)\right\}e^{\alpha a}\right] \end{aligned} \tag{A.14}$$

Now $\frac{k}{\alpha} = \sqrt{\frac{E}{V_0 - E}}$. In the case of α decay, $E \sim$ a few MeV and the barrier height $V_0 >> E$. Thus $\frac{k}{\alpha} << \frac{\alpha}{k}$ and $\frac{\alpha}{k} - \frac{k}{\alpha} \approx \frac{\alpha}{k}$.

Using this approximation, Eq. (A.14) becomes

$$\begin{aligned} A_1 &\approx \frac{A_3}{4}e^{ika}\left[(2 - i\frac{\alpha}{k})e^{-\alpha a} + (2 + i\frac{\alpha}{k})e^{\alpha a}\right] \\ &= \frac{A_3}{4}e^{ika}\left[2(e^{\alpha a} + e^{-\alpha a}) + i\frac{\alpha}{k}(e^{\alpha a} - e^{-\alpha a}\right] \end{aligned} \tag{A.15}$$

In the case of α decay, we found earlier that $\alpha a \sim 10^2$. Therefore, Eq. (A.15) can be approximated as

$$A_1 \approx \frac{A_3}{4}e^{ika}e^{\alpha a}\left[2(1 + e^{-2\alpha a}) + i\frac{\alpha}{k}(1 - e^{-2\alpha a}\right] \approx \frac{A_3}{4}e^{ika}e^{\alpha a}\left(2 + i\frac{\alpha}{k}\right) \tag{A.16}$$

Therefore $\dfrac{A_3}{A_1} \approx e^{-\alpha a}\dfrac{4e^{-ika}}{2+i\frac{\alpha}{k}}$; $\left|\dfrac{A_3}{A_1}\right|^2 \approx \dfrac{16}{4+\frac{\alpha^2}{k^2}}e^{-2\alpha a}$ (A.17)

The term in front of the exponential is not significant, as its variation with respect to α is negligible as compared to the variation of the exponential term itself. Thus, the transmission probability is given as

$$P = \frac{\text{Transmitted intensity}}{\text{Incident intensity}} = \left|\frac{A_3}{A_1}\right|^2 \sim e^{-2\alpha a}, \tag{A.18}$$

where $\alpha = \dfrac{1}{\hbar}\sqrt{2m(V_0 - E)}$.

Note that as $\hbar \to 0$, $\alpha \to \infty$ and P approaches the classical limit of zero transparency. Also, P is larger for particles with smaller m.

APPENDIX B

Parity

Parity transformation or space inversion is a transformation where all three coordinate axes in the Cartesian system change sign. If the location of a point is given by (x, y, z), then the coordinate of the same point under parity transformation will be $(-x, -y, -z)$. Under parity

$$(x, y, z) \xrightarrow{P} (-x, -y, -z)$$

The parity operation can be represented as a reflection on the $z = 0$ plane, followed by a rotation about the z axis by π

$$(x, y, z) \xrightarrow{\text{Reflection}} (x, y, -z) \xrightarrow{\text{Rotation about the z axis by } \pi} (-x, -y, -z)$$

Such a transformation takes us from a right-handed coordinate system to a left-handed one. It cannot be achieved by any combination of rotations. We can verify that the determinant of the transformation matrix for rotation is $+1$, while for parity it is -1.

Illustrative Example B.1:

Calculate the Jacobian (J) for the transformation (reflection)

$$x' = X; \;\; y' = y; \;\; z' = -z$$

Solution $J = \begin{vmatrix} 1 & 0 & 0 \\ 0 & 1 & 0 \\ 0 & 0 & -1 \end{vmatrix} = -1$

The transformed coordinate is left-handed, with $J = -1$.

Illustrative Example B.2:

Calculate the Jacobian (J) for the transformation (rotation about the z axis by π)

$$x' = -x; \;\; y' = -y; \;\; z' = z$$

Solution $J = \begin{vmatrix} -1 & 0 & 0 \\ 0 & -1 & 0 \\ 0 & 0 & 1 \end{vmatrix} = +1$

In this case, inverting any two axes is equivalent to rotation of the coordinate about the third axis by 180°. Thus, under such operations, a right-handed system remains right-handed.

Illustrative Example B.3:

Calculate the Jacobian (J) for the transformation (reflection + rotation)

$$x' = -x;\ y' = -y;\ z' = -z$$

Solution $J = \begin{vmatrix} -1 & 0 & 0 \\ 0 & -1 & 0 \\ 0 & 0 & -1 \end{vmatrix} = -1$

Again, the transformed coordinate is left-handed, with $J = -1$.

Under parity operation

Position vector $\vec{r} \xrightarrow{P} -\vec{r}$

Linear momentum $\vec{p} \xrightarrow{P} -\vec{p}$

$$r = \sqrt{\vec{r}.\vec{r}} \xrightarrow{P} \sqrt{(\vec{-r}).(\vec{-r})} = r$$

Similarly $p \xrightarrow{P} p$.

Thus, ordinary scalars remain unchanged under space inversion or parity operation, but vectors change sign. There are, however, some scalars and vectors that do not transform under parity, as shown above. For example, the orbital angular momentum

$$\vec{L} = \vec{r} \times \vec{p} \xrightarrow{P} (\vec{-r}) \times (\vec{-p}) = \vec{r} \times \vec{p} = \vec{L}$$

Thus, $\vec{L}$ behaves as a scalar under space inversion and is known as *axial vector* or *pseudo vector*. Similarly, there is a class of scalars that changes sign under parity, like vectors. For example

$$\vec{a}.(\vec{b} \times \vec{c}) \xrightarrow{P} \vec{-a}.(\vec{-b} \times \vec{-c}) = -\vec{a}.(\vec{b} \times \vec{c})$$

Such quantities are called *pseudo scalars*.

Illustrative Example B.4:

Suppose a point particle of mass m and charge q is placed in an electric field $\vec{E}$. Write down the equation of motion and explain how it behaves under parity.

Solution The equation of motion for the particle is

$$m\frac{d^2\vec{r}}{dt^2} = q\vec{E} \tag{B.1}$$

The electric field[1] $\vec{E}$ is a polar vector and changes sign under parity operation. Thus, under parity operation, both the left-hand side and the right-hand side of Eq. (B.1) will change sign. Therefore, electrostatic interaction is invariant under parity transformation. Similarly, gravitational interaction is also invariant under parity.

[1] $\vec{E}$ is in the form, $\vec{E} = \frac{c}{r^3}\vec{r}$.

Illustrative Example B.5:

Suppose a point particle of mass m and charge q is moving with velocity $\vec{v}$ in a magnetic field $\vec{B}$. Write down the equation of motion and explain how it behaves under parity.

Solution The equation of motion for the particle is

$$m\frac{d^2\vec{r}}{dt^2} = q\vec{v}\times\vec{B} \tag{B.2}$$

The magnetic field[2] $\vec{B}$ is an axial vector, and thus, does not change sign under parity operation. However, $\vec{v}$ being a polar vector changes sign. Thus, under parity operation, both the left-hand side and the right-hand side of Eq. (B.2) will change sign. Therefore, magnetic interaction is also invariant under parity transformation.

In quantum mechanics, the probability density $|\psi(x,y,z)|^2$ is observable and its value cannot depend on whether we have chosen the left-handed or right-handed system. Thus

$$|\psi(-x,-y,-z)|^2 = |\psi(x,y,z)|^2$$

This requirement will be satisfied if $\psi(-x,-y,-z) = \psi(x,y,z)$ even function or $\psi(-x,-y,-z)$ $-\psi(x,y,z)$ odd function.

We can express the above result in terms of the following eigenvalue equation:

$$P\psi(x,y,z) = \lambda\,\psi(x,y,z),$$

where $P^2\psi(x,y,z) = \lambda^2\psi(x,y,z) = \psi(x,y,z)$, as two successive parity operations must bring the system back to its original form. Thus, $\lambda^2 = 1$ or $\lambda = \pm 1$. The eigenvalue of the parity operator is ± 1.

Illustrative Example B.6:

Show that $[H,P] = 0$.

Solution $P\{H(x)\psi(x)\} = H(-x)\psi(-x) = H(x)\psi(-x)$, where we assume $V(-x) = V(x)$.

Therefore, $\{PH - HP\}\psi = 0$. Thus $[H,P] = 0$.

If the Hamiltonian is invariant under parity, that is, if $H(-x) = H(x)$, then $[H,P] = 0$. In that case, the eigenfunctions of P are also the eigenfunctions of H with eigenvalues ± 1.

Illustrative Example B.7:

Show that the parity operator P is Hermitian, $P^\dagger = P$.

Solution $\int_{-\infty}^{\infty}(P\psi(x))^*\phi\;dx = \int_{-\infty}^{\infty}\psi^*(-x)\phi(x)\;dx \;= \int_{-\infty}^{\infty}\psi^*(y)\phi(-y)\;dy$

$$= \int_{-\infty}^{\infty}\psi^*(x)\phi(-x)\;dx = \int_{-\infty}^{\infty}\psi^*(x)P\phi(x)\;dx$$

[2]Recall the Biot–Savart law that involves the cross-product of two polar vectors.

Illustrative Example B.8:

Show that the parity operator is unitary.

Solution As two successive parity operations must bring the system back to its original form

$$P^2 = 1 = PP^{-1}$$

Therefore, $P = P^{-1}$. Also $P^\dagger = P$ and thus $P^\dagger = P^{-1}$.

Illustrative Example B.9:

Explain how the Hamiltonian of a one-dimensional harmonic oscillator behaves under parity.

Solution The Hamiltonian of a one-dimensional harmonic oscillator is $H(x) = \frac{p_x^2}{2m} + \frac{1}{2}mw^2x^2$ and under parity, $\frac{p_x^2}{2m} + \frac{1}{2}mw^2x^2 \xrightarrow{P} \frac{(-p_x)^2}{2m} + \frac{1}{2}mw^2(-x)^2 = H(x)$.

Thus $PH(x) = H(x)$.

The energy eigenfunctions are thus either even or odd functions of x, but never a mixture of even and odd. If the Hamiltonian is invariant under parity, then $[H, P] = 0$ and the energy eigenfunctions are also the eigenfunctions of the parity operator.

For a spherically symmetric potential, $\psi_{nlm}(r, \theta, \phi) = R_n^l(r)Y_m^l(\theta, \phi)$.

Under parity, it transforms as

$$(r, \theta, \phi) \xrightarrow{P} (r, \pi - \theta, \pi + \phi) \text{ and } P\psi_{nlm}(r, \theta, \phi) = (-1)^l \psi_{nlm}(r, \theta, \phi),$$

where l is the orbital angular momentum.

The notion of *intrinsic parity* is applied to all elementary particles. The parity of a state described by ψ_{nlm} is given by

$$P\psi_{nlm} = \eta_\psi(-1)^l \psi_{nlm}, \quad \text{(B.3)}$$

where η_ψ is the intrinsic parity of the quantum state. Since $P^2\psi_{nlm} = \psi_{nlm}$, the intrinsic parity satisfies the condition

$$\eta_\psi^2 = 1 \quad \text{(B.4)}$$

Therefore, the total parity of the state described by ψ_{nlm} is given by $\eta_\psi(-1)^l$.

Parity of a complex system: Let us consider a system comprising A and B. The parity of such a system is

$$P_{A+B} = \eta_A \eta_B (-1)^{l_A}(-1)^{l_B}$$

If the intrinsic parities of A and B are known, then the parity of the system can be determined. The absolute value of the intrinsic parity cannot be determined. By convention, pions and kaons are assigned $-ve$ parity and baryons have $+ve$ parity. Parity of the antifermions is the opposite of that of the fermions, but bosons have the same parity for particles and antiparticles. Overall, parity is violated in weak interaction.

Intrinsic parity of pions: The intrinsic parity of pions may be determined from the reaction

$$\pi^- + d \longrightarrow n + n$$

The pion is captured almost at rest by the deuteron, and thus, the relative angular momentum of the initial state is $l = 0$. Total parity of the initial state is

$$P_{\text{initial}} = \eta_\pi \times \eta_d \times (-1)^l = \eta_\pi \times \eta_d$$

In the initial state, spin of $\pi^- = 0$; spin of $d = 1$.
Therefore, the total angular momentum of the initial state is $J = l + s_\pi + s_d = 1$.

In the final state, there are two identical fermions, and thus, the total wave function must satisfy the requirement that

$$\Psi_{\text{total}} = \Psi_{\text{space}} \times \Psi_{\text{spin}} \Rightarrow \text{antisymmetric}$$

Since the neutron is a spin-$\frac{1}{2}$ particle, the total spin of the final state is

$$s = 0 \quad \text{and} \quad 1$$

The spin wave function is antisymmetric for $s = 0$ and symmetric for $s = 1$. The space wave function is symmetric for $l = even$.

The possible values of the orbital angular momentum L and total angular momentum J, satisfying $\vec{L} + \vec{s} = \vec{1}$, will be

$s = 0, L = 1, J = 1 \Rightarrow \Psi_{\text{total}} = \text{symmetric}$
$s = 1, L = 0, J = 1 \Rightarrow \Psi_{\text{total}} = \text{symmetric}$
$s = 1, L = 1, J = 1 \Rightarrow \Psi_{\text{total}} = \text{antisymmetric}$
$s = 1, L = 2, J = 1 \Rightarrow \Psi_{\text{total}} = \text{symmetric}$

Therefore, the requirement of the antisymmetric wave function is satisfied only for $s = 1, L = 1$.
Total parity of the final state is $P_{\text{final}} = \eta_n \times \eta_n \times (-1)^L = (-1)^1 = -1$
Using the condition $P_{\text{initial}} = P_{\text{final}}$

$$\eta_\pi \times \eta_d = -1$$

As the intrinsic parity of deuteron is $+1$, the intrinsic parity of the pion is –ve.

Illustrative Example B.10:

Consider the following reactions: $\pi^- + p \longrightarrow n + \pi^0$, $\pi^0 \longrightarrow 2\gamma$, $\pi^- + p \longrightarrow n + \gamma$. Show that the intrinsic parity of π^- and π^0 are the same and that it is odd.

Solution The pion is captured almost at rest by the proton, and thus, the relative angular momentum of the initial state is $l = 0$. In the initial state

$$\text{spin of } \pi^- = 0; \text{ spin of } p = \frac{1}{2}$$

Therefore, the total angular momentum of the initial state is $J = l + s_\pi + s_p = \frac{1}{2}$.
In the final state

$$\text{spin of } \pi^0 = 0; \text{ spin of } n = \frac{1}{2}$$

Therefore, the total spin of the final state is $\frac{1}{2}$ and the relative angular momentum of the final state will be $l = 0$, and the total angular momentum $J = l + s_\pi + s_n = \frac{1}{2}$.

Therefore, $l_{\text{initial}} = l_{\text{final}} = 0$, and the spatial parities $(-1)^l$ of $(\pi^- + p)$ and $(n + \pi^0)$ are the same.

Considering the total parity on both sides $\eta_{\pi^-} \times \eta_p = \eta_{\pi^0} \times \eta_n$, we get $\eta_{\pi^-} = \eta_{\pi^0}$, since $\eta_p = \eta_n$.

APPENDIX C

List of Physical Constants

Constants

Boltzmann constant	k_B	=	1.3807×10^{-23} J/K
		=	8.6174×10^{-5} eV/K
Planck constant	h	=	6.62618×10^{-34} J·s
		=	4.13570×10^{-15} eV·s
	hc	=	12.40 keV·Å
	$\hbar c$	=	197.326 MeV·fm
	$\frac{e^2}{4\pi\varepsilon_0}$	=	1.44 MeV·fm
Compton Wavelength	λ_e	=	2.426×10^{-12} m
Bohr Magneton	μ_B	=	9.274×10^{-24} J/T
Nuclear Magneton	μ_N	=	5.051×10^{-27} J/T
Gravitational constant	G	=	6.673×10^{-11} N·m^2/kg^2

Rest Masses

Electron	5.4858×10^{-4} u	0.511 MeV/c^2
Proton	1.007276 u	938.28 MeV/c^2
Neutron	1.008665 u	939.57 MeV/c^2

Bibliography

Burcham, WE, and Jobes, M. 1955. *Nuclear and Particle Physics*, Pearson Education Limited.

Clayton, D. 1983. *Principles of Stellar Evolution and Nucleosynthesis,* The University of Chicago Press.

Cohen, BL. 1971. *Concepts of Nuclear Physics*, McGraw-Hill.

Das, A, and Ferbel, T. 2003. *Introduction to Nuclear and Particle Physics, Second Edition*, World Scientific Publishing Company.

Enrico, F. 1950. *Nuclear Physics, Revised Edition*, The University of Chicago Press.

Evans, RD. 1955. *The Atomic Nucleus*, McGraw-Hill.

Gautreau, R, and Savin, W. 1999. *Schaum's Outline of Theory and Problems of Modern Physics (Schaum's Outline Series),* McGraw-Hill Education.

Griffiths, D. 1987. *Introduction to Elementary Particles*, John Wiley & Sons.

Kamal, AA. 2010.*1000 Solved Problems in Modern Physics*, Springer-Verlag.

Kaplan, I. 1962. *Nuclear Physics*, Addison-Wesley Publishing Company.

Knoll, GF. 2000. *Radiation Detection and Measurement, Third Edition*, John Wiley & Sons.

Krane, KS. 1987. *Introductory Nuclear Physics*, John Wiley & Sons.

Lee, SY. 2004. *Accelerator Physics, Second Edition*, World Scientific Publishing Company.

Leo, WR. 1994. *Techniques for Nuclear and Particle Physics Experiments, Second Revised Edition*, Springer-Verlag.

Lim, YK (Ed.). 2002. *Problems and Solutions on Atomic and Nuclear Physics*, Sarat Book Distributors.

Mittal, VK, Verma, RC, and Gupta, SC. 2009. *Introduction to Nuclear and Particle Physics*, PHI Learning Private Ltd.

Mukhin, KN. 1987. *Experimental Nuclear Physics, Volumes I and II*, Mir Publishers.

Patel, SB. 2011. *Nuclear Physics, An Introduction, Second Edition,* New Age International Pvt. Ltd Publishers.

Perkins, DH. 2000. *Introduction to High Energy Physics, Fourth Edition,* Cambridge University Press.

Phillips, AC. 1996. *The Physics of Stars,* John Wiley & Sons.

Raine, D, and Thomas, T. 2001. *An Introduction to the Science of Cosmology,* Institute of Physics Publishing, Bristol and Philadelphia.

Rangacharyulu, C. 2014. *Physics of Nuclear Radiations, Concepts, Techniques and Applications,* CRC Press.

Rogers, P, and Stephens, GA. 1967. *Worked Examples in Modern Physics, Volume 1,* Iliffe & Sons Limited.

Roy, RR, and Nigam, BP. 1967. *Nuclear Physics, Theory and Experiment,* John Wiley & Sons.

Segre, E. 1977. *Nuclei and Particles, Second Edition,* WA Benjamin Inc., Advanced Book Program.

Tsoulfanidis, N. 1995. *Measurement and Detection of Radiation, Second Edition,* Taylor & Francis.

Turner, JE. 2007. *Atoms, Radiation and Radiation Protection,* Wiley-VCH Verlag GmbH & Co. KGaA.

Index

A

actinium 77, 78
activation energy 155, 158
age of specimen
  biological 90
  geological 91
antineutrino 106, 107, 114
antiparticle 107, 244, 294, 297
antiquark 271
Aston 9
asymmetry term 47
atomic mass 21, 93

B

Bainbridge mass spectrograph 9, 10, 11
Bartlett force 37
baryon
  about 244, 245, 246, 269, 272
  conservation of number 254, 259
Batzel 163
Becker 146
Becquerel, Henri 73
betatron
  average energy
    gained per cycle 235
    of electrons 235
  condition 234
  principle of operation 233
Bethe
  carbon–nitrogen (CN) cycle 303
  formula for stopping power 186
Big Bang
  definition 285
  first few seconds after 293
  hot 288
binding energy (BE)
  about 15, 46
  abundance of stable nuclei 25
  charge symmetry 29
  constancy of curve and saturation of nuclear force 19
  Coulomb energy difference of mirror nuclei 28
  Coulomb energy of the nucleus 27
  curve 18, 20, 33, 170
  fall of curve at small and large values of A 20
  magic nuclei 19
  magic number 19
  mass defect 21
  nuclear separation energy 23
  packing fraction 22
  release of energy in fission and fusion 20
black-body spectrum 298
Bohr 181, 189
  compound nucleus theory 142
  hypothesis of independence 143, 144
  magneton 3
  –Wheeler theory of nuclear fission 156
Boltzmann factor 296, 300
Bose–Einstein statistics 244
boson 243, 244
Bothe 146
Bragg
  curve 188
  –Kleeman rule 191
branching
  about 79
  ratio for alpha decay 79
breeder reactor 169
bremsstrahlung 191

C

carbon–nitrogen (CN) cycle 303
carbon–nitrogen–oxygen (CNO) cycle 173
Cavendish Laboratory, Cambridge 9
Chadwick 3, 148
chain reaction 163
charge
  conjugation 266

independence 30
symmetry 30
colour charge 273
compound nucleus
decay 143
energy levels 143
formation 142
mechanism 130
theory 142
Compton
effect 196, 200
scattering 146, 197
Condon 97
conservation laws
about 129, 246
violation of 259
conservation of
angular momentum 5, 106, 131, 247
baryon number 247, 254
charge 131, 247
energy 4, 105, 130, 247
lepton number 247, 252
linear momentum 106, 130, 247
cosmic background explorer 290
Coulomb
barrier 98, 149, 155, 156, 300, 304
force 5, 6, 21, 26, 156, 181, 182, 190, 194
law 156
repulsion 14, 21, 98, 157, 300
term 46, 50
Coulomb energy
about 21, 30, 50, 53, 157
difference of mirror nuclei 28, 53, 257
nucleus 27
cyclotron
about 224
decrease in frequency due to relativistic correction 226
limitations of 225
resonance condition 225
resonance frequency 225
synchrocyclotron 226
Curie 104, 146

D

de Broglie wavelength 6, 130, 184, 220
decay, alpha 92
alpha-ray spectrum 102
basic experimental results 96
Geiger–Nuttal law 97
kinetic energy and half-life 96
range and half-life 97
energetics of 93
energy released in BE 94
properties of alpha particles 92
range of particles 95
theory of 97
decay, beta 104
beta spectrum 105
difference between neutrino and antineutrino 107
electron capture 104
energetics of 110
neutrino hypothesis 105
selection rules 113
violation of parity 108
β^- 104
β^+ 104
decay, gamma 114
energetics of 114
internal conversion 117
selection rule 116
dees 224
deuteron
about 3, 16, 34, 45, 298, 302, 318
maximum energy 225
photo disintegration of 17, 296
Doppler effect 283

E

Einstein
general theory of relativity 286
electron–proton model 2, 3
endpoint energy 105
energetics
in the centre-of-mass frame 137
in the laboratory frame 131
of alpha decay 93
of beta decay 110
of gamma decay 114
of nuclear reactions 131
expanding universe 283

F

factor
fast fission 166
multiplication 164
reproduction 164
thermal utilisation 167
Fermi, Enrico
about 164
–Dirac statistics 244
distribution 7
energy 64, 65

- momentum 64, 65
- National Accelerator Laboratory (Fermilab) 221
- nuclear gas model 64
- selection rule 113

fermion 30, 64, 106, 244, 272, 318
frame
- centre-of-mass (CM) 137
- laboratory 131

Friedmann equation 286, 288

G

Gamow
- alpha emission 97
- energy 300
- –Teller 113

gas amplification 202
gas-filled detectors, regions
- Geiger–Müller 202
- ionisation 201
- limited proportionality 202
- proportional 202
- recombination 201

Geiger–Müller (GM)
- counter 207
- region 202

Geiger–Müller counter 206
- advantages 212
- characteristics 211
- dead time 207
- disadvantages 212
- discharge quenching 211
- recovery time 207
- resolving time 207
- Townsend avalanche 206

Geiger–Nuttall law 97
Gell-Mann, Murray
- eightfold way 267
- –Nishijima relation 257
- quarks 271
- strangeness 256

Ghoshal, SN
- about 144
- experiment 144, 146

gravitational force 242
Gurney 97

H

hadron 245, 270, 273
Hahn 151
half-integral spin 3, 113, 244, 272
half-lifc 76
Hamiltonian 30, 60, 317
Heisenberg force 37
helicity 107
helium mass fraction 298
Hoyle 304
Hubble, Edwin
- about 283
- constant 283
- law 283
- plot 284

hypercharge 258, 270

I

inconsistency with
- magnetic moment 3
- nuclear spin 3
- uncertainty principle 2

intrinsic parity 317
ionisation
- chamber 203
- energy 56, 187, 191
- region 201

isospin 257

J

Jensen 60
Joliot 104, 146

K

K-absorption edge 195
kaon 255
kinematics 131
Kleeman 191

L

Lawrence 220, 224
Lee 108
lepton
- about 244, 270
- number 244, 266
- number conservation 259

linear attenuation coefficient 200
linear energy transfer (LET) see *stopping power*
linear particle accelerator (LINAC)
- about 221
- advantages 223
- disadvantages 223

liquid-drop nuclear model
- applicability of 48
  - beta disintegration energy of mirror nuclei 54
  - binding energy of nuclei 48
  - energy released in alpha decay 55

mass difference of mirror nuclei 52
mass parabola 49
most stable isobar 49
assumptions 46
asymmetry term 47
Coulomb term 46
pairing term 48
semi-empirical mass formula 48
surface term 46
volume term 46

M

magic
nuclei 19, 58, 94
number 19, 55, 57, 60
magnetic moment 32, 33, 55
inconsistency with 3
main sequence stars 303
Majorana force 37
many-body problem 45
mass
atomic 21, 93
defect 21
number 1
parabola 49, 50
spectrograph 9
Bainbridge 10
spectrometer 9
spectrometry 9
Mayer, MG 58, 60
mean life 77
meson 37, 244, 245
Milky Way 283
mirror nuclei
Coulomb energy difference
disintegration energy 54
mass difference 52
moderators 149, 164, 169
moment
dipole 31, 107
electric 32
magnetic 3, 31, 35, 108
monopole 32
quadrupole 32, 34, 58
most stable isobar 49

N

neptunium 77, 78
neutron
cycle and four-factor formula 165
delayed 162
discovery 146
emission in fission 161
fast 162
multiplication factor 164
production of 149
prompt 162
properties 149
reproduction factor 164
neutron–proton model 4
non-integral spin 245
Nordheim rules 61
nuclear astrophysics **283–309**
application of Newtonian mechanics 286
cosmic microwave background radiation 289
and expansion 292
expanding universe 283
Hubble's constant 283
Hubble's law 283
red shift 283
first few seconds after Big Bang 293
primordial nucleosynthesis 297
hot Big Bang 288
stellar nucleosynthesis 299
fusion in stars 299
hydrogen burning 302
for $A < 60$ 304
for $A > 60$ 305
rough estimate of age of the universe 285
nuclear model **45–72**
Fermi gas 64
liquid-drop 45
shell 55
nuclear pile 164
nuclear radiation, gas-filled detectors
principle 201
types
Geiger–Müller counter 206
ionisation chamber 203
proportional counter 204
nuclear radiation, interaction with matter **180–219**
detection of 200
gas-filled detectors 200
methods 200
electrons 189
bremsstrahlung 190
energy transfer in elastic collision 180
heavy charged particles 181
Bethe formula for stopping power 186
photons 193
attenuation of gamma rays 198
Compton effect 195
pair production 196
photoelectric effect 193

range of charged particles190
alpha 191
Bragg's experiment 191
scintillation detector 212
advantages 215
basic process 213
characteristics 214
features 214
inorganic crystal 213
organic 213
nuclear reactions **129–179**
and conservation laws 129
conserved quantities 130
representation 129
types of 129
energetics of 131
compound nucleus 142
cross-section 140
in centre-of-mass frame 137
in laboratory frame 131
neutron discovery 146
fission
about 151
at high energy 163
Bohr–Wheeler theory 156
energy released 153
mass distribution of fragments 151
neutron emission 161
spontaneous 154
utilisation of energy 163
fusion
about 170
solar 172
nuclear reactions, energetics in laboratory frame
about 131
Q equation 132
reactions
endoergic 132, 133
exoergic 132, 134
threshold energy 132
nuclear reactions, types
compound nucleus 130
Bohr hypothesis of independence 143
decay of 143
energy levels 143
formation of 142
Ghoshal experiment 144
direct 130
endoergic 132, 133
exoergic 132, 134
fission 151
radiative capture 130
scattering
definition 129
elastic 130
inelastic 130
transfer reaction
definition 130
pick-up 130
stripping 130
nuclear reactor
definition 164
features 168
types of
fast 168
heterogeneous 168
homogenous 168
intermediate 168
thermal 168
nucleus
definition 1
properties of **1–44**
nucleus, properties
atomic mass 8
mass spectrometry 9
binding energy 15
constituents of 1
electron–proton model 2
inconsistency with magnetic moment 3
inconsistency with nuclear spin 3
inconsistency with uncertainty principle 2
neutron–proton model 4
density 14
moments
electric 31
magnetic 32
parity 30
properties of nuclear force 33
size estimation/observation 18
from alpha-ray scattering experiment 4
from other scattering experiments 6
spin 30

O

oblate shape 32
ordinary force 37

P

Pais, Abraham 256
parity 30, 55, 61, 108, 116
particle accelerators **220–241**
about 220
need for higher energy 220

types
betatron 233
cyclotron 224
linear (LINAC) 221
magnetic focussing 230
synchrocyclotron 231
particle physics **242–282**
conservation laws 246
baryon number 254
basic 247
charge conjugation 266
isospin 257
lepton number 252
strangeness 255
violation of 259
elementary particles 244
hadrons 245
leptons 244
eightfold way 266
fundamental interactions 242
quark model 271
Pauli Exclusion Principle 56, 58, 59, 61, 64, 244, 272
Penzias 289
photoelectric effect
about 117, 193, 199, 214
features 194
photomultiplier tube 213
pion 37, 245, 255, 257, 294, 318
potential 31
dipole moment 31
monopole moment 31
quadrupole moment 31
primordial nucleosynthesis 297
prolate shape 32
proportional counter 204
proton–proton
chain 302
cycle 172

Q

Q equation 132
Q value 102, 132
quark 271

R

radiative capture 130, 165
radioactive dating
age of specimen
biological 90
geological 91
radioactive equilibrium
no 83
secular 83
transient 83
radiocarbon dating 90
radioactivity **73–128**
activity rate 75
alpha decay 92
beta decay 104
branching 79
dating 90
decay constant 74
decay equation 73
decay law 74
decay rate 75
equilibrium 80
gamma decay 114
half-life 76
mean life 77
production of element by nuclear bombardment 80
series 77
successive disintegration 80
unit of activity 75
red giant phase 304
red shift 283
relativistic effect 225
resonance escape probability 167
rest mass energy 130, 186
Rutherford
about 1, 104, 129, 212
scattering experiment 2
scattering formula 5, 6

S

scattering
alpha ray 4
Compton 146, 195
definition 129
other experiments 6, 257
Rutherford 2, 5
types
elastic 130
inelastic 130
Schrödinger equation 30, 45, 59
scintillation detector 212
Seaborg 163
Segre chart 25
selection rule
Fermi (F) 113
Gamow–Teller (GT) 113
semi-empirical mass formula 48, 153
shell nuclear model
assumptions 58

choice of potential 59
drawbacks of 63
evidence for 56
in atomic case 56
inclusion of spin-orbit coupling 60
introduction to 58
predictions of 60
size estimation from alpha-ray scattering experiment 4
conservation of angular momentum 5
conservation of energy 4
solar fusion
about 172
carbon–nitrogen–oxygen (CNO) cycle 173
proton–proton cycle 172
Soddy 104
space exchange 37
spallation 163
spin
antiparallel 34, 113
exchange 37
half-integral 3, 113, 244, 272
integral 3
non-integral 245
nuclear 3, 30, 34
parallel 34, 109, 114
zero 244
statistics
Bose–Einstein 244
Fermi–Dirac 67, 244
Stefan–Boltzmann constant 289
stellar nucleosynthesis 299
stopping power
definition 184
Bethe formula for 186
straggling 96, 188
strangeness 255, 257, 268
Strassmann 151
stripping 130
strong force 242, 243, 257, 260
synchronous
orbit 231, 232
particle 231, 232

T

Taylor series expansion 301
tensor
force 36
interaction 35
term
asymmetry 47
Coulomb 46
pairing 48
surface 46
volume 46
Tevatron 221
thermal utilisation factor 167
Thomson, JJ
about 9
method 9
thorium 77
three-nucleon system 45
Townsend avalanche 206
transfer reaction 130
triple-alpha reaction 304
two-nucleon system 45

U

unit of activity 75
uranium 77, 151, 163, 168

V

Van de Graaff 220
velocity filter 10
volume term 46

W

wavelength shifter 215
weak force/interaction 242, 243, 257, 260, 296, 317
Weizsäcker 48, 302
Wheeler 156
whole number rule 9
Wideroe, Rolf 220
Wigner force 37
Wilson 289

Y

Young 108
Yukawa 245

Z

Zweig 271